SLICING SPACES

PERFORMANCE OF ARCHITECTURE IN CINEMA

SLICING SPACES

PERFORMANCE OF ARCHITECTURE IN CINEMA

GUL KACMAZ ERK AND REBECCA – JANE MCCONNELL

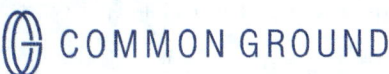 COMMON GROUND

First published in 2023
as part of the *Arts in Society* Book Imprint
doi: 10.18848/978-1-957792-11-8/CGP (Full Book)

Common Ground Research Networks
University of Illinois Research Park
2001 South First St, Suite 201 L
Champaign, IL 61820 USA

Library of Congress Cataloging-in-Publication Data

Names: Kacmaz Erk, Gul, editor. | McConnell, Rebecca-Jane, editor.
Title: Slicing Spaces: Performance of Architecture in Cinema / edited by
  Gul Kacmaz Erk and Rebecca-Jane McConnell.
Description: Champaign: Common Ground Research Networks, 2022. | Includes
  bibliographical references and index. | Summary: "As suggested in the
  title, Slicing Spaces: Performance of Architecture in Cinema, this
  project slices through the multifaceted layers of film space. The text
  investigates how architecture performs as an altruist, proving that
  environed space is not merely a backdrop in film scenes, but an active
  performing character. The substantial spectrum of opinions from
  contributing authors allows the reader to absorb the diverse
  relationships of architecture in cinema, inviting the reader to form
  their own opinions on the topic and inspiring a new way of thinking.
  Slicing Spaces explores the interconnected relationship between
  architecture and film via distinct approaches to spaces of the city,
  confinement, actuality, the psyche and the imagination. The book
  uncovers a path to look at lived spaces of architectural design from an
  alternative perspective, focusing on the authoritative contribution of
  architecture to the realm of filmmaking"-- Provided by publisher.
Identifiers: LCCN 2022013888 (print) | LCCN 2022013889 (ebook) | ISBN
  9781957792095 (hardback) | ISBN 9781957792101 (paperback) | ISBN
  9781957792118 (pdf)
Subjects: LCSH: Motion pictures and architecture. | Architecture in motion
  pictures. | Space (Architecture)--Psychological aspects.
Classification: LCC NA2588 .S55 2022 (print) | LCC NA2588 (ebook) | DDC
  720.1--dc23/eng/20220509
LC record available at https://lccn.loc.gov/2022013888
LC ebook record available at https://lccn.loc.gov/2022013889

Cover and Chapter Images Credit: Rebecca-Jane McConnell

To Nehir

To Loraine, Adrian, Max & Mark

TABLE OF CONTENTS

Spaces of Confinement:

Inside the Architecture Inside the Film

Spaces of the Psyche:

Psychology in Film Architecture

Spaces of the City:

Cinematic Urbanism in the Past, Present, and Future

Spaces of the Imagination:

Dystopian Cities and Fantastic Places in Film

Spaces of the Imagination:

The Affinity of Film and the Tangible

ACKNOWLEDGEMENTS

Many thanks to our contributors for their hard work. We would also like to thank our colleagues in Architecture at Queen's University Belfast as well as Dr. Jan Frohburg of University of Limerick. Special thanks go to our families who kindly put up with our long hours.

INTRODUCTION

The 125-Year Relationship between Architecture and Cinema

Rebecca-Jane McConnell and Gul Kacmaz Erk

As Jeff glares longingly out of his rear window, as Oh Dae-Su feels powerless in his longstanding prison cell, and as Kelvin slips in and out of lucidity in the Solaris Space Station, it is evident that these characters are shaped largely by the built environment. The films in question have a trail of directors and production designers whose vision was to manifest a setting that makes the viewer *feel* something: afraid, anxious, relieved, or tense. In Alfred Hitchcock's *Rear Window* (1954), Jeff observes a curation of colourfully-inhabited apartments, each one with a distinct sense of its occupant. In several scenes of the film, the photographer sits in position motionless, consumed with the observation of his neighbours. Similarly, the collection of colour, patterns, light, and careful positioning of objects in *Oldboy* (2003) has been systemised to project a feeling of unease. Although more violent in nature, the film follows a similar concept of containment of a person in an architectural space. Kris Kelvin is comparably trapped in *Solaris* (1972), with the characters suffering from paranoia and confusion in the space station's tight confines. People position their feelings, impulses, and deepest fears in buildings and human-made structures. As architect and writer Juhani Pallasmaa (2001) explains, someone who is scared of the dark has no logical reason to dread darkness; they are purely fearful of projecting their own thoughts and suppressed fantasies.

The chronicles of architecture, therefore, do not solely consist of conventional built (and unbuilt) structures; it also embraces the creations and depictions of architecture in their non-traditional forms. Performances of architecture can be found in painting, literature, theatre, fashion, video games, television, and certainly, film. Cinema was a ground-breaking innovation in the twentieth century, and one that changed the course of the arts forever; as film-architecture scholar Steven Jacobs (2013, 20) explains, "the medium of film has offered designers possibilities to create visionary buildings and utopian cities that could not be built in reality." Starting with Georges Méliès's *A Trip to the Moon* (1902) in the first decade of cinema, the preliminary instinct was to document everything. This manifested in two distinct trends: the city and urban living. These movements ran parallel to one another, and unveiled ways in which architecture and the real world could be represented in film.

Two decades later, visual artists Charles Sheeler and Paul Strand created *Manhatta* (1921) in which architecture performs in a different way. This culturally-significant documentary depicts the borough of Manhattan as its subject, with each shot framing a different perspective of the neighbourhood's urban life. The eleven-minute film has an objective of emphasising the scale of the dense borough of New York City and the imposing monumentality of skyscrapers, as designer and researcher Cecilia Mouat (2014, 22) describes, "people walking in front of a façade where the scale of the building's windows miniaturize people; or a high-angle camera with foreground composed by a solid balustrade that suggests at the distance, a street full of cars, moving like ants." It was thus from the beginning that the interconnected and interdependent relationship of film and architecture was formed.

The architect and the filmmaker draw many parallels; architecture critic Mark Lamster (2000) emphasises that the two professions demand bravery and resolution to allow the creator to impose their personal vision onto the world. However, the marrying of the two is a relationship that is sometimes ignored. When thinking of influential participants in film production, set design is often overlooked, which to an elementary extent provides the background and setting to complement the narrative of the film. At a deeper level, the set, be it a real place or in a studio, distinguishes characters and their psychology, along with setting the atmosphere of a scene. Elements such as lighting, sound, and placement of objects and camera all contribute to production design, fashioning a sense of place with their ambience, inducing emotions of terror, admiration, joy, sadness, or anger (Bergfelder et al, 2007). In fact, some filmmakers, such as 'master of suspense' Alfred Hitchcock, have debated that the setting is the most important aspect of a scene (Paglia, 1998). The architectural setting of not only film, but everyday life, can arguably become the most influential aspect of human existence.

Soviet filmmaker and theorist Dziga Vertov coined the term 'Kino-Eye' in the 1920s. Also known as Cine-Eye, this is a film technique, which Vertov described as a method of capturing what was inaccessible to the naked eye (Hicks, 2007). His aim was to depict and express the emotions of the society by using the camera as a more flawless tool than the human eye. The orchestration of this method opened up a whole new realm of possibilities, further diversifying and crystallising the relationship of film and the built environment, as can be observed in his *Man with a Movie Camera* (1929).

By forming an alliance with directors, production designers have been fabricating spaces that stimulate the viewer, encouraging them to enter a realm of fantasy. When watching a film, the viewer naturally empathises with that scenario. The set is designed to strategically encourage their empathy to take over – perhaps it reminds people of a childhood home, a negative work environment, or a feeling of joy or shame. Architectural theorist Robert Mugerauer speaks of how people can use these expressions of life through artwork as a reflective tool, and how to look back at the event in retrospect and assess reactions and decisions. He states:

> We can learn, then, from artworks that witness what also has happened to other people in other times and places and that, whether actual or imaginary, open a realm for us to reflect [...] on [how] what is given in testimony [...] bears on our own lives (Mugerauer 2015, 17).

Reflecting back to the nineteenth-century theories of art critic John Ruskin, architectural theorist Katherine Shonfield (2000, 8) argues in her book, *Walls Have Feelings: Architecture, Film and the City*, that an architect has the chance to be moral with their structures, stating, "the architect has a choice between an aesthetic of hiding, covering up how the building is put together, and one of revealing it." She describes architectural structures as potentially pure and honest, speaking with almost anthropomorphic adjectives. It is with such descriptions that the emotion and personalisation of a building come into play in film: a building is not just a building; it is a character in both the real world and the fictional one.

In cinema, architecture is used as a tool to express emotion and opinion on the scene. As Jacobs (2013, 10) enlightens, "Screen architecture demonstrates the ways people have put meaning on the notions of home, domestic culture, public spaces, landscapes, monuments, the difference between inside and outside, and so forth." The setting is orchestrated to provoke a sensation in the viewer; it is done in a sophisticated manner that alludes to the senses. He continues that architecture can express opinions and feelings through buildings shown on screen. It is with this method that some of the most prominent film scenes of all time have taken advantage of the architecture surrounding them. Oliver Stone's *World Trade Center* (2006) is about the survival of the mind, rather than the catastrophic obliteration of skyscrapers. This follows the emotional journey of selected families surrounding the 9/11 disaster, and explores the relationship between buildings and people, and the blurred lines between real life and the cinematic performance of architecture. This portrayal of the historical event is depicted as a private journey with the background noise of additional characters, and even the event itself is omitted. The twin towers are only seen briefly on screen, even though the story surrounding them is the focus of the storyline, as discussed by architecture-film scholar Merrill Schleier eight years later in *Skyscraper Cinema* (2009).

In this context, this book is organised into five sections, each questioning and exploring one aspect of the relationship between architecture and cinema, from the use of the interior to strolling an entire city, from the perception of the suburban dweller to the view of the cinemagoer, and from actual spaces to imaginary environments. The reader is led on a journey weaving through the horrors of Hitchcock, the fantastical imagery of Wes Anderson, and a more tangible city symphony of modern Berlin, which makes the performance of architecture visible by slicing spaces framed in films. Ultimately, the aim of this edited collection is to investigate and generate novel understandings of the perennial intertwined marriage of architecture and film. It hopes to spark debates around the analysis of film from an architectural point of view and celebrates the beauty in the unification of these two art forms.

Spaces of Confinement: Inside the Architecture Inside the Film

In the first section of the book, **Blayne Fulton** aims to prove that the settings in Andrei Tarkovsky's *Solaris* (1972) are used to provoke and convey feelings to the audience through architectonic space by analysing the city, library, home, and objects of the home such as paintings and mirrors. The rooms portrayed in the film are filled with symbolism and detail. They are imbued with a poetic quality rarely seen in cinema.

The investigation draws parallels with the writing of **Christopher Rooney**, who investigates the importance of the unacknowledged corridor. In both cinema and architecture, corridors often go unappreciated; in cinema their scenes are often the first to be cut and left on the cutting room floor, but these long and unseemly spaces are essential to film and architecture, and for more than just the obvious reasons. Corridors, along with other seemingly insignificant elements of architecture, have the power to either ground a film in reality, or push it beyond the realms of all possibility and expectation. This exploration proves the importance of the corridor in architecture and in film and that corridors should be investigated and seen, not ignored.

One can argue that the protagonist in *Truman Show* (1998) is directly influenced by his surroundings. **Matthew McGibbon** looks at this fake utopian world, created specifically for Truman Burbank, questioning the reality of perfect suburban life. Truman has a deep fear of water, which is mainly due to his scripted cast mates insisting his father died at sea. This confines Truman even more to his places of daily routine in the same house, streets, and office. The film draws parallels between the cardboard scenery of the island town of Seahaven and the phony life of Truman. In turn, it analyses his psyche to discover if there is a correlation between the demise of his sanity and the involuntary containment he has experienced his whole life.

In *Spaces of Confinement*, the authors focus on the performance of architecture as a vessel; in other words, a space that can contain or ensnare a person. As demonstrated in these chapters, this is not necessarily limited to a small interior, as in macro scales such as the city, one can also feel trapped. The text probes a selection of films that demonstrate characters that are heavily influenced by their confines.

Spaces of the Psyche: Psychology in Film Architecture

Film portrays complex stories through a language which is expressive, has emotional impact, and resonates in memory. **Cliona Brady** probes the elements of this immersive medium, asking if it can be used to portray the psychological state of a character through occupying and engaging with the space they inhabit. What is shown on screen is selected for its atmospheric qualities or its symbolic significance to a character's psychological condition. The storytelling structure of film also provides an accessibility, which renders it an appropriate medium to communicate the significance that architectural space can have in people's daily lives. It takes them directly into the intimate and subjective way a character inhabits space.

Rebecca-Jane McConnell also looks at the psyche, attempting to identify the psychological fusion between a person and their environment. She examines how the idea is introduced in selected Alfred Hitchcock films, influencing the viewer's perception and emotions of the screen. Architectural surroundings can trigger emotion. Environment creates a certain subconscious nostalgia, positive or negative, leaving an imprint on the experiencer. When this type of architecture is applied, it can take on a personality. The building or context becomes not just another element in the backdrop, but an actual character.

Jack Torrance is strongly influenced by his architectural milieu. **Hayden Allen** explores *The Shining* (1980), and how it weaves gestures of claustrophobia and cabin fever at The Overlook Hotel in the Southern Rocky Mountains. The hotel poses as a vessel for psychological torture for the writer, his wife, and five-year-old son over the winter months. Jack suffers from irritability, lethargy, and hallucinations while trapped in this isolated and compressed environment. In this film, the hotel becomes a character rather than a backdrop or set. With its confusing layout, the lodging is not easy to figure out for the viewer. Alongside his filmic investigation, Hayden also carries out a personal experiential study of abandoned spaces, examining the role of fear in the day-to-day routine, its effect on everyday life, and how it may corrupt perspective of space.

Psychological condition is a prominent theme in this and other chapters in *Spaces of the Psyche*, relating to filmmaking and the design of interior spaces. This section speaks about the main characters and the spaces they inhabit, causing magnified consciousness of the rooms, homes, and workplaces in question. A series of vacant, anonymous, dark, or even lively spaces are analysed to lead the spectator on an intimate passage, showing the subjective and instinctive way in which a character inhabits or occupies a space.

Spaces of the City: Cinematic Urbanism in the Past, Present and Future

Berlin: Symphony of a Great City (1927) pioneers avant-garde cinematic techniques to capture and represent urban life on screen. In his chapter, **Ciaran Magee** argues that, although there is no conventional story structure, as the day goes by from dusk to dawn, *Berlin Symphony* presents the viewer with a series of "intertwining fragmented images of the urban landscape," depicting a city progressing towards modernity (Penz and Lu 2011, 10). These fragments are merged together as a whole, representing vivid recollections and memories of a city. It is through the idea of cinematic memory that we see films such as *Berlin Symphony* beyond a piece of media, but also as a relic capturing the city's spirit. Films have historically been one of the most important mediums exhibiting the spaces of the city.

As displayed in all areas of this book, cities usually become actual characters in films, rather than simple backgrounds. There is a vast range of studies on the cinematic representations of the built environment and their role in the narrative, but **Ece Sila Bora**'s study particularly focuses on the real locations in the city of Belfast and their representation in cinema. Belfast and its surroundings have been highly valued as film locations because of the city's growing film industry, nationally and internationally, in recent years. It has a unique potential that allows a retrospective discussion.

Gul Kacmaz Erk analyses the future noir environment of Alex Proyas' *Dark City* (1998) from a spatial perspective. This science fiction film puts forth questions about the construction process of a city. The aliens in the film constantly alter each street, building, and room to create the right environment for humans to dwell. These 'strangers' believe that they need to study humans in their authentic spaces to understand human nature. Using bits and pieces of people's memories, they reconstruct a worldless city. On another note, architect and theorist Christian Norberg-Schulz identifies four elements of space: physical, perceptual, existential, and conceptual, and the chapter revolves around these concepts.

Spaces of the City focuses on the physical and emotional interactions people have with the urban landscape. In recent years, the city has prevailed as the choice of residence for the majority of people worldwide. Accordingly, location films shot in an urban setting have more presence in contemporary film history. This section therefore looks at the point where film meets the city, and their ongoing relationship since 1895.

Spaces of the Imagination: Dystopian Cities and Fantastic Places in Film

In *Blade Runner* (1982) Ridley Scott illustrates how atmosphere and cityscape play in unison to represent a particular setting on the big screen. **Cormac McAteer** looks at how the film builds upon dystopian themes and environments, based in an imagined future of Los Angeles. The city has an aura of doom and yet is filled with bright lights; it is busy and yet abandoned, flourishing with technologies and yet decaying. This complex topic belongs solely to cinema, the city, and the imagination. This chapter —and section— seeks to explore how and why real architecture is imperative to the portrayal of a dark, ominous, dystopian world, and what it means for a society outside the screen.

Andrew Bryce studies this milestone film from a different angle, to unfold the influence and ideologies of postmodernism in architecture, and its paralleled exploration through film. Postmodernity and its influence on architectural theory is discussed via the literature review of critical sources. The postmodern city is examined initially through an understanding of the voices and motivating forces that gave rise to this stylistic movement in the late 1970s. The style is further examined by research of its repercussions in the perception of city space and its potential to influence social structure. This underlying study is supported and referenced by a case study of the urban and architectural aesthetics and narratives of the original *Blade Runner* (1982). The retrofitted future city is examined through a top-down approach of filmic analysis, from urban hierarchy to the ornament of interior space; cinematography and *mise-en-scène* are decoded into a reading of the postmodern future city.

Liam Corcoran examines the work of Wes Anderson, best known for his quirky, brightly coloured, symmetrical films. The Texan director started a renaissance in modern American cinema in the twenty-first century, inspiring a new wave of young filmmakers showing how diverse and creative one can be when designing a film. With a patent knowledge of spatial logic, Anderson presents his cinema through meticulous set design, cinematography, and ensemble of reappearing actors. This chapter cuts to the core of Anderson's cinema to show how much of an influence architecture has to play in his films.

Meanwhile, **Lara Clifford** looks at another larger-than-life director, Hayao Miyazaki and Studio Ghibli through cultural context, conflict with nature and emotional presence. Her work explores the development of the studio, the films, and eventually of the museum as a tactile, real life example encapsulating the spirit of their ethos. This chapter strives to establish the frames of reference that are the driving force through which Miyazaki conceptualises his architecture – his childhood, background, and his passions. References are made to the extensive work of Susan Napier in documenting his life, while drawing on Miyazaki's own writings in an attempt to understand what shaped his architectural view.

Spaces of the Imagination argues that architecture has always had a relationship with fantasy and science fiction. Since the silent era, architecture is often the main feature in these genres, with strong imagery deployed to depict the unimaginable and unfathomable. The purposeful performance of architecture has cemented notions of utopia and dystopia through the cinematic lens. The approach, in this section, is examined through research of its repercussions in the perception of city space, along with its potential to impact and inspire social structure.

Spaces of Actuality: The Affinity of Film and the Tangible

This section can be portrayed as a study into the physical relationship of film and architecture. Both share multiple similarities, such as the employment of space, time, framing, and light. Themes within this section include movement, narrative, character, and perception of space. It focuses less on the spatial analysis of film, and more on actual spaces, both indoor and outdoor, alongside their relationship to film. This appears in the form of, for instance, experiencing a place via the human eye versus the lens of the film camera, or researching historical cinema buildings. Ultimately, this section demonstrates how film can be utilised to present, analyse, and transform space.

Spaces of Actuality looks to explore the affiliation of architecture and film in an experiential manner. It attracts discussions on neighbourhoods, towns, and cities, and their changeable liaison with the screen. It offers film as a medium that critically analyses complex environments, assessing spatial qualities and the influence of media. **Daniel Savage** looks in particular at how skateboarders perceive the space they inhabit. They see the city as a pleasure ground and a place for the expression of energy, movement, and representation. They are concerned with addressing the physical architecture of the city and responding to this with a dynamic presence.

Antoine Trallero-Mindan develops arguments to support the preservation of heritage buildings in a sustainable way, with a specific analysis of movie palaces. The preservation of this heritage is treated as its influence on the surroundings and the urban scale of the city, not only as the architecture of the building itself.

Clarissa Moore aims to give a more in-depth understanding of the design process of set design, and how set designs can be created using architectural techniques. The use of techniques such as orthographic drawings and models are studied as methods to develop these concepts into a final form.

Fergal Rainey focuses on the 'curious case' of Berlin and the undesirable hereditament created by the fall of the Third Reich and the Nazi Party in Germany after World War II. Through a cinematic methodology, these snapshots inform our understanding, over space and time, of Berlin in relation to undesirable hereditament.

In *Slicing Spaces*, architecture is a performer that portrays emotion, nostalgia, and even fantasy in film. This introduction explains how the book has been structured to proceed from inquiry at a small scale (dealing with confinement and psychoanalysis), to large scale (looking at the city and imagination), with wavering levels of both in-between. As such, the book attempts to provide a systematic format to the analysis of a broad, abiding, and complex relationship of architecture and film.

The book presents the authors' work accompanied by visual representations. Architecture and film both rely heavily on a strong visual culture, meaning these illustrations are imperative to explaining the message behind the text. The book also employs observation and critique through drawings and film still analysis. This allows the reader to use their gaze as part of the communication of ideas, while also developing a further level of examination and critique on the subject. Accordingly, a series of analytical drawings, diagrams, storyboards, film stills, and experiential photographs feature in the book as a creative and performative style of communication. Fittingly, the book makes use of visual analysis, appreciating that the fields of both architecture and cinema rely inordinately on ocular representation and reasoning. The use of graphical illustrations as a supplementary form of investigation not only makes this book pleasant to look at, but it adds an extra dimension of critical thinking to the overall outlook.

This book is an architectural filmic investigation that will peak the interest of professionals within these fields, and also people with an avocational interest. It brings together films from diverse genres, and varying timelines from 1927 to 2015, and connects each in a specific way through recurring themes. Accordingly, it targets a range of readers from divergent age groups, prompting the reader to track down films they have not watched previously. *Slicing Spaces* exhibits the meaningful connection of the analyses found, and furthermore, shows the power of architecture's performance in the cinematic world. The text emphasises how their relationship is a robust one, and takes into consideration not only the obvious contributing factors, such as built environment and composition, but hidden ones too, such as the realm of the psyche. This book will be an effective tool for students, professionals, academics, and people with a general interest in architecture and film. In this way, it is hoped that it will continue to be a useful publication well into the future.

REFERENCES

Books and Articles

BERGFELDER, TIM, HARRIS, SUE, and STREET, SARAH, (2007) *Film a Architecture and the Transitional Imagination: Set Design in the 1930s European Cinema*, 1st edn., Amsterdam: Amsterdam University Press.

BROOKES, XAN, (2012) 'Shining a light inside Room 237', *The Guardian*, [online] Available at: https://www.theguardian.com/film/2012/oct/18/inside-room-237-the-shining (Accessed: October 2020)

HICKS, JEREMY, (2007) *Dziga Vertov: Defining Documentary Film*, 1st edn., London: I.B. Tauris.

JACOBS, STEVEN, (2013) *The Wrong House: The Architecture of Alfred Hitchcock*, 1st edn., Rotterdam: Nai010 Publishers.

KOECK, RICHARD, (2013) *Cine-scapes: Cinematic Spaces in Architecture and Cities*, 1st edn., London: Routledge.

KUHN, ANNETTE, (1999) *Alien Zone II: The Spaces of Science Fiction Cinema*, 1st edn., London: Verso.

LAMSTER, MARK, (2000) *Architecture and Film*, 1st edn., New York: Princeton Architectural Press.

MOUAT, CECILIA, ROCKWOOD, DAVID., and SARVIMAKI, MARJA., (2014) *Including Film Analysis to Investigate History of Design. Beyond Architecture, New Connections and Intersections*, 1st edn., Honolulu: ARCC/EAAE.

MUGERAUER, ROBERT, (2015) *Responding to Loss: Heideggerian Reflections on Literature, Architecture, and Film*, 1st edn., New York: Fordham University Press.

NEUMANN, DIETRICH, (1996) *Film Architecture: Set Designs from Metropolis to Blade Runner*, 1st edn., Prestel Publishing.

PAGLIA, CAMILLE, (1998) *The Birds*, 1st edn., London: BFI Publishing.

PALLASMAA, JUHANI, (2001) *The Architecture of Image: Existential Space in Cinema*, 1st edn., Rakennustieto Publishing.

PALLASMAA, JUHANI, (2012) 'The Existential Image: Lived Space and Architecture.' *Phainomenon*, (25), 157 – 173 [online]. Available at: http://phainomenon-journal.pt/index.php/phainomenon/article/view/327 (Accessed: October 2020)

PENZ, FRANCOIS, and LU, ANDONG. eds. (2011) *Urban Cinematics*, 1st edn., Bristol: Intellect.

SCHLEIER, MERRILL, (2009) *Skyscraper Cinema: Architecture and Gender in American Film*, 1st edn., Minneapolis: University of Minnesota Press.

SHONFIELD, KATHERINE, (2000) *Walls Have Feelings: Architecture, Film, and the City*, 1st edn., London; New York; Routledge.

Filmography

2001: A Space Odyssey (1968) Film. Directed by – Stanley Kubrick. [DVD] USA: Stanley Kubrick Studios.

28 Days Later (2002) Film. Directed by – Danny Boyle. [DVD] UK: Fox Searchlight Pictures.

Alien (1979) Film. Directed by – Ridley Scott. [DVD] USA: 20th Century Fox.

Berlin: Symphony of a Great City (1927) Film. Directed by – Walter Ruttmann. [DVD] Weimar Republic: Fox Film Corporation (US)

Blade Runner (1982) Film. Directed by – Ridley Scott. [DVD] USA: Warner Bros.

Castle in the Sky (1986) Film. Directed by – Hayao Miyazaki. [DVD] Japan: Toei Company.

The Darjeeling Limited (2007) Film. Directed by – Wes Anderson. [DVD] USA: Fox Searchlight Pictures.

Dark City (1998) Film. Directed by – Alex Proyas. [DVD] USA: New Line Cinema.

Fantastic Mr. Fox (2009) Film. Directed by – Wes Anderson. [DVD] USA: 20th Century Fox.

Hitchcock (2012) Film. Directed by - Sacha Gervasi. [DVD] USA: Fox Searchlight Pictures.

Hitchcock/Truffaut (2015) Film. Directed by - Kent Jones. [DVD] Cannes: Cohen Media Group.

High Rise (2015) Film. Directed by – Ben Wheatley. [DVD] UK: StudioCanal.

The Life Aquatic with Steve Zissou (2004) Film. Directed by – Wes Anderson. [DVD] USA: Buena Vista Pictures.

Memento (2000) Film. Directed by – Christopher Nolan. [DVD] USA: Newmarket.

Mon Oncle (1958) Film. Directed by – Jacques Tati. [DVD] France: Gaumont.

Moonrise Kingdom (2012) Film. Directed by – Wes Anderson. [DVD] USA: Focus Features.

Oldboy (2003) Film. Directed by – Park Chan-Wook. [DVD] South Korea: Show East.

Ponyo (2008) Film. Directed by – Hayao Miyazaki. [DVD] Japan: Toho.

Psycho (1960) Film. Directed by - Alfred Hitchcock. [DVD] USA: Universal Pictures.

Rear Window (1954) Film. Directed by - Alfred Hitchcock. [DVD] USA: Universal Pictures.

Rebecca (1940) Film. Directed by - Alfred Hitchcock. [DVD] USA: Anchor Bay Entertainment.

Rope (1948) Film. Directed by - Alfred Hitchcock. [DVD] USA: Universal Pictures.

The Royal Tenenbaums (2001) Film. Directed by – Wes Anderson. [DVD] USA: Buena Vista Pictures.

Rushmore (1998) Film. Directed by – Wes Anderson. [DVD] USA: Buena Vista Pictures.

The Shining (1980) Film. Directed by – Stanley Kubrick. [DVD] USA: Warner Bros.

Singin' in the Rain (1952) Film. Directed by - Gene Kelly, Stanley Donen. [DVD] USA: Warner Home Video.

Solaris (1972) Film. Directed by - Andrei Tarkovsky. [DVD] New York: The Criterion Collection, 2011.

The Sound of Hitchcock (2008) Documentary. Directed by - Gary Leva. [online] Vimeo: https://vimeo. com/143186463.

Total Recall (1990) Film. Directed by – Paul Verhoeven. [DVD] USA: TriStar Pictures.

Trainspotting (1996) Film. Directed by – Danny Boyle. [DVD] UK: PolyGram Filmed Entertainment.

The Truman Show (1998) Film. Directed by – Peter Weir. [DVD] USA: Paramount Pictures.

SPACES OF
CONFINEMENT

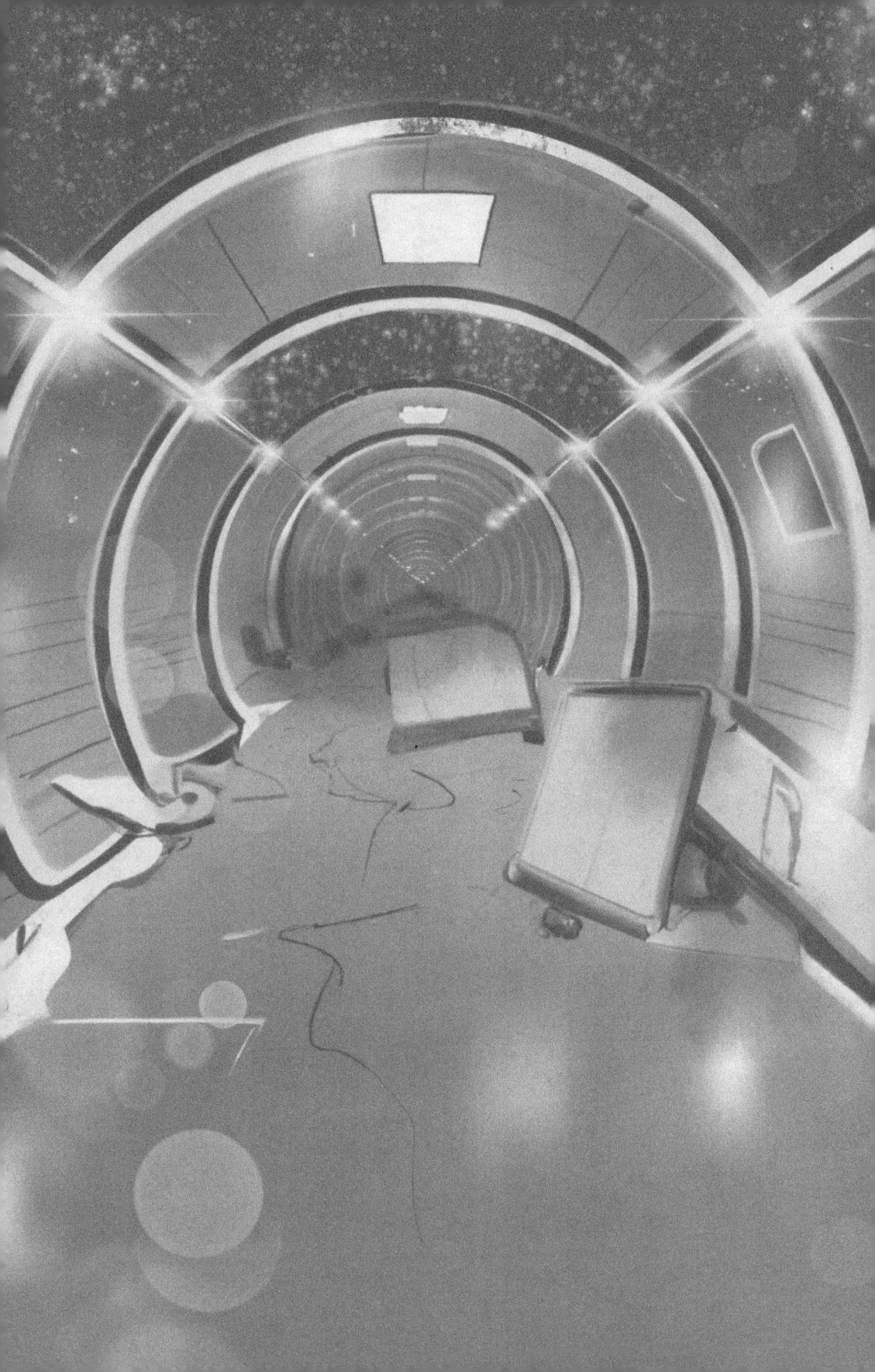

Cinematic and Architectonic Space: Tarkovsky's *Solaris*

Blayne Fulton

BLAYNE FULTON received his Bachelor of Science and Master of Architecture degrees at Queen's University Belfast and previously worked as an architectural assistant in Bucharest, Romania. His Masters dissertation, *Sensing Architecture in Space—Solaris*, was written under the supervision of Dr. Gul Kacmaz Erk and focused on the relationship between cinema and architectural space.

Architecture plays an important role in the films of the Russian film-maker Andrei Tarkovsky, which are widely considered to be some of the most important films of the twentieth century. Architecture in these films is no mere backdrop set, as it defines the atmosphere of a space and the memory of a place. *Solaris* (1972), which is based on a science-fiction novel by Polish writer Stanislaw Lem, published in 1961, is Tarkovsky's third film. In this film, the director confronts universal ideas such as the nature of love, memory, dreams, mortality, perception, and reality. In this chapter, we look at how the settings in *Solaris* are used to provoke and convey feelings to the audience through 'architectural images' (Pallasmaa, 2007, 7) in five categories of 'cinematic and architectonic space,' including outer-space, inner-space, city, home, and library. The primary aim is to gain a better understanding of the link between the art forms of architecture and cinema.

Solaris is an anomaly among Tarkovsky's other films in that the majority of the film's action takes place in an enclosed constructed set. Rarely do Tarkovsky spaces exert so much control over the actors' movements within a meticulously designed and detailed set. Most of his films take place in existing landscapes with the actors and the director free to improvise with their setting (Ibid, 8). This is one of the reasons why we have chosen to analyse this film in terms of its architectural settings.

Most of the film takes place on a research space station orbiting a planet known as Solaris. The team aboard the station have been analysing the planet's ocean and its atmosphere, but have barely made any progress with their studies. Most of the team have been suffering from emotional breakdowns of various sorts. Psychologist Kris Kelvin from Earth is sent to the Solaris Station to investigate the mental states of the research crew. The station's personnel consists of three scientists, Dr. Gibarian, Dr. Snaut, and Dr. Sartorius. The ocean on the planet has caused each of them to be called upon by a 'Visitor' or guest, which is a materialised being created from their memories, thoughts, and feelings of someone on Earth. Each Visitor exists as a living reflection of the individual crew member's subconscious.

Figure 1

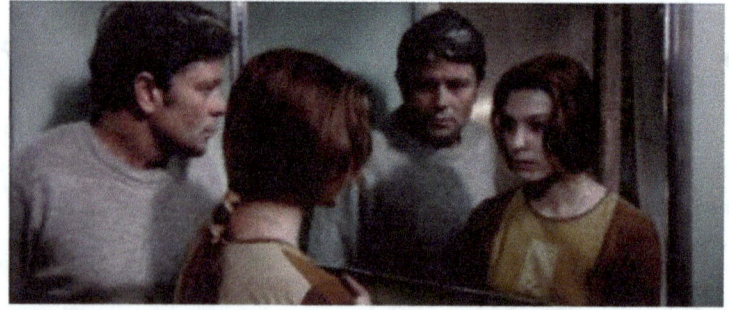

Upon Kelvin's arrival at the space station, it is clear that Dr. Gibarian has committed suicide, but under mysterious circumstances. During the rotation of the space station around Solaris, the fluctuations in the planet's ocean cause Kelvin to begin hallucinating about his dead wife Hari (Fig. 1). She appears as a physical manifestation of Kelvin's perceived memory of her and his feelings of guilt surrounding her death.

While science-fiction is often adopted by directors to explore ideas about the possible future, Tarkovsky, similar to Stanley Kubrick in *2001: A Space Odyssey* (1968), uses the genre to explore deeper ideas which would not usually be confronted in realistic stories on screen, "Both the Eastern European Lem and Tarkovsky were critical of what they saw as Western science-fiction's shallowness and wanted to invest the form with intellectual and emotional depth" (Lopate, 2011, 11).

Outer Space

"We place our feelings, desires and fears in buildings. A person who is afraid of the dark has no factual reason to fear darkness as such; he is afraid of his own imagination, or more precisely of the contents that his repressed fantasy may project into the darkness" (Pallasmaa, 2007, 31). The terms 'claustrophobia' and 'cabin fever' are related, and the latter is referenced in Kubrick's film *The Shining* (1980). The dictionary definition of claustrophobia is an "abnormal dread of being in closed or narrow spaces" (merriam-webster.com). This makes it clear why enclosed spaces are particularly suited to horror and science-fiction films, where characters often suffer from delusions or hallucinations while trapped in confined or vast spaces. The term 'cabin fever' is referred to at the beginning of *The Shining* by the hotel manager as a prelude to the events that follow, and Oxford Dictionaries (oxforddictionaries.com) define it as "lassitude, irritability, and similar symptoms resulting from long confinement or isolation indoors during the winter".

In *Solaris*, each of the characters suffer from aspects of paranoia and confusion within the tight confines of a space station. This is characteristic of many films set in outer-space, such as Ridley Scott's *Alien* (1979). Claustrophobic spaces in film are often depicted as spaces enclosed or enveloped by an element of nature like snow or rain. These spaces are often characterised by long corridors, with seemingly endless corners and tight living quarters. The spaces of claustrophobia are especially suited to characters who suffer from a fear of small spaces. The architecture of claustrophobia can be seen in many buildings depicted in horror films such as The Overlook Hotel in *The Shining*, which narrates the story of a family trapped within the snow covered mountain hotel, and in Outpost 31 of John Carpenter's *The Thing* (1982), which is set in an isolated research station. In both films, the inhabitants are cut off by snow in isolated regions of the world. In *The Thing*, Carpenter established himself as a master of using the tight framing of both the camera and perimeter darkness of the walls of a room to increase tension. As in Alfred Hitchcock films, the claustrophobic rooms of *The Thing* are emptied of their emotional content, which allows them to be filled with terror (Pallasmaa, 2007, 27).

This type of claustrophobic space is also characteristic of science-fiction films where a story is set on a spaceship enveloped by outer-space. Notable examples of this genre are *2001*, where a group of astronauts are trapped under the control of a deviant computer known as HAL, and *Alien* which contains similar themes, such as out of control artificial-intelligence and a spaceship which contains numerous rooms of claustrophobia. These rooms include a huge cathedral-like hanger and tight air vents where the alien creature is hiding. There is also an obvious analogy between outer-space and the ocean, which means that there are films set underwater that exhibit claustrophobic spaces, notably Wolfgang Petersen's film *Das Boot* (1981) and James Cameron's *The Abyss* (1989). These are often spaces designed for practicality rather than for occupants to live in and are characterised by narrow corridors filled with pipes and machinery.

Inner-Space

The renowned Japanese director Akira Kurosawa was invited on a rare visit around the set of *Solaris* in 1971; here he describes the set of the space station with wonder (2011, 14):

> [T]he space station was an incredibly expensive, very detailed set, made out of thick duralumin. The cold metallic light was gleaming in silver, red, blue and green beams intricately blinked and twisted from the lights of the various gauges lined up in a row. And above that ran two duralumin rails, from which hung a camera on small wheels, completely free to move about the entire space station set.

Tarkovsky worked closely with his art director, Mikhail Romadin, in creating the set for the space station. Romadin produced a series of paintings that formed the basis of which sets were built, while working closely with engineers and other specialists. It is remarkable how similar Romadin's original artwork is to the final set which was eventually built (2011):

We began working on Solaris, at first we didn't know how it was going to look. They even gave me a subscription to an American science magazine. But science was not for me. I am an artist. I proceed from aesthetics. I think of something – let's say a mobile. Then it's the scientist's job to make it work. And that is how we proceeded.

It was important for Tarkovsky and Romadin that the technology in the film did not overtake the relationship between Hari and Kelvin portrayed on screen. But it was also important for the space station to contrast with the nostalgic Earth scenes. In the film, it is clear that the science-fiction element is only a backdrop to the human story at its centre.

We know Tarkovsky had seen Kubrick's *2001*, and disliked it as cold and sterile. The media played up the cold-war angle of the Soviet director's determination to make an 'anti-*2001*,' and certainly Tarkovsky used more intensely individual characters and a more passionate human drama at the centre than Kubrick. Still, hindsight allows us to observe that the two masterworks are more cousins than opposites. Both set up their narratives in a leisurely, languid manner, spending considerable time tracking around the space sets. Both films employ a wide-screen *mise-en-scène* approach that draws on superior art direction, and both generate an air of mystery that invites countless explanations (Lopate, 2011, 8).

There are similarities to how Tarkovsky depicted the space station in *Solaris* and how Kubrick depicted the spaceship Discovery One in *2001*. Both are dominated by the primary shape of a circle with interiors designed as circular sets to reveal the idea of centrifugal motion. More importantly, they reveal aspects of the characters' actions and thoughts. With *2001*, Kubrick uses the spaceship similarly to how he uses the vast hotel soundstage sets in *The Shining* as an endless maze that reflects the characters' repetitive daily routines; most famously, the tracking shot following an astronaut jogging like a hamster trapped in a cage.

Similarly, the long narrow corridors in *Solaris* make it impossible for Kelvin to witness what awaits him around corners (Fig. 2). This lack of visibility gives the station a claustrophobic quality similar to the circular 'hamster's wheel' corridor of *2001*. It is particularly suited to the atmosphere of confusion and paranoia among the occupants of the station when Kelvin arrives. All of the rooms and corridors in the space station (except the library) have vertically concave walls (Fig. 3). This gives the feeling that the walls are pressing in on the inhabitants. Similar to how the tight submarine set in *Das Boot*, where confined spaces create the illusion of deep sea pressure, there is the atmosphere that outer-space is exerting pressure on the inner-space of the Solaris Space Station, and this gives the audience a sense of isolation in the research crew's current situation.

Figure 2   Figure 3

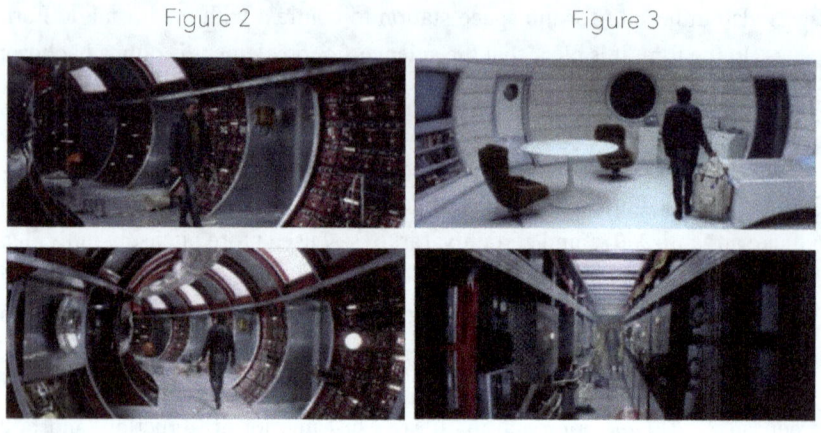

Figure 4   Figure 5

The influence of Rembrandt's painting technique can be seen in many of Tarkovsky's films in terms of light and darkness. E.H. Gombrich (1960, 73) notes that Rembrandt paintings "provide an astounding object lesson in reliance on dark tones and subdued contrasts." This is an apt description of many subdued naturally-lit scenes in *Solaris*. Tarkovsky's use of perspective and symmetry, on the other hand, was directly influenced by his admiration for the work of early-Renaissance painters (Hughes, 1991, 17):

> Perspective is a form of abstraction. It simplifies the relationship between eye, brain and object. It is an ideal view, imagined as being seen by a one-eyed motionless person who is clearly detached from what he sees. It makes a god of the spectator, who becomes the person on whom the whole world converges.

In *Solaris*, the camera often pans ninety degrees following a character from a wide ratio of a concave corridor (Fig. 4) to an adjacent corridor symmetrically showing the machinery within the walls of the space station (Fig. 5). The wide aspect ratio 2.35:1 of the film images in *Solaris* (which is the same as *2001*) is used well to make the corridors feel more circular and enclosing (to the audience) than they would seem to feel in reality. This adds to the overall claustrophobic atmosphere of the film and gives the sense that Kelvin is constantly being watched or followed along corridors and around corners. It gives the impression to the audience that they are not aware of the space behind the scene being revealed on screen.

> For science fiction writers and directors, the dome was the ideal metaphor for a world blind to the realities of the outside (as well as, in some cases, a viable solution for future living). Inside the dome, the city becomes a giant, multi-levelled American-style mall, bathed in constant artificial light, with vast gardens and a network of tube-style monorails. (Mahleb, 2005)

In Lem's (1991, 45) novel of Solaris, the space station is described as a dome: "I was at the summit of the Station, beneath the actual shell of the superstructure; the walls were concave and sloping, with oblong windows a few yards apart". The space station, like all buildings which provoke claustrophobic feelings, acts like a miniature city or doll's house with endless corridors acting like streets.

In *Solaris*, the space station's endless maze of circular rooms reveal to us the protagonist Kelvin's limitless love and memory of his dead wife, "I was going around in circles; there seemed to be no escape" (Ibid, 56). Even the 'room of knowledge', the space station's library, is depicted as an oak panelled circular space. This creates an atmosphere which often disorientates the viewer into losing a grasp of spatial awareness and time passing. In the same way, as Kelvin loses his grasp of reality, his obsession grows. Through the course of the film, the viewer, like the on screen character of Kelvin, becomes lost in the familiarity of the circular maze made up of non-existent corners to escape around.

City

*The image is not a certain meaning, expressed by the director, but the entire
world reflected as in a drop of water.*
Andrei Tarkovsky

J.G. Ballard (2008, 36) refers to: "The endless landscape of concrete and structural steel that extended from the motorways." Tarkovsky's depiction of the
'city of the future' in *Solaris* is effective but minimal compared to other
visions of the future we have seen in, for instance, Ridley Scott's *Blade Runner*
(1982), with its cyberpunk imagery evocative of a neon, street level Tokyo or
Hong Kong. In *Solaris*, Tarkovsky uses footage of a motorway (Fig. 6) in Aka-
saka and Iikura in Tokyo, Japan. While we do not get the level of detail seen in
other science-fiction films, it is a highly successful way to show the future using
the continuous lines of cars driving along a motorway (Fig. 7).

Many 'future' scenes in films usually are evoked by constant rain, loud airborne
noises, and the continuous movement of public transport. Science-fiction films
often reveal the future as a place where time speeds up and still moments of
tranquillity do not exist. "I had the extraordinary feeling that all these cars were
gathering for some special reason I didn't understand. There seemed to be ten
times as much traffic" (Ibid, 56). Tarkovsky's vision of the 'city of the future'
evokes images of Ballard's realist, science-fiction novel *Crash*, which deals
with the influence of twentieth century technology on the human psyche. The
night time, neon images in *Solaris* of endless streams of traffic recall this passage in Ballard's novel, where the wheelchair-bound protagonist obsessively
observes traffic flowing from a London airport after being involved in a near
fatal car accident. "I gazed down at this immense motion sculpture, whose traffic deck seemed almost higher that the balcony rail" (Ballard, 2008, 36).

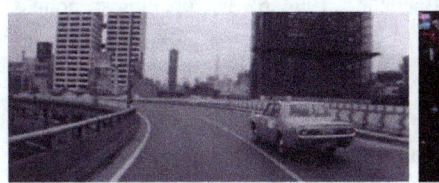
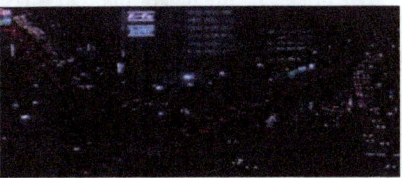

Figure 6   Figure 7

During the 1970s and 1980s, Tokyo was the one city in the world where the amount of technology being used every day surpassed even the public's image of the future. "In his haunting shots of freeways, Tarkovsky disdains from showing anything but contemporary cars, just as the French film-maker Jean-Luc Godard did with the buildings in *Alphaville* (1965): why bother clothing the present world in sci-fi garb when the estranging future has already arrived?" (Lopate, 2011, 9). In Godard's film, according to Mahleb (2005), the city of Paris "is turned into a cold, modernist island where buildings of glass and concrete stand as an effigy to scince and dehumanization." In contrast, Tarkovsky's sequence of concrete and glass buildings seen from the motorway acts as a transition between the ethereal scenes of nature and the technology-orientated scenes set on the space station. It reveals a passage of time where science has evolved around, and eventually as in *2001*, beyond man's control.

Home

The American film-maker Steven Soderbergh directed his own adaptation of the Solaris novel in 2002. One of the similarities between Tarkovsky's and Soderbergh's films is the 'home' theme which is not present in the novel, and which the author would no doubt have disagreed with, as they both end with an illusory dream sequence related to Kelvin's last memories of being at home on Earth before journeying to Solaris. In the latter, he greets Rheya in his apartment, and in Tarkovsky's film, Kelvin is reunited with his father at his home (Fig. 8). "Tarkovsky's *Solaris* concludes with the space station's claustrophobic concavities yielding to the rain-sodden beauty of this island Earth, and the returning Kris embracing his father's knee" (Lopate, 2011, 11).

[T]he house is one of the greatest powers of integration for the thoughts, memories, and dreams of mankind" (Bachelard, 1994, 6). The opening scene in *Solaris* and the final sequence form an underlining thread through Tarkovsky's depiction of the concept of home in his films, and they are closely related to his childhood memories of Russian rural life. It is often this nostalgic feeling that resonates with many viewers who find Tarkovsky's films both familiar and inspiring, "In all my pictures, the theme of roots was always of great importance: links with family house, childhood, country. Earth. I always felt it important to establish that I myself belong to a particular tradition, culture, and circle of people or ideas (1986, 193).

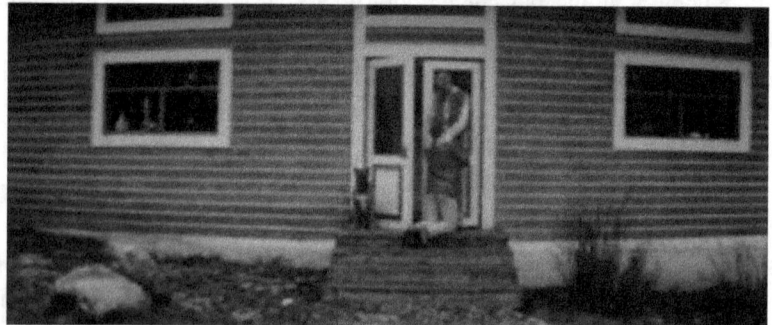

Figure 8

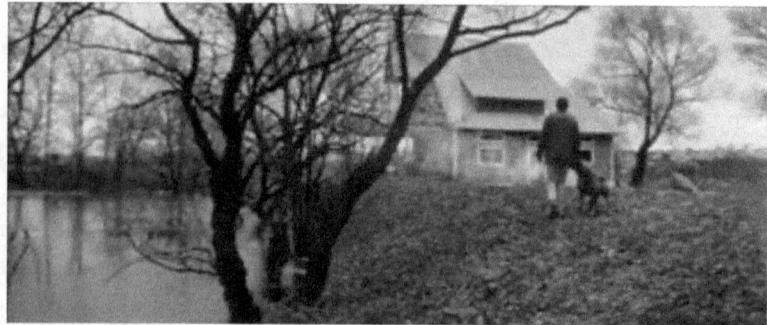

Figure 9

Tarkovsky's most autobiographical film, *The Mirror* (1975), is very much a close sibling to his *Solaris*; it was written before but filmed after *Solaris*. Most of the film is set within the confines of the protagonist's childhood home. The film consists of Tarkovsky's own projected feelings and memories of his life there and how it relates to his memory of his mother and his relationship with his wife. This could be taken as the roots of Tarkovsky's personal connection with Stanislaw Lem's novel.

In the first thirty minutes of *Solaris*, Tarkovsky depicts the house of Kelvin's father as a timber clad vernacular house (Fig. 9). It appears similarly to the pitched timber houses in both *The Mirror* and *The Sacrifice* (1986). It is also evocative of the steep pitched timber houses depicted in Bruegel's painting *The Hunters in the Snow* which is shown in detail during the library sequence in *Solaris*. The scenery of Kelvin's family home, which sits among trees next to a river, is very similar to the backdrop landscape depicted in Bruegel's masterpiece. These family home scenes are important as they evoke the feeling of nostalgia for home later in the film. A scene at the family house with a black horse in a stable is referenced later by photograph of a black horse in Gibanian's living quarters; this evokes remorse and empathy in Kelvin when discovering Gibanian's fate.

The depiction of a house in miniature form in Tarkovsky's films is perhaps indicating the director's longing for his childhood home. The structure of a house is sometimes shown within a larger structure; this relates to how the director's image of home appears in his mind's eye.

Tarkovsky's *Solaris* ends with three shots showing Kelvin's family home. A crane shot morphs into an aerial shot which morphs into an atmosphere shot showing the house sitting on an island within the sea of Solaris. This gives the film an unnerving end, and reveals Kelvin's inner turmoil of living among his memories of home on Earth.

Library

The library of the Solaris Space Station is described in Lem's novel as a place of solitude, tranquillity, and knowledge. In Tarkovsky's film, in contrast to the other spaces of the station, it evokes a sense of reason and sanity, as Lem (1991, 110) stated, "Situated right at the centre of the Station, the library had no windows: It was the most isolated area in the great steel shell, and made me feel relaxed in spite of finding my researches held up".

The library of the space station contains numerous details, including a head bust of Socrates, a leather bound copy of *Don Quixote* by Miguel de Cervantes, most of Bruegel's 1565 paintings (*The Hunters in the Snow*, *The Hay Harvest*, *The Harvesters* and *The Return of the Herd*), and The Tower of Babel set into an oak veneer panelled alcove with leather seating. Many of Lem's scientific, Solarist theory referencing was cast aside for more poetic referencing, which could better aid the visual ideas. *Don Quixote* is often thought to be one of the greatest novels ever written and the greatest piece of literature written in the Spanish language.

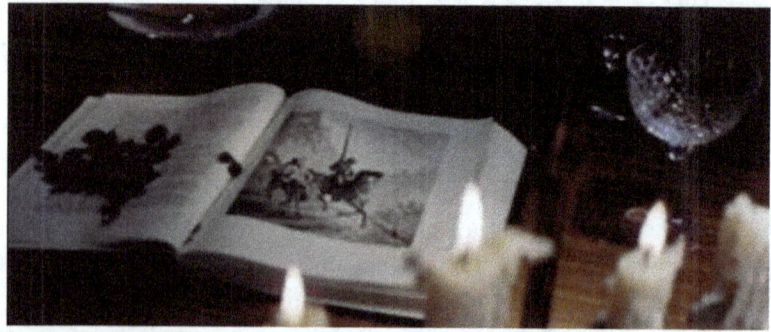

Figure 10

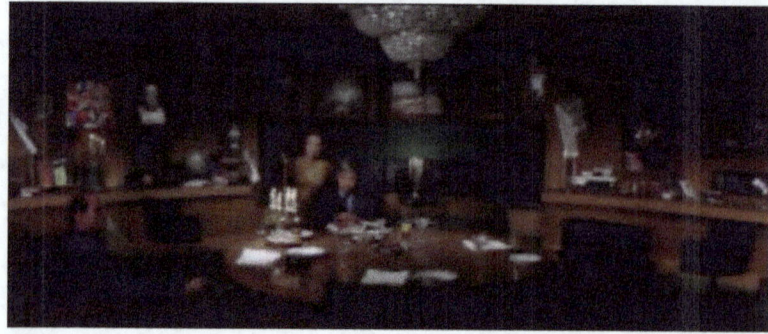

Figure 11

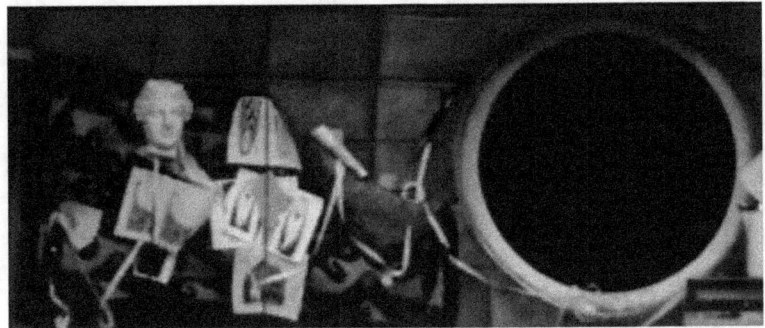

Figure 12

There is a rich feel to how the library is depicted in *Solaris* as seen through these details, and there is a nautical feel to the room, another analogy to sea ships. This contrasts with how spaces are portrayed in other science-fiction films, for example, the white bottom-lit bedroom (which does resemble the mirror room sequence in *Solaris*) as seen in Kubrick's *2001*, or in stark contrast to George Lucas' film *THX 1138* (1971).

In Lem's novel, there is one brief reference to *Don Quixote* when Kelvin describes Dr Satorious, "His thin face, entirely composed of vertical planes, exactly as I had imagined Don Quixote's, was expressionless. This blank mask did not help me to find the right words" (Ibid, 43). Tarkovsky and Romadin were obviously aware of this minute reference in the novel, and both would have been familiar with French illustrator Gustave Doré's pictorial work for the 1863 French translation of *Don Quixote*, as indeed the leather-bound copy of the novel in the film belonged to the art director himself (Fig. 10). These engravings obviously influenced the spatial atmosphere of both the library (Fig. 11) and Sartorious' quarters (Fig. 12), as they resemble his wood engraving of Don Quixote's private library and chaotic lair   .

These depictions of chaotic spaces reflect the lives of the scientists who inhabit the space station. Many of the scientists' behaviours, especially Kelvin's and Gibrarian's, resemble the delusional Don Quixote, who has spent so long studying tales and folklore that he is under the illusion of being a courageous knight. The phrase, 'Tilt at Windmills,' which can be defined as 'to go on a wild goose chase or to persistently engage in a futile activity,' clearly defines Kelvin's entire mission to Solaris. It reflects his behaviour of suspecting and attacking imaginary enemies, such as when he destroys the first incarnation of Hari by luring her into a rocket set for outer space.

Cinematic and Architectonic Space

While Tarkovsky considers *Solaris* unsuccessful and a slave to genre, it is an interesting film to study in terms of 'cinematic and architectonic space' in that it provides a distinct contrast between the natural forms of nature and the artificial forms created and manufactured by man. "A useful building addresses our reason whereas a ruined building awakens our imagination and unconscious fantasies" (Pallasmaa, 2007, 27).

Spatially and materially, the scenes set on Earth at Kelvin's childhood home and the scenes shot at the space station orbiting Solaris are radically different. Tarkovsky uses this contrast between outward (home) and inward (station) spaces to provide a sense of nostalgia and longing for home. Feelings of homeliness are evoked by the protagonist's memories of being on Earth at his father's home, while at the space station there is a feeling of confusion and paranoia evoked by a sterile enclosed environment. "Humans seem in thrall to machinery and TV images, cut off from the nature surrounding them (underwater reeds, a thoroughbred horse, a farm dog)" (Lopate, 2011, 9).

There is an endless surface quality that cannot be penetrated by the senses in the Solaris Station, with its continuous surface of glass, metal, and mirrors. With the Earth scenes, one can feel and sense the wood grain that covers Kelvin's father's home. The atmosphere of freedom within nature is underlined by Tarkovsky himself with the endless drawings and photographs of balloons that decorate the interior. There is a sense of tradition and family in how the house is presented to have been built with a traditional roof pitch and idyllic setting.

Like all great directors, Tarkovsky uses the science-fiction element simply as a backdrop to investigate ideas of humans' place in the world and their sense of that place in Solaris. Similar to a great building, the merit of a great film that transcends genre or style is one which makes us feel. "The artistic value of great architecture is not its material existence but the images and emotions that it evokes in the observer" (Pallasmaa, 2007, 36). There is a similarity between how some directors use technology excessively in science-fiction films, and how architects often overuse technology and structure. "A filmmaker, consequently, often recognises the mental ground of architectural impact more subtly than an architect" (Ibid, 33). Architects can reflect upon and learn about space, perception and architecture from Tarkovsky's films, but especially from Solaris, as the allusion to technology and material, and the difference between house and home have never been clearer.

REFERENCES

Bachelard, G. *The Poetics of Space*. London: Beacon Press, 1994.

Ballard, J.G. *Crash*. London: Harper Perennial, 2008. Lem, S.

Gombrich, E.H. *Art and Illusion: A Study in the Psychology of Pictorial Representation*. Kingsport, Tennesse: Kingsport Press, 1960.

Hughes, R. *The Shock of the New: Art and the Century of Change*. United Kingdom: Thames & Hudson, 1991.

Kurosawa, A., (2011)., "Tarkovsky and Solaris," *Solaris. The Criterion Collection*

Lem, S., (1991)., *Solaris*, London: Faber and Faber

Lopate P., "Inner Space," *Solaris. The Criterion Collection* (2011), 11.

Pallasmaa, J. *The Architecture of Image: Existential Space in Cinema*. Helsinki: Rakennustieto Publishing, 2007.

Mahleb, E., (2005). *Architectural Representations of the City in Science Fiction Cinema* (posted June 30)

Romadin, M., (2011)., Quoted in "Video interview with Mikhail Romadin," *Solaris. The Criterion Collection*

Gombrich, E.H. *Art and Illusion: A Study in the Psychology of Pictorial Representation* (Kingsport, Tennesse: Kingsport Press, 1960), 73.

Solaris. London: Faber and Faber, 1991.

Tarkovsky, A. *Sculpting in Time: The Great Russian Filmmaker Discusses His Art.* Austin, Texas: University of Texas Press, 1986.

Available at: <http://www.merriam-webster.com/dictionary/claustrophobia>

Available at: <http://oxforddictionaries.com/definition/cabin+fever>

Available at: <http://www.yume.co.uk/architectural-representations-of-the-city-in-science-fiction-cinema>

Available at: <http://www.yume.co.uk/architectural-representations-of-the-city-in-science-fiction-cinema>

Stills of *Solaris* (1972) have been captured by the author from Andrei Tarkovsky's Solaris (New York: The Criterion Collection, 2011).

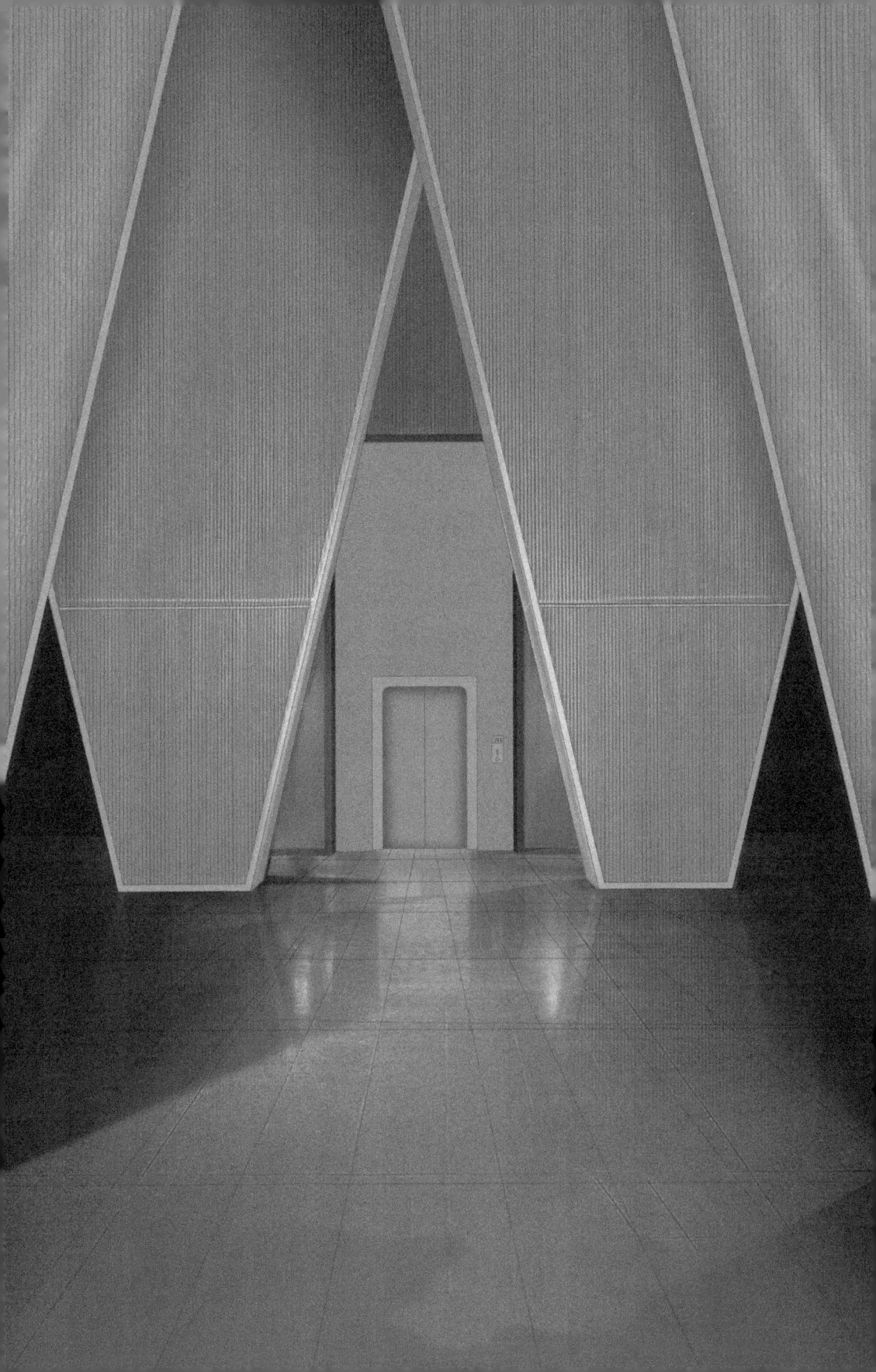

Corridors: Architecture, Film, and the Metaphysical

Christopher A. Rooney

CHRISTOPHER ALEXANDER ROONEY is a qualified architect with experience working on varied, international projects across the full range of Royal Institute of British Architects (RIBA) stages. Upon graduating from Queen's University Belfast in 2014, he began his career working for Maccreanor Lavington Architects in Rotterdam before moving to work in the United States. He returned to the UK in 2019, completing his RIBA Part Three with distinction, and is currently practicing in London.

Most of us will walk down multiple corridors every day, whether in our own homes, at the office, or in a public building. They are a part of our everyday lives, and as Mark Jarzombek notes (2010, 726), "one can hardly imagine that they played anything other than a relatively trivial part in the history of architecture." However, by understanding the history of the corridor, and the socio-economic and political upheavals that shaped them, the corridor's importance as a powerful symbolic and practical element of architecture is brought to the surface.

Historical records of corridors, as we know them, do not begin to appear until the seventeenth century. Prior to their invention, circulation through buildings either flowed from one room to the next, or via a central courtyard. As Robin Evans (1978, 60) notes in his analysis of Villa Madama in Rome (1525), there was no "systematic division of circulation space from occupied space." Etymologically speaking, the term *corridore* (Italian for runner) was originally used to describe the job of a courier rather than an architectural space. This is what Dante's *Inferno* refers to in the line *'corridore vidi per la terra vostra'* which translates to 'corridors I have seen upon your land.' As time passed, the word was gradually replaced by *courier*, and the meaning of *corridore* evolved. Initially, it was used to describe the secret passages that ran underneath defensive fortresses that were used to carry messengers or for a rapid escape. A notable example of this is the Passetto di Borgo, an elevated passage connecting the Vatican to Castel Sant'Angelo. Outside of this, corridors were not typically found in domestic settings, where a courtyard was often used as a means of linking rooms. In the seventeenth century, this began to change, and a 1644 sketch by the Roman architect Felice Della Grecian illustrates this in his villa design, where he replaces an *andito* with a *coritore*. Here, it was not hidden away as a secret passage, but displayed prominently as a kind of status symbol. The ultimate example of this is Francesco Boromini's 1635 corridor at the Palazzo Spada, which employs forced perspective (an optical illusion) to create the impression that the corridor is longer than it really is.

Whilst these corridors may have impressed visitors, they did not serve any practical purpose. It was not until Boromini designed the Oratory of Saint Philip Neri in Rome (1650) that the corridor was properly integrated into the architectural program. Here, corridors circle around a chapel, simultaneously linking and separating the oratory and the pre-existing church. This design set an important precedent, and more corridors began appearing in floor plans for churches and colleges, and importantly, they were being consistently labelled as corridors in the drawings. These corridors were not just for circulation, but a means of linking institutions with the outside world, both symbolically and literally. But the corridor had an even more profound impact on social order. In the previous arrangements of room-to-room circulation, everyone had access to every room due to the necessity of circulation. However, with the corridor, the rich nobility could reside in their private rooms while their servants circulated through the corridors out of sight and out of mind (Evans 1978, 267). As such, the corridor provided a new paradigm for privacy, instigating an architecturally-defined physical separation between social classes.

It would be some time before this architectural shift away from courtyards would carry over to England's institutions. John Soane's 1788 Bank of England had no corridors, despite being designed almost a century later.

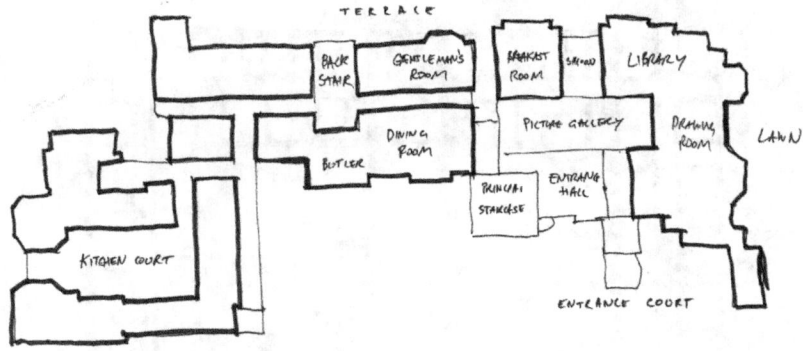

Figure 1. Sketch plan of Bearwood designed by Robert Kerr. Note that all the corridors are named for specific servants (all drawings by author)

Up to and including the early nineteenth century, English speaking architects were resistant to the corridor, and incorporated them only in prisons such as Dublin's Kilmainham Gaol (1796). This reinforced their image as dark, lonely, and dangerous (qualities that would later lend themselves well to cinematic purposes). In the end, it was the military that brought the corridor into architectural legitimacy in England via a new type of building: the barracks. These buildings were defined by their corridors so much so that until the nineteenth century, the German term Barrackenstil was used to refer to buildings with inner corridors, such as schools or hospitals. These buildings all had a specific function, and it was here that corridors first found their home in purpose-driven buildings.

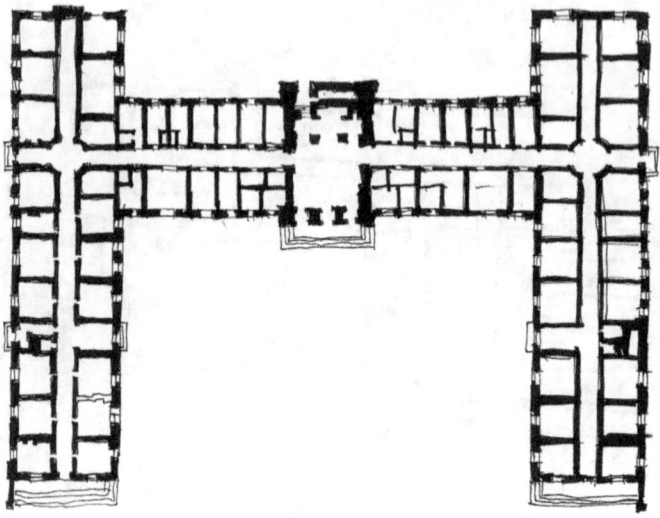

Figure 2. Sketch of Saumur Barracks, 1765

The nineteenth century English Houses of Parliament feature several extravagantly decorated, named corridors. Here corridors become more than just a means of getting somewhere; they become a destination in their own right. The corridors also provide a solution to an increasing problem of social separation in nineteenth century society, allowing different classes to spatially coexist within the same building. They provide a spatial means of social stability in the increasingly complex structure of Victorian society, again proving to be important socially, as well as practically.

The corridor was a firm part of the architectural language of buildings. However, the Modern movement's disdain for decoration, combined with an increasing reliance on new materials like concrete, put an end to the era of lavishly decorated corridors. Post WWII, the corridor was stripped of its paintings, arches, statues, and vaults. It became an afterthought as one of the most maligned parts of modernism, as noted in the 1970s:

> The ugly long repetitive corridors of the machine age have so far infected the
> word 'corridor' that it is hard to imagine that a corridor could ever be a place of
> beauty, a moment in your passage from room to room, which means as much as

all the moments you spend in the rooms themselves (Alexander, Ishikawa and Silverstein, 1977).

The historian Robin Evans even encouraged architects to return to the idea of the courtyard in the Palladian Villa, blaming corridors for the "obliterat[ion of] vast areas of social experience." Carlos Teixeira agrees (2016), and maligns the corridor as inefficient, advocating for a "Circulation area: 0%; functional area: 100%" approach. To this day, many architects feel the same, and prefer open plan designs. However, the varied historic examples of the corridor show that when properly considered, they also can provide valuable spaces for social integration rather than social separation.

This brief history of the corridor demonstrates how these spaces are more important than they may seem at first glance. Over the centuries, they have evolved from purely functional and practical spaces to those which have wide social implications. This notion is eloquently summarised by Jarzonbeck (2010, 767), who states that "the corridor from its inception was an instrument of modernity, relating first to speed, then to power... then to social structures and finally... industrialisation and the corporatisation of life." Over time, corridors have moved from obscurity into the mainstream, playing no small part in the social and architectural progress of civilisation. The range of symbolic and social implications is, in large, responsible for the potency of a great corridor scene in cinema.

Corridors that Control

The 2014 Venice Biennale has the theme of the 'fundamentals' of architecture, of which there were fifteen. One of them was the corridor, presented via a research project conducted by Stephen Trüby (2014). His research, which explored the hierarchy of space and social order, was criticised by Léopold Lambert who states that it is regrettable that [Trüby's] study does not go back to the 'fundamentals' of the corridor itself' (2016). These 'fundamentals' are essential to understanding our perception of the corridor as a space, and the dramatic power it has on film.

Perhaps the most fundamental reading of architecture is that it simply organises bodies in space. The corridor does this differently to other spaces because of its floor-to-wall surface ratio. For instance, as Lambert notes, 'a 100-square-foot square room has 40 linear feet of walls, whereas a 100-square-foot corridor might count 200 linear feet of walls.' Therefore, if the corridor has a higher ratio of wall to floor (the wall being the architectural element that organises bodies within space), then the corridor space exerts more control over its inhabitants than a normal room, by restricting the user's movements to 'forwards' and 'backwards,' and eliminating their ability to move side-to side.

The corridor's physical exertion of power over inhabitants is demonstrated by animal scientist Temple Grandin's designs for a slaughterhouse cattle forcing pen. The design utilises the herding instinct of cattle to calmly funnel the cows towards their fate. The curving walls of the cattle corridor facilitate a direction-ality of movement as it constricts around the animals, gradually separating and singling out each cow without causing panic.

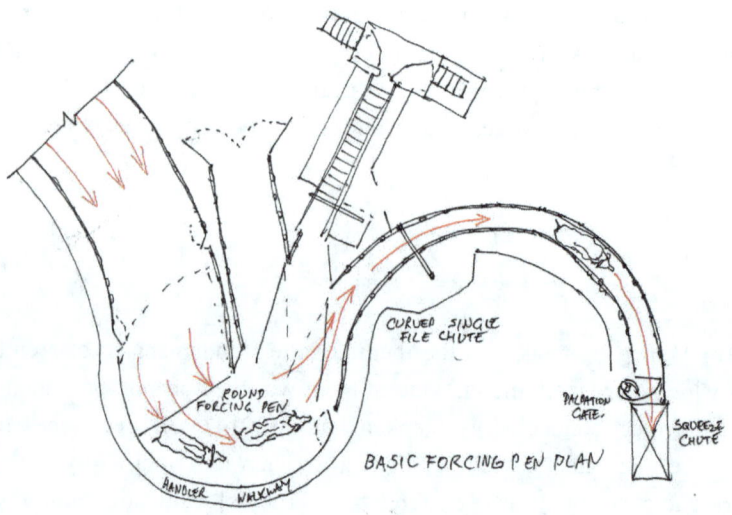

Figure 3. Sketch of Temple Grandin, 'Basic Forcing Pen Plan'

Disconcertingly, many of these same principles can be observed in the design of military checkpoints, such as the 150-foot-long Checkpoint 300 in Israel. As early as 3.30 am, the queue begins outside (Morgan 2016), with Palestinian workers queuing up to get into the city of Jerusalem. In this case, the corridor has been weaponised by designing the checkpoint's walls to press in on the user in order "to crush the Palestinian bodies crossing it" (Weizman 2007, 151).

A highly criticised incident in 2012 also illustrates this phenomenon: twenty Eritrean refugees were trapped for almost a week inside the security fences at the Israeli-Egyptian border and imprisoned on a long thin strip of land between the two countries in a frightening corridor-like no-man's land (Sherwood 2012). Even more extreme than this architectural immurement is the use of the corridor as a form of capital punishment. In *Indiana Jones and the Temple of Doom* (1984), there is a famous scene where the protagonist finds himself in a room whose walls are closing in on him (with added spikes for good measure); the bones scattered around the room imply that these walls have become a tomb for previous explorers. At various points throughout history, people have been executed in similar ways, most recently in Mongolia at the start of the twentieth century. The most vivid depiction of such a death is in the Romanian ballad, *Meșterul Manole*. The story depicts an architect who, upon making a pact with an evil spirit, must imprison his wife within the walls of the monastery he is constructing. The viewer is introduced to the violence that architecture is capable of imposing when wielded as a weapon as she desperately pleads for help: "Manole, Manole, Master Manole! The wall presses me too hard and breaks my little body!" (Leach 2006, 189). This violent side of architecture is something which films can exploit to great effect, and the corridor is one of the most powerful means of doing so. However, corridors and architecture can inspire feelings of wonder and joy as well as fear or oppression.

Jean Nouvel uses the corridor to surprise and delight the users of his architecture. He is inspired by film, which he uses as a means to understand how humans perceive space. Film provides a source of visual tropes that can be exploited by the architect to create their own form of drama. As a result, his architecture is complex and often contradictory: he applies the filmic notion of a sequence of cuts to the layout of architectural space. The point in which we transfer from one architectural space to another becomes the 'cut' from one scene to another, imbuing the threshold between these spaces with a cinematic potential. Therefore, both the architect and the filmmaker craft experiences in time as well as space.

The cinematic cut can also move the viewer closer or further away from any given object, forcing the filmmaker to consider scale as well as sequence. After a cut, the subject of a shot that had previously been dwarfed by its surroundings can suddenly fill the frame. Nouvel's architecture often juxtaposes spaces with radically different proportions and sizes, altering the user's perception as they move through the spaces. In Nouvel's Culture and Congress centre in Lucerne, the architectural 'cut' is employed at the entrance to the building's main performance space: a long corridor (mimicking the cinematic long take) ends in a dark, low-ceilinged space before cinematically erupting into a grand performance space (Cairns 2016). This use of a corridor provides the user with an exciting and theatrical experience.

The unique spatial quality of the corridor can have an exerting influence over its users. It can be harnessed violently and maliciously to evoke horror and desperation or used benevolently to summon feelings of wonder; these spatial and affective qualities are invaluable to both film and architecture.

Perceiving the Corridors

This section explores how the mind responds to space in both film and reality, and how space can come to symbolise certain aspects of our mental state, including our fears, hopes and dreams. Film, much like the corridor throughout history, traverses the strange territory between symbolism and practicality. However, film is unique in its ability to unshackle its creator from the restraints of reality, the only limits being those set by the imagination. It is no coincidence then, that some of the most extraordinary corridors can only exist within the realms of science fiction, and it is often these extraordinary and impossible spaces that transfix us the most.

A common supposition is that for a film to have a profound meaning or impact, it must exist within the bounds of believability. However, the genre of science fiction often transcends these boundaries and manages to make the impossible seem real. The term science fiction is in itself contradictory as 'reality' cannot simultaneously be 'fiction.' This oxymoronic duality is at the heart of film's ability to thrill and inspire. Films, notably science fiction films, portray reality in a way that assumes experiential subjectivity, creating multiple realities for different viewers based on their own perception of the world. As such, someone who has experienced Checkpoint 300 may have a drastically different psychological reaction to a corridor space than someone who has never been subjected to its oppressive qualities.

For a viewer to enjoy a film, they must be able to ignore the fact that they are viewing two-dimensional moving images on a screen. Samuel Taylor Coleridge calls this "the willing suspension of disbelief" and suggests that a viewer will only suspend judgement if a "human interest and semblance of truth" is fabricated into a piece of fiction (2009, 442-445). This 'semblance of truth' can be provided by architecture, and in many films a key component of this is the corridor, which can ground the fantastical and "make science-fiction believable" (Anderson 2016). In this way, film subverts the viewer's own experience, just as Borromini's illusory corridor did in 1650.

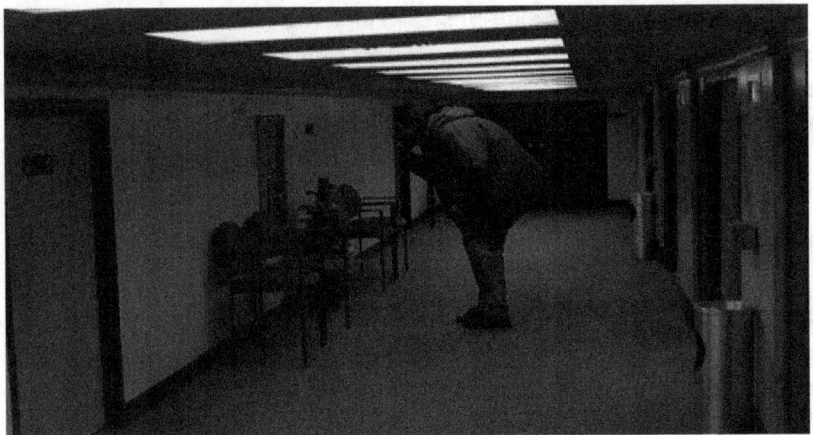

Figure 4. *Being John Malkovich* (all film stills captured by the author)

In *Being John Malkovich* (1999), the protagonist discovers a portal into John Malkovich's head, allowing him to effectively 'step into his shoes.' This absurd premise works because its world and architecture are grounded in realism. Of note is one scene, which takes place in an unusual office on the 7½ th floor with an extremely low ceiling. It is explained that this floor was designed for a 'low-statured' woman who complains that architecture was "not built with [her] in mind... doorknobs are too high, chairs are unwieldy and high-ceilinged rooms mock [her] stature" (21:38:00). The entirety of the floor was designed to be viewed and operated from her perspective, with proportionally-sized furniture, doors and appliances (Gabbard 2009, 229-233). When viewed without any inhabitants, the space looks just as a viewer would expect. However, when the space is inhabited by a typically sized person, the illusion is shattered, just as the illusion of forced perspective can be broken in Borromini's corridor.

Christopher Nolan goes to extreme lengths in his psychoanalytic thriller *Inception* (2010) to subvert the audience's expectations. One particularly impressive scene features a hotel corridor that rotates throughout the scene, requiring the characters to constantly change their position in relation to the constantly changing floor. The wall becomes the floor, the floor becomes the ceiling and vice versa. This architectural subversion of the corridor takes everything that the viewer takes for granted and literally turns it on its head. To film the scene, Nolan and a team of 500 crew members constructed a 100ft revolving set inside a WWI era hanger in Bedfordshire, England. The camera itself was installed on a mounted track, to make it independent from the rotating set. This means that the viewer is anchored within the rotating corridor while the actors and the space rotate around them (Total Film Magazine 2012, 44-45). This is almost an inversion of Borromini's corridor, as in this way, the viewer experiences a 'real' space in an impossible way. This gives the space a hallucinatory effect because the corridor simultaneously appears real and unreal.

Jaques Lacan states that "Architecture...like painting...is organised around emptiness," and in the seemingly objective practice of architecture, interpretation becomes all about the subjectivity of space. Jacques Lacan devotes much of his thought towards human perception, and as Lorens Holm notes, there are striking similarities between Lacan's diagram of the visual field (1964) and a diagram one might draw of Brunelleschi's demonstration of linear perspective (1420). In the demonstration, Brunelleschi viewed the famous Florence Baptistery using a screen and mirrors to sketch it in perfect perspective. This enabled the mathematical calculation of the scale of objects and visual relationships within a drawing in order to make them appear realistic. Ultimately, as Holm notes, "that's what subjectivity is... a distributed array of screen and positions"

(2010). Not unlike the placement of an individual within the film or the orientation of a camera within space. The converging lines of a corridor are a physical manifestation of this linear perspective, which is why scenes like the one in *Inception* are so powerful; they take advantage of this subjectivity by altering the viewer's perspective.

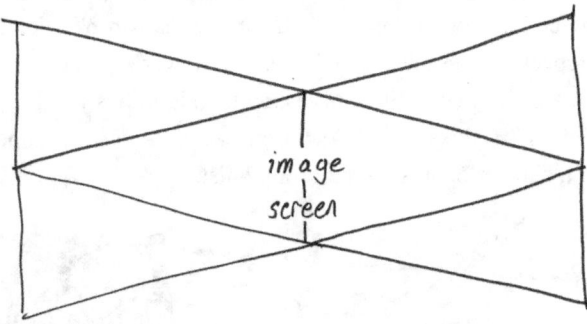

Figure 5. Sketch of Jacques Lacan's 1964 diagram of the visual field

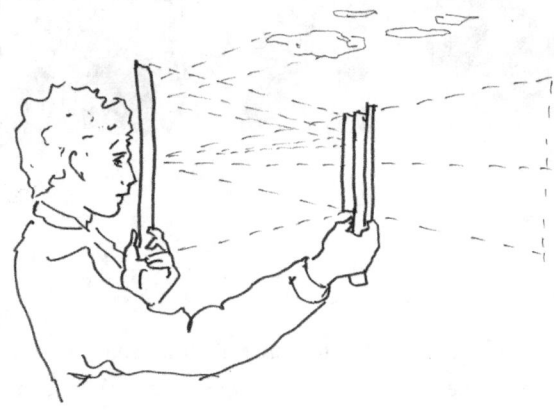

Figure 6. Illustration of Brunelleschi's 1420 demonstration of linearperspective

The perspective and scale of the corridor and other spaces are also masterfully subverted by Orson Welles in his 1962 adaptation of Franz Kafka's *The Trial*. The prologue states that its logic is based on a dream, which Welles uses to justify the rich texture and stylistic excess of how the film was shot. As the film progresses, the architecture constantly presses in on the protagonist, despite much of the film being shot inside huge spaces like le Gare d'Orsay in Paris (Wheldon 1962, 43). By altering the elevation and camera angle, Welles transforms open space into something more linear and claustrophobic. This manipulation of perspective completely changes the viewer's perception of a space where "angles are sharpened like knives, and… sightlines [are] slanting symmetrical perfection" (Hinkson, 2015). In this way, Welles anthropomorphised the space into a sinister enemy of the protagonist.

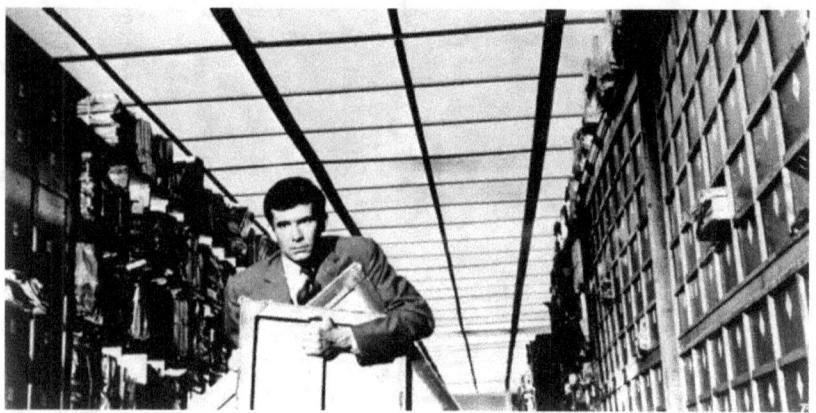

Figure 7. *The Trial*

Corridor, Camera, Action

Filmmakers operate and orientate the camera within space by focusing on, perhaps, the most technical of filming challenges: the action scene. The corridor lends itself well to these scenes, with the linearity of the space creating backdrops full of sharp angles and striking geometry. The simplicity of the space also helps to keep the viewer orientated when the action becomes particularly frantic.

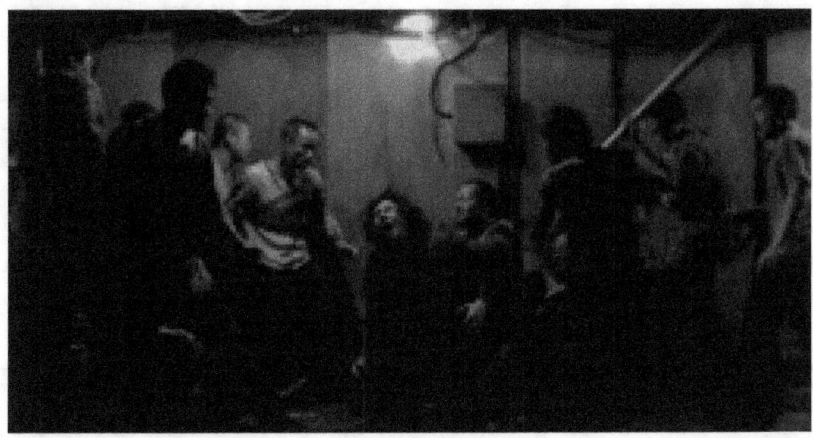

Figure 8. *Oldboy*

Oldboy (2003), directed by Park Chan Wook, contains what is often cited as one of the greatest action scenes of all time (Film4). In it, the protagonist fights his way through a corridor of opponents in one continuous three and a half minute tracking shot. As the figures move through the space, the perpendicular camera slowly pans along the corridor, making it appear as though the corridor is cut in a sectional view, the tension building with every second of unbroken footage. The linear nature of the corridor is used to compress the space in which the sequence is filmed, emphasising the number of opponents within the space, and removing any opportunity for the protagonist (or the audience) to flee. As the camera moves on a single axis, the actions sways to and from, using the linearity of the space as a literal representation of the character's progress. The simple presentation of the space allows the viewer to view the action and the prowess of the actors and stuntmen involved, uninhibited by intrusive cuts or angle changes.

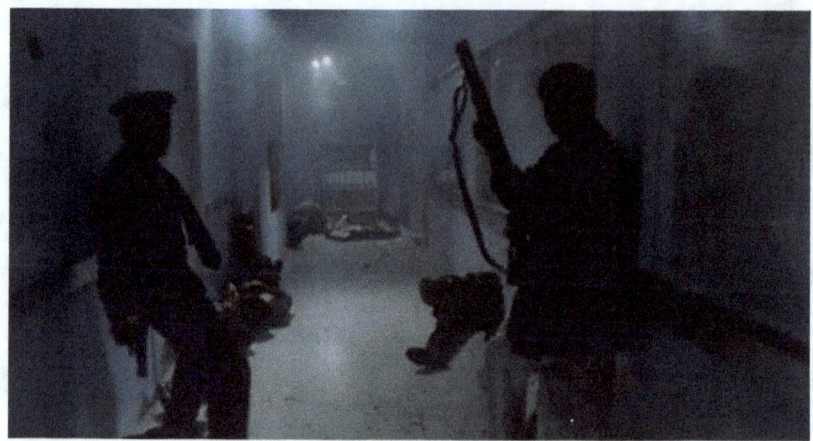

Figure 9. *Hard Boiled*

Another corridor-based scene, shot in one unbroken tracking shot, comes from John Woo's *Hard Boiled*, in which the characters fight their way through a series of hospital corridors, pause briefly in an elevator (while the crew re-dress the entire set to look like a different floor), and then fight through the floor above, all in one continuous tracking shot. All around them, bits of rubble and glass fly as the walls explode around them. The linearity of the corridor is exploited as they switch sides and move rapidly along towards their destination. In this scene, the idea of turning a corner in a corridor is also exploited. The nature of the perpendicular shift in perspective means that whatever is around the corner is obstructed from the camera's view. This builds tension as Tequila and his partner peek around corners, unsure of what lies around them.

Here one can see how filming techniques can contribute to the drama and excitement of an action scene. The restricted nature of the corridor used in such scenes presents unique challenges to filmmakers, but when they are approached creatively, they can produce some of the most memorable scenes in cinema.

The Horror Corridor

In *Alien* (1979), long before we even meet the protagonist, the audience is introduced to the real main character of the movie, the Nostromo. After a series of sweeping panoramic shots, the hulking outline of a spaceship looms out of the darkness of deep space. As we cut to inside the ship, and the camera pans and creeps slowly along the deserted corridors, metal grating lies underfoot, and industrial pipes shrouded in shadow line the walls. All this comes together to form our first impression of the Nostromo. By evoking a gritty, grimy, industrial reality while simultaneously instilling feelings of claustrophobic dread in the viewer, the director uses the corridor to foreshadow the impending horror.

The director Ridley Scott lingers over these corridors lovingly in the film's opening moments, acknowledging the admirable work of the set designer Roger Christian (influenced by the concept designs by Ron Cobb). Each corridor has a distinctly different feel, enabling the viewers to orientate themselves within the ship when things get hectic on screen. The corridor leading to the hyper sleep chamber, where we first meet the crew, has padded walls and a clinical white colour scheme that is just as unnerving as the gritty industrial corridors on the engineering levels. These linear, narrow spaces play a pivotal role by hosting a deadly game of hide and seek for an alien on the prowl. This is in stark contrast with the alien environments we see in the film, most of which were designed by H.R Giger (who also happens to have been a student of architecture and industrial design). Giger plays on human insecurities with his design of the alien creature as well as in the strange organic architecture which these creatures inhabit. The derelict alien ship has three openings at ground level between the two horns of the craft, through one of which the crew of the Nostromo enter. The interior resembles that of an organic, living organism rather than the industrial craft that we were first introduced to in the film's opening minutes. The walls and ceilings of its labyrinthine corridors are seemingly made of bone, with ducts as veins or tendons, and organic shapes and embellishments around its doorways and rooms. These organic forms continue the imagery playing on the viewers' fears, making it seem as if the corridors the crew have entered are the veins of some huge living creature.

Many members of *Alien*'s design team previously worked on the failed adaptation of Frank Herbert's science fiction novel, *Dune*, directed by Alejandro Jo dorowsky. He handpicked his team for *Dune*, hiring H.R Giger, Chris Foss, and Jean Giraud, amongst others. Although it was never filmed, its influence can be seen in many of the iconic science fiction films that followed. Giraud, Foss and Ginger all went on to create *Alien*. Like Giger, Foss trained as an architect before focusing his career on art.

The success of *Alien* by the end of the 1970s made the 1986 sequel, *Aliens*, inevitable. James Cameron took over from Ridley Scott as director, and what is considered to be one of the greatest sequels ever made came into being. The visual style of the original film was preserved, and Ron Cobb was brought back to design the colony, atmosphere processor, and all the interiors. The industrial corridors returned on a larger scale. If *Alien* was a haunted house story, then *Aliens* was a war movie. As such, there were much bigger set pieces, like the face-off with the alien queen in the cargo bay, where the corridors were dispensed with in favour of large aircraft hangars for the final fight to take place. Cameron explained that he wanted "to have really huge air ducts–taller, in fact, than the corridors in the ship — so that when Dallas first sees it there, it's standing on the roof of this giant wind tunnel, suspended upside down. Then I was going to have it roar down the tunnel toward him, running and jumping full-circle around the walls" (Shay 1980, 60). These visual effects were something that could not be achieved in the original film due to the technical limitations of the time. However, *Aliens* was able to show the creature rushing and leaping towards its victims. As such, the film was able to fully utilise the corridor's propensity for movement. Because of this, *Aliens* feels much more like an action film than the original.

Both *Alien* and *Aliens* are examples of how a film can use the corridor to provide an exciting and atmospheric setting. The differences between the films showcase the versatility of the corridor's ability to play host to multiple genres of film. Each director approaches the technicalities of filming the corridor differently, and thus adapts the space to their specific purpose.

The 'Ballardian' Corridor

The novelist J.G. Ballard's favourite building was the Hilton hotel at Heathrow airport in London, where he "was always supremely happy sitting in its vast atrium, where one becomes, briefly, a more advanced kind of human being [where] one feels no emotions and could never fall in love, or need to" (Hall 2009). This callous, yet also liberating form of architecture is explored in his 1975 novel, *High Rise*, which was recently adapted for the screen by British director Ben Wheatley. *High Rise* (2015) is defined by its architecture, and the eponymous skyscraper embodies Ballard's social-surrealist vision.

The film was mainly shot in Bangor, Northern Ireland in a soon-to-be demolished brutalist leisure centre. This provided the majority of the interior scenes in the film, including several scenes shot in its dark corridors. The CGI scenes of the entire tower are clearly reminiscent of brutalist icons such as the Barbican or Trellis Tower. In the multitude of scenes shot in the building's dark and decaying corridors, the viewer begins to see why these "ugly long repetitive corridors of the machine age" (Wainwright 2016) fell out of favour. As the film progresses, the corridors gradually begin to fill with rubbish and detritus, becoming more like war zones than luxurious apartment hallways.

The fictional architect of the high rise is Antony Royal who, like the Trellis Tower's Erno Goldfinger, presides triumphantly in his penthouse apartment. He, rather conspicuously, is rarely seen in the corridors of 'his' tower. For most of the film, he is in a walled garden on top of the building (shot in the eighteenth century walled garden of Bangor Castle) or at lavish parties in his penthouse, where his guests dress as eighteenth century French aristocrats. In the only scene where he is in one of the corridors, he is not recognised by the other occupants of the building. Given the social symbolism of the corridor discussed earlier, Royal has become like one of the nobles, living in privacy while his 'servants' traverse the corridors out of sight and out of mind. This is only the beginning of the madness that descends upon the high rise as the film progresses. This madness is in stark contrast to the supposed 'sanity' of the modernist architecture it inhabits. Ballard used this as an analogy for the disillusioned youth he saw growing up in Britain in the 1960s and 1970s.

Wheatley's adaptation is successful because, as in Ballard's novel, the built environment serves not just as a backdrop, but exists as a character in itself, "integral and distinctive in its recurring imagery" (Hall 2015). In *High Rise*, and in much of Ballard's other work, he explores the latent psychology of our surroundings, and how it can often come to define the people that inhabit them. The corridors here are the most obvious manifestation of this, and their slide into disrepair and chaos mirrors their inhabitants' own descent into madness. Another literal example of this is the physical manifestation of class hierarchy imposed upon the residents, making the phrase 'upper class' quite literal. Interestingly, the upper class of the rises inhabit more open-plan spaces in their apartments, whereas the 'lower class' inhabit the more cellular apartments connected by corridors. This may be Wheatley's means of advocating the superiority of open plan design.

Ballard himself was influenced by the work of Oscar Newman who, like Jane Jacobs (1961), believed that violence in cities could be mitigated by designing open spaces which facilitates natural surveillance. This is something that the oppressive, tight corridors and cellular rooms of a high rise cannot provide. Conversely, the protagonist in *High Rise* values privacy above all, and ultimately it is this that allows him to survive everything that the high rise has in store. Perhaps then, *High Rise* is not the scathing critique of this corridor design that it first seems to be. Indeed, Ballard himself wondered if "human beings perhaps haven't evolved sufficiently to be able to enjoy living in high rise blocks... something like Corbusier's radiant city seems much too regimented" (Gale 1998). The multi-million-pound penthouses being built all over London symbolise the city's growing social divide which makes the social themes explored in *High Rise* more relevant than ever. As identified earlier in the chapter, the introduction of the corridor into architectural design created a novel form of social separation. The 'Ballardian corridor' is what happens when class separation is taken to the extreme; *High Rise* sends a powerful message to architects, urging them to consider the wider implications of how they design and organise space.

REFERENCES

Alexander, C., Ishikawa, S. and Silverstein, M. (1977). *A pattern language*. New York: Oxford University Press.

Anderson, M., (2016). "In praise of the sci-fi corridor" online *Den of Geek*. Available at http//www.denofgeek.com/movies/313130/in_praise_of_the_scifi_corridor.html (Accessed 12 Apr 2016).

Ballard, J. G., (1966). *New Worlds* October Issue.

Battersby, M., (2011). "A Science Fiction Visionary" online *The Independent*. Available at http//www.independent.co.uk/arts-entertainment/books/features/a-science-fiction-visionary-2318750.html (Accessed 5 Apr 2016).

Bazin, A. and Gray, H., (1967). *What is cinema?* Berkeley University of California Press.

Packer, S., (2002). *Dreams in myth medicine and movies*. Westport Conn Praeger.

Benjamin, W. and Underwood, J., (2008). *The work of art in the age of mechanical reproduction*. London Penguin.

Borromini, F., (1720). "Opera del Caval", Francesco Boromino. In *Roma: Data in luce da Sebastiani Giannini*, p.27.

Cairns, J., (2016). *Cinematic Phenomenology in Architecture Akademeia*, Vol 2 Issue 1.

Chapelle, D., (2014). *Whiplash*. USA Sony Pictures Classics.

Chapman, T., (2005). *Heathrow Hilton* online Ballardian.com Available at http //www ballardian com/heathrow-hilton (Accessed 5 Apr 2016).

Coleridge S 2009 Biographia literaria Auckland N Z Floating Press p.442- 445.

Creed B 1993 The monstrous-feminine London Routledge.

Czarny, A. (2009). Alien and Aliens. [online] Jamescarononline.com. Available at: http://www.jamescarononline.com/AlienandAliens.htm [Accessed 22 Apr. 2016].

Ditzian, E. (2010). 'Inception' Hallway Scene: How Filmmakers Pulled It Off. [online] MTV News. Available at: http://www.mtv.com/news/1643947/inception-hallway-scene-how-filmmakers-pulled-it-off/ [Accessed 20 Apr. 2016].

Film4 (2016) The 25 Greatest Action Movie Scenes online Available at http //www film4 com/special-features/top-lists/top-25-action-movie- scenes (Accessed 10 Apr 2016).

Foster A, O'Bannon D, Shussett R and Roberts H 1979 Alien New York Warner Books SCANLON P and GROSS M The Book of Alien London Titan Publishing Group.

Frick T (2016) Paris Review - The Art of Fiction No 85 J G Ballard online Theparisreview org Available at http //www theparisreview org/inter- views/2929/the-art-of-fiction-no-85-j-g-ballard (Accessed 24 Mar 2016).

Freud S and Falzeder E. 2002. The complete correspondence of Sig- mund Freud and Karl Abraham 1907-1925 London Karnac.

Freud S McLintock D and Haughton H 2003 The uncanny New York Penguin Books.

Fuller. S. 1963 Shock Corridor USA Allied Artists Pictures Corporation

Gabbard G 2001 Psychoanalysis and Film London GB Karnac Books p. 229-233.

Gabbard G Litowitz B and Williams P 2012 Textbook of psychoanalysis Washington DC American Psychiatric Pub p. 540.

Garrigou Grandchamp, P., Olmer, P., Arnold, P., Giraud, P. and Rous- seau, B. 2005. Saumur, l''école de cavalerie. Paris: Monum, Éditions du patrimoine.

Hall G. 2013 Disentanglement and Gates online DesignIntelligence Available at http // www di net/articles/disentanglement-and-gates/ (Accessed 6 Apr 2016).

Hall Chris. 2015 Why JG Ballard's High-Rise takes dystopian science fiction to a new level The Guardian October 2015.

Hinkson J. 2015 Orson Welles at 100 The Trial 1962 by Jake Hinkson online Crim- inalelement com Available at http //www criminalelement com/blogs/2015/05/orson- welles-at-100-the-trial-1962-kafka-jake-hinkson (Accessed 12 Apr 2016).

Holm L 2010 Brunelleschi Lacan Le Corbusier London Routledge

Jacobs, J. 1961. The Death and Life of Great American Cities New York Random House.

Jonze, S 1999 Being John Malkovich USA Focus Features

Jung C and Dell S 1940 The integration of the personality London K Paul Trench Trub- ner & Co. Kaplan E 1990 Psychoanalysis & cinema New York Routledge.

Kerr, R. 1972. The gentleman's house. New York: Johnson Reprint Corp. Leach, N. (2006). Camouflage. Cambridge, Mass.: MIT Press.

Lambert, L. (2016). The Politics of Narrowness: When Walls Tighten on Bodies. [online] Averyreview.com. Available at: http://www.averyreview. com/issues/11/the-politics-of- narrowness-when-walls-tighten-on-bodies [Accessed 21 Apr. 2016].

Lebeau V 2001 Psychoanalysis and cinema London Wallflower.

Lacan, J. and Miller, J. 1990. Les quatre concepts fondamentaux de la psychanalyse, 1964. Paris: Seuil.

Lewis, C. 1956. Surprised by joy. New York: Harcourt, Brace, p.10.

Morgan, P. (2016). Visualizing Check Point 300: A Photo Essay. [on- line] Blog.eappi. org. Available at: https://blog.eappi.org/2016/02/22/ visualizing-check-point-300-a-pho- to-essay/ [Accessed 21 Apr. 2016]. SCI-FI CORRIDOR ARCHIVE 2015 online Avail- able from http //scificor- ridorarchive com/ Accessed 19 Nov 2015

McGinn Paul 2005 The Power of Movies How Screen and Mind Interact United States Vintage Books pp 192-3 202-3.

New York Times, The 2014 'Whiplash,' Anatomy of a Scene. Available at: https://www. youtube.com/watch?v=gHEiqYYrZeg (Accessed: 24 March 2016)

Nolan, C. Inception USA Warner Bros Motion Pictures

Pavich, F. 2013 Jodorosky's Dune USA Sony Pictures Classics

Sherwood, H. (2012). Eritrean refugees trapped by security fence at Israeli-Egyptian border. [online] the Guardian. Available at: http://www. theguardian.com/world/2012/sep/05/eritrean-refugees-at-israeli-egyp- tian-border [Accessed 21 Apr. 2016].

Scott, Ridley 1979 Alien. USA 20th Century Fox

Scanlon P Gross M and Lippincott C 1993 The book of Alien London Titan.

Shay, D. and Duncan, J. 1997. Cinefex. Riverside, CA: Don Shay, p.60.

Sklarew B. 1999 Freud and Film Encounters in the Weltgeist Journal of the American Psychoanalytic Association 47 4 pp 1239-1248

Stuckman, C. 2015. The Problem with Action Movies Today. Available at: https://www. youtube.com/watch?v=eac0lXfMs9c

Teixeira, C. 2016. History of the Corridor – Vazio S/A. [online] Vazio. com.br. Available at: http://www.vazio.com.br/ensaios/historia-do- corredor/?lang=en [Accessed 21 Apr. 2016].

Total Film 2012. Grappling Gravity. Total Film Magazine, (200), pp.44-45.

Toy M. 1994 Architecture & film London Academy Editions pp 7 11-13 91 CAIRNS G PENZ F and ROSE H n d The architecture of the screen pp 35-41.

Wachowskis 1999 The Matrix USA Warner Bros

Wallis V 2011 Introduction Socialism and Democracy Journal April 6 Wheldon H (1962) BBC Radio 3 Interview

Wainwright O. 2016. A long way down the nightmare of JG Ballard's towering vision online The Guardian Available at http //www theguard- ian com/artanddesign/2016/mar/13/high-rise-jg-ballard-towering-vision- film-tom-hiddleston Accessed 24 Mar 2016.

Weizman, E. 2007 Hollow Land: Israel's Architecture of Occupation. London: Verso, p. 151.

Welles O. 1962 The Trial USA Astor Pictures Corporation

Wheatley, Ben. 2016 High Rise UK StudioCanal

Woo, John. 1992 Hard Boiled Hong Kong Golden Princess Film Production Zizek S. 1993 ''The Thing that Thinks' The Kantian Background of the Noir Subject ' In Shades of Noir ed Joan Copjec London Verso.

Containment Architecture:
Oldboy and *The Truman Show*

Matthew McGibbon

MATTHEW McGIBBON is an architect who received his qualifications from Ulster University and Queen's University Belfast with work/life experience in the UK, Ireland, and the Netherlands. Before undertaking his career as a freelance architect and artist, he worked extensively in professional practice, specialising in residential architecture. This experience allowed him to work on multiple urban and rural-based new build, conversion, and refurbishment projects, building a close working relationship with many clientele and other industry experts within Northern Ireland. A keen traveller, currently based in the Netherlands, he hopes to bring the skills he developed in a UK based professional practice and expand on them within a European context.

C ontainment is defined as 'the action of keeping something harmful under control or within limits.' An individual who serves time in prison does so to be disciplined because he or she has committed a crime or has harmed another individual and is deemed a risk to society. When describing discipline in the form of imprisonment Micheal Foucault (1995, 141) states, "Discipline sometimes requires enclosure, the specification of a place heterogeneous to all others and closed in upon itself. It is the protected place of disciplinary monotony." Although over the centuries, judicial corporal punishment has either been abolished or practised with less frequency in western society, the core principles of punishment through the form of containment have remained much the same.

This chapter aims to analyse and discuss the qualitative issues that forced containment within architecture generates, and what psychological disorders people can develop when they are contained against their will. The scale of the architectural entities within which these people become enclosed is of importance too, as this study looks at whether there are differentiations between the psychological traumas caused by being contained in either a large or small space. This is done through the analysis of two films that, although having differing levels of extremity, and representing contrasting cultural identities between the east and west, have the same underlying concept of forced containment. These two films are *Oldboy* by Park Chan-wook (2003) and *The Truman Show* by Peter Weir (1998).

Real-life investigations into the differing scopes of the penal system, and how prisoners cope with issues such as solitary confinement and the more traditional forms of incarceration are also used to supplement the analysis between the two films. As more often than not 'Hollywood' films depict a certain degree of unrealistic positive outcomes, or the complete opposite where every outcome is negative or too intense, the line is thus blurred between representation and realism.

The difference between impending freedom and actual freedom is another important subject covered in this study, as generally, prisoners feel differently when thinking about as opposed to experiencing the latter. This, in a perverse way, is frequently true when they have been imprisoned for a long period and have gotten accustomed to prison's rigorous routines and architectural arrangement.

Containment Through Film Analysis: *Oldboy*

Oldboy by Park Chan-wook (Show East, 2003) is a South Korean film adapted from the Japanese manga of the same name by Garon Tsuchiya, which was published between 1996 and 1998. The main themes present in the film are that of containment, freedom, revenge, love, suspense, and brutality, as there are high levels of violence showcased throughout the film. Besides these concepts, the film is, at its core, a revenge film, with these other concepts acting as supplementary parts to the film's main premise. The film initially takes place in 1988, and continues through to 2003, with its setting being the large metropolitan city of Seoul. It follows the story of the main protagonist Oh Dae-su, a stereotypical drunk businessman who regularly goes on drinking binges before returning home to his disgruntled wife and four-year-old daughter.

The film begins with an intoxicated Oh Dae-su held up in a small police station due to his disorderly behaviour. At this early point of the film, we see that he does not react well to being 'contained' in a small enclosed area, with him repeatedly arguing and physically threatening the police. Oh Dae-su's mental state is clearly on edge as he states, "My name, Oh Dae-su, means... getting through one day at a time but, God.... why can't I get through this day? Let me go!!"

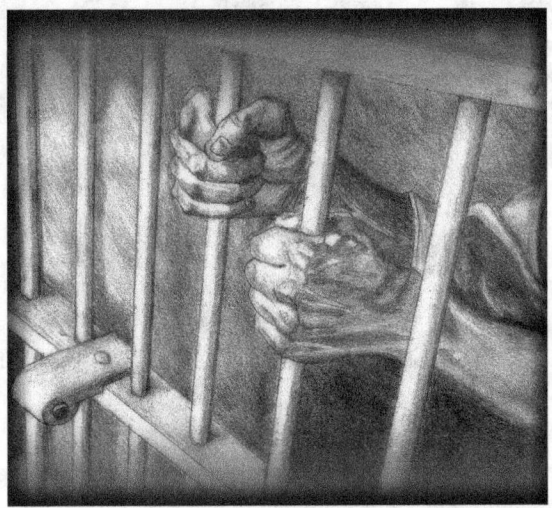

Figure 1. Sketch of Oh Dae-su's pleading for freedom
(Sketch by the author)

This statement in itself is almost like a prelude of what is to come later in the film, even though Oh Dae-su and the audience do not know it yet. The situation does not improve either, as after changing his rhetorical stance, albeit through a put-on apologetic-like charade, the police continue to ignore his pleas. This leads to him partaking in further erratic behaviour as he starts stripping his clothes off and contorting on the ground. His mood changes and becomes more subdued again, once he is surrounded by other temporary inmates, as shown in Figure 2. After these events, he is bailed out by his friend No Joo-hwan, and they proceed to use a payphone so Oh Dae-su can phone his daughter. As he passes the telephone to Joo-hwan, Oh Dae-su walks outside the payphone and the camera starts rotating until he is completely out of the scene. At this point, Joo-hwan tries to hand the phone back to a now non-present Oh Dae-su.

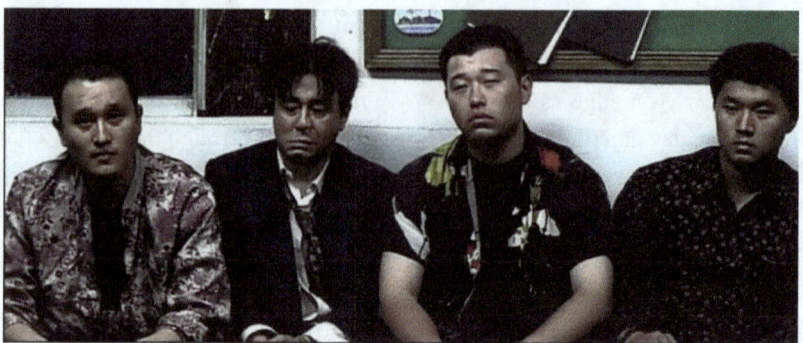

Figure 2. Oh Dae-su (second from the left) sitting beside other inmates (all illustrations are film stills captured by the author unless indicated otherwise)

The setting then changes to a poorly lit, sinister corridor, and the camera is placed at ground level whilst focusing on what appears to be the opening flap to a prison door. We see an unknown person open the flap with his foot, with Oh Dae-su at ground level and positioned close to the opening. In this scene, it is implied that he has been waiting on the floor for the flap to open for a lengthy period of time, as there is visible movement between the small gap between the door and its opening flap, with his behaviour that of desperation and urgency once opened.

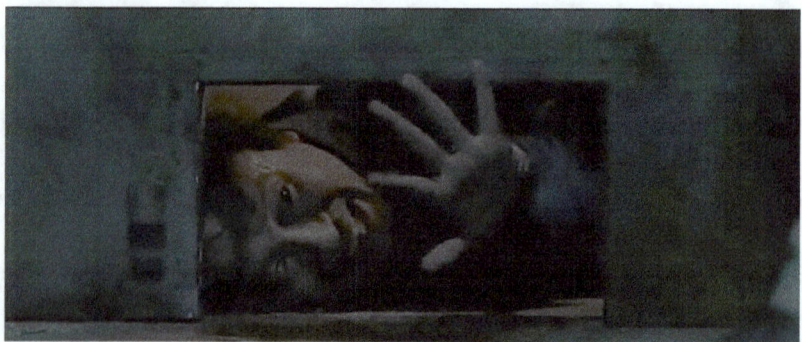

Figure 3. Oh Dae-Su at the prison door opening flap, asking why he has been imprisoned

In some ways, this scene is very reminiscent of the one preceding it when he was in the police station, as Oh Dae-su changes from having a panicked, but mannerly attitude to a very abusive, insulting one when he knows he is not going to get his desired response, although this time the change is related to his fear and not intoxication.

As the door flap opens, Oh Dae-su pleads, "Sir, sir, I won't ask you to let me go again, just tell me why I am here, just tell me how long I have to stay here." This is quite a contrast to when the unknown person who opened the door flap starts forcing his foot on Oh Dae-su's head so he can push him back into his 'cell.' At this point Oh Dae-Su starts reciting, "Fuck you, come here you asshole, son of a bitch, I saw your face, asshole! You're dead when I get out!" This is only for Oh Dea-su to yet again change his tone once he realises that he will be alone for presumably another day as the reason the unknown man comes to the door is to slide in a meal, reminiscent of how a prisoner would receive one. As the unknown man is leaving, Oh Dae-su pleads one last time and says, "I'm sorry! I won't swear at you again, just tell me how much longer. One month? Two, three?" This scene shows us that his mental state at this point is extremely fickle, and his desperation is starting to manifest through physical actions as he franticly tries to grab onto the unknown man's leg and shoe as he is leaving. The low positioned camera work in conjunction with his low positioning to the ground is symbolic, as it temporarily brings the viewers down to his level, which can be interpreted to be quite grim for the reasons described above.

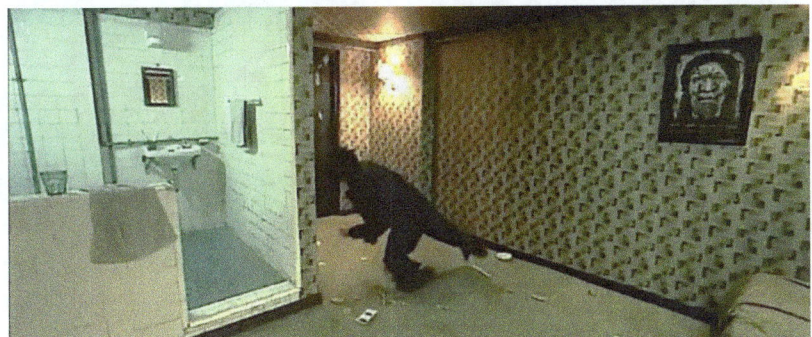

Figure 4. Oh Dae-su in a fit of rage, throwing crockery at his 'prison' door and showcasing his descent into madness

At this point, the camera enters the 'prison' in which Oh Dae-su is being held captive for the first time. From looking at Figure 6, we see the room is very similar to what a low-quality hotel room would look like and has a dull appearance with almost all of the décor being an earthy brown or yellow colour. The brown patterned wallpaper that covers the room consists of monotonous geometric shapes dimly lit by lampshades, as well as there being an 'open' bathroom that is surrounded by aged and dirty white tiles. There is no apparent natural lighting in the room, as the only window is quite small and has an artificially-lit image of a European windmill and grass landscape behind it, completely out of context as to what is on the other side of the window.

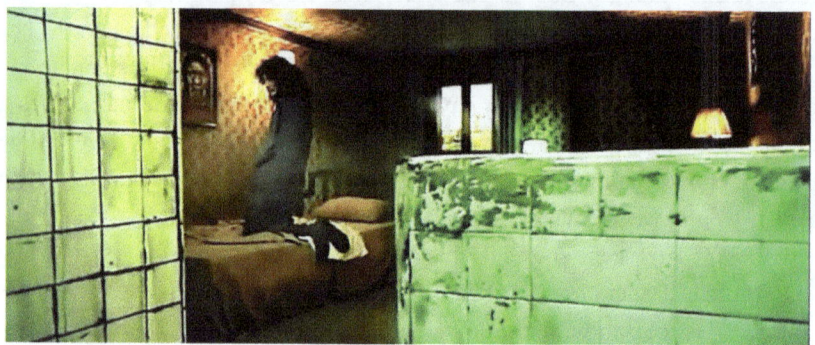

Figure 5. The artificially-lit window from the perspective of the bathroom in Oh Dae-su's 'prison'

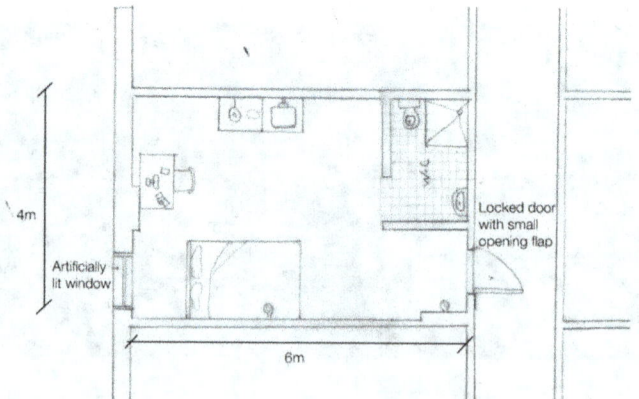

Figure 6. Plan of Oh Dae-su's room as it appears for the first time in the film (Sketch by the author)

As Oh Dae-su states through a first-person narrative, "If they had told me it would have been 15 years... would it have been easier to endure?" We quickly and unexpectedly learn the scope of how long he is to be in this room or 'prison,' without knowing how or why he gets out at this point.

Analysing what mental conditions he has or develops during his containment is hard to identify with certainty, although he shows signs of having two types of disorders, the first being 'seasonal affective disorder.' As described by the NHS online (2014), this disorder is where people experience episodes of depression, notably during winter, with the person affected being low in mood and having a lack of interest in life. The exact cause is unknown; however, lack of direct sunlight over long periods of time is thought to be a contributing factor, as the theory is that the hypothalamus area of the brain that is stimulated by sunlight stops functioning at its maximum potential, with it normally controlling people's mood, appetite, and sleep. As there is no natural light entering Oh Dae-su's room, with the only light coming from dimly lit lampshades and an artificially-lit window, he likely suffers from this condition at some point during his fifteen year period of containment. The fact that he also tries to take his own life on multiple occasions is also a testament to this theory.

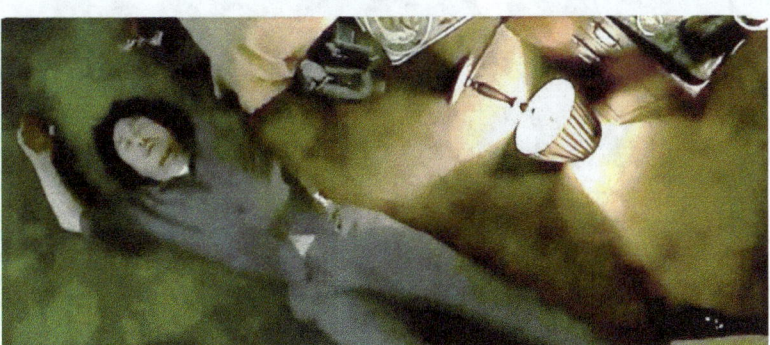

Figure 7. Oh Dae-su being dragged away by his captors after a suicide attempt

The other disorder he likely suffers from, hallucinations, as described by the Merriam-Webster Dictionary (2014) is "a perception of something (as a visual image or a sound) with no external cause usually arising from a disorder of the nervous system (as in delirium tremens or in functional psychosis without known neurological disease) or in response to drugs."

We are shown in a scene that his captors occasionally release sleeping gas into the room so they can enter without confrontation. Within this time, they inject him with what appears to be a hallucinogenic drug, as thereafter he starts to have violent hallucinations if faced with something distressing. The trigger for his first violent hallucinogenic outburst comes through watching the news on the small TV in his room. The news report is about the murder of his estranged wife, with him being the primary suspect due to his sudden disappearance a year before the murder took place, and because his fingerprints were found at the scene, implying that he has been set up, possibly by the people who have imprisoned him.   While he watches the news report with a stoic expression on his face he starts to hallucinate as he sees an ant burrowing from inside his arm and coming out through his skin. His hallucinations escalate dramatically as we are shown an image of his agonis   ed face covered in ants as well as him writhing in agony.

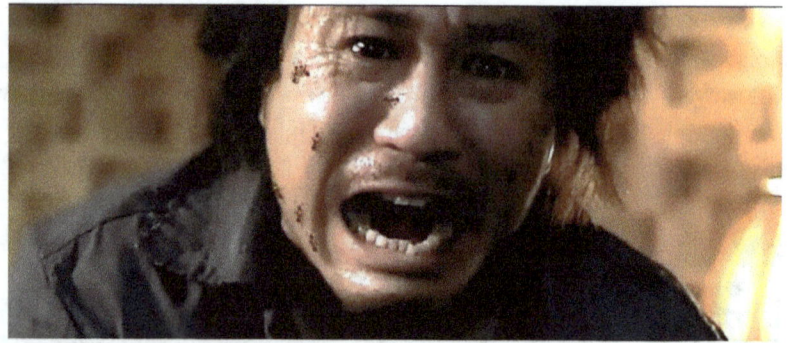

Figure 8. Oh Dae-Su hallucinating

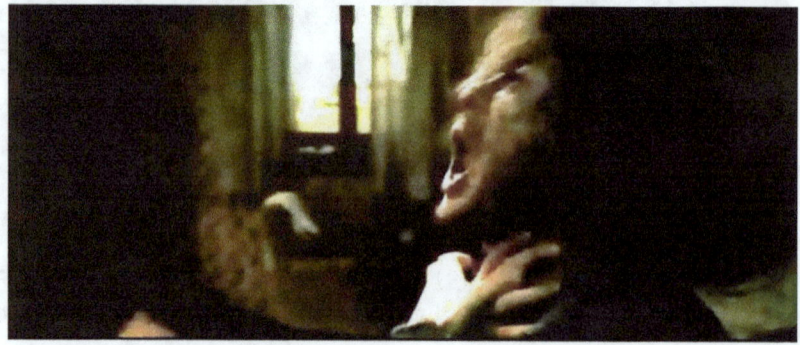

Figure 9. Oh Dae-Su writhing in agony during his hallucination

There are multiple interpretations behind the meaning of this scene and whether it is more than just a drug-related hallucination. One such interpretation by Aaron Ellis (2013) is that ants always move in colonies and are therefore never 'lonely.' The hallucinations of ants can consequently be interpreted as a product of Oh Dae-su's psyche, implying that he has a desire to be a part of society again. It is a violent remedy of sorts to his loneliness.

Whilst not actually a diagnosed medical disorder, 'cabin fever' is another condition that can be attributed to Oh Dae-su's mental state and actions at this point. When describing cabin fever, Bertha Muzzy Bower (2005, 1) states:

> There is a certain malady of the mind induced by too much of one thing; (…) the mind fed too long upon monotony succumbs to the insidious mental ailment which the West calls "cabin fever," and it may drive you to commit peccadillos and indiscretions of various sorts. It will betray your little, hidden weaknesses.

Throughout Oh Dae-su's forced containment he is repeatedly shown in a bad light through his choice of actions. This is quite apparent when, before another suicide attempt, he is shown partaking in manual stimulation while he is watching a female signer on his small television. He does so in quite an indecorous and indiscreet manner even though he knows his unknown captors are watching him. Kelly Y. Jeong, (2013, 169) suggests that Oh Dae-su's most profound loss is that of his stable self, and how through imprisonment the loss of self-identity implicates one's humanity, "as the self becomes no longer recognizable and turns abject." To quote Julia Kristeva (1982, 2) when she is describing abjectness, she states, "it is a massive and sudden emergence of uncanniness, which familiar as it might have been in an opaque and forgotten life, now harries me as radically separate, loathsome."

Oh Dae-su's previous life outside this 'prison' may be a distant memory, but we are reminded through scenes such as the previous one that he was not always a respectable member of society, as we are clearly shown at the beginning of the film. It is, however, after these multiple indecorous events, Oh Dae-su starts to change and seems to be in a more positive state of mind that craves freedom. As Bower (2005, 1) states when describing what can be seen as the positive effects of cabin fever, "It can cut and polish your undiscovered virtues, reveal you in all your glory." Oh Dae-su's panicked and erratic behaviour is now of a more reflective and serious tone as he starts writing what he calls "the autobiography of all my evil deeds," a journal detailing all the people he has ever hurt. This prompts him to say, "I thought I had lived a normal life…but there was too much wrongdoing." Through writing these lengthy journals and listing all his potential enemies, he starts trying to decipher who it could have been that imprisoned him, which seems to reignite one emotion that he has not lost at this point, his anger.

He uses it as motivation to start physically training himself and practicing shadowboxing, as he states in an austere manner, "Who had imprisoned me? Whoever it was, wait. Just you wait. I'll rip your body limb from limb, and your remains will never be found." Julian Darius's (2013) interpretation of Oh Dae-su's newfound hobby of shadowboxing is that he explicitly does it so that someday he will be able to exact his revenge on his captors. It is also probable that Oh Dae-su gains an interest in boxing in general, as he is shown watching it multiple times on his television. Regardless of this, revenge is the clear motive for his changed demeanour.

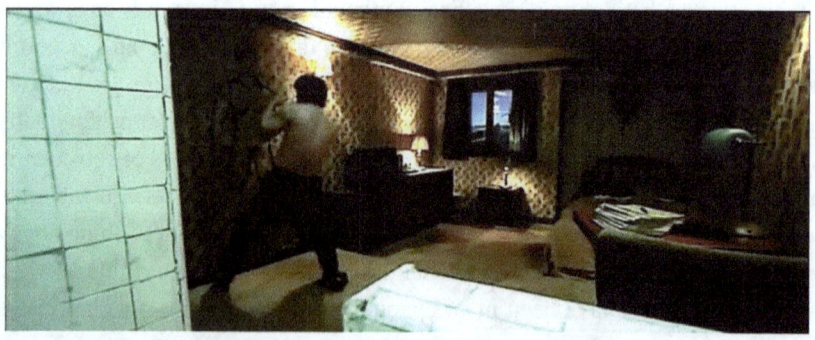

Figure 10. Oh Dae-su shadowboxing and punching
a drawn on human target on the wall

An interesting aspect of Oh Dae-su's imprisonment up until this point is that although he is being punished harshly for something that he is not aware of, at no time is he physically abused by his captor. This is not too dissimilar to Foucault's (1995, 16) description of the penal system of the last two centuries where he states:

> If the penalty in its most severe forms no longer addresses itself to the body, on what does it lay hold? The answer of the theoreticians is simple, almost obvious. It seems to be contained in the question itself: since it is no longer the body, it must be the soul. The expiation that once rained down upon the body must be replaced by a punishment that acts in depth on the heart, the thoughts, the will.

This is precisely what Oh Dae-su experiences. Not physiological punishment but punishment of the soul whereby over time, his captors are seemingly trying to break him mentally rather than physically.

After six years of being in his prison, and around the time of his changed frame of mind, Oh Dae-su gives himself 'tally' like tattoos on his hand as a symbolic reminder of how many years he has been imprisoned by his captors. Stating, "One line for each year, when I start doing this. I am already six lines behind... so next year will be easier." This shows us that he has resigned himself to the idea that he will not be released, and that perhaps he has, in a perverse way come to consider this prison a place of atonement with which he has to comply.

When discussing the hierarchy of power and imprisonment in society, Foucault (1978, 93) has stated "power is not an institution and not a structure (...); it is the name one attributes to a complex strategical situation in a particular society." This is somewhat relevant to Oh Dae-su's form of imprisonment. It is clearly not governed by legal authority, nor is it legally structured or even ethical; however, it is still allowed to occur for over a decade as it is implied that his captors seem to have greater power than legal authorities of that time and era. One thing that is apparent at this point is that Oh Dae-su has developed an obsession with time that also accompanies his obsession with being free; this in turn distorts his perception of reality.

It is not in the same manner as before, however, as he does not have violent outbursts or hallucinations during this period; it is more his common sense and judgement that becomes clouded. This obsession begins when after his captors accidentally give him an extra chopstick with his daily meal, he realises that he can use it as a 'tool' in which he can carve his way out of the prison, in a literal sense. "The more tattoos I have, the shorter the chopstick becomes." This statement encapsulates the immense task he has undertaken, and that he is not complying with his namesake anymore, which loosely translates to 'getting through one day at a time.' He is now counting time in years rather than days. Georg Lukacs' description of time can be extrapolated and applied to Oh Dae-su's situation when he says:

> The great discrepancy between idea and reality is time: the process of time is duration. The most profound and most humiliating impotence of subjectivity consists not so much in its hopeless struggle against the lack of idea in social forms, as in the fact that it cannot resist the sluggish, yet consistent process of time; that it must slip down, slowly yet inexorably, from the peaks it has laboriously scaled (1974, 54).

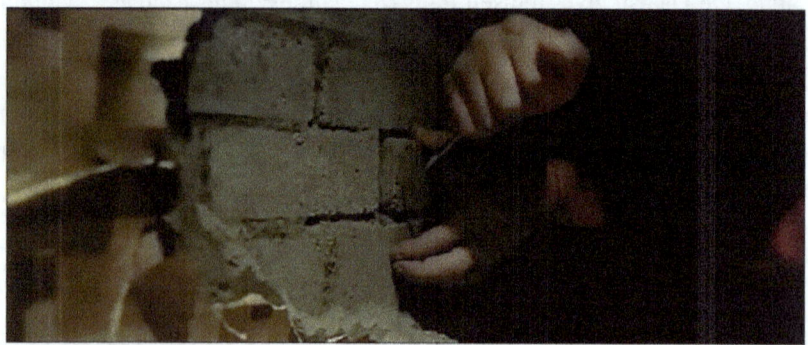

Figure 11. Oh Dae-su carving the mortar between the bricks away
with the 'annually shortened' chopstick

The reality that Oh Dae-su has seemed to have forgotten over time, perhaps subconsciously, is that he is being watched. Even if he hides the chopstick under his mattress and moves his bed to hide the side of the wall that he has been slowly carving away at, his captors are still aware of what he is doing, and perhaps allowing him to do so for their amusement. It can be argued that there is a notable discrepancy between his wishful thinking and rationality, with prolonged time in solitary confinement seemingly attributing to this wil   ful blindness.

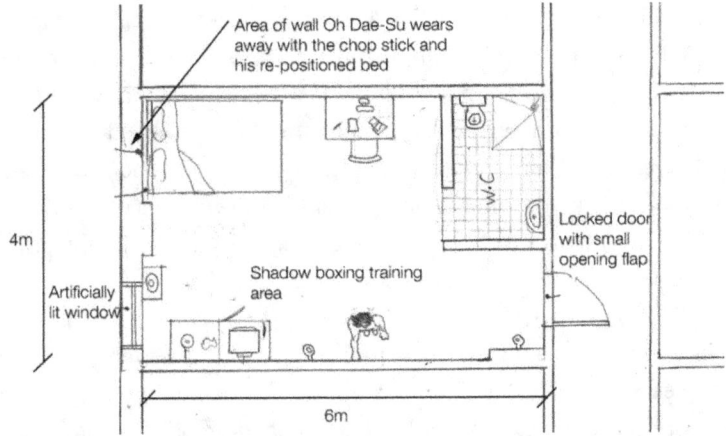

Figure 12. Plan of Oh Dae-Su's room – altered furniture arrangement
to comply with training and escape plan (Sketch by the author)

Professor David Alexander (2013) from The Aberdeen Centre for Trauma Research states that in cases of solitary confinement, you should get a system going as you do at home. He suggests, "Anything you do to try and impose order and structure on your world, which helps your identity and helps you to try and counter what the bad guys want you to experience." What they want, he says, is for prisoners to slip into what clinicians refer to as "learned helplessness." This is the feeling that whatever prisoners do will ultimately end in failure, and what Oh Dae-su does at this point of the film battles this 'learned helplessness' concept. His newfound 'hope,' resulting from increased levels of endorphins entering his brain through his regular shadowboxing regime may also be a possible reason for his more focused, albeit ignorant mood.

His perception of reality starts coming back to him once he finally breaks through to the exterior of the building. Granted, the opening is only the size of a single brick, and it took nine years of persistent carving to get to this stage. It is evident that he still has a fixation with time, though, as he repeats, "I'll be out of here in one month's time, I'll be out in a month, in exactly one month." He is still oblivious to the fact that his captors are watching him, and at this point oddly not stopping him until they suddenly start releasing sleeping gas into his room.

Regardless of this, he starts thinking of worldly things irrelevant to prison as he recites while falling asleep: "I'll need money when I get out, so what should I do? Should I steal or rob?" And "But where am I? With all the car horns it must be the city. The most important thing is what floor I'm on. What if I break through the wall and I'm on the fifty-second floor?" These are things which we would have expected him to have considered beforehand and are a testament to the distortion of his rational thinking over his fifteen years of imprisonment. "Even if I plunge to my death, I'll still be getting out," are the final words recited by Oh Dae-su as the sleeping gas submerges over him.

This tells us that even though the potential reality of his situation has dawned on him, he does not care; the idea of freedom and overcoming his captor's mental hold on him has overtaken all other thoughts and emotions, with him again reciting the words "in one month I'm getting out!"

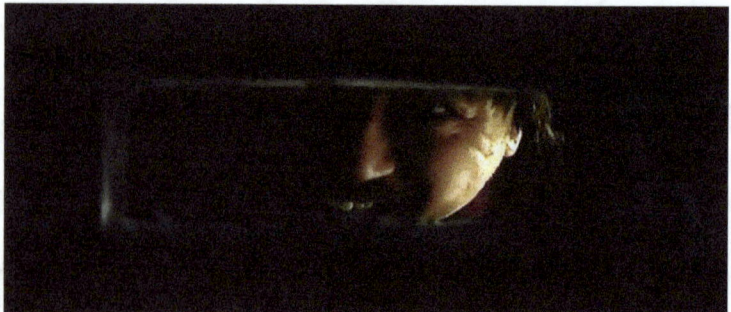

Figure 13. A smiling Oh Dae-su looking through the hole he carved away from the wall

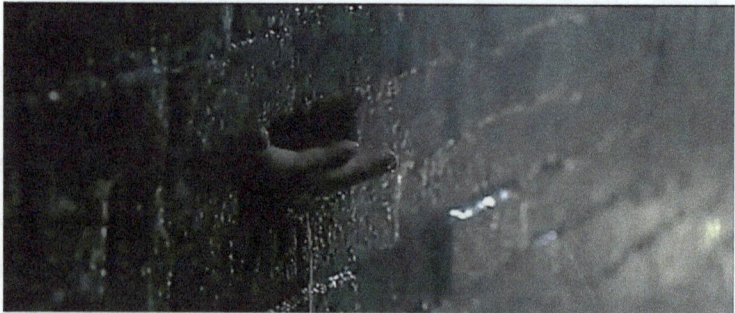

Figure 14. Oh Dae-su's hand as it passes through the hole and touches the rain for the first time in fifteen years

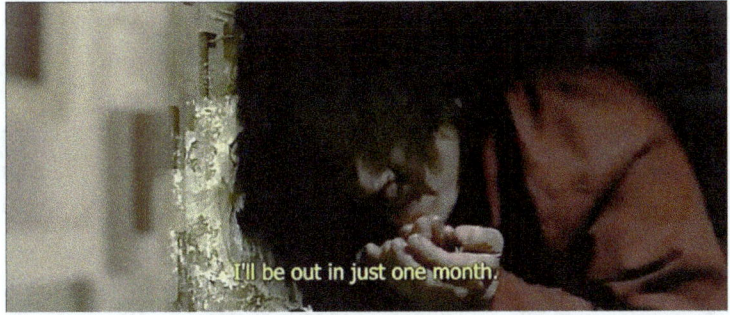

Figure 15. Oh Dae-su drinking the rainwater whilst reciting how long it will be before he escapes

To best describe Oh Dae-su's duration of imprisonment within this 'room' is to look at the three forms of 'detention' that Foucault (1995, 117) discusses. The first of which is the 'cachot', whereby the penalty of imprisonment is augmented by various measures, solitude, a deprivation of light and restriction on food; the 'gene' in which these ancillary measures are attenuated (reduced), and 'imprisonment proper', which is reduced to simple confinement. The one 'luxury' Oh Dae-su has is his television, however, it is arguable that this also contributes to the loss of his sanity as he can see what is happening in a world in which he does not belong anymore, until of course, his sudden freedom.

Containment Through Film Analysis:
The Truman Show

The Truman Show by Peter Weir (Scott Rudin Productions, 1998) is an original story and an American drama that on the surface feels like a light-hearted, comedic film that sometimes diverts away from its more serious undertones of containment, physiological trauma, and paranoia. This is influenced somewhat by Jim Carrey's intentionally preposterous style of acting, with him portraying the main protagonist throughout the film. This protagonist, Truman Burbank, is your everyday 'nice guy' in his early 30s who appears at first to live with a very high standard of living in his home town of 'Seahaven'. He has all the assets that one would attribute to a so-called 'perfect life' such as a conventionally pretty wife, a nice house, a modern car, a best friend, many politely mannered acquaintances, a well-paid job, and all the amenities that he would need close by. However, at the very beginning of the film, it is quite apparent that there is an odd undertone to all of this, as the premise of the entire film is revealed to us through an unknown man at this point (Christof). He states, while looking directly at the camera, "We've become bored with actors giving us phoney emotions, we are tired of pyrotechnics and special effects…, while the world he inhabits, is in some respects counterfeit… there's nothing fake about Truman himself, no scripts, no cue cards, (…) it's genuine… it's a life."

After this, the screen cuts to Truman for the first time; he is looking directly at the camera and his face is shown on what seems to be the small display screen that a camera would have, with the word 'live' digitally stamped onto the bottom right of the image.

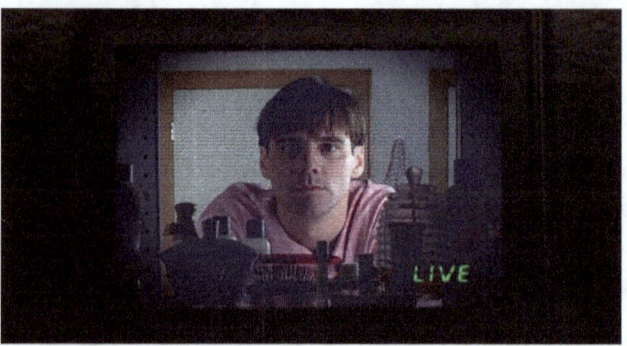

Figure 16. Truman staring directly at the camera, from his perspective he is staring at his bathroom mirror, from the viewer's perspective we are looking at the display screen of a camera

As the opening credits continue to roll, a number of other unnamed characters are speaking to the camera in a manner as if they are being interviewed. They also confirm the idea that this 'world' of Seahaven is structured. One person states, "It's all true, it's all real…nothing here is fake…nothing you see, on this show, is fake…its merely controlled." The words 'show' and 'controlled' have a seemingly odd fitting to the film's initial bright and happy visual settings, but at the same time make sense when analysing the other characters' mannerisms and many peculiar camera angles used.

This odd combination is shown when Truman first walks out his front door in the morning to go to work, as he is instantly greeted by his adjacent neighbours, and is playfully targeted by a neighbouring dog. This particular scene seems almost staged as the neighbours are already perfectly positioned before he walks out his door, and the order of events seem to enable the changing of camera angles that range from chest height angles and angles that are positioned within objects such as a bin for medium height or garden gnomes for a low 'worm's eye view.'

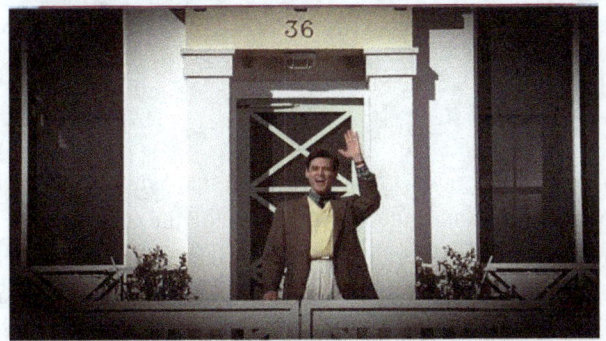

Figure 17. The chest height camera view coming from a member of the adjacent neighbours that greet Truman every morning; the camera lens is visible along the corners.

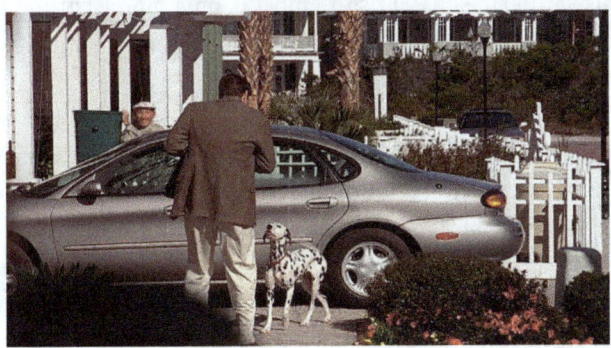

Figure 18. A camera angle coming from the kitchen window of Truman's home, a camera is also visible on the green bin that is being held by a neighbour.

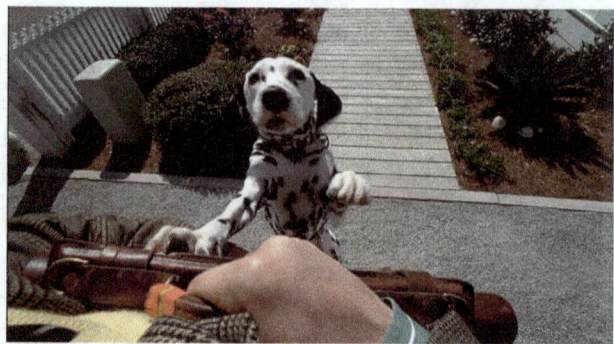

Figure 19. A camera angle coming from Truman himself, presumably from an item of his clothing.

The images shown in Figures 17 to 20 confirm that Truman's life and daily interactions are recorded and staged, with him being the only one that is ignorant to it; the question at this point is why? When discussing sociological theories, Erving Goffman (2005) states that everybody unconsciously plays out particular roles in their environment. People are actors, and the human experience is 'our performance in society.' Society exists to protect people, and one of the ways is to make sure they know how to respond correctly to other people at the right time. Referring to Goffman, Robert Castle (2005) states, "*The Truman Show* tests the limits of a performance world. Unwittingly, by creating a private utopia for his surrogate son, Christof embarks on a more startling project. He literally creates a world of entertainment, Seaville, in which all of the society is acting except Truman."

Christof himself is the man who speaks directly to the camera at the beginning of the movie, and the creator of this fictional world within which Truman is contained. Another interesting point is when Castle discusses the potential meaning behind Truman's name when he states, "Put together the hero's name and we get the 'True man' of the 'Burbank' world. Burbank itself is a city in where many large-scale movie studios such as the Warner Brothers and Disney studios are based. This analysis of Truman's name somehow encapsulates a metaphorical meaning behind his identity and his arguably constructed and controlled personality, as his name is essentially a 'play on words,' and everybody is in on it, except him.

There is a series of points within the film where Truman becomes aware that there is something amiss with the reality that he is accustomed to, and that his attempts to try new things unfamiliar to his usual routine or the initiative to travel beyond the constraints of his hometown are usually stifled. When he tries to investigate odd events that occur around him, other people, be it his wife, best friend, or even the local radio and TV stations try to convince him that there is a logical explanation for it. All these explanations are to prevent him from questioning his identity and to keep him in the dark over his actual constructed reality, which, in short, is a reality TV programme that he has been the main attraction of for his entire life.

This is revealed to him briefly by his former love interest 'Lauren.' When Truman was in high school, she was a paid actress on the 'show,' but as Tony Jackson (2010, 147) puts it, 'Lauren looks at Truman as a real human being, rather than as the unwitting star of a show.' After sharing a passionate kiss on a beach where they had fled to, she states, much to Truman's bewilderment, "Truman, everybody knows about you! Everybody knows everything you do! They're pretending, Truman. My name is not Lauren; it's Sylvia!" After this, a man who claims to be Lauren's father ushers her away as she pleads to Truman to come and find her, with her supposed father saying "Fiji, we're going to Fiji," stating she has a series of mental problems. It is implied that the man is not her father and is just another paid actor that has been forced to go to the beach to prevent Lauren from revealing the truth to Truman, with Lauren herself stating she has never met the man before.

It is suggested that Lauren believes this 'utopia' that Christof has created for Truman is more of a dystopia, completely void of all the regularities and pain that would constitute a 'normal' life. When observing this aspect of Truman's life, Jackson (2010, 147) states:

> this experiment involves reducing randomness to a minimum; providing comfortable living conditions; regulating economic, political, and social forces so that they have only predictable and positive effects, and doing all this unknown to the experimental subject. All this done, then we can observe, precisely, 'a life' as if it were an exemplar of life in general, apart from all the random vicissitudes that constantly beset an actual existence.

The first odd incident in the film that makes Truman question his surroundings is when he sees a mechanical object fall from the sky and land beside him. He tentatively walks over and inspects the object to find that it is a high-powered studio light. Immediately after this, when he is driving to work, a news report on the radio states, that it was as an aircraft shedding some of its components as it passed over Seahaven. This is followed by the reporter saying, "Thinking of flying anywhere!?" to which Truman replies with a quick "Nope!", conveniently tying in well with the effort to keep Truman contained on the island.

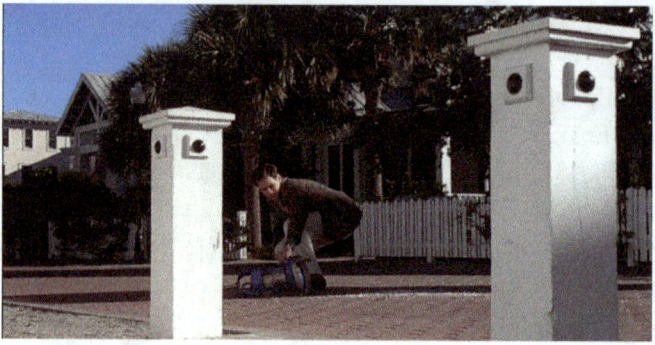

Figure 20. Truman inspecting the object that fell from the sky.

Another incident is when Truman is asked to visit a nearby island for work-related matters. He is seen walking towards the ferry along the sea deck only to come to a trembling stop and exhibit feelings of hesitation and panic once he sees the water and a partially sunken rowboat. After this, he walks back in the direction he came from, and asks for the ferry to go on without him. It is shown in a slightly later scene that his apparent fear of the water comes from when he and his father went on a fishing trip when he was a child, only for his father to drown after falling out of the boat during stormy conditions. This has resulted in Truman showing signs of post-traumatic stress disorder, which, as described by the NHS (2014), is when a person exhibits visible forms of anxiety caused by a very stressful or frightening past event.

The partially sunken rowboat acts as a trigger for Truman to have flashbacks of his father's sudden death, and therefore turns him off the idea of leaving the island. The behaviour Truman exhibits at this time is quite a stark contrast to his usual cheerful and happy persona, and he has likely been forced into this scenario by Christof as an attempt to yet again stifle his wish to explore the world beyond Seahaven. It is also around this point of the film when Truman shows increasing eagerness to do so, and to specifically visit the Island of Fiji where he believes Lauren, 'Sylvia,' is located.

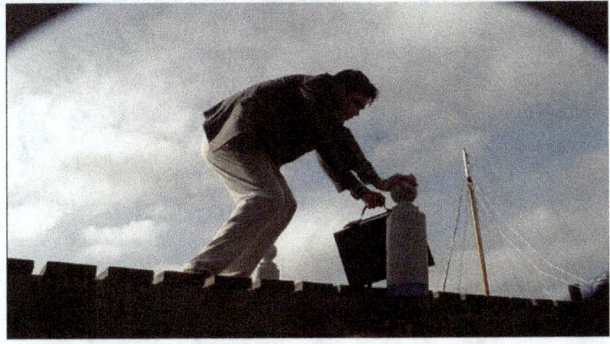

Figure 21. Truman trembling in fear as he walks over the sea decking, camera view from the partially sunken rowboat.

To further understand the artificial world that Truman inhabits, we are shown that Seahaven is actually 'the world's largest studio set,' with this set's external shell resembling an extremely large geodesic dome that can be seen from space.

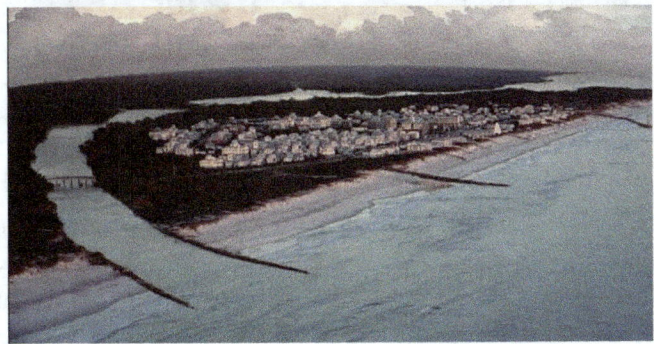

Figure 22. A view of the island of Seahaven, showing that it is not that much bigger than a large town.

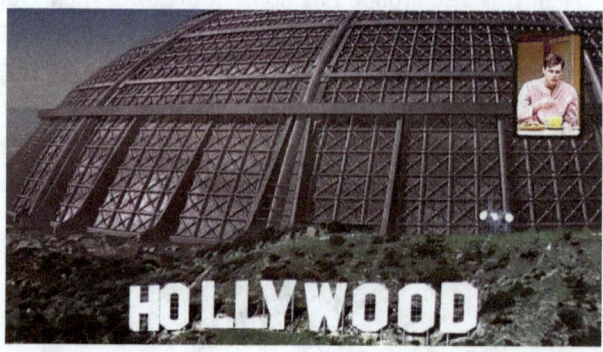

Figure 23. An exterior view of the geodesic dome that Seahaven is contained within. The Hollywood sign lets us know that the dome is situated in Los Angeles, California.

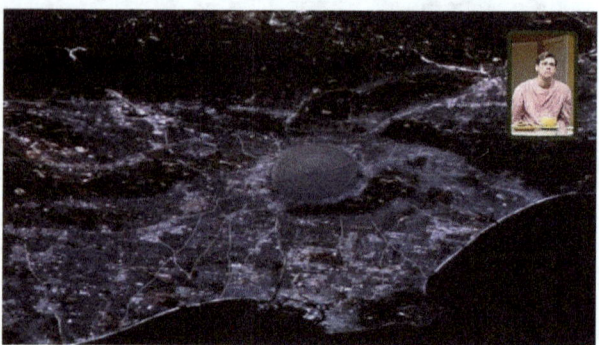

Figure 24. View of the geodesic dome that contains Seahaven from outer space, showing us its massive scale.

The reason for this dome being so large in scale is because it contains a large portion of the sea, or more accurately, a strategically placed artificial sea to add to the realism of the 'set.' Its interior walls project a phoney sky that usually portrays beautiful sunsets reminiscent of what you would see in a tropical climate. This, of course, is another mechanism to persuade Truman to stay on the island. The weather is also artificial and controlled by Christof and the other producers that run the 'Truman Show.' A prime example of this is when Truman is sitting on a beach and it suddenly starts to rain heavily, however it only rains on him and not around him. He notices this and becomes quite perplexed, and even amused by it. It is likely to have been a mistake in the artificial weather's programming, as soon after it starts to rain everywhere in a normal fashion.

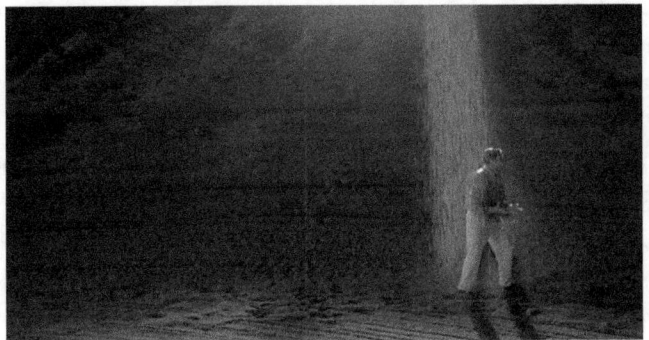

Figure 25. The patch of rain that only falls on Truman.

When Truman is fairly certain that either people are watching him or that he is 'trapped' on the island, he shows signs of potentially having 'paranoid personality disorder.' Although research on this disorder is ongoing, John Livelsey (1995, 45) states an unwarranted mistrust of others has been considered the defining feature of the disorder. Other clinical characteristics of the disorder are the individual being hypersensitive to criticism from others, acting with antagonism, aggressiveness, rigidity, and hypervigilance. The writings of Robert G. Harper (2010, 1-3) explain these contributing factors further. He states this unwarranted mistrust and suspiciousness of others' actions or intentions due to the belief that they seek to cause harm or ill will to them, are the embodiment of the term 'paranoid.' He continues by saying anyone can have such worrying concerns for a time, but when it becomes a pervasive and enduring feature of a person's way of dealing with reality, this can constitute a paranoid personality disorder.

This previous statement can be applied to the analysis of Truman's continued 'paranoid' behaviour when he feels that he is being 'contained' within Seahaven. Harper explains that among mental health scholars, there is consensual agreement reflected in the Diagnostic and Statistical Manual (DSM, the gold standard for diagnosis of psychiatric disorders) that a 'personality disorder' is an enduring, inflexible pattern of behaviour across a broad range of functional contexts that produces either clinically significant personal distress or disrup-

tion and impairment in a person's social, occupational, or other important areas
of functioning. Some of these areas have been previously discussed, such as
how Truman's actions affect his occupational roles, but one particular scene
encapsulates these behavioural patterns documented by Livesley and Harper.
This scene begins when Truman's wife, Meryl, spots Truman waiting in his car
as she comes home from work. Judging from the neighbours' and her reaction
to seeing him sitting stationary in the car there is a notion that something peculiar is going on. When she gets into the car with him, he demands that she looks
in the front rear-view mirror and states, "I predict... in just a moment, we will
see a lady on a red bike... followed by a man with flowers... and a Volkswagen
Beetle, with a dented fender."

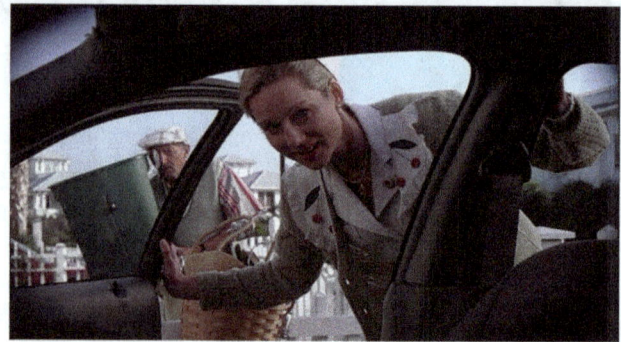

Figure 26. Truman's wife, Meryl, looking into the car and
asking him if everything is ok.

The interesting aspect of this scene is that Meryl tries to discount Truman's
increasingly intense proclamations by dismissing them as his imagination or
just an illusion by stating "Truman... oh please..." as he is explaining his findings to her. In certain ways, which at this point are ill-advised and unknown to
her, she is dismissing one disorder (paranoid personality disorder) with another, this being 'sensory perception disorder.' Defined by John C. Eagles (1980,
51), this is a disorder connected to visual illusions which arise because of the
self-conscious mind striving for a meaningful interpretation of an ongoing activity.

R. Jung (1980, 53) stressed the importance of meaning and action in perception, and how physiological experience demonstrate two essential integrative
effects of sensory perception. The first is the sensory stimuli that are effective

in a person, mainly for their meaning and less by their intensity, quality, or modality. The second is that the person learns from perceptions mainly during action on the basis of emotional and instinctive motivations. Both of these involve anticipation of the sensory stimulus, similar to Truman's findings involving anticipation for these 'activities' or moments to occur repeatedly. As Meryl dismisses these activities, and the proposed synced regularity of them to be a figment of Truman's imagination, he reacts with considerable irritation towards her, as a person suffering from paranoid personality disorder would if their concerns are disregarded.

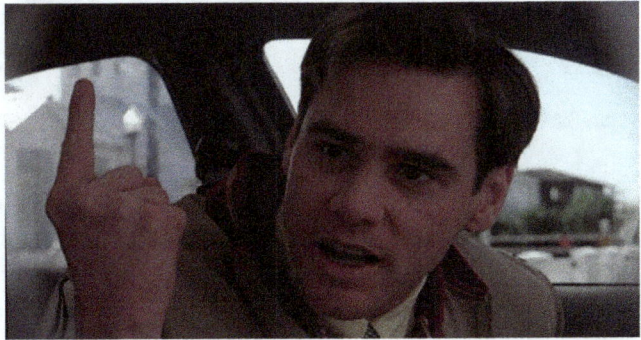

Figure 27. Truman looking more defensive and aggressive than usual after defending his belief that the people that occupy his street are on a 'constant loop' just so the street looks civilised.

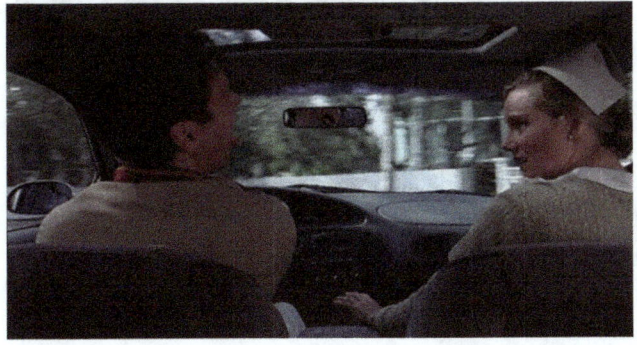

Figure 28. Truman driving in circles, deliberately shouting and screaming in somewhat of a humorous manner to try and frighten Meryl, making it clear at this point that he wants to drive off the Island.

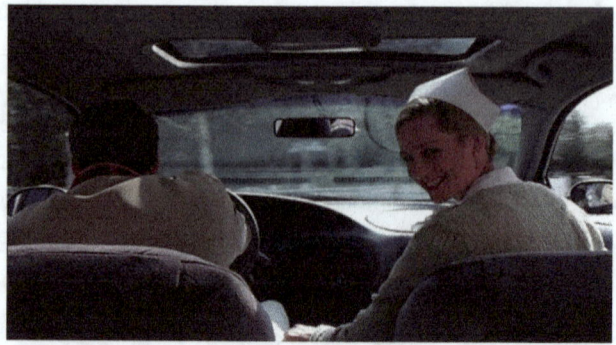

Figure 29. Meryl deliberately looking at the camera that is in the back of the car with a look of concern on her face to let the producers of the show know she needs help or a constructed diversion to stop Truman.

As it would be predicted, a series of quickly assembled 'obstructions' are put in place to prevent Truman from leaving the island again. These range from large amounts of traffic to deal with his fear of the sea again by driving over a bridge. Once they are off the island, several signs are signalling a forest fire is up ahead, with Truman ignoring them and even driving through an artificial fire that is ignited across the road. Eventually, he has to come to a stop once he arrives at a nuclear power station that is having a meltdown due to a leak.

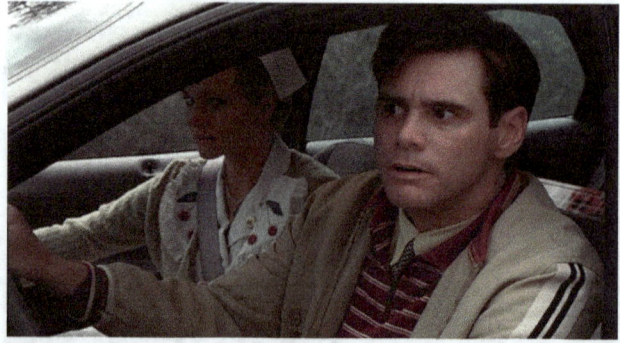

Figure 30. Truman and Meryl's reaction to a police officer that Truman had never met before, calling him by name when telling them they have to evacuate the area due to the nuclear leak.

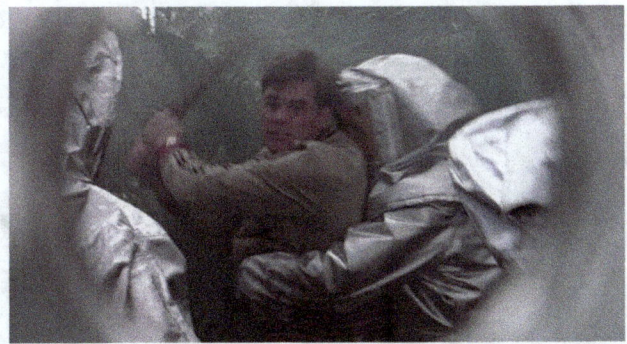

Figure 31. The 'nuclear power plant workers' apprehending Truman as he tries to fight them off with a stick.

Once the officer calls Truman by name, it all but affirms his many suspicions. He proceeds to dash out of his car and tackles those who try and stop him until he is circled and intercepted by several men in the woods who are wearing protective radioactive gear. It is during and after these events that Truman's symptoms of paranoid personality disorder reach their peak destructiveness, which prompts Meryl to leave him, and effectively 'The Truman Show,' as he becomes more physical in his frustrations towards her.

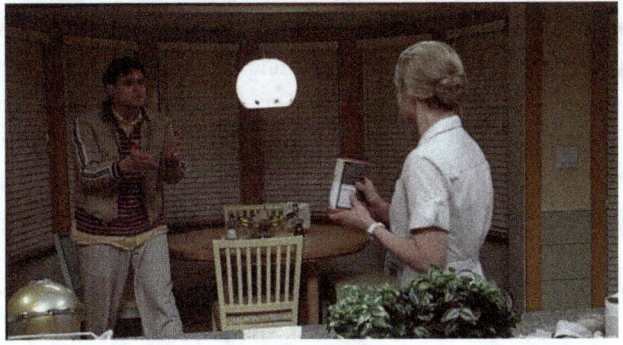

Figure 32. Truman asking Meryl if she loves him. Her reply is in the form of a 'sales pitch' by offering Truman some cocoa, with Truman asking "who the hell are you talking to, what has this got to do with anything!?"

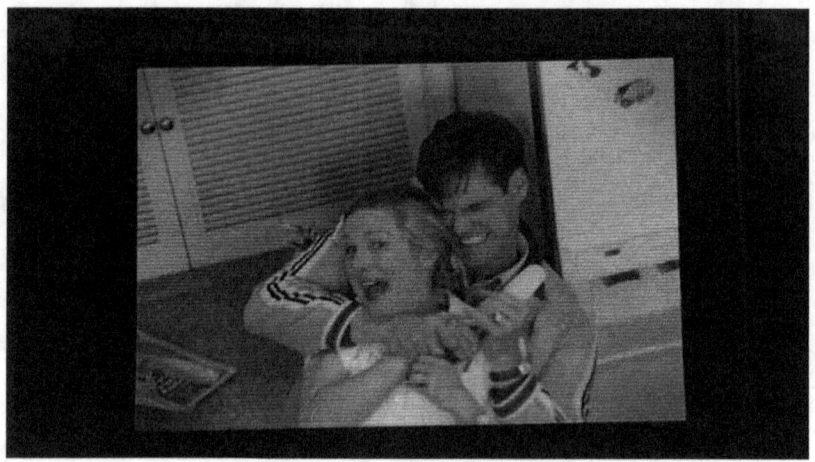

Figure 33. Truman grabbing Meryl after she threatens him with a knife, whilst she screams "do something!" in the direction of a main camera.

Further writings from the American Psychiatric Association (2000) in regards to paranoid personality disorder continue to describe the many actions carried out by Truman. It is stated that there is a preoccupation with unjustified doubts about the loyalty or trustworthiness of family, friends, or associates, and due to this, there is a reluctance to confide in others because of this unwarranted fear that the information will be used maliciously against him or her. In effect, Truman feels that he is alone, and that the only person that he can confide in is not his wife, but is his best friend Marlon, who is the only person that does not 'doubt' him in an insulting or unconstructive manner. This, of course, is all part of Christof's plan, as Marlon is constantly told what to say through an earpiece, effectively becoming Christof's most useful asset at this point to subdue Truman's emotions. When analysing the hierarchy of power within this constructed world, it is arguable that Christof's 'vantage point' is in essence not too dissimilar to a watchmen's view of prisoners from their position in a 'panopticon.'

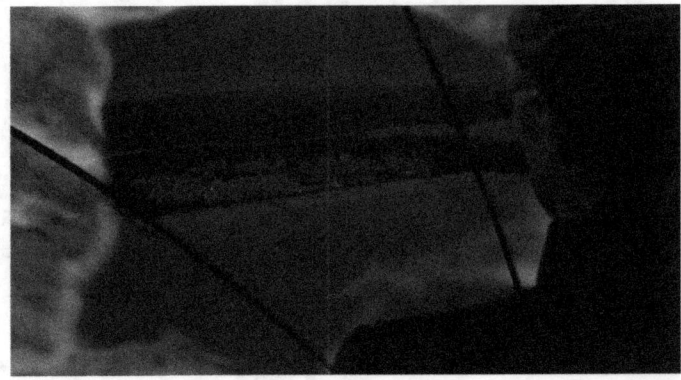

Figure 34. Christof looking down upon Seahaven from his 'lunar room on the 221st floor' of the dome that contains Seahaven.

Foucault (1995, 201) wrote about the panopticon as being a metaphor for society. He states its major effect was to induce in the inmate a state of conscious and permanent visibility that assures the automatic functioning of power; however, they do not know when or if they are being watched. Foucault redefined the panopticon to address the tendency of modern society to normalise itself. No longer were despots needed to exercise complete control; rather, permanent visibility forces members of a society to comply by a common set of rules. These 'rules,' for better or worse, are not questioned by the 'cast' of 'The Truman Show,' and are ones which Truman was unknowingly following his entire life.

Boghani (2014, 54) argues that it was up until this point that Christof rarely had to rely on physical barriers to keep Truman contained within Seahaven because the most powerful weapon he wielded was Truman's own fear. In this latter section of the film, however, Truman starts to overcome his fears of the unknown and, more literally, his fear of the sea when trying to break away from the confines of his constructed life by sailing off the Island. Now, as Boghani puts it 'Christof must engage his full arsenal, and succeeds in blocking Truman at every turn.' This is until Truman manages to, for the first time, escape the watchful eyes of Christof and his entire crew of producers that run the show, and the thousands of cameras within Seahaven in his final pursuit of 'freedom.'

A Comparison

Throughout both films, regardless of their genre or underlying motifs, the theme of 'containment' is the most prevalent. The protagonists' 'prison' is their world and something from which they both desperately try to escape by any means necessary, even at the potential cost of their life. As discussed before, once Oh Dae-su breaks through the wall of his prison, he does not care if he is on the '52nd' floor and falls to his death; in his mind, he believes that he has overcome his captors' hold on him, and that is all that matters. As for Truman, he not only overcomes his fear of the water by trying to sail off the island, but he also does not care if he drowns when Christof creates an artificial storm to capsize his sailboat. As documented by Boghani (2014, 56), Christof is ready to watch Truman die at sea rather than let him out of his grasp. Part of the reason that Christof is so content in his desire to prevent Truman from leaving the island is that even if his decisions cause Truman to die, he knows that people will still be watching his creation up until the end.

The protagonists make these life-changing decisions because their reality has become unbearable and has effectively turned into a life prison sentence. Foucault (1995, 122) describes the mindset of a prisoner when they realise that they will be in detention for life:

> A life sentence throws them into despair; (...) they become concerned only with plans to escape and to rebel; and since the judgements that were passed on them did not deprive them of life, why should one seek to render it unbearable for them?

The defining similarity between Oh Dae-su and Truman is that at some period during their containment, be it known or unknown to them is that their newly formed change of personality is related to the built environment that they are in. Deborah Welch Larson (1985, 24) discusses the psychological theories of attitude change by stating that psychology has been accompanied by an altered view of humans as active agents who shape their own behaviour by constructing meaning from their environment. Oh Dae-su changes from being a drunken businessman who acts with little grace into a more reflective and serious man during his time of containment, which was in the form of solitary confinement. Considering that his duration of imprisonment lasted fifteen years in a 'room' no bigger than 6x4 meters, it is natural that he had a lot of time to think and 'reform.' Foucault (1995, 237) states, while discussing solitary confinement, "through the reflection that it gives rise to, and the remorse that cannot fail to follow, solitude must be a positive instrument of reform: 'Thrown into solitude, the convict reflects.'"

For Truman however, it was his feeling of being trapped (albeit within a fairly large area) and his suspicions of being under constant surveillance that caused his naturally cheerful attitude to change into a more paranoid and aggressive state. Foucault's theorisation on how an individual's attitude is altered when they believe they are under constant surveillance is revolved around forced adaptation, as he states:

> Perhaps, but more certainly and more immediately it was an effort to adjust to the mechanisms of power that frame the everyday lives of individuals; an adaptation and a refinement of the machinery that assumes responsibility for and places under surveillance their everyday behaviour, their identity, their activity and their apparently unimportant gestures (1995, 77).

In a parallel to Oh Dae-su's surroundings, Truman spends arbitrary lengths of time in a room of similar dimensions and lacking natural lighting, in this case, it is his basement. This space, however, is a form of retreat for Truman, and one in which he likes spending time. It is also within this room where he begins his last attempt to escape from the Island, notably through a similar method to Oh Dae-Su by literally carving through the architecture he is contained within.

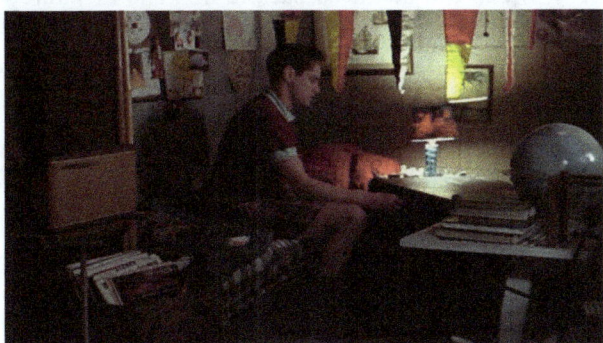

Figure 35. Truman's private room and place of retreat located in the basement of his house.

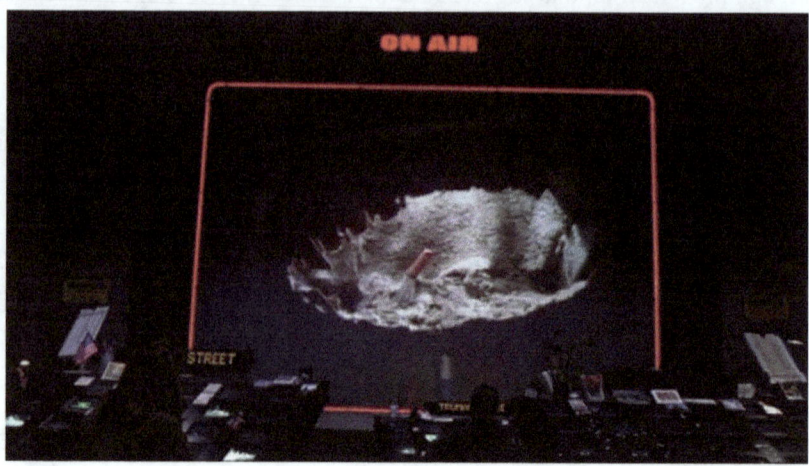

Figure 36. Camera view of the hole Truman creates by carving through
the floorboards of his house, done so in a similar level of secrecy to
that of Oh Dae-Su's attempt.

As previously mentioned, the architectural entities that both protagonists are
contained within are contrasting in scale. However, one of the main differences
between the films is the overall atmosphere and setting. When discussing the
urban setting of *Oldboy*, Jeong (2013, 179) mentions that the classical vision
of the inner city, which can be traced back to film and literature of the colo-
nial era, represents an urban landscape that can be a space of violence, trage-
dy, and moral corruption, themes which occur regularly within the film. This
is in comparison to the more tranquil nature of the countryside or a small to
medium-sized town, like that of Seahaven. Boghani (2014, 29) suggests that
these settings within Seahaven are based on a utopian ideal that comes from
post-WWII American idealism. Shows like *The Honeymooners*, *Lassie*, and *My
Three Sons* were the first to portray this vision of middle-class suburbia. This
'utopia,' consisting of streets laden with old fashioned, white-picket-fences,
where everyone is happy and has meaning in their lives, is something which
Christof tried to transfer over to his creation of Seahaven.

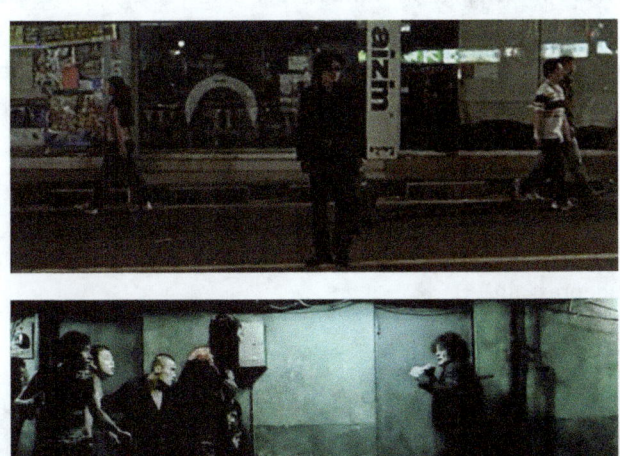

Figure 37. The general setting and lighting in *Oldboy*, once Oh Dae-Su is released.

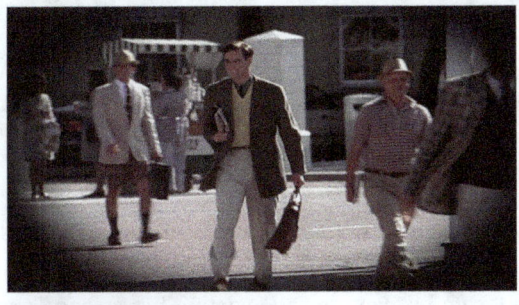

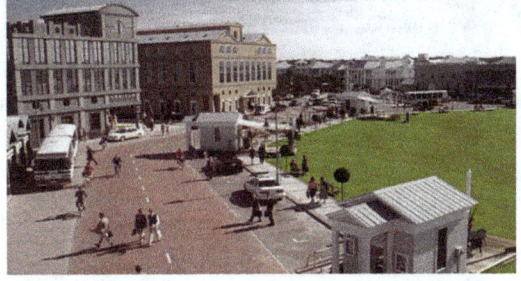

Figure 38. The general setting and atmosphere within Seahaven in *The Truman Show*.

When analysing the change of attitude that both protagonists go through, it is obvious that Oh Dae-Su becomes a more 'well rounded' person during his period of containment, in comparison to Truman who loses much of his humble nature and humanity the more he becomes convinced of his suspicions. These factors are all the more peculiar as the architectural settings that Truman is living within would initially make you assume the opposite, as he is situated within a bright and happy environment, albeit contained within it. The same conditions are not provided for Oh Dae-su, as his architectural surroundings are much more depressing.

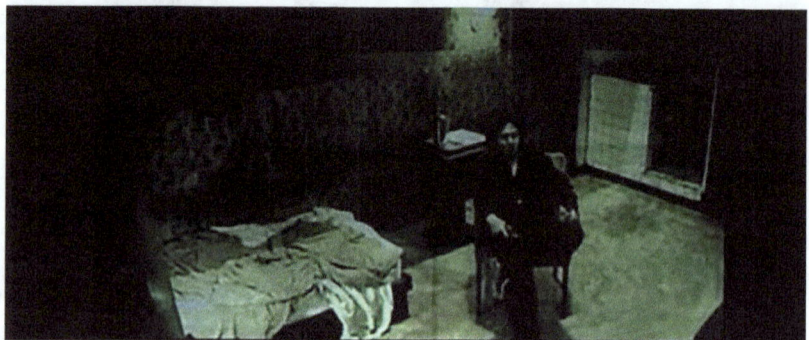

Figure 39. A security camera view of Oh Dae-su revisiting his former prison later in the film, its harsh conditions remaining much the same as they were at the time of his imprisonment.

The core difference between both films' theme of containment is that in *Oldboy* we get to see Oh Dae-Su released from his prison. The rest of the film consists of him trying to locate his captors and exacting his revenge upon them, whilst dealing with the psychological trauma that he incurred in prison. As for the *Truman Show*, we are left with somewhat of an ambiguous ending where in the last scenes we see Truman being able to walk around and through the constructed dome of Seahaven and out into the real world for the first time. What happens after this is entirely up to the viewer's interpretation.

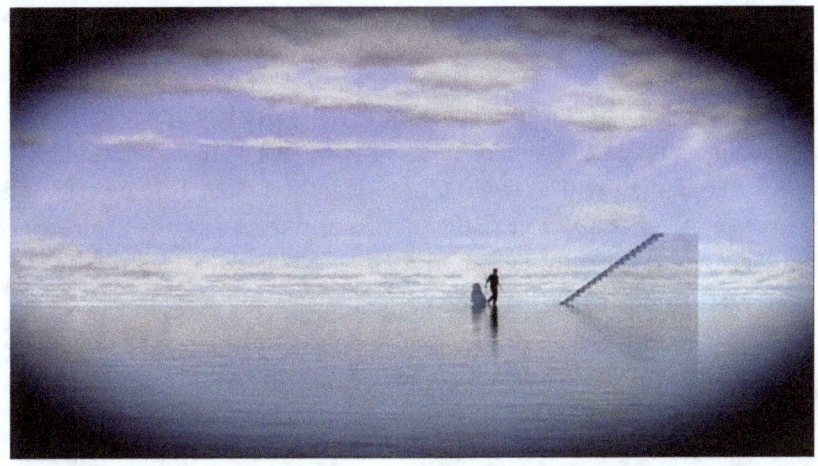

Figure 40. Truman circling the interior edge of the geodesic dome that he is contained within.

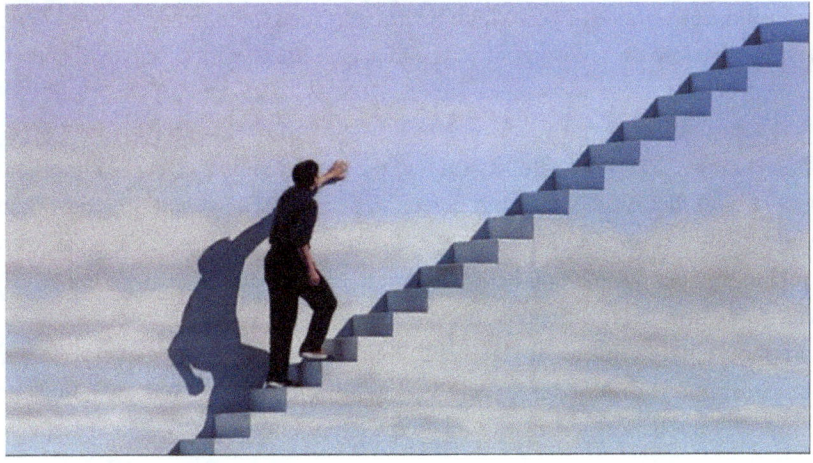

Figure 41. Closer view of Truman inspecting the interior edge of the geodesic dome while he is walking up to the door labelled 'exit'.

Post Imprisonment Freedom and Human
Reaction to Freedom

The predicticted feeling that someone would have once free after a long period of containment is perhaps elation, but more often than not it is confusion as the 'new world' is presented to them. Ozay Rinpoche (2008, 141) describes his initial reactions after he was released from a prison sentence that he received after going AWOL from the British Army:

> Now was the time of deliverance, I was out of prison and beginning a new phase of my life. My first impression of the outside world was how strange it felt to see women as well as men, and having the freedom to walk around wherever I wanted to go, this must be how everyone feels having been institutionalized and then set free.

This form of confusion can lead to a condition called institutionalisation or institutional syndrome. This is when the real world that is absent of the routines of daily prison life may be too much for a newly released prisoner to handle, and they can struggle to manage the demands of having a normal life. Their confusion can become anger, which in turn may lead them to commit an offence just to go back to the rigorous structure of prison life to which they had become adapted.

Craig Haney (2002, 79), who has studied the psychological effects of imprisonment, argues that it can vary from person to person. "The adaptation to containment within a prison is almost always difficult and, at times, creates habits of thinking and acting that can be dysfunctional in periods of post-prison adjustment." He goes on to say, "Yet, the psychological effects of incarceration vary from individual to individual, and are often reversible; (…) not everyone who is incarcerated is disabled or psychologically harmed by it. But few people are completely unchanged or unscathed by the experience."

In his documentary titled, *Louis Theroux: Behind Bars* (2008), Louis speaks with several guards and prisoners who have become institutionalised at San Quentin prison in San Francisco. Many of the prisoners have become so used to prison life they ignore its limitations and instead focus on what is available and even demonstrating the mindset of not wanting to be released. When asked by Louis, "Do you feel you've got a life in here?" one inmate serving a life sentence states, "you can make a life as comfortable as it can get in here if you put your mind to it, you can say I'm on my 401k (pension), I'm always gonna have food, I'm always gonna have shelter, I ain't gotta think about the stresses of losing my job,… I'm gonna be taken care of until I die."

Alternatively, when speaking with an experienced guard at the prison about the release of twenty-seven prisoners on a particular day, Louis asks how many of them he believes will "stay out and not come back," to which the guard replies, "with twenty-seven guys going out today, I would probably see about…more than half come back (…) it could be a matter of days or a matter of months." He goes on to say, "All human beings are creatures of habit, they go back to their old neighbourhoods, they tend to fall into the same groups of people that still disobey the law… and they get caught up." When asked how they feel about their impending freedom, one of the twenty-seven inmates says, "I'm nervous, because I haven't had no human contact for three years, I've been in this cell by myself, no windows, no sunlight…just locked up"

Going by these real-life studies of prisoners who have either gotten used to being institutionalis ed or are awaiting release, it is apparent that after a long duration of imprisonment, a person may consider 'freedom' a paradox of sorts, as they are now about to live their life autonomously, something which they have not experienced in years. Louis Theroux formulates his final opinion on the matter by proclaiming,

> I realized that so many prisoners have been institutionalized that San Quentin was now their home, with little contact with family and friends, their real relationships were here, and as much as prison walls kept others out, it also forced those on the inside together.

The Protagonist's Reaction to Freedom

Once Oh Dae-su is released from his prison, he does not exhibit elation, as it comes as a complete surprise to him. His newly found freedom has not come as a result of all the years of carving away at his prison walls, but it is his captors who have surprisingly released him. He wakes up and emerges from a suitcase on a rooftop in the inner-city area of Seoul with him struggling to breathe the fresh air and immediately shielding his eyes from direct sunlight as he has been exposed to neither in fifteen years.

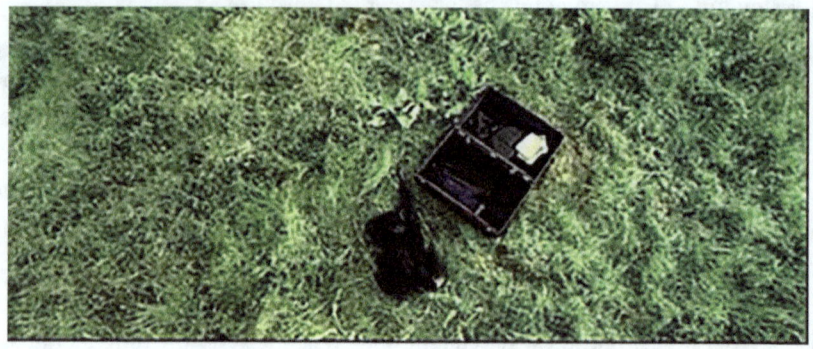

Figure 42. Oh Dae-su emerging from the suitcase that he was contained within.

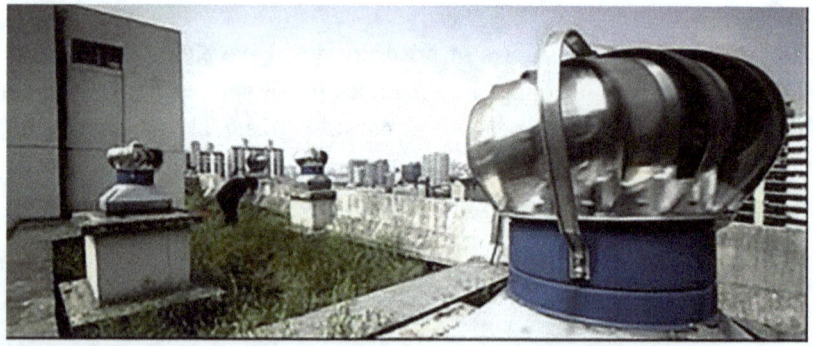

Figure 43. The rooftop that Oh Dae-su is released on top of.

Coincidentally, there is another unnamed man on the rooftop when Oh Dae-su is released; however, he is there because he is contemplating suicide by jumping off the building. After seeing this man, Oh Dae-su acts as if he is experiencing 'sensory overload' as he tentatively walks over to the man and addresses him by caressing and smelling him, presumably to see if he is not just having another hallucination or experiencing delirium.

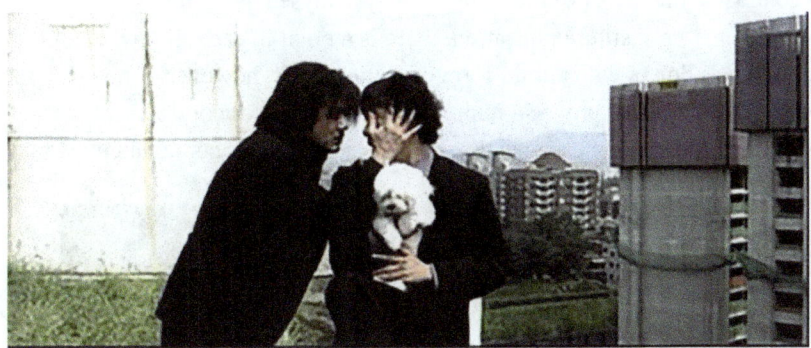

Figure 44. Oh Dae-Su embracing the unknown man on the rooftop in an odd manner.

It is possible to link this scene back to the story told by Ozay Rinpoche where after his release from solitary confinement, he thought that everyday occurrences such as a man and woman walking down the street was a strange sight. For Oh Dae-su, however, seeing another tangible human being was enough to make him act in a disbelieving manner. The case is different with Truman, as we do not see what happens to him after his 'release'; however, the film suggests that the main reason why Truman would leave the island is to pursue his former love interest Lauren, or 'Sylvia.' In terms of a reaction, as soon as Truman thinks that he is about to step into the 'real' world, or at least escape the reality that he has come to know, we see a final glimpse of his former humorous self. He does this by ironically turning around and saying "in case I don't see ya!, good afternoon, good evening and good night!" when directly prompted to say something to the world by Christof.

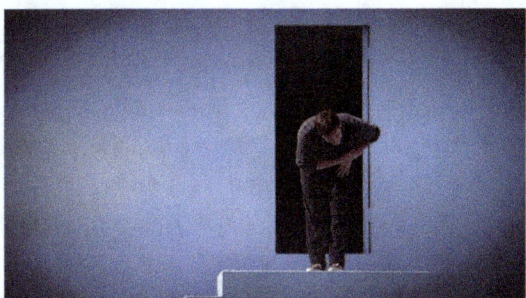

Figure 45. Truman addressing the viewer's directly just before he walks through the door that leads out past his enclosed world into the real world.

In contrast to the real-life studies previously analysed, particularly the prisoners who suffer from institutionalisation, there is a point in each film where the two protagonists do act with a mild form of elation. This, however, is not after they are released from the physical realm of their structure of containment, but once they believe they have escaped the mental realm of their containment.

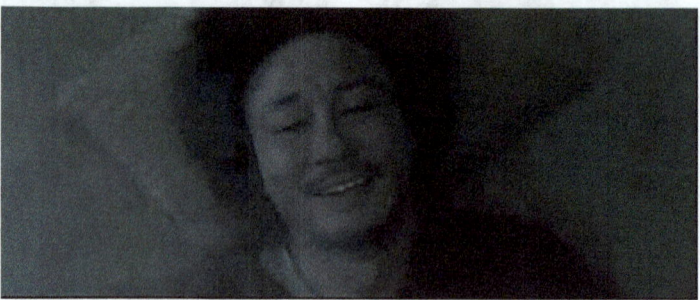

Figure 46. Oh Dae-su drifting off to sleep with a happy expression on his face after breaking through the walls of his prison to the outside world.

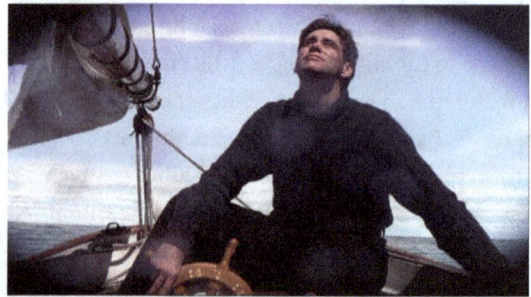

Figure 47. Truman continuing his attempt to sail off the Island of Seahaven after surviving the artificial storm created by Christof in an attempt to stop him.

Both scenes are set during their impending freedom; however, it is arguable that at this point they are happier than what they are and would be once free, which begs the question, does the idea of freedom evoke more pronounced happiness than actual freedom? In the case of both films, you could argue that it does. Oh Dae-su's post imprisonment mood is anything but happy, as his sole purpose is to find and punish those who imprisoned him once he gets past his initial disbelief that he is actually 'free.' For Truman, it is less uncertain, as we are left with an ambiguous ending that does not show us the aftermath of his escape.

Christof, however, speaks an element of truth when communicating directly with Truman when he is about to step through the exit, and he says, "Listen to me Truman! There's no more truth out there than there is in the world I created for you, the same lies, the same deceit, but in my world… you have nothing to fear." This statement echoes the principle of what is said by the prisoner serving a life sentence to whom Theroux speaks, as he states "I'm gonna be taken care of until I die."

In a different approach, Haney (2002, 79) states that the consensus on the most negative effects of containment is that most people who have spent time in the best-run and designed prisons return to the free world with little or no permanent and diagnosable psychological disorders as a result. The conditions of Oh Dae-su's prison are poor and spatially designed to not only contain, but also to restrain normal human activity. After a long duration of time, even the most strong-minded person would arguably lose some degree of sanity in such poor architectural settings. The suburban settings that Truman was contained within were of a conceived luxury, as he had everything that he needed to survive, and lived in comfort, not too dissimilar to prisoners who are placed under 'house arrest.' This did not suffice in the end, as it was still a form of forced containment that ultimately led to him suffering from psychological disorders. Haney's statement on how the psychological ramifications of prolonged containment vary from person to person is applicable. However, the idea of a prisoner who returns to the 'free world' with little or no psychological damage after being contained in a 'well run' environment may not always be true, Truman being the archetype of this theory.

Conclusion

Regardless of the difference between the scale and setting of a 'prison,' it is clear from the analysis of these films and the portrayal of the two main characters that a human being can feel trapped and can develop psychological problems in any architectural setting. This setting does not have to follow the perceived notion of containment relating to a space of captivity being micro in scale as the definition of 'containment' is 'to hold, restrain or keep someone or something within limits.' In the case of both films, Oh Dae-su's limits were a 4x6m room and Truman's were a moderately sized town.

In addition to this, human input, be it through prison authorities or simply the volume of accompanying inhabitants also plays a great deal on the level and type of psychological trauma a prisoner, or newly freed prisoner can tolerate, as neither too little nor too many have been shown to be the most advantageous. As Haney (2002, 80) states, "Prisons do not, in general, make people crazy." However, researchers who are openly sceptical about whether the miseries caused by imprisonment commonly convert into psychological harm concede that, for some people, prison can produce adverse, prolonged changes. Most people concur that the more drawn-out, extreme, dangerous, or psychologically demanding the nature of the containment, the greater the number of people who will likely suffer and the deeper the psychological damage that they will incur.

The final stages of imprisonment, just before release, are typically thought to be moments of euphoria for a prisoner as portrayed by the two films studied, but the reality is often different to this if the prisoner has spent much of their life in a form of containment. Once released, the 'free world,' void of the systematic setup that a prison consists of, can worsen, or create incurable psychological trauma the prisoner has incurred whilst incarcerated. This asks the question, is there a point in which real freedom is unobtainable to those who have become institutionalised? Or would the prisoner find the solace that the 'free world' is meant to deliver if they simply remained in containment?

REFERENCES

American Psychiatric Association. 2000. Diagnostic and Statistical Manual of Mental Disorders, 4th Edition, Text Revision (DSM-IV-TR, 4th edn., Texas: American Psychiatric Association.

Beaumont, Matthew & Dart, Gregory. 2010. Restless Cities, London: Verso.

Boghani, Ami. 2014. GradeSaver (TM) ClassicNotes: The Truman Show, Boston: GradeSaver LLC.

Bower, Bertha Muzzy. 2005. Cabin Fever, Connecticut: 1st World Library - Literary Society

Castle, Robert. 2005. "Performance World: The Truman Show's Sociology," BRIGHT LIGHTS Film Journal. Accessed February 2015. http://brightlightsfilm.com/performance-world-truman-shows-sociology/#footnote_0_16269.

Chan-wook, Park, (director). 2003. Old boy (DVD). South Korea: Show East.

Cabb, Stuart, dir. Louis Theroux: Behind Bars, BBC, 2008.

Craighead, Edward. 2010. The Corsini Encyclopedia of Psychology (Corsini Encyclopedia of Psychology and Behavioral Science), 4th edn., New York: John Wiley & Sons

Darius, Julian. 2013. "Revenge, Hypnotism, and Oedipus in Oldboy (2003)," Sequart organisation. Accessed January 2015. http://sequart.org/magazine/30991/revenge-hypnotism-and-oedipus-in-oldboy-2003/.

"Diagnostic criteria for 301.0 Paranoid Personality Disorder," BehaveNet. Accessed March 2015. http://behavenet.com/node/21647.

Eccles. C. John. 1980. The Human Psyche, Berlin: Springer-Verlag.

Ellis, Aaron. 2013. "Oldboy (2003 movie): What does the hallucination of ants symbolise or mean during Oh Dae-su's fifteen-year imprisonment?," Quora. Accessed January 2015. https://www.quora.com/Oldboy-2003-movie/What-does-the-hallucination-of-ants-symbolise-or-:mean-during-Oh-Dae-sus-fifteen-year-imprisonment

Foucault, Michel. 1995. Discipline & Punish: the Birth of the Prison. 2nd ed. New York: Vintage Books.

Foucault, Michel. 1978. The History of Sexuality Volume I: An Introduction, New York: Random House.

Haney, Craig. 2002. "The Psychological Impact of Incarceration: Implications for Post-Prison Adjustment". Paper presented at From Prison to Home conference, California, 30-31 January 2002, p77 -92.

Jackson, Tony. "Televisual Realism: The Truman Show." Mosaic: A Journal for the Interdisciplinary Study of Literature Volume 43, no. 3 (September 2010): 147.

Jeong, Y, Kelly. "Towards humanity and redemption: The world of Park Chan-wook's revenge film trilogy." Journal of Japanese & Korean Cinema Volume 4, no.2 (January 2014): 169. https://doi.org/10.1386/jjkc.4.2.169_1

Kristeva, Julia. 1982. Powers of Horror: An Essay on Abjection, New York: Columbia University Press.

Kremer, William & Hammond, Claudia. 2013. "How do people survive solitary confinement?," BBC World Service. Accessed January 2015. http://www.bbc.co.uk/news/magazine-22878268.

Larson. W. Deborah. 1985. Origins of Containment, New Jersey: Princeton University Press.

Livesley, John. 1995. The DSM-IV Personality Disorders (Diagnosis & Treatment of Mental Dsorders), New York: Guilford Press.

Lukacs, Georg. 1974. The Theory of the Novel, Massachusetts: The MIT Press.

Merriam Webster. 2014 "Hallucination," Accessed: December 2014. http://www.merriam- webster.com/medical/hallucination.

NHS. 2015. "Post-traumatic stress disorder (PTSD)," Accessed February 2015. http://www.nhs.uk/conditions/Post-traumatic-stress-disorder/Pages/Introduction.aspx.

NHS. 2014. "Seasonal affective disorder," Accessed December 2014. http://www.nhs.uk/conditions/Seasonal-affective-disorder/Pages/Introduction.aspx

Rinpoche, Ozay. 2008. Freedom! Escaping the Prison of the Mind, Washington: Eremitical Press.

Weir, Peter, (director). 2003. The Truman Show (DVD). USA: Paramount Pictures.

SPACES OF THE
PSYCHE

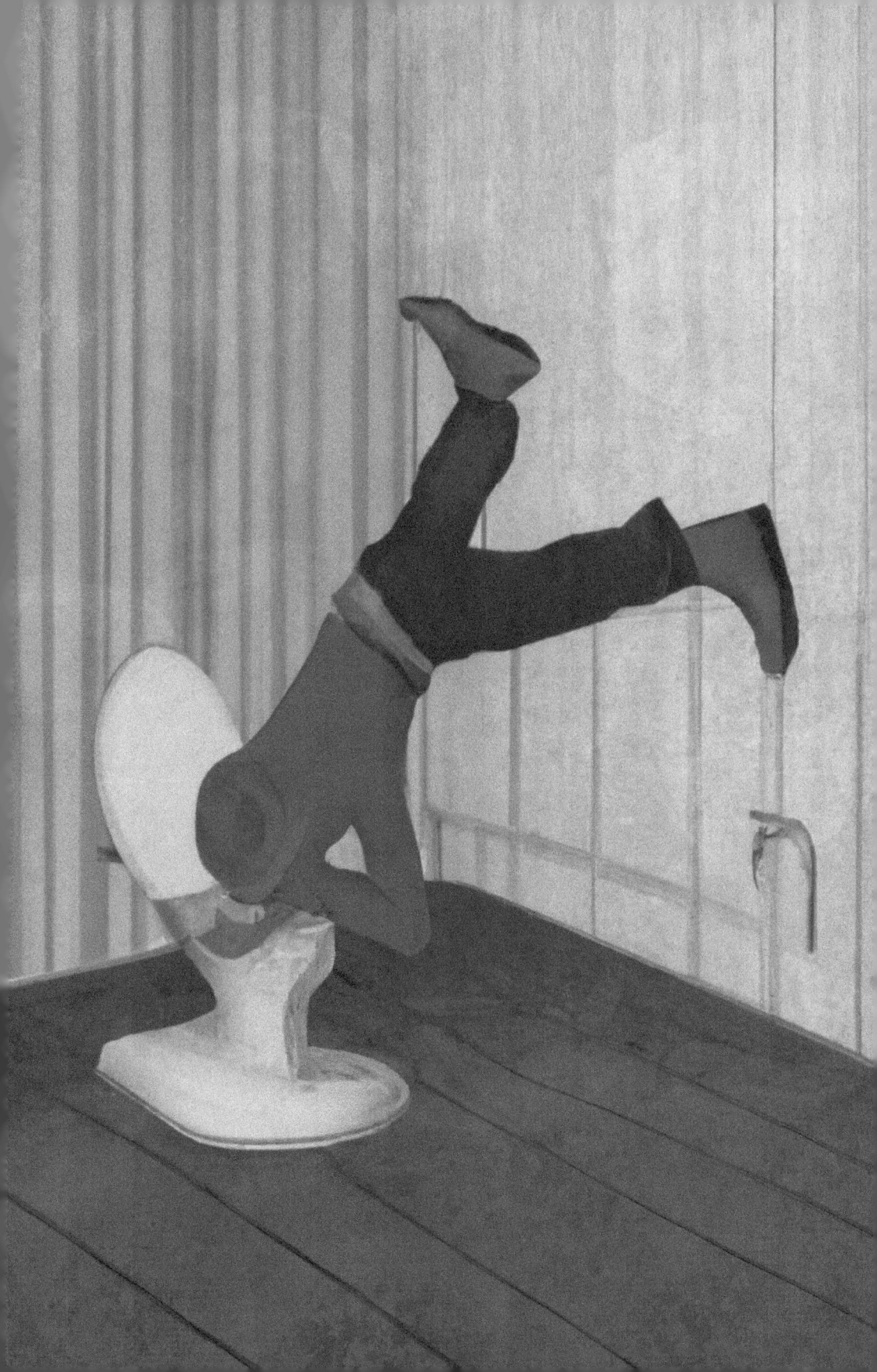

Amnesia and Addiction:
Housing the Psyche in *Memento*
and *Trainspotting*

Clíona Brady

CLÍONA BRADY has been a lecturer in Architecture at the Yeats' Academy of Arts, Design and Architecture at the Institute of Technology Sligo since 2004. Her research and teaching interests focus on architecture and film, and the psychological presence and impact of interior space. She completed an MA thesis in Education in 2011 entitled *Dialectics of Theory and Praxis in Architectural Education: The role of the physical model in the relationship between creative intention and intuitive action*, which explored the use of photography and film in communicating architectural ideas through the physical model. She completed her PhD at the School of Natural and Built Environment, Queen's University Belfast. Her doctoral thesis, *Permeable Boundaries: Exploring the Architecture of the Psyche in Cinematic Spaces through Collage*, proposes a new method of rendering the psychological content of interior space visible. She is a member of CACity: Cinema and Architecture in the City Collaborative Research Group (www.cacity.org).

This chapter focuses on the psychological content of space as communicated in film. It begins with a brief overview of psychological film and examines how architecture frequently plays a dominant role in its expression. The use of interior space in this role is then analysed in more depth in two examples of contemporary film: *Trainspotting* (1996), directed by Danny Boyle and *Memento* (2000), directed by Christopher Nolan. The main character in each suffers from some form of psychological disruption and is preoccupied with issues of identity and memory, respectively. Both films stand out as having a strong visual and psychological presence that has resonated over time. In each, my aim was to compile stills and sequences, which conveyed the protagonist's psychological state through the setting, and to both record and analyse this expressive occupation of space through storyboards.

Physical and psychological condition invariably influences both perception of interior space and the impact that spaces have upon those who inhabit them, affecting observation, disrupting encounters, and rendering space laden with association. Examining the highly personal, subjective experience of an individual's encounter with architecture can imbue spaces with a significance that as an integral and unavoidable part of most people's daily lives, has the potential to provide both support and inspiration to its inhabitants. Film portrays complex stories through a language, which is expressive, has emotional impact, and resonates in memory. The expressive elements of this immersive medium can be used to portray the psychological state of a character through the way they occupy and engage with the spaces they inhabit. What is shown on screen is selected for its atmospheric qualities or its symbolic significance to the character's psychological condition. The storytelling structure of film also provides an accessibility, which renders it an appropriate medium to communicate the significance that architectural space can have in our daily lives. It takes us directly into the intimate and subjective way a character inhabits space. As well as contributing to a deeper consideration of the spaces we inhabit, analysing ways in which space may be represented through the expressive language of film can potentially contribute to extracting more from the communicative tools of architecture.

The relationship between film and psychology has been a close one since the earliest years of each discipline and has resurfaced periodically as a condition of human existence and as such, persists as a primary topic of interest. There are examples spanning film's lifetime, from the expressionistic representation in *The Cabinet of Dr Caligari* (1920), conveying the escalating insanity of the hero to the present day. There have been many examples across a range of film genres in which psychological instability or disorder was the subject matter such as: film noir (*The Lost Weekend* (Billy Wilder, 1945)); drama (*Brighton Rock* (John Boulting, 1948), *One Flew over the Cuckoo's Nest* (Miloš Forman, 1975), *Rain Man* (Barry Levinson, 1988), *Good Will Hunting* (Gus Van Sant, 1997), and *Girl Interrupted* (James Mangold, 1999); psychological thriller (*Rope* (Alfred Hitchcock, 1948), *Taxi Driver* (Martin Scorsese, 1976), *The Machinist* (Brad Anderson, 2004), *Shutter Island* (Martin Scorsese, 2010) and *Black Swan* (Darren Aronofsky, 2010)); dystopian sci-fi (*A Clockwork Orange* (Stanley Kubrick, 1971) and *12 Monkeys* (Terry Gilliam, 1995)); biographical drama (*Shine* (Scott Hicks, 1996), *A Beautiful Mind* (Ron Howard, 2001) and *The Aviator* (Martin Scorsese, 2004)); comedy-drama (*What About Bob?* (Frank Oz, 1991), *As Good as it Gets* (James L. Brooks, 1997), *Silver Linings Playbook* (David O. Russell, 2012) and *The Skeleton Twins* (Craig Johnson, 2014)) and even the animated Pixar production *Inside Out* (Pete Docter, 2015). The 1990s decade opened with Martin Scorsese's *Goodfellas* (1990), introducing a new slant on the mobster film, through outward depiction of affluent lifestyle and concurrently the internal psychological breakdown of its hero, Henry Hill, a perspective which would be subsequently and repeatedly emulated, giving the action film a new depth through character development. Sense of place strongly exudes the grim tone of both *The Silence of the Lambs* (Jonathan Demme, 1991) and the darkly comic, neo-noir *Fargo* (Joel and Ethan Coen, 1996). In the early 1990s, independent film experienced a resurgence with Quentin Tarantino's *Reservoir Dogs* (1992) and *Pulp Fiction* (1994), both of which redefined the style of independent film making through non-linear plotlines and multiple interlinked characters and predominantly interior locations, while being steeped in cinematic historical reference.

The selected films represent two approaches to using architectural space to convey disrupted psychological conditions. Danny Boyle's *Trainspotting* (1996) based on Irvine Welsh's 1993 novel of the same name, deals with a group in their twenties engaged in a lifestyle of recreational heroin use and the struggle of one member to extract himself and stay clean. His triumphs and setbacks are documented through a narrative conveying themes of alienation, and conflicts between self-identity and loyalty to the people and place one comes from. The narrative is linear, punctuated by surreal intrusions in the dealer's flat. Both the film style and the soundtrack reflect the zeitgeist of a particular time in life and in the world. *Memento* (2000) directed by Christopher Nolan and based on his brother Jonathan's short story, *Memento Mori* (published after the film in 2002) portrays a very different world. The narrative follows a man who has anterograde amnesia: Leonard Shelby can form no new memories since an accident in which his wife was killed and spends his days trying to piece together his missing memories, seeking her retribution. The reversed narrative structure intertwined with real time parallels the confusion he feels in dealing with the complexities of loss, identity, and belonging. The role of space is in some cases translated directly from the source texts, since the spaces in which the characters function are intrinsic in conveying their mental condition. Filmmaker and critic Mark Cousins cites control of space, magnifying detail, and awareness of time as essential cinematic elements (2016, 15), which is used here as mechanisms with which to analyse the expressive content of each film.

Trainspotting: Control of Space

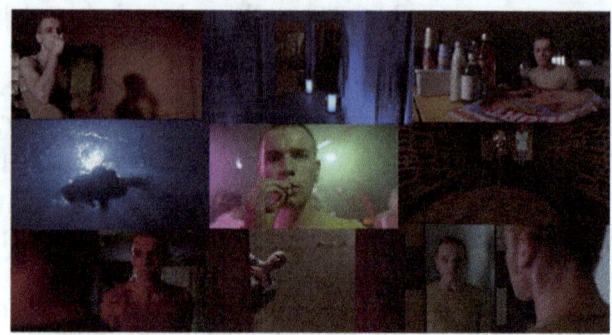

Figure 1: The Language of Trainspotting (all film stills captured by the author unless indicated otherwise.)

The look of *Trainspotting* is drawn from real life but very much exaggerated" (Westbrook, 2017). Inhabited spaces are experienced in high colour when Renton is under the influence of heroin, with floating elevated angles contrasting with the straight point of view blandness of his apartment on an 'unamplified' day. Stylistic techniques include:

> [S]urreal…imagery, a view into characters' mental states (often through point-of-view shots, narration, and dream sequences), use of very high/low angle shots. A series of very short, frenetic shots juxtaposed with long shots, Generally fast-paced, energetic storytelling (accompanied and enhanced by fast-paced editing), disorienting camera placement, and use of strong, bright colors, either through lighting or set decoration (Matthew Jones, 2017).

A series of stills and sequences observe both how the protagonist is shown in space and how he uses the space, moving through it in a particular direction, position within framing, and other cinematic techniques. The film opens with a chase through the streets of Edinburgh, much like Boyle's earlier film *Shallow Grave* (1994), although this time instead of speeding in a vehicle, we are running with pedestrians. Renton (Ewan MacGregor), Sick Boy (Jonny Lee Miller) and Spud (Ewen Bremner) sprint over the cobbles and down alleyways with two security guards hot on their heels. The city becomes a three-dimensional snakes and ladders game board through which they slip and slide and manoeuvre speedily but awkwardly through gateways and over railings. Intimate knowledge of these backstreets is apparent; this is his territory.

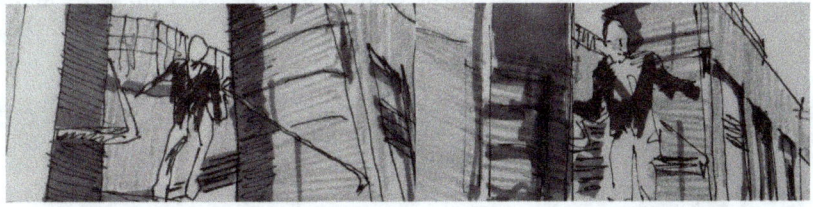

Figure 2: Renton describes the backstreets of Edinburgh (all sketches and storyboards have been created by the author unless indicated otherwise.)

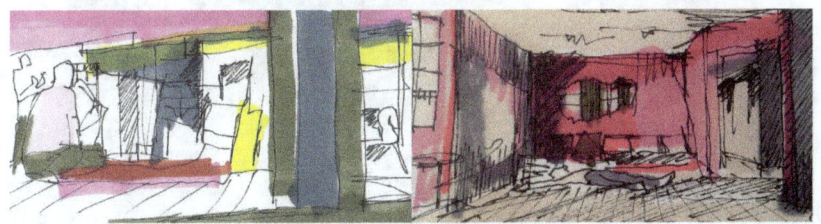

Figure 3: Enhanced interior space in Swanney's flat.

[M]uch of the narrative resembles that of the classical Hollywood cinema, the visual style is also heavily influenced by American cinema and pop culture. In particular, the editing and camera movement resemble the look of a Hollywood action movie…The camera is almost constantly moving to capture all the kinetic energy on screen, giving this brief moment a greater sense of urgency. The narration continues over several different places, including a soccer field where the gang is playing and a beat up apartment where they cook heroin (Matthew Jones, 2014).

Tracing their individual passage through the city, we then follow the protagonists inside, where both physical and psychological space are presented in all their filth, paranoia, wonder and distortion, agony and ecstasy. The architecture of the film is that of the everyday encounter, modest family homes, squalid shared flats with makeshift furniture. The realism portrayed in the 'ugliness' of these everyday spaces contribute to a clearer understanding of the mental condition of the inhabitant. In contrast to the grey streets, the interiors of the dealer, Swanney's flat are lit up and filled with open doorways and bright, vibrant colours (Figure 3). Time slows and a suspension of reality can be felt, based on both the event and its association. The camera stays low and aligned with the floor level, which is a visual mechanism used throughout the film.

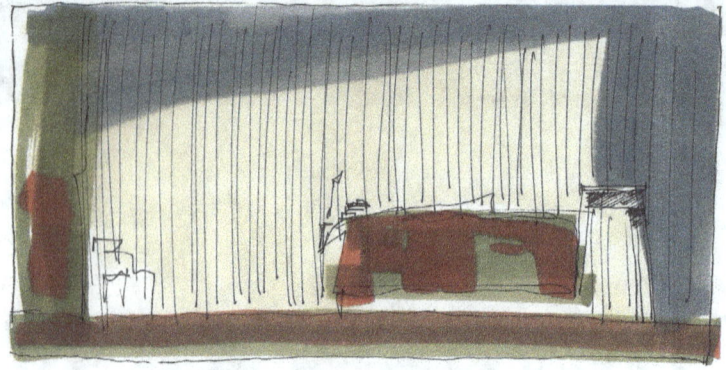

Figure 4: Low camera portrays steadiness and balance.

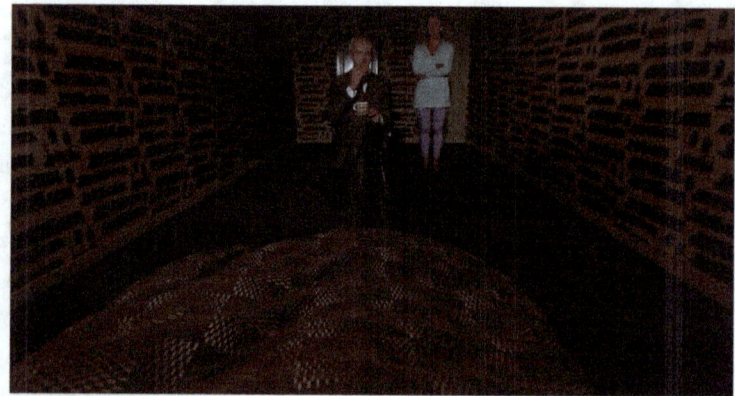

Figure 5: Elongation, distortion and alienation from the external world prevails as withdrawal sets in.

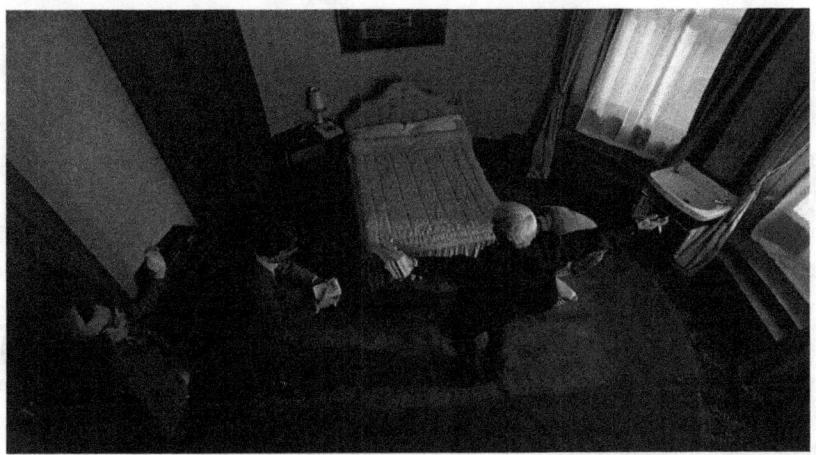

Figure 6: Hotel room portrayed as an arena.

When Renton decides to get clean, the camera level elevates. He returns with his supplies to his dim, sparsely furnished room, which is presented with a certain stoic balance in its bleakness (Figure 4), conveying determination in facing the challenge ahead. This control is lost entirely during his withdrawal sequence in his childhood bedroom (Figure 5). Proportions are distorted, the room appears grotesquely elongated conveying his isolation from the external world. Sick Boy leers with his teacup and biscuits from the far end of the room, while Renton's mother stands silently by the door, her arms crossed judgmentally.

In the hotel room scene, after the drug deal takes place, the camera angle changes again. The viewer's perspective from above conveys the gang's misconception of their control of the situation. The circular room with its alternate vertical red and white stripes is reminiscent of a circus tent, giving the scene a surreal atmosphere of everything not being quite as it appears and trickery lurking behind the many doors.

Magnified Detail

The detail in the film is reserved for the subject of most interest to the protagonist as a young addict. Early in the film, he plans his detoxification method, which he has calculated with precision going through the well-practiced motions. At various points in the film, certain aspects of the drug-taking process are magnified in increasing detail. Use of strong, bright colours, through lighting or colourful set decoration amplifies the heightened reality the inhabitant perceives (Jones, 2017). High-energy storytelling accompanied and enhanced by fast-paced editing combines with disorienting camera placement to communicate a powerful sense of perceiving a world suddenly disrupted. I analysed the scenes through hand drawing storyboards of sequences and individual shots, which necessitated a deeper reading of Mark Renton's physical and psychological environment.

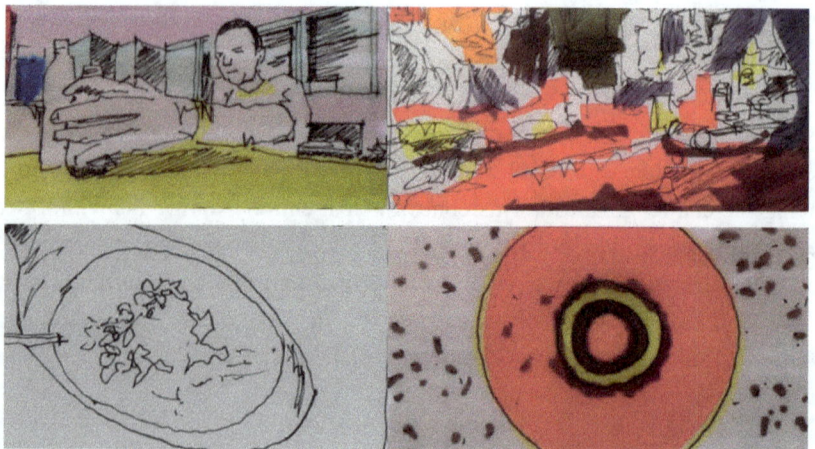

Figure 7: Meticulous detail and process: Renton's detox method.

At several points in the film, certain aspects of the drug-taking process are magnified in increasing detail. When Renton decides to get clean, the camera level elevates. He has calculated his actions with precision, going through well-practiced motions. He returns with his supplies to his dim, sparsely furnished room, which is presented with a certain stoic balance in its bleakness (Figure 6), conveying determination in facing the challenge ahead. This control is lost entirely during his withdrawal sequence in his childhood bedroom (Figure 7). Proportions are distorted, the room appears grotesquely elongated conveying his isolation from the external world. Sick Boy leers with his teacup from the far end of the room, while Renton's mother stands silently by the door, her arms crossed judgmentally.

Awareness of Time

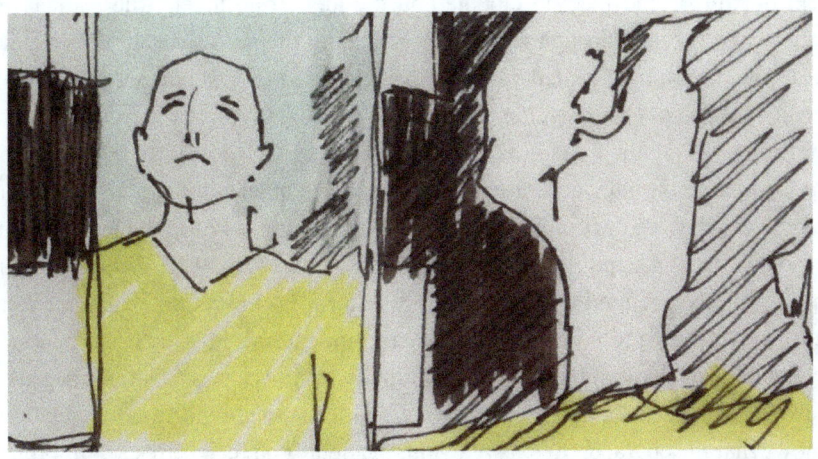

Figure 8: Looking to the past.

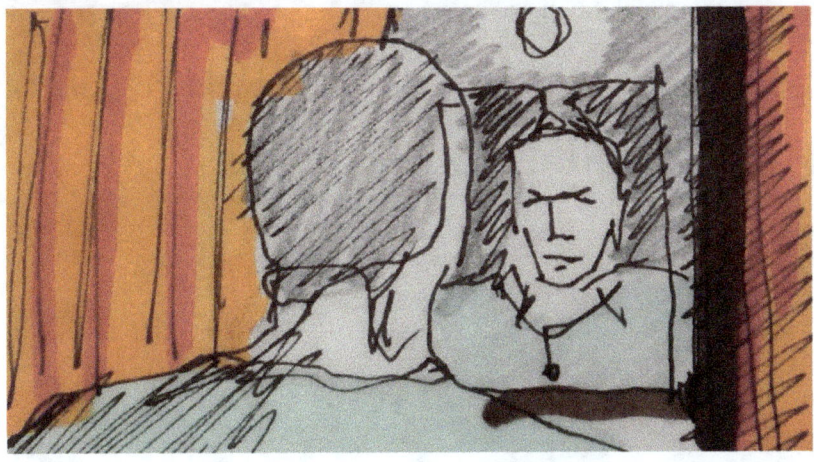

Figure 9: Facing the future.

Early in the film, Renton stands before the mirror, framed looking backwards
to the past (Figure 8). He confronts his own gaze in the mirror in a domestic setting. The interior setting is unkempt and is falling into a state of decay, in stark
contrast to the clarity of the reflected image. Another side of the character looks
back from the mirror, revealing the interior of the protagonist's other nature.
In the final scene, he confronts his gaze head on in the mirror, the naked light
bulb leaving nothing unseen. He faces his future with determination, pointed
and direct (Figure 9). Elsaesser and Hagener discuss the tradition of the concept of 'mirror and face' in cinema and the idea of an inner 'truer' image of
self being revealed through reflection, extending this to discuss how the spectator may see himself reflected back through the mirror of cinema (2010, 61).
Renton's voiceover also guides us on this journey, giving us a unique insight
into his psychological state as it ranges from agony to ecstasy. The case of
the unreliable narrator accentuates the subjective manner in which each of us
perceives what we encounter. It undeniably adds intricacy to the narrative, but
to some extent it exposes the fact that everyone sees the world from a singular perspective, tainted by personal impressions, upbringing, past encounters,
stories overheard, relationships, the media, the culture in which one happens
to live. All of this renders personal outlooks laden with association, people's
lies to themselves about who they are. As a mechanism it allows the viewer to
know what the character deems relevant, the details he recognises as important.
It also, as Slavoj Žižek notes, calls attention to the significance of what is not
noted. This is the magic of film; presenting the apparently insignificant in a way
that possesses a high emotional impact.

Memento: Control of Space

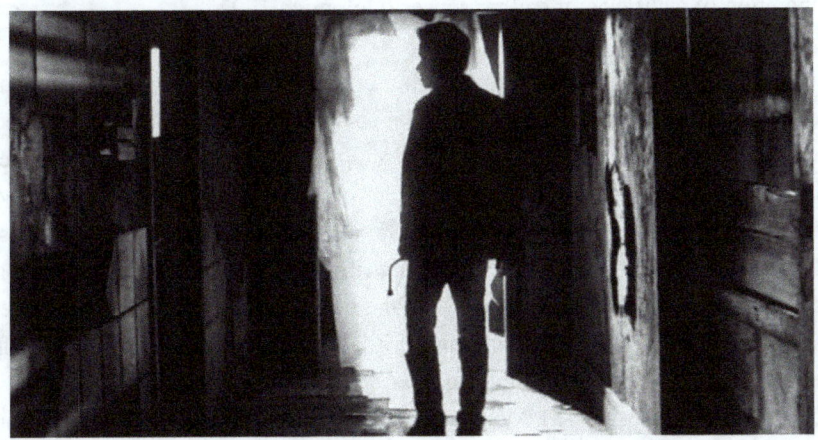

Figure 10: *Chiaroscuro* interior as Leonard confronts forgotten memories.

The human body in space takes a primary role in reflecting identity in *Memento*, where the reflected image communicates information to the protagonist about who he is and what he is searching for. His body is used as the medium of communication, as a kind of map with messages tattooed across it, rendering it unavoidable in his reflection. Leonard notices his reflection in the mirror, and through his tattoos, his story is revealed to both himself and to us all at once.

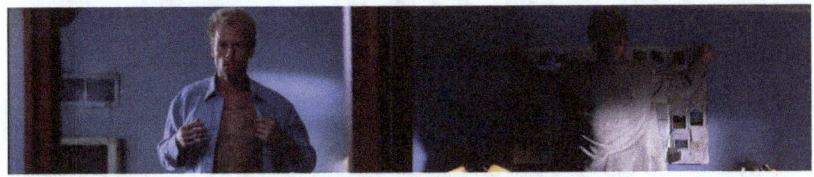

Figure 11: Mapping of memory on the body and creating a visual memory map.

In Freudian theory the mirror represents the psyche. The reflection in the mirror is also a self-portrait projected onto the outside world. The placement of Freud's mirror on the boundary between interior and exterior undermines the status of the boundary as a fixed limit. Inside and outside cannot simply be separated…mirrors promote the interplay between reality and illusion, between the actual and virtual, undermining the status of the boundary between inside and outside…This ambiguity between inside and outside is intensified by the separation of sight from the other senses (Colomina,1992, 8).

Leonard does not question the truth of the image, although we later realise that he has manipulated both himself and the spectator by transmitting fabricated memories and instructions through his visual narration to his damaged psyche. He explains his strategy for keeping track of everything to an unidentified phone caller. Tattoos are his permanent way of recording important memories. He mentions that he trusts his own handwriting, subjective visual affirmation of his actions. Forgettable locations like the motel reflect his loss. In the motel room's anonymity and predictable interior layout everything has its place; his reflection within this anonymous context helps him to locate his own identity and purpose (figures 12-13). Memories are focused, but incomplete, mapped on wall and body. The empty space ensures he will notice his messages to himself.

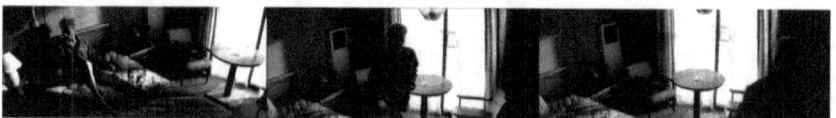

Figure 12: Observed anonymously from above.

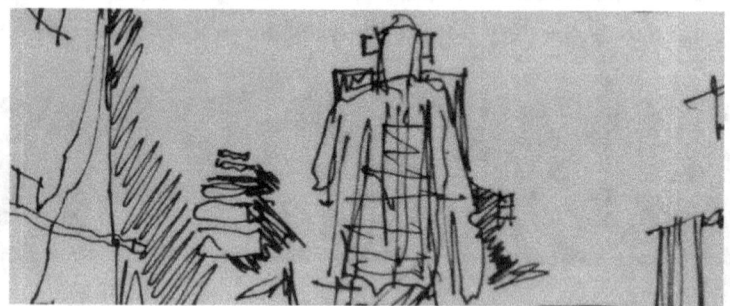

Figure 13: Empty interior.

The character–driven nature of much film necessitates consideration of in-habitation or interior occupation. In Memento self-made maps and annotated polaroids re–educate Leonard each time he sees them, of his situation, both geographical and psychological. Like Benjamin's description of the "dialectical

tension between…order and disorder" (1968, 60), Leonard attempts to maintain an ordered existence, but unknowingly fails because his system is flawed
through his own sabotage. His description of discipline seems plausible in the
confines of the dim motel room but is contrasted sharply in the setting of the
diner where Natalie has arranged to meet him. The space is busy and noisy with
daily activity. Windows run the length of the walls and distraction is all around.
The viewer, like Leonard, feels disorientated and finds it hard to concentrate.
Background sound is implicit in communicating Leonard's inner state of mind.
Repetitive banging sounds occur frequently in the background of the black and
white scenes. Phone ringing and security alarms add to the tension he feels.

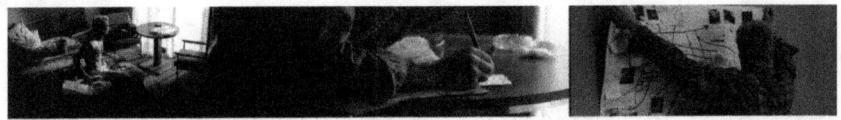

Figure 14: Methods of recording memories in his environment.

His use of hand-drawn wall maps, polaroid photographs annotated to identify
characters, notes, possessions, images, locations, and most crucially, the tattoos
he has imprinted on his skin, are unavoidable, relentlessly insisting on his direction. The fact that Leonard lives in anonymous, empty motel rooms means
he has free reign over creating his own past. There are no objects of association
and memory, which would be present in the house he lived in with his wife.
Sutton describes this use of habit to dissociate with actual memory "the smooth
exercise of established skills and habits operates along autonomous and automated embodied lines, independent of attention, awareness, control, delibera-
tion, and explicit memory" (2009, 70). Much like the disruption which occurs
when the process of a skilled action is questioned, Leonard's control of his everyday patterns have become so routine that the "absorbed action is the smooth
direct engagements of body and world, so that conscious access to the causes or
mechanisms, the processes or principles involved, can only interfere with the
grooved routines: 'mindedness is the enemy of embodied coping'" (Dreyfus in
Sutton, 2009, 70). Real objects with associated memories could therefore interfere with the new reality he has so meticulously constructed to give him purpose.

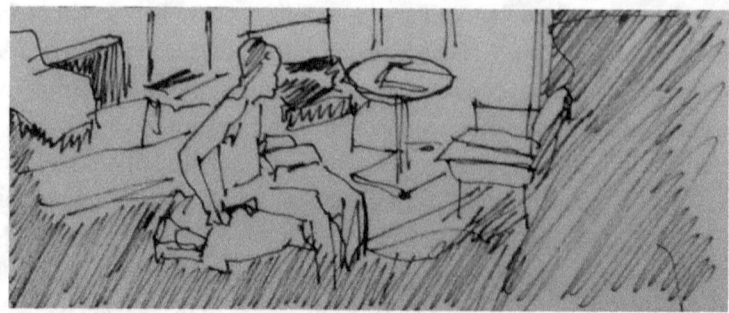

Figure 15: Anonymous motel room: no memory.

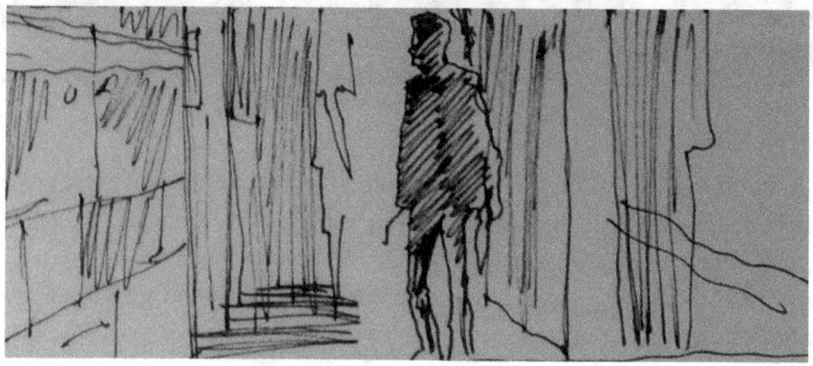

Figure 16: Abandoned warehouse: reinvention of self.

Magnified Detail

Architecture can often be focused on the macro to the detriment of the detail, particularly the interior. The aim of this analysis is to cast a light on ways we can connect with the interior through subjective perception. In *Memento*, Leonard Shelby is very consciously preoccupied with detail. However, as the story progresses, the viewer learns that it has become highly selective. He chooses certain details to remember in order to re-structure his concept of the present. The tattoos that cover his body for example, which he has selected as the key directions leading to his wife's killer are a constant reminder of what his purpose is. This becomes all he is. He annotates polaroid photographs and collates them on a map to guide his future actions (Figure 18). He has re-shaped his own identity based on his redefined priorities, turning himself into his own pawn. The details he notices are all assimilated into the narrative he has created, fitting into places he has assigned.

Figure 17: Detail noticed, generic objects.

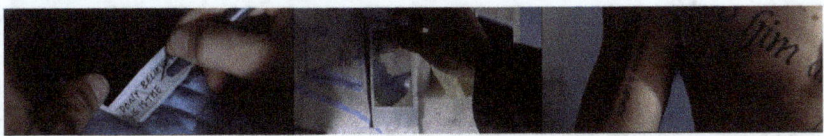

Figure 18: Creating a new present to direct the future.

Colour –and its absence– is used as a tool to differentiate between past and present (Figure 17-18; Table 1). Black and white sequences move in a forward direction and serve to explain Leonard's mindset. Much of it is set in the interior of a relatively empty motel room. Camera angles are generally high and distant, emphasising his isolation. Audio is almost continuous, with Leonard's incessant commentary explaining his situation, his past, his ways of dealing with the present. Movement also tends to be slower in the black and white scenes. In contrast, colour scenes spell out the story from end to beginning. Time has moved backward in each successive scene, until the final scene, when present and past coincide, and colour filters in as the photographic image appears in the polaroid. Linearity dominates the settings, and extreme close-ups are used. Unlike the black and white sequences, Leonard speaks more hesitantly, but moves more quickly. The colour scenes are more dynamic overall, as well as being mainly exterior.

Table 1: Key characteristics of Black and White/Colour Sequences.

Black and White Sequences	Colour Sequences
Time moves forward	Time moves backwards
Empty room	Blue, white
Camera angle high	Linear
Distant camera, isolating	Close-ups
Continuous audio	Silent
Incessant vocal commentary	Speaks slowly
Slow movement	Fast movement
Handwriting	A lot of movement
Tattoos	Tattoos
Disciplined, organised	Memory - no sound
Ringing (in head?)	Extreme close-ups
Memory versus instinct	Sound/touch as certainties
Mainly interior	Mainly exterior

Awareness of Time

From an architectural point of view, time may be the element most often over-looked. Reflection on time immediately takes us out of the everyday. Seeing the bigger picture, by zooming out from our current situation to view it in a broader context immediately changes our perspective, reducing the importance of the present moment. In *Memento* (2000), time is the most notable tool that is played around with both in the narrative and throughout the visuals in the film. The opening scene is of an image slowly disappearing off a polaroid photograph, reversing into its camera.

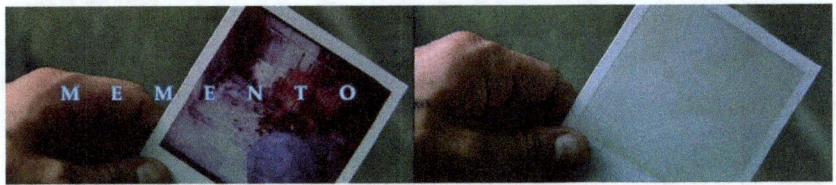

Figure 19: Reversing time/erasing memory.

Returning to the opening scene (Figure 19): time almost stands still, blood flows slowly, a spent shell lies on the pale tile. A pair of bloodstained glasses sits alongside it, their owner next to them, face down in a spray of blood. As the viewer recognises that things are moving in reverse, they see a bullet slide back into the barrel of a gun and a dead man return to life, all within ten seconds. Even in this scene slow–motion has been employed, aligned with the gradual disappearance of the photographic image and the urgency of the reverse gunshot and the spinning victim. The viewer learns that Leonard Shelby has suffered a head wound leaving him unable to form new memories. His wife was killed in the same incident and he is searching for her killer. He recalls her in short flashbacks throughout the film, describing his memories through an assemblage of images revealing his fragmented thoughts and isolated recollections that come together to describe how he felt about her:

> You can just feel details, and bits and pieces you never bothered to put into words. And you can feel these extreme moments even if you don't want to. Put these together and you get the feel of a person (Leonard Shelby, *Memento*, 2000).

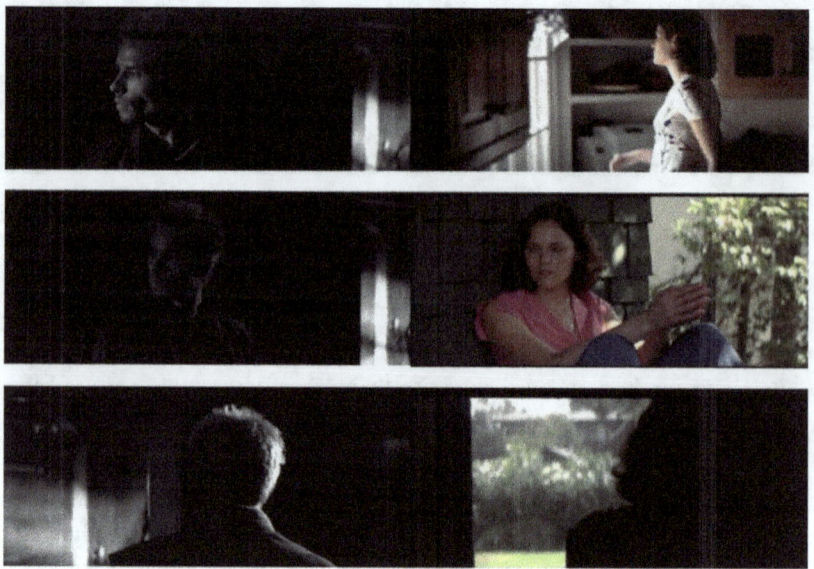

Figure 20: The past leaking into the present.

Leonard's movement reflects his wife's in this sequence (Figure 20). All context and space around Leonard fades to black as his memories of his wife appear in rich colour and sunlight. He has not remained living in the house he had shared with his wife. He stays in motel rooms, collaging the walls and writing on polaroids to re-establish his narrative, and keep himself on the path he has chosen. These visual tools define the film as a collage of means of communicating and how "history and meaning can be absorbed and retained" (Sutton, 2009, 75). These fragmented flashbacks colour Leonard's perception of everything else and have become the driving force motivating his every move (Sutton, 2009, 75). In the film, memory is both associated with and affected by space, with memories of a place intertwined with both real and remembered experience. Truth and fiction are not clearly identified and combine to form a 'complete' memory of place, raising the issue of the subjectivity of experience of space and also of memory, articulated in his speech about unreliable memory:

> Memory can change the shape of a room, it can change the colour of a car;
> Memories can be distorted, they're just an interpretation, they're not a record
> (Leonard Shelby, Memento, 2000)

This interpretation of remembering indicates that on some level, Leonard is aware of his manipulation of his own memories.

Conclusion

The encounters between a character and the spaces they inhabit involve both the body and the mind, qualities that are apparent in this study of the films *Trainspotting* and *Memento*. Memory and identity are key elements connecting human experience to the surrounding world and they are crucial in exploring a subjective interpretation of space. Aspects of architectural language, such as material finish and surfaces, use of colour and texture and ingress of light and reflection, are given new function in film in establishing identity. Our physical and psychological condition invariably influences both our perception of interior space and the impact our spaces have upon us, affecting observation, disrupting encounters and rendering space laden with association. Examining the highly personal, subjective experience of an individual's encounter with architecture can imbue our spaces with a significance that as an integral and unavoidable part of our daily lives, has the potential to provide both support and inspiration to us as its inhabitants. Psychological condition is a driving force both in the cinematography and the production design of the interior spaces in the films discussed in this chapter, resulting in amplified perception of the spaces inhabited by the protagonist in each case. Visuals and sound in each allow access to acutely intimate points of view through close-up shots revealing extreme detail of individuals and objects, through the location within the frame and point of view of the protagonist and through voiceover, which provides invaluable insight into the psychological state of the protagonist.

In the realm of architecture, it has proved extremely difficult to materialise the intangible psychological qualities of interior space. Although the experiential components from a sensorial point of view have come to the fore in architectural discourse, there is still a lack of research and design practice which considers the psychological impact of the interior. In order to have access to multiple examples of experiential space, I have reached outside the boundaries of architecture to the realm of film. The interior in film is frequently engaged to contribute to the narrative and give a context and background to a character. This study aimed to show that analysing examples of acutely subjective perception of ordinary spaces in *Trainspotting* and *Memento* can reveal aspects of film language that may be adopted to potentially inform a richer definition of lived space in architecture.

The spaces we are familiar with become almost invisible to us, as we go through our daily motions in autopilot, without noticing anything in particular for more than a moment. Most of our attention is in our minds, focused on the job at hand or on past or future concerns. How can we change our way of seeing? The medium of film, in this context, is invaluable in providing myriad examples of the inhabited and atmospheric interior. Emotive forces are inherent within the narrative, and this storytelling power is what makes film such an accessible medium. Diverse scenarios and storytelling techniques portray respective perceptions of space, through awareness of inside and outside, concepts of enclosure, artificial and natural light and human presence in space. Taking Finnish architectural theorist and educator Juhani Pallasmaa's description of filmic events as "inseparable from the architecture of space, place and time" (2007, 20), the experiences, encounters and imagination of characters on screen are similarly fused with the filmic space they occupy. The material content of space therefore reflects identity as well as emotional condition, through indicating what the protagonists find themselves surrounded by, or what they choose to have in their environment. Professor for the History of Modern Architecture and director of Urban Studies at Brown University Dietrich Neumann identifies the dialogue between film and architecture "as a realm in which a different approach to the art and practice of architecture can be realized" (1999, 7), which describes the incentive for this study and a potential approach to addressing the frequent oversight of psychological engagement with architectural representations of space.

REFERENCES

Barnwell, Jane. 2004. *Production Design: Architects of the screen*. New York: Columbia University Press.

Benjamin, Walter. 1968. "Unpacking my Library". *Illuminations*. New York: Schocken Books.

Colomina, Beatriz. 1992. "The Split Wall: Domestic Voyeurism." *Sexuality and Space*. New York: Princeton Architectural Press.

Cousins, Mark. 2016. "Crash, Bang, Wallop." *Sight and Sound*, May 2016, Vol.26, Issue 5.

Elsaesser, Thomas, and Hagener, Malte. 2014. *Film Theory: an introduction through the senses*. London: Routledge.

Jones, Matthew. 2017. "The Rise and Fall of Danny Boyle: from Shallow Grave to T2". *Philosophy in Film: a philosophical approach to cinema*. Oct. 15, 2017. https://philosophyinfilm.com/2017/10/15/the-rise-and-fall-of-danny-boyle-from-shallow-grave-to-t2/

Joy, Stuart. 2020. *The Traumatic Screen: The Films of Christopher Nolan*. Bristol: Intellect.

Kania, Andrew. 2009. *Memento*. London: Routledge.

McGowan, Todd. 2012. *The Fictional Christopher Nolan*. Austin: University of Texas Press.

Mottram, James. 2002. *The Making of Memento*. London: Faber and Faber.

Murphy, J.J. 2007. *Me and You and Memento and Fargo: How independent screenplays work*. London: Bloomsbury.

Neumann, Dietrich. 1999. ed. *Film Architecture: From Metropolis to Blade Runner*. New York: Prestel.

Nolan, Jonathan. 2002. *Memento Mori*. In Mottram. 2002. *The Making of Memento*. London: Faber and Faber. (Audiobook read by Jonathan Nolan). https://soundcloud.com/mappingtheterritory/memento-mori-by-jonathan-nolan)

Pallasmaa, Juhani. 2007. *The Architecture of Image: existential space in cinema*. Helsinki: Rakennustieto.

Smith, Murray. 2002. *Trainspotting*. London: BFI Publishing.

Sutton, John. 2009. "The Feel of the World: Exograms, Habits, and the Confusion of Types of Memory." In Kania, 2009. *Memento*. London: Routledge.

Welsh, Irving. 1993. *Trainspotting*. London: Secker and Warburg.

Westbrook, Caroline. 2021. "Trainspotting: The Complete Behind-the-Scenes History." *Empire Magazine*, issue #81. March 1996. https://www.empireonline.com/movies/features/trainspotting-behind-scenes-history/

Young, Skip Dine. 2012. *Psychology at the Movies*. Chichester: Wiley-Blackwell.

Žižek, Slavoj. 2014. *Event*. Philosophy in Transit, London: Penguin.

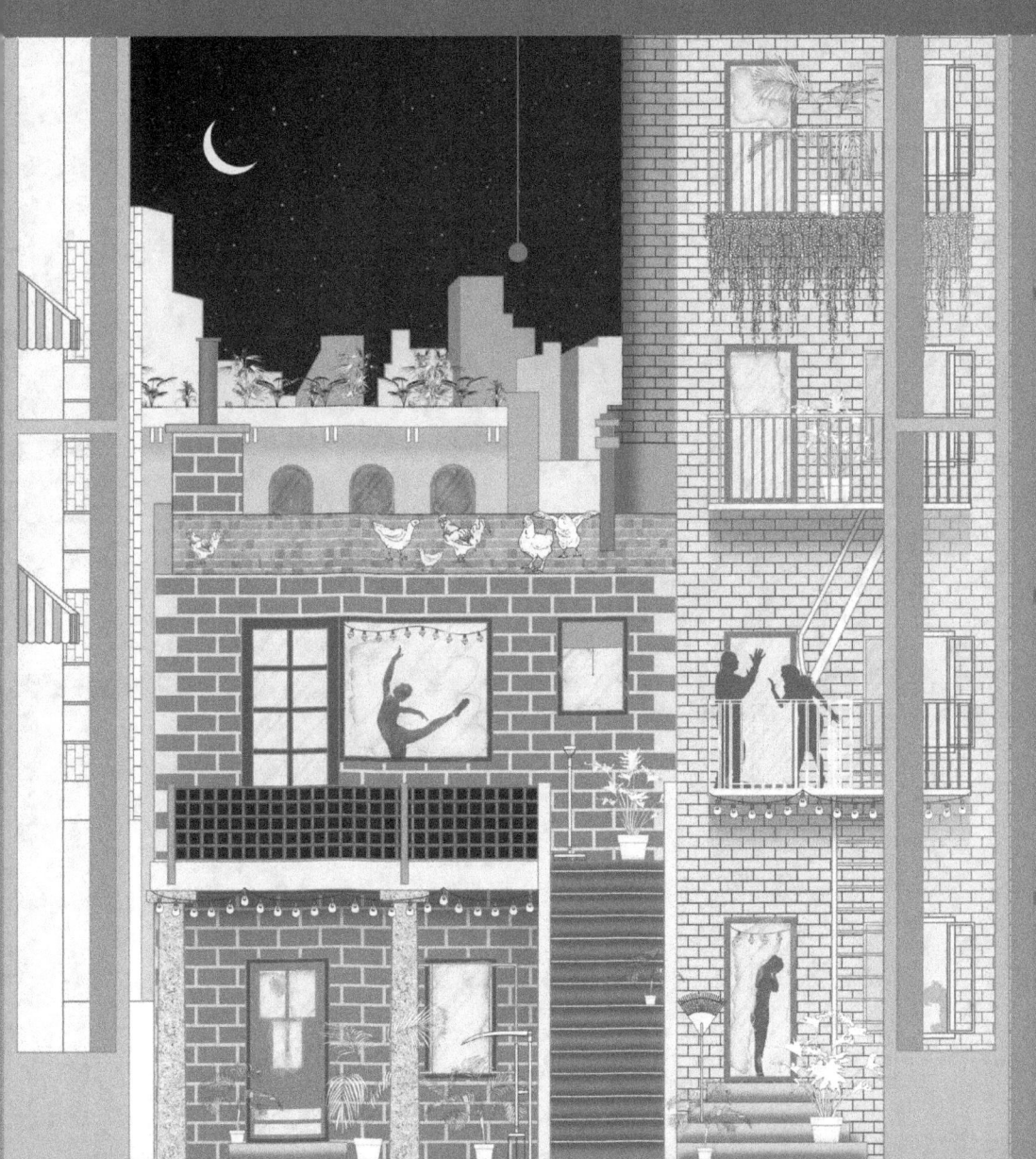

Hitched: Architectural Psychology in Hitchcockian Cinema

Rebecca-Jane McConnell

REBECCA-JANE MCCONNELL is an architect and PhD candidate at Queen's University Belfast. With work/life experience in Ireland, UK, New Zealand, and Southeast Asia, she has been progressing her career in two interdisciplinary areas: 'architecture and cinema' and 'architecture and climate change.' Before undertaking her PhD, Rebecca worked in professional practice in both residential and commercial architecture. Rebecca currently teaches part time in the School of Architecture at Queen's University Belfast. She shares her research regularly via Instagram @thefutureblueprint.

Sir Alfred J. Hitchcock, born in August 1899, was a popular film director and producer from Essex, England. His collective works were categorised as psychological thrillers, and he even earned himself the nickname 'master of suspense.' Throughout his career, Hitchcock continuously denied the application of psychological theory in his filmmaking; however, in analysing his work, we can draw distinctive parallels between his techniques and the likes of neurologists Sigmund Freud and Jacques Lacan. Freud and Lacan worked on theories of the mind, debating how our brain interacts with the environment of daily life. This chapter looks at the research on various hypotheses for psychology and the built environment, then it applies this knowledge to an analytical overview of a selection of films directed by Alfred Hitchcock. This investigation into Hitchcockian cinema studies the application of Freudian and Lacanian psychoanalytic theories to Hitchcock's work through architectural settings. The scope for this investigation includes many Hitchcockian films, while focusing on three films in particular: *Rebecca* (1940), *Rear Window* (1954), and *Psycho* (1960).

Theorists such as art historian Steven Jacobs have previously explored the idea of Alfred Hitchcock as an architect by scrupulously dissecting his set designs (2013). By developing the floor plans, sections and elevations of the context, scholars have successfully depicted considerations in Hitchcock's set design to be of great architectural significance. There are surveys of Hitchcock's design of gothic manners, suburban dwellings, modernist villas, urban mansions, and penthouse suites, while also examining the use of objects and people. Even though Hitchcockian blueprints sometimes fail to make architectural sense, it is argued they work flawlessly for their purpose in film, and the inconsistencies are near impossible to spot. At a contrasting research viewpoint, Professor of Philosophy Constantine Sandis (2009) has explored Hitchcock's use of psychoanalytic theory, contrary to his statements on the matter. Sandis declares that Hitchcock appreciated the magnetism of the psychoanalytic process and general charm of Freud's conceptual world; it is for this reason that he kept returning to Freudian aesthetics throughout his cinematic career. This study intends to entertain Hitchcock as both an architect and an employer of psychoanalysis. It assesses the deployment of architectural surroundings in film, and their psychological effect on the viewer. In turn, the aim is to prove that Alfred Hitchcock is in fact playing a game with us through his architectonic creations, toying with our emotional reactions in whatever way he desires.

This investigation is ultimately about how architecture can influence our mind. Architectural spaces influence our understanding of films; it is a finessed tool that formulates a relationship between viewer and screen. Environmental arrangement in scene composition is an instrument that can be applied by directors to build that relationship. Hitchcock in particular exercises this custom, reviewing his use of everyday architecture and its psychological consequences meticulously. As Alfred Hitchcock famously stated, "Some of our most exquisite murders have been domestic, performed with tenderness in simple, homey places like the kitchen table" (Sloan 1995, 412). The director reportedly told scriptwriter Ernest Lehman he plays the audience "like an organ" (Business Insider, 2016). Mischievous thoughts such as this even led to his own cameo appearances, of which thirty-seven were confirmed over his career. Beyond that, there are rumoured additional appearances that are too far away or too short to be conclusively Hitchcock, and he keeps the audience guessing, 'is it him?'.

This chapter initially introduces environmental psychology — primarily focusing on how surrounding architecture shapes our actions and reactions of day-to-day life. The psychological positions to be discussed are as follows; the theory of the unconscious, wish fulfilment, neurosis, hysteria, psychosis, the Oedipus complex, the interpretation of jokes, psychic reality, guilt transference, and displacement theory. Following this, these theories are applied to the involvement in Alfred Hitchcock's films, focusing on architectural elements; sound, camera, lighting, spaces and confined environments. His numerous tactics are poised to purposely set the viewer on edge, proving the right to his throne as the master of suspense. Ultimately, this chapter measures Hitchcock's architectural influences, to discuss the psychological effect on the viewer.

Evolutionary psychology is defined in *The Dictionary of the English Language* (2011, 45) as, "The branch of psychology in which aspects of brain structure, cognition, and behaviour are interpreted as evolutionary adaptations to the physical or social environment." According to psychologist Leda Cosmides and anthropologist John Tooby, it is a theoretical approach to psychology that attempts to explain useful mental and psychological traits —such as memory, perception, or language— as adaptations, i.e., as the functional products of natural selection (2000, 6). Professor and psychologist Robert Plutchik's 'psycho-evolutionary theory of emotion' states that human beings have eight primary emotions; sadness, fear, anger, disgust, surprise, trust, anticipation, and joy — other emotions are derived from, or a combination of, these prototypes (1980, 92). These feelings come to light in situations involving both cognition and behaviour. For example, if a subject is approached by an attacker with a knife (threatening behaviour), they would deduce that they are in danger (cognition), causing a feeling of fear (emotion). Within evolutionary psychology lies environmental psychology, which is the study of emotional interactions between people and their physical settings (Gifford, 2007). When individuals move through various spaces, behavioural changes occur and in turn, experiences are changed by their surroundings. This theory has a direct relationship with architectural psychology, which can be considered a branch of environmental psychology. Architectural psychology deals with the psychological processes of interaction between a person and their environment, for example, spatial perception, spatial thinking, orientation behaviour, spatial experience, or territorial behaviour. Hitchcock applies this theory to his films, using the architectural creations and choreography of character to manifest emotional engagement in the spectator.

Human beings naturally identify with their surroundings before they construct their own personal identity within those spaces, allowing the built environment to engineer thoughts, feelings, and actions. This can be exploited in a psycho-therapeutic way, for example in hospitals or rehabilitation domains. In film, it can be applied to prompt emotion and memories. When this is exercised in a powerful fashion it can take on a personality — the building or context becomes not just a background element, but an actual character in the movie. People are part of the continuous creation of space, moving through it, altering it.

Dr. Sigmund Freud is understood as 'the father of psychoanalysis;' he carried out studies on patients who could talk freely, usually under hypnosis, in order to produce clues to the source of their symptoms. As academic Paula Marantz Cohen states, "unconscious information could be brought to the surface and made available for interpretation. In the gaps and patterns produced by talk, the therapist could help the patient piece together a repressed story and, in doing [so], effect a cure." (1995, 56). Freud excavated repressed thoughts and feelings to rehabilitate his patients. In Hitchcockian film, the notion of a character's repressed memories are revealed carefully and gradually, and usually pivotal to the plot. Sometimes Hitchcock will permit the viewer to come to a realisa-tion before the character, which stimulates a sense of involvement, gaining our trust. Through plot twists and revelations however, we never truly know what is about to happen. Hitchcock tends to imply doubt, demanding our attention, therefore retaining his reputation as 'the master of suspense.'

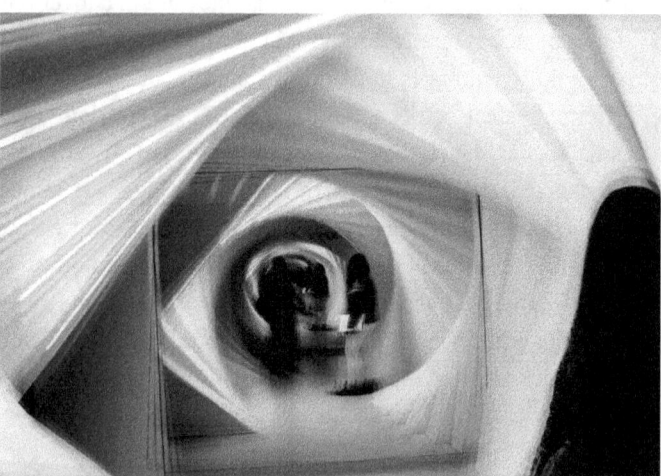

Figure 1: Connecting with your architectural surroundings (photography by Hayden Allen).

Freud claims we rarely act for the reasons we believe. It is this type of influential and yet simple everyday life analysis that may have attracted Hitchcock to Freud's work. Many of today's psychological theories can be linked to Freud's academic research: wish fulfilment, neurosis, hysteria, psychosis, the Oedipus complex, the interpretation of jokes, psychic reality, guilt transference, and displacement theory (Sandis, 2009, 90). Freud's 'Theory of the Unconscious' (a universally known theory explored by Freud in psychoanalytic theory, in which unconscious processes are understood to be expressed in dreams in a symbolical form, as well as in slips of the tongue and jokes) explains that our subconscious mind is where some of our emotions, thoughts, and memories are stationed. Behaviour will change depending on the management of the subconscious and can even lead to mental illness if too forceful. Freud believes feelings and thoughts rest in our 'preconscious' mind, which is a space in cognition that only when required, can be accessed.

Freud divided the mind into three parts: the id, the ego, and the superego (White 2021). The id is the subconscious mind at an unconscious level. Here resides hopes, fears, desires, dreams, urges, repressed emotions, etc., and it is usually this part of the mind that drives thoughts and actions in life. The ego is a part of the brain that develops from a young age; it provides a sense of reality and somewhat constrains the id, taking environmental considerations into account. The superego contains the conscience, i.e moral and social values. Overall, the majority of our mind belongs to the unconscious. Hitchcock targets the unconscious of the audience, often presenting the protagonist to be cold (Jeff in *Rear Window* and Rebecca in *Rebecca*), but as the film develops, we discover repressed emotions and desires, allowing empathy and connection with the character.

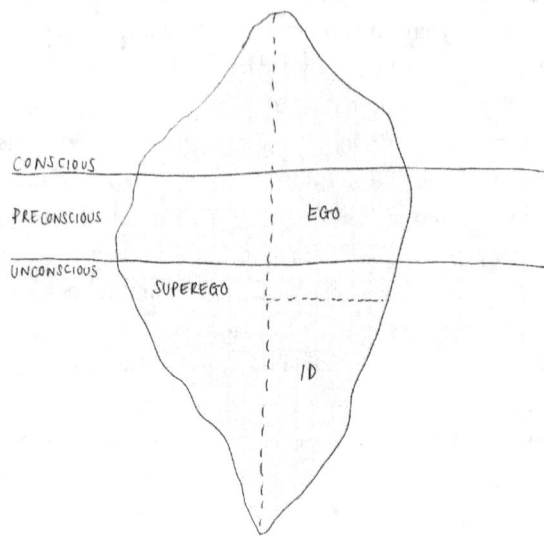

Figure 2: How Freud divides the mind for his psychoanalytical theories (all sketches and storyboards have been created by the author
unless indicated otherwise).

Psychoanalyst Jacques Lacan, predecessor of Freud, somewhat followed in 'the father's' footsteps, and is known to be equally controversial with his theoretical thinking. At one point he was even excommunicated from official psychoanalytical circles (Lacan, 1978, 13). Nevertheless, his interest in the development of psychoanalysis earned him an esteemed role in today's psychiatric schooling. Lacan's 'Mirror Stage' theory is defined as "the psychological description of a child's reactions when faced with its reflection in a mirror" (Macey, 1997, 34). Lacan argued that a child is born without a sense of physical entirety until it identifies with an image of itself, resulting in the articulation of its subjectivity.

In contrast to Freud, Lacan pursued the idea of the ego as the process of identification with an external image or subject. As the mind develops, the theory identifies with the mother figure (an external form) through the relation of the physical and psychic. Thus, a sense of identification is generated by the child who experiences his/her body being mirrored in the environment. In contrast to Freud, Lacan perceived the ego as an 'illusion,' an externally shaped entity that could be manipulated or controlled:

Lacan's Mirror Stage formed the ego as dependent upon another external object, the mother, who exists within a particular society and culture that has a linguistic framework. Unlike the Freudian notion of the ego, Lacanian subject is not interior to the psyche but transindividual to mean that it shifts with context just like speech and language (Nyauma, 2014, 2).

Real and imaginary undertones are explored by Hitchcock throughout his works through dreaming, fantasising, and suggestive settings, slipping in and out of the unbelievable and yet relatable, forging a provocative relationship with his spectators. Hitchcock generates identifiable environments and scenarios through which the spectator can connect, leading to the branding of the character's personality as 'relatable.' In *Rear Window*, we empathise with Jeff stuck in his apartment; in *Rebecca*, we have compassion for Maxim in Manderley who has lost his wife, and in *Psycho*, we have a sense of apprehension for Marion as she runs away from home.

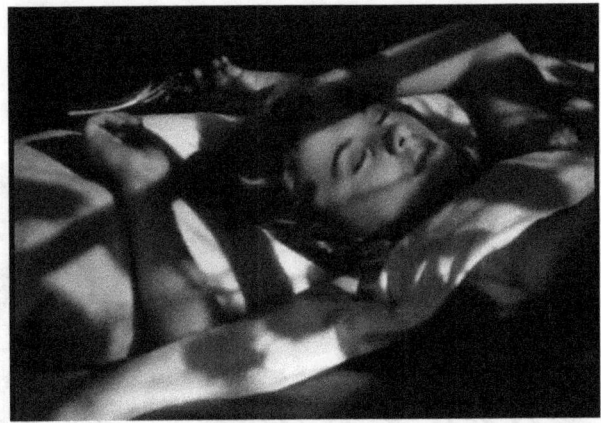

Figure 3: The anonymous character dreaming in Rebecca (0:12:29)
(all film stills captured by the author unless indicated otherwise).

The realm of film has an undeniable connection with architecture. In cinema, people can form relationships with the screen through the architectural context. Film offers us as designers the chance to fabricate the fantastical and impossible. Directors can operate architecture to enhance the mood and formulate an elusive dialogue between person and setting. Architecture can construct a metaphorical representation and even can be used as an operational character. Directors such as Hitchcock generate settings to capture and immerse the viewer in a cinematic experience.

Dr. Penelope Haralambidou, coordinator at The Bartlett School of Architecture, argues that film is a vital tool for communication. She explains how film operates on many levels, allowing thought in space and time, not merely a static plan or section (2016). Spatial experience is connected to time; it relates to the past and memories, but also allows imagination of the future. Through film, we have the potential to encounter architecture as an extension of self. It offers an innate level of engagement with the architectural object and somehow comes alive.

Sir Alfred Hitchcock saw an architectural opportunity within his artistic cinema direction and production design. Throughout his career, he directed over fifty films, expressing his own personal perceptions through the built environment, projecting thoughts and feelings on to his sets. He was considered an architect as well as a director of cinema. As Camille Paglia noted, "Hitchcock's vision of architecture as the grand but eternally provisional frame of human meaning is evident everywhere in his major films" (1998, 66).

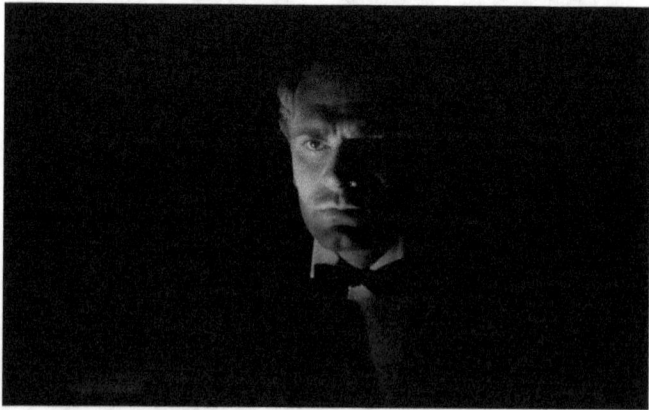

Figure 4: The male protagonist *Rebecca* (1:00:15).

It is important to note how Hitchcock denies the employment of psychology in his direction of films, which probably is another way to mess with our minds. Regardless, we can pinpoint a moment in his career that might have struck an interest in psychoanalysis. In the early 1940s, Hitchcock was asked to create a movie based on David O. Selznick's real-life experience with psychotherapy (he was a patient suffering from depression). In an edited collection of Hitchcock's interviews, he states, "Never use a setting simply as a background. Use it one hundred percent. You've got to make the setting work dramatically... In other words, the locale must be functional" (Hitchcock,1995, 351). Every aspect of the set was not coincidental, but calculated and precise. Hitchcock did not solely rely on the production of physical set designed buildings to gain these reactions, but also considered colour, light, everyday sound, music, framing, people, and objects to conjure an emotive architectural setting. It is palpably obvious that Alfred Hitchcock was consumed by his career, to the point of borderline obsession. He was a heartfelt workaholic with precise attention to detail, and loved toying with the viewer (Trauffaut 1967, Jacobs 2013, Nyauma 2014). He was highly intelligent and exploited this for his mischievous gestures.

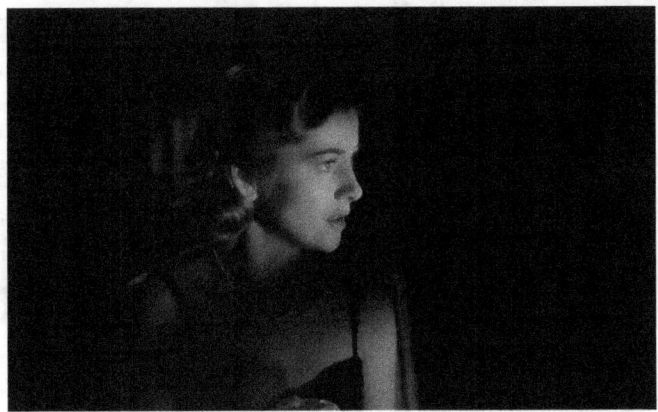

Figure 5: The new Mrs. de Winter (1:00:09).

Hitchcock exploits our weaknesses through his psychologically charged sets. It is important to investigate sound as an invisible means of architectural representation of place. Film could be argued as the sole architectural medium which can be exploited through sound. Unlike drawing or photography, sound offers a further dimension into the exploration of space. As Hitchcock's earliest films were void of sound, this is an important component to reflect upon. When he transitioned from silent film, this led to extreme cautiousness of the involvement of any noise — making every sound count. It is through this movement to sound that Hitchcock became somewhat of a foley artist, (an artist that recreates sound effects for film, television and radio productions on a Foley Stage in a Post Production Studio) using various props and utensils — car fenders, plates, glasses, chairs, and just about anything they can find — the original sound is then replaced or augment to create a richer track (The Art of Foley 2008). It is the invisible architecture Hitchcock uses precisely in his art to promote a reaction.

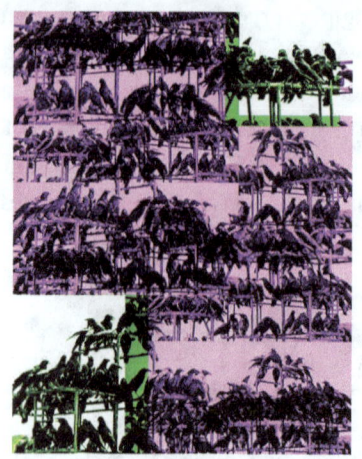

Figure 6: *The Birds*, illustration by the author.

Sound is an integral component of *Rear Window*. Imagery and dialogue alone fail to tell the story, and it is the use of this further dimension that promotes a mood. Thirty-five percent of *Rear Window* constitutes a zero-dialogue movie, showing how Hitchcock uses silence and 'white noise' as a tool to represent space — the lack and presence of sound are of equal importance (The Sound of Hitchcock 2008). This is exercised in *The Birds* (1963), where the opening credits are initiated with typical seagull sounds, calm and reassuring (almost reminiscent of an afternoon at the seaside). This eventually morphs into an attacking sound of unnatural threatening birds, as if they are from another planet.

Hitchcock was an expressionist; the background noise of everyday life was a necessity in his opinion — the New York background buzz, the sirens of a nearby police car, and the dog in the courtyard add to off-screen realism. Viewers may not pay conscious attention to it, but we feel it nevertheless. Gary Leva's *The Sound of Hitchcock* (2008) documentary interviews a group of Hollywood directors, who argue this technique adds to the 'storytelling' power. Sound designer to *Jurassic Park* (1993), Gary Rydstrom, states that Hitchcock expanded recordings from the real outside world, with noise bouncing off neighbouring buildings, to maintain an understanding of surroundings for the audience. In *Rear Window*, the lead protagonist Jeff is primarily stationary in his chair from the beginning of the feature. The camera pans the courtyard simultaneously with Jeff's eyes, and the sound is specifically stylised to describe each apartment or space. In each window, a muffled choice of sound is heard to depict the characters and their space. The man playing his piano, the couple fighting, the composer and his latest writings, the newlyweds and their loving calls to each other and the tearful cries of 'Miss Lonely Hearts.' Each sound subconsciously changes our opinion of the space that is occupied; it allows us to think of the spatial arrangement of the apartments from Jeff's window view.

Interestingly, Hitchcock uses a sound bridge in *Rear Window* to connect Jeff in his apartment and the composer in his. This is a running theme in the film, we hear the composer before we see him, visualising the room in our minds before actually seeing it. This is a particularly important method of spatial representation, as the sound is the sole illustrator, something that cannot be explored in a two-dimensional architectural drawing or photograph.

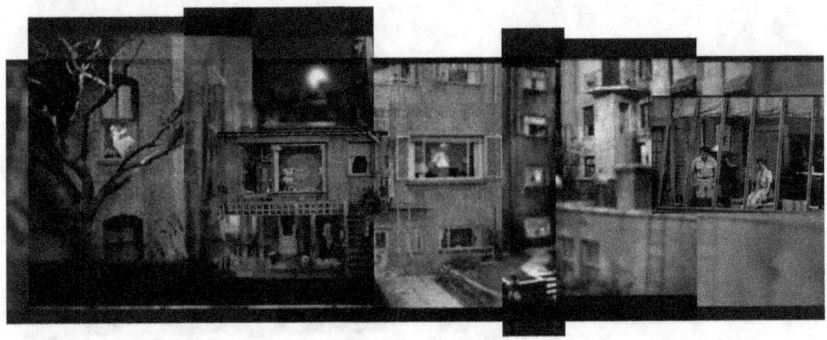

Figure 7: Collage showing the general arrangement of Jeff's neighbours.

Sound plays an important role in the building of suspense in the attack scene. Everything is silent, as Jeff looks at the door motionless and in fear. Then begins the repeated thud of footsteps from the outside corridor. Hitchcock focuses our minds with this subjective sound to visualise the corridor - a long room with the killer approaching closer. Hitchcock directed the absence of sound and light in this scene to amplify the spectator's anxiety. He manipulates everyday sound such as footsteps to construct an image of a dramatic and eerie corridor. Suddenly the footsteps stop, the apartment door creaks open, and silence and darkness enter the screen again. Hitchcock constantly uses silence as a tool of fear in his murder scenes, stating: "There is no terror in the bang, only in the anticipation of it" (*The New Yorker*, 2011).

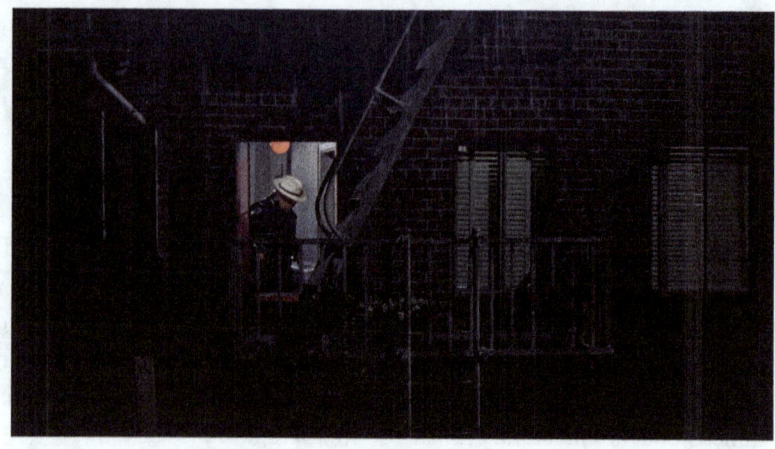

Figure 8: Killer Thorwald leaves his apartment in *Rear Window* (00:27:30).

Figure 9: Elevational fenestration study from Jeff's courtyard
view in *Rear Window*.

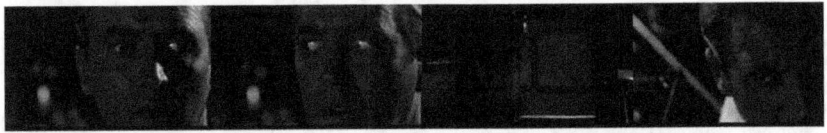

Figure 10: Sequence images of Jeff as he hears killer Thorwald approaching.

Rebecca uses both diegetic and non-diegetic sound. During the opening scene, which takes place at the gate to Manderley estate, the mood is eerie, disquieting, surreal. In a voice-over, we hear the anonymous heroine, Mrs. de Winter (Joan Fontaine) say, "Last night I dreamed I went to Manderley again....I stopped at the gate, and then, like all dreams, I was possessed as by a sudden supernatural power and passed like a spirit through its bars" (*Rebecca* 1940 0:01:37). With this quote, Hitchcock steps away from realism to induce a sense of elusiveness, drawing parallels with the previously-mentioned Freudian theory of psychic reality. The opening dialogue is used to stress a strong association with place at Manderley, a haunting spiritual place. Hitchcock specified, "Dialogue should simply be a sound among other sounds, just something that comes out of the mouths of people whose eyes tell the story in visual terms" (Truffaut, 1967, 222).

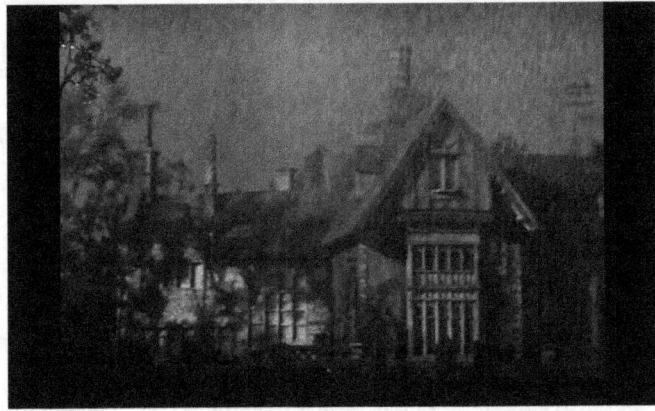

Figure 11: Rainy arrival at Manderley Estate in *Rebecca* (0:29:05).

Music is famously celebrated in *Psycho*. It is 'larger than life,' and the movie is relatively dependent on sound. Frequently Hitchcock would create complimentary tension between the visual and the sound, not continuously keeping one in sync with the other (Sullivan 2008). In the illustrious 'shower scene,' it is not the literal sound of each knife thrust we hear, but instead shrill high shrieking musical chords along with screams in the background from Marion. William Friedkin, the director of *The Exorcist* (1973) states hat Hitchcock's lack of literal sound works immaculately to accentuate the dramatics of the murder (*The Sound of Hitchcock* 2008).

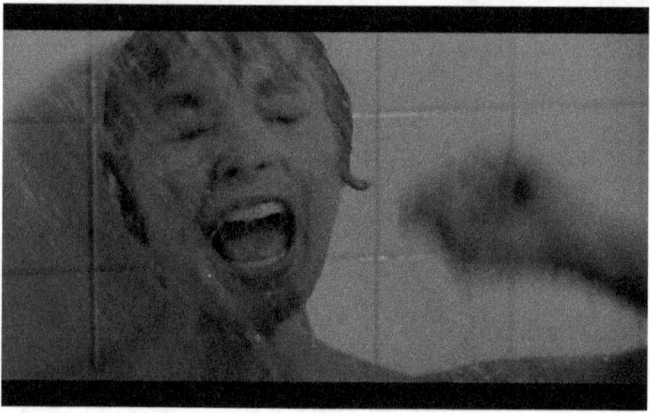

Figure 12: Marion shrieking in the shower in *Psycho* (0:47:00).

Sound is central to architectural representation in film, and Hitchcock recognised this. Architects and writers such as Reyner Banham (1984) studied how heat, light, air, and materiality produce atmosphere that influence our experience of buildings. He emphasised that such contemplations are "naturally subsumed into the normal working methods of the architect" (Banham 1984, 111). He also argues that this list should include sound. In a recent article, *The New York Times* (2015) used three-dimensional audio online to explore the effect of sound in space. It looked at what would be considered 'silent space' such as an office or a library, and highlighted how audible these places actually are. The article aims to prove the importance of distinguishing location according to the sound it produces, stating:

> Sound may be invisible or only unconsciously perceived, but that doesn't make it any less an architectural material than wood, glass, concrete, stone or light... albeit most architects rarely think much about it, except when their task is to come up with a pleasing concert hall or a raucous restaurant — and then acousticians are called in. That said, you don't need to be a specialist to differentiate spaces according to the sounds they make.

Sound is a principal contextual factor to consider. Occasionally architects defy discussion on sound in space, and how it makes the user feel. Hitchcock recognised that sound was crucial and applied it as a representation of architectural space with the intention of stimulating emotion.

Hitchcock worked the camera, perspective, and light to capture the ambience. Communications specialist Paige Driscoll (2013, 4) states that in Hitchcock's

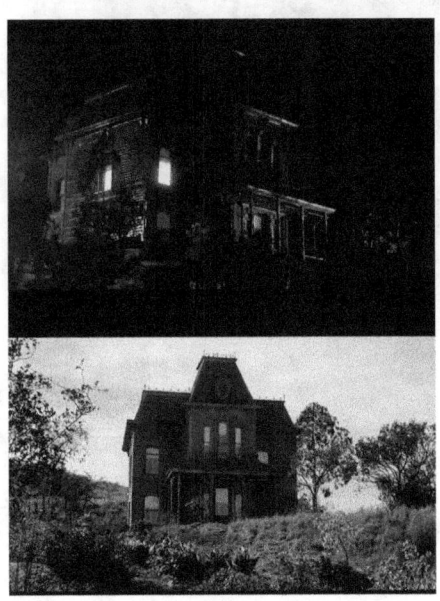

Figure 13: Night and Day - House on the hill in *Psycho* (0:32:55) (1:35:16).

work, "attributes like low-key and edge lighting create mood. Odd angles and voyeuristic perspectives and themes place the audience members in a place they do not normally find themselves and alert them of what they may not have noticed otherwise." Hitchcock studied German set design which helped with his unique approach. Through his studies he knew that the configuration 'on set' did not matter as much as what was framed on screen (Mc-Gilligan 2003, 63). Hitchcock was scrutinous with his precision of placement of characters and objects to fulfil the composition of frame.

Ultimately, the architecture of the film is "architecture that has been depicted, photographed, turned into an image" (Dieter Schaal 2010, 16) and is not
necessarily 'real.' However, as argued by architectural historian Beatriz Colomina (1996, 70), by containing architecture to an object and assimilating that
object within its image, it becomes relatable to the viewer. Although architects
may consider this exploitation of architecture fictitious, it is worth noting that
Le Corbusier published 'doctored' photographs of his projects (Wolfe-Murray
2005, 12). This implies Le Corbusier composed a somewhat emphasised illustration of his ideas than alternatively the authentic demonstration of the genuine
built work. Hitchcock adheres to a similar notion; he wishes to denote the film's
setting rather than reproduce the city. This approach is reminiscent of Lacan's
idea previously discussed of 'imaginary as a field of imagery,' as Hitchcock is
utilising fantasy to paint a picture in our minds.

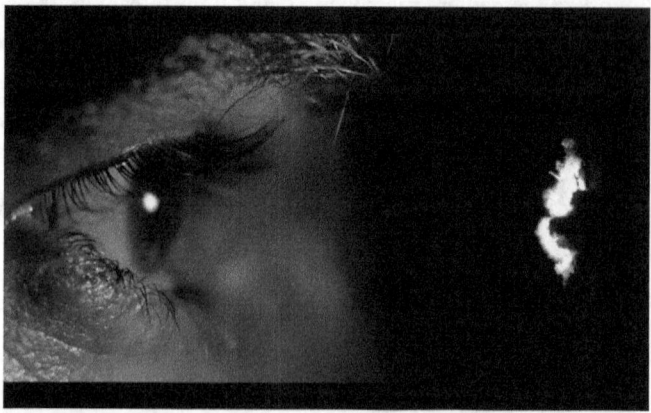

Figure 14: Norman's peep hole. *Psycho* (0:44:45).

Hitchcock uses a recurring voyeuristic undertone in *Rear Window*, depicting the
interior space of people's homes from a distance. Jeff's view is of a courtyard
and the rear side of his neighbours apartments. The camera pans the elevational
view of the surrounding apartments, letting our minds map the surroundings.
The viewpoint framed by the window is proportional to the camera, seducing
us further into the intimate enclosure of the fictitious community (Jacobs 2013,
282). Hitchcock emphasises the emotion of each individual residence through
colour, sound, light, thusdemanding the association of the interior with the occupant. The informality of a back window evolves his characters; for example,

if the stance was directed toward a front window, we would not see the same liberal attitude the residents have. The people become the environment and the architecture. The characters are positioned to illuminate space. The personalities portray Freud's psychic reality throughout the film, with the supporting characters continuously hinting at ideas in Jeff's mind through their movement, actions, and behaviours. The film plays on our surveillance of Jeff, and Jeff's surveillance of his neighbours.

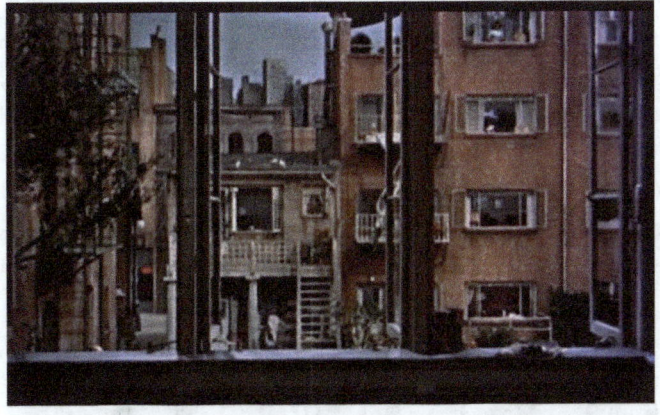

Figure 15: Introduction to *Rear Window* (0:01:29).

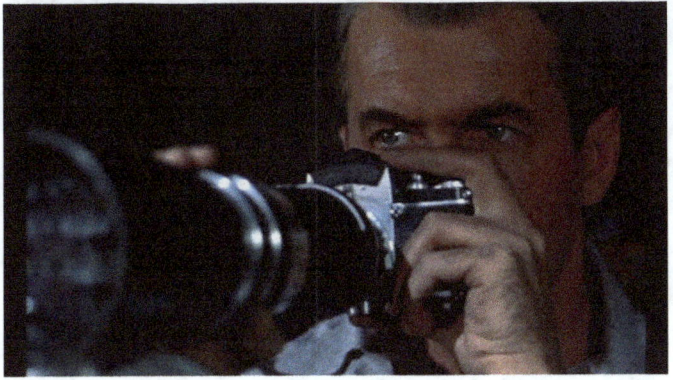

Figure 16: Jeffries using his photography equipment to spy on his neighbours. *Rear Window* (1:37:18).

here is a scream as the discovery of the murder of a pet dog is unveiled. Thorwald's apartment can be seen in pitch black, with a glowing cigarette the only clue to his occupancy. The view into this window of darkness is an extremely evocative scene, the absence of light and lack of the physical appearance of Thorwald's figure only adds to his sense of presence. Hitchcock engages with a technique reminiscent of Caravaggio, who used the orientation of bodies and direction of light in his paintings to define a strong architectural setting, even though the background to his work was typically minimal, conventionally consisting of a single wall (Saggio 2010, 28). The camera is poised in a single wide angle shot, from the perspective of the strangled dog in the courtyard. This is quite uncharacteristic of the film, intensifying anticipation. The dog is said to be killed because it 'knew too much' - this is a play on Hitchcock's previous film *The Man Who Knew Too Much* (1934). When Thorwald enters the dark room at the climax of the film, Hitchcock uses lighting to promote isolation and tension. A similar technique is used in *Rebecca*, when the fire at Manderley takes place and Mrs. Danvers rises through the flames.

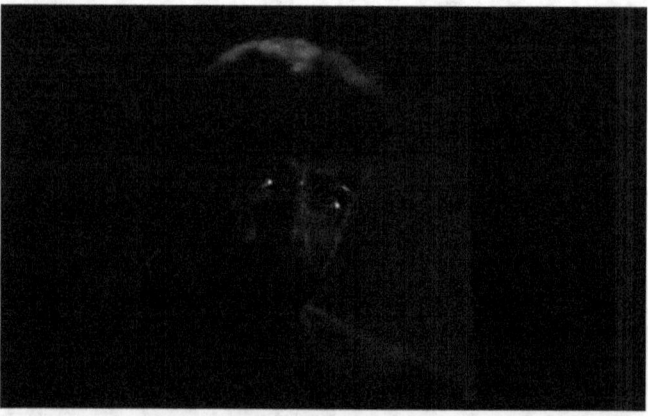

Figure 17: Murderer Thorwald emerging from the shadows.
Rear Window (1:42:54).

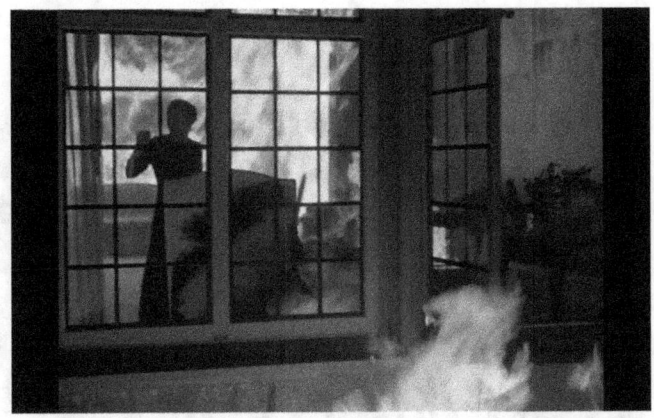

Figure 18: Mrs. Danvers in the fire at Manderley in *Rebecca* (2:09:00).

The shadows and lighting in *Psycho* play a fundamental role in the eminent shower scene, with the forty-five second clip astounding viewers at the time. An ambiguous figure creeps up on Marion in the shower. We are not quite sure how things will unfold. Hitchcock plays with light and shadow, while zooming in with the camera to suggest movement outside the shower. We sense that something is not right, while slowly the killer's blurred outline descends upon the character. Interestingly, the bathroom, where the infamous murder takes place is captured by not only showing the shower, but the whole room, and this is communicated through a single sweep of the en suite. After the murder, there is a closeup of unresponsive Marion's eye, portraying her lifelessness. The camera then glides along the floor of the bathroom, past the toilet and out to the bedroom, zooming into the stolen money wrapped in a newspaper. When Hitchcock probes a focus on a particular object or person, the audience obey. Every movement is theatrical and dramatic, filled with the purpose of formulating suspense. It is patent that Hitchcock controlled the camera, shadow, light, and framing of space to generate a response.

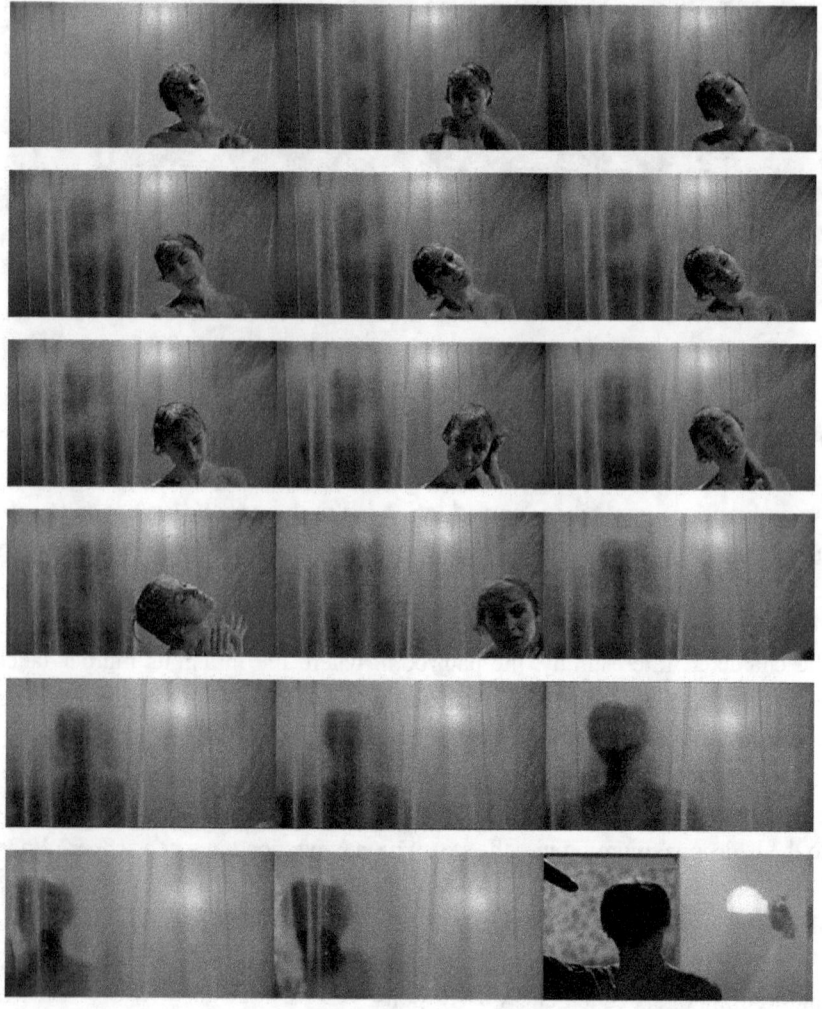

Figure 19: Camera and shadow movement in *Psycho*.

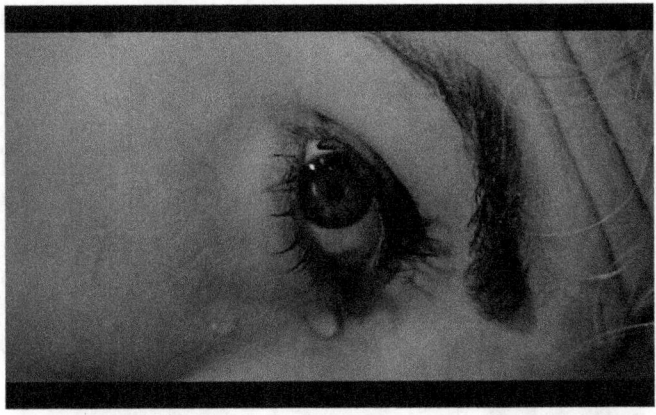

Figure 20 Marion's murder. *Psycho* (0:49:19).

Hitchcock also used physical entities such as architectural space, rooms, and objects as symbolically charged entities. As discussed previously, Freud had a theory concerning wish fulfilment, and this could be manifested through symbolisms and representational spaces or objects within the dream. He states these representations are a result of repressed thoughts, the unconscious, fear, anger, aspirations, and compulsion, all of which strive to express themselves in sleep when the conscious guard is at its lowest. Freud claims the unconscious appears in a camouflaged way in these illusions. Thus, every subject within that dream essentially has a hidden meaning. Hitchcock places symbols and scatters clues throughout the story to hack into our subconscious, disguising hidden meanings in object form and insinuating subliminal messages (Jacobs 2013, 26). Hitchcock consistently considered the audience in the production of his sets, collaborating the *mise-en-scène* with our own projected thoughts and feelings onto objects, turning them into characters (Douchet 1999, 65).

Hitchcock was fascinated by the house as a series of spaces with secrets and concealment, and the Manderley estate in Rebecca is no exception. Jacobs (2013, 34) states that the houses in Hitchcockian film are projections of the ego (the previously discussed Freudian concept), that each piece of furniture is an image of self-worship, conveying inklings into the character through their furnished space. The objects featuring in Manderley are in abundance, imprinting the history and magnetism of the deceased Rebecca. The decoration illustrates the wealth and power, making the unpretentious newlywed Mrs. de Winter II feel uncomfortable. In *Psycho*, the use of taxidermy in Norman's motel is a subtle nod towards the creepy impression of death.

Andre Bazin (1971, 11-37) studied 'Door Knob Cinema,' exploring how architectural and domestic objects are used in film as symbolism of suggestions and emotions. In *Rear Window*, Hitchcock determines the single entrance door to Jeff's apartment as the only authoritative structure standing between Jeff and his fate (killer Thorwald), and colossal fear is projected on to the object. In *Rebecca*, the repeated appearance of the door to Rebecca de Winter's room is a psychological threshold between Mrs. de Winter II and her predecessor. The nameless new bride builds an idea in her mind of possibilities behind the door. This is further inferred through the tracking shot of the closed door, or the close-up shot of her hand on the forbidden handle. This establishes an augmented reality in the anonymous lead's head. When she finally crosses the threshold, housekeeper Mrs. Danvers (whose loyalties lie with the deceased) catches her in Rebecca's room, prying, "You've always wanted to see this room, haven't you madam?" (*Rebecca*, 1:05:15).

Windows are dominant features in many Hitchcockian works, playing a part in films such as *Rebecca* (1940), *Shadow of a Doubt* (1943), *Rope* (1948), *I Confess* (1953), *Rear Window* (1954) and *Psycho* (1960). *Rear Window*, as the title suggests, is the pioneer example of this representation. The window is formulated to absorb the spectator; we use the opening to peer out as an onlooker alongside Jeff. The fact that the viewer experiences the 'rear' window activities brands the experience as personal. Hitchcock realised that people were not as comfortable in their rooms with a front window, where they would keep up appearances; instead he focuses on the characters' casual liberties of their rear living space.

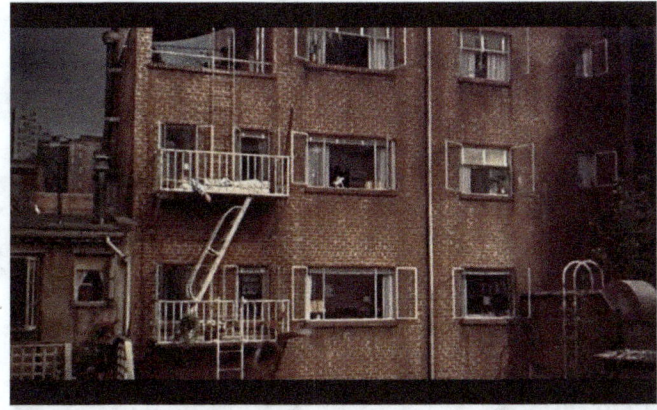

Figure 21: Still from the opening scene to Rear Window, showing the
view from Jeff's apartment. *Rear Window* (0:02:43).

The dimensions of 'the staircase' are a Hitchcockian trademark, which has been discussed by scholars such as Lesley Brill (1991), Dan Babineau (2003), Michael Walker (2006), and Maurice Yacowar (2010) to name a few. The intricacy of staircase architecture in Hitchcock's manifestations prove the cruciality of their role, from *Rebecca* demonstrating an impressive gothic fine detailed fabrication, to *Psycho* displaying a domestic traditional design. The change of level suggests the character will explore the space, as if something is waiting to be discovered, tapping into Freud's theory of the aforementioned 'urges' buried in our unconscious. The stair can be used to seclude people and their interaction with surrounding space, as Jacobs (2013, 28) proclaims:

A central spine of domestic space, the staircase presents itself as an arena for psychological tensions. Furthermore, in Hitchcock's films, staircases lead to trouble since they accompany the cognitive hubris of the characters. Inquisitiveness drives characters upstairs or downstairs. In addition, Hitchcock integrates his staircases perfectly into his technique of suspense: each step advances but also delays the denouncement.

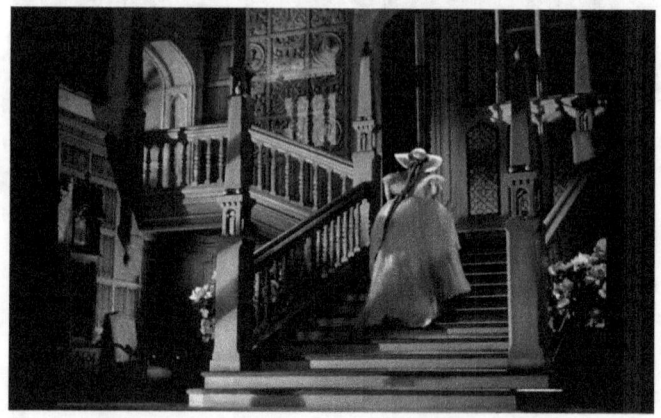

Figure 22: Staircase at the Manderley estate in *Rebecca*. (01:21:27).

The theme of ascending and descending materialises in *Rear Window* when
Lisa nervously climbs the fire escape to sneak into the murderer's apartment,
and again when Thorwald creeps up the stairs to reach Jeff. In *Rebecca*, Mrs.
de Winters slowly travels upwards to invade Rebecca's room. In *Psycho*, the
stairs are the divide that separates Bates' deceased mother from the outside
world. Hitchcock continuously uses stairs as a psychological threshold. This
constructs tension and suspense, and it provokes the viewer anxiety through
establishing an uncertainty to the character's fate.

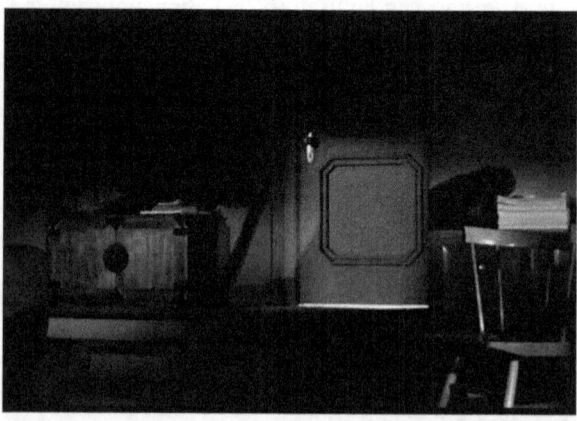

Figure 23: *Rear Window* - Door.

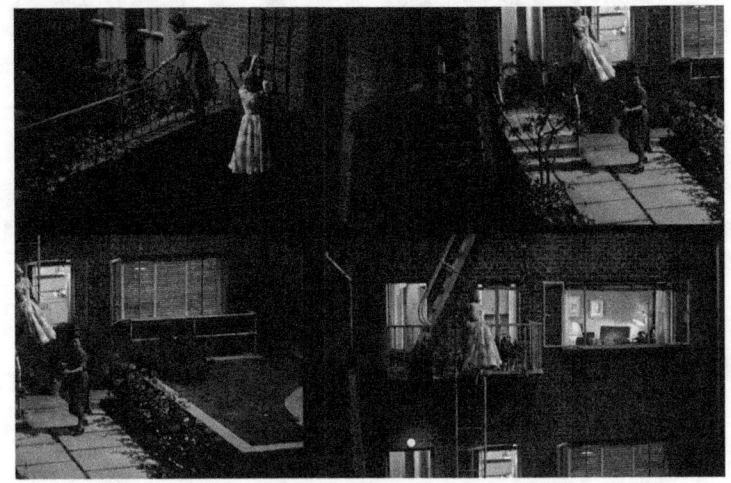

Figure 24: *Rear Window* - Stairs.

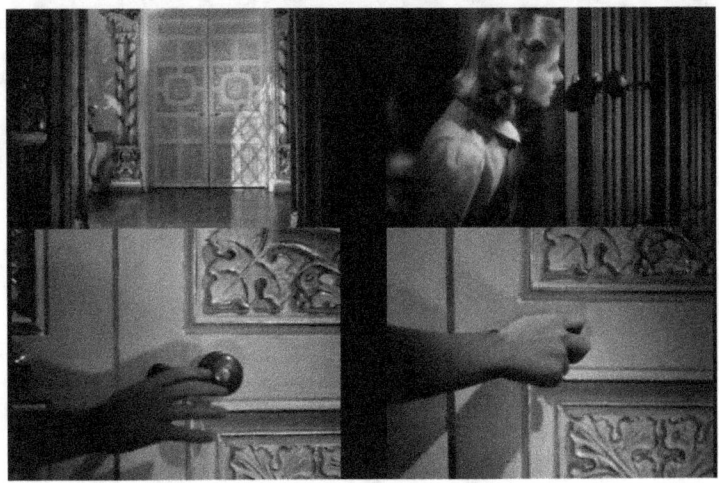

Figure 25: *Rebecca* - Doors.

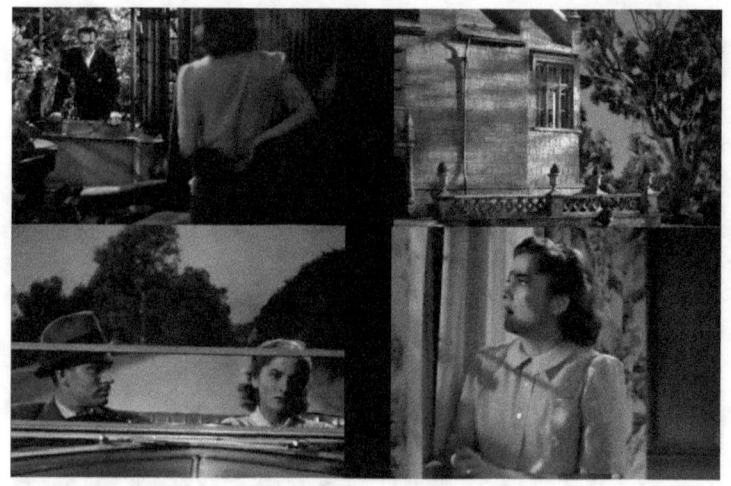

Figure 26: *Rebecca* - Doors.

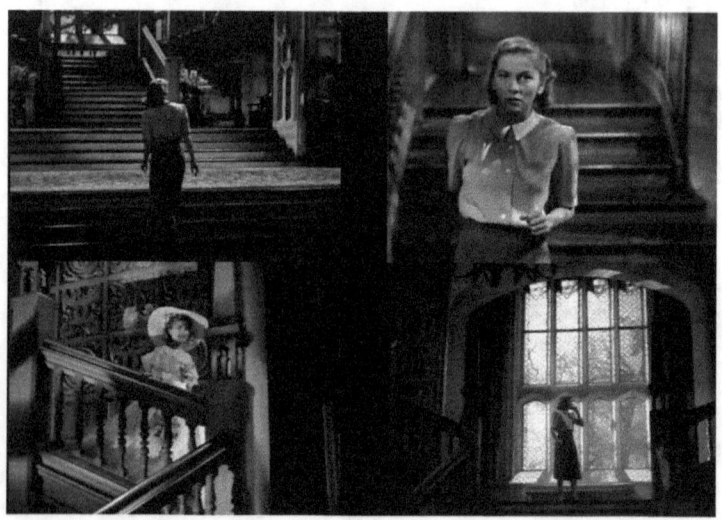

Figure 27: *Rebecca* - Stairs.

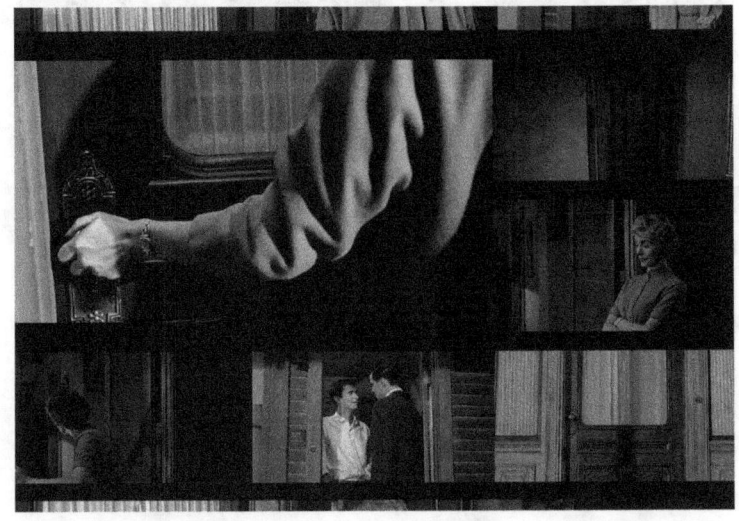

Figure 28: *Psycho* - Doors.

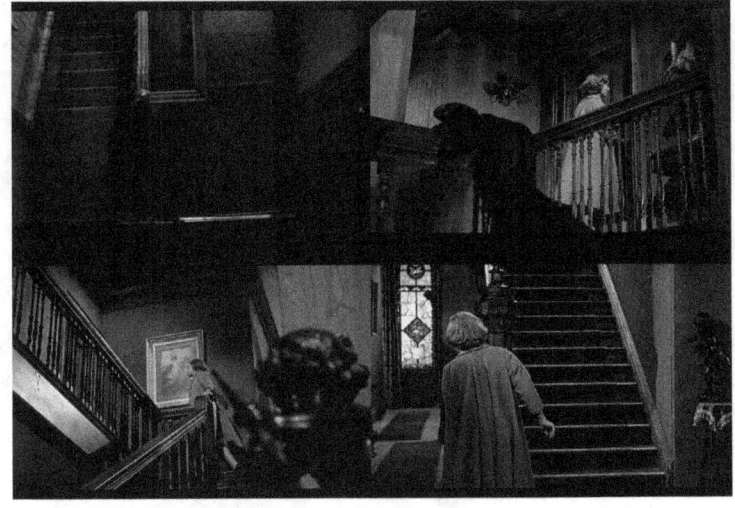

Figure 29: *Psycho* - Stairs.

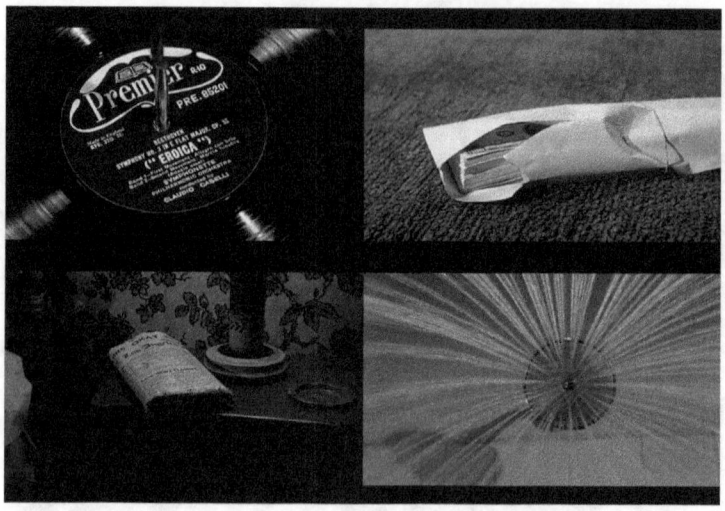

Figure 30: *Psycho* - Objects.

The unexpectedness of Marion's murder in *Psycho* was classic of Hitchcockian style, as he stated, "The first part of the story was a red herring" (Truffaut
1967, 269). This unanticipated death is compared with that of private investigator, Arbogast, whose murder is remembered as somewhat predictable. Notably, we can speculate that a contributing factor to the opposing reactions is
due to the architectural setting of each killing. Hitchcock's primary locations
within *Psycho* are predominately private spaces, from Marion's hotel room in
the opening scene, to the bathroom of her murder. One of the significant dis-
tinctions between Marion's and Arbogast's murders is that Marion is killed in
the privacy of her restroom whilst the private investigator is killed in a more
public space (Wolfe-Murray 2005, 22). The Bates Motel bathroom is exploited
by Hitchcock, using the seemingly private safe space to deter our mind "as far
as possible from what's actually going to happen" (Truffaut 1967, 269). The
association of the en suite is one of security; it is typically the least public room
of the archetypal house, a room within a room. Hitchcock has purposefully selected a recognisable and relatable venue for the sake of the audience. There is a
conventional simplicity to the white walls and floor tiles (Wolfe-Murray 2005,
23), and the bathroom adheres to a principle of familiarity; hence, the viewer
feels safe and secure in the establishment of the 'homely' bathroom (Fear 2000,
40). Hitchcock first abuses the privacy of her room with the hole in the wall

for Bates to peer through, then goes further by creeping into the en suite. This contrasts with Arbogast's murder, taking place in the entrance hall of Bates dwelling, a relatively public room in the house, therefore "Hitchcock is able to displace the terror and fear of the film, by means of the architecture, to the banal and everyday world of the viewer" (Wolfe-Murray 2005, 32). Hitchcock's objects are representational, with the ambition of tapping into our unconscious mind — puppeteering his audience.

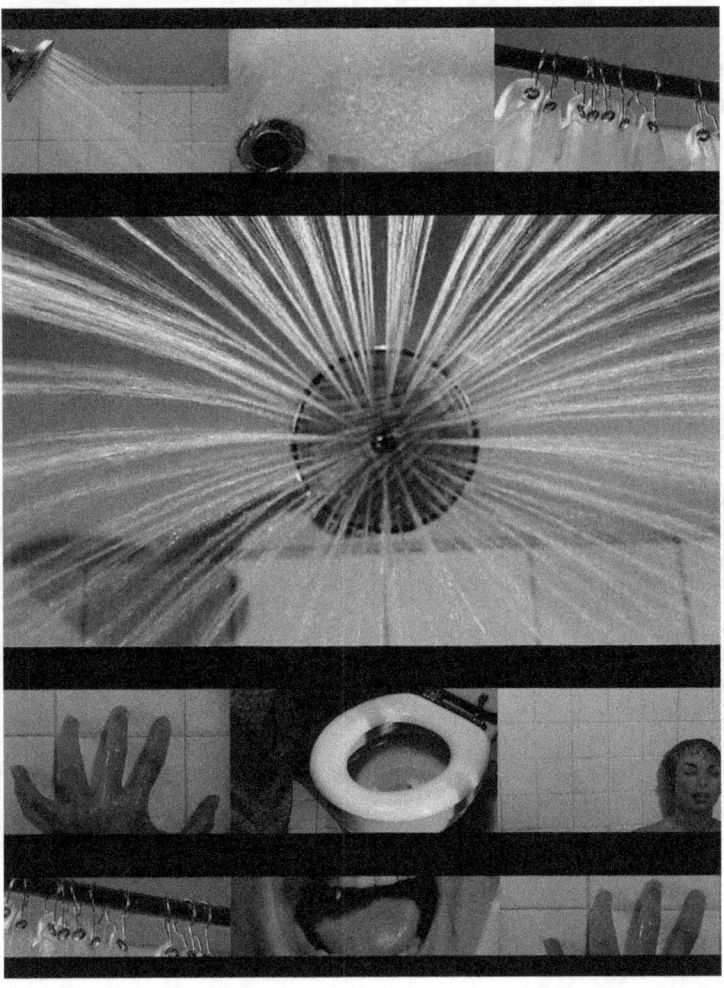

Figure 31: Study of Bates Motel bathroom in *Psycho*.

Psycho could be argued to be the most Freudian of all the Hitchcock films, dealing with the repressed memory of a traumatising incident, along with transference of guilt, two Freudian theories that have a strong role in the plot (Sandis 2009, 70). Here Hitchcock has taken the neurosis of Bates and used it to guide us through the architectural setting of the story. The journey we undertake with the Bates' house, and the gradual revelation of the maze-like rooms, runs parallel with the exposé of Bates' compartmentalised mind. The household is a vital piece of architecture in the film, and was inspired by the 1925 painting, 'House by the Railroad' by Edward Hopper. The light shining in the painting is bright enough to cast deep shadows on the stately Victorian mansion, but not to rid it of its negativity, as 'Picturing America' (2014) analysed, "Instead of happy, anecdotal pictures celebrating the energy and prosperity of the Roaring Twenties, Hopper portrayed modern life with unsentimental scenes of either physical or psychological isolation." This could be why Hitchcock chose this painting as the inspiration behind his 'house on the hill' for psycho-killer Norman Bates.

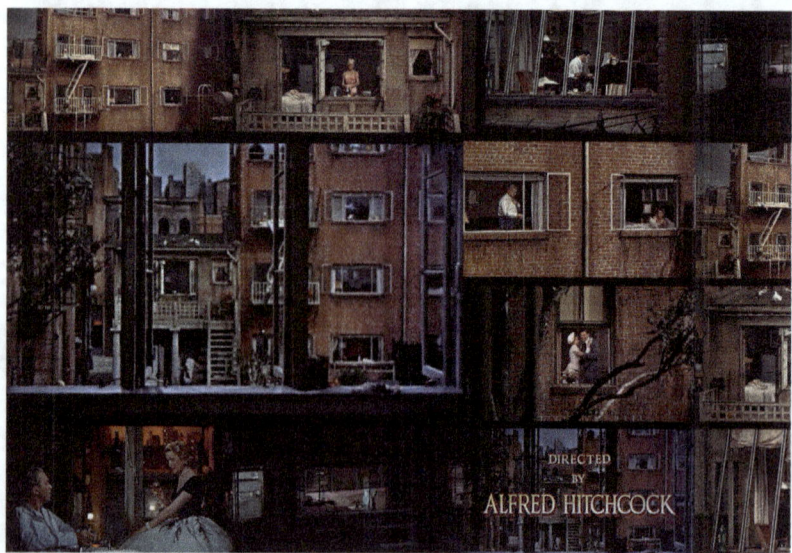

Figure 32: *Rear Window* Collage.

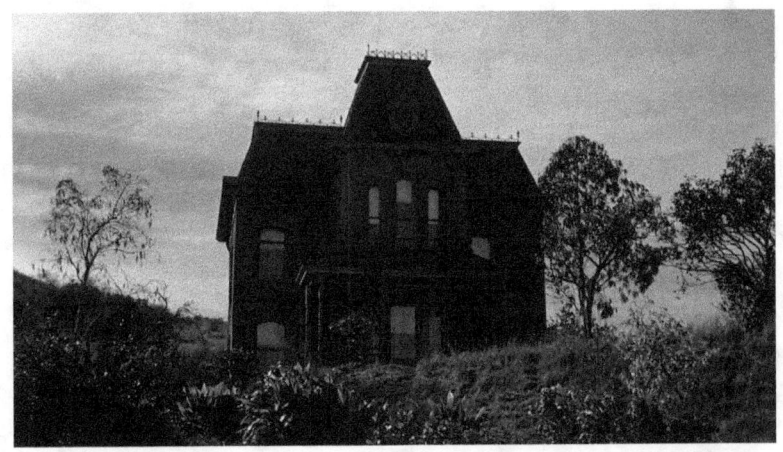

Figure 33: House on the hill in *Psycho* (1:35:20).

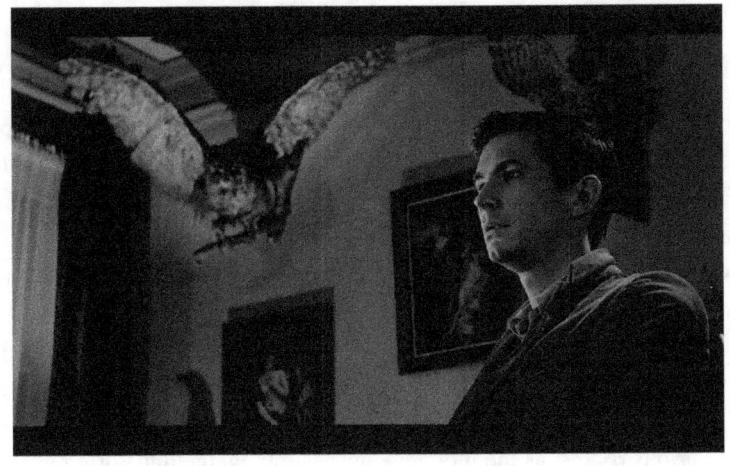

Figure 34: Bates and his birds in *Psycho* (0:39:02).

After greeting Marion, Bates disappears into his eerie Victorian house to have discussions with his mother. The house acts as an anthropomorphic entity of his mother, and Hitchcock initially hides the inside from the audience, as if it holds secrets. Hitchcock is triumphant in characterising the house as spiritual, a concept that is performed by architects such as Louis Kahn, who famously said that every building essentially has "its own soul." The Freudian diagnosis of 'repressed guilt' is indicative of Bates, and possibly why he blames his mother for the murders he committed. The neurosis of Bates leads him to experience Lacan's mirror image, wanting to be his mother because he yearns for a sense of identity, which he struggles with due to schizophrenia.

In *Psycho*, Bates early on indicates a dangerous imprisonment, "We're all in our private traps, clamped in them, and none of us can ever get out. We scratch and claw but only at the air, only at each other. And for all of it, we never budge an inch" (*Psycho* 0:38:00). Even the decor of the motel features dead stuffed birds, as if they are trapped and cannot move. The confinement of *Rope* shows a similar approach and is exaggerated due to its spatial restrictions as a single-set film. The film was shot between 7.30am and 9.15pm, and Hitchcock used close-ups of dark items to hide the cuts from swapping the reel. These extensive takes lead to a feeling of enclosure, leaving the viewer with an uneasy sensation.

Rear Window is filmed from the window of one apartment, mainly through the eyes of one character. Jeff is confined to a wheelchair, which limits the spaces we experience throughout the film. The story has a limited setting: a courtyard and the standpoint of a set of apartments. These spatial restrictions alone provide a sense that the character is trapped, one viewpoint from one immobile character from a single room is unnerving to the viewer, serving a feeling of discomfort. Manderley estate spawned a classic Hitchcockian labyrinth. It is a mansion also full of forbidden rooms and mysterious chambers, to which the anonymous newly-wed Mrs. de Winter II is not accustomed, portraying the home as a place of isolation and imprisonment. Again, we see a gradual revelation of various rooms, as the plot develops. The fundamental 'forbidden room' symbolises the repressed longings of the new Mrs. de Winter, as the novel bride perceives Manderley as a house of alienation and fear. This leads to a loss of identity on her part as she loses contact with her ego, trying to mimic her legendary predecessor. The incessant theme of confinement and claustrophobia, alongside the typical labyrinth layout, puts the viewer on edge. The restricted setting of the story could initially trick the observer into a sense of safety — a suggestion executed in jest when it comes to Hitchcock's direction. The spaces are set up as a trap, eventually projecting the fear of the imprisoned character onto his spectator's psyche.

Rear Window, *Rebecca*, and *Psycho* demonstrate how Sir Alfred Hitchcock can alter one's mental state through control of architectural influences in cinematography. Symbolically charged spaces, buildings, characters, and objects augment emotional reactions. The visual and audible effects operate in parallel. Hitchcock is playful with the sentiment of his spectators, and he somewhat abused his power as an influential figure of the 1920s, when film was a relatively foreign concept to the public. He was a perfectionist and obtained a deep understanding of his psychotic killers to sell stories. It is apparent that he employed Freudian and Lacanian theories of psychoanalysis to his work, and as an advocate for architecture, he projected this psychoanalytical conjecture on to his sets. "These architectural motifs," Jacobs (2013, 26) explains, "often relate to specific narratives or plot constructions such as a secret that is hidden within the confines of the house and the family." A window, for example, can illuminate the interior of a domestic setting, while also promoting or even seducing the addictive voyeurism that drives Jeff to his near-death experience in Rear Window. Similarly, a staircase not only connects public and private space within a house, but also threatens danger when it acts as a threshold.

Hitchcock's bank of copious art proves how passionate he was in his profession. His aim was to entertain the viewer, and in that he succeeded. Through his early role in set design in the 1920s, he established a position that the *emotion* of the surroundings is integral. He found intuitive methods that manipulated the built environment, and therefore the audience. Elements in space such as a room, object or sound are not an afterthought. The strong visual presence on screen took priority in his films, constantly insinuating sentiments such as suspense, suspicion, or fear. This thinking can drive the design by constantly considering the repercussions on the viewer's state of mind. The use of emotion in architecture is not a new concept, and has been applied for centuries, as Ma Yansong (of MAD Architects) affirms, "I see architecture as an environment where you can have emotion and contact, you can feel happy, be optimistic and use your imagination" (Yansong 2013 0:02:30). Ultimately, this imagination is what Hitchcock envisioned and executed. With his passion for the craft, playful character, and undeniable talent, Hitchcock established an arguably legendary influence in the trajectory of architecture in cinema.

REFERENCES

academia.edu. 2015. Freudian and Lacanian Psychoanalysis: A Comparison and Contrast. Accessed Mar 2016. https://www.academia.edu/8904743/FREUDIAN_AND_LACANIAN_PSYCHOANALYSES_A_COMPARISON_AND_CONTRAST

American heritage. 2011. Dictionary of the English Language. Accessed Nov 2015. http://www.thefreedictionary.com/evolutionary+psychology

Archdaily. 2008. AD Interviews: Ma Yansong. Accessed Mar 2016. http://www.archdaily.com/318140/ad-interviews-ma-yansong-mad

Archdaily. 2008. The Architecture of Alfred Hitchcock. Accessed Nov 2015. http://www.archdaily.com/470191/the-architecture-of-alfred-hitchcock/.

The art of foley. 2008. What is a Foley Artist? Accessed Mar 2016. http://www.marblehead.net/foley/whatisitman.html

Babineau, Dan. 2003. *Stairs in Cinema: A Formal and Thematic Investigation.* Thesis. Concordia University, Quebec, Canada.

Banham, Reyner. 1984. *The Architecture of the Well-Tempered Environment.* Illinois: The University of Chicago Press.

Bazin, Andre. 1971. *What is cinema?* Berkley: University of California Press.

Brill, Lesley. 1991. *The Hitchcock Romance: Love and Irony in Hitchcock's films.* NJ: Princeton University Press.

Business insider. 2016. *Horror movies do something strange and incredible to your brain - Ernest Lehman.* Accessed Mar 2016. http://www.businessinsider.com/horror-movies-do-something-incredible-to-your-brain-2016-3/?r=AU&IR=T.

Colomnia, Beatriz. 1996. *Privacy and Publicity: Modern Architecture as Mass Media.* Massachusetts: The MIT Press.

Cosmides, Leda. & Tooby, John. 2000. *Evolutionary Psychology and the Emotions.* NY: Guilford.

Dieter Schall, Hans. 2010. *Learning from Hollywood: Architecture and Film. 2nd edition.* Germany: Edition Axel Menges.

Douchet, Jean. 1999. *Alfred Hitchcock.* Paris: Cahiers du Cinema.

Driscoll, Paige. 2013. *The Hitchcock Touch: Visual Techniques in the Work of Alfred Hitchcock.* International ResearchScape Journal: Volume 1 (Article 4). p4-22. https://scholarworks.bgsu.edu/irj/vol1/iss1/4

Friedman, William. 1973. *The Exorcist*. DVD. Directed by - William Friedman. California: Warner Bros

Fear, Bob. 2000. *Architecture and Film*. Architectural Design: Volume 2. North Carolina: Academy Press.

Gervasi, Sacha. 2012. *Hitchcock*. DVD. Directed by - Sacha Gervasi. USA: Fox Searchlight Pictures.

Gifford, Robert. 2007. *Environmental Psychology. Principles and practice*. 4th edition. Colville, WA: Optimal Books.

Haralambidou, Penelope. 2015. *Success through architecture interview*. (firsthand study — interview: Rebecca Jane McConnell, Alice Gordon, Youhong Lin, Adam Moore).

Hitchcock, Alfred. 1934. *The Man Who Knew Too Much*. DVD. Directed by – Alfred Hitchcock. UK: Universal Pictures UK

Hitchcock, Alfred. 1940. *Rebecca*. DVD. Directed by - Alfred Hitchcock. USA: Anchor Bay Entertainment.

Hitchcock, Alfred. 1943. *Shadow of A Doubt*. DVD. Directed by - Alfred Hitchcock. USA: Universal Pictures.

Hitchcock, Alfred. 1948. *Rope*. DVD. Directed by - Alfred Hitchcock. USA: Universal Pictures.

Hitchcock, Alfred. 1953. *I Confess*. DVD. Directed by - Alfred Hitchcock. USA: Universal Pictures.

Hitchcock, Alfred. 1954. *Rear Window*. DVD. Directed by - Alfred Hitchcock. USA: Universal Pictures.

Hitchcock, Alfred. 1960. *Psycho*. DVD. Directed by - Alfred Hitchcock. USA: Universal Pictures.

Hitchcock, Alfred. 1963. *The Birds*. DVD. Directed by - Alfred Hitchcock. USA: Universal Pictures.

Hitchcock, Alfred. and Gottlieb, Sidney. 1995. *Hitchcock on Hitchcock: Selected writings and interviews. Interview by Herb Lightman - Hitchcock talks about lights, camera, action*. Berkeley: University of California Press.

Jacobs, Steven. 2013. *The Wrong House: The Architecture of Alfred Hitchcock*. Rotterdam: 010 Publishers.

Jones, Kent. 2015. *Hitchcock/truffaut*. DVD. Directed by - Kent Jones. Cannes: Dogwoof Studio.

Lacan, Jacques. 1978. *The Four Fundamental Concepts of Psycho-Analysis*. 11th Seminar. Toronto: Parasitic Ventures Press.

Leva, Gary. 2008. *The Sound of Hitchcock*. Documentary. Directed by - Gary Leva. Vimeo: https://vimeo.com/143186463.

Macey, David. 1997. *Dictionary of Cultural and Critical Theory*. 'Mirror-stage'. Payne, Michael edition. Hoboken: Wiley-Blackwell Publishing.

Marantz Cohen, Paula. 1995. *The Legacy of Victorianism: Alfred Hitchcock*. Lexington: The University Press of Kentucky.

McGilligan, Patrick. 2003. *Alfred Hitchcock: A Life in Darkness and Light*. New York: Regan Books.

The New York Times. 2015. *Dear Architects: Sound matters*. Accessed: Mar 2016. http://www.nytimes.com/interactive/2015/12/29/arts/design/sound-architecture.html?_r=0.

The New Yorker. 2011. *The Exchange: Karen Russell on "Swamplandia!"* Accessed: Feb 2016. http://www.newyorker.com/books/page-turner/the-exchange-karen-russell-on-swamplandia

Nyauma, Mokaya. 2014. *Freudian and Lacanian Psychoanalyses: A Comparison and Contrast*. Essay. https://www.academia.edu/8904743/FREUDIAN_AND_LACANIAN_PSYCHOANALYSES_A_COMPARISON_AND_CONTRAST.

Picturing America. 2014. *House By the Railroad*. Accessed: Mar 2016. http://picturingamerica.neh.gov/downloads/pdfs/Resource_Guide_Chapters/PictAmer_Resource_Book_Chapter_16A.pdf.

Plutchik, Robert. 1980. *Emotion. A Psychoevolutionary Synthesis*. The University of Michigan: Harper & Row Publishers.

Saggio, Antonio. 2010. *The Instrument of Caravaggio*. First English Edition. North Carolina: lulu.com.

Sandis, Constantine. 2009. *Hitchcock's Conscious Use of Freud's Unconscious*. Europe's Journal of Psychology. Volume 3. Oxford: Oxford Brookes University. p56-81.

Sloan, Jane. 1995. *Alfred Hitchcock: A Filmography and Bibliography*. California: University of California Press

Spielberg Steven. 1993. *Jurassic Park*. DVD. Directed by – Steven Spielberg. UK: Universal Pictures UK.

Sullivan, Jack. 2008. *Hitchcock's Music*. Usa: Yale University Press.

Truffaut, Francois. 1967. *Hitchcock/Truffaut*. France: Simon & Schuster.

Walker, Michael. 2006. *Hitchcock's Motifs*: Film Culture in Transition. Holland: Amsterdam University Press.

White, Edward. 2021. *The Twelve Lives of Alfred Hitchcock: Anatomy Of The Master Of Suspense*. New York: W.W Norton & Company

Wolfe, Tom. 2009. *From Bauhaus To Our House*. Uk: Picador.

Wolfe-Murray, Tim. 2005. *Psychoanalysis: The Architecture Of Alfred J. Hitchcock*. Thesis. University Of Greenwich, London, UK

Yacowar, Maurice. 2010. *Hitchcock's British Films: Contemporary Approaches To Film And Media Series*. Second Edition. Mi: Wayne State University Press.

Yansong, M. 2013. 'Ad Interviews: Ma Yansong'. Accessed May 2021. http://www.archdaily.com/318140/Ad-Interviews-Ma-Yansong-Mad

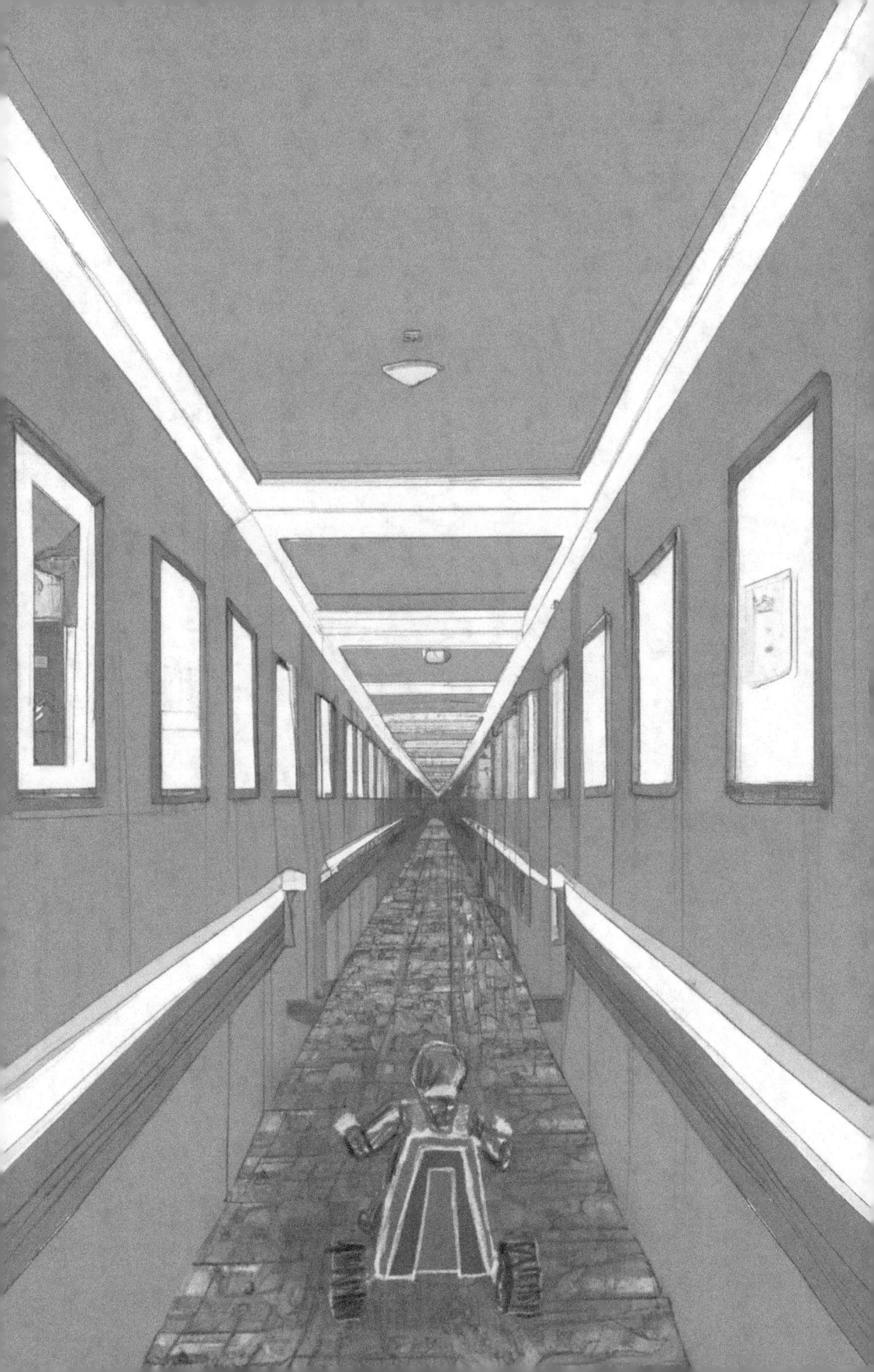

Fear of Spaces: How Abandoned Space Seduces the Imagination

Hayden Allen

HAYDEN ALLEN is an architect with experience working on both commercial and small scale projects across conception to completion. He graduated from Queen's University Belfast in 2017 and began his career working for Taro Architects in London. He is currently working with award winning practice Maccreanor Lavington Architects.

A successful horror film must play on the emotions of the audience to conjure fear. This investigation includes an analysis of how directors evoke terror in the cinematic world, which prompted a study into how emotions change within specific spaces. The expansive term, 'abandoned space,' probed an inquiry into its architectural definition, and namely how it can be differentiated from other terms, such as 'unoccupied space.' Engrossed with the concept of fear within these spaces, and their portrayal in film, this research explores how media characterises these spaces, in an attempt to determine whether an abandoned space can ever truly be abandoned. With an endless newsfeed of horrific stories available in the palm of your hand, feeding constant stories of murder, violence and rape, this chapter scrutinises the role of fear in our day-to-day routine, its impact on our everyday lives, and how it may corrupt our perspective of spaces. The intention of this exploration is to answer such questions as: What makes a space abandoned? Why are abandoned buildings constantly associated with horror and fear? And can a space ever be truly abandoned? Ultimately, this is a study into the role of architectural spaces in the context of horror films.

This analysis seeks a profound understanding of the term 'abandoned space.' It considers spatial characteristics, lighting, and materiality while simultaneously considering the psychology of the space, including how human senses inspire undeniable emotional responses. Abandoned space is seldom explored, but it has become a term that conveys a dark demeanour. A person, having never had a bad experience regarding an unoccupied or neglected space, may still choose to avoid it based on an assumption of danger that is manipulated by media and film. Analysing various forms of media, this work questions the representation of spatial setting, and how it alters the audience's perceptions. Intermittent horror inflicted on a small percentage of the population seems to be actively distorting our experience of the world and encouraging avoidance behaviour.

To successfully examine the role of abandoned space within the horror film genre, this study focuses on two case studies that depict a contrasting sense of abandonment. Danny Boyle's *28 Days Later* (2002) captures an almost stereotypical post-apocalyptic experience of abandoned space, utilising dramatic visuals as a fear-driving device. In contract to this, Stanley Kubrick's *The Shining* (1980) explores a more psychological approach to the proposition of abandoned space. The narrative revolves around the psychology of isolation, as the audience watches a man descend into madness while living in an abandoned hotel, shut off from the outside world.

Delving into works by neurologist Sigmund Freud and philosopher Aristotle, this research looks at the psychology of spaces, and their power in promoting a fearful response. This involves a study of Aristotle's work on the definition of 'human nature' in order to understand the role of our natural animalistic responses, and Freud's essay *Uncanny*, which investigates the psychology of fear. Both texts led to a deeper understanding of human psychology within abandoned spaces, which are relatable to personal experience within an abandoned space.

This topic could not be entirely investigated without first-hand exploration of an abandoned space. To understand the architectural aesthetics of decay, alongside our fascination with horror, a first hand experience was documented within an abandoned prison. Photographs and videos were utilised to provide the reader an insight into the space. Acquiring a deeper understanding of abandoned space allowed the research to connect experience to the senses, film, media, and psychological theories to determine if somewhere can ever truly be 'abandoned.'

In an attempt to determine whether an abandoned space truly is abandoned, it is important to first understand what qualities exist in forsaken territory. Within the first section here, an architectural definition is determined for an abandoned space, in conjunction with psychological studies into fear and human nature. Having acquired background knowledge of fear from analysing the works of Aristotle and Freud, the study observes the evolution of fear in today's society. The text explains how certain architectural spaces, in particular abandoned spaces, are portrayed in horror films, in an attempt to understand how this may alter our perception of a space. The study examines how directors Boyle and Kubrick manipulate sets, colour, light, and framework to exaggerate space and evoke a fearful response from the audience. The research looks at an abandoned Belfast building - Crumlin Road Gaol. It contains a detailed account of a personal experience wandering around the abandoned wings of the prison. With the help of photography and video recording, the explorations provide a first-hand experience, which can be linked to the theories examined.

Abandoned Spaces and Fear

This section investigates the role of architecture in decaying spaces. The materiality, light, and sensitivity of the space slowly evolve over time, not only to affect the physical characteristics of the space but also its spiritual atmosphere. Considering the role of the senses in abandoned spaces, in conjunction with psychological theories on fear, I attempt to find out what makes an abandoned space and why a fear of these spaces exists.

The architectural decay of an abandoned space often appeals to the imagination. The formerly maintained building has been rejected by society, and over time it has slowly decayed fading from memory. A key factor in defining an abandoned space is the absence of a human routine. Without the presence of people, the building is allowed to evolve into a decayed ruin. Paint separates from walls, peeling onto the floor, over time exposing a crumbling structure. Without a sense of ownership, the building struggles against the elements and will often fall victim to leakages, resulting in large puddles of stagnant water, while abandoned objects act as pieces of debris. The evolution of decay continues to follow Kelling and Wilson's (1982) broken-window theory, which hypothesised that a broken window, if not repaired, attracts vandals to break a few more windows, which may lead to breakages into the building, which later may lead to squatters or fires lit inside.

"The way spaces feel, the sound and smell of these places, has equal weight to the way things look." Steven Holl (Pallasmaa, 2005, p.7)

Space is a sensual experience. It allows its occupier to generate a range of emotions, from absolute comfort to crippling fear. The materials appeal to our basic human instincts. They control the light, texture, smell, and sound to become familiar to us. Abandoned materials decay over time, mimicking our own mortality, evolving into a new material. In relation to the five senses, if a blind person occupies an abandoned space, without obvious signs of decay, would they know it was abandoned by using all their other senses, and would their experience of the space differ as a result?

With an obvious lack of the human sounds of footsteps, talking and movement, at first the abandoned space would appear peaceful to the blind occupier. When mundane sounds of wind, creaks and echoes fill the space, perhaps it would be identified as an unoccupied space. Therefore, sound may not be a key sense in identifying abandoned spaces; however, when the abandoned nature has been established, similar to film, sound plays a vital role regarding the emotional associations. Acclaimed French film director Robert Bresson stated that, "A sound always evokes an image; an image never evokes a sound" (1975, 23). Mundane sounds, such as wailing winds and slowly creaking doors, do not go unnoticed and contribute to the occupier's fear and anxiety. The smallest of sounds can play on the mind when alone, especially in an abandoned space. A fear of the unknown sets the imagination wild as it struggles to identify mundane noises, regarding them as looming dangers rather than common occurrences.

Why do abandoned houses always have the same hollow smell: is it because the particular smell is stimulated by emptiness observed by the eye? (Juhani Pallasmaa, 2005, p.59)

Juhani Pallasmaa, finish architect, educator and critic, argues that, "the most persistent memory of any space is often its smell" (2005, 58), as smell acts as a trigger, stimulating comparable emotional responses that identify the occupier with another time and place. The smell of dust and damp lingers inside abandoned spaces, with an uncanny familiarity to spaces within the home that house little human activity. Similar to abandoned buildings, eaves cupboards and under-stair cupboards become a graveyard for unwanted objects that are left to decay, over time accruing a layer of dust, producing a similar smell. In the case of our blind occupier, the smell would identify itself as an abandoned space, then exaggerating the mundane sounds, changing the atmosphere of the space.

> The hands are the sculptor's eyes.
> (Juhani Pallasmaa, 2005, p.60)

As the space sits absent from routine or time, a layer of dust accumulates over every surface, acting as a thin barrier that dramatically changes the occupier's relationship with the materials. The dust acts as a pest, changing elements of the material, for example a dust-covered floor becomes slippery. Losing a sense of stability one must alter their pace to avoid falling. Other dust-covered materials feel dirty and are avoided, resulting in the vulnerable positioning of the hands. In the case of our blind occupier, the sense of touch is not a defining sense — its avoidance is an outcome of the other senses.

Abandoned space accords with the role of the senses, each playing their role to arouse a fear response from the occupier. Pallasmaa states, "architecture has to address all the senses simultaneously" (2005, 12). In a similar way, the senses address all of the architectural elements of abandoned space simultaneously. Each sense accumulates to form the complete atmosphere of a space and an occupier's emotional response, resulting in a blind person and any other occupier ultimately sharing a similar experience. With an absence of one sense, the other senses heighten, allowing the occupier to fill in the gaps and resulting in a similar experience. This is evident in film, as the absence of smell or touch is exaggerated by the sounds and visuals, in an attempt to recreate the other senses in the audience's mind.

Abandoned space typically radiates an eerie atmosphere, creating a sense of anxiety and fear. The fear of space directly relates to both the absence of people and the presence of people. Investigating deeper into the role of psychology in abandoned spaces, one must examine how a disconnection from society and lack of human routine affects the mind. Reading the work of Greek philosopher Aristotle offered a deeper understanding of human nature that could be applied within the spatial qualities of abandoned space. Aristotle states:

Man is a conjugal animal – meaning an animal which is born to couple when
an adult, thus building a household and, in more successful cases, a clan or
small village still run upon patriarchal lines. (Nicomachean Ethics, VIII. 1162a;
Politics, 1252a)

By nature, we are social beings that have become reliant on, and bound to, other
beings. With security in numbers, a social culture has been embedded into our
society, from the city scale to the community scale, and to a family scale, establishing social interactions as an everyday occurrence. Fear of abandoned spaces
can be directly linked to the detachment of human routine; whilst inhabiting
an abandoned space, the social aspect of the civil world is lost, leaving you
completely detached. An oxymoron exists: fear of an abandoned space due to
the absence of a human presence, yet fearful about the possibility of a human
presence. The imagination foresees possible horrors embedded in our minds by
film and mass media. Arthur C. Doyle, the British writer and physician, states:
"Where there is no imagination there is no horror" (1888). With an absence of
man, the imagination, led through the senses, begins to repopulate the space
with horror.

Aristotle (*Poetics*, 1148b) continues to say that man is a "mimetic animal" that
loves to use the imagination and not only to make laws and run town coun-
cils. He states, "we enjoy looking at accurate likenesses of things which are
themselves painful to see, obscene beasts, for instance, and corpses." And the
"reason why we enjoy seeing likenesses is that, as we look, we learn and infer
what each is;" Aristotle's hypothesis continues to prove accurate to the present
day, as we take pleasure in reading terrifying news stories and watching graphic
horror films, which Aristotle believes allows people the chance to purge their
negative emotions in a process called catharsis, releasing built-up aggression.
There is an entity of horror that speaks directly and instinctively to the human
animal, when inhabiting an abandoned space: it is the horrors we have read and
watched exaggerated in our mind. We place ourselves as the protagonist of the
story, generating our natural fear reflex, negatively altering our perception of
the space. In a sense we contribute to our own fear.

Sigmund Freud, an Austrian neurologist and the father of psychoanalysis,
proposed that with horror comes the 'uncanny,' the surfacing of thoughts and
images of the primitive id that are suppressed by the civilised ego. "What is

feared is thus a secret intention of harming someone, and certain signs are taken to mean that such an intention is capable of becoming an act" (1919, 12). Freud continues to say, "the uncanny is that class of the terrifying which leads back to something long known to us, once very familiar" (1919, 1). The familiarity of an abandoned space may seem 'uncanny' in the detection of familiar senses. Similar to Pallasmaa's theories, they act as a trigger, stimulating familiar emotional responses.

In the 1970s, Roger Harp, an environmental psychologist, carried out an investigation to find out what children do when they are alone. A small town in Vermont was selected with eighty-six participating children ranging from the ages of three to twelve. Harp proceeded to examine the children's behaviour for over two and a half years. By following the children throughout the day, Harp secretly monitored how they behaved when they thought they were absent from adult supervision. The children would show Harp their favourite hiding places, places they believed to be 'scary,' and generally any place they were allowed to go by themselves. Using the data, Harp created maps and worked out the average radius each child was able to travel from their home for each age group, showing that the children had remarkable freedom of the town, with children as young as five having access to the lake located on the very edge of town. Forty years later, Harp continued his research and proceeded to revisit the small town in Vermont, this time to document the children of the original children he had once examined, and to carry out similar experiments. Harp found that the children were not allowed to stray far from the house, and most of the places the children took him to were within close proximity of their house or within the garden, leaving places such as the lake as out of bounds, as parents wanted to 'keep an eye on them' at all times. The parents, who themselves had freely roamed the town, had denied their own children this privilege. This is because parents nowadays are more aware of child abductions and murders, due to this information-rich world, and are burdened by the fear of crime when in fact crime in America is at an all time low since the 1950s.

Ralph Adolphs, a professor of psychology and neuroscience, argues that in modern society, our fear threshold is set to an unnecessarily high level. Modern life is constantly triggering our fear emotion, which the natural world does not. He argues that the horror inflicted upon other people, thanks to the media, has distorted our experience of the world, activating our sense of fear when we do not need it.

> You know, if I just hear a slight creak in my house at night, I feel fear, and 99.9 percent of the time, there's no burglar in the house. And it's all safe. But nonetheless, I felt fear. So you have a lot of false positives (Adolphs, as cited in Miller and Spiegel, 2015).

In these situations, the mind begins to populate a space with our own fears, placing images of murderers and buglers in the space to rationalise the noise, again asking the question: can a space ever be truly abandoned? The imagery of horrors provides a similar emotional response when alone in these spaces, one that would not be as heightened in the familiarity of human routine, determining that it will never be truly abandoned. The abandonment exists in the physical state but proves populated in a psychological state.

> "I can't read fiction without visualizing every scene. The result is it becomes a series of pictures rather than a book." Alfred Hitchcock (Rebello, 1990, 19)

In 1971, Herbert A. Simon, one of the most influential social scientists of the twentieth century, stated that we live in an 'information-rich world.' The statement is even more true today; with the use of the Internet, billions of people have access to more information than ever before in human history. Simon continues to explain that:

> The wealth of information means a dearth of something else: a scarcity of whatever it is that information consumes. What information consumes is rather obvious: it consumes the attention of its recipients (1971, 40-41).

New reports and social media sites are designed to prey on the attention of people. Without attention, they cease to exist, which is why they go to excessive lengths in order to seize attention. Fear generates attention and helps to create an audience; fearful headlines draw people in, and stories are often exaggerated to provoke a reaction. Hitchcock was reputed to have said, "Television has brought back murder into the home" (Elkind, 1984, 103). With the constant bombardment of graphic films and horrific news stories, there is an assumption that crime rates are increasing, resulting in the audience overestimating the likelihood of becoming a victim. Bad things happen, they have always happened and always will happen; as a society we are becoming more 'scared,' shedding light on the quote, "the only thing we have to fear is fear itself," coined by President Franklin D. Roosevelt in his first Inaugural Address on 4 March 1933.

With an investigation into how the media can influence an audience's perception of certain spaces, I documented the most popular news articles over the course of a week by monitoring the UK's biggest news source: the BBC. Daily the BBC showcases the top ten most-read articles on its home page, giving me an insight into what engrosses the majority of people. The articles fell into two categories, either fearful or non-fearful. Fearful stories included themes of murder, assault, attack, kidnapping, and threat to safety — for example, 'Mother guilty of toddler murder,' leaving the remaining stories to fall under the non-fearful category, stories that provoke a neutral response, such as, 'Bridge to link Saudi Arabia and Egypt.' After accumulating fifty articles over the week, I discovered that 64% of the articles fell under 'fearful,' leaving only 36% under the 'non-fearful' category (see next page). Accompanying the previously discussed hypothesis made by Aristotle, this study shows that we do read more horrific stories than pleasant stories. Chiricos et al. (2000), on the topic of fear and mass media, has claimed that, "the frequency of news consumption is significantly related to fear." In light of this, it is easy to understand why fear is the natural response within an abandoned space. We witness so much horror and violence in the media and film that fear subconsciously is our natural response to anything. When thinking about rollercoasters, we picture malfunctions; when thinking of flying, we picture planes crashing; and when we think about abandoned buildings, we picture murderers and criminals. A surge in fearful stories has moulded a fearful society.

Filmic Case Study: *28 Days Later* (2002) and *The Shining* (1980)

This section investigates the role of abandoned space within film, which involves an analysis of two films that each portrays a contrasting sense of abandonment. Danny Boyle's *28 Days Later* (2002) captures an almost stereotypical post-apocalyptic imitation of abandoned space, using dramatic visuals that exaggerate the space to create tension and fear, whereas Kubrick's film *The Shin-*

ing (1980) explores a deeper psychological experience of abandoned spaces centring on isolation and the lack of human routine.

The film *28 Days Later* (2002), written by Alex Garland, follows protagonist Jim, twenty-eight days after a deadly virus spreads throughout the UK. The first scenes of the film perfectly depict a desolate London. The director first introduces the audience to Jim as he awakes from a coma, only to discover that all has been abandoned. Boyle mirrors Jim's journey of discovery with the audience, as we are brought through a range of scales to show the extent of the abandonment.

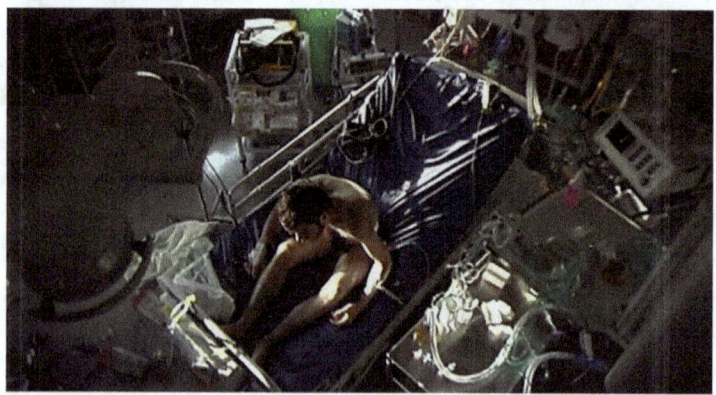

Figure 1: Jim wakes up in *28 Days Later* (all film stills are captured by the author unless indicated otherwise).

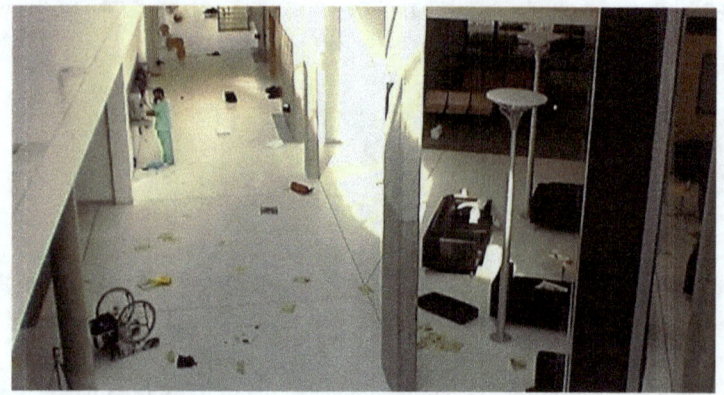

Figure 2: Jim explores an empty hospital in *28 Days Later*.

Micro

> We pull back to see that Jim is lying on a hospital bed, in a private room. Con-
> nected to his arms are multiple drips, a full row of four or five on each side of his
> bed. Most of the bags are empty. (Alex Garland, *28 Days Later* Script, 2002, 6).

Jim awakes to find a chaotic hospital room. Confused and disorientated, he
begins to rationalise what is happening and why he is there. Furniture and
hospital equipment lie scattered throughout the room, exaggerating a sense of
disorientation and confusion. Naked and alone, Jim is vulnerable. He finds a
nearby hospital gown to cover himself up and moves towards the door. He cries
out to anyone that may be listening. Echoing through the corridors, his calls are
met with complete silence.

Meso

> All the wards and corridors are deserted. Medical notes and equipment lie
> strewn over the floors, trolleys are upended, glass partition doors are smashed.
> In a couple of places, splashes of dried blood arc up the walls. (Alex Garland,
> *28 Days Later* Script, 2002, 7)

Jim proceeds through the empty corridors, venturing further into the hospital. T
he corridors mimic the hospital room, as he follows the trail-like path of scattered debris and hospital equipment. Crying out again for a similar response,
Jim cautiously moves down a set of stairs to discover a group of pay phones;
however, upon investigating he finds that the phones are disconnected. During
the payphone scene, Boyle uses the symbolism of disconnected payphones to
enforce the premise of abandonment. Phones, which are usually connected to
every phone across the globe, prove to be disconnected, exaggerating the scale
and sense of abandonment. As Jim continues his journey, he discovers a broken
vending machine that has discharged drink cans onto the floor. After checking
that no one is watching, Jim takes a few drink cans from the machine, drinks one
and bags the rest for later. Boyle is considering the social psychology of abandoned spaces. Jim has to check whether anyone is watching before he steals the
cans. His sense of morality remains even when a civil world seems abandoned.
Jim's animalistic alter ego surfaces, reinforcing the idea that humans act differently in the absence of a social presence.

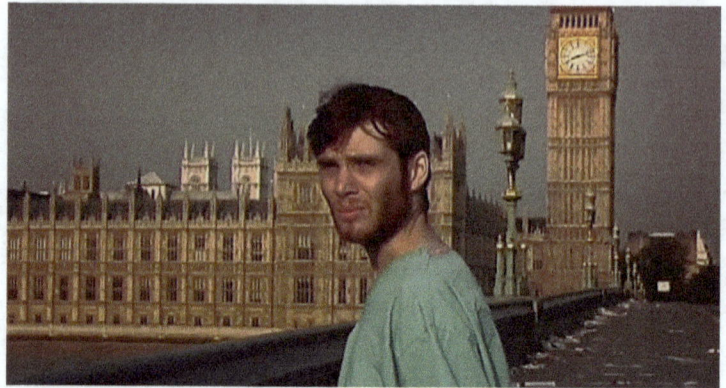

Figure 3: Jim explores empty landmarks *28 Days Later.*

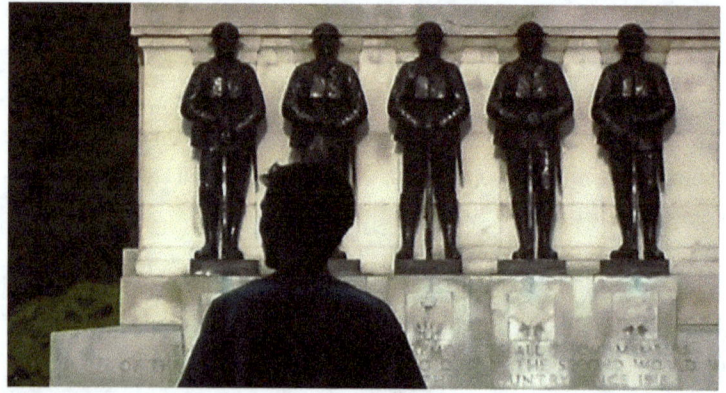

Figure 4: Jim walks past The Guards Memorial in London *28 Days Later.*

Macro

> Aside from a quiet rush of wind, there is silence. No traffic, no engines, no
> movement. Not even birdsong. (Alex Garland, 2002, 8)

Venturing beyond the hospital, Jim proceeds out into the empty streets of an
abandoned London. Moving through the deserted streets, Boyle utilises beautiful wide-angle shots of abandoned iconic landmarks. In the film script, Garland
writes that there is just silence; there is no traffic, no engines and no movement.

Jim moves through the normally bustling streets of London unopposed by pedestrians, cars or buses, having free roam of the city. Boyle uses the scale of London to mimic the scale of abandonment, adding eeriness to the scene. Frequently overlooked, the people and figures observed on billboards, advertisements, and statues (Figs. 4-5) seem uncanny — they seem alive as they follow Jim's journey through the empty streets. Populated with the imagery and memories of a past life, the billboards and statues exaggerate a lack of regular human routine. Eventually, Jim approaches a wall covered in photographs of missing people (Figure 6). In silence they stare at him as a newspaper caught in the wind flies past, and only after reading it does he discover the scale of the pandemic.

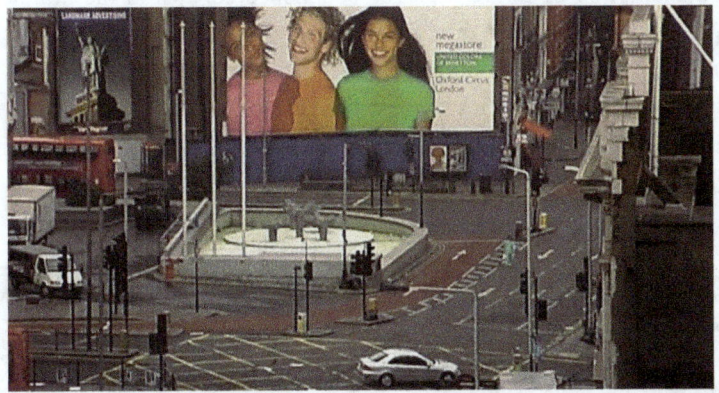

Figure 5: Jim roams the empty streets of London in *28 Days Later*.

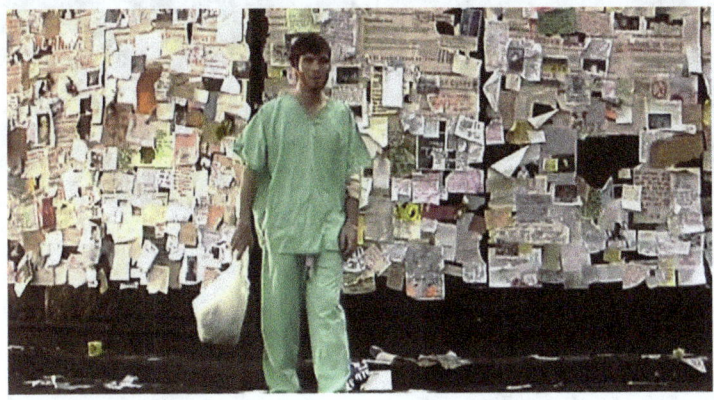

Figure 6: Jim discovers the missing persons wall in *28 Days Later*.

As part of everyday life, we come across unoccupied spaces quite regularly. They may take the form of an empty street or an empty corridor. All the physical characteristics of an abandoned space may be the same as an unoccupied space, as they both have an absence of human interaction. The difference between them is that an unoccupied space hosts a routine of human interaction, but at a particular point in time it has become vacant, with an assumption that it will be used again. An abandoned space has been disowned with the assumption that it will not be used again, leaving slight irregularities. Analysing the empty street (Figure 5) shows an irrational placement of a car. This irrational sense is what differentiates an abandoned space from an unoccupied space — the car looks abandoned never to be used again rather than strategically placed in the presumption of future use. The abandoned car lies in the middle of a junction, specifically within the restricted yellow zone amplifying its position, one that the civil world would never allow. These types of irregularities exist in abandoned spaces. They invite pressing questions about the origin, user and position, which trigger the imagination to fill in the blanks, usually resulting in fearful rationalisation.

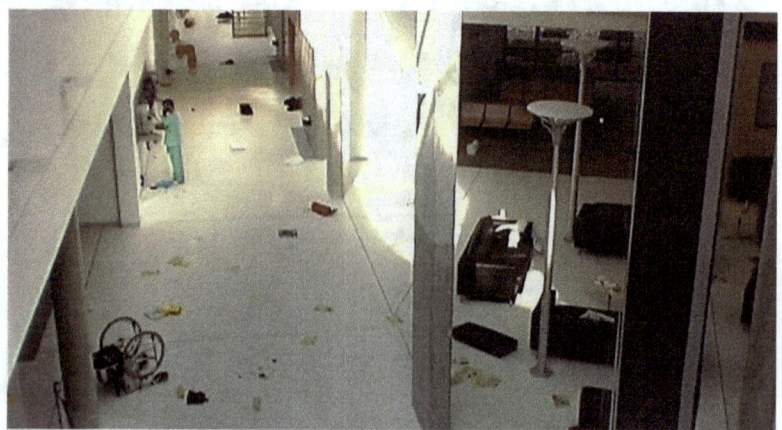

Figure 7: Hospital corridor with debris in *28 Days Later.*

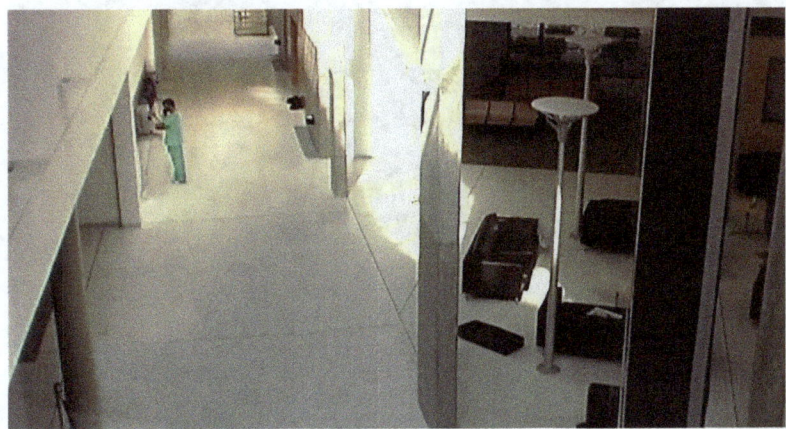

Figure 8: Hospital corridor without debris in *28 Days Later.*

The opening scenes of *28 Days Later* are used to set the atmosphere for the film. The chaotic sets and lack of human companionship give the audience a sense of abandonment. Boyle exaggerates debris during the opening scenes. The simple use of mundane objects scattered irrationally throughout the set presents the audience with the imagery of chaos. The irrational placement of things proves significant to the perception of abandoned spaces, simply because we are not familiar with them, because they would never coexist alongside human routine, like the uncanny placement of the car or debris throughout the hospital corridors. Without the debris scattered throughout the corridor, the hospital looks normal and functional. This one simple addition to the set adds a deeper psychological dimension to the scene, similar to the objects in abandoned spaces.

28 Days Later (2002) captures a stereotypical approach to abandoned spaces on a wider city scale. To gain a more psychological understanding of abandoned spaces, I have introduced Stanley Kubrick's The Shining (1980) to the investigation, which explores more the lack of human routine within a space. Kubrick's Overlook Hotel relies on techniques unrelated to the typical characteristics of abandoned space, focusing more on the uncanny nature of the spaces within, in conjunction with a lack of human routine.

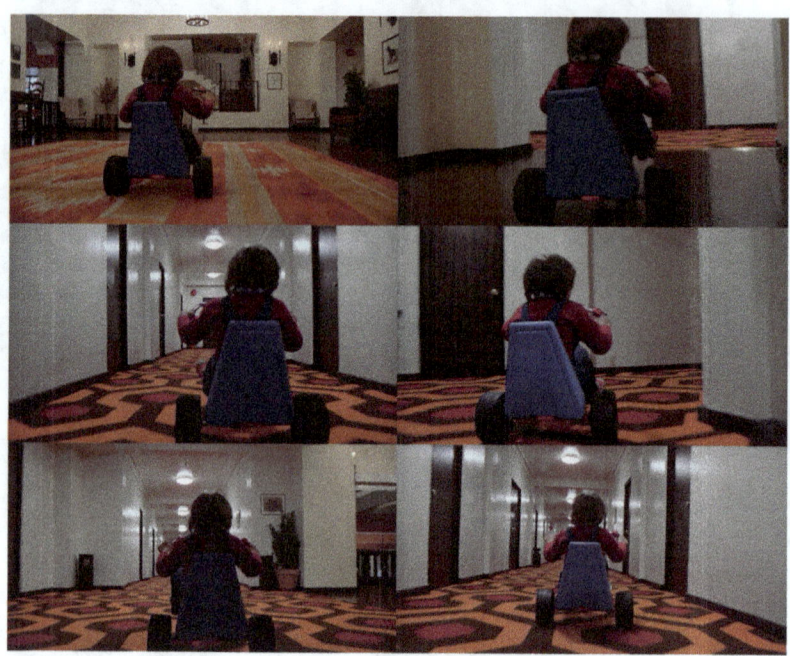

Figure 9: Danny's second loop in *The Shining*.

The Shining (1980) begins as Jack Torrance, his wife Wendy and son Danny embark towards the Overlook Hotel, where Jack is to be interviewed for the position of caretaker for the winter months, as the hotel cannot be left unattended. The hotel manager, Ullman, who is aware that Jack is a recovering alcoholic who has been dismissed from his previous teaching job for losing his temper, expresses concern about hiring him. Ullman explains that during the winter of 1970–1971, Delbert Grady, the then caretaker, had murdered his wife and two daughters in a drunken rage in the ghostly room 237 before killing himself. Jack recognises his concerns, but nevertheless accepts the job. Upon meeting the family, the hotel's chef, Dick Hallorann, recognises Danny's capacity for extrasensory perception (EP), or as he calls it, the 'shining.' Danny's EP warns him of the hotel's evil, through blood-soaked visions of the past and warnings from room 237.

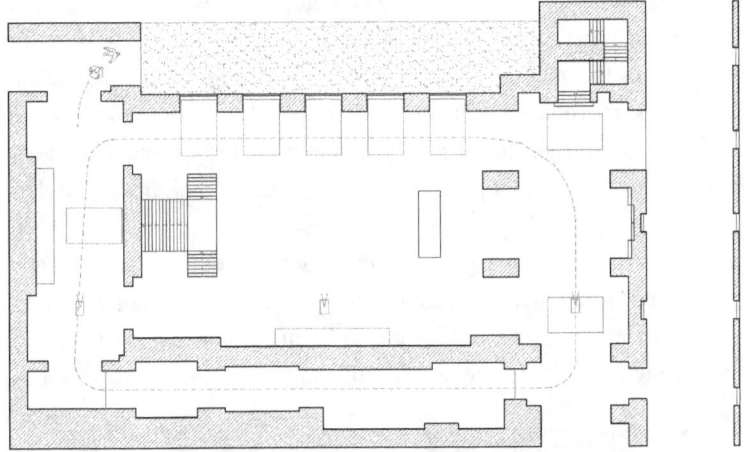

Figure 10: Plan of the Colorado Lounge (all illustrations are by the author).

As the Torrance family settle into the hotel, Jack (a would-be writer) sets up his office in the large Colorado lounge with strict orders not to be disturbed, as he proceeds to write his play. Danny is seen cruising around the hotel on his Big Wheel and going for walks in the hedge maze with Wendy. As Danny is cruising around the corridors of the hotel, a red ball rolls towards him, appearing to come from room 237. He enters the room. At that moment, we hear Jack screaming. Wendy comforts him, as he tells of his nightmare in which he says he killed them both with an axe. Danny appears, looking disorientated and bruised, and Wendy accuses Jack of being the cause. Furious, Jack walks towards the Gold Ballroom, where he meets bartender Lloyd. Jack explains to Lloyd about Wendy's concerns for Danny, as three years ago Jack had hit him. Following this, Jack decides to investigate room 237 for himself. Upon entering he is greeted by a beautiful woman who suddenly turns into a decaying old woman. Frightened, Jack leaves and locks the door. When reporting to Wendy, Jack lies and claims the room is empty. Following this, Wendy expresses her concerns and considers leaving the hotel at which Jack loses his temper and proceeds to the Gold Ballroom where he is persuaded by Grady, the previous caretaker, to 'correct' his family. Hallorann, while on vacation, receives signals from Danny and begins to make his way back to the hotel. Threatened by

Jack's behaviour, Wendy fears for her life. She hits Jack with a baseball bat and locks his unconscious body in the storage room. With the help of Grady, Jack escapes and attacks the bathroom Wendy and Danny are taking refuge in. Danny manages to squeeze out the window and head for the maze. Distracted by Hallorann's arrival, Jack kills him and follows Danny into the hedge maze. Danny lures Jack deeper into the maze and manages to escape with Wendy on Hallorann's snowmobile. Hopelessly lost in the maze, Jack freezes to death.

In *The Shining*, we see the Torrance family, abandoned in a large asylum-like hotel, in such a large space in which the characters are often alone. Jack is busy trying to write his play and wishes not to be disturbed, Wendy is playing the role of housewife, while Danny is often playing in different parts of the hotel.

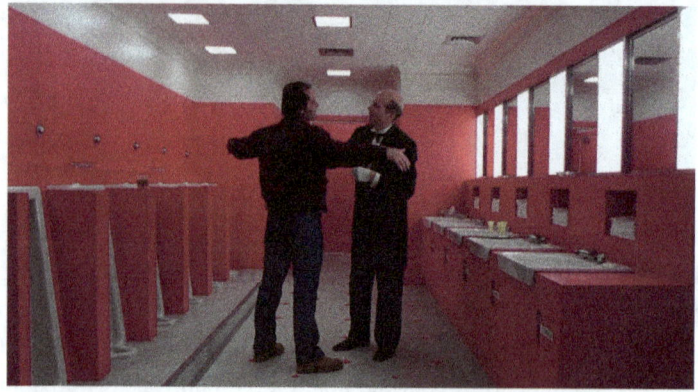

Figure 11: The red bathroom scene in *The Shining*.

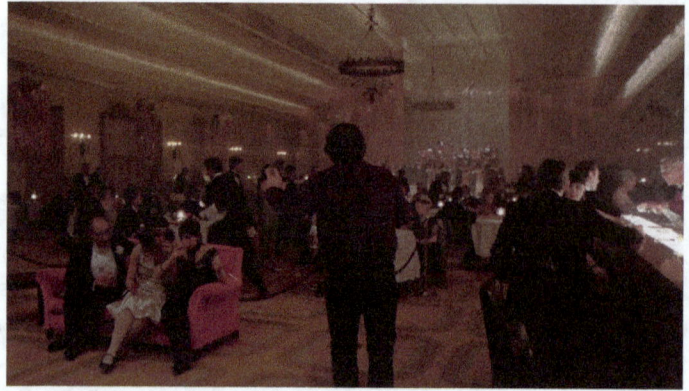

Figure 12: The gold ballroom scene in *The Shining*.

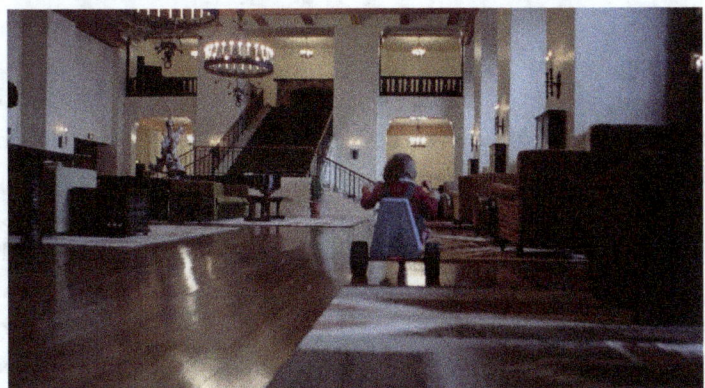

Figure 13: Danny's Colorado Lounge loop in *The Shining*.

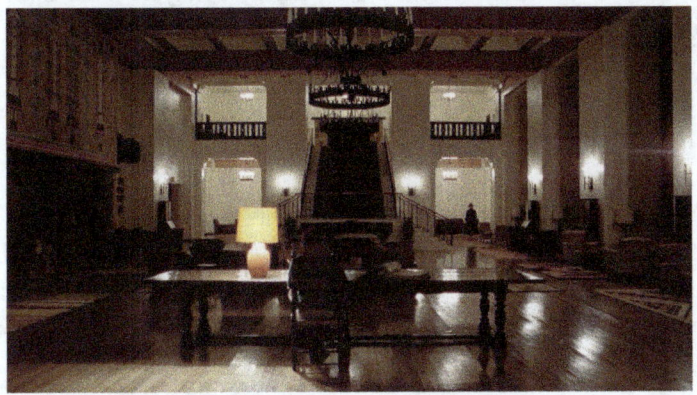

Figure 14: Jack typing in *The Shining*.

In a period when most horror films were imitations of *The Exorcist* (1973) and *The Omen* (1976), Kubrick felt the need for a different take on the cliché horror genre for his adaptation of the Stephen King novel. Interviewed by Ciment (1980), Kubrick stated that he wanted the hotel to look "authentic rather than like a traditionally spooky movie hotel. The hotel's labyrinthine layout and huge rooms, I believed, would alone provide an eerie enough atmosphere." Drawn to the idea of the evil side of human personality, Kubrick continued that he was interested in our brutal and violent nature because it is a true picture of human beings. And any attempt to create social institutions on a false view of human nature is probably doomed to failure (Interviewed by Ciment, 1980).

This is similar to the Freudian theory regarding humans' inner animalistic nature being suppressed by a civilised ego. The Overlook Hotel becomes the most important character throughout the film. It is mundane and ordinary, but with careful attention to architectural detail and spatial arrangement it manages to portray a sense of evil. The enormous scale of the hotel portrays an impression of dominance over the Torrance family and over-scaled spaces such as the Colorado Lounge and the Golden Ball Room make them appear small and powerless. When spatially trying to determine a general arrangement, there is a realisation that the hotel's layout appears absurd, and that spatially the hotel cannot exist, as rooms, halls and doorways begin to overlap with one another. Giving Kubrick's rigorous work ethic and attention to fine detail, one can only presume that these spatial anomalies do not occur by chance, but are strategically thought-out designs that are intended to disorientate the audience. These spatial anomalies are most evident during Danny's tricycle loops through the maze-like corridors of the hotel. Danny's first loop reveals the overall arrangement of the ground floor to the audience, circling the double-height Colorado Room, a significantly over-scaled space where Jack struggles with his writer's block.

Danny's second loop flows through the corridors on the first floor. Proceeding past the elevator, Danny turns right, coming back on himself moving through a corridor. The audience will recognise doors to the right, doors that lead to nowhere as spatially the room cannot exist because the thin wall is not thick enough. Continuing the loop, Danny moves past a landing that overlooks the Colorado Lounge. As he progresses further down the corridor, more doors are placed on the wall adjacent to the double-height Colorado Lounge, doors that, again, cannot spatially exist.

When carefully analysing the ground floor plan of the Colorado Lounge, spatial inconsistencies become evident. During a scene in the director's cut of *The Shining* (1980), the Torrance family are shown around by the hotel manager, Ullman. As the camera pans, the audience is aware of five large double-height windows that highlight the exterior of the hotel; however, as the camera moves, people can be seen entering from a corridor that could not exist.

Given Kubrick's attention to detail, it can be assumed that the doors were placed there deliberately, to escalate the sense of confusion. Moore et al. on the subject of physiological responses define anxiety as "places from which escape might be difficult or in which help might not be available" (2002, 197). Using this spatial confusion, Kubrick creates suspense through anxiety, as the irrational and unfamiliar layout of the hotel's ever-changing corridors and layout suggests that "escape might be difficult" and the hotel's isolated abandonment due to barricaded roads suggest that help may not be available.

In contrast to most horror films, *The Shining* is largely well lit, allowing Kubrick to use the vivid symbolism of colour to convey traits about the characters. The light exaggerates colossal spaces, lavish ballrooms, cold sterile bathrooms and tight sinister corridors, to give the mundane hotel spaces a sense of uncanniness.

At the start of the film, Jack is seen wearing a grey suit during his interview with Ullman. Grey is normally branded as a bland colour, symbolising Jack's 'dull' life; an abusive husband with a drinking problem, a failed teacher and an unaccomplished writer. As the film progresses, and the hotel begins to take control of Jack, he is seen wearing a dark velvet jacket, the red imagery coinciding with Jack's unstable mental state. Red is a common theme in many of Kubrick's films. It is used for an atmospheric purpose to convey a certain mood. In *The Shining*, red represents blood, danger, rage, and anger. Figure 11 shows former caretaker Grady speaking with Jack in the vivid, well-lit, red bathroom, where he speaks for the hotel urging Jack to 'correct' his family. The gold ballroom's earthy tones and soft lighting completely contradict the modernist style of the red bathroom. The bathroom is unlike any other room in the hotel. It is as if the audience has left the hotel, and entered Jack's mind. The pure white floor and ceiling accentuate the red walls, depicting Jack's rage and anger.

Upon hearing of Garrett Brown's Steadicam invention in 1974, Kubrick asked Brown to assist him in filming the famous continuous shots that seem to glide effortlessly behind the characters, creating beautiful seamless scenes through endless corridors. The camera followed directly behind the characters from a low vantage point, in a serpent-like manner indicating the hotel's looming evil, preying on the Torrance family. Kubrick's approach mimics our own behaviour in certain spaces, when alone. At times we may feel we are being followed, a sensation that generates anxiety, which Kubrick uses for suspense.

Film is essentially a visual experience; however, it is important not to under-estimate the role of sound. Sound is everything we hear throughout the film; it can be in the form of dialogue, sound effects or music. It is used to build atmosphere, provide us with information about the scene, advance the plot and tell us more about a character. Sound can be broken into two categories: di-egetic and non-diegetic. Diegetic sounds come from the world we see through the screen: character, dialogue, footsteps, etc. Non-diegetic sounds refer to ele-ments that are not part of this fictional world, such as musical scores and sound effects. Kubrick often plays against our expectations by using sound in various ways. He often takes everyday sounds related to the scene and exaggerates them. Figure 13 shows Danny cycling around the Colorado Lounge, the camera following close behind him like a predator trailing its prey. The most disturbing element of the scene is the pulsing sound created from the contrasting surfaces that come into contact with the tricycle's wheels — the hard thunderous roar of the hard wooden surface contrasts with the mute silence of the soft carpet, unsettling the audience and leaving them in suspense. During the scene where Jack is typing (Figure 14), Kubrick expresses the oversized scale of the Colora-do Lounge. The hard-surfaced space intensifies every tap of Jack's typewriter; the uncanny tap of every key thunders around the room, creating an eerie atmo-sphere. The sound generated sets the tone of the scene as Wendy enters. As she draws closer, the music escalates. Long stretched tones create suspense, which mimic Wendy's and the audience's fear, as she approaches an erratic Jack.

In the film, Danny's 'shining' warns him of the hotel's evil by showing him visions of blood and death, which is much like our own minds. When alone in an eerie space a sense of fear arises. Much like Danny's 'shining,' we engage our primal instincts and begin to imagine the potential threats we fear the most, confirming Aristotle's theory that we take pleasure in envisioning horrific scenes, which results in the mind essentially scaring itself.

When considering what abandoned buildings to investigate, I started my search for buildings in Belfast, only to discover that the Crumlin Road Gaol has been inactive and abandoned, with parts of the prison untouched, for over twenty years. I found the idea of exploring a prison fascinating, as most of us have never experienced the inside of a prison, gleaning all our knowledge from sto-ries, news reports and film. Having never been in a prison either, I felt a need to explore it and document my findings.

Case Study: Crumlin Road Gaol

> I am a product of long corridors, empty sunlit rooms, upstairs indoor silences,
> attics explored in solitude, distant noises of gurgling cisterns and pipes, and the
> noise of the wind under the tiles. (Lewis, 1965, 10)

Crumlin Road Gaol, situated in North Belfast, is the only remaining Victorian
prison in Northern Ireland. The prison, designed by Sir Charles Lanyon, was
built between 1843 and 1845 to operate as one of the most advanced prisons of
its day, holding over 550 inmates. Over its lengthy history, the gaol imprisoned
murderers, suffragettes, loyalists and republicans, and witnessed births, deaths,
marriages, escapes, riots, and, between 1854 and 1961, seventeen judicial hangings within the grounds. Lanyon had not considered a space for hanging, resulting
in the earlier inmates' hangings occurring on the roof and the bodies left on display in full view of the street. With a design based on the successful HM Prison
Pentonville in London, the gaol consisted of four radiating wings spanning off a
central watchtower, allowing each wing to be visible from the guards at all times.

Since its closure in 1996, the prison has been out of service, leaving three of
the wings completely abandoned for over twenty years. Recently one of the
wings has been restored to its original Victorian style, becoming a small tourist
attraction. The staff at Crumlin Road Gaol granted me permission to explore
the three abandoned wings of the prison alone, allowing me to document a first-
hand experience of an abandoned space.

> There may be some spaces—the endless room, the empty room, the dark ascend-
> ing or descending stair, tight spaces (between wall, up the chimney, etc.), the door
> that should not be opened, sounding walls of unknown thickness, or uncomfort-
> able proportion—that are archetypically horrifying. (Ellin, 1997, 151)

Looking up, I saw peeling paint falling from the ceiling onto the floor — what
remains catches the light from a nearby window, casting scattered shadows that
mimics a colony of bats hanging in a cave. I did not recall ever seeing a bat up close
in reality; however, I was able to establish an image based on television and the
Internet. Bat imagery, in pop-culture, generally falls into the horror genre, associated with the supernatural. There is "[s]omething about their erratic, indirect flight
and their squat, fanged faces send shivers through our collective consciousness"

(Wigley, 2014). Bachelard says, "A roof tells its raison d'être right away: it gives mankind shelter from the rain and sun he fears." However, passing under this roof threshold, I felt as though I was entering a dangerous space, leaving the safety of the bright outside, to descend into the darkness of the decaying prison.

Advancing through the rusted bars, which in a past life prevented criminals from escaping, a feeling of claustrophobia arose as I imagined the scenario of the bars being locked on my return. As stated above, Moore et al. speak of the anxiety that comes from "being in places from which escape might be difficult or in which help might not be available" (2002, 197). Conscious that this was my only way out, I moved deeper into the d-wing. At this point, I had cast myself as the protagonist of a horror film.

> Deep shadows and darkness are essential, because they dim the sharpness of vision, make depth and distance ambiguous, and invite unconscious peripheral vision and tactile fantasy. (Juhani Pallasmaa, 2005, 50)

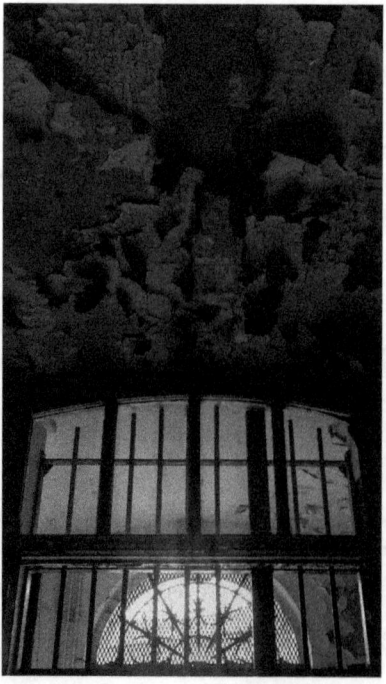

Figure 15: The entrance to D-wing, Crumlin Road Gaol.

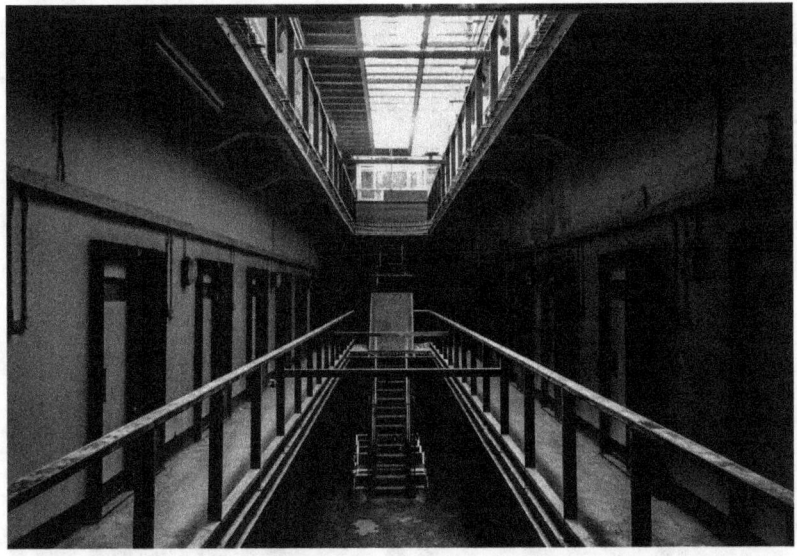

Figure 16: Atrium, Crumlin Road Gaol.

Probing deeper into the ever-darkening d-wing, I noticed a slight relief from the darkness. A peculiarly placed roof light flooded the atrium with much-desired light. As my eyes adjusted to the transition from dark to light, it became harder to see into the darkness of the cells. The long narrow design of the space was meant to allow guards to see the full-length wing to monitor the inmates; however, without any artificial lighting and hampered by the boarded-up windows, looking down the wing was difficult. It appeared to be swallowed up by absolute darkness, suggesting an endless corridor with countless cells.

Awkwardly squeezed through a narrow steel walkway between the prisoners' cells and the atrium, the feeling of claustrophobia arose again, which was amplified by my close proximity to cells when walking past each cell door, especially opened ones. Almost all of the cell doors were closed. Each door contained a narrow horizontal window that allowed views into the space. It was hard to see what occupied each cell, as the glass was full of scratches. I peered into each cell window, curious about what was inside, but not lingering long for fear of what was inside. The cells were generally typical, a 12 by 7-foot room with a window to the rear. The walls in almost all the cells showed evidence of decay. The discoloured cream paint had begun to peel, exposing crumbling walls and blockwork behind. Paint flakes, dust and assorted litter make up the floor finish, hiding the scuffed marks on the worn-out floor and engravings of names and gangs covered walls, indicating their previous occupiers.

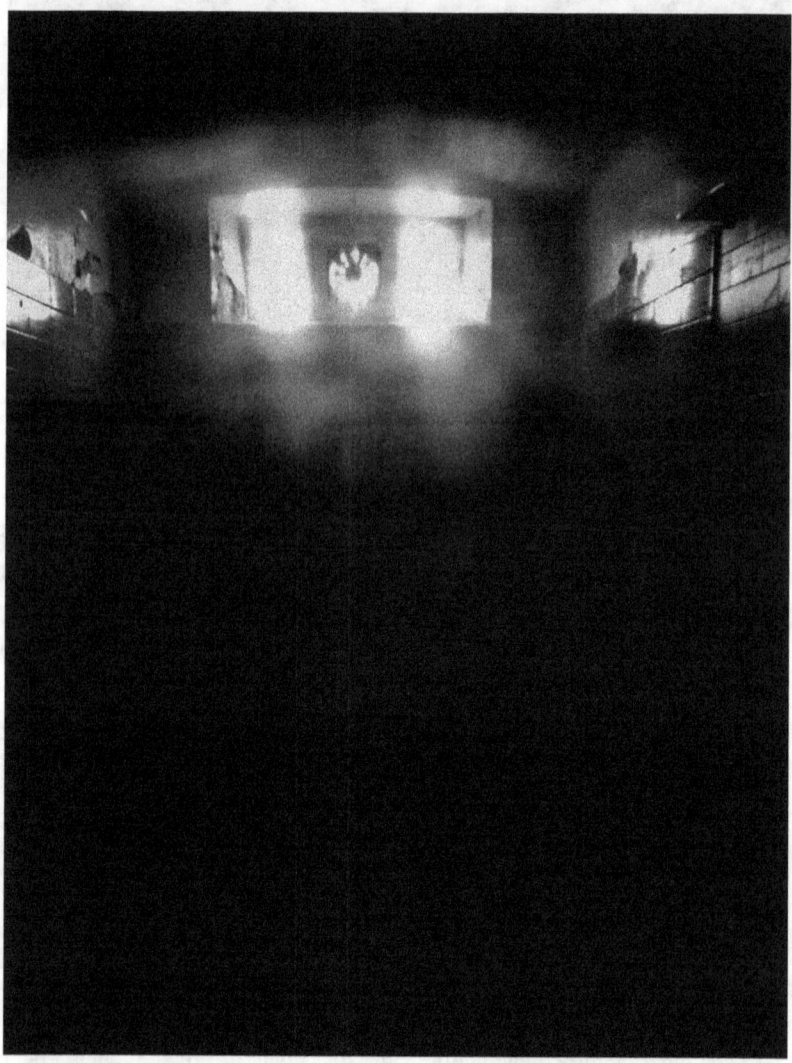

Figure 17: View into cell, Crumlin Road Gaol.

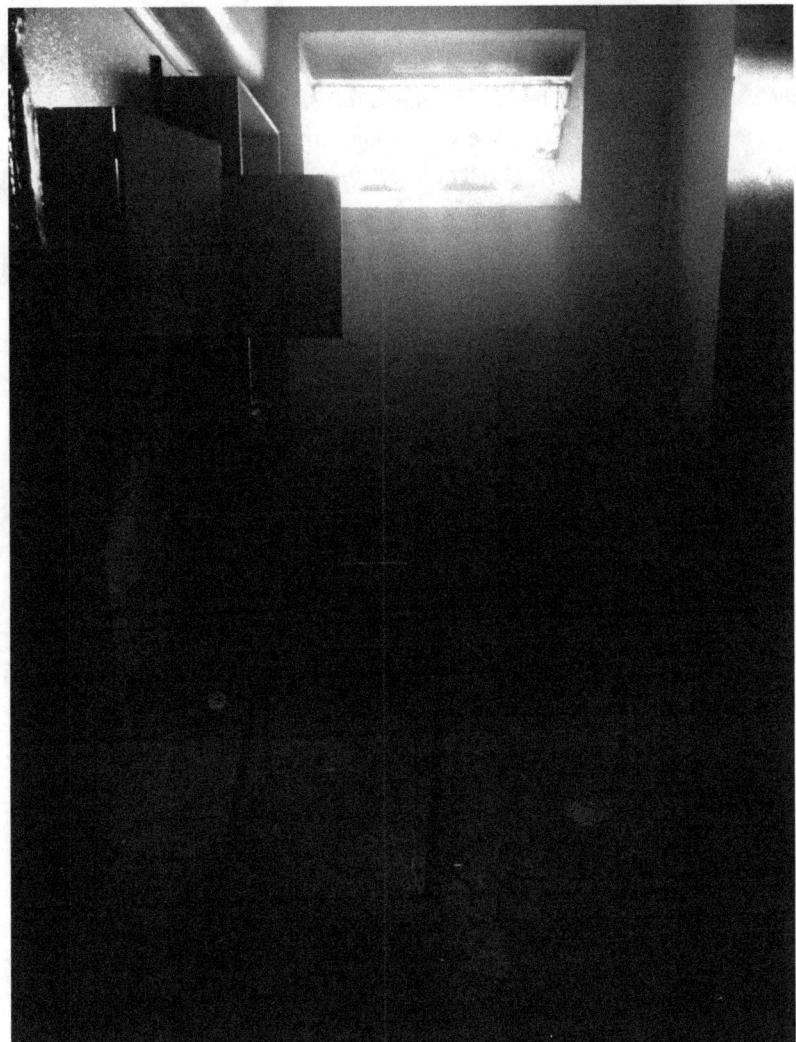

Figure 18: Empty chair, Crumlin Road Gaol.

Approaching a particular cell, I noted that the door was neither open nor fully closed. With a surprising struggle I forced it open to find yet another empty cell but containing a strangely placed chair in the centre of the room, facing the window with its back towards the door. The emptiness of the room amplified the chair's presence. The chair did not seem to be abandoned. It gave the impression that someone had placed it there intentionally. On closer inspection the cell seemed to be less abandoned than the previous cells I had explored. The paint on the walls was largely intact, the floor relatively clean, and there were even cupboards fixed to the wall. It was strange. It was the same dimensions as the other cells and it had the same door, which made me speculate about why it was different. Why was it in better condition than the rest? Has it been occupied since the prison was shut down?

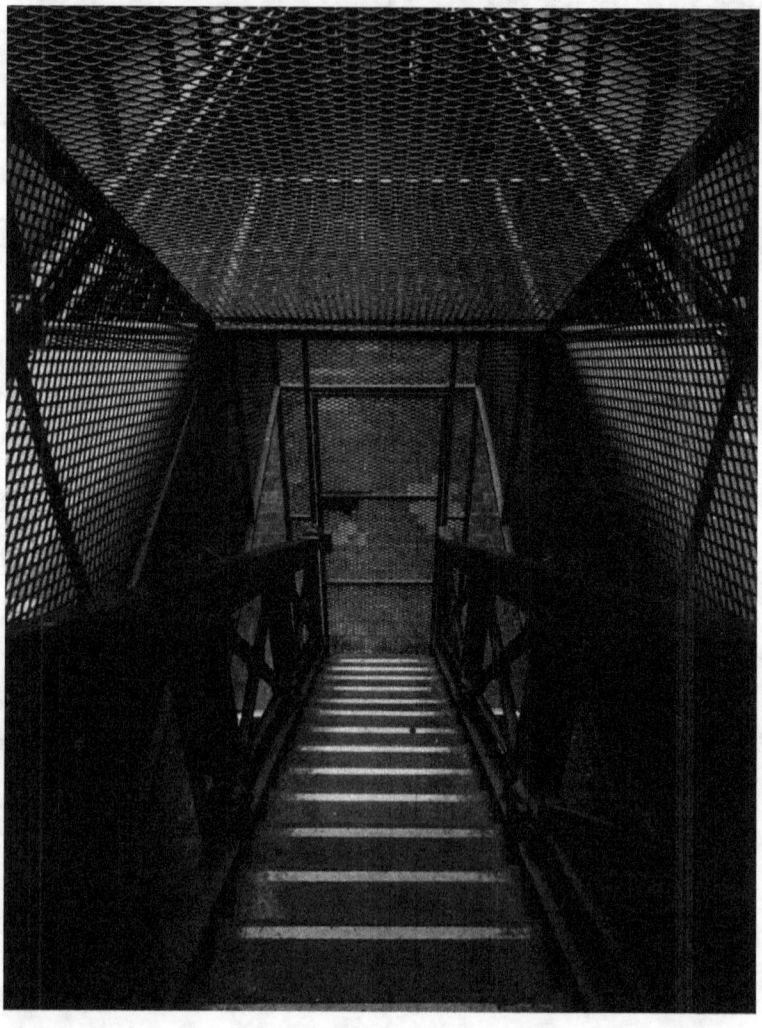

Figure 19: D-wing stair, Crumlin Road Gaol.

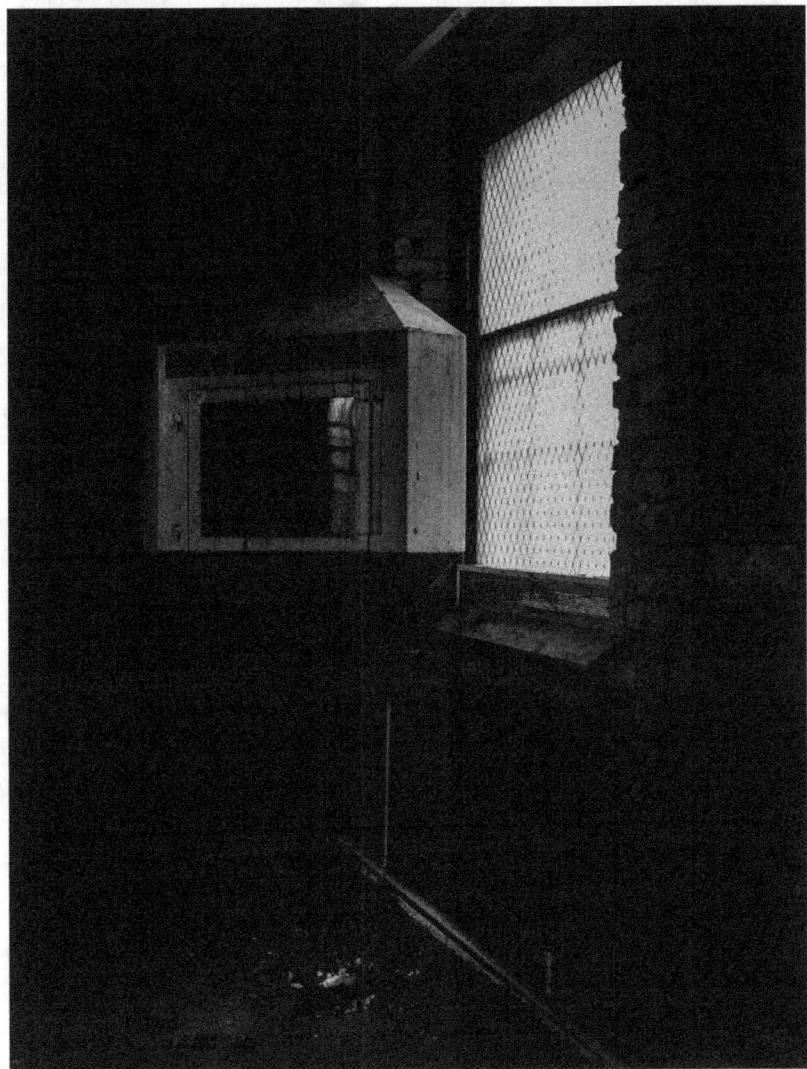

Figure 20: Common room, Crumlin Road Gaol.

The sound of footsteps populated the space. Amplified by the steel walkway, they echoed off the hard steel surfaces that surrounded me. The echo created multiple footsteps that mimicked multiple people walking. Was I alone? I began to count each footstep to ensure every sound and accompanying echo was accounted for, to ensure that they were just my own. The narrow steel walkway abruptly ended, delivering me to a caged metal stairway. I stepped down the awkwardly steep steps to the very bottom to find that the cage door at the bottom was locked. The space changed from a threshold space to a caged cell. Claustrophobia and anxiety arose at the bottom. Feeling trapped and vulnerable, I lost my high vantage point. Scaling back up the stairs, the overly steep riser made the ascent seem higher than it actually was. Avoiding the rusted steel railing, I had no leverage to assist my climb.

> It is no matter for surprise that the primitive fear of the dead is still so strong within us and always ready to come to the surface at any opportunity. (Freud, 1919, 14).

At the end of the corridor, a thick door laid open, presenting a well-lit room inside. Two large fogged glass windows on opposite sides of the room illuminated the space, offering restricted views out of the prison. A large steel cabinet that looked to have housed a television set sat in the corner. Under the cabinet, there was a dead pigeon — disturbingly, it looked like it had been killed rather than simply died. The body had been hacked, as ruffled feathers lay scattered across the floor. The imagery of death changed the atmosphere. The idea of predators inhabiting the prison evoked a sense of fear. In the other corner, there was a timber box with a discoloured circle patch and a lonely dart sticking from it. I imagined this might have been a fun space, or a treat for well-behaved criminals, where they could watch television, play darts and exchange stories, but now it felt like a punishment.

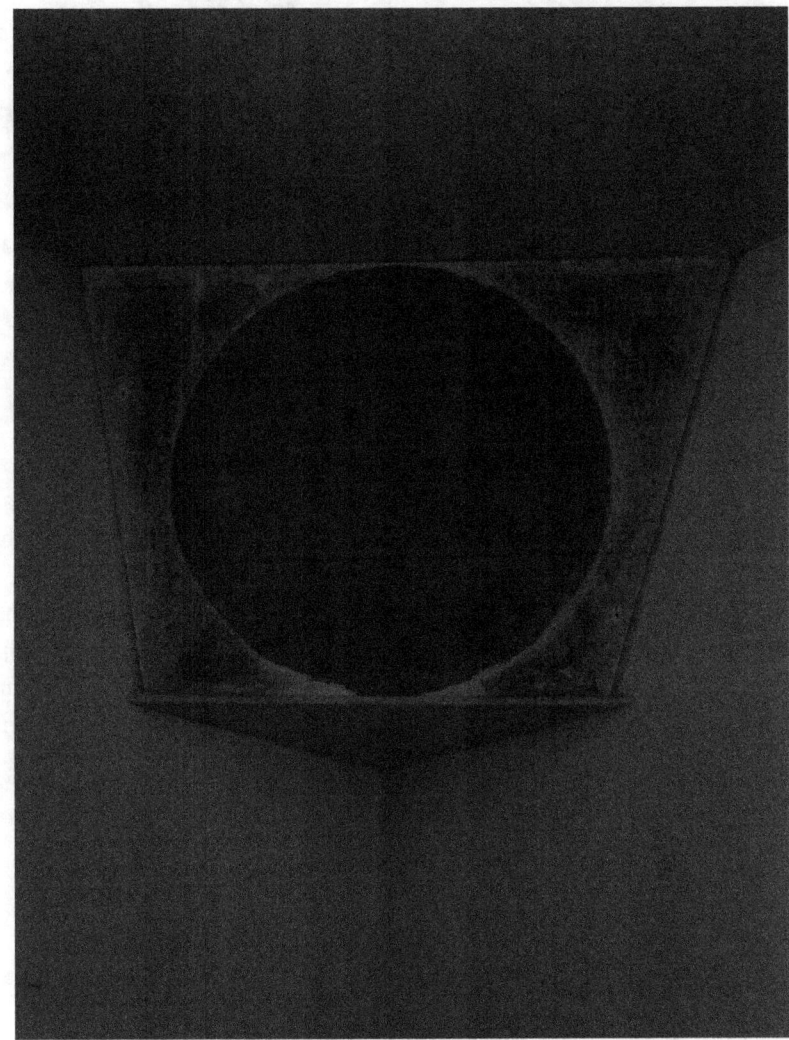

Figure 21: Dart board, Crumlin Road Gaol.

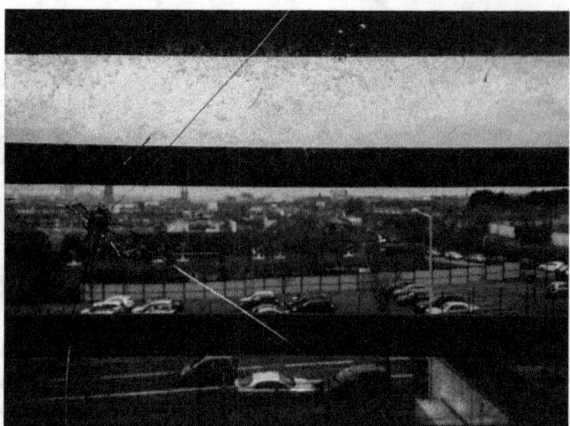

Figure 22: Watch tower window, Crumlin Road Gaol.

Most of the cell windows had been boarded up, sealing them in absolute darkness. At the end of the wing, I reached a ladder, the space above emitting light onto the ground below. Above was a circular room with long horizontal windows that towered over the prison, providing views to the grounds and the street to the west. Light was generous here, which was a pleasant relief from the darkness of the wings below. A sense of safety existed — I had gained human companions from the adjacent street. Strangely, the sense of claustrophobia was absent, which was uncanny, as it was the peak of my exploration, before the long journey back through the wing to get out of the prison.

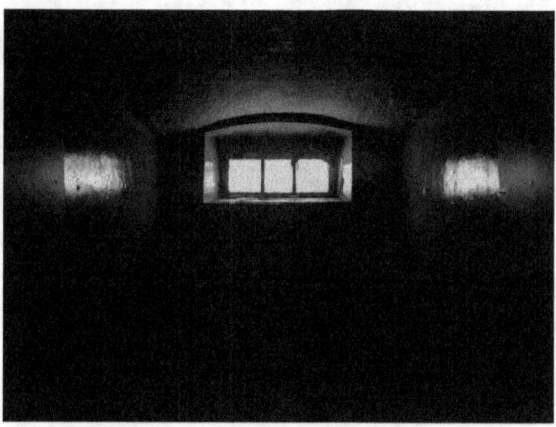

Figure 23: Cell window, Crumlin Road Gaol.

The prison proved to be a very sensual space. Vision, sound, touch, and smell all played vital roles and added to the atmosphere. The shadows and infrequent light competed with each other, which had an effect on my sight, requiring constant readjustments and leaving me visionless for short periods. Footsteps would echo, mimicking another person and the dust that covered everything resulted in my avoiding touching anything, leaving my hands in an awkward vulnerable position. A lack of social presence was obvious. Windows were scarce, permitting very little light and minimising views out. In a sense, it felt like another world wherein both Freud's and Aristotle's theories came to life, as a sense of unwelcoming presence that followed me throughout my exploration, prompting me to picture images reminiscent of a gruesome horror scene from a film. However, the prison proved to be ultimately abandoned and my imagined scenarios faded away.

> There is no terror in the bang, only in the anticipation of it.
> (Alfred Hitchcock, Gunman, 1955)

Conclusion

An abandoned space is one lacking in human routine. This lack of routine allows the physical space to evolve over time; however, it is not the physical change in the decay of materials that defines the space, but more a disconnection from the civil world. An abandoned space evokes a sense of anxiety and fear upon the occupier, allowing our animalistic id to populate the scene with fearful image ry reminiscent of horror films and frightful stories. The space becomes the set in which our animalistic fears and imagination portray the actors. The mind is essentially scaring itself.

The psychological change in atmosphere heightens our animalistic senses and exaggerates our fear response unnecessarily. With a constant news feed of hor-rific stories found on social media, people have become more aware of other people's horrors and tragedies. This increase in awareness is mistaken for an increase in instances, creating a society influenced by fear. In these spaces we often place ourselves as the protagonist in a horror scene. Harp's experiments conducted in the 1970s and early 2000s give evidence of this. The children who once had an unrestricted right to roam the town do not permit their own children to do the same, even though crime rates are at an all time low. With a quick insight into the mass media, a study of the BBC's most-read stories suggests that our tendency to indulge in the horrors inflicted on other people has created a society that constantly lives in fear.

Like in the media, fear is the core element used in horror films to entertain their audience. With horror the spatial nature of a film often acts as a main character that generates suspense and fear, as seen in *28 Days Later* and *The Shining*. Film sets, created to mimic space that is familiar to the audience, often include features that are uncanny (often as a nod from the director) to indicate that the film is not in fact real, and the events on screen would not transpire in the civil world. Abandoned spaces, similar to film, contain these uncanny features, indicating that the space is not real but another world where all social interaction has been removed. Film mimics our emotional response in these spaces, as it is the anticipation of fear that frightens us. Ultimately, we are aware that what we fear is not real, supporting Freud's theory that our animalistic nature comes alive within these spaces, due to a lack of social camaraderie.

Is an abandoned space ever truly abandoned? It is a paradox. The building is simultaneously both abandoned and not abandoned. The imagination will re-populate a space with fear in the event of abandonment, demonstrating that a space is never truly abandoned. In the novel *The Director's Cut* (2000), author Nicholas Royle described abandoned spaces as "dead" spaces that lived on in a kind of spatial after-life. Imprisoned in limbo, the building lives on through the imagination of the occupier.

REFERENCES

Bachelard, G. 1969. *The Poetics of Space*. Boston: Beacon Press.

Bresson, R. 1975. *Notes on the Cinematographer*. London: Quartet Books Limited.

Cavallari, D. 2002. *Gothic Vision: Three Centuries of Horror, Terror and Fear*. London: Continuum International Publishing.

Chibnall, S & Petley, J. 2002. *British Horror Cinema*. Oxon: Routledge.

Cocks, G. 2004. *The Wolf at the Door*. New York: Peter Lang Publishing Inc.

Doyle, A C. 1988. *A Study in Scarlet: A Sherlock Holmes Murder Mystery*. London: Ward, Lock and Co.

Ellin, N. 1997. *Architecture of Fear*. New York: Princeton Architectural Press

Falsetto, M. 2001. *Stanley Kubrick: A Narrative and Stylistic Analysis*. Westport: Praeger Publishers.

Freud, S. 1919. *The 'Uncanny'*. The Standard Edition of the Complete Psychological Works of Sigmund Freud, Volume XVII (1917-1919): An Infantile Neurosis and Other Works. London: The Hogarth Press and the Institute of Psycho-Analysis.

Goffman, E. 1963. *Behaviour in Public Places: Notes on the social Organisation of Gatherings*. New York: Free Press of Glencoe.

Hills, M. 2005. *The Pleasures of Horror*. London: Bloomsbury Publishing.

Jancovich, M. 2002. *Horror, The Film Reader*. London: Routledge.

Kagan, N. 1995. *The Cinema of Stanley Kubrick*. Oxford: Roundhouse Publishing Ltd.

Lewis, C.S. 1965. *Surprised by Joy*. New York: Harvest

McRoy, J. 2005. *Japanese Horror Cinema*. Hawai'i: University of Hawai'i Press.

Muthesius, H. 1979. The English House. New York: Rizzoli.

Pallasmaa, J. 2005. *Eyes of the Skin: Architecture and the Senses*. Sussex: Wiley-Academy.

Pallasmaa, J. 2007. *The Architecture of Image: Existential Space in Cinema*. Helsinki: Rakennustieto Publishing.

Rebello, S. 1990. *Alfred Hitchcock and the making of Psycho*. New York: Dembner Books.

Simon, H.A. 1971. 'Designing Organizations for an Information-Rich World', in Martin Greenberger, *Computers, communication and the Public Intrest*. Baltimore, MD: The Johns Hopkins Press.

Taylor, J. 1991. *Hospital and Asylum Architecture in England 1840 - 1914: Building for Health Care*. London: Mansell Publishing Limited.

Usai, P Cherchi. 1998. *Revue d'études Cinématographiques / Cinémas: Journal of Film Studies*, vol. 9, n° 1.

Website

Ciment, M. 1981. *Kubrick on The Shining: An interview with Michel Ciment*. [online] Available at: http://www.visual-memory.co.uk/amk/doc/interview.ts.html [Accessed 24 Dec. 2015].

Garland, A. 2002. *28 Days Later, shooting script*. Fox Searchlight Pictures. [online] Available at: http://www.scribd.com/doc/243169873/28-Days-Later [Accessed 14 Jan. 2016].

Gunman, P.L. 1955. *Wit and Wisdom of Alfred Hitchcock*. Alfred Hitchcock: The Master of Suspense. [online] Available at: http://hitchcock.tv/quotes/quotes.html [Accessed 14 Jan. 2016].

Hess, J P. 2013. The Psychology of Scary Movies. *Filmmaker IQ*. [online] Available at: http://filmmakeriq.com/lessons/the-psychology-of-scary-movies/ [Accessed 14 Apr. 2016].

Kelling, G.L & Wilson, J.Q. 1982. 'Broken Windows: The police and neighborhood safety'. *The Atlantic*. [online] Available at: http://www.theatlantic.com/magazine/archive/1982/03/broken-windows/304465/ [Accessed 4 Apr. 2016].

McGregor, C. 1972. Nice Boy from the Bronx? *The New York Times*. [online] Available at: http://partners.nytimes.com/library/film/013072kubrick-profile.html [Accessed 22 Nov. 2015].

Totten, C. 2011. Designing Better Levels Through Human Survival Instincts. *Gamasutra*. [online] Available at: http://www.gamasutra.com/view/feature/134779/designing_better_levels_through_.php [Accessed 17 Feb. 2016].

Wigley, S. 2014. 10 Great Bat Films. *BFI*. [online] Available at: http://www.bfi.org.uk/news-opinion/news-bfi/lists/10-great-bat-films [Accessed 8 Apr. 2016].

Podcast

Miller, Lulu, and Spiegel, Alix. 2015. *Fearless*. [Podcast] Invisibilia. 16th January. [online] Available at: http://www.npr.org/programs/invisibilia/377515477/fearless [Accessed 17 Feb. 2016].

Journals

Moore, K. et al. 2002. *Panic and Agoraphobia in a Virtual World:* Cyber Psychology & Behavior, 5 (3): 197-202. [Online] Available at: http://www.ncbi.nlm.nih.gov/pubmed/12123240 [Accessed 17 Apr. 2016].

Franklin, F.D. 1933. "Only Thing We Have To Fear Is Fear Itself": FDR's First Inaugural Address". *The Public Papers of Franklin D. Roosevelt, Volume Two: The Year of Crisis*. New York: Random House.

Film

28 Days Later. 2002. Film. Directed by - Danny Boyle [DVD] UK: Fox Searchlight Pictures.

The Exorcist. 1973. Film. Directed by - William Friedkin [DVD] USA: Warner Bros. Entertainment Inc.

The Omen. 1976. Film. Directed by - Richard Donner [DVD] USA: Twentieth Century Fox Film Corporation.

The Shining. 1980. Film. Directed by - Stanley Kubrick [DVD] USA: Warner Bros. Entertainment Inc.

List of Illustrations

SPACES OF THE

CITY

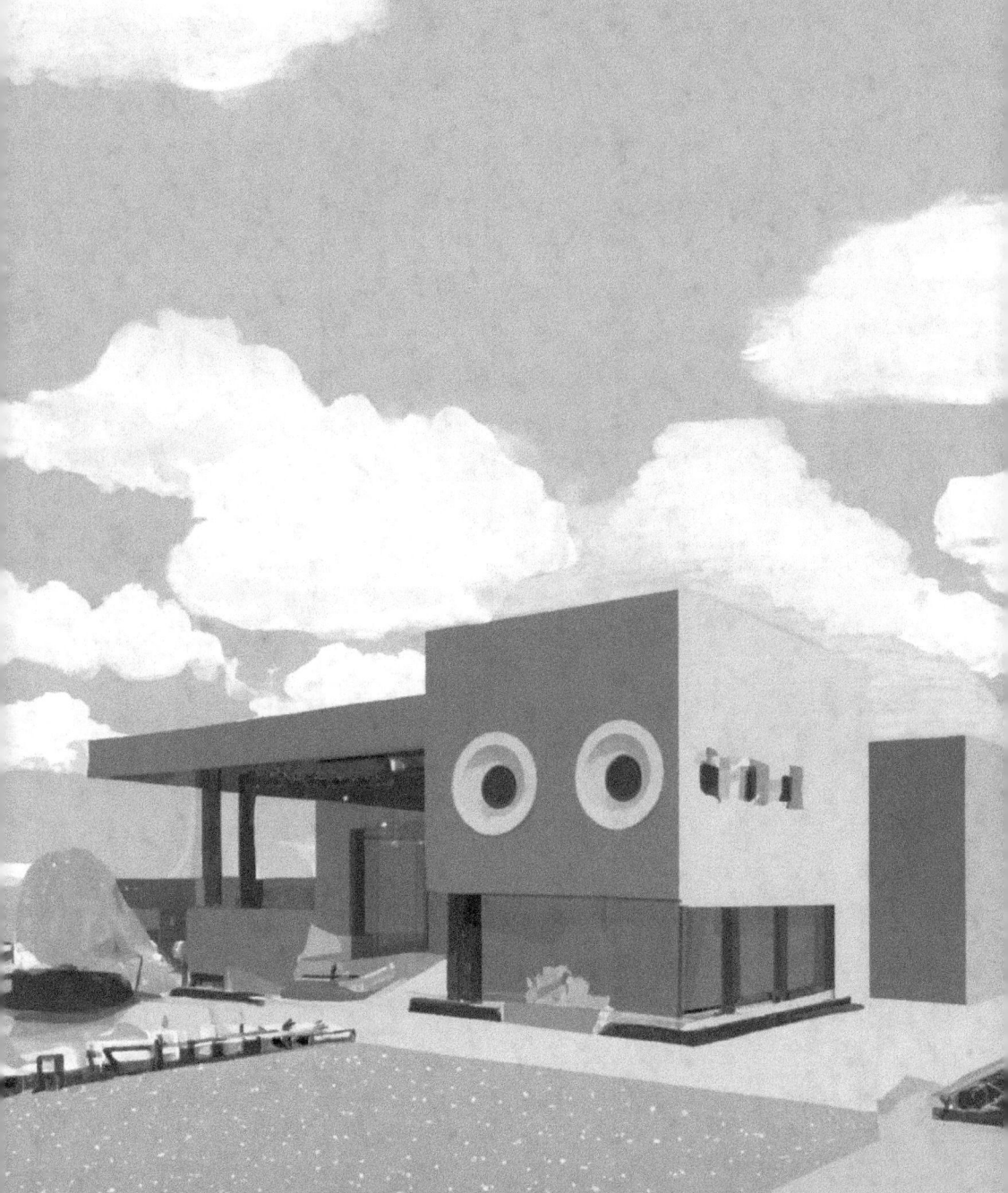

Symphony of the Modern City

Ciaran Magee

CIARAN MAGEE is a Part 2 architectural assistant with Reed Watts Architects. Originally from Kilclief, Northern Ireland, he completed both his undergraduate and masters' studies at Queen's University Belfast where he was a fellow of the British Pavilion at the 2017 Venice Art Biennale and represented Northern Ireland at the 2018 European Architecture Students Assembly (EASA) in Rijeka, Croatia. He has previously worked with Hall Black Douglas Architects in Belfast and on urban master planning schemes with Allies and Morrison in London.

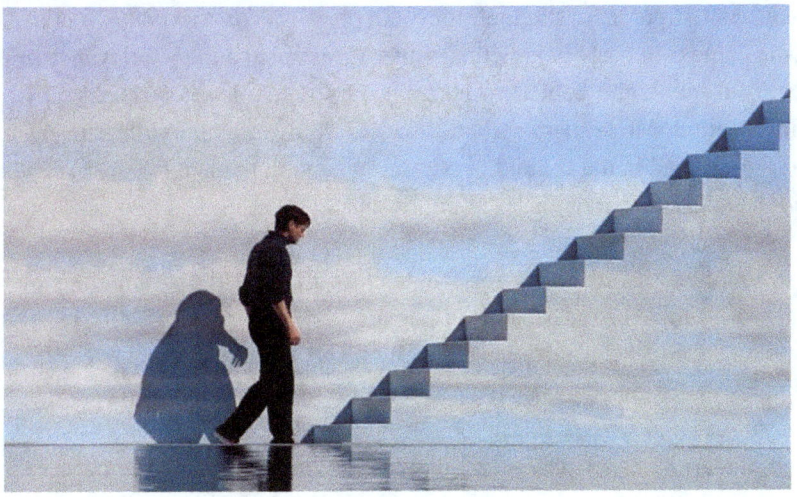

Figure 1: A panoptic exodus. *The Truman Show* (1:31:47).

In her seminal work, *The Death and Life of Great American Cities*, Jane Jacobs describes the modern metropolis as an 'organised complexity' (1961, 143), terminology readily applicable to cinema. Through a bombardment of audio-visual media, we observe the illusion of motion and interpret narrative through *mise-en-scène* and montage. In cinema, as in the city, we witness in fragments that, which we subconsciously consolidate into a perceived whole (Pallasmaa 2007, 31). From the inception of cinematic representation, film and urbanism have informed each other symbiotically. The urban landscape offers a kaleidoscope of visual and narrative opportunities, whereby ideas and philosophies 'form an apercu of urban life and moderni- ty' (Weihsmann 2011, 27). Bridging the twentieth and twenty-first centuries, and emerging concurrently with the idea of modernity, we look to cinematic media for an analysis of urban life and the repercussions of modernity on the urban fabric.

This text interrogates cinema's capability of capturing and representing an urban zeitgeist. Analysis focuses on films that either overtly or subtextually reference the city, and comment on the state of urbanism and modernity. The three chosen films are *Berlin: Symphony of a Great City* (1927), *Mon Oncle* (1967), and *The Truman Show* (1998); each of which is used to analyse a specific aspect of modernity through literature reviews of key texts and move- ments contemporaneous to their time and place. *Berlin Symphony* is analysed in the context of early twentieth century Modernism and the relevance of the literary trope of the flâneur to cinema; *Mon Oncle* is interpreted as part of mid-twentieth Modernism and the situationist movement; while *The Truman Show* is studied in the context of New Urbanism in the late twentieth century, and the evolving panopticism of public space.

The common thread running through these films is the chronicling of the real-world impact Modernism can have on urban life through a form of cin- ematic synecdoche. By looking at fragments, cinema that engages the city attempts to achieve the urbanist goals of 'observing and, in some sense, 'ex- plaining' the 'nature' of it (Bullock 2011, 90). The main contextualisation of each modernist era expands on the question of the role of 'the observer' in understanding the city from an urbanist perspective. This text builds upon a foundation of research into a broad range of areas, thematically establishes links between them, and uses a contemporary reading of the cinematic city to investigate how 'the imagined city of film' can contribute to the comprehen- sion of the urban landscape.

First Movement

Early 20th Century Modernism, the Modern Flâneur, and Walter

Ruttmann's Berlin: Symphony Of A Great City *(1927)*

The turn of the twentieth century marked the beginning of a period of profound societal metamorphosis. The 'horrors' of the slum cities of the nineteenth century had reached a critical mass, erupting into a time of reactionary development and social change (Hall 2014, 50). In 1885, Alan Foreman described the city in the *American Magazine* as a 'seething mass of humanity. So ignorant, so vicious, so depraved that they hardly seemed human' (Ford 1936, 174). This, at the time prevailing, ideology towards the urban populace became the justification for how cities were to be structured and restructured, guiding approaches towards housing and public space. With advances in technology and media, the modern city became a 'rapid crowding of changing images' normalising 'discontinuity in the grasp of a single glance' (Simmel, 1903, 94). This new urban modernity was characterised by a uniform genius loci of the city; one which traversed culture globally, and created a commonality between varying metropolitan contexts.

This 'climate of overstimulation, distraction, and sensation' (Charney and Schwartz 1995, 278) would act as a catalyst for a reaction that would influence every aspect of contemporary life. Progress was the focus of the era, often in neglect of the social for the material. Henry George wrote in *Progress and Poverty*, a treatise which helped initiate the Progressive Era in the United States as well as a global movement for social reform; 'Man is the only animal whose desires increase as they are fed, the only animal that is never satisfied' (1886, 94). This understanding of the human condition would be prophetic for what modernity would cultivate, and the social implication it would have on class division. Modernism became synonymous with material progress, a developmental process which George describes as not only a failure to relieve poverty, but one which 'actually produces it' (1886, 6).

Advances in transportation technology continued to drive physical and social change in the urban sphere, as such, the city required an evolution to meet the needs of a new street devolved to the mechanical. In *Towards a New Archi-*

tecture, Le Corbusier writes that 'Modern life demands, and is waiting for, a new kind of plan, both for the house and the city' (1931, 3). However, Le Corbusier's tabula rasa philosophy would later be criticised for embracing 'every feature of the contemporary city except its essential social and civic character' (Mumford, 1968, 119), an issue which infected the early urbanist ideas of the twentieth century.

The transitional modern era would also initiate a 'change in the structure of experience' (Benjamin, 1969, 156). With inventions in the field of representation, including both the photographic and cinematic camera, the modern epoch embraced the instantaneous, the momentary, and the fragmentary. The nature of these images is, however, that they are always reflective. As soon as the image is captured, it becomes a moment in and of the past. Henri Bergson writes in his essay, *Matter and Memory*, that we 'perceive only the past, the pure present being the invisible progress of the past gnawing into the future' (1988, 150). A collection of photographs, i.e., cinema, can only be such a fragmented, momentary representation of the past.

In its typical permutations, the literary architype of the flâneur would take the form of an urban wanderer, displaying a voyeuristic tendency embodying the 'covetous and erotic… gaze of modernity' (Pollock 1988, 67). Although continuing to exist as a literary device, and later appearing in the developing language of film, the flâneur would re-emerge as an object of scholarship in the 1970s due to the translation of Walter Benjamin's writings on the poetry of Charles Baudelaire into English (Coates 2017, 28). In *Charles Baudelaire: A Lyric Poet in the Era of High Capitalism* (1973), Benjamin notes the origins of the flâneur in eighteenth century French physiologies, short textual studies of archetyp al characters. It is here where Benjamin recognises the act of flânerie as 'botanizing on the asphalt' (1973, 36), introducing an analytical and scientific aspect to the literary trope, one which has been since adopted by scholars across the humanities and social sciences (Coates 2017, 28). Baudelaire's flâneur, according to Benjamin, was a tool for representing, analysing, and participating in the city.

The flâneur has since evolved into a model for understanding the relationship between the 'individual, modernity and the city,' acting as a figure used in 'mobile urban ethnographies' (Coates 2017, 28), quietly observing and establishing an understanding of an area's genius loci, or spirit of place. Benjamin writes of the flaneur's 'quick grasp' (1973, 41), language that echoes in the quick grasp of the film camera, whereby the cinematographer too could develop reactions 'in keeping with the pace of a big city' (1973, 41). The ephemerality of representation links the nature of the observer and the camera, whereby the camera is a tool for reframing how we view the city.

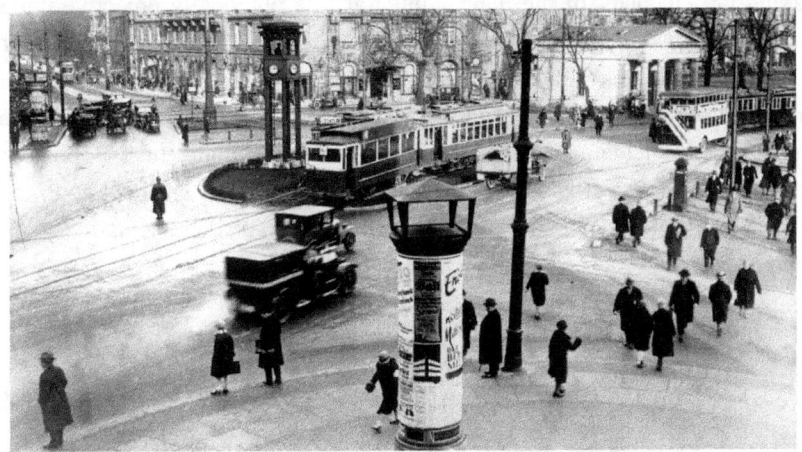

Figure 2: The emergence of modern urbanism.
Berlin: Symphony of a Great City (0:05:32).

Released in 1927, *Berlin: Symphony of a Great City* is an archetypical film of the city symphony genre. Alongside other notable works such as *Manhatta* (1921), *Études sur Paris* (1928), and *Man with a Movie Camera* (1929), the film pioneered avant-garde cinematic techniques to record and present city life on screen. By eschewing plot and focusing on an almost stream-of-conscious montage style, the film paints a broad picture of early twentieth century urbanity. Although there is no traditional narrative structure, *Berlin* presents us with a series of 'intertwining fragmented images of the urban landscape' depicting a city on the cusp of modernity (Penz and Lu, 2011, 10). It is through an idea of cinematic memory that we see films such as *Berlin Symphony* and other city symphonies beyond the scope of isolated works, but as time capsules preserving an urban zeitgeist. City symphonies are intrinsically linked with the passive observations of the Baudelairean flâneur, both being 'emblematic archetypes of urban, modern experience' (Shaya 2004, 10).

Berlin Symphony opens with a scene traditionally associated with the literary flâneur, the arrival to a city. Here, the approach of a series of trains establishes *Berlin Symphony*'s position in its representation of a city, 'emphasising the locale' as a 'unified space to be visited' (Bernstein 1984, 7). The use of locomotives in a film of this era specifically represents the industrial modern city, one where mass urban transportation unifies the landscape. This journey to the city establishes a theme of the observation of participation with the modern city, making the character of the flâneur integral to a potentially objective understanding. In *Berlin: Symphony of a Great City*, it is the inquisitive gaze of the camera that undertakes the role of the flâneur-protagonist, observing and maturing as it witnesses the dawn of the modern city. By establishing the camera as an arriving outsider, detached from participation, the character can 'botanise' with a sense of objectivity, gradually encroaching on the physical and metaphorical heart of the city, represented through the recurring cinematic motif of the spiral.

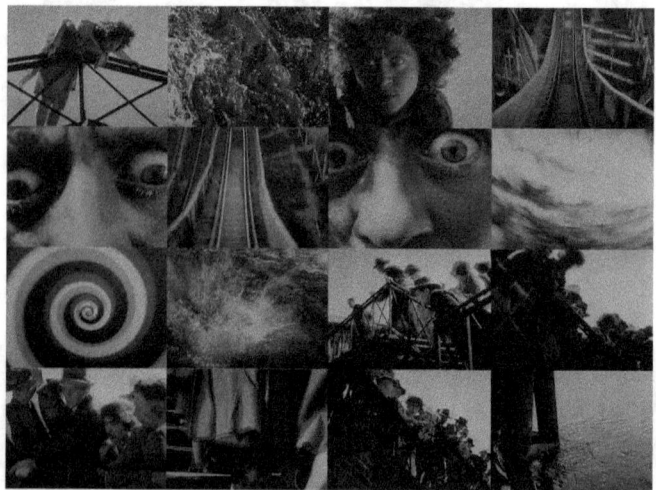

Figure 3: The suicide scene.
Berlin: Symphony of a Great City (0:46:02-0:46:31).

One particularly interesting aspect of *Berlin Symphony* is its temporary mid-film departure from its documentary format. In a brief scene, we see a woman die by suicide by jumping into a river, while a crowd of gesturing but ultimately passive onlookers watch (Figure3). The suicide is unusual also in that it departs from Ruttmann's largely celebratory portrayal of a city, which has embraced industrial modern life. In *Berlin Symphony*, the tight symphonic timing and rhythm presents a Taylorist production line, where the city's occupants are brought into the city, carry out their work, consume, participate in social and leisure activities, and leave on the train again. In the suicide scene, fast paced visual metaphors allude to the accelerating frantic pace of the industrial city, edited into the scene to reinforce the theme. As the word *krise*, in English 'crisis', jumps out of a newspaper, the woman leaps into the water and the film immediately falls back into its documentary format, now emphasised due to the 'momentarily un-documentary scene just enacted' (Hunter 2013, 203). We are left without answers as to why this woman chose to kill herself, as the explanation is 'hidden in a past which the documentary camera cannot show and therefore we cannot learn (Hunter 2013, 204).

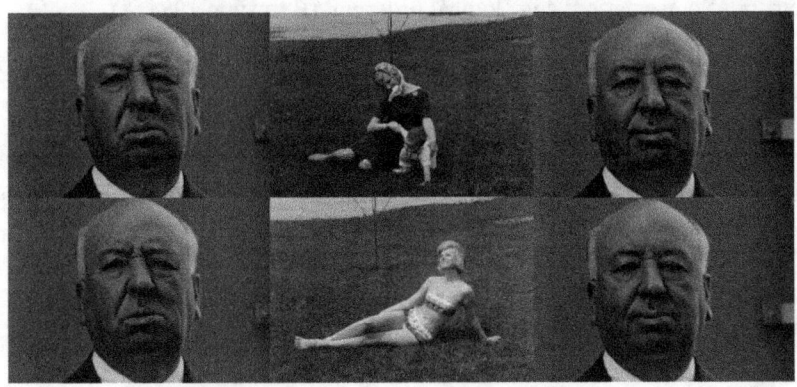

Figure 4: Hitchcock's demonstration of 'Pure Cinematics.'
Telescope: A Talk with Hitchcock (0.18.17).

Non-narrative films of the city symphony form can be considered demonstrations of the Kuleshov effect, a montage method whereby a sequence of shots derives a meaning, which would potentially not be considered from the shots in isolation. Sir Alfred Hitchcock called this 'Pure Cinematics' in his 1968 interview in *Telescope: A Talk with Hitchcock*, describing the intercutting of two shots of a man (Hitchcock) observing something off-screen and smiling. This sequence was interspliced with a shot of a baby playing, and then in a second form, a woman wearing a bikini. In the first sequence, we see a 'benign gentleman who loves babies,' transforming into a 'dirty old man' in the second instance (Figure4). The interplay of shots as described here calls into question the authenticity of something being considered non-narrative. Although perhaps lacking in typical ideas of plot. Any montage of cinematic material can subconsciously establish thematic connections. Although *Berlin Symphony* lacks such a formal plot, it still presents an interpretation of a 'day in the life of a great city' as William Empson titled his 1928 review. Utilising principles which Christian Metz termed 'bracket syntagma' (1974, 124), whereby the Kuleshov effect is perceived not only to infer meaning from a sequence, but also to establish individual shots as related, the assemblage of visuals produces an overall sense of urban life. This editing technique is used to present the 'messy inclusivity and nervous simultaneity' of the early twentieth century city's apparently 'hidden organisation' (Hunter 2013, 189). Throughout the film, this bracket syntagma alludes to the everyday occurrence of its depictions in the city, emphasised by their 'brief presentation' and 'logical ordering' (Bernstein 1984, 8).

Although utilising the visual documentation of *Berlin Symphony* to present the spirit of the early modern city, it is in the film's editing where the conceptual themes become apparent, and Walter Ruttmann becomes the 'real auteur of the film' (Hunter 2013, 195). Ruttmann is presenting his version of Berlin as a living breathing place, using short shot length and a long and medium shot scale to emphasise the mechanisation of a high tempo urban world.

Second Movement

Mid-20th Century Modernism, the Psychogeographic City,

and Jacques Tati's Mon Oncle

Provocatively opening her repudiation of modernist urban planning, Jane Jacobs describes her book, *The Death and Life of Great American Cities*, as an attack on her contemporary architectural theorists' approach to city planning and rebuilding (1961, 3). Denouncing the Garden City movement (as applied to existing urban contexts), as well as theories pioneered by architects such as Le Corbusier, she mourns cities as 'sacrificial victims' to an orthodox and over-simplified way of thinking, reduced to the geometric (1961, 25). Her critique echoes Bachelard, where he writes 'we are far removed from any reference to simple geometrical forms... inhabited space transcends geometrical space' (1969, 47).

Acknowledging the intentions of thinkers such as Lewis Mumford, Clarence Stein, Henry Wright, and Catherine Bauer amongst others – collectively referred to as 'Decentrists' – one of Jacobs' lamentations was that city authorities looking to 'strengthen their great cities' had chosen to adopt ideas specifically designed to undercut their economies (1961, 20). In attempting to apply overly simplified principles to such a complex entity, the city suffers from a restriction on its ability to organically thrive as a working and living environment.

Jacobs' view on the requirement of historic buildings in a city is in direct opposition to Le Corbusier's unbuilt modernist proposals for Ville Radieuse and his Plan Voisin. While Plan Voisin called for the razing of Paris' third and fourth arrondissements, Jacobs considered historical urban artefacts such a necessity that it would be 'impossible for vigorous streets and districts to grow without them' (1961, 187). Le Corbusier's tabula rasa approach to the city is symptomatic of a philosophy Walter Benjamin referred to as 'the destructive character', the mindset of someone who 'knows only one watchword: make room. And only one activity: clearing away' (Jennings 1999, 541). Le Corbusier saw the modern city as an entity devoid of history, while Jacobs envisions an integration between memory and progress.

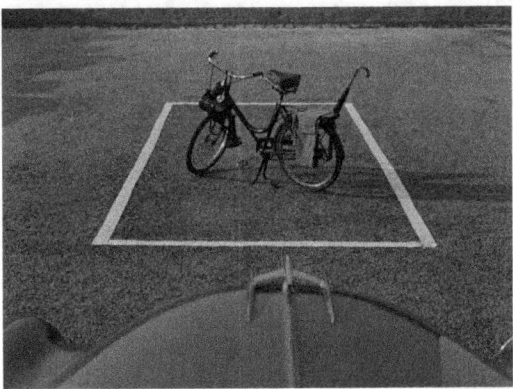

Figure 5: In defiance of a modern world. *Mon Oncle* (1:22:49).

In *The Urban Prospect*, Decentrist Lewis Mumford criticises the mark left on
our cities due to 'bureaucratic ideals of standardisation, regimentation, and
centralised control' (1968, 128). He bemoans the transformation of the city
as a habitable space into a mechanised world he proclaimed 'anti-city' (1968,
131), a super-metropolis devoid of urban markers and inhospitable to a varied
combination of uses. This capitalist landscape would provide incubation for
reactionary movements opposed to the intrusion of, and the alienation caused
by, mass media and the commodification of cities.

The Situationist International (SI) was an art-political movement for social revolution in the city active between 1957 to 1972. Fundamentally, it was a methodology for understanding the city as host to 'situations,' categorised by the SI
as moments of 'life concretely and deliberately constructed by the collective
organization of a unitary ambiance and a game of events' (1958), while 'situationists' were those members of the organisation, or more broadly anyone who
actively engaged with the construction of 'situations' (Debord 1958). Emerging
with the first release of *Situationiste Internationale* (1958), the formal organisation would dissolve in 1972, due to a programme described as 'so ambitious
and uncompromising that it condemned itself to failure' (Sadler 1999, 106).

Integral to the situationist understanding of the city was the act of 'dérive', as
instructed by Guy Debord in his first contribution to *Situationniste Internationale* (1958). Citing social geographer Chombart de Lauwe who, after mapping
a Parisian student's journeys over a year in his study *Paris et l'Agglomération
Parisienne* (1952), found that most of her traversed city formed a triangle between her home, her school, and her piano lessons. Debord interpreted this as
being indicative of 'the narrowness of the real Paris in which the individual
lives' (Debord, 1958). His solution, dérive, was a practice of engaging with
geographical factors and ambiance of the city and was developed as an antithesis to this perceived 'narrowness'. Evolving from, and yet firmly opposed to,
the passive observations of the flâneur, dérive was to involve exploration utilising a methodology of detaching oneself from relations and activities, using
personal geographic markers and the attractions of situations to lead the way.
Debord proposed that cities contained 'psychogeographical contours, with
constant currents, fixed points and vortexes that strongly discourage entry into
or exit from certain zones' (1958); and that dérive was an analytical method

of mapping them to uncover the 'natural connections between places' (Mc-Donough 2010, 7).

The primary outcome of Debord's experiments with dérive was a series of psychogeographic maps, illustrating the connected ambiances of the urban fabric. Represented by large arrows connecting collages of historic maps (utilising the situationist technique of détournement), Debord describes such arrows as 'slopes that naturally link the different unities of ambiance' (Sadler 1999, 88). These maps were visual representations of 'class struggle, the quest for equilibrium, and the sovereign decision of the individual' (Ross 1988, 101); a rejection of the perceived modern notion of the individual's role in the urban landscape, and the antithesis of the mediated landscape Debord called 'the spectacle', i.e., 'the concrete inversion of life, and as such, the autonomous movement of non-life' (1967, 5).

As a film director, French auteur Jacques Tati commented on Modernism so predominantly that, to an extent, it became a recurring character in his work. In films such as *Mon Oncle* (1958), his magnum opus *Playtime* (1967), and *Traffic* (1971), modernity is the driving force behind the follies of his characters. Tati described the world as 'becoming one vast clinic' consisting of a 'lost' populace (Harding, 1984, 24), and his films reflected that perception.

Tati's oeuvre cements his personal attitude towards modernity, with *Playtime* especially acting as a 'defence of the individual in the face of a mechanical world' (Penz 1994, 39). This is achieved through a combination of visual gags, slapstick humour, and absurdist situations. In Tati's version of the modern city, daily routines become tasks of Sisyphean proportions; colour is drained from the world in favour of a cold and sterile cityscape, modern interiors become a labyrinth of identical office spaces, and a trade exhibition is indistinguishable from domestic space. Although his films share many themes and concepts regarding modernity, this text will focus primarily on *Mon Oncle* (1958), Tati's comedic statement on the dichotomy between traditional Parisian incremental urbanity, and the modernist planned Paris streetscape.

The first of Tati's films to be released in colour, *Mon Oncle* consists of a loosely connected sequence of scenes with minimal plot. The film is a satire of what Tati considered to be the absurdness in everyday modern life. The modernist

brother-in-law of *Mon Oncle*, M. Arpel, seemingly derives his identity from his
car, his job in a plastics factory, and his automated house. By focusing on these
three 'prime icons of fifties Modernism', and revolving his comedies around
them, Tati establishes his stance towards the human impact of technology. One
of the key ways in which Tati structures his films is the 'parallel anthropomor-
phosis of objects and the mechanisation of individuals' (O'Donoghue 2013,
16), a device in opposition to Le Corbusier's 'machines for living'. Rather than
approach modernity with fascination towards the new, Tati recognises an object's ability to be flawed.

A common thread through Tati's four key films on modernity is the character
of Monsieur Hulot. Featured in *Le Vacances de Monsieur Hulot* (1953), *Mon
Oncle* (1958), *Playtime* (1967), and *Trafic* (1971), and portrayed by Tati himself, Hulot acts as an avatar for Tati to express his frustrations with the absurdity
of the modern world. In *Mon Oncle* we are shown the confrontation between
Hulot's traditional, incrementalistic, ad-hoc, Parisian locale, and that of the
modernist development in which M. and Mme. Arpel reside - two vastly psychogeographic ambiances, of which we are shown the threshold (Figure 6). In
this scene depicting Monsieur Hulot traversing the boundary between old and
new, he replaces a fallen brick on the traditional masonry wall. Symbolic of the
character's link to an antiquated way of life, Hulot is futilely holding on. One
could imagine this is where Debord would place his arrow on a psychographic
map.

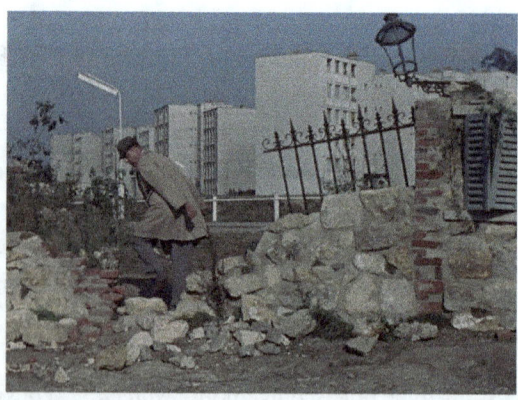

Figure 6: A marker of ambient boundary. *Mon Oncle* (0:14:34).

The unconcerned strolling of Tati's Hulot evokes both the Baudelairean flâneur and the Situationist act of dérive. As with a typical flâneur, Hulot operates outside of the capitalist system, existing with no apparent 'economic need to make a living' (O'Donoghue 2015, 12), fumbling his way through modern life while his nephew Gérard takes every opportunity to subvert it. Hulot's obvious disconnect with modern life is rooted in his residence in the historic part of town, depicted with richly occupied public spaces, 'colours of community life', and 'warm sounds' (Alsayyad 2006, 102). Hulot's dismissal from the factory cements his incompatibility with modern life, as the remnants of the old Paris are demolished at the conclusion of the film, Monsieur Hulot finds himself in exile.

Despite ostensibly being the main character of the film, the title *Mon Oncle* reframes the story as one from the perspective of Hulot's nine-year-old nephew, Gérard Arpel. Both are comparable in their dissatisfaction with their environs and are symbolically depicted as kindred spirits. It is here we understand Tati as portraying the childlike qualities of Monsieur Hulot and its link with the flâneur's child-like inquisitiveness. As an ethnographical tool, Tati utilised Hulot's interpretation of the city to present his critique of Modernist urban design.

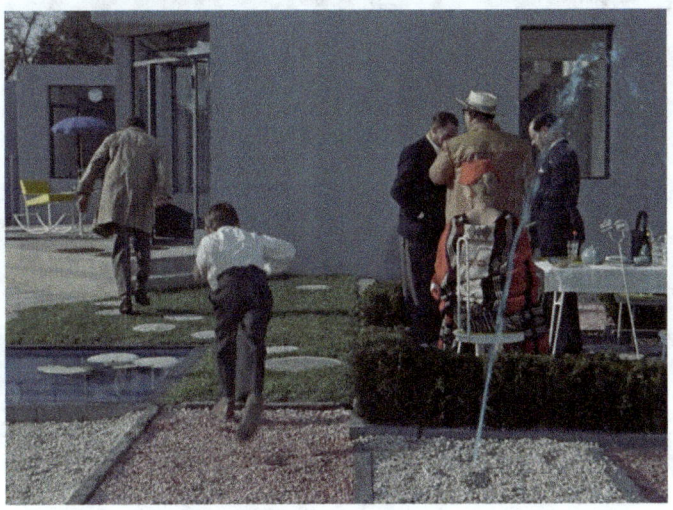

Figure 7: Kindred spirits. *Mon Oncle* (1:09:58).

Comparable to the observational nature of the flâneur, Tati introduces an aspect of voyeurism and paranoia into the thematic construct of *Mon Oncle*. Noting the recurring image of the circular window, we first see this appear during Monsieur Hulot's job interview. While waiting for the interviewer to appear, Hulot accidentally transfers paint from his shoe onto the office desk. The woman misunderstands the situation as Hulot attempts to view into the next room while she changes and expels him from the office. He is later chastised by his sister and brother-in-law for this, who ironically spy on their next-door neighbour's garden through similarly styled windows, evoking in the image of watching eyes. This later culminates in the visual gag of Hulot hiding from the gaze of the home (Figure 9).

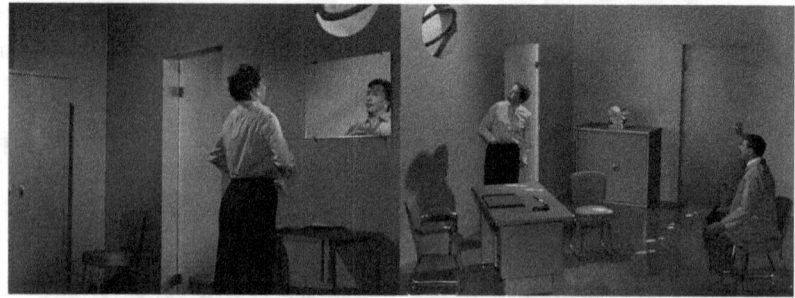

Figure 8: Monsieur Hulot's interview. *Mon Oncle* (0:28:40) (0:28:29).

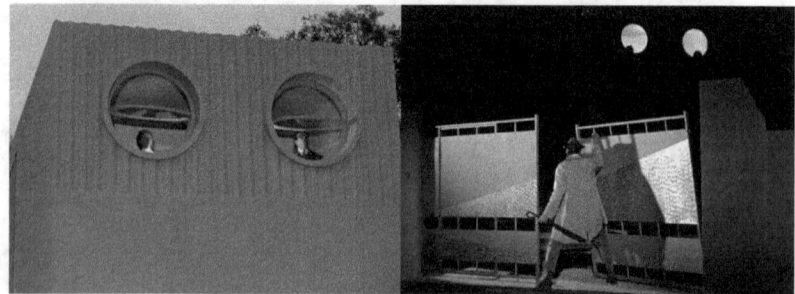

Figure 9: The anthropomorphic house. *Mon Oncle* (0.48.18) (1:19:13).

Tati's later films revolve around themes of the imposition upon the 'free movement of the individual' through 'architecture, urban planning, street furniture, signage, advertising, and the mass media' (O'Donoghue 2015, 12), which Guy Debord would consider as 'Spectacle'. Although not directly influenced by the Situationists, as the movement was still in its infancy at the release of *Mon Oncle*, it is possible to draw the conclusion that both the Situationist Internationale and Jacques Tati were exploring resonating concepts, derived from their shared perception of modernity. In *Playtime*, a film more likely to have been influenced by the Situationists due to its release after the May 1968 riots, Monsieur Hulot inhabits a Paris which has seemingly succumbed to a destructive modern urbanism. Only hints of the historic Paris can be seen in the character of the florist, and in a fleeting scene in which the character of Barbara catches a glimpse of the Eiffel Tower in the reflection of a modern glass door. The denouement of *Playtime* sees Tati's characters leaving the city, echoing the ending of *Berlin: Symphony of a Great City*, although presented with a more sombre tone.

THIRD MOVEMENT

Late 20th Century Modernism, the Public Realm Panopticon, and Peter Weir's The Truman Show

New Urbanism as a form of urban design first came to prominence in the late twentieth century, although it is one which has been 'evolving in America for over a century' (Talen 2005, 1). A reaction to modernist urban planning, New Urbanism is rooted in an American adoption of Sir Ebenezer Howard's *Garden City principles as outlined in his text To-morrow: A Peaceful Path to Real Reform* (1898), later released as *Garden Cities of To-morrow*. As a reactionary movement, New Urbanists emerged as architects, planners, and social theorists in opposition to the urban sprawl of the modern city, which effectively destroyed the concept of a 'walkable city.' The Congress for New Urbanism (CNU) outlines their aims in their charter for a new urban thinking:

> We stand for the restoration of existing urban centres and towns within coherent metropolitan regions, the reconfiguration of sprawling suburbs into communi-

ties of real neighbourhoods and diverse districts, the conservation of natural environments, and the preservation of our built legacy (1898-1993).

Focusing on the consolidation of function around urban centres, the key components of the movement can be distilled down to 'the neighbourhood, the district, and the corridor'. This has been outlined by architects, and two co-founders of the CNU, Andres Duany and Elizabeth Plater-Zyberk in their contribution to Peter Katz' volume *The New Urbanism: Toward an architecture of community* (1994):

> A single neighbourhood standing free in the landscape is a village. Cities and towns are made up of multiple neighbourhoods and districts, organised by corridors of transportation or open space. Neighbourhoods, districts, and corridors are urban elements. By contrast, suburbia, which is the result of zoning laws that separate uses, is comprised of pods, highways and interstitial spaces. (1994, p. xvii)

In this text, Duany and Plater-Zyberk refer to the separation of uses due to zoning laws, an outcome antithetical to New Urbanism. The New Urbanist movement follows an underlying principle that it is the 'combinations of mixtures of activities, not separate uses, [that] are the key to successful urban places' (Montgomery 1998, 98).

Although apparently adverse to strict municipal zoning, the nature of New Urbanism's identity as a methodology for planning communities, requires strict planning codes. Much in the same way incremental development can fail to consider the 'larger context of civic proposals,' glorifying non-beneficial 'chaotic urbanism'; New Urbanism's dogmatic approach to planning and rejection of incremental growth can fail to create a more socially equal urbanism (Talen 2005, 253). Kim Dovey states in *Becoming Places: Urbanism/Architecture/Identity* that 'all places are in a state of continuous change,' and that the conscious attempts of designers to prescribe a sense of place easily produces a 'manipulative corporate formulae or nostalgic ideologies written literally into space' (2009, 3). It is in this regard that New Urbanism has found its detractors, having been decried as a 'mimicry' of nineteenth century streetcar neighbourhoods and 'a grand fraud' by writers such as Alex Marshall (1996). Accusing developments of an architectural dishonesty, they criticise a pastiche style that relies on nostalgia and 'flatly reject the contention that there is an overriding universal spatial or physical aesthetic of urban form' (Webber 1963, 52). Jane Jacobs wrote critically of what she called 'Garden City nonsense' (1961, 289), for much of the same reason Lewis Mumford decried the 'anti-city' (1968, 128). Both denounced the abstract calculations and segregation of urbanism into compartments.

With the strict implementation of planning codes, the New Urbanist tradition reveals its need for control to achieve its goals. In the book *Planning the Good Community: New Urbanism in Theory and Practice*, Jill Grant identifies the New Urbanist aim of implementing 'the panopticon as Foucault explains it' with the intent of establishing spaces in which 'everyone believes that someone may be watching, and adjusts their behaviours accordingly' (2005, 196). Initially proposed by English philosopher and social theorist Jeremy Bentham, and later re-established by French Philosopher Michel Foucault in his 1977 work *Discipline and Punish: The Birth of the Prison*, the panopticon is a hypothetical prison system whereby a circle of prison cells surround a single 'inspection house'. Key to the success of Bentham's panopticon was that the central guards were somehow concealed from the view of the inmates, who were to be kept unaware of whether they were being observed, creating a need for self-regulating behaviour. Bentham recognised that power should be both 'visible and unverifiable', with the inmate never aware if they are being observed 'at any one moment (Foucault 1977, 200).

Foucault adopted this prison concept as a metaphor for disciplinary power in societies, a social theory he called Panopticism. Panopticism was theorised as a method of social control relying on self-regulating behaviour, in a similar vein to Bentham's prison design, through a permanent visibility assuring automatic power. Foucault considered invisibility to be the 'guarantee of power', seeing the prison cells as 'cages' and 'theatres' (1977, p200). Panopticism was to be rooted in the 'formation of a disciplinary society ... that stretches from the enclosed disciplines, a sort of social quarantine, to an indefinitely generalised mechanism of 'panopticism' (Foucault, 1977, 216).

Much like Grant, Dean MacCannel in his essay *'New Urbanism' and its Discontents* opposes what he describes as an authoritarian approach to urban design, derived from nostalgia (1999, 133). He criticises the town of Celebration on an

individual residential unit level as being 'panoptic', calling the designs a 'totalitarian attempt to remove habitability' (1999, 114). With the layout facing criticism even from proponents of New Urbanism, Robert A.M. Stern labelled it
'horrendous' on an architectural level (Rymer 1996, 70); MacCannel describes
a seeming 'nostalgia for a central authority that penetrates the most intimate
details of life' (1999, 113).

An underlying totalitarian tone is prevalent in the writings of some of the key
proponents of New Urbanism, describing how 'the new urban form plays a
disciplinary role' (Grant 2005, 196). Writing about the town of Seaside,
Florida, Vincent Scully identifies the role of the building code or pattern as one
with which 'to keep the city civilised, exactly as laws are intended to do' (1991,
20). While Duany supports this, calling the code 'a proactive vision… shaping
public space to achieve it' (Duany *et al* 2000).

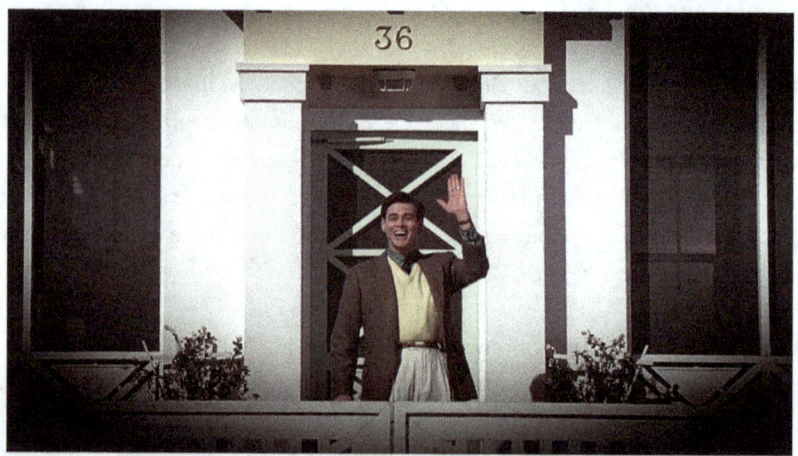

Figure 10: "And in case I don't see you, good afternoon, good evening,
and goodnight." *The Truman Show* (0.02.47)

Released to critical and commercial success in 1998, Peter Weir's *The Truman
Show* stars Jim Carrey as the titular Truman (true-man) Burbank, the unknow-
ing star of a reality television show chronicling his seemingly ordinary life. At
the hands of the show's omniscient and omnipotent creator Christof, a name
with religious allusions, Truman has been reduced to a commodified product,
designed to entertain a mass of 'virtual flâneurs' (AlSayyad 2006, 14). The

film depicts the final few weeks of the eponymous 'The Truman Show,' a TV show which relies on what Henri Lefebvre described as 'the power concealed in everyday life's apparent banality' akin to the flâneurs observations of the 'extraordinary in [life's] very ordinariness' (2003, 37).

Adopted at birth by the television studio, Truman was brought up in the idyllic 1950s style suburban island town of Seahaven. The town, enclosed in an arcological dome, is a simulacrum whereby Truman's family, friends, and wider society are actors. The producers of the show exert control over every aspect of Truman's life, filming and producing the 'The Truman Show' for record audiences. The control exerted over Truman extends to who he is designed to fall in love with; his fear of water manufactured through the traumatic, and scripted, experience of watching his father drown; and the engineering of phenomena designed to keep him isolated on the island of Seahaven. This primes the film as an embodiment of what Gilles Deleuze termed a 'society of control' (1992), primarily through the inverted panoptic view of the television audience. The main themes of *The Truman Show* open it up to interpretation as an 'indeterminate postmodern critique of modernist hegemony and commodi-fication' (Lavoie 2011, 55).

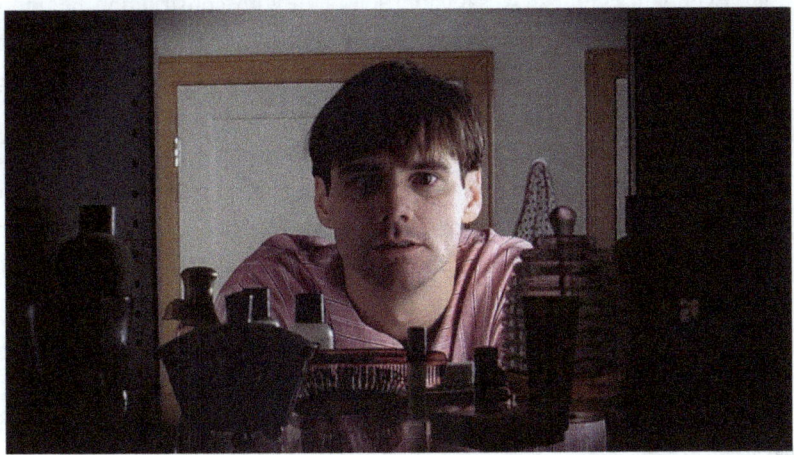

Figure 11: An unaware Truman carries out his morning routine. *The Truman Show* (0:02:23).

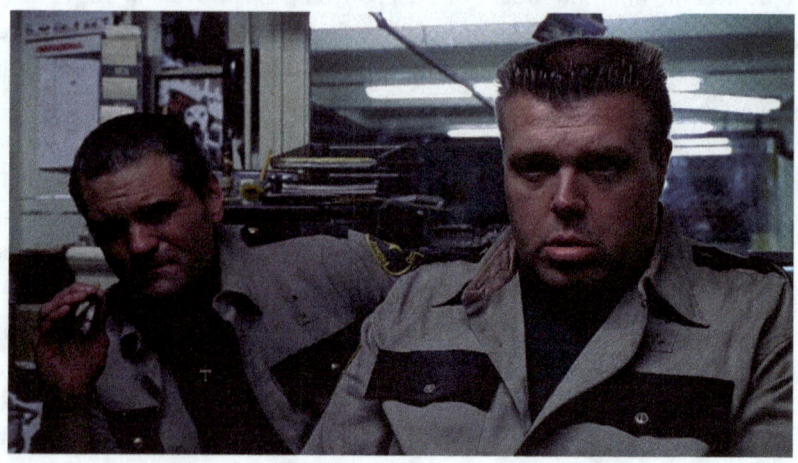

Figure 12: Truman's voyeuristic audience. *The Truman Show* (1:22:16).

To depict the theme of unsettling perfection and voyeurism, *The Truman Show* found its spatial language in the Florida town of Seaside. Repurposed as the island town of Seahaven for the film, Seaside is a prominent 'manicured post-modern New Urbanist settlement' indicative of the movement's goals during the late twentieth century (AlSayyad 2006, 14), with construction beginning 17 years prior to the release of The Truman Show. New Urbanist writer Peter Katz has described Seaside as being of 'great importance' to American urban-ism, distilling designers Andres Duany and Elizabeth Plater-Zyberk's aims of 'fostering a strong sense of community,' one which places greater importance on the public realm over the private (1994, 3). The intentions of Duany and Plater-Zyberk follow the New Urbanist reactions to modern urban design, cre-ating walkable nostalgic spaces in defiance of the perceived alienation of dense city life. Although held in high regard by the New Urbanists, Seaside has its de-tractors amongst the wider architectural profession. Fredric Jameson critiques Seahaven from a Marxist perspective as displaying New Urbanism's desire for 'empty, dead nostalgia' (1991, 156) in the form of a 'pre-postmodernist fantasy' (Lavoie 2011, 54).

The typical panoptic sense of observation has been inverted by *The Truman Show*, making Truman the centrepiece to be watched by concealed eyes. In set-ting the film in the neo-traditionalist town of Seaside, Weir makes a statement on the urbanism of the late twentie   th century as that which demands 'ultimate scopic control and paranoid security' only achievable through 'anti-urban environments which double as stage sets' (AlSayyad 2006, 14). As demonstrated by Seaside/Seahaven, 'public space and public architecture have been constructed with a purpose of control since Paris was renovated in the nineteenth century, or more recently the campus riots of 1968' (Wise 2002, 36). Most perverse however, is the intrusion of the observer (the show's audience) into Truman's most intimate and private spaces. To hide his innermost secrets, Truman recedes to his basement, where he has enshrined his memories and dreams. These dramatic moments of vulnerability are what makes the show so popular, and what makes Truman 'a valuable commodity' (AlSayyad 2006, 226).

Although we have yet to reach *The Truman Show*'s level of depravity with regards to reality television, the film is considered significantly prophetic with regards to its depiction of a 'techno-voyeuristic-entertainment scheme' that we now consider 'endemic in contemporary media and representation' (Lavoie 2011, 57). As the film depicts a 'commodification of the watched', it simultaneously 'parodies our own obsession with watching' (Lavoie 2011, 57). The fact that the 'monstrous fabrication' that is the in-universe '*The Truman Show*' is financed through 'corporate advertising' (Sharpe 1998, 121) opens itself to analysis in terms of the Debordian spectacle. As previously referenced, Debord's spectacle is embodied in mass media and its encroachment on our everyday lives. The mediated life of Truman Burbank has been rendered the 'epitome of a commodity that has become image or spectacle' (McGregor 2004, 113).

Despite a physical panoptic space relying on the prisoner being simultaneously aware that they are being watched and yet unaware when they are being watched, Truman's character arc is that of someone becoming aware of this pervasive voyeurism. As he understands himself to be part of a television show, he also becomes aware of his place as a Debordian spectacle. Truman is a combination of both an 'unwitting spectacle and an uninformed prisoner' (Lavoie 2011, 63). As Truman is unaware of his imprisonment, he cannot be controlled. Instead of utilising the 'brute force of a disciplinary regime' Truman is managed through 'the shaping of the social space in which he is embedded', just as the television show's audience is controlled by 'fostering habits of consumption' (Wise 2002, 38).

As the film concludes, Truman escapes from the panopticism and hegemony that is his world and enters ours in which a hypermediated urbanity and surveillance state design still exists. As Wise writes in his analysis of *The Truman Show*'s climactic scene, 'he is not leaving the society of control, he merely exits from one institution' (Wise 2002, 42). The panoptic design of New Urbanist settlements, and their emphasis on the public over private space echoes the commodification and panopticism of Truman Burbank — a planned city for a planned life.

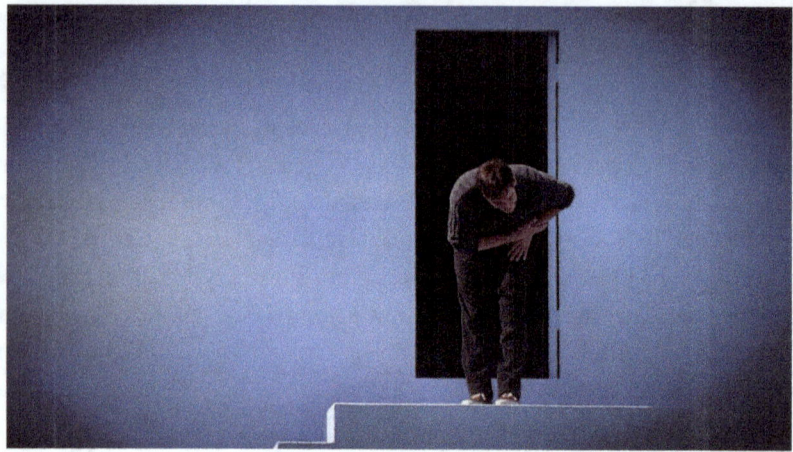

Figure 13: Truman's final bow. *The Truman Show* (1:35:05).

With cinema and the moving image firmly ingrained into our daily lives, we can observe both how our built environment influences film, and how film influences our environment. Our society is one which now mass produces these so-called 'poetic images' for 'commercial exploitation, political and ideological conditioning, entertainment, instruction, and learning' (Pallasmaa, 2007, 9).

As a field of study, urbanism at its core should observe and explain the nature of the city. In any of the multitude of forms that that explanation could take, the three films presented here illustrate the medium's intrinsic ability to capture the 'essence of the modern city' (Bullock 2011, 90). From the optimistic embrace of Modernism portrayed in city symphonies such as *Berlin: Symphony of a Great City*, to the voyeuristic science fiction of *The Truman Show*, via the comedic and absurd in *Mon Oncle*; we are not only seeing the influence architecture and the city has on film, but a capturing of the 'flux of the city' (Bullock 2011, 90).

This illustrative investigation has strived to analyse the symbiotic relationship between cinema and the city throughout the twentieth century. Highlighting the role of the observer in the city, through closely linked themes of the flâneur, dérive, and panopticism, this text has sought to contextualise urban Modernism through the analysis of films displaying characteristics of their time. As cinema has been understood as both 'expressive and constitutive of the experience and sensibility of modernity' (Brunsdon 2012, 220), it is befitting to analyse a medium so intrinsically linked with the city and modernity.

Cities are not simple constructs and should not be given simple solutions. Jacobs writes of 'the immense number of parts that make up a city, and the immense diversity of those parts' (1961, 143); it is through this diversity that the city gains its genius loci. It is the reading of the part and the whole which constructs our perception of urbanity, and while cinema is a successful method of capturing and influencing an urban spirit, the city continues to be 'a phenomenon that exceeds all our capacity of description, representation and recording and, consequentially, it is experientially infinite' (Pallasmaa, 2007, 22).

REFERENCES

AlSayyad, Nezar. 2006. *Cinematic Urbanism: A History of the Modern from Reel to Reel*. New York: Routledge.

Bachelard, Gaston. 1969. *The Poetics of Space*. Boston: Beacon Press.

Benjamin, Walter. 2002. "On Some Motifs in Baudelaire" in *Illuminations*, edited by Hannah Arendt. London: Pimlico.

Benjamin, Walter. 1973. *Charles Baudelaire: A Lyric Poet in the Era of High Capitalism*. London: NLB.

Benjamin, Walter. 1999. *Walter Benjamin: Selected Writings, Volume 2, part 2*, 1931–1934, edited by Michael Jennings, Cambridge: Belknap Press.

Bergson, Henri. 1912. *Matter and Memory*. Translated by William Scott Palmer and Nancy Margaret Paul. London: G. Allen & Co ltd.

Bernstein, Matthew. 1984. *Visual Style and Spatial Articulations in Berlin, Symphony of a City* (1927). Journal of Film and Video 36 (4): 5-12.

Brunsdon, Charlotte. 2012. *The Attractions of the Cinematic City*. Screen 53 (3): 209-227.

Bullock, Nicholas. 2011. "Aids to Objectivity? Photography, Film and the New 'Science' of Urbanism" in *Urban Cinematics*, edited by Francois Penz and Andong Lu. Bristol: Intellect.

Charney, Leo. and Schwartz, Vanessa. eds. 1995. *Cinema and the Invention of Modern Life*. Berkeley: University of California Press.

Coates, Jamie. 2017. *Key Figure of Mobility: The flâneur*. Social Anthropology 25, no 1, February 2017: 28-41.

Congress for the New Urbanism. 1993. *The Charter of the New Urbanism*. Washington, DC: Congress for the New Urbanism. Accessed November 23, 2016. https://www.cnu.org/who-we-are/charter-new-urbanism

Corbusier, Le. 1931. *Towards a New Architecture*. New York: Dover.

Cosgrove, Ben. *LIFE at the Movies: When 3D Was New*, LIFE Magazine, December 15, 1952.

Debord, Guy. 1955. *Psychogeographic Guide of Paris*. Denmark: Permild & Rosengreen.

Debord, Guy. 1958. "Definitions" in *Internationale Situationniste 1*. Accessed May 10, 2017. http://www.cddc.vt.edu/sionline/si/definitions.html

Debord, Guy. 1958. "Theory of the Dérive" in *Internationale Situationniste 2*. Accessed May 10, 2017. http://www.cddc.vt.edu/sionline/si/theory.html

Debord, Guy. 1967, *The Society of the Spectacle*. Paris: Buchet-Chastel.

Deleuze, Gilles. 1992. *Postscript on the Societies of Control*. October 59 (Winter): 3-7.

Dovey, Kim. 2009. *Becoming Places: Urbanism/Architecture/Identity*. London: Routledge

Duany, Andrés and Plater-Zyberk, Elizabeth. 2000. *Suburban Nation*. New York: North Point Press

Foucault, Michel. 1977. *Discipline and Punish: The Birth of the Prison*. Translated by Alan Sheridan. London: Penguin.

Ford, James. 1936. *Slums and Housing, with Special Reference to New York City: History, Conditions, Policy*. Cambridge, MA: Harvard University Press

George, Henry. 1886. *Progress and Poverty*. London: Kegan Paul, Trench & Co.

Grant, Jill. 2006. *Planning the Good Community: New Urbanism in Theory and Practice*. New York: Routledge.

Hall, Peter. 2014. *Cities of Tomorrow: An intellectual history of urban planning and design since 1880*. Chichester: John Wiley & Sons.

Harding, James. 1984. *Jacques Tati: Frame by frame*. London: Secker and Warburg

Howard, Ebenezer. 1945. *Garden Cities of To-morrow*. London: Faber and Faber.

Hunter, Jefferson. 2013. *James Joyce, Walther Ruttmann, and City Symphonies*. The Kenyon Review 35 (2): 186-205

Jacobs, Jane. 1961. *The Death and Life of Great American Cities*. New York: Random House

Jameson, Frederic. 1991. *Postmodernism, or, the Cultural Logic of Late Capitalism*. Durham: Duke University Press.

Katz, Peter. 1994. *The New Urbanism: Towards and Architecture of Community*. London: McGraw-Hill.

Lavoie, Dusty. 2011. *Escaping the Panopticon: Utopia, Hegemony, and Performance in Peter Weir's The Truman Show*. Utopian Studies 22 (1): 52-73.

Lefebvre, Henri. 2003. *The Urban Revolution*. Minneapolis: University of Minnesota Press.

MacCannell, Dean. 1999. "New Urbanism and its Discontents" in *Giving Ground: The politics of propinquity*, edited by Joan Copjec and Michael Sorkin. New York: Verso Books.

Markle, Fletcher. 1964. *Telescope: A talk with Hitchcock. Television Series*. Fletcher Markle. Canada: Canadian Broadcasting Corporation. Accessed May 31, 2021. https://the.hitchcock.zone/wiki/Telescope:_A_Talk_with_Hitchcock_(CBC,_1964)

Marshall, Alex. 1996. "Putting some 'City' back in the suburbs." *The Washington Post*, September 1, 1996. Accessed May 31, 2021. http://www.washingtonpost.com/wp-srv/local/longterm/library/growth/solutions/nokent.htm

McDonough, Tom. 2010. *The Situationists and the City: A reader*. New York: Verso Books.

McGregor, Peter. 2004. *The Truman Show as a Study of 'the Society of the Spectacle'*. Australian Screen Education 32 (Spring): 112-115.

Metz, Christian. 1974. *Film Language: A semiotics of the cinema*. Chicago: University of Chicago Press.

Montgomery, John. 1998. *Making a City: Urbanity, Vitality, and Urban Design*. Journal of Urban Design 3 (1): 93-116.

Mumford, Lewis. 1961. *The City in History: Its origins, its transformations, and its prospects*. London: Secker and Warburg.

Mumford, Lewis. 1968. *The Urban Prospect*. London: Secker and Warburg.

O'Donoghue, Darragh. 2015. *Monsieur Hulot's History: Jacques Tati Pictures Modern France*. Cineate 40 (2): 12-17

Pallasmaa, Juhani. 2007. *The Architecture of Image: Existential space in cinema*. Hameenlinna: Karisto Oy.

Penz, Francois. 1994. "Cinema and Architecture." In *Architecture and Film. Architectural Design*. Edited by Maggie Toy. Hoboken: John Wiley and Sons

Penz, Francois and Lu, Andong. 2011. *Urban Cinematics*. Bristol: Intellect.

Ross, Kristin. 1988. *The Emergence of Social Space*. Minneapolis: University of Minnesota Press.

Ruttmann, Walter. 1927. *Berlin: Symphony of a Great City*. DVD. Directed by - Walter Ruttmann. USA: Fox Film Corporation.

Rymer, Russ. 1996. "Back to the Future." *Harper's Magazine*. October 1996.

Sadler, Simon, 1999. *The Situationist City*. London: MIT Press.

Scully, Vincent. 1991. *Architecture: The natural and the Manmade*. New York: St Martins Press.

Sharpe, M.E. 1998. *The Truman Show*. Challenge 41 (5): 121-129

Shaya, Gregory. 2004. *The Flâneur, the Baudad and the Making of a Mass Public in France circa 1860-1910*. The American Historical Review 109 (1): 41-77.

Simmel, Georg. 1976. *The Metropolis and Mental Life*. New York: Free Press.

Talen, Emily. 2005. *New Urbanism and American Planning: The Conflict of Cultures*. New York: Routledge.

Tati, Jacques. 1958. *Mon Oncle*. DVD. Directed by – Jacque Tati. France: Gaumont.

Webber, Melvin. 1963. "Order in Diversity: Community Without Propinquity." in *Cities and Space: The Future Use of Urban Land*. edited by Lowdon Wingo Jr. Baltimore: The John Hopkins Press.

Weihsmann, Helmut. 2011. "Ciné-City Strolls: Imagery, Form, Language and Meaning of the City Film." in *Urban Cinematics*, edited by Francois Penz and Andong Lu. Bristol: Intellect. Ch.1

Weir, Peter. 1999. *The Truman Show*. DVD. Directed by – Peter Weir. USA: Paramount Pictures.

Wise, John Macgregor. 2002. *Mapping the Culture of Control: Seeing Through The Truman Show*. Television and New Media 3 (1): 29-47.

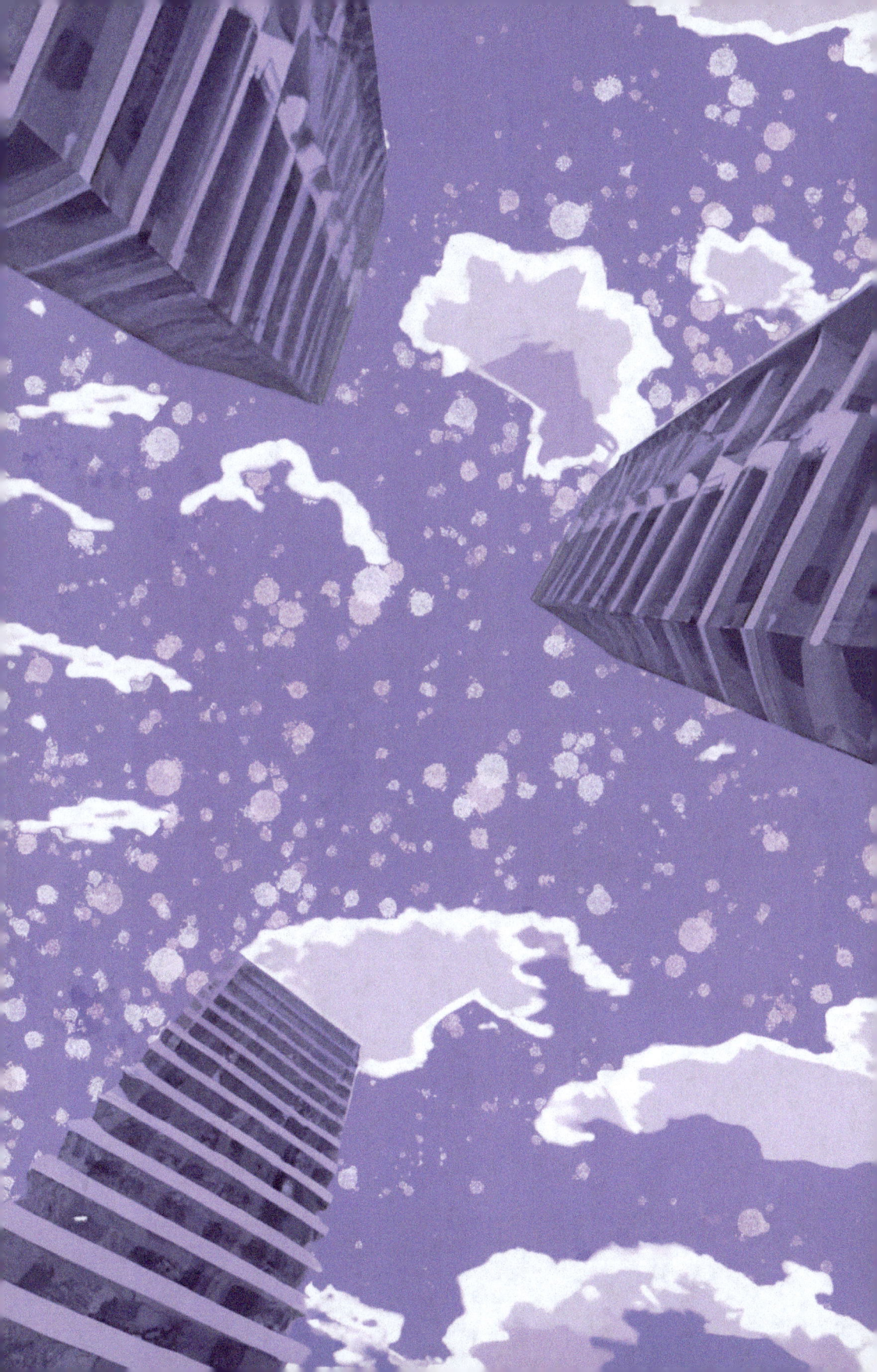

Exploring the City: Belfast in Films

Ece Sila Bora

Ece Sila Bora is an architect and PhD candidate at Queen's University   Belfast. With work/life experience in Turkey, France, Portugal, and Northern Ireland, she has been conducting research on 'architecture and cinema.' She studied a double major, Architecture and Landscape Architecture, at Istanbul Technical University. Before joining Queen's in 2021, she worked as a professional architect and teaching assistant in İstanbul. In addition, she acted as a production designer and art director in short films about the built environment. She is a fellow in CITI-GENS, a Horizon2020 funded Marie Skłodowska-Curie doctoral training program.

S ince its early times, cinema has been concerned with the representation of space, lifestyles, and human conditions within the city. Films could be pursued as an exploration tool to understand the multi-layered and often ambiguous urban environment. They had a striking and distinctive ability to capture and express the spatial complexity, diversity, and social dynamism of the city (Shiel and Fitzmaurice 2011). It is hard to comprehend the emergence of cinema separately from the urban environment. Since the 'city symphonies' at the beginning of the twentieth century, film has been the tool of both representing and orientating with the astounding speed of modernism. The modern mode of living and the rhythm of these modern cities have been extensively recorded and documented through cinematic techniques.

This claim is also valid for the city of Belfast, which has been one of the prominent cities of the film industry. Belfast has been frequently framed in films because of being one of two capitals representing the Irish identity. That is why there is a great potential for a retrospective reading of the city via cinema. Thus, this study attempts to understand the complex urban environment of Belfast through film. It discusses mapping as a creative method to analyse the city and film settings in cities from a cinematic perspective. The research also shows how real locations in film play an important role to shape our knowledge about cities in a broader sense. The city has always been a major actor in cinematic narratives beyond merely being a backdrop or a décor. To put it in a different way, the city performs, shapes and directs the events in the plot. The study investigates the relation of cinema with the built environment, especially concentrating on real locations and their representation in film. Moreover, it shows that mapping and digitising film locations could provide new perspectives and visions about the space. This framework is used to make a comparative analysis of two films that are set in Belfast: *Odd Man Out* (1947) and *I am Belfast* (2015).

There is a growing body of literature about the intersection of city, architecture, and cinema in recent years. The transformation of film as a 'medium' has influenced the city. In return, as the urban environment has changed, the relationship of the cinematic image with the built reality has also evolved. That expanding discourse has a variety of discussions around some themes, such as cinematic geography, cinematic cartography, movie mapping, city in film, and cinematic city. They all refer to research areas related to spatial aspects, and they all have some competing and overlapping claims (Roberts and Hallam 2013). This chapter introduces some of the researchers working on these topics, with a particular focus on location mapping.

In *The Cinematic City*, geographer David B. Clarke mentions the conceptualisation of the cityscape as a 'screenscape.' He argues that the birth of cinema has irreversibly transformed our visual perception and individual experience of cities. He explains "the city has undeniably been shaped by the cinematic forms, just as cinema owes much of its nature to the historical development of the city" (2005). In accordance with Clarke, film-architecture scholar François Penz states that cinema metaphorised modernism, and cities became more comprehensible with films. Cinema has the power of revealing things that we could not conceive in daily life. In short, film has changed our perception of cities and liberated us (2020). As depicted, cinema does not only represent the urban environment but also reconstructs our apprehension of it. Cinematic tools, such as editing and montage, attempt various ways to depict and reconstruct existing locations in the city, beyond merely recording them. Architect and filmmaker Patrick Keiller claims that especially after the introduction of narrative, space and time in films have been reconstructed by cutting and assembling individual shots

(2007). Film practice has become a more fragmented form of representation since then. That allows the viewers to see the city from a different perspective by reconstructing the given reality, their perception and memories. So, the concept of cinematic city overall expresses the intertwined relationship and co-evolution of city and cinema. To illustrate, the alteration of ways we perceive and reconstruct cities, artificial and built cinematic spaces, their reflection on societies, cinematic-urban spectatorship are a few of the related subjects.

'Cinematic cartography' is a term more related to the geographic aspects and locational analysis of the cinematic spaces. Architect Richard Koeck and media scholar Les Roberts state that both cinema and cartography are spatial practices framing epistemological, ideological, aesthetic or perceptual modes of urban participation (2010). That is why, one of the emerging fields in that study area is the 'mapping' practices. Although architects have long been working at the intersection of cinema and space in various scales, their major focus was not primarily on the documentation and mapping of 'real' film locations. Hence, there is still an undiscovered area related to the architectural point of view. Mediated city images of urban life constitute a rich source to understand the dynamics of urban life. Mapping these locations allows us to place that information on a definite base, to turn it into the quantitative type of knowledge and to see relationships between them. On the other hand, the act of mapping has also the power to reveal the invisible qualities of the surrounding. To clarify, mappings are usually expected to be measurable, objective and rational, but they also have the potential to reflect the cognitive, emotional and immanent aspects of the terrain and the mapper subject. In accordance with that, landscape architect James Corner claims that the act of mapping is a productive tool and an unfolding practice. Due to its highly subjective and open-ended features, each act could conclude with separate outputs. In his words, "mappings discover new worlds within past and present ones; they inaugurate new grounds upon the hidden traces of a living context" (2011). So, mapping becomes a new method to rediscover the environment from individual perspectives. It also provides a base to categorise that particular knowledge into layers. Film maps could be classified and stratified with spatial and temporal inputs, such as architectural and urban features, film stills, current images, and historical maps. Therefore, mapping establishes a versatile and open-ended work ground for further projections with the stratification of knowledge.

After addressing the potentials of mapping, it is beneficial to investigate how mapping is theorised and performed by various disciplines related to cinema. Some researchers focus on the existence of maps in films, such as philologist Tom Conley. He claims that since the emergence of the narrative, maps are indispensable in the field of the image to reveal the place of action (2011). In his book, *Cartographic Cinema*, he discusses the efforts of films to reorient the audience through their imagination. According to Conley, even though a film does not involve a visual of a map, it still orients the audience through geographic and representational cartographies (2007). Following this, Teresa Castro, a film and media scholar in Paris, argues that cinema's exploration of urban space is driven by a 'mapping impulse and it results with different cartographies in films, such as panoramas, atlases, and aerial views of the space' (2009). She claims that 'mapping impulse' cannot simply be reduced to outputs. It is more related to a particular way of thinking and strategies to represent the space. In other words, mapping as action must be discussed separately from maps as objects. A well-known example of it is Charles Joseph Minard's map of Napoleon's Russian Campaign, which depicts Napoleon's march to Moscow in 1812. In that representation, Minard processes various layers of data, such as topological information, number of troops, temperature changes, and specific locations at different times into a single map. The map is one of the early instances that represents the act of mapping as a process, not only as an output or final product. To put it another way, mapping is an action that constantly evolves and that is not necessarily fixed in certain depictions.

Another major research topic in the field is the mapping of film production and consumption. That study area focuses on the geographies of the film industry and distribution. One of the prevailing formations is the HOMER Network (History of Moviegoing, Exhibition and Reception). It initiates the research on the geographies of film distribution and cinema locations in different cities. The network brings together many studies in this field, using historical maps to retrace film distributions, sites of exhibition, and cinemagoing experience in different periods and cities. It includes an interactive mapping of various projects around the world, consisting of databases, local mappings, oral histories, digitalisation and software. Studies under this theme are concerned with mapping the 'screening spaces' rather than the locations where films are set. Still, the work in that field constitutes a large proportion of mappings made within the scope of film and space studies.

When mapping actual film locations is considered, there is less variety. An important part of research conducted in this context is related to tourism and place marketing. There are researchers focusing on how film and tourism industries shape each other, for instance Alfio Leotta who is a media scholar interested in the touristic aspects of film consumption. In his article "Navigating Movie (M)apps: Film Locations, Tourism and Digital Mapping Tools," Leotta studies movie maps compatible with software applications that enable users to identify the geographical position of film locations. He discusses the topic with different aspects such as the relationship of movie maps with film tourism, media consumption and its effect on place (2016). In addition to these academic surveys, it is possible to find online location maps for various cities created by state organisations, film institutions, web developers, and film audiences. An example of online mapping in the UK is the "Britain in Film" project created by the British Film Institute. In this interactive-online map, films are pinned according to region, city and approximate location in the city and classified in genres, such as documentary, newsreel, short film, and campaign film.

Apart from the studies outlined above, there is only minimal research that utilises mapping as a method to produce architectural or spatial knowledge. Media scholars Julia Hallam and Les Roberts at the University of Liverpool are among them. They conduct research on the concept of spatiality in film studies and new navigations in the field. Hallam and Roberts analyse the concept of the cinematic city with digital tools including GIS and discuss the mapping of film locations as an emerging research practice in urban and film studies. They have a research project entitled "Mapping the City in Film," which is an interdisciplinary study that combines the expertise of scholars from architecture, film studies, communication studies and social anthropology. The project examines Liverpool's changing urban landscape and its representation in films. It locates a range of film and video depicting the urban environment and architecture from the early days to the present. They have created a database, over 1700 film and video recordings made in

and about the city, which allows them to make both quantitative and qualitative analyses of the changing urban environment (2013).

Cartographer Sébastien Caquard is another researcher who focuses on film
locations. In their research project with Daniel Naud, entitled "The Cyber-
cartographic Atlas of Canadian Cinema," they work on mapping film locations in various cities and the connections between them. They use selected
variables, including the duration of the scene, the level of accuracy of location, and the way the place is materialised, as inputs to visualise maps. With
the evolving narrative, they process all the actions and relocations as points
and lines. Their output and analysis focus on the cartographic forms generated by these connections (2014). They do not intend to make spatial claims
about how these changing networks affect the built environment of the city.
Still, their research constitutes a good example because of its technicality
and considering time as an input of the mapping process.

After framing the theoretical background on cinema and mapping, this
framework could be used to analyse selected film settings in Belfast. In
a broader perspective, Irish cinema has successfully reflected the social
conditions, the city and the built environment with changing perspectives
throughout film history. Identified with 'emigration narratives' in the early
twentieth century, Irish films played an important role in the establishment
of national identity after independence. In the following decades, new
images are produced regarding religious and political conflicts, the criticism of the church and the state as well as economic fluctuations. Belfast,
as a city where the Troubles are intensely felt, has become the natural set of
many conflict-themed films. Even in the post-Troubles period, UK and Irish
films based in Belfast continued to depict social traumas. Recently, the city
has become one of the fastest-growing creative industry sectors in the UK
economy. Belfast has hosted many TV series and film productions such as
Game of Thrones, *Line of Duty*, *The Fall*, *Highrise*, and *Good Vibrations*.
However, research about the city's portrayal in film is still limited.

The main discussion of this chapter is based on two films set in Belfast in
different decades, *Odd Man Out*, a 1947 film directed by Carol Reed, and *I
Am Belfast*, directed by Mark Cousins in 2015. Although there seems to be
no connection between the two at first glance, there are many similarities

and differences in their depiction of Belfast. The main reason for the selection is their powerful representation of the city in different historical periods. While the former exemplifies an industrial city in the mid-twentieth century, the latter   depicts the present state and the transformation of the urban environment over time. Reed's film is a fictional crime drama, which includes both real locations and constructed set designs, whereas Cousins' film is a documentary that represents the city as it is, without any physical constructions. *Odd Man Out* is a story about an illegal organisation leader who rebelled against the authorities. He gets injured in a gunfight in a robbery attempt and runs from the police. He suffers a blur of consciousness due to his wound and gets lost in the streets. While following him wandering and getting detained by strangers, we also have a chance to observe the everyday life and movement in the city. Some streets are dark and desolate, while others are lively and full of crowds. Although it is never stated that the story takes place in Belfast, we see an introduction declaring "the film is about a political unrest in a city of Northern Ireland." Anyhow, the city is easily recognisable from the aerial views and the images of the public space.

Odd Man Out uses various locations in Belfast and London as well as set constructions. Although it is not possible to distinguish all of the exact locations, some online resources and film databases are utilised to identify and compare visuals. Many of these sources refer to "Reelstreet," an online platform that documents film locations in various movies. While these locations were processed on Google Earth, city maps corresponding to setting years were placed as a base to observe the changes in the cityscape. For this, the Public Record Office of Northern Ireland (PRONI) maps were employed. For the area covering most of the city center, "OSNI Six Inch to One Mile Irish Grid (1952-1967)" map was applied. For other locations on the periphery not covered by this map, "OSNI Historical Fourth Edition (1905-1957)" map was used.

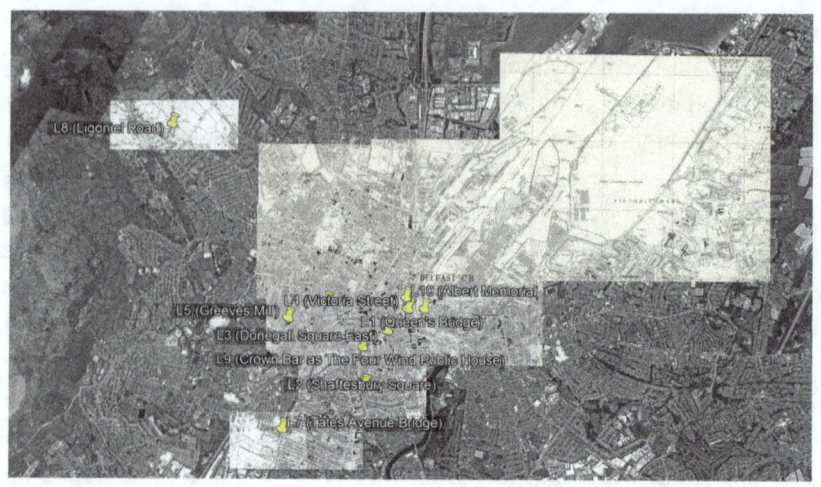

Figure 1: *Odd Man Out* film location map
(all maps and illustrations are by the author.)

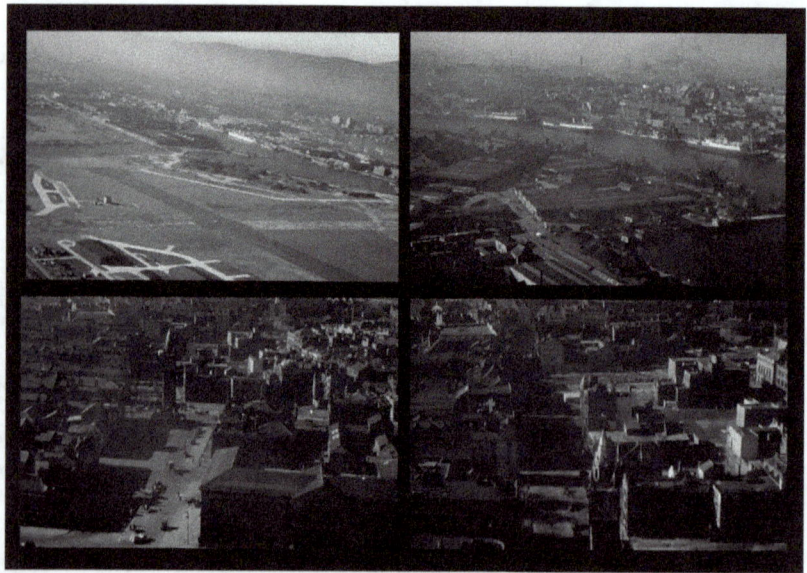

Figure 2: *Odd Man Out* aerial views
(all film stills are captured by the author.)

A comparison to the present day could be made by discussing one of the scenes set in Queens' Bridge. In that scene, the bridge is seen with some buildings by the river. Looking at the OSNI map, it is clear that there were structures adjacent to the bridge at that time. Comparing the old map and the current one, it could be noted that some arrangements about the highways and landscape have been made throughout the years.

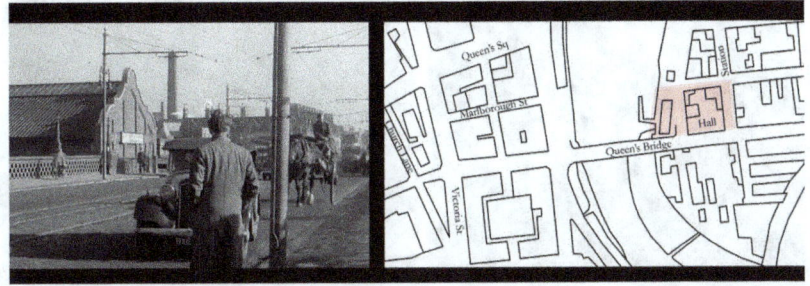

Figure 3: Queen's Bridge in *Odd Man Out* and map for the same period.

In the scene of Shaftesbury Square, this public space is a nodal urban point with pedestrians crossing the street, cars, movement and chaos. It was a juncture in the city although the architecture has quite changed. This inference could be confirmed by analysing OSNI maps. It seems that the urban fabric has mostly been preserved with minor changes since those years.

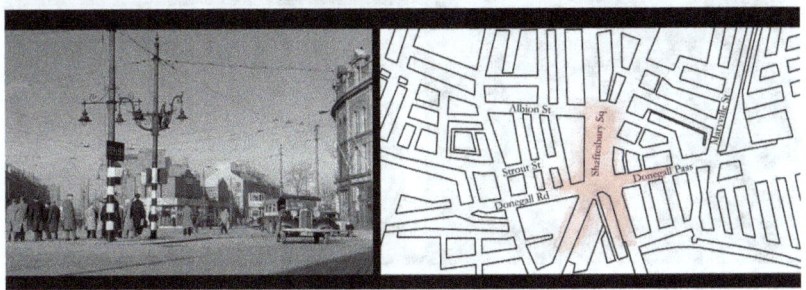

Figure 4: Shaftesbury Square in *Odd Man Out* and map for the same period.

Odd Man Out also contains some elements that have changed or disappeared in the urban fabric throughout the years. Following the robbery scene, a short display of a factory building and its chimney is seen. According to the comments in 'Reelstreet,' this image might belong to the long-demolished Greeves Mill building, which was destroyed during civil unrest in August 1969. The shot seems to be taken from Balaclava Street, which no longer exists.

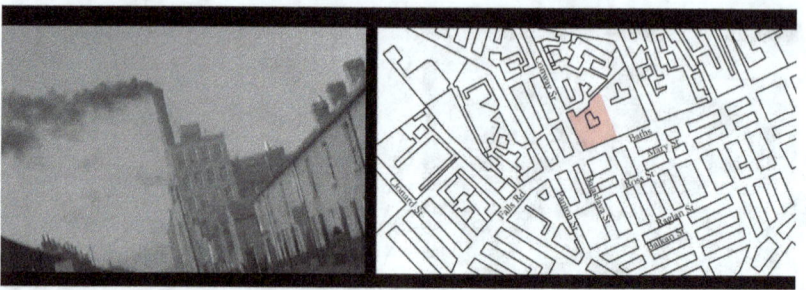

Figure 5: Greeves Mill building in *Odd Man Out* and map for the same period.

Another urban element that disappeared is Boomer Street, which was located close to Boundary Street. In the film, there is a narrow street with a small square with a shop on the corner. This whole area went through redevelopment, and the street pattern has changed completely, as seen in the maps.

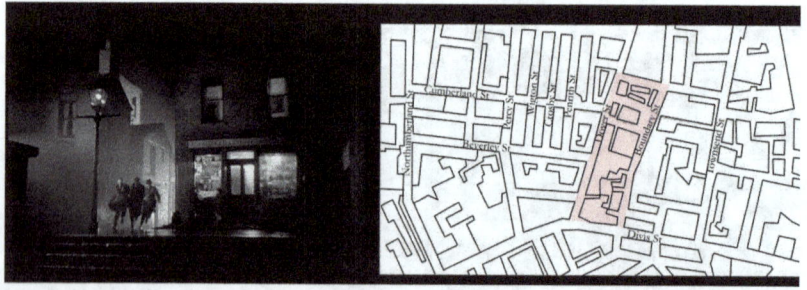

Figure 6: Boomer Street in *Odd Man Out* and map for the same period.

Among the landmarks in the city, Crown Bar in Great Victoria Street is represented in the film. Although the actual interior space was not used in the shooting, 'Four Winds Bar' in the film was influenced by the Crown Bar. Similarly, the images of Albert Memorial Clocktower in Belfast are used in *Odd Man Out*. However, most of the images are based on set design, and the original memorial's form is slightly distorted to fit camera angles.

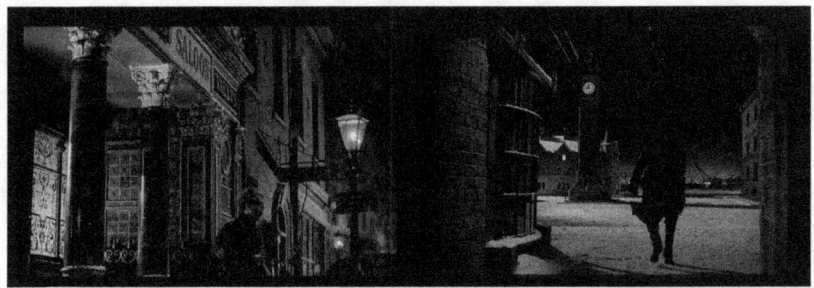

Figure 7: Four Winds Bar and Clock tower in *Odd Man Out*.

Reed's *Odd Man Out* gives important insights into the transformation of the city since the 1940s. It is also a beneficial example of how the city is represented through the eyes of a filmmaker during a period of internal conflict.

The second case study, *I am Belfast*, is a more recent film and director Mark Cousins' tribute to his hometown. Similar to early black and white recordings of the city, Cousins wanders in streets to capture architecture, people, the surrounding landscape and everyday objects. The director is not alone during his wanderings in the city; he talks with a fictional senior citizen who introduces herself as the literal 'Belfast.' Throughout the dialogue, mnemonic information is given about Belfast's history, milestones, sociological structure and conflicts. But the film is not a didactic documentary; it is rather a conversation with the city represented as an elderly person. Due to the filming angles, scene durations and the progress of the script, the identification of locations has been challenging. Various objects in the frame, such as murals, street signs, or names in the dialogue, are traced to mark the places. The film also employs historical footage in some scenes. For example, the City Hall building appears in various scenes with its historical and contemporary images. Likewise, the cranes at city ports from different periods are featured. Moreover, shipbuilding, especially the Titanic's construction and its subsequent sinking is mentioned as an important milestone in the history of the city. In addition to those collective memories, social conflicts and political unrest are discussed in various scenes. The city's

memory of violence could be read through the traces left on the built environment. Images of memorials, peace walls and murals are frequently used to
represent the conflict and survival from it.

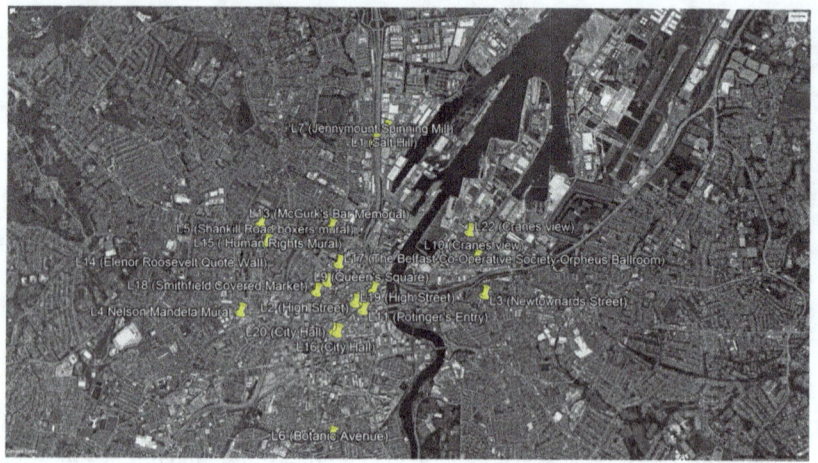

Figure 8: *I am Belfast* film location map.

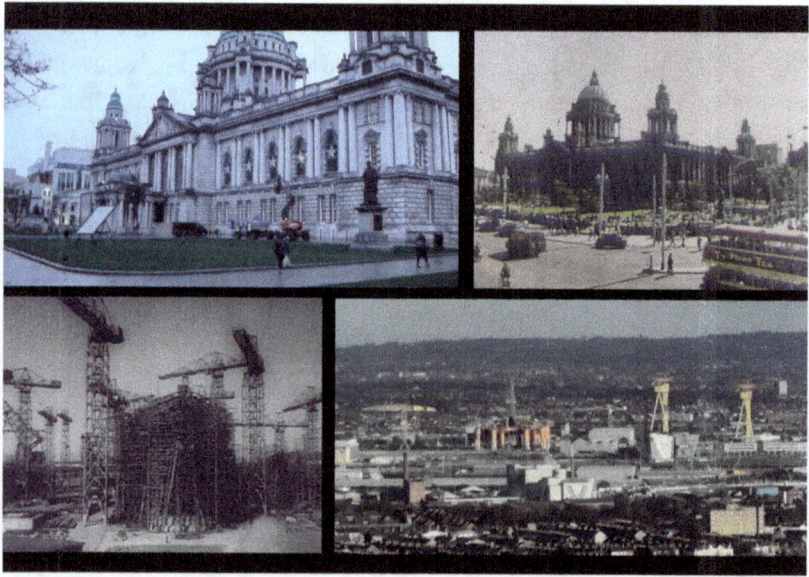

Figure 9: Various film stills from *I am Belfast*.

I am Belfast also reveals some of the landmarks that are concealed in the chaotic urban environment, such as the legacies of Belfast industrial heritage: Linen Mill Buildings. They are not as popular or known by tourists as other structures in the city, however these industrial buildings are among the architectural heritage of Belfast. One of the many others, as an example, is Jennymount Spinning Mill, just across the port area. The elderly woman tells stories about linen production while featuring images of the ruined building in the film. It is one of the few intact structures still standing as a relic of the great age of local industry associated with textiles.

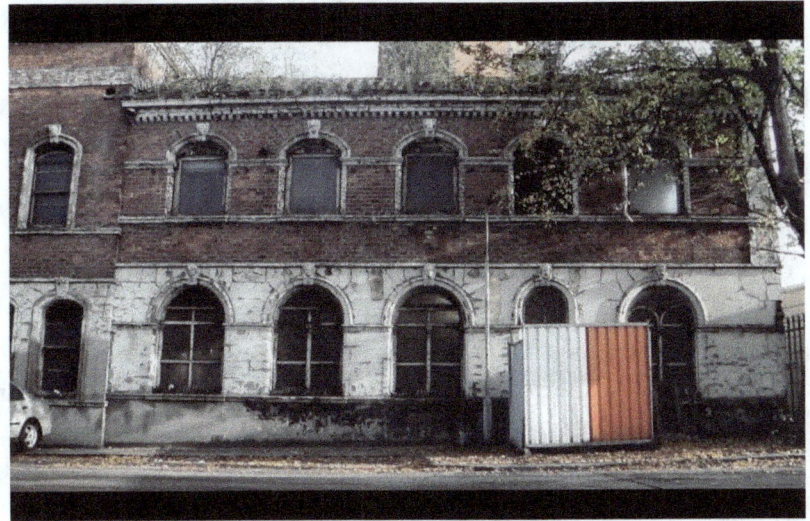

Figure 10: Jennymount Spinning Mill in *I am Belfast*.

A disappeared architectural piece is the Belfast Co-operative Society building. The original building was constructed in 1932. In the 1970s, a part of its historical façade was covered to turn it into a modern shopping centre. During the Troubles, it was bombed multiple times and mostly destroyed. In the following years, although the structure continued to be used as a shopping centre, it was completely demolished in 2015. The film gives clues about all these stages the building has gradually gone through. The structure witnessed most of the recent history of the city, including the Troubles. That is why one might argue that the building itself was layered like a city with traces behind its façade. In the film, some images of its demolition are displayed, which signifies an important change in spatial memory.

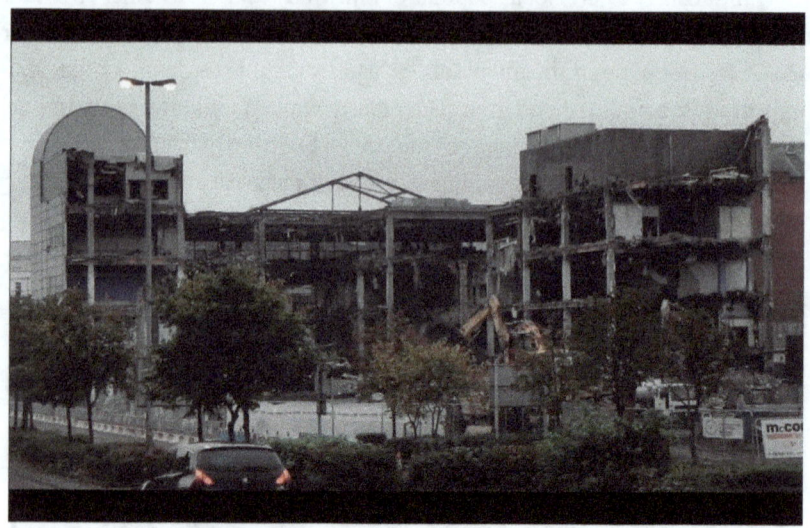

Figure 11: Belfast Co-operative Society building in *I am Belfast*.

Salt Hill, which appears at the beginning of the film, could be seen as another landmark of the city. The significance of Salt Hill is its temporariness. It is in fact not unique; there are other hills that consist of coal, stone and other industrial raw materials, which give shape to the landscape of the harbour area. As is the nature of the work, these materials are piled up, stored and they gradually disappear as they are distributed to different locations. Over time, new hills appear in different places. Thus, the appearance of Belfast's port area is constantly changing.

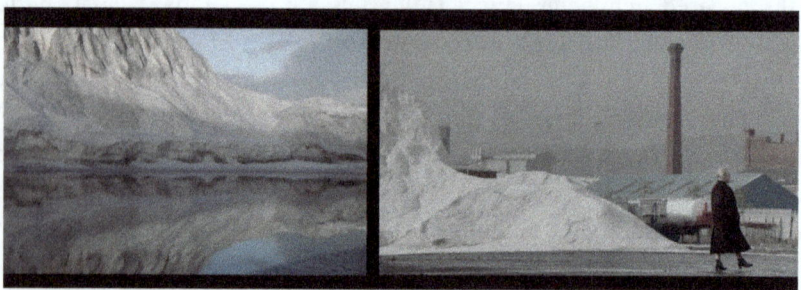

Figure 12: Salt Hill in *I am Belfast*.

The colours of the city are displayed as an important element in *I am Belfast*. Murals, in particular, are one of the remarkable aspects, which stand out in the built environment with their masterful use of colour. The film creates a colour palette of Belfast out of small details, material patinas, street images and urban elements.

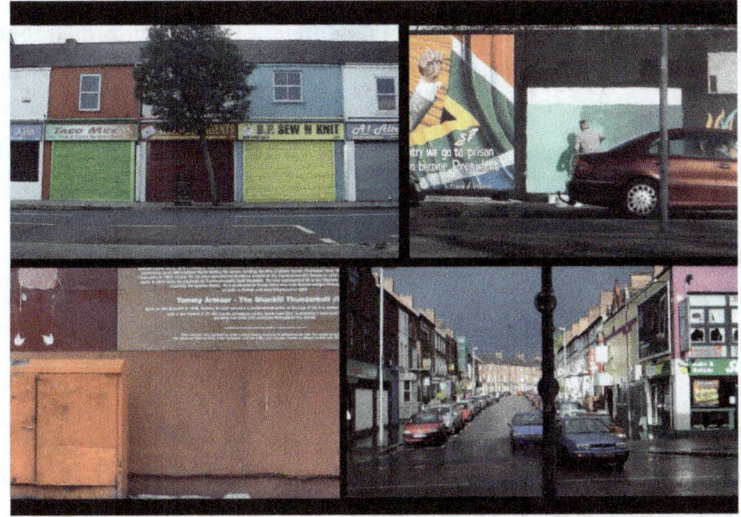

Figure 13: Belfast colours in *I am Belfast*.

Films use metaphors. To illustrate, Belfast itself is represented by a senior and sophisticated woman telling stories. In one scene, she talks about how theatrical the city and its inhabitants are, by referring to social conflict. Then she defines herself as *mise-en-scène* in which events take place. This allows seeing Belfast as a stage framed by urban elements such as yellow cranes, passages and gates.

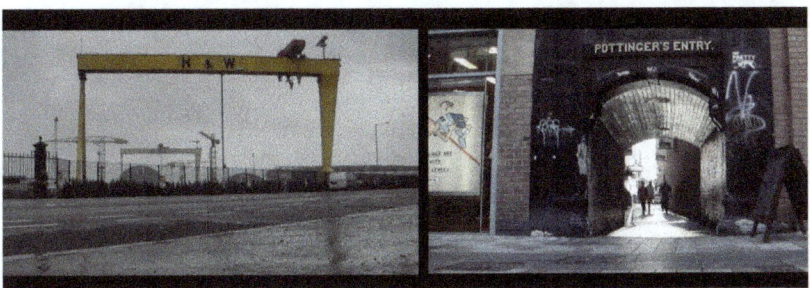

Figure 14: Frames in the city in *I am Belfast*.

The mapping of *I am Belfast* allows us to observe the present state of the city in the light of new notions and perspectives. The neighbourhoods of the city where the murals are concentrated, the widely known and lesser known landmarks as well as the architectural pieces that have a significant role in the collective memory could be detected in the map.

Mapping provides a unique database that different types of information could be stratified and overlapped. It enables one to analyse and compare various films' unique representations of the city. In line with these analyses and the mapping of *Odd Man Out* and *I am Belfast*, an analogical reading could be made depicting various interpretations of urban characteristics.

To begin with, both films enable the viewer to experience the city through   the eyes of walking characters, however, their perspective and the representation of the city are divergent. In *Odd Man Out*, with the effect of artistic concerns of 'film noir,' the city is represented as a 'city noir.' While following Johnny McQueen wandering in the streets and running away from the police, the viewer is exposed to the labyrinths of Belfast. That is why, the city is reflected as dark, detained and fragmented. This aspect of the city is also repeated in many films about the IRA and in escape scenes. We observe the city as a place of flow and velocity with the effect of escape scenes. On the other hand, in *I am Belfast*, the spectator is invited to walk the city with its reification, an elderly woman. This time, one could observe the locations of the city as they are, without any reconstructions. The female "Belfast" tells and reveals herself in all her nakedness. In the film, the city is represented as a place built from memories, more settled and less surprising. Unlike the uncanny urban representation in *Odd Man Out*, this portrayal of Belfast depicts a city of colours. That does not mean that the city is in less conflict. On the contrary, the peace is rebuilt every day by the efforts of its residents. Belfast here is represented not through flow, but rather through inertia and the small details in its stillness. The audience constructs a holistic image of the city from fragments by induction.

Odd Man Out and *I am Belfast* establish two unique interpretations of Belfast. One is darker, uncanny, and full of movement under the influence of the Troubles, and the other is a mature, settled and serene city. As the films frame the urban space with a particular cinematographic approach, they also reshape our perception of the urban environment. Mapping acts as a creative method to explore this reframing process. The active use of mapping enables the process of different types of data collection and stratify the knowledge about film locations in the city. Hence, the act of mapping becomes an open-ended process triggering the prospective architectural discussions and interpretations.

REFERENCES

British Film Institute. *Britain on Film*. Accessed 29 May 2021. https://www2.bfi.org.uk/britain-on-film.

Caquard, Sébastien & Naud, Daniel. 2014. "A Spatial Typology of Cinematographic Narratives". *Modern Cartography Series 5* (December): 161–74. https://doi.org/10.1016/B978-0-444-62713-1.00011-8.

Castro, Teresa. 2009. "Cinema's Mapping Impulse: Questioning Visual Culture". *Cartographic Journal*, The 46 (February): 9–15. https://doi.org/10.1179/000870409X415598.

Clarke, David. 2005. *The Cinematic City*. Routledge.

Conley, Tom. 2007. *Cartographic Cinema*. Minneapolis, US: University of Minnesota Press. http://ebookcentral.proquest.com/lib/qub/detail.action?docID=331684.

Conley, Tom. 2011. "The 39 Steps and the Mental Map of Classical Cinema". In *Rethinking Maps*. Routledge. https://doi.org/10.4324/9780203876848-14.

Corner, James. 2011. "The Agency of Mapping: Speculation, Critique and Invention". In *The Map Reader*, edited by Martin Dodge, Rob Kitchin, and Chris Perkins, 89–101. Chichester, UK: John Wiley & Sons, Ltd. https://doi.org/10.1002/9780470979587.ch12.

Cousins, Mark. *I am Belfast*. 2015. BFI Player. Directed by Mark Cousins. UK: Canderblinks Film and Music, Hopscotch Films

Culture Northern Ireland. "Famous Belfast Stores: The Co-Op". Accessed 20 May 2021.

Keiller, Patrick. 2007. "Film as Spatial Critique". In *Critical Architecture*, edited by Jane Rendell, Jonathan Hill, Mark Dorrian, and Murray Fraser, 1st edition. Routledge.

Koeck, Richard & Roberts, Les, eds. 2010. *The City and the Moving Image: Urban Projections*. Houndmills, Basingstoke, Hampshire; New York: Palgrave Macmillan.

Leotta, Alfio. 2016. "Navigating Movie (M)Apps: Film Locations, Tourism and Digital Mapping Tools". *M/C Journal* 19 (3). https://doi.org/10.5204/mcj.1084.

Mapping Cinematographic Territories. Accessed 20 April 2021. https://atlascineproject.wordpress.com/.

Penz, François. 2020. "Foreword". *In Narrating the City Mediated Representations of Architecture*, Urban Forms and Social Life, edited by Ayşegül Akçay Kavakoğlu, Türkan Nihan Haciömeroğlu, and Lisa Landrum.

PRONI Historical Maps. Accessed 25 April 2021. https://apps.spatialni.gov.uk/PRONI-Application/.

Reed, Carol. *Odd Man Out*. 1947. DVD. Directed by Carol Reed. UK: Two Cities Films.

Reelstreet. *Odd Man Out*. Accessed 20 April 2021. https://www.reelstreets.com/films/odd-man-out/.

Roberts, Les & Hallam, Julia. 2013. "Film and Spatiality: Outline of a New Empiricism". In *Locating the Moving Image: New Approaches to Film and Place*, January 1–30.

Shiel, Mark & Fitzmaurice, Tony. 2011. *Cinema and the City: Film and Urban Societies in a Global Context*. John Wiley & Sons.

The HoMER Network. Accessed 20 April 2021. http://homernetwork.org/.

Thoughtbot. 2014. "Analyzing Minard's Visualization of Napoleon's 1812 March". Accessed 20 May 2021. https://thoughtbot.com/blog/analyzing-minards-visualization-of-napoleons-1812-march.

Ulster Architectural Heritage. "Jennymount Spinning Mill". Accessed 29 May 2021. https://www.ulsterarchitecturalheritage.org.uk/case-studies/jennymount-spinning-mill/.

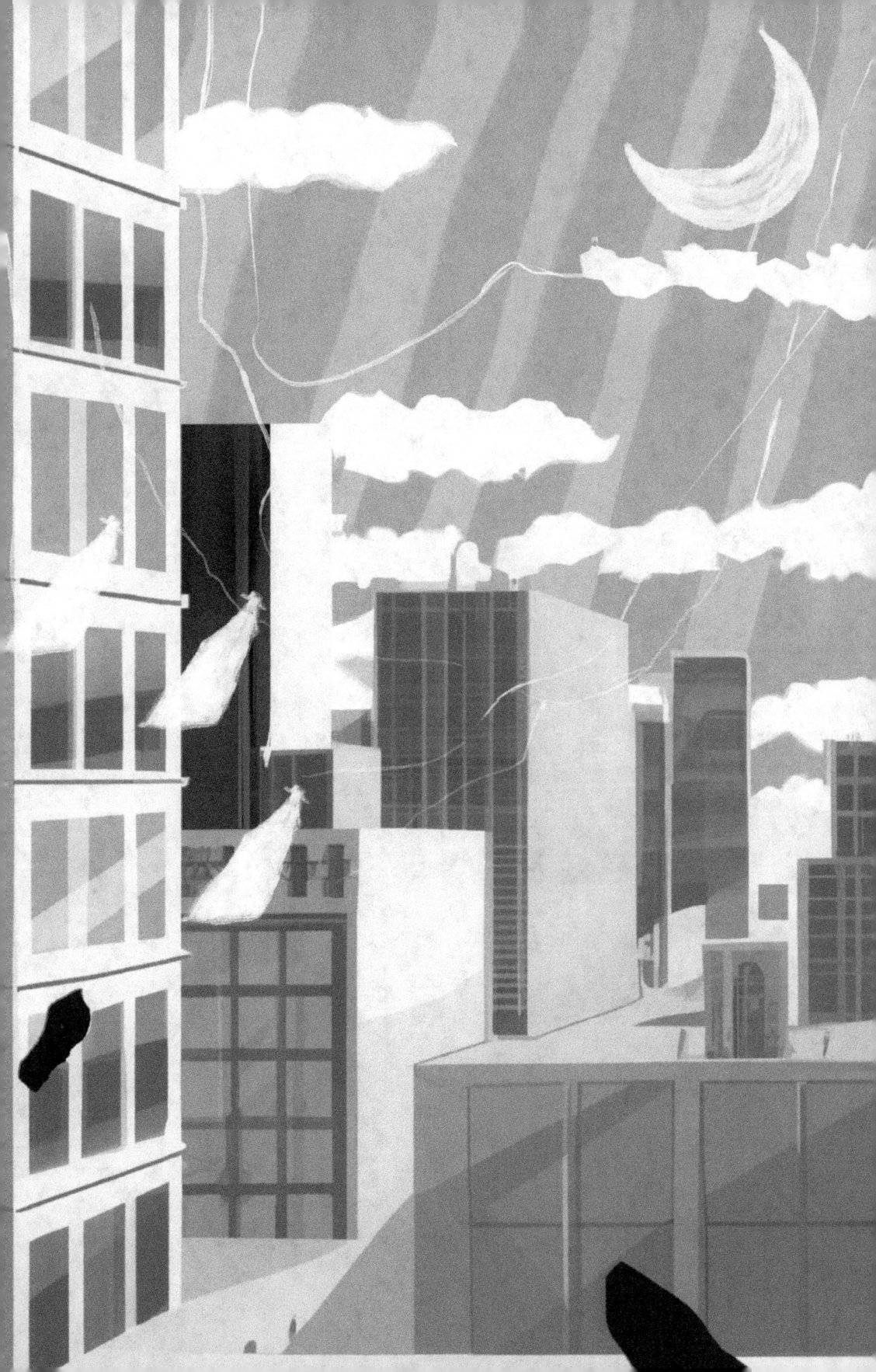

Norberg-Schulz' Elements of Space
in *Dark City*

Gul Kacmaz Erk

GUL KACMAZ ERK is a senior lecturer and programme director in Architecture at Queen's University Belfast. With work/life experience in Ireland, Netherlands, Turkey, UK and USA, she has been conducting research in two interdisciplinary areas: cinematic architecture and humanitarian architecture. Before joining Queen's in 2011, she worked professionally as an architect in Istanbul and Amsterdam, researched at the University of Pennsylvania, University College Dublin and ZK/U Berlin, and taught at Philadelphia University, Delft University of Technology and Izmir University of Economics in the areas of Architectural Design, and History, Theory and Criticism. Gul studied Architecture at Istanbul Technical University and Middle East Technical University. She leads CACity: Cinema and Architecture in the City Research Group (www.cacity.org), organises Walled Cities film festivals and conducts urban filmmaking workshops: https://pure.qub.ac.uk/en/persons/gul-kacmaz-erk.

As a spatial and temporal art, cinema includes representational space. With a critical gaze at the existing norms of architecture, science fiction films create new spatial horizons. They extend the borders of the concept by envisioning the space of the future or of the non-existent. Depicting what is to come, sci-fi is a critique of existing spatial ideas, which are driven from the physical limitations of Earth such as gravity, proximity to the sun, available materials, and changes in light and temperature. Science fiction reflects its time, not the future. Film architecture has been a laboratory for the exploration of architecture and the city (Vidler 2000, 99). In a world where what is imagined is realised, the spaces designed for films do not wait long to find their places in real life. With this observation in view, SF cinema is introduced as a medium to open up a discussion about architectural space. This chapter explores futuristic (or historical?) spaces represented in Alex Proyas' 1998 science fiction film *Dark City*. The traces of Christian Norberg-Schulz' elements of space are identified in the film. The connection between the philosophies of Norberg-Schulz and Martin Heidegger frames the discussion.

Norberg-Schulz' Conception of Space

The concept of space first appeared in architectural theory as late as 1893, and Christian Norberg-Schulz (1926-2000) is one of the leading space theorists of the twentieth century. He is a Norwegian architect, historian and theorist, and a follower of German philosopher Martin Heidegger. He was a student of Swiss art historian Sigfried Giedion; Norberg-Schulz' interest in space stems from Giedion. In his studies, Norberg-Schulz deals with existentialism, psychology, phenomenology of environment, and behavioural sciences. He was a student of German architect Walter Gropius in Harvard and of another Modernist German architect, Mies van der Rohe, in Chicago. He worked with engineer Luici Nervi in Italy. He was a professor of architecture in Oslo School of Architecture. He edited *Byggekunst*, the national architectural journal of Norway. Apart from phenomenology, he was interested in the Italian Baroque, Modern Architecture and Norwegian Architecture.

In *Genius Loci: Towards a Phenomenology of Architecture* published in 1979, Norberg-Schulz defines space as a system of places. Place/locality is an integral part of existence and a concrete term for the environment. A place is a space with a distinct character, not abstract, scientific or mentally constructed, but qualitative and phenomenological. Places are the spaces where life occurs.

Dwelling on the other hand is the purpose of architecture; the architect's task is to create meaningful places and help people to dwell. When people dwell, they are located in space and exposed to a certain environment. The characteristics of this environment influence them, and the place contributes to the development of people's identities. Without places, life could not take place. 'A work of architecture is therefore not an abstract organization of space; … it brings the inhabited landscape close to man, and lets him dwell poetically, which is the ultimate aim of architecture' (Norberg-Schulz 1988, 48). A person's identity depends on their belonging to a place (Norberg-Schulz 1988, 16; 1984, 5-6). This idea is crucial in the discussion of *Dark City*.

The philosophy of Heidegger (1889-1976) is the foundation of Norberg-Schulz' understanding of architecture. Accordingly, before moving on to his elements of space, the chapter will focus on Heidegger's approach to architecture, which is introduced to architectural theory by Norberg-Schulz himself. Heidegger did not only influence Norberg-Schulz but also many other thinkers including Hans-Georg Gadamer, Jean-Paul Sartre, Maurice Merleau-Ponty, Jacques Derrida and Michel Foucault. His work became key to the growth of existentialism, hermeneutics, deconstruction, and postmodernism. Being and Time (*Sein und Zeit*) published in 1927 is considered as his best piece of work. Some of the architectural concepts he focuses on in his writings are being, *da-sein* (being-(t) here), existence, thingness of things, and time.

In his well-known article, 'Building Dwelling Thinking' (*Bauen Wohnen Denken*), first presented in 1951, Heidegger argues that building is really dwelling, which is the basic character of being. He explains his argument through language (Heidegger, 1978, 324-25): 'The Old High German word for building, *buan*, means to dwell. This signifies to remain, to stay in a place... *Bauen* originally means to dwell... What then does *ich bin* mean? The old word *bauen*, to which the *bin* belongs, answers: *ich bin, du bist* means I dwell, you dwell... To be a human being means to be on the earth as a mortal. It means to dwell.' Hence etymologically building, dwelling, and being are the same (Heidegger, 1978, 324-38).

This is how Norberg-Schulz derives the concept of place from Heidegger's philosophy. Heidegger (1978, 332) explains, 'Only something *that is itself a location* can make space for a site. The location is not already there before the bridge is...Thus the bridge does not first come to a location to stand in it; rather, a location comes into existence only by virtue of the bridge.' Thus one cannot say that there is a site to build on, rather the building defines and creates a location. Norberg-Schulz quotes Heidegger: 'The bridge ... does not just connect banks that are already there. The banks emerge as banks only as the bridge crosses the stream.' He continues: 'The bridge thus makes a *place* come into presence, at the same time as its elements emerge as what they are' (Norberg-Schulz 1988, 42); 'the landscape as such gets its value *through* the bridge. Before, the meaning of the landscape was 'hidden,' and the building of the bridge brings it out into the open' (Norberg-Schulz 1984, 18). Therefore, the essence of a space comes not from the void itself but from the place, which is the site, or the location, of the building. Spaces receive their essential being from locations (Heidegger, 1978, 332).

For Heidegger (1978, 331), a building is a thing: "Gathering or assembly, by an ancient word of our language, is called 'thing.' The bridge is a thing." And the space, *raum*, is a void, an emptiness: '*Raum, Rum*, means a place cleared or freed for settlement and lodging. A space is something that has been made room for, something that is cleared and free, namely, within a boundary, Greek *peras*. A boundary is not that at which something stops but, as the Greeks recognized, the boundary is that from which something *begins its essential unfolding*' (Heidegger, 1978, 332). Accordingly, there is a strong tie between space and its boundaries which are defined by both the building and the site.

There is a link between the dweller and the space. For Heidegger, a three-dimensional mathematical construction of space (devoid of people and place/location) is markedly abstract: 'space is not something that faces man. It is neither an external object nor an inner experience. It is not that there are men, and over and above them *space*' (1978, 334). Heidegger sees people and space as one and links them through dwelling; "because it produces things as locations, building is closer to the essence of spaces and to the essential origins of 'space' than any geometry and mathematics" (1978, 336). As a result, architecture captures the essence of space much better than maths since buildings create places (Heidegger, 1978, 333-36). Norberg-Schulz explains the link between his and Heidegger's architectural theories (1984, 5):

> I owe to Heidegger the concept of *dwelling*; … 'dwelling', in an existential sense, is the purpose of architecture. Man dwells when he can orientate himself within and identifies himself with an environment, or, in short, when he experiences the environment as meaningful. Dwelling therefore implies something more than 'shelter' … the task of the architect is to create meaningful places, whereby he helps man to dwell.

In *Architecture: Meaning and Place*, first published in 1986, Norberg-Schulz talks about four elements of space: The first is physical space that is physical existence as it is. This is a quantitative (mathematical) space concept, which can be measured. The second is perceptual space which is the temporary space the user perceives. Perceptual space is related to experience and has a subjective value. It changes as to the perceiver and as to the mood of the perceiver. Norberg-Schulz (1974, 30) articulates 'we all have *different* worlds. When we *judge* the house in front of us, it often seems as if we were looking at completely different objects.' The idea that a similar world is given to all of us a *priori*, Norberg-Schulz believes, is a misunderstanding. The third element is existential space that is related to the basic relation of a person and their environment. Existential space, for instance, the meaning of the concept of home, is abstract and permanent; it does not change with the immediate situation or changing conditions. It has its own stability and order. It stands for one's concept or image of the environment. For that reason, Louis Kahn asks what a building wants to be. Architecture is a concretisation of existential space. Finally, Norberg-Schulz defines conceptual space that is the space concept of specialists like architects, economists, and mathematicians. The conceptual space of an architect is different, say, from the conceptual space of a physicist or filmmaker (1974, 31, 97; 1984, 5; 1988, 14-29).

Proyas' *Dark City*

Dark City is Alex Proyas' (1963-) third feature film, which he made in Sydney, Australia in 1998. Proyas was born in Egypt, and his parents are Greek. When he was three, they moved to Sydney where he grew up. His other well-known films are *I, Robot* (2004) which is an adaptation from an Isaac Asimov book, and *The Crow* (1994) that he adapted from a popular underground comic book. Bruce Lee's son Brandon Lee who was the main character of *The Crow* sadly lost his life in an accident during the shooting. *Dark City* is based on a story by Proyas himself; he wrote the screenplay with Lem Dobbs and David Goyer.

Dark City is a science fiction film. It is also categorised as a *future noir* that is a contemporary version of *film noir*. *Film noir* (literally black movie) is a Hollywood genre of the 1940s and 1950s that is influenced by German Expressionism of the 1920s. It is a dark, typically black-and-white crime film that takes place in an urban setting. It usually includes a murder and crime investigation. People are trapped in unwanted situations, and the city is designed as a labyrinth or maze. Sharp angles, strong light-dark contrasts, and dramatic shadow patterning are important characteristics of *film noir* and *Dark City* (Figure 1).

Some scenes and spaces of the film inspired the Wachowskis for *The Matrix* which was shot a year later. The staircase where Neo mentions 'deja vu' is the staircase of Murdoch's apartment building. The roof chase scene of Trinity has similarities to Murdoch's roof chase.

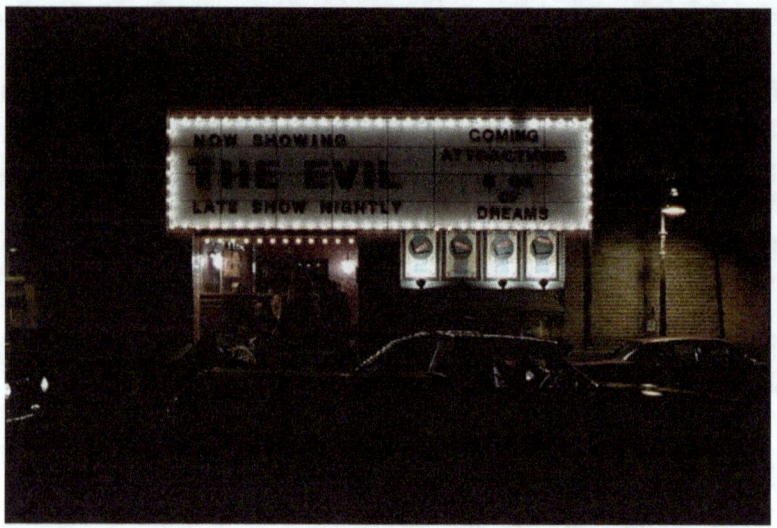

Figure 1: The urban *film noir* environment of *Dark City.*

Dark City is also a thought-provoking example of urban exospace cinema. In 2004, I proposed the term exospace in my doctoral thesis to define extra-terrestrial spaces. Exospace is a space designed by humans, or aliens, for living beyond Earth's atmosphere (Kacmaz Erk 2014). Labels like science fiction, future noir and exospace film however are not enough to define a complex movie like *Dark City*. Just like Fritz Lang's *Metropolis* (1926) and Ridley Scott's *Blade Runner* (1982), *Dark City* has multiple layers, which make it more than an exemplar of sci-fi or noir cinema. The official website of the film (http://www.darkcity.com) told its story as follows:

> *Dark City* is a tale of mythic proportions about one man's battle to reclaim his destiny. John Murdoch awakens alone in a strange hotel to find that he is wanted for a series of brutal murders. The problem is that he cannot remember whether he committed the murders or not. In fact, most of his memories have completely vanished, and for one brief moment, he is convinced that he has gone

stark raving mad. Pursued by Detective Bumstead, Murdoch seeks to unravel the twisted riddle of his identity. As he edges closer to solving the mystery, he stumbles upon a fiendish underworld controlled by a group of ominous beings collectively known as The Strangers. These shadow-like figures possess the ability to stop time and alter people's perceptions -- a process known as Tuning. Through an evolutionary anomaly, Murdoch is also imbued with this power and thus, he alone is able to resist The Strangers' control over his mind. And for that, he must be destroyed. With the help of the inscrutable Doctor Schreber, Murdoch is able to stay a step ahead of his adversaries while he slowly pieces together the labyrinthine puzzle of his past -- his bittersweet childhood, his love for his estranged wife Emma and the key to a hideous series of murders which he is suspected of committing.

One crucial aspect that the synopsis above does not reveal is that *Dark City* is constantly built, un-built and rebuilt, and as Heidegger says, 'The buildings bring the earth as the inhabited landscape close to man' (in Norberg-Schulz 1988, 44). Proyas had the inspiration for a morphing city on the set of *The Crow* when they moved around scale models for a roof-top scene:

> I remember exactly when I got the idea. I was standing on the set of *The Crow* and we had built this roof-top set because we did not have a great budget we just build these one-third scale buildings that we moved around on wheels so after we did a shot, we'd move them all around so we could make the background look different so we could shoot different scenes and you would not see the same building in the background all the time. I remember standing there on the set and watching these buildings just move, because you could not see the guys moving them, so all you could see was just the building sliding across the set. And I just remember thinking that was really cool and I'd have to use that in some way. So I stuck it into this movie… I loved a city where you could open a door and there would not be a building on the other side' (Proyas 1988).

Gathering, a concept Norberg-Schulz derives from Heidegger, is beneficial to appreciate *Dark City*: 'Gathering' means that things are brought together, that is, that they are moved from one place to another. This transportation is in general done by means of symbolization, but it may also consist in a concrete displacement of buildings and things' (Norberg-Schulz 1984, 169). The strangers *gather* information using *gathered* buildings via *gathered* memories. They study the memories of humans to piece together a city that will help them to understand what makes them human.

Dark City Through Norberg-Schulz' Elements of Space

For Norberg-Schulz, space is an integral part of existence. As humans live, they are simultaneously located in space and exposed to a certain spatial character. Experienced spaces influence people; they transform their identities. Architects' job is to create meaningful spaces and help people to dwell. In *Dark City*, the strangers experiment with how memories affect character, psyche and emotions. For their investigation, they not only rebuild memories humans possess (new memories are 'injected' into their brains every night) but also the setting they live in. They simulate environments, including rooms, buildings, streets, even a whole city, to study human nature. After all, as Norberg-Schulz believes, without understanding it in a spatial and temporal context, it is not possible to arrive at any cognition. Accordingly, the strangers constantly un build and rebuild the city to provide places for humans to dwell. Although their aim is not to study the human-space relationship, they are aware that to understand human nature they need to study them in their own spaces. Since they use bits and pieces of humans' memories to assemble buildings, *Dark City* is a random collage of past times (Figure 2) (Norberg-Schulz 1984, 19; 1988, 29).

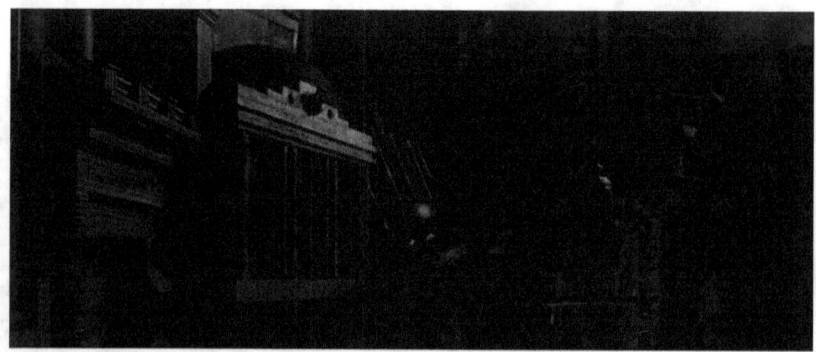

Figure 2: The city as a collage of past times in *Dark City*.

To be a human being, Heidegger believes, is to be on the earth as a mortal. To be human means to dwell/live. For that reason, the strangers are building a city for humans. By doing so, they hope to understand what it means to be a human being. 'We do not dwell because [they] have built, but [they] build and have built because we dwell, that is, because we are *dwellers*' (I took the liberty to change 'we' to 'they' in Heidegger, 1978, 326). Accordingly, the action of building is in itself already an action of dwelling. In order to build (for humans) the strangers have to think like humans, and dwell like humans. As a result, they start living in the dead bodies of human beings. A human head becomes the space for the alien body of a stranger. They are, after all, incompatible with the habitat that is suitable for humans (Figure 3) (Heidegger, 1978, 324-26).

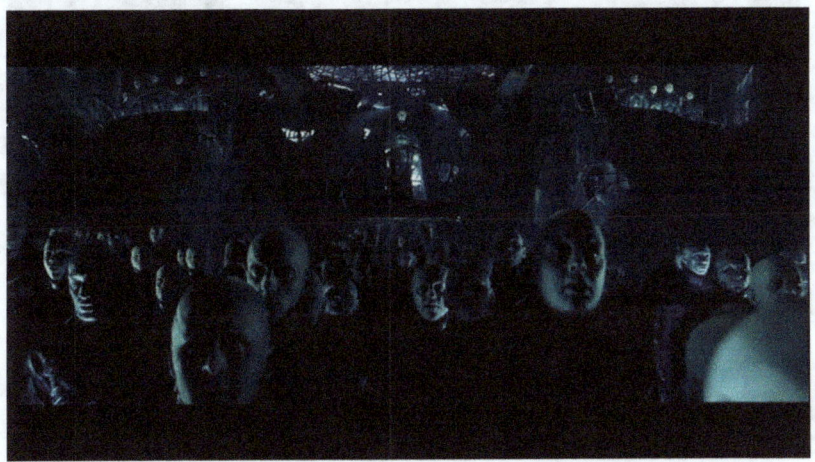

Figure 3: Strangers living in human bodies in *Dark City*.

Norberg-Schulz proposes identification as a psychological function of architecture. Identification is the basis for one's sense of belonging; people have to identify themselves with their environment. For the environment to become a meaningful *milieu*, it has to offer rich possibilities of identification. Dwelling means belonging to a concrete place. Meaning 'depends on *identification*, and implies a sense of 'belonging.' It therefore constitutes the basis of dwelling; … man's most fundamental need is to experience his existence as meaningful' (Norberg-Schulz 1988, 166). Alienation is a result of one's loss of identification with the natural and human-made things that form their environment. Murdoch feels lost. He is lost in space because firstly he lost his memory and he cannot identify himself with the city, and secondly, he witnesses the tuning of the city. Therefore, there is no city left for him to identify with. His sense of belonging has disappeared. He cannot reach the beach he remembers from his childhood. He cannot recall the people around him. He does not know the shops, the streets, and the city (Figure 4) (Norberg-Schulz 1988, 22-24, 168; 1984, 19).

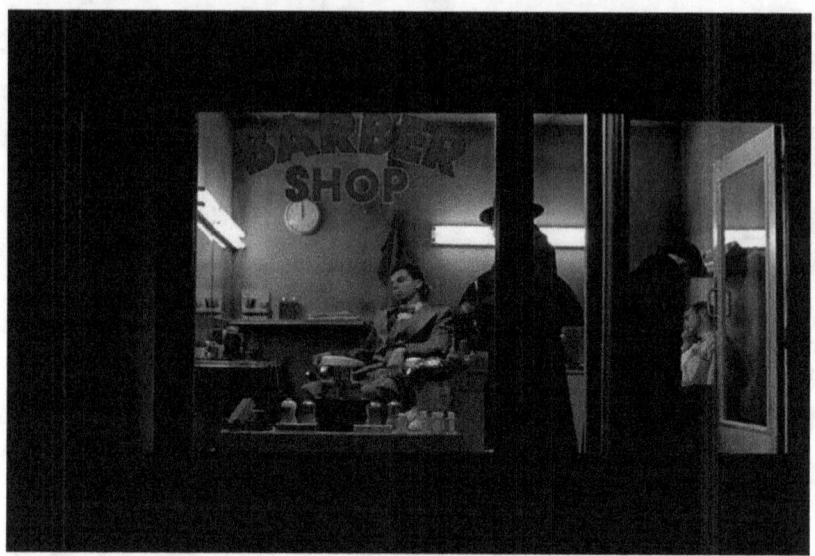

Figure 4: The barber shop around the corner in *Dark City*, or the sense of familiarity and belonging.

Norberg-Schulz claims that 'the human environment is two-dimensional; ... the third dimension is basically *different* from horizontal extension. [It is] hidden behind the visual or intellectual horizon of the individual' (1988, 31). Only when the detective is sacrificed by 'falling out' of the city, the third dimension is revealed, and the audience is able to grasp the nature of *Dark City*. They get the answers to Murdoch's questions when they see what is above and below the constantly rebuilt horizontal maze since a "work of architecture is hence characterized by 'what it is' in relation to its surroundings" (Norberg-Schulz 1988, p. 33). The city is not on Earth; it is not even part of a planet. It is a flat outerspace habitat supported with an infrastructure underneath. It floats miserably in the darkness of outerspace all by itself (Figs. 5-6).

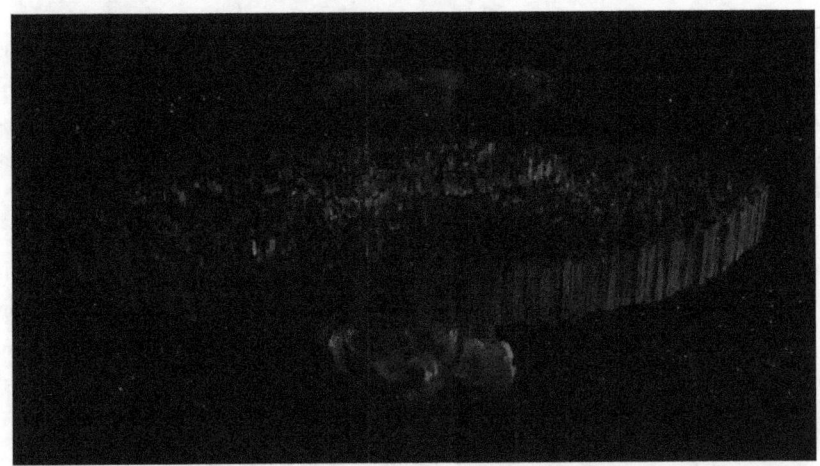

Figure 5: A 'worldless' city in *Dark City*.

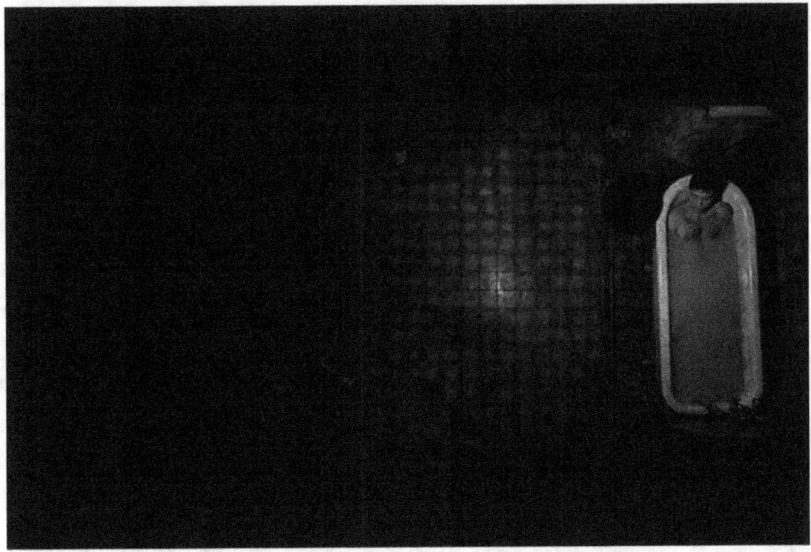

Figure 6: A 'homeless' man in *Dark City*.

Physical Space

The strangers in *Dark City* examine tangible 'things' by studying the personal belongings of humans to comprehend their nature (Figure 7). Referring
to Heidegger's writings, Norberg-Schulz talks about how things tell several stories and reveal truth. In 'Thinking on Architecture,' he writes 'Hie-
degger wants to remind us of the fact that our everyday life-world really
consists of concrete 'things,' rather than the abstractions of science' (1988,
42). In that sense, it is possible to say, the strangers follow a Heideggerian approach in their experiments (Norberg-Schulz 1984, 185). Following
Heidegger, and opposing to a scientific and abstract approach to architecture,
Norberg-Schulz (1988, 13-14) debates returning to the things themselves:

> Life in fact does not consist of quantities and numbers, but of concrete things
> such as people, animals, flowers and trees, of stone, earth, wood and water, of
> towns, streets and houses, of sun, moon and stars, of clouds, of night and day
> and changing seasons… What we need is therefore first of all a better aware-
> ness, a better understanding of the world.

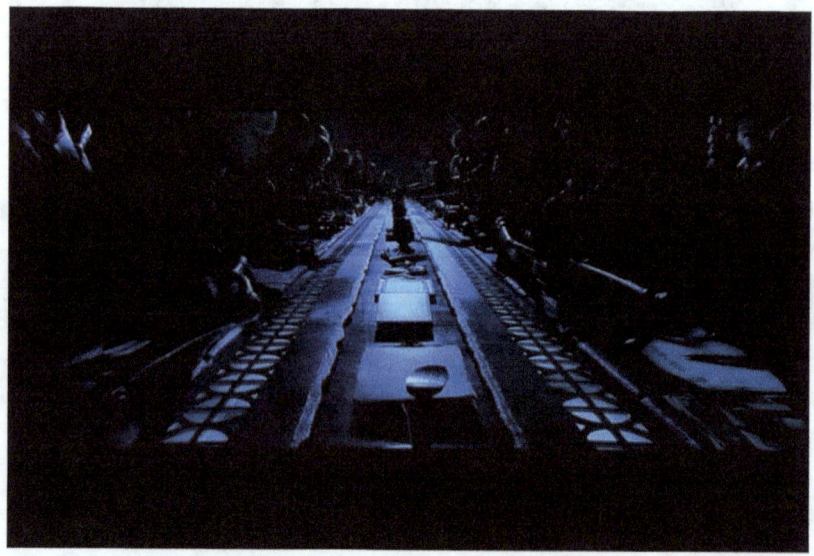

Figure 7: Strangers examining the personal belongings of humans on
an assembly line in *Dark City*.

If physical space is physical existence as it is, most of the spaces in *Dark City*, houses, offices, and streets, are simulated spaces. They look real, however they are part of the staged architecture 'tuned' by the strangers for humans to dwell. Therefore, no part of the morphing city is a real physical space in the conventional meaning of the term. The whole city is a platform that is rebuilt every single night using the strangers' collective psychokinetic powers and underground machines. Their underworld, on the other hand, is a physical space, as Norberg-Schulz defines it, and an exospace. The duality between the simulated human city and alien underground city is emphasised using different colour plates, yellow-green for the humans and blue-green for the strangers (Figs. 8-9).

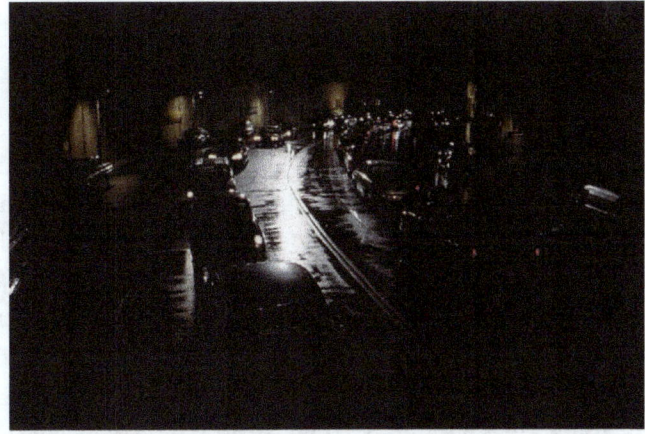

Figure 8: The fake human city in *Dark City*.

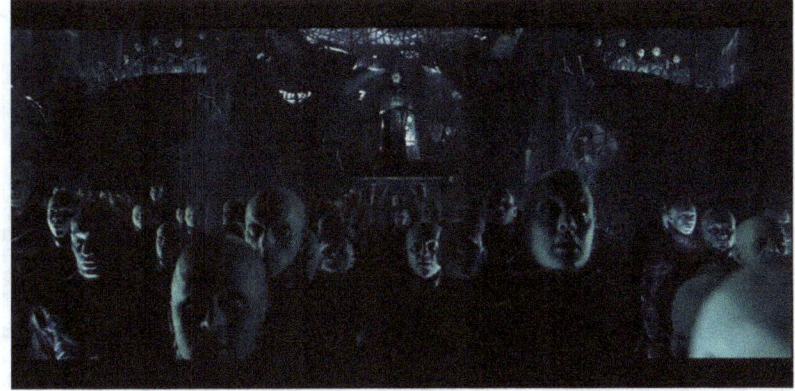

Figure 9: The underground city of aliens in *Dark City*.

Everything starts with physical space. We understand and give a meaning to Norberg-Schulz' other elements of space as to our comprehension of the physical. In *Dark City*, by changing the norms of the physical world, Proyas provides a foundation to question the meaning of physical, perceptual, existential, and conceptual spaces.

Perceptual Space

Throughout the film, John Murdoch knows that what he perceives is not physical reality. The film is the story of his hunt for the truth, a search for the real physical space. As to Norberg-Schulz, perceptual space is a temporary space that the user perceives. However, not only perceptual space but also physical space is temporary in *Dark City*. The film proposes multiple perceptual spaces for humans to see and to experience urban living. It depicts how space perception can be altered and misled. This constant resetting and endless tabula rasa cause alienation. Norberg-Schulz refers to an Italian film, Federico Fellini's *Orchestra Rehearsal* (1978), to discuss the concept of alienation. He links the film, in which the rehearsal of a chamber orchestra ends up with the collapse of the medieval chapel they play in, to disintegration and confusion. Fellini's and Proyas' films have commonalities within this context; in both films the sense of belonging and identity are lost. This loss is represented by a world going into pieces (Figure 10) (Norberg-Schulz 1984, 11).

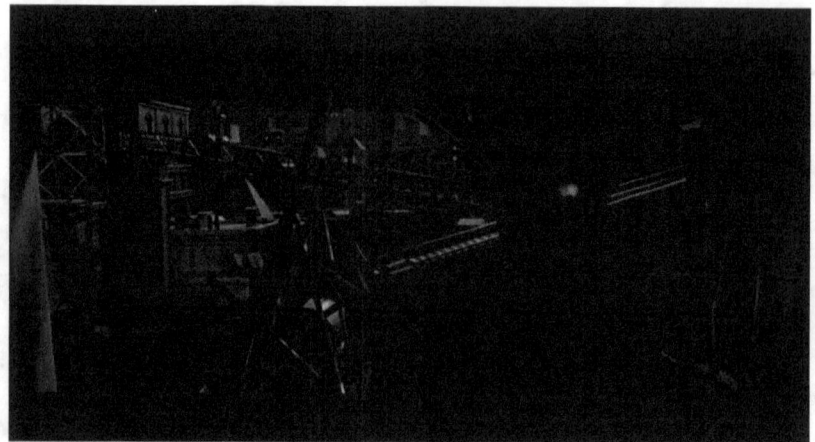

Figure 10: A city going into pieces in *Dark City*.

'We see and hear what we expect, and in this way the given stimulus be-comes meaningful' (Norberg-Schulz 1974, 50). This is how the citizens of *Dark City* survive. Based on their limited, rather shallow memory re-freshed at midnight, they tend to believe in what they see. Perception is in-adequate in front of the unknown. It 'is an unreliable companion who does not mediate an objective and simple world' (Norberg-Schulz 1974, 28, 37).

The physical changes of the city Murdoch experiences make existence 'mean-ingless' for him. He feels 'homeless' because 'he does not any longer belong to a meaningful totality' (Norberg-Schulz 1988, 12). He has lost his sense of belonging and his identity. He does not have a world that has a qualitative to-tality and that he feels a part of (Norberg-Schulz 1988, 11-12). Only by the end of the film the audience realises *Dark City* is not a city on Earth but an artificial world. Murdoch and the detective tear down the wall behind the Shell Beach illustration to discover what is beyond the limits of the city, a theme the film shares with *The Truman Show* shot in the States by Peter Weir the same year. The rootless and limited presence of the metropolis, which resembles a reck-lessly uprooted plant, is breath-taking (Figure 5).

Existential Space

As Norberg-Schulz puts it, existential space is about one's relation to their environment; it is an image of the environmental structure. Human life de-pends on the establishment of an existential space. It is an abstract and perma-nent concept that does not change as to different examples. The film revolves around several houses, Murdoch and Emma's home, Uncle Karl's home, the prostitute's home and the one that is converted from a small house to a large mansion in the tuning scene. Though these dwellings are all different in ap-pearance and content, they all evoke the same feeling, a private space for an individual to live; 'home is still connected with those values which are known to us and give us security' (Norberg-Schulz 1988, 24, 37; 1984, 5). French philosopher Gaston Bachelard (1958, 5) also focuses on the notion of home:

> [T]he sheltered being gives perceptible limits to his shelter. He experiences
> the house in its reality and in its virtuality, by means of thought and dreams.
> ... An entire past comes to dwell in a new house. ... Through dreams, the vari-

ous dwelling-places in our lives co-penetrate and retain the treasures of former days. And after we are in the new house, when memories of other places we have lived in come back to us, we travel to the land of Motionless Childhood.

In the tuning scene, as time stops and the city is rebuilt, the strangers start to convert the house that belongs to a working-class family into an upper-class mansion. The little dining table gets bigger; delicious food and candles are added. The modest fireplace and the room get larger and tall. Architectural materials and the size of the house change in front of our eyes. As a result, physicality and perceptual space change. However, the existential space, the concept of home, stays the same. The same conversation continues at the dining table after the tuning (Figs. 11-12).

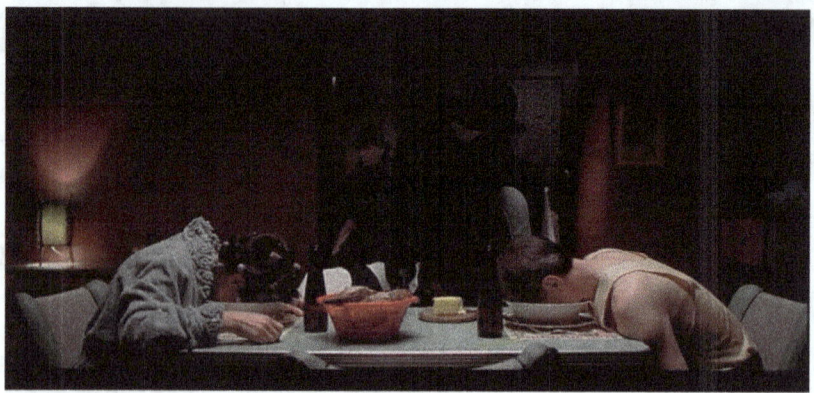

Figure 11: Un-building a 'home' for a working-class family in *Dark City*.

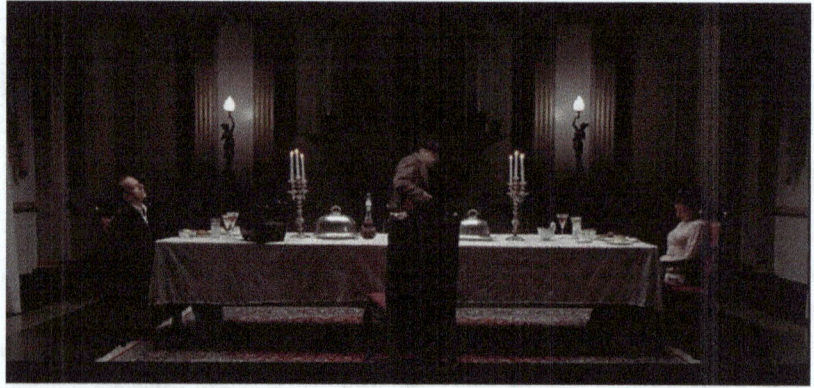

Figure 12: Re-building a 'home' for an upper-class family in *Dark City*.

Shell Beach, defined as a sea-side town where Murdoch grew up, is an 'image' of an existential space. It is a beautiful piece of nature and a missed place to go. It is an escape from urban life, a happy place. It is a destination to have fun and to enjoy nature and life. It is not significant that it is a beach, forest or mountain. It is *that particular place* that one would go to escape from the troubles of their daily routine (Figure 13).

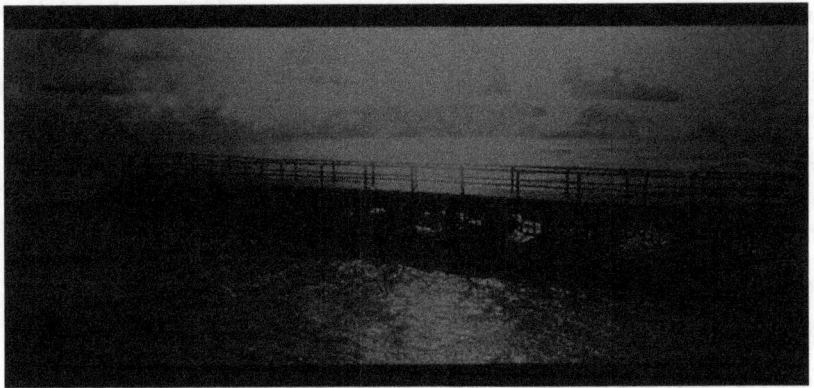

Figure 13: Shell Beach in *Dark City*.

Cinema, as a medium, makes use of existential spaces. Using quite few signifiers, film can evoke the image of a barber shop, night club, or hospital. Without the concept of existential space, it would be hard to tell a story in two hours. Unlike literature, cinema does not say that the characters are in an airport, cinema *shows* them in an airport using audio-visual signifiers of an airport like big signs, check-in counters and regular announcements. Cinematic narration is built upon the concept of existential space.

Conceptual Space

Norberg-Schulz defines conceptual space as the space concept of specialists like architects, economists and mathematicians. When one reviews the literature on space in architectural theory and in film studies, they easily see that the space concept of architects is different from the space concept of filmmakers. Architects talk about various philosophical aspects of space, whereas in film studies, the physical conditions of a set are the primary spatial concern. Film space is theorised elsewhere; it would be fair to say space is not seen as a major filmic element in film theory.

Dark City represents the opposing space concepts of strangers and humans. Physically the strangers are alien creatures, and their spatial needs and conventions are different. Unlike humans, they do not like daylight, water and moisture. They are not bound to gravity; they can fly. They can alter physical reality using their brain power. What they do with their power is to create perceptual spaces for humans according to humans' existential spaces. For that reason, *Dark City* looks like a human city (from the past), whereas the underground city of the strangers has its own rules and looks. Proyas (1998) states: 'The city was designed based on (the inhabitants') memories, so the retro feel to it was very strong because they used elements from all different ages of memory and blended them together' (Figs. 2, 14).

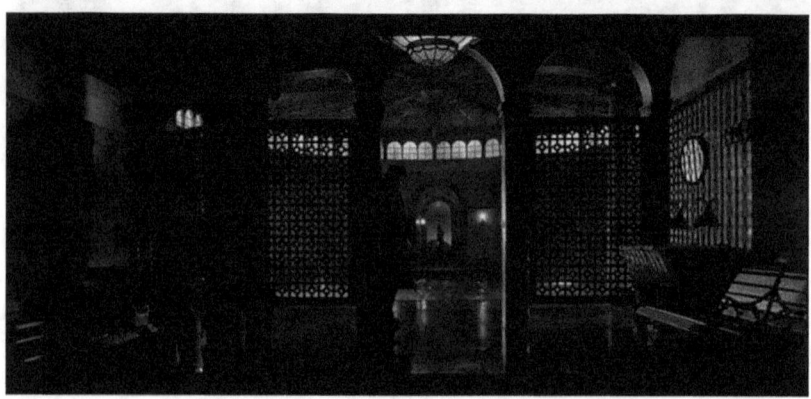

Figure 14: The strangers' city in *Dark City*.

To conclude, films have many actors, and space is one of them. Architecture is not merely a backdrop filling the gaps between the actors. When used effectively, space acts. Few directors including Wes Anderson, Terry Gilliam, Peter Greenaway, Alfred Hitchcock, Stanley Kubrick and Andrei Tarkovsky benefit from the potential of film space. This study has brought forth the imagined architectural designs of *Dark City*. Analysing this film in which space performs like an actor shows how sci-fi set design adds to cinematic narration and helps architects question the concept of space. Both Norberg-Schulz and Heidegger would enjoy *Dark City* in which the borders of the concept of space are questioned and extended.

Proyas' *Dark City* and its analysis from a spatial perspective provide a new perspective to the discussion regarding humans' relationship to the environment they live in. Asking (futuristic) questions starting with 'what if', the film investigates norms taken for granted. What if you wake up to a different life every morning? What if your house, workplace and entire city change at midnight? What if your memories are altered? How would you exist in such conditions? Would you belong to this place, or would you feel like a lab rat?

As Giedion, Bruno Zevi and Henri Lefebvre so well put it, a mere scientific understanding of architectural space does not provide a coherent and complete conception of space. For that reason, the conceptual space of architects is different from that of mathematicians. Norberg-Schulz proposes four different spaces. For him, a conception of space is possible when these spaces come together and are understood thoroughly. This is necessary for a better understanding of the world, since it is not possible to experience or describe reality as it is. Since the strangers design rooms, buildings, and cities by assuming architecture is merely physical space, they are mistaken. Its citizens accept *Dark City* as a physical space; as a result, they are alienated from this 'synthetic' environment (Norberg-Schulz 1988, 20).

In the end, what matters is people's conception of existential spaces; they are what they believe in. They come together and make up their conceptual space, through which people conceive and interact with the world. Existential space is an altered accumulation of perceptual spaces. For someone who has lived on the top floor of a high-rise building all their life, a farmhouse would not feel like home. Perceptual space, on the other hand, is at the intersection of what is actually out there (physical space) and one's past -their memories, hopes, and dreams. While one exists in (physical) space, conception of (perceptual) space exists within them. That is crucial for a sense of belonging and identification. *Dark City* brings forth questions of identity by simply shifting reality as we know it. What Norberg-Schulz (1988, 12) says about the modern world seems like the summary of the life in *Dark City*:

> [T]he loss of things and places makes up a loss of 'world.' Modern man becomes 'worldless,' and thus loses his own identity, as well as the sense of communication and participation. Existence is experienced as 'meaningless,' and man becomes 'homeless' because he does not any longer belong to a meaningful totality. Moreover he becomes 'careless,' since he does not feel the urge to protect and cultivate a world anymore.

REFERENCES

Bachelard, Gaston. 1958. *Poetics of Space*. Boston: Beacon Press.

Dark City Official Website. <http://www.darkcity.com> [accessed 19 March 2008].

Heidegger, Martin. 1978. *Basic Writings: Nine Key Essays plus the Introduction to Being and Time*. London: Routledge and Kegan Paul.

Kacmaz Erk, Gul. 2014. "Living in Exospace: ISS and Discovery 1." *The International Journal of Critical Cultural Studies*, 11 (1): 11-22. <https://cgscholar.com/bookstore/works/living-in-exospace>

Norberg-Schulz, Christian. 1988 [1986]. *Architecture: Meaning and Place*. New York: Electa/Rizzoli.

Norberg-Schulz, Christian. 1984 [1979]. *Genius Loci: Towards a Phenomenology of Architecture*. New York: Rizzoli.

Norberg-Schulz, Christian. 1974 [1965]. *Intensions in Architecture*. Cambridge, Massachusetts: MIT Press.

Proyas, Alex. 1998. *Dark City*. DVD. Directed by Alex Proyas. USA: Warner Bros.

Proyas, Alex. 1998. 'Visions of 'Strangers' Dance in his Head', interview with Rob Blackwelder, 13 February, *SPLICEDwire*, <http://www.splicedonline.com/features/proyas.html> [accessed 30 June 2012].

Vidler, Anthony. 2000. *Warped Space: Art, Architecture and Anxiety in Modern Culture*. Cambridge, London: The MIT Press.

SPACES OF THE
IMAGINATION

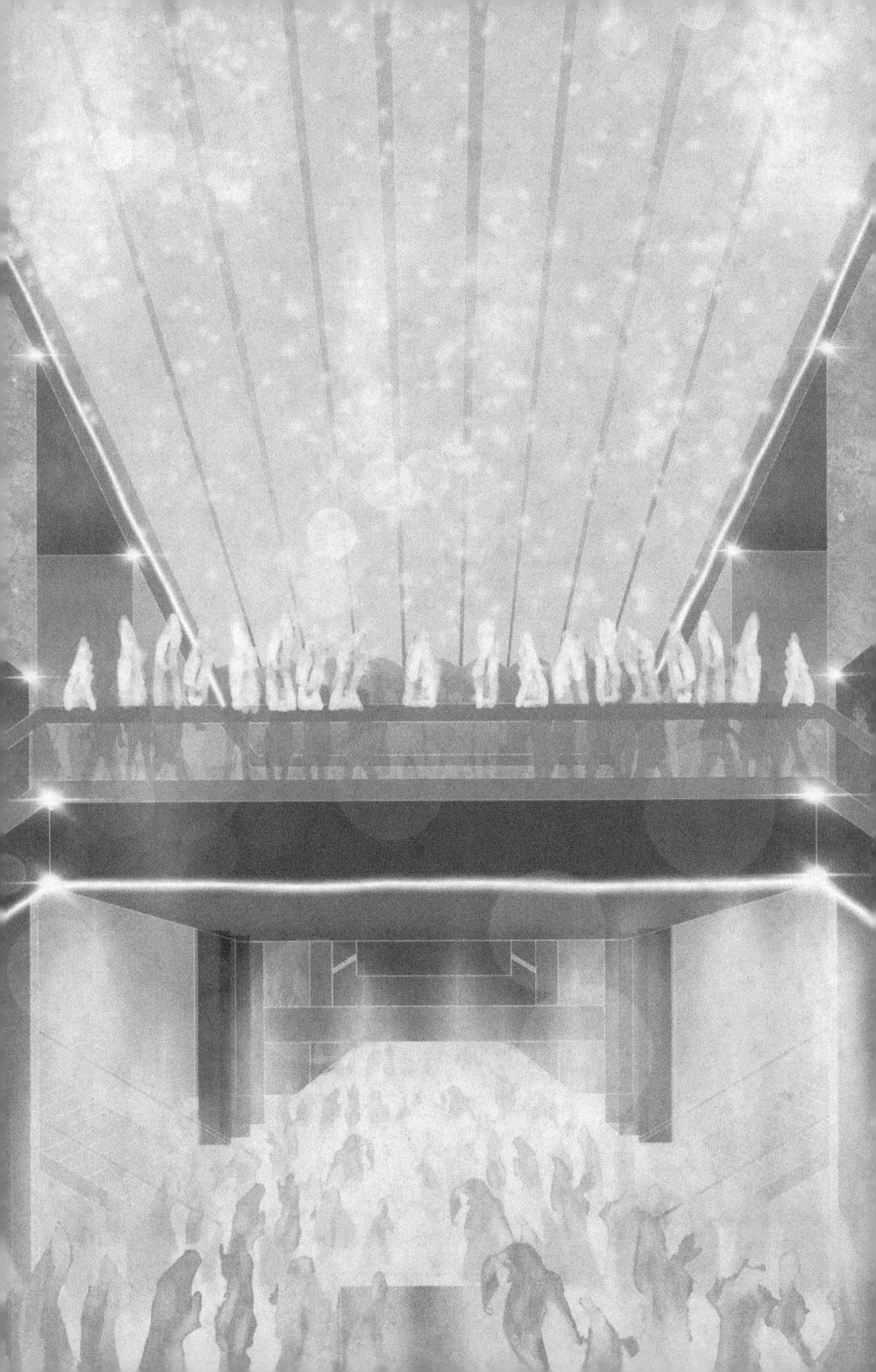

Plastic Realities:
Future Portrayed Through Architecture

Cormac McAteer

CORMAC MCATEER is an architect and former student of the School of Architecture at Queen's University Belfast. His career in the UK has thus far found Cormac involved in the design of commercial architecture, most notably the construction of a new central campus in the centre of Belfast for Ulster University. Cormac is an art and cinema enthusiast and has been inspired by a love of film and its inspirational imagery since childhood. He feels privileged to contribute to this book and would like to thank Dr. Gul Kacmaz Erk and Dr. Tom Hulme for all their support and guidance.

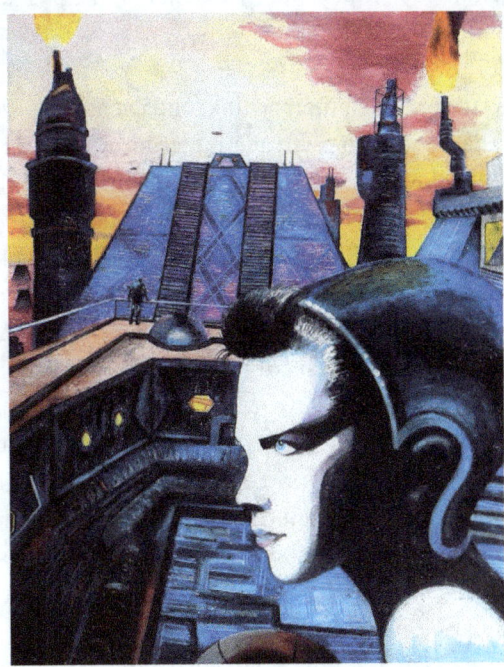

Figure 1: *Do Androids Dream of Electric Sheep*, 1968 Book Cover Oil Pastel (all illustrations are by the author)

Introduction

W hen future environments are shown in science fiction adaptations, they often portray a believably dystopian picture. Through
the investigation of architecture presented in film, and this architecture's connections with twentieth century design culture, this chapter
considers the relationship between imagined and real space. In doing so,
it considers why the believability of a dystopian future could be found in
past architecture. I reflect on the real-world influence of twentieth century
Modernist and Brutalist ideology on *Blade Runner* (1982) and *Total Recall*
(1990), considering how the forward-looking ideas and philosophies of
these movements informed later cinematic narrative ambitions. The chapter
also examines how the drawings and design imagery of these movements
filtered into representations on screen, and how the spatial relationships
between room, city and street connect to the character of futuristic environments. The aim is thus to appreciate why we, as audiences, identify with
dystopian surroundings in films and, by extension, the past architecture that
supposedly embodies that dystopia.

The films in this study share a literary link, chosen as they are on account of
their cinematic adaptation from written material by Philip K. Dick. Dick's
work is widely valued for its storytelling and his insightful social and moral
depictions of potential future societies. Ridley Scott's *Blade Runner* was
adapted from 'Do Androids Dream of Electric Sheep?' (1968) and Paul
Verhoeven's *Total Recall* from 'We Can Remember it for You Wholesale'
(1966). Exploring the Modernist societal visions that gave rise to new architectural forms aids my analysis of the built situations composed in both
films. Analysis of 1920s and 1930s Modernist backdrops, along with the
later 1960s and1970s postmodern developments, also situates each film's
architecture in its relevant real-world context. Attention is given to: American architects and designs, particularly those of Frank Lloyd Wright; examples of major European influence, such as Le Corbusier; inspirations from
the East, notably Japan; and the use of Brutalism in Latin America, specifically Mexico City. This contextual approach provides a background in
which to assess the cinematic urbanity of these films.

The Science Fiction Writing of Philip K. Dick
and Cinematic Adaptations

Science fiction writing came to fruition during the twentieth century, but few authors achieved such an impact on the genre as the American writer Philip K. Dick. Dick invented unreal accounts of future societies in his work, creating textual landscapes that expanded forth from the evolving reality in which he lived. The sense of actuality and truth contained in his literature is, for the most part, derived from everyday circumstances. Critics have commended his ability to explore often intangible connections to existential issues. It is Dick's mixture of reality and fiction - a distorted reality - that encouraged the use of his literary work in film adaptations. In related literary stratums, the movement defined as Cyberpunk materialised in the 1980s. As a specialised sub-genre of science fiction writing, it held an affiliation with Dick (despite his death in 1982) because of ideas realised and continued from themes of his 1960s work. With more specific yet also fantastical subject matter, such as violently troubled and nihilistic storylines, Cyberpunk emphasised an incorporation of virtual reality with pop culture and our relationships with technology, both artificial and essential. Cyberpunk expanded on earlier ideas of individual interaction with technology by focusing on system networks, connectivity and globalised information control. This in turn related to Modernist and Postmodern modes of architecture and thought, with Modernism representing the adherence to a singular style and Postmodernism assembling many different conditions together. Architecture has always had a productive relationship with science fiction literature; used as a central descriptive tool for cinematic situations, it often visualises an atmosphere for the literary mind's eye. The imagery deployed by architecture's depiction in film has thus subsequently linked notions of intimacy with built styles that aspired to represent emotions of dystopian and utopic future conditions: "sci-fi understands its use of fiction as a device for addressing the present, architecture believes its own fiction." Jacob (2011, Architects Journal) Like parallel conditions, twentieth century Modernist change and Dick's 1960s writing highlighted problematic living situations and future responses to their effects. On this, Gold states:

Grand Narratives are most plausible when validated by events taking place in the outside world. Widespread adoption of modernist principles in urban reconstruction programmes seemingly authenticated the historic triumph of modernism. Twenty years later popular discontent with the products of those principles made that position untenable (Gold 1997, 3).

Blade Runner depicts a dystopian society set in a future Los Angeles (year 2019). The main themes centre on humanity and our ability to empathise with the perceived limits of human existence. Its plausibly dystopian atmosphere is reflected in the vague disorder of the film's built landscape - the primary visual element in illustrating a society's future functioning. The real architecture within this film centres on the domestic spaces and interior homes of Frank Lloyd Wright. The depiction of disorder, however, is reminiscent of Philip K. Dick's 'Kipple': an all-encompassing term, coined in 'Do Androids Dream of Electric Sheep?', that is used to describe the age, decay, and condition that all matter and material move towards. 'Kipple' thus aims to demonstrate humanity's accumulation of outdated ideas; a terminal depreciation of possessions and property that ultimately are neglected with time. *Total Recall* is a slightly later science fiction film, but still firmly in the same cinematic era as *Blade Runner*. This film places the viewer in a controlled totalitarian future, the setting of which frames more recognisable societal infrastructures such as methods of transport. Verhoeven's focus on more formal architectural systems, and their management of human movement, is the visual impression that brings dystopia to an otherwise perceived utopian condition. In comparison to *Blade Runner*, the real architecture of *Total Recall* focuses on institutional buildings and public designed spaces, partially using buildings from Mexico City. 'Runnels,' another literary invention by Dick used in 'We Can Remember It for You Wholesale,' suggests a system of transport that promotes movement and order in the film's future world. *Total Recall*, as I demonstrate, teases an interpretation of these 'Runnels' using real architecture and infrastructure for the future society.

Modernist Movements in the early 20th Century

Modernism, and the mechanical motivation that first formed its ideology, was geared toward a single unifying architecture that aimed to create a systematic urbanism that, in turn, reflected a new technologically-conscious era. Renyer

Banham, a comprehensive twentieth century commentator and theorist, neatly summarises the movement's aims and shortcomings: "Based on the model of scientific method and its emphasis on calculated originality, the architecture of efficiency and standardisation replaced values of style and comfort developed in the bourgeois home" (Fortin, 2011). Modernism's minimalist intentions, with rules defined by Le Corbusier and the international group CAIM, were intended to be a necessary replacement for the cultural affectations of décor. The conventions of the 'International Modern Architecture Congress' paved the way for the International Style with its emphasis on complete urban renewal. Ornament, in the eyes of European schools of architectural thought, was a pursuit that clouded the design needed to better humanity.

John R. Gold, in *Modern Architecture and the Future City*, describes the lasting efforts of the Modernist imagination in the social housing programmes of postwar Europe. He condemns many of the later century products, such as the isolated tower blocks that spawned from supposed machine utopias. A lack of concern about existing environments and their contexts fixated modernism, making it focus and reflect on its superiority over previous architectural periods. As Brookes suggests, the French architect Le Corbusier's "early schemes portrayed not cities, but ideas about cities; he outlined possibilities, simplifying the complexity of urban function, frequently having unfilled the gap between image and reality" (1987, 242). The re-envisioning of the nineteenth century 'open paradigm' by Le Corbusier, best articulated in his 'Radiant City' proposals, presented a new all-encompassing vision of city planning.

The design values of Modernism were not truly introduced on a large scale until the postwar reconstruction period, when Modernism's simplicity could be monopolised to rebuild society, as per the promise of earlier visions and images. Walter Gropius, founder of the Bauhaus School, coined the description of Modernism as 'total architecture' and 'total vision' in its tradition of larger than life, collectively similar means of habitation for society. When such an emphasis is compared with utopian ideals, and the circumstances of dystopian situations, it could be argued that Modernist visions are ironically a promoter of both. Firstly, Modernist values insist on change in societal living conditions for the better, but in that change appears the emergence of non-descript uniformity —a fear realised in later master-planned housing schemes. In turn, Bauhaus teaching informed the likes of Paul Rudolf, who can more readily be described as an originator of early Brutalist work: "Machine age architecture only in the sense that its monuments were built in a machine age, and [that it] expresses an attitude to machinery in the sense that one might stand on French soil and discuss French politics, and still be speaking English." Braham (2013, 139).

Modernism had an unrealistic belief in its own ability to transform every aspect of contemporary societies, neglecting to explain how it would stitch together the historic fabric with a total vision of planning for cities. Banham's account of architectural evolution through the twentieth century critically peels back Modernist misinterpretations of solutions, describing its only relevance as being a facade trying to match a world changing in unprecedented technological ways. Modernism, in its heyday, created images of wonder and ideas of positivity for living, through the promise of a responsive architecture that reflected an increasingly technologically-directed future. When compared with its eventual products, however, these often-wondrous images can leave a negative impression, or at least a suspicion of what they show compared to our own built realities. Many science fiction films embody this disconnected feeling of urban living, while at the same time showcasing the Postmodern complexity of any given cityscape (Fortin, 2011).

Early 20th Century Los Angeles

Los Angeles (LA) forms the geographical backdrop for *Blade Runner*'s imagined futuristic setting and, as the home of Hollywood, the real-life locality for the film's creation. It is therefore no coincidence that LA is the place from which much of the film's architectural content is drawn. In the 1920s and 1930s, LA was a relatively new yet rapidly growing city, with little architectural history. As a developing culture, it was therefore well-set to embrace new ideas of liberated urban development. Forms of expression in architecture, popular culture and commercialism made it a place suitable for architects who were less seriously concerned with being advocates of the International Style or strict Modernism. (Banham, 1971) Hispanic and Mexican traditions underpinned LA's original townscape, character, and footprint. Many architects, such as Frank Lloyd Wright, found inspiration from these backgrounds, creating 'modern' architecture with ethnic idiosyncrasies that acknowledged other cultural heritages. Banham emphasises this employment of heritage in LA's architecture against Modernism's purist advocates. LA's urbanism and development as a young city made it an enigma when compared to European contemporary 'new city' conceptions. Architecture can often express individuality through separate buildings, yet even with LA's variety, a local typology was formed, with low slung suburban sprawl that surrounded the young cityscapes impulsive modernism. In 'Los Angeles', Banham describes the city's relevance in the following way: "Such architecture should never be brushed off as mere fancy dress; in Los Angeles it makes both ancestral and environmental sense, and much of the best modern architecture there owes much to its example" Banham (1971, 9). It is noteworthy how this city developed so spontaneously in the twentieth century, and yet so inadvertently different from the more mainstream European Modernist backdrop at large. From a seemingly Postmodern position, it mixed different conversations in architecture; the city simply seemed to do as it wished, an embodiment of the human desire to prosper and grow. LA maintained a connection with Modernist utopia in that it sold itself: as an image, an urban idea and an ideal of American culture. A relevant consideration by science fiction film is thus reminiscent of how LA's architecture was portrayed, correlating identity with commercialism in future cities (Fortin, 2011).

Frank Lloyd Wright's Alternative Modern Living

Frank Lloyd Wright's career brought an abundance of ideas in architecture that few others have surpassed. European Modernism's edited doctrine of form, as in the work of Le Corbusier, is loosely apparent in Wright's designs and plans c. 1910-1930. Although unlike the harsh Marxist teaching of Walter Gropius's Bauhaus, Wright's architecture continually created new ideas by absorbing and building on prior ones. The Broadacre City scheme was Wright's planning concept and equivalent of the 'Radiant City.' Its model for urban management swings closely toward the principles of a Postmodern city. Although rules and ideas of uniformity bounded his acre-conceived plots, the possibilities of what could architecturally grow in each were more open ended. The dislocation of Modernist cityscapes, and their ability to be placeless and adapted for any context, is seen by many as an impersonal approach that disconnects life from the complexities of real urban situations. A contextual responsiveness, or rather acknowledgement of site, in Wright's work is again one of the bigger differences between him and his European contemporaries.

Not absorbed by Modernism's rigid detachment from ornament and classical embellishment, Wright continued to try and alter the effect of design through new emotions found in material expression. His concern was perhaps embedded in the human qualities of architecture, or, as Fortin paraphrases: "What it means to be human through the design of the built environment" Fortin (2011, 163). In *Writings on Wright*, it is noted how the monumentality of ruin was captured in a domestic scale through many of Wright's residential designs during the 1920s and 1930s. Typically, spaces created often framed an interior spectacle through interlinking rooms and unfolding views. This is especially apparent in his domestic standalone Los Angeles housing projects that occupied an otherwise light period in his celebrated career. Through the lens of film, monumentality is often attached to moments of spectacle. Thus to see how Wright's architecture is used on-screen in the film *Blade Runner* to showcase the future, and to such successful effect, is instructive (Brooks, 1970).

Wright's delicate concrete 'textile blocks' emerged following trips he made in Latin America. At first, they appear as a test form without reason; an impulse to provide detailing in an otherwise featureless building material. When Wright's travels and visits to other places and cultures are considered, it is easy to see these inspirations at work. These singular residences, such as the Freeman and the Ennis House, are an aesthetic product of Wright's own exploration in Mayan and Latin American heritage, and yet they contain, like much of his previous work, that Modernist exaggeration of extended form and wall tectonics. The Ennis House, second of Wright's block constructions, again formed a heavy dexterous mass. Perched on the LA hills like a contemporarily conceived ruin, it is this house that informed the illustrations for Ridley Scott's portrayal of the future in *Blade Runner*. This is why the construction, character, form and principal notions that shaped Wright's architecture are so important; his ornate distinction to Modernism's machine smooth ideals is all too evident. In Wright's own words:

> Concrete was the inert mass and would take compression... a plastic material —susceptible to the impress of imagination... I saw a kind of weaving coming out of it. Why not weave a kind of building? Then I saw the shell. Shells with steel inlay in them. So his imagination was carried along on a wave of poetry: one image followed another and little by little a design emerged that was both scientific and artistic, Frank Lloyd Wright (2005, 235).

Postmodern Architecture and the Brutalist Movement

Planned futurist visions of mechanised utopia with patented replicas were proposed by Modernists like Le Corbusier, the functional fulfilment of which would never require change for the societal infrastructure they supported. These ideas rarely materialised at city scale however, and urbanisation in the Western world continued to develop in reactive and haphazard ways. It is perhaps interesting to consider that these pre-planned environments were not realised because their grid rational order often already existed —at least in some form. A city often expands from two dimensionally ordered plans, but, with time, varying building identities manifest, too diverse to be rationalised by the simplicities of Modernist preparation. This is the less uniform and more complex condition of Postmodern change and thought. The architecture of the city turned from being a homogenous ambition of Modernism to an insular concern with built identities of a singular form. As Schrijver suggests: "Postmodern critics in particular think that the notion of unity, totality or a 'centre' is an artifice, an arbitrarily constructed narrative" Schrijver (2005, 32).

Coinciding with this new urban Postmodern picture was the introduction of a new movement in concrete architecture. The movement and form of Brutalist architecture is thus a development that superseded Modernism's earlier domestic concerns with a plain surface. These superficial concerns were not present, as its character oppositely sought to express mass, density, and the honesty of concrete, as an originally raw manmade material. Le Corbusier was one of the first prominent architects who reproached his own ideas of a clean machine aestheticism. The Unite d'Habitation residential complex in Marseille began Corbusier's new sense of sculptural wholeness through the materials he used. As Croft summarises: "Le Corbusier conjured concrete almost as a new material, exploiting its crudities and those of the wooden formwork, to produce an architectural surface of a rugged grandeur that seems to echo that of the well-weathered Doric columns of temples in Magna Graecia – it was not a question of 'architecture is that which makes magnificent ruins' " Croft (2004, 20).

Serban Cantacuzino's *Compendium of 20th Century Modern Architecture* posits the development of reinforced concrete, by European and American designers in the 1960s, as a moment that Japan sought the adoption of this flexibly appropriate construction material as an alternative to its adobe construction tradition.

From this moment onwards, Western buildings sculpted from concrete became equally infused with Eastern cultural influences, just as those in Japan began to adopt the Brutalist character of construction. "It was," as Collins puts it, "more than anything else, the fact that Le Corbusier had abandoned the pre-war fiction that reinforced concrete was a precise, 'machine age' material" Collins (2004, 326). One architect whose work represents Brutalism, before the term 'New Brutalist' was coined, is Paul Rudolf. As a US-based architect, his work grew with design peer influence from Wright and Corbusier in the 1940s and 1950s, the result being very textural buildings that elevated the heavy mass of his concrete and brick construction. Renyer Banham again reflects contemporary critical commentary about Rudolf's work in his 1965 article, 'A Home is not a House,' summarising the conceit of these heavy forms still pretending to wrap the ever-evolving dependence of technology in societal culture:

> When your house contains such a complex of piping, flues, ducts, wires, lights, inlets, outlets, ovens, sinks, refuse disposers, hi-fi reverberators, antennae, conduits, freezers, heaters- when it contains so many services that the hardware could stand up by itself without any assistance from the house, why have a house to hold it up? (Renyer Banham as quoted by Whiteley, 2002, 190)

In the same era, the think-tank Archigram pursued architecture through image, the results projecting a new structure and theory to the urban situations they imagined. Archigrams image rational was based on responses to production and time, creating urban representations at a parallel speed to society's new communicative and technological standards. A group under the leadership of Peter Cook collaborated for the 1963 'living City exhibition,'   Renyer Banham was one of the groups most avid supporters, and provided an esteemed recognition to the work produced. This work often explored themes of commercialism, depicting concept cityscapes that are as much marketing devices in graphic image as new spontaneous systems for urban living (Allison, 2007). Instant City, one of Archigrams renowned projects, was less concerned with architecture than it was with modern technology, but was nonetheless still effective for popularising broader considerations with urban design. As Alison puts it, "Instant City consummates the disappearance of architecture, which has transformed into environment. Architecture gives ways to the image, the event, the audiovisual, to gadgets and to other environmental simulators" Alison, (2007, 281). More recently, the architectural critic and documentary producer Jonathan Meades has commented:

> It is accretive, ostentatious, hyperbolic in its asymmetries and protracted voids, composed of parts that do not connect or are in fragmentary state, dramatically vertiginous, geometrically farouche, extravagantly cantilevered, discomforting, aggressive (in so far as an inanimate object can be aggressive). There is no desire to please with prettiness or even beauty. Meades (2014, Guardian).

Latin America and Mexico City's Modern Architecture

An awareness of the other cultural influences and backdrops behind the architecture of both *Blade Runner* and *Total Recall* helps reveal the character that is instilled in the urban spaces shown on screen. 'New Brutalism' was embraced as the vehicle for urban development in Mexico City's centre between the 1960s and 1970s. New public spaces sought to express a simplicity with their base material form, unlike Frank Lloyd Wright's houses, where the relief and pattern of Latin American culture read more clearly. It is, more than anything, curious how the juxtaposed influences of Modernism and Brutalism converged together in a Latin American context. In the late twentieth century, the systems of governance in Mexico fashioned many urban schemes in this image. The transference and emergence of international styles with a national difference in this culture was apparently repeated from early Modernism through the New Brutalism. (Banham, 1965) Brutalist expression often trod the boundary between architecture and sculpture, taking form in symmetrical order and other more hyperbolic compositions.

Following Le Corbusier's influence, Brutalist architects and engineers began pushing for more ordered space arrangements in the public domain. Corbusier's visit to Mexico City in 1929 provided an energy to this direction by the new Vargas regime, bringing a comparable pre-eminence with technocracy and corporatism. "The reception of modernist architecture in Latin America," as Guillen argues, "thus corroborates the general pattern that foreign influences, while attractive at first, are ultimately refracted through the lens of local peculiarities and institutions" Guillen (2004, 27). International proponents of these Brutalist manipulations included Gottfried Bohm, Walter Forderer and Fritz Wotruba, the work of whom provided relative definition for 'brut' character in aspiring Latin American cities in the mid-century. As Herzog summarises: "Mexicans embrace there past; the modern Mexican political system built its power base in part around nationalism and the celebration of history and culture. Public spaces served well as symbolic places to implement the national government agenda." Herzog (2010, 139).

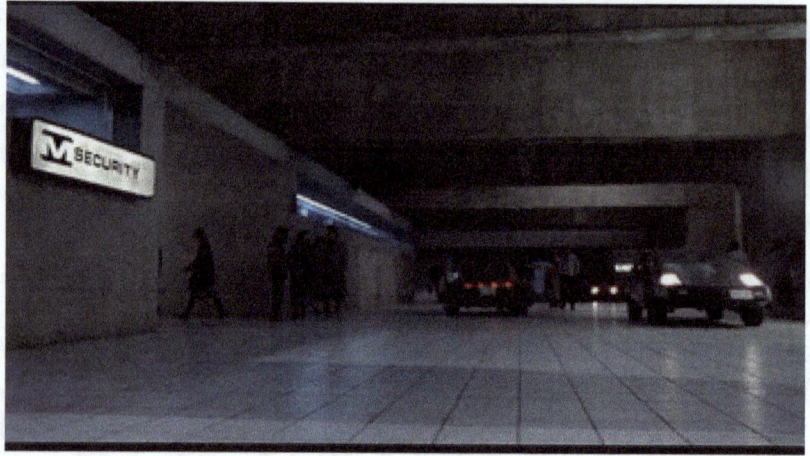

Figure 2: *Total Recall* (all film stills captured by the author)

It is easy to relate an architectural race for change in society with an institutional or governmental intention to reposition its influence with the imposition of new urban character; this is why architecture is one of the clearest signifiers and markers of change in society. The use of Brutalism in institutional building types in Mexico City, such as the military institute and metro underground, exemplifies how a totalitarian connection and character was entwined in built typologies in this period. Such an entwining is an interesting difference to the way that heritage and culture was retrieved for Frank Lloyd Wright's architecture, and shows how we recognize architecture for an intended provocative image and memory as much as a lived experience. As Guillen puts it:

> Still this Mexicanized modernism produced a rational architecture that sought to cater the needs of the population, promote the (shifting) goals of the revolution, and enhance the regimes domestic and international stature. Guillen (2004, 98).

Cinematography and Architecture

The architecture of the twentieth-century Modernist movement was well-defined by the striking photography that sold the promise of its new style. Photography graphically dehumanised space by depicting empty interiors and spaces void of habitation. Admiration of Modernism's built forms, cast in a defined light, set up a distinct visual promotion for modernity's sense of self. As Higgott advises in *Camera Constructs*, spatial properties are subtly difficult to capture with photography: "The medium favours and promotes an abstracted vision of architecture that assumes far more significance in the photographic representation than in built r.eality" Higgott, Wray (2012, 2). Properties of space, materiality and day-to-day experience are, as Holl adds, particularly difficult to define through photography:

> As buildings lose their plasticity and their connection with the language ... they become isolated in the cool and distant realm of vision. With the loss of tactility and the scale and details crafted for the human body and hand, our structures become repulsively flat, sharp edged, immaterial and unreal. The detachment of construction from the realities of matter and craft turns architecture into sets for the eye, devoid of the authenticity of material and tectonic logic. Holl (2007, 29).

In an analysis of three architectural scene scales from each film, I explore the spatial qualities captured and communicated to the viewer. Five visual characteristics are used: 1) light; 2) perspective; 3) scale; 4) material; and 5) occupation, which combine to form qualitative comparisons about the selected spaces shown. Spatial contrasts captured through light and shadow are of particular interest, as they emphasise the graphic presentation of modern design and how these spaces were represented cinematically. *Total Recall* and *Blade Runner* utilise this approach in different ways: *Blade Runner* using scenes set at night and an absence of natural light to impose a sense of unknown when experiencing environments on scene; and *Total Recall*, in reverse, using daylight to create contrast and more awareness of the spatial structure and activity shown. As cinema cannot convey touch, taste, and smell to us, any sensory interpretation relies on the visual and the human ability to apply memory to create more complete and complex experiences, given every past experience of architecture involves several sensory qualities. It is the involvement of the senses that allows

us to remember and compare new experiences, or to discern differences or fa-
miliarities with spaces. Theory suggests that buildings, like paintings, present
a canvas of emotive experience for us to process and remember. The controlled
and distilled use of architecture in film can thus focus the viewer's attention to
certain features on-screen to reconcile them with our own experiences. As Holl
summarises:

> The timeless task of architecture is to create embodied existential metaphors
> that concretize and structure man's being in the world. Images of architecture
> reflect and externalize ideas and images of life; architecture materializes our
> images of ideal life. Buildings and towns enable us to structure, understand
> and remember the shapeless flow of reality and, ultimately, to recognize and
> remember who we are. Architecture enables us to place ourselves in the contin-
> uum of culture. Holl (2006, 37).

The legibility to the eye of surface materials can be heightened on screen with
the control of light. Light changes our perception of what is seen, often making
set situations and environments more spectacular. The use of light in cinema
can be extreme, especially in science fiction situations, and can exaggerate limited film set constructions (both real and scale model). Often what lies in darkness or overexposure cannot be distinguished, but these areas can still impart
an idea. This often allows the viewer to imagine that which cannot be seen, and
a non-descript extension of the texture and form to be revealed "Deep shadows
and darkness are essential," then, "because they dim the sharpness of vision and
invite unconscious peripheral vision and tactile fantasy" (*Questions of Perception*). By considering these principles within a focus on architectural qualities
of scale, geometry, and material, we can grasp the feelings of inertia caused by
urban dystopian pictures.

Blade Runner's Cityscape and *Total Recall*'s
Public Terminal Scenes

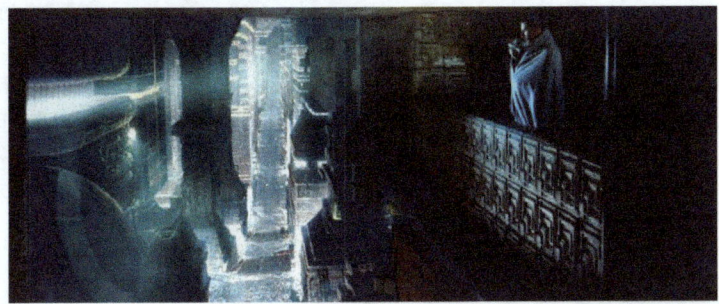

Figure 3: *Blade Runner.*

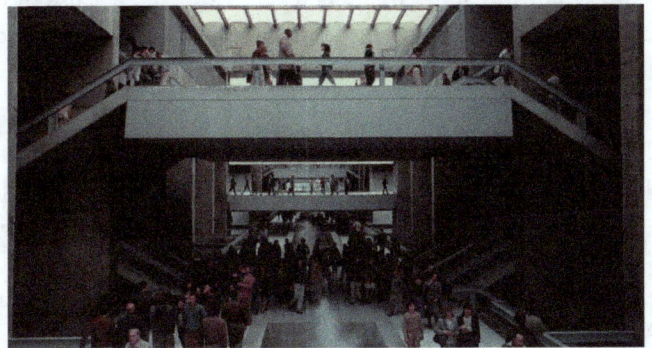

Figure 4: *Total Recall.*

Light and Shadow

For *Blade Runner*, an absence of natural lighting permeates the entire film. In the scene above, a transition occurs between the interior room and the outside space. A gradient of light illuminates a vertical axis from ground to centre frame, the focus of which draws the view to the streetscape elevations beyond. A sense of activity is implied at street level, with inactivity apparent in the higher levels of the building. Colourful artificial lighting is the focal element, and at ground level is exaggerated horizontally, drawing our view into the distance. The overall lack of light also brings a gloomy atmosphere to the setting. In *Total Recall*'s opening public realm scene, shown above, we have moved from an interior home to a transportation system that presents an instant sense of linear direction. Natural lighting frames suspended level walks in both light and shadow underneath, presenting a layered intersectional space. The broken edge that shapes the continuing path has a lateral depth of shadow and darkness, indicating movement away from daylight and toward an environment with more artificial needs. This depth and sense of darkness is also gained from the space indicated under the central walkway, an example of Dick's 'runnel.'

View and Perspective

In *Blade Runner*, the camera angle mimics the character's viewpoint from a greater vantage. This angle illustrates distance in long view more than the raised position from which the frame is taken. However, a sense of enclosure is achieved with the dwelling space encompassing the protagonist and half the scene; an almost sectional view relationship. In *Total Recall*, meanwhile, the camera pans in a descending vertical path, showing bridged walkways crossing separately in horizontal breaks. The position of these bridges in relation to one another implies separate routes of movement from the larger central elevated path, a system of movement designed to control pedestrian flows in space. An undefined end to this central system is hard to gauge; again, this implies a continuity to the space beyond what can be seen, a feeling gained from repeating Modernist city plans.

Scale and Geometry

None of the perspective elevations in the *Blade Runner* scene have a consistency of form or relief on their facade. Although effects of light and texture create a homogenous style in built form, the lack of uniform profile is a reference to postmodern cityscapes, with every building expressing its own intent and not conjoining to achieve a unified style or language. Interestingly, a roof is almost perceived over the exterior street, which again brings an idea of interior enclosure or 'room' to an exterior space. The geometry is longitudinal, dense, and, it could be assumed, continuous. This emphasises overdevelopment and undermines the architectural importance of this small terrace in the great city expanse.

A sense of interior monumentality is formed in *Total Recall* with this 'runnel,' mainly because of the distinct balance between known ground and space that is indicated but not shown. The stretched rectilinear arrangement again reinforces the impression that activity on the paths is controlled and essential. The lateral intersections centre this space into a notion of collectiveness, allowing us to believe in a much bigger network of which this architecture is a part.

Material and Texture

In *Blade Runner*, a great deal of the built form has a nondescript outline along planar surfaces. The foreground composition incorporates the block work previously explored in Frank Lloyd Wright's Ennis House, providing the tonal and textural knowledge that projects onto the more ambiguous dark areas of the landscape. Warmth and the depth of the block work bring an entropic placement to other contextual elements in the scene. It is the balcony's material character that brings solidity and permeance to the architecture. The concrete enclosure of the main walkway in *Total Recall* presents a density and solid boundary in the space, a material form that gives stability and apparent bracing for floors suspended between vertical concrete stratums. Concrete frames the immediate view, vertically distinguishing the more polished horizontal floors that suspend between. The monotonality of material also compounds the scene, forming a utilitarian sense of system and uniform coordination for the architecture of the space.

Use

Only one person occupies this scene in *Blade Runner*. Emptiness between the living environment and the street below is created again by distance and scale. In contrast with the 'street' scale urban scenes, this singular occupancy brings emptiness to the space, making it adverse to place oneself — or anyone else — in the city at large. In *Total Recall* the directed view suggests the walkway does not comfortably support the crowd in this public space. This machine architecture thus suggests a societal pressure, by visually not providing any excess room or space of release from the movement routes shown. This is not a space to dwell, stop or rest; it is by observation a pedestrian motorway to fulfil function, reflecting, therefore, the ideals of Modernism.

Blade Runner's Cityscape and *Total Recall*'s

Transport Route Movement Scenes

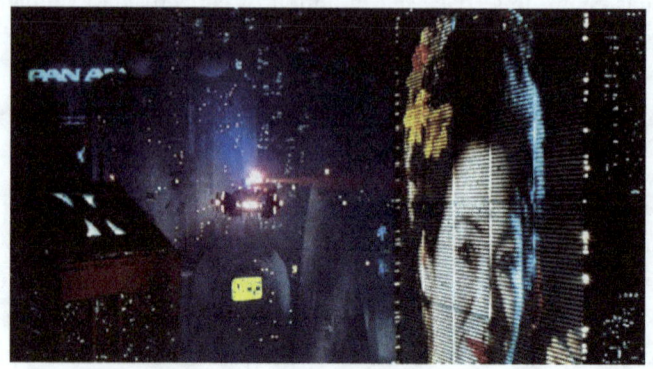

Figure 5: *Blade Runner.*

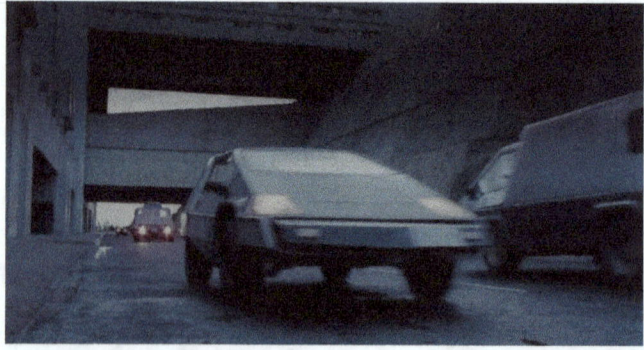

Figure 6: *Total Recall.*

Light and Shadow

As a night scene in *Blade Runner*, the composition of architecture is undefined, especially vague in the more distant buildings. Artificial advertising, as a lighting source, overshadows the less focal light sources from building facades and the unknown spaces within. Highlight and focus on the advertisement displays covering built forms is especially clear. This lighting contrast not only takes attention away from the architecture, but conveys a hierarchy of civic importance, where apparently older neo-classical style buildings are only shadows in this future cityscape. Again, in this external situation in *Total Recall*, the use of daylight is brought into play, with a clear view of sky used to silhouette the large Brutalist style buildings that act as bounding enclosure to the transportation route. This evidence of natural colour and soft light in the backdrop brings a dark impression and shadow between each road edifice into clear view. Artificial lighting from vehicles again juxtaposes with the visible natural light and environment created by the concrete street.

View and Perspective

Unlike the previous street vantage, this angle of view in *Blade Runner* sits on a vertical middle ground between floor and skyline. As the view does not include a scope of complete building size or ground position, it is difficult to gain any relative position in the city, even as the camera slowly pans to reveal more clustered building compositions and non-linear endpoints. In *Total Recall*, the low viewpoint exaggerates the setting and vertical extent of the building form. It also brings a closer inspection of the road, edging out of the visible end point because of the upward perspective. The foreground of the built environment consistently projects into the frame's distance, with little visible distortion. An assured sense of monumentality is thus gained from views underneath the bridge structure and spanning across the roadway. Again, the built form is acting and implying a civic system and necessity.

Scale and Geometry

In *Blade Runner* the scale of this space is hard to define since colours are dark and unsaturated by natural light. In comparison to vehicle size, the buildings extend far beyond the point at which the camera pans on the horizontal plane. The indeterminate size of the window openings and facade detail again limits our interpretation of scale. Geometric built form is juxtaposed with the infrastructure of piping and terminals. Furthermore, each building form appears to situate its own space, not relating in any obvious relationship to the next. This confounds the idea that any of this urban terrain is planned. Using vehicles and road as measures of space in *Total Recall*, we can understand the dramatic drop to the road level from the highest brut building form edge. The sloped face of the wall forms a pressure and movement to the road below, creating an acute angled space in its connection with the bridge element. Planer angles of the monolithic concrete offsets the vertical and horizontal planes to produce over-lapping-built identities with an attached sense of function.

Material and Texture

The main texture in *Blade Runner* is created through the pattern of light from interiors on exterior building surfaces. Little indication of material is shown, which informs the built environment with an unknown aesthetic character; building constructions could, then, be young or old. It is perhaps the heavy urban density that indicates an association of designed infill or addition over time. Surface tone is dark, and again contrasts with colourful superficial attach-ments to the built form. Akin to Brutalism, this architecture and its character-isation is impossible to place because of an ascetic lack of detail. This lack of detail presents an air of timelessness to the cityscape. In *Total Recall*, a palette of mono-tonality is brought through this setting. Much like the interior trans-port room looked at previously, the exterior extends the same truth of expres-sion in material form. The brut-stained texture, which homogeneously covers the majority of on screen image, increases both the sense of architectural scale and our ability to interpret its continuity. Simplicity of detail is another aspect that creates a Brutalist quality within this transit route.

Use

The central focus of this view in *Blade Runner* is the flying vehicle that moves towards the frame of the camera. This singular motive object shows both how little activity is visible beyond the facades of constructed buildings, and how undetermined the system of movement is within the urban cluster. In *Total Recall*, more than one vehicle can be seen in movement, thus reinforcing the road's activity; infrastructure and the function of space thus have an under-standable link. Once again, the number of occupants or vehicles shown in the scene diminishes any vacant space between architecture and habitation, remov-ing any sense of comfort or personal resonance.

Blade Runner's Home Interior and *Total Recall*'s Work Interior Scenes

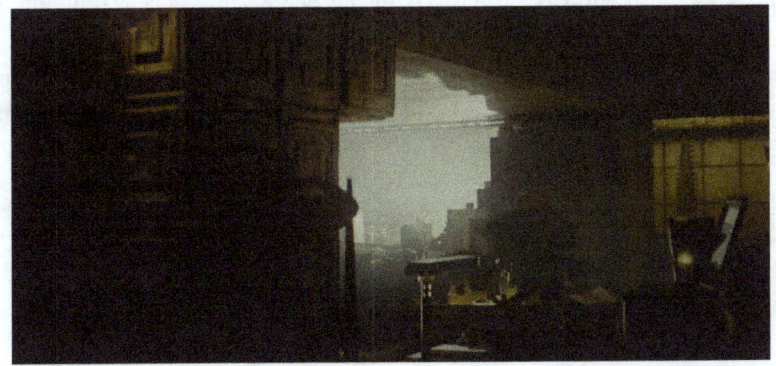

Figure 7: *Blade Runner.*

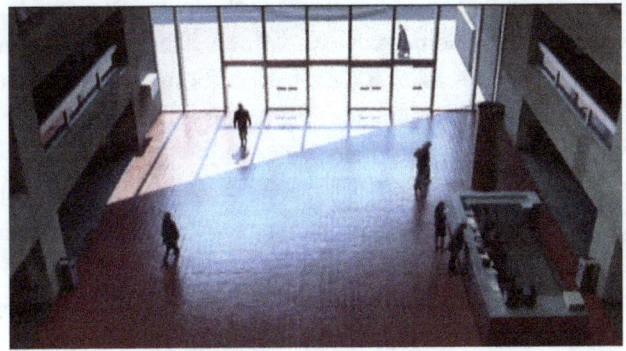

Figure 8: *Total Recall*

Light and Shadow

This interior room in *Blade Runner* is cast with soft artificial light from above. The position of light sources change between different sub-spaces in the apparently interconnected open home. The illumination cast on the wall's surface is of key focus for observing its material decoration. From the perspective of the camera, the light gradient changes from objects in focus to areas where light levels blur the viewer's impression and distinction of darker areas. This adds an unknown quality to brighter spaces, and better balances a glimpse into other areas cast in dim light. The colour and texture of the light varies, but collectively maintains a warmth akin to light pollution. Natural light, used again here in *Total Recall*, contrasts instantly with the perceived exterior situation and the concrete enclosed space within. The large, glazed frontage that separates the two indicates how much the interior triple height space absorbs this light, meaning the space remains in relative shadow. Office spaces in darkness that assemble around the foyer are how we gauge the little impact of daylight on this solid, heavy interior world. An extremely white colour tone and intensity of light, combining with the mono-tonality of concrete within, produces a cold atmospheric feeling. This sensation relates in turn to a planned sense of control and power to the body that governs such a space.

View and Perspective

In this scene in *Blade Runner*, the camera sits at a level just above the furniture from which we gain a standing sense of position. This angle also includes the walls, ceiling, and fixtures that, in combination, bring a restricted atmosphere to the size of the living space. As the camera pans right to left on the room, we gain a better sense of scale and the containment of smaller spaces within the open arrangement. Panning motion by camera viewpoint is often broken by columns and other structural piers, bringing an unknown interpretation of how the entire area works together. In an opposite way, the camera pans from above in this scene in *Total Recall*. The elevated position thus provides spectacle and oversight to the building's function. When viewing this transition, a complete overview is disturbed by the observer not knowing its function, which might have been revealed with a more pedestrian approach.

Scale and Geometry

The vertical scale of this interior space in *Blade Runner* is limited, and initially illustrated by the position of characters in the background, with any vertical height distorted by the long horizontal panning motion that occurs. The shape of the space is largely rectilinear, a depiction that is reasoned by the square block construction made up in the surface construction. Orthogonal arrangement, in combination with height constraints, provides a real spatial limitation to the home. In *Total Recall*, the public building is realised from the centred orthogonal triple height space that is presented on entrance; such architectural design resonates with us as a programme used in many institutional buildings. Our identification, and yet lack of awareness to the buildings purpose, is enhanced by the elevated-but-concealed balcony levels above. The rigour of a grid ordered concrete structure, and its thickness in comparison to the bays behind, again brings a modern sensibility to the way this open central space is framed and enclosed.

Material and Texture

Possibly the most inherent quality of this sequence in *Blade Runner* is the Frank Lloyd Wright blockwork lining the surface elements and presumably-structural columns. This decorated concrete in combination with warm light creates a worn character aesthetic, brought forth from the walls. The depth of one pattern line casting shadow above the next engages classical ornament connections, and again a notion of aging construct within its circuit-inspired design. The surface texture completes the atmosphere of space in the apartment and, in combination with hazy lighting, casts visible space in a layer of dust and dirt. Tonality of space in the *Total Recall* composition, meanwhile, is broken by the application of concrete to the walls and the textured red floor finish on the horizontal. This split of material texture changes our focus of image from the centre to the surrounding edges with darker areas. The concrete vertical columns and balcony edges provides the monolithic element, visualising a density and weight that is separate from the red tiled floor below. Its Brutalist concrete character is evident, therefore, but controlled by the order of structural elements shown, maintaining sensibility and awareness in its coordination.

Use

Two characters occupy the background space in this *Blade Runner* scene, with their presence in the surroundings again cast into blur and shadow with high levels of light from their position; this location also emphasises the amount of free area between sub-spaces. In *Total Recall*, the elevated viewpoint, against the bright glazed curtain wall, throws into silhouette the few people who populate the space below. This effect, along with distance, helps disconnect their necessity within the space, or at least places the viewer's perception of them beneath the surrounding building. A similar effect of shadow again enforces a totality of system against individual resonance.

Spatial Links and Movement Between Room, City, Street

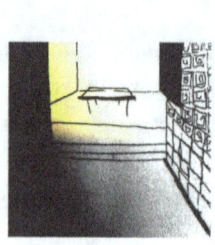 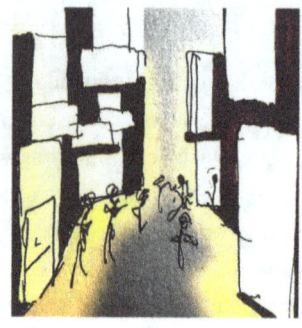 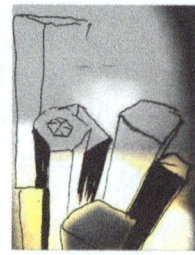

Figure 9: Room, City, Street.

After exploring the architectural movements and cultural backgrounds for the architecture used in each film, and comparing the architectural qualities demonstrated, this chapter now focuses on *Blade Runner* to consider the spatial relationships between room, city and street. Such an approach is useful in understanding the intrinsic ideas connecting spaces and urban fabrics together. Our human relationships with interior rooms are important in science fiction; the room expresses the most personal indications and quirks of future living. In film, this relationship often reflects the most truth from a wider situation and illustrates compatibility with how architecture accommodates different means of life. The larger external city environments of both films are often used as links from one place of activity to another, representing movement, but not a resonance with or rest within any space. Are the compositions of the future cityscape framed purely by imagination? And like the real urban space between room and city, is the street framed by both reality and imagination?

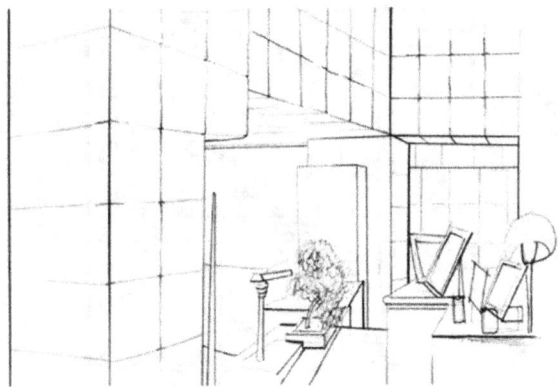

Figure 10: *Blade Runner* Apartment.

When looking at the living space and interior formwork that insulate the protagonist in *Blade Runner*, there is a clear continuity between the permanencies of wall, roof, opening, and objects that construct these borders. Most of these elements are constructed from the textile blockwork of Wright's Ennis House. As mentioned earlier, these blocks incorporate real cultural ornament and yet somehow, in this film's environment, also conjure technological influences with their circuit board-like pattern. When viewed under the film's dimmed lighting, an overlap occurs with our perception of this decoration as both a thing of identity and forgotten meaning. This textural relevance and decay of solid form is perhaps what gives an element of age to this home for the watching audience. In addition to pattern, the rough texture of the plaster-based block work links with Dick's depiction of 'Kipple': an accumulation of dirt and disarray that transforms any environment that yields to the effects of time. As Dick describes:

> Silence. It flashed from the woodwork and the walls; It rose from the floor, up out of the tattered grey wall-to-wall carpeting. It unleashed itself from the broken and semi-broken appliances in the kitchen, the dead machines which hadn't worked in all the time Isidore had lived here. From the useless pole lamp in the living room it oozed out, meshing with the empty and wordless descent of itself from the fly-specked ceiling. It managed in fact to emerge from every object within his range of vision, as if it—the silence—meant to supplant all things tangible... The silence of the world could not rein back its greed. Not any longer. Not when it had virtually won. (Dick 1968).

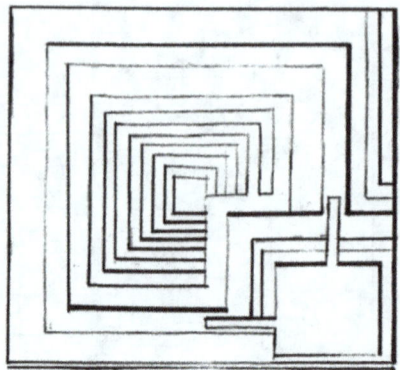

Figure 11: Ennis House Textile Block.

Like any home, the personality within is created through a mix of articulations, some personal artefacts, and other culturally specific suggestions. More
evidence of how life is lived in the space is shared through its populating with
furniture and material possessions. Conveyed by this assemblage is how little
leftover space exists between walls, tectonic formwork, objects, and any room
for circulation, made apparent by the dense array of items that exist between
the built environment's solid boundary forms. Any hope of this architecture's
effectiveness for lifestyle and living standards is diminished by the spatial limitations shown, which make the viewer presume that this room, with such inherent problems, cannot be transformed to satisfy the needs of its occupants.

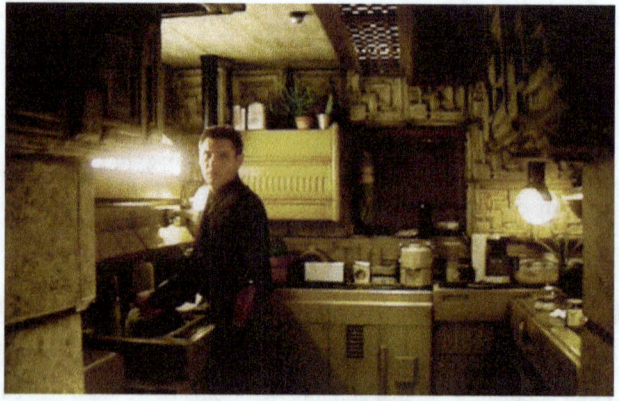

Figure 12: *Blade Runner.*

The intrinsic technological decoration that builds out from walls to kitchen appliances is also an ornament of this future. Technology resting on every surface cannot help but indicate a disparity between it and the effectiveness of the surrounding architecture. As the film switches from one apartment to another, visual motifs that imply feelings of age and past are again expanded, connecting the disrepair of the home in future living. A supposition that past ideologies do not accommodate new ideas is the downfall and starting point for the disarray and congregation of dirt in this home. The future, not showing the products of any one style but the evolved mix of many, reinforces an assumption that society has become ignorant to change, and that those ideas forgotten are left to erode one by one, creating a cascade of inevitable mess. The depreciation of architectural permanence in favour of more contemporary technological wallpaper is perhaps the underlying disregard to which the viewer can relate.

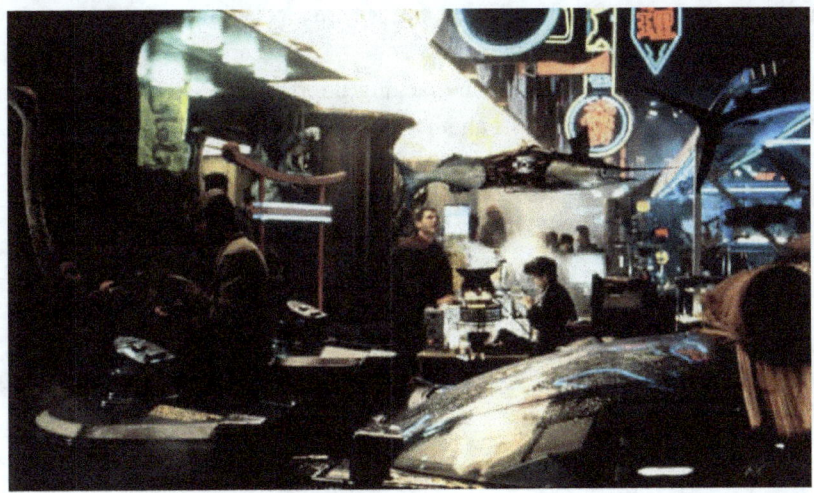

Figure 13: *Blade Runner.*

When moving from room to city, in both life and film, a true change in scale occurs. In *Blade Runner*, many buildings are overlaid in shadow, removing any certainty about style. This is a distinct difference to the interior apartment, and yet an illusion of internally-lit spaces, connecting across built facades, mimics an intricacy of the very same internal block work. This gives each structure a circuit like design. Movement and navigation through the neon cityscape places more emphasis on electronic lighting, conveying less a sense of need and more a promotion of added things. A sense of architectural flatness is gained from the building edifices cast in darkness with adorning advertised signs, much like the elevations of twentieth century Los Angeles, which built its urban form and commercialised strips on a shallow facade.

Constantly moving in this sporadic network, but not resting in any one place, projects a sensation of not belonging, or, at least, not feeling comfortable. Each building's apparent lack of individuality connects to the totality that runs through many Modernist ideals, such as Le Corbusier's Plan Voisin. It is contradictory to see that the presence of many different things can at some stage collect to form an impression of one thing; this partly resembles the Archigram 'instant city' re-appropriation of civic theory. It is another shortcoming of the future to see that all these lights fail to illuminate much of their surroundings, maintaining that isolated and retracted interior life. Since movement through the cityscape is generally one of descent, we are blocked from the street below and are instead confronted with the range of service pipes and mechanical pieces that emerge from roofs. The lacking impression of free space running between buildings thus projects another constrained sense of space.

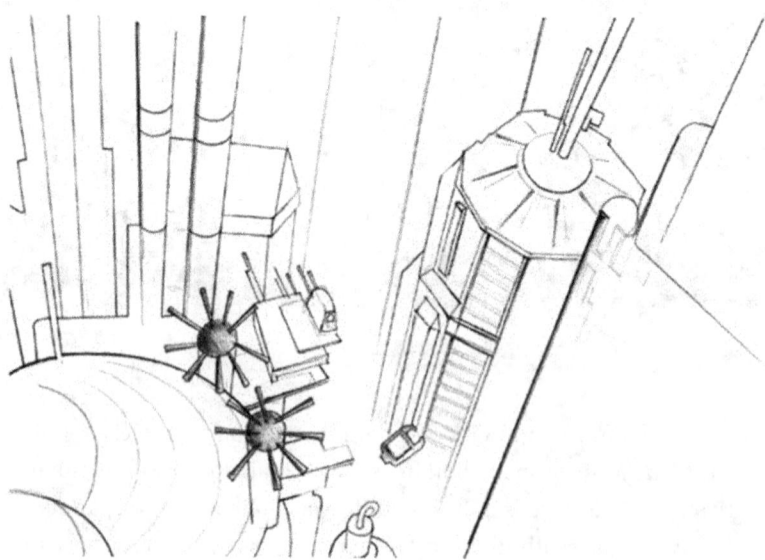

Figure 14: *Blade Runner* Cityscape.

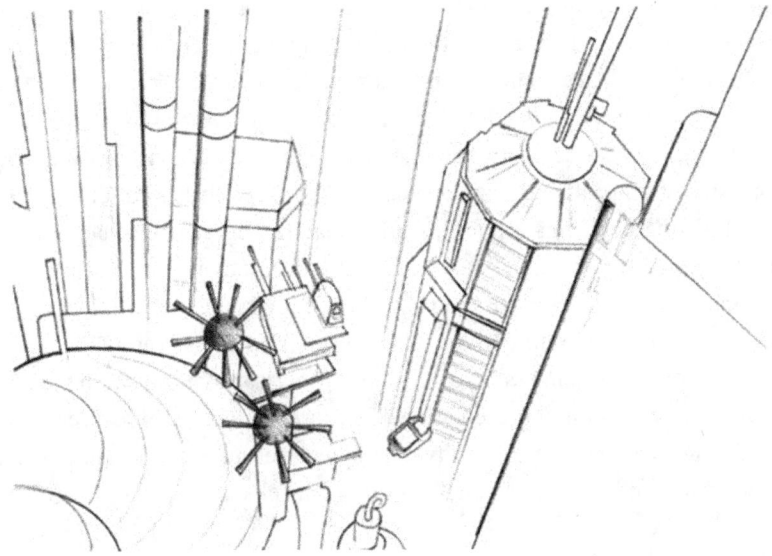

Figure 15: *Blade Runner* Streetscape.

In the physical portrayal of the future city, an exaggeration of twentieth century constructs can be seen. It is the logical and plausible excesses of built form, along with subsequent additions to the material architecture, that make this dystopian feeling feasible. The by-product of overpopulated ground space, and the inability to integrate Modernism within an existing cityscape, is perhaps a theme that has always dominated modern motivations for change. Images constructed for LA 2019 in 1982 evenly mixes two modernities together, with a poetic temper gained from Postmodern reaction to the hard International Style that held technology as its catalyst. The transition into the populated streetscape of *Blade Runner* contrasts with the isolated interior living situation. The hustle and bustle of the street is something familiar to most of us; expectations for a transient ever-changing space is likely what allows the viewer's comprehension of this space the most effectively. Unlike the isolated domestic apartment, a crowd moves, flows and mixes in the street environment. This streetscape is thus an interesting comparison to that of *Total Recall*, which displays order with pedestrian movement and a successful sense of control in urban function.

The Postmodern complexities of *Blade Runner* act on multiple design para-digms produced during the twentieth century. The backdrop almost resembles a neoclassical Western street, but the advertising on the surface speaks louder. The attachment of electronic appliances to architectural fabric reinforces the suffocation of future life, much like the interior homes in the film. A superficial amalgamation of service ducts and misplaced pipe work is a visual feature seen in domesticity, one which Reynar Banham sought to exalt as a condition of nor-mality. Existing buildings around us often feature upgrades that lack the care coordinated in their original creation. The all-encompassing use of technology as decoration in *Blade Runner* shows just how inevitable the results of such an environment can be. Cultural imbuement in glittering signs is another language that crosses over environments. Just as Latin American symbolism in the apart-ment resonates with the representation of culture, so too do these streetscapes, using signage to add modern identity to architecture and masking useful change with decoration of an original shell. As Dick thus observes:

> Kipple is useless objects, like junk mail or match folders after you use the last match or gum wrappers or yesterday's homeopape. When nobody's around, kipple reproduces itself. For instance, if you go to bed leaving any kipple around your apartment, when you wake up the next morning there's twice as much of it. It always gets more and more. Dick (1968, 52)

Conclusion: For the Future

This chapter has explored how architectural realities can filter into film, and how some of the original twentieth century ideals of Modernism and Brutalism have been used in filmic visions to make the future more believable. The scenes from each film compared here indicate two distinct approaches to framing fu-ture-built environments. *Blade Runner* presents disorder; an architectural syn-thesis of past, present and future ideas, indicative of Postmodern philosophy. *Total Recall*, conversely, uses Modernist principles, displaying visible control and architectural consistency to sustain society as a system of order. As Wor-pole states:

> Films such as Ridley Scott's *Blade Runner* (1982)... have shaped the way we think about the modern city in a period of social crisis. Moving images now

count for more than drawings and elevations, or artists' impressions. When we dream about cities we dream of teeming and amorphous emotions, of powerful currents, force-fields and dark eddies, not of plans, grids or clear sightlines. Worpole (2000, 22)

Our appreciation for changing architecture does not yet demand a greater flexibility in accommodating more consistently evolving technological norms. Technology and its integration are in constant flux, always improving, and it is important for good architectural examples to be recognised for their reliance and ability to stay viable for future change. Within the medium of film, architectural placement has continued to serve as universal ornament to the permanency of architectural form. The future is always supported by the past; in this we may find comfort, but by better balancing commitments for innovation with adaptation, the future might not necessarily look too different so soon.

The intrinsic nature of dirt, and its ability to collect and stick, is something that is rarely designed or planned. *Blade Runner*'s grounded synthesis of aging structures again mirrors the battle that all materials and surfaces face. This understanding should not encourage us to perpetuate perfect computer renders for new design proposals. Modernism, in that sense, continues to inspire an image deception, with new architectures sold as perfect finished products. Architecture starts with its ideology but accrues more interesting qualities with the advent of time. Although the process of architectural construction and design understanding will maintain a strong relationship with the 2D drawing line, pursuits for more compelling means of representation must continue to evolve. Architecture's portrayal through 3D experiences will be a continuing direction for design solutions; the future, of course, is the product and integration of past and present ideas. It is therefore useful to see the messy environments of science fiction for the intensified truth they portray; to do so will enhance the reality of imagined future designs.

REFERENCES

Blade Runner: the Final Cut (2007) DVD, Ridley Scott. Warner Bros Pictures.

Total Recall: Special Edition (2005) DVD, Paul Verho.Even. Momentum Pictures.

Alison, J. (2007) *Future City: Experiment and Utopia in Architecture*, Thames & Hudson.

Banham, R. *The New Brutalism.*

Banham, R. (1955) *The New Brutalism, Essay.*

Banham, R. (1980) *Theory and Design in the First Machine Age.* 1st edn. Butterworth-Heinemann Ltd.

Banham, R. (1965) *A House is Not a Home*, Art in America Issue 2, April.

Banham, R. (1971) *Los Angeles: The Architecture of Four Ecologies.* 1st edn. The Penguin Press.

Banham, R. *Design by Choice* (1981) academy editions.

Brooks, H. A. (1970) *Writings on Wright.*

Braham, W. W, Hale, J. A (2013) *Rethinking Architectural Technology.* 1stedn. Taylor & Francis Publishing.

Dick, P. K. (1968) *Do Androids Dream of Electric Sheep?.* 3rd edn. Gollancz: Oxford-Bookwork's Library.

Dick, P. K. (2012) *Total Recall: What is Real Collected Stories.* 1st edn. Orion Publishing.

Dick, P. K. (1968) *Do Androids Dream of Electric Sheep?.* 1st edn. Orion Publishing.

Fortin, D. T. (2011) *Architecture and Science Fiction Film: Philip K. Dick and the Spectacle of Home.* Ashgate Publishing ltd.

Gebhard. D (1997) *The California Architecture of Frank Lloyd Wright*, 1st edn Chronicle Books.

Gold R. J. (1997) *The Experience of Modernism: Modern Architects and the Future City.* 1st edn. University Press Cambridge.

Higgot A. & Wray T. (2012) *Camera Constructs: Photography Architecture and the Modern City.* 1st edn. Ashgate Publishing ltd.

Jacob, S. (2011) *Architecture, Philip K. Dick and Science-fiction Film*, Architecture Journal.

Holl S, J Pallasmaa, A Perez Gomez (2006) *Questions of Perception: Phenomenology of Architecture* 2nd edn, William Stout Publishing.

Lawrence, A. (2006) *Return to the centre: Culture, Public Space, and City Building in a Global Era.* Ist edn, University of Texas Press.

Meades, J. (2014) *Brutalism*, The Guardian.

R, Fishman. (1985) *Companion to Urban Design*.

Worple, K. (2000) *Here Comes the Sun: Architecture and Public Space in Twentieth Century European Culture*. 1st edn. Reaktion Books ltd.

Spade, R. (1971) *Paul Rudolph*. 1st edn, Thames and Hudson.

Sant'Elia, A. (1914)' *L'Architettura Futurista*.

Trieber D. (2008) Frank Lloyd Wright, Birkhäuser GmbH; 2nd Revised edition.

Wright L. F. (2005) *Frank Lloyd Wright: A Primer of Architectural Principles*. 1st edn. Phaidon Press Inc.

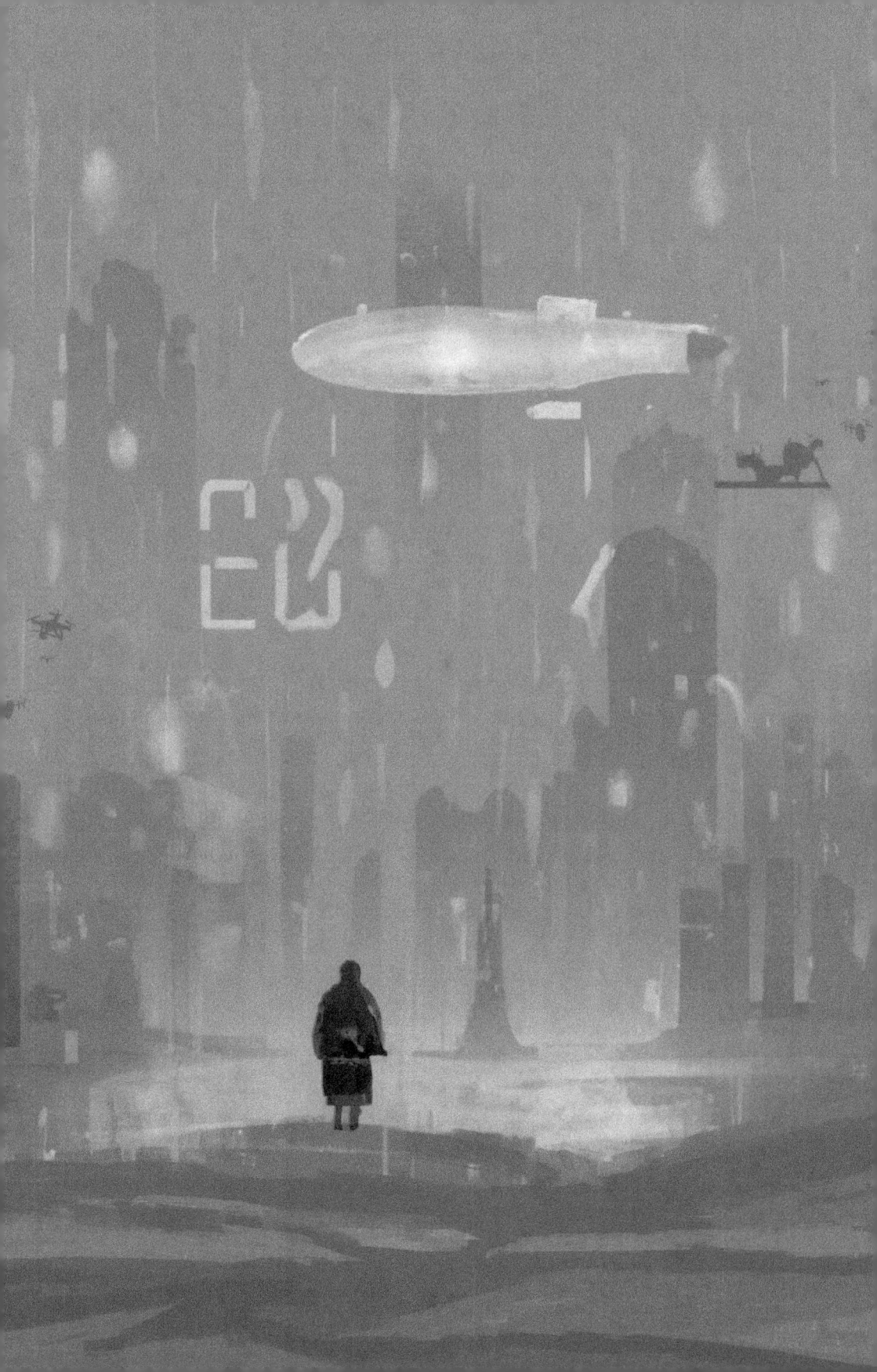

Replicating Modernism:
Dreaming of a Postmodern Future

Andrew Bryce

ANDREW BRYCE is a Part II Architectural Assistant currently living and working in Belfast. Andrew graduated from Queen's University Belfast in 2019 with a Master's degree in Architecture and a Bachelor's degree in 2014. During his studies, Andrew used his dissertation to develop an existing interest in cinema, architectural ornament and the role of fictional urban dystopias in conveying social complexities. His thesis project expanded on these themes, focusing on Belfast's 'Queer Quarter' in an attempt to understand the role of identity, struggle and visibility in space making. Having subsequently gained employment in professional practice, Andrew is working towards his qualifications to become an architect, with a particular focus on conservation, heritage and meaningful regeneration.

This chapter explores the stylistic and ideological rupture of postmodernism with modernism, following the latter's figurative end in the 1970s, and through this research presents a reading of the consequential postmodern future city. Fragmentation, pluralism, and eclecticism, the key design reflexes and arguably corrective motivations, which have come to define the movement, are observed through the optic of social, cultural and political discourse. In doing so, the discussion engages in a critique of postmodernism that finds its place among present day issues concerning the future of rapidly changing city space and its determining effect on society.

Having established an existing foundation of academic theory, the research moves to film as an analytical tool for urban, architectural and spatial dissection. The moving image finds particular ease in echoing the constructed montage of the postmodern and foregrounds the familiarised spaces of everyday life; "all these things are part of us like our skin, and because we know them by heart we do not know them with the eye. Once integrated into our existence, they cease to be objects of perception [...] the cinema performs a kind of critique of the material world by teaching its viewers once more how to see" (Koeck 2010, 117). Ridley Scott's *Blade Runner: The Final Cut* (2007) is used as an exemplar of postmodern cinematography, and a film which undoubtedly falls into this category of reawakening perception of lived space. Moreover, in this neo-noir classic, architecture is not in the film, it is the film; rising above the mere spectacle of the visual to become a mechanism for reflection and discovery in an indeterminate world. While the filmic analysis in this chapter makes reference to the already existing and extensive body of work surrounding the cult hit, which has been studied *ad nauseum*, the context and content of the research evinces an original argument through unexplored interpretations of cinematic space.

Research is presented in a two part structure of literature review followed by case study. As the case study is that of filmic in nature, visual accompaniments aid in explaining and decoding themes discussed in the text. These take the form of film stills and a series of original drawings, captured and generated by the author respectively.

In order to reasonably define the scope of this chapter, it is necessary at its outset to establish both its research boundaries and its underlying assumptions. Firstly, while it is the approach of this study to examine *Blade Runner* as an intertext with broader implications that reach out to other disciplines, it is not the subject of journalistic criticism; that is to say, the author does not assume the role of the 'film critic' and reserves judgement on plot, direction, and acting. Secondly, as previously noted, the version of the film to be analysed is the 2007 re-release, *Blade Runner: The Final Cut*. Although an argument stands that the multitude of versions that exist of this film reflect the inherently schizoid nature of postmodernism, their minute differences bear little consequence compared to the effort required in listing them. Of the five major cuts of the film, this most recent version is the only one in which director Ridley Scott assumes complete artistic and directorial control; therefore, this is arguably the most accurate edition in its conviction of the postmodern city. Finally, the filmic representation of Los Angeles 2019 is not compared to the real-world city. Despite several academic writings which do make associations between the two, this research understands LA 2019 as a significant divorcement from the real, instead reading it as a hypothesised abstraction of the urban, detached from specific place and time.

Redefining the City from a 'Total Space' to One
of Localised Narratives

This section discusses the stylistic and ideological disparities between the total-ising restraints of modernism and the fragmented liberalism of postmodernism, and the implications of this transition in redefining architectural and urban city spaces. Postmodernism in architecture was and continues to be a reaction to and rejection of modernism. The relationship between these conflicting ideologies is described by modernist architect Ludwig Mies van der Rohe (1886-1969) and postmodernist architect and theorist Robert Venturi (1925-2018) in their summations of modernism and postmodernism respectively.

Less is more
Less is a bore

Venturi, being at the forefront of the postmodern movement, was here arguing that the modernist aesthetic of formalism, minimalism and rationale, even in their apparent neutrality, were themselves subjective architectural treatments.

Postmodern architecture began to emerge as early as the 1950s but did not take hold as an established stylistic movement until the late 1970s. It is easy to imagine the disapproving glares of modernists towards such designs as the AT&T building in New York designed by Philip Johnson in 1984 or the Port-land Building in Oregon by Michael Graves built in 1982.

These iconic buildings embody the essence of postmodern values in their rein-troduction of colour and symbolism, architectural ornament and form adopted for its own sake. As architect and historian Paolo Portoghesi explains, "Post-modern in architecture can be generally read as the re-emerging of the arche-types and the reintegrations of the architectural conventions and thus as the premise for the creation of an architecture of communication, an architecture of the visual, for a culture of the visual" (As quoted by Shepherdson 2003, 212).

Modernism was driven, in no small part, by progress born out of a Western culture in the midst of industrial revolution, capitalism, secularisation of art practices and advances in technology. This mechanised and clinical cultural environment articulated changes in architectural design and was cemented by the dictum "Form ever follows function. *This is the law*" (Sullivan 1896, 407). But the belief in enlightenment and emancipation through 'rational' thought, science and technology could not be sustained. In the wake of two world wars and the advent of the nuclear bomb, society understandably began to question and reject the dictatorial monotony of modernism, as Sigfried Giedion writes of the time, "A certain confusion exists in contemporary architecture, as in painting; a kind of pause, even a kind of exhaustion" (2008, 32). Political theorist Frederic Jameson also alludes to the exhaustive narrative of modernism "abstract expressionism in painting, existentialism in philosophy, the final forms of representation in the novel, the films of the great auteurs, or the modernist school of poetry all are now seen as the final, extraordinary flowering of a high-modernist impulse which is spent and exhausted with them" (1992, 23).

Postmodernity then is the rejection of a universal truth and prescriptive architecture generated by purity, logic and rationale, such as Le Corbusier's Villa Savoye (1931) or Mies' Farnsworth House (1951). Instead it understands the world through smaller, localised narratives or what French sociologist Jean-François Lyotard calls *petit récit*, which take events in their context and emphasise the diversity of human experience rather than its singularity (1984, 60). The comparatively fragmented aesthetic of postmodern architecture contains a plurality of meanings and truths, each as valid as the other. While to the observer these may seem paradoxical, they serve as a more accurate reflection of the intricacies and discontinuities of lived space; "A building cannot be a human building unless it is a complex of still smaller buildings or smaller parts which manifest its own internal social facts [...] any monolithic building is denying the facts of its own social structure, and in denying these facts it is asserting other facts of a less human kind and forcing people to adapt their lives to them instead" (Alexander 1977, 469).

Similarly, postmodernist film was also a reaction to the modernist tendencies within its own field. The egocentrism with which Le Corbusier or Wright sought to plan entire cities was also evident in the auteurism of modernist cinema. Of course, the indulgences of the *auteur* are not exclusively limited to modernist cinema, and are evident in the works of many of the most popular and recognised directors of postmodern film, such as Quentin Tarantino or David Lynch. Modernist film however invested more faith in the author than it did the viewer, "To investigate the transparency of the image is modernist but to undermine its reference to reality is to engage with the aesthetics of postmodernism" (Wilson 1990, 390). Both in architecture and cinema, the reading of the piece should reveal no single individual, but should rather be a reflexive experience through which one experiences self. In his seminal essay *The Death of the Author*, literary theorist and semiotician Roland Barthes advocates that "the author is never anything more than the man who writes, just as I is no more than the man who says I: language knows a 'subject,' not a 'person,' [...] to restore to writing its future, we must reverse its myth: the birth of the reader must be ransomed by the death of the Author" (1967, 3-6).

Postmodern cinema makes use of liminal space, the transitional space between dialogues. In placing the viewer along the transition of colliding spaces, the filmic plot is heightened through a less controlled, more powerful cinematographic style, as Bergson writes "there is more in the transition than the series of states" (1922, 344). As in other disciplines, postmodern film typically engages in extensive use of homage and pastiche through assimilation of temporality; the story often unfolds out of chronological order, fragmenting and subverting mainstream boundaries of representation, emphasising that the screen represents a constructed space. Out-dated artistic styles are also combined in the postmodern frame resulting in a kind of tonal montage; the mixing of 'high' and 'low' art forms is typical of postmodernism. The constructed nature of the image is further highlighted in the self-referential and reflexive quality of postmodern film; images are understood in relation to other images in media.

It is worth indicating that postmodernism emerged, unlike modernism, during a time not characterised by war or revolution but by media culture. In the populist movement of postmodernism, the world is only ever captured through the eye of the individual, it can only manifest with any meaning through personal perception. As Baudrillard suggests, we have lost the connection between signifier and signified; we are in a recursive process of signification in search of true meaning. Above all, the postmodern embraces contradiction, whether it is in the transitional space of cinema or the collision of styles in architecture, the articulation of the contradictory is crucial.

> I am for richness of meaning rather than clarity of meaning... I prefer 'both-and' to 'either-or,' [...] A valid architecture evokes many levels of meaning and combinations of focus [...] But an architecture of complexity and contradiction has a special obligation toward the whole: its truth must be in its totality or its implications of totality. It must embody the difficult unity of inclusion rather than the easy unity of exclusion. More is not less (Venturi 1984, 16).

Italian architect Aldo Rossi writes that "The history of architecture is always the history of the ruling classes" (As quoted by Ellin 1999, 26). The city is an embodiment of power relations and a communicator of social distinction through its pageantry of symbol and status. As modernism, which includes modernist urbanism, took its last breath in the early 1970s, it is pertinent to study what effect, if any, the transition to postmodernism had in addressing the issues created by its predecessor.

Modernist urban planning in the twentieth century emerged largely as a problem-solving exercise in reaction to the rapid and apparently disorganized growth of the nineteenth century industrial metropolis. An emphasis was placed on the imposition of rational order, as well as the unity of art and technology, as a means to bring about freedom and liberation in the contemporary city. To evade the mounting chaos and squalor of cities, houses were to be designed as 'machines for living in,' with this notion extending to the design of entire cities as machines that housed human society (Thomas 1987). In 1922, Le Corbusier drafted his proposal for the *Ville contemporaine*, an imagined city that would house three million inhabitants and although unrealized, every major city is marked by its ideas. Offices were to be contained in sixty-storey skyscrapers and housing in twelve-storey blocks allowing dense population whilst also creating large open green spaces. Ornament was to be avoided in favour of clean, straight lines, windows were to be in horizontal strips, roofs should be flat and modern construction methods were to be exploited and maximised. Similarly, his later proposals of the *Plan Voisin* (1925) and the *Ville radieuse* (1930) built upon the use of high-rise housing, free circulation, abundant green spaces and mono-functional zoning practices, a recurrent attribute of subsequent modernist urbanism. These schemes, along with the publication of the Athens Charter and conversations held within the *Congrès Internationaux d'Architecture Moderne* (CIAM) in the 1930s, set rigid and restrictive constraints for urban planning veiled under the guise of egalitarianism and universality.

When modernism was in its infancy in the 1920s, it was briefly but decidedly linked to left-wing ideologies, "It was the Bolshevik government in the USSR, and left Social-Democratic local authorities in Germany, Austria and the Netherlands, who commissioned big blocks of flats for workers in the space, clean-cut modern style" (Thomas 1987, 20). The early motivations of the modern movement worked towards publicly-provided, mass-produced housing for the working class many, condemning monumental constructions for the rich few. Early modernists also pressed for city planning to take control out of the hands of individual property owners and as a response to social and economic asymmetry being created by an unregulated free market.

One of the first attempts at showcasing these egalitarian ideals was *Cité de la Muette*, 1934, in Paris. Set at the edge of the city, it was conceived as a *cité-jardin* development and championed those notions set out by contemporary modernist urbanism; function-based zones, green belt planning, freestanding high-density housing and community. However, after Paris succumbed to Nazi invasion during World War II, the complex was vacated for military use. Ironically, this modernist vision of progress and humanity was used as an interim prison for Parisian Jews before they were deported to concentration camps. The meticulously framed open green space was envisioned to be sunlit and blissful but instead served as a round-up arena for the condemned; "The clinical and reductive pragmatism and universal anonymity of the modernist expression suddenly became palpable in its blind interchangeability between a signifier of progress and a medium for inhumanity" (Becker and Chen 2015, 131).

The unforeseen malleability of early modernist aspirations, in the ensuing decades, enabled it to be repurposed to suit other ends. Modern principles in the 1950s for example had not be adopted for any of the ideals associated with it in the 1920s, but rather because they suited the economic motivations of corporations, property developers and governments; large developments like office towers, blocks of flats and shopping centres made more financial sense than piecemeal jobs (Thomas 1987).

Throughout the 1960s and 1970s, the naive utopian socialism of the early modernist movement had hardened into bureaucratic regimentation. The city had fallen into the hands of planners and corporate elites dealing in totalities in an

effort to redevelop and rebuild their cities quickly and cheaply, after the dev-
astation left by World War II. This panicked era of rebuilding failed to recognise the complex social topographies of the city; a 'telescopic urbanism' which
overlooked the everyday lives of ordinary people who inhabit the multitudinous
city, the endless city (Murray 2017).

> [T]he ordinary and indistinct terrains occupied by urban dwellers who are sim-
> ply 'making do' in a social world defined by survivalist economics- just 'blurs
> out of focus', glossed over as an annoying encumbrance that appears 'out of
> place.' [...] 'one city yet two separate worlds' (Murray 2017, 37).

As cities polarised, an enduring critique emerged that modernist urban planning
was a fool proof approach for ensuring and perpetuating social stratification,
impersonal and inflexible spaces, anonymity and placelessness. As social ac-
tivist and urban theorist Jane Jacobs articulates, "This is not the rebuilding of
cities. This is the sacking of cities" (1992, 1). The oversight of modernism was
visually exemplified at 3.32pm on 15 July 1972, when the Pruitt-Igoe housing
development in St Louis, Missouri, which was modelled on Le Corbusier's
'machine for modern living', was dynamited after being deemed uninhabitable.
Cultural theorist and architectural historian Charles Jencks marks this event as
the symbolic end of modernism and the passage to the postmodern (Harvey
1990).

As a fitting visual follow-on, French sociologist Jean Baudrillard writes of modernism, "It has all been done. The extreme limit of these possibilities has been
reached. It has destroyed itself. So all that are left are pieces. All that remains to
be done is to play with the pieces. Playing with the pieces- that is postmodern"
(As quoted by Ellin 1999, 141). Modernism's implosion and resulting transition
to the postmodern characterised a break with existing attitudes. Where modernism troubled itself with a political stance towards a *laissez-faire* economy, private property ownership and class relations, postmodern urbanism considered
these matters to be beyond the line of duty. As a result, the role of the urban
designer shifted from that of the Corbusian social engineer to a more humble
position; attempting simply to accommodate rather than organise (Ellin 1999).

The turn to postmodernism recognised that the city was impossible to command, or even comprehend, except in bits and pieces. In recognising that the

modernist city had become saturated with automated systems of mass production and consumption of material goods, postmodernism began to operate in the
aesthetic currency of signs and images. The division of cities by occupation,
class or capital could instead adopt an "individualism and entrepreneurialism
in which the marks of social distinction were broadly conferred by possessions
and appearances" (Harvey 1990, 5).

However just as with the potential that early modernism held, postmodern urbanism is, if for different reasons, subject to many of the same pitfalls. For
example, "postmodernism in architecture and urban design tends to be shame-
lessly market-orientated because that is the primary language of communication in our society" (Harvey 1990, 77). Inherent in this 'mass marketing' is the
risk of catering to and thus empowering the rich private consumer, rather than
upholding the best interests of society. The on the surface populist intentions
of the free market system elevates the middle class into the enclosed isolation
of shopping complexes while simultaneously plunging the poor into a new
and nightmarish landscape of homelessness (Harvey 1990). Novelist Jonathon
Raban, author of *Soft City*, describes the mechanics of this urban unpredictabil-
ity; "the very plastic qualities which make the great city the liberator of human
identity also cause it to be especially vulnerable to psychosis and totalitarian
nightmare" (As quoted by Harvey 1990, 6).

Ultimately, it may be the case that these conditions are something that the architect is powerless to change, at least not in any predictable or controlled manner.
The conceited endeavours of the past illustrate the futility of such actions and
their potential to become demoralised and subverted. The designer should not
desire for any artificial societal order or fetishize the architectural object, but
rather embrace the capacity to contribute to the composed chaos that is the
city. In *Collage City*, architectural historian Colin Rowe argues that the city
is a place which inevitably contains contradiction, past and future, utopia and
anti-utopia and that it is the dialectic tension held between these extremes that
give force (Rowe and Koetter 1984).

> The postmodernist mixing and borrowing of diverse themes from scattered con-
> texts ensures that no one can ever distinguish fully the sinister from the benign
> themes. In responding to the popular media, we laugh at the same time that we

are filled with horror. Much the same difficulty exists in everyday relationships among persons (Mestrovic as quoted by Ellin 1999, 137).

As previously discussed, postmodern design makes use of pastiche as one of its main narratives. This stylistic revivalism brings to light the importance of history and memory in the perception of city space. Seemingly interchangeable terms, but in the context of experiencing the urban, they exist as polar opposites. As urban historian Christine Boyer differentiates, history is "manipulable and re-presentable in a play of lost significance" while memory is "plural, alive, and cannot be appropriated" (1994, 67). History understands past 'facts' through an abstracted fragmentation of time periods into a categorised, encyclopaedic chronology that excludes the present. The continuum of the city is dissolved into smaller parts that do not represent the whole. It is an 'imaginary history' "that wilfully ignores the city's complex and competing actual pasts" (Bastéa 2005, 13).

The embodiment of history through architecture is meaningless; history by its very nature evades viewing and can never be directly perceived; "History is hysterical: it is constituted only if we consider it, only if we look at it- and in order to look at it, we must be excluded from it" (Barthes 1981, 65). The danger of history, or what could be seen as 'imposed memory', is the synthesis of many subjective recollections and experiences into a totalising whole that becomes translated into architectural space, "As if the past was in the past with a distinct barrier" (Yüksel 2014, 3).

Where the city is restricted by the imposition of history, memory permeates its streets in dynamic, individualised fragments. Memory acts as an 'antimuseum'; it is not found in a single space but finds its power through surprises, tears and collisions in the perceived space of the spectator's imagination (Boyer 1994, 68). Memories are a product of the body's sensory interaction with architectural space and the process by which we differentiate space from place; a process of continuous reconstructive imagination situated in the context of present realities. It is the decidedness of modernist rhetoric that resists attachment to memory, "The homogeneous and undifferentiated character of modern cities kills all variety of life styles and arrests the growth of individual character" (Alexander 1977, 43). The postmodern city demythologises the dead styles of the past, freeing them to form new attachments, new interpretations of meaning and encourages a culture of choice. The urban and the architectural are mnemonic frameworks through which sensual cues facilitate formation and retrieval of past experiences.

Memory is directly experienced, recalled and relived through the experiential fragments of postmodern urban space. In film, montage induces an impression of reality through what Juhani Pallasmaa describes as the "utilization of the properties and deficiencies of human perceptual mechanisms" (1999, p15). The products of space or screen are not meaningful of themselves, but it is their mode of operation and our perception of them that imparts value. The richly textured postmodern city, more than the anaemic modern, bears information in the "weaving and unravelling of its fabric" (Boyer 1994, 31).

Temporal representation, in the city as in cinema, defines our perception of reality. The past is our identity and as Yüksel writes, "the formation of identity is not possible without the existence of memory" (2014, 4). Drawing from itself in a continually additive process, "Memory becomes constitutive of the self- its continuity implies a kind of immortality, and the vicissitudes of the flesh become irrelevant" (Bukatman 1997, 78).

Filmic Examination of the Postmodern City in
Blade Runner: The Final Cut

Like any significant cultural movement, postmodernism established footings in other disciplines, none more pervasively than film. Along with other examples such as *Pulp Fiction* (1994), *Ghost in the Shell* (1995), *The Matrix Trilogy* (1999-2003), *Mulholland Drive* (2001) and *Synecdoche, New York* (2008), *Blade Runner* exemplifies postmodernist cinematography. Loosely based on Philip K. Dick's 1968 novel *Do Androids Dream of Electric Sheep?,* the original 1982 filmic version envisioned Los Angeles in 2019 as a polluted and glittering urban landscape, as terrifying as it is magnificent in its prediction of the future city.

This section analyses Ridley Scott's *Blade Runner: The Final Cut* (2007) edition of the neo-noir cult classic in terms of its postmodern imagery and cinematography, from the scale of the urban to the architectural, and aims to understand

the implications and intricacies of the postmodern future city through its filmic
representation.

Acting as a speculative, cautionary treatise on the future of cities, Los Angeles
2019 presents a discourse on a socially, economically and spatially fragmented
megalopolis; an established and frequently used theme in social realist film
making, evinced in other science fiction classics such as *Soylent Green* (1973),
Things to Come (1936) and of course Fritz Lang's *Metropolis* (1927). In this
sense, film reflects on social and political trends and attitudes at the time of their
making, and in doing so participates in broader intertexts of cultural practices,
as Boyer describes, "theatrical and architectural space are both cultural prisms
through which the spectator experiences social reality, viewing mechanisms
that metaphorically spatialize reality, establishing the scene as authentic and
truthful, or fanciful and spectacular" (1994, 74). *Blade Runner*, for example,
was shot during the dawn of Reaganism in the early 1980s and is, at least in
some small part, an unconscious reaction to its real world political context.
Furthermore, filmic ties between what has been referred to as the real versus
the reel city are not limited only to the time surrounding their production, but
through representing a reality ever external to itself and by the individualised
habitation of cinematic space, continue to engage in debates about the present
day; "Searching for exotic unreality, realms that lie beyond our everyday life,
the stroller meanders through the corridors and containers of city places hoping
to encounter the strange effect where illusion and reality collide" (Boyer 1994,
471). While the extrapolated realities of science fiction film may present an at
times uncertain and unsettling view of the future, they also present the opportunity to be critical of such potential realities.

The postmodern urbanism of *Blade Runner* is a representation of a physically
stratified city, exploring not only the inequality inherent in socio-spatial separation, but how it is intensified by it (Coiacetto 2005). But as Koeck asks in *The
City and the Moving Image*, how can one "articulate a coherent and meaningful
critique of the city when the object of analysis appears fragmented, ungrasp-
able in its totality by any single attempt to define it"? (2010, 114). The answer,
Lefebvre argues, lies in analysing the fragments, to treat the phenomenon of
the urban as an unquantifiable virtuality, rooted strongly in reality but never
entering 'the realm of the concrete' (2003).

The urban scale of Los Angeles 2019 confronts the viewer with a trichotomous socio-spatial arrangement; the gradient variation of humanity has been synthesised into a ternary urban condition. These layers which can be simplified to the 'above', the 'interstitial' and the 'below', do not intersect and it is this separation of urban space that accounts for much of the tension and thematic narratives that run throughout the film. As AlSayyad accounts, "each class has created its own city within a city" (2006, 13); a complex, self-similar space that manifests as a fractal social and urban environment where "Infinite complexity structures urban reality" (Bukatman 1997, 59).

As the opening shot of the film materializes on screen a vast cityscape emerges as what William Gibson, in his 1984 cyberpunk novel *Neuromancer*, came to term 'The Sprawl' (Figure 1). Also nicknamed the 'Hades landscape' during the films production, its imagery is reminiscent of the paintings of Hieronymus Bosch and in literary terms is comparable to Dante Alighieri's description of hell in his fourteenth century epic poem *Inferno*.

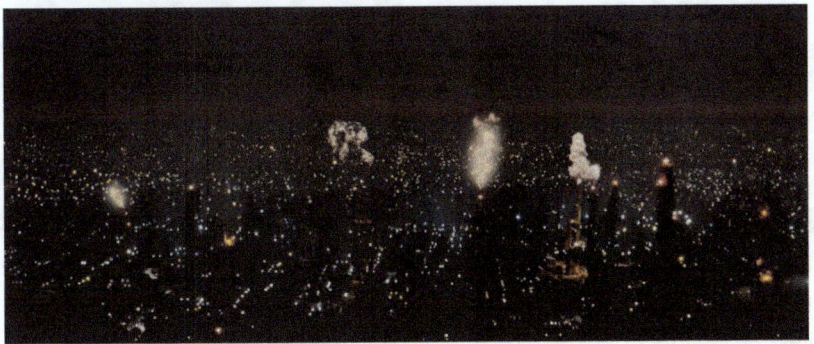

Figure 1: Opening scene, 'The Hades Landscape'. *Blade Runner*, 00.03.07 (all film stills captured by author)

As has been previously noted, similarities between *Metropolis* and *Blade Runner* are vast, so much so that a comparative study of the two could amount to an essay in its own right. Both present their respective urban environments as 'total' spaces, as Bukatman attests, "The only constant was the view that revealed everything in a single glance; a view both panoramic and kaleidoscopic [...] both micro and macrocosm: imploded yet still monumental" (1997, 45) (Figure 2).

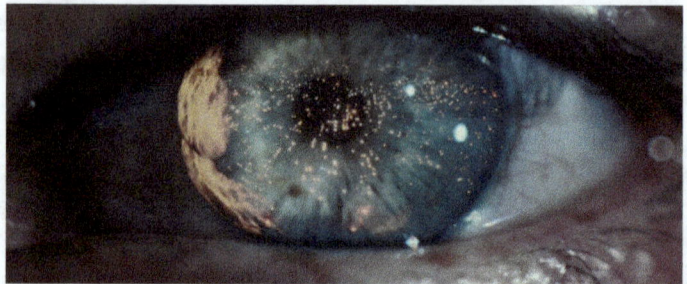

Figure 2: The city in a single glance. *Blade Runner*, 00.04.04

[T]he only thing that seems to separate one space from another is a depthless surface, an *interface*. Under these conditions, the concepts of here and now are no longer meaningful, and chronological or historical time is replaced by a time that exposes itself instantaneously. This is the moment when the city becomes exposed in all its vulnerability, and the eye can see it all. This is the particular moment that connects modernity to postmodernity (AlSayyad 2006, 11).

At the highest level of the city, a capitalist monopoly watches on from the safety of its towers, in this case the gargantuan high-tech, Mayan inspired pyramids of the Tyrell Corporation (Figure 3). Again, nodding back to *Metropolis*, whose city is also punctuated with a monumental building, in this case the Fredersen's headquarters, influenced by Bruno Taut's *Die Stadtkrone* and reminiscent of Dutch painter Pieter Bruegel the Elder's 1563 *The Tower of Babel*. The scene introduces the idea of a hierarchical or vertical urbanism through the presence of these corporate landmarks and the implied subsurface city that underpins them.

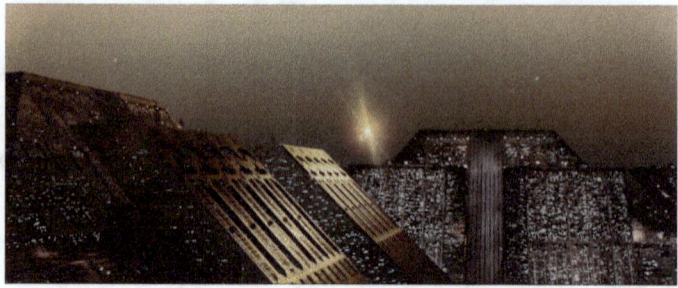

Figure 3: The Tyrell Corporation. *Blade Runner,* 00.16.24

The practice of layering produces landscapes which resemble an extended 'territorial ecosystem' of externally alienated, but internally homogenized, enclave spaces 'located next to, within, above, or below each other.' The vertical dimension of urban life reifies superiority and privilege by endowing it with certain spatial properties. Urban verticality quite literally means security from the insecurities below (Murray 2017, 131).

In this heterogeneous city, gigantic splinters in the urban dynamic (Figure 4) challenge the 'rationality' of the centrally planned cities of modernism, yet simultaneously exhibit that same unmistakable traits of late modernism which expressed political and corporate dominance through blinding urban visibility; epitomising the economic disparities and social vacuums among its inhabitants. These monuments, which may be anywhere between 600 and 900 storeys tall (Sammon 1996) and whose footprint occupies the space of a small city, demonstrate the capitalist colonization of space (with the meaning of space here also extending to the existence of the off-world colonies) which sustains and expands the process of capital accumulation. Space, therefore, becomes the currency that drives both urbanization and the commoditization of labour-power under a capitalist technocracy.

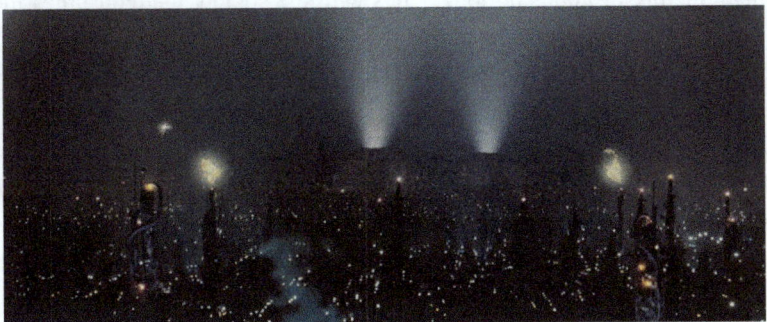

Figure 4: Dominance of Tyrell Corporation mega-structures in cityscape.
Blade Runner, 00.03.51.

Acting as a postmodern *flâneur* whose gaze has become spectatorial rather than participatory, we descend into and traverse, via the shielded confines of a Police Spinner, the liminal or interstitial layer between 'the above' and 'the below.' As opposed to the clearly binary extremes of the city, whose boundaries are determined by geological limits of night sky or earth, and whose position in urban space is absolute, this layer floats somewhere ambiguously between as a disconnected entity. A digitised limbo constituted of an infinite array of vertical planes of illuminated façades (Figure 5), this is an inverted panopticon of consumerism where "we live as spectators in an unreal society in which the individual is reduced to a passive consumer of, among other things, the commodified spectacle of urban space" (AlSayyad 2006, 137).

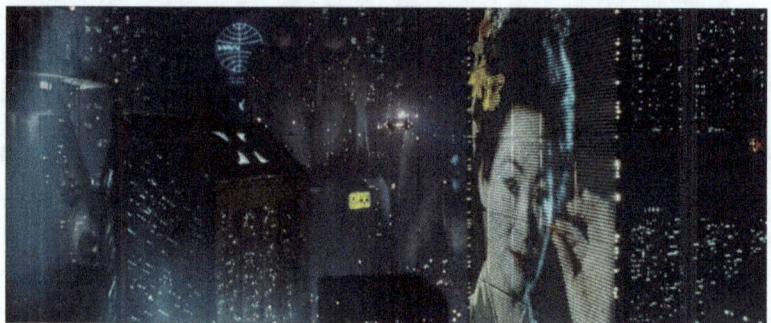

Figure 5: Commercialised city space. *Blade Runner*, 00.07.22

This hyper-commercialism is the mark of a post-industrial civilisation, where the manufacture of goods no longer lies with the society that consumes them. Instead, production is outsourced, perhaps to the extra-terrestrial off-world colonies, creating a system where individuals can at best choose from, but never influence. Targeted at only those who can afford it, the overwhelming presence of advertising in this expansive consumerscape acts as a control of social mobility, keeping the poor in their designated place, and making the rich richer. Capital then, becomes the only thing able to move freely between these disconnected worlds. Interestingly, this calls into question the humanity of the detective protagonist, Rick Deckard, a point of strong contention amongst fans of the notoriously ambiguous classic. This character, whose apartment lies on this intermediate urbanity (Figure 6), is able to move uninhibited through the city throughout the duration of the plot and could therefore be viewed as capital, potentially as a replicant, "the canyons between skyscrapers in which we first find Deckard can be seen as both the confined realm of the noir detective and as *Mitzrayim*, The Hebrew term for the 'narrow place' of slaves and 'little people' (Brooker 2006, 3).

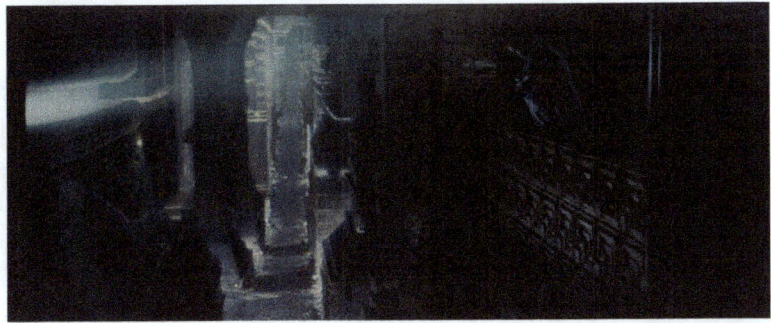

Figure 6: Deckard's confined space as Mitzrayim. *Blade Runner*, 00.34.57

In concluding this analysis of the urban hierarchy, we reach the dark underside of the city. Here, the similarities to *Metropolis* must again be recognised. In Lang's silent film, workers reside in a subterranean city and operate great machines that support it and its affluent inhabitants above. Conversely in *Blade Runner*, it is 'street level' that becomes the setting of a multicultural bazaar in which crime, disorder and decay pervade. However, as the films visual futurist describes, the spatial experience here is not recognisable as that of the street, rather it is a view from below; "with these enormous structures going up 2000, 3000ft, decent people never went beneath the 60th floor, so you've got these big pylons supporting the architecture, and the street then became like a basement essentially, an urban basement" (Mead 2000) (Figure 7).

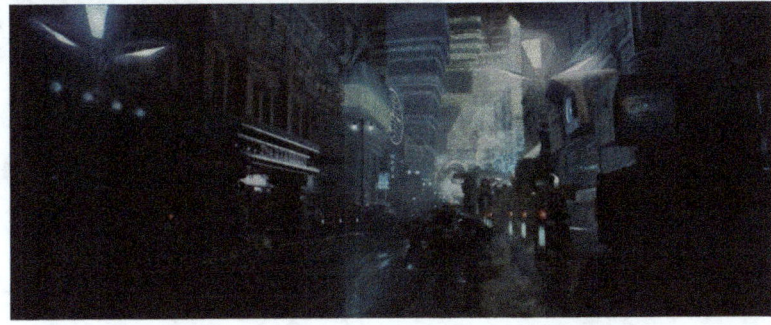

Figure 7: The urban basement. *Blade Runner*, 00.35.34

As is common in the depiction of both postmodern dystopias and the cyber-punk genre as a whole, this space of the everyday is stylistically marked by the confluence of high tech and 'low life', "In the postindustrial city the explosion of urbanization, melting the futuristic high-tech look into an intercultural sce-nario, recreates the third world inside the first" (Shepherdson 2003, 211). The prevalence of a multicultural society is paralleled by the multitudinous sprawl it inhabits, reflecting social and urban homogenisation respectively. This loss of identity is deepened by the use of a hybrid language known as 'cityspeak', which also references back to the *Tower of Babel* and the 'confusion of tongues' fable, following construction of the tower.

In this microcity, the subject of race also carries significance. The upper world of this future civilisation is shown as entirely Caucasian, and whether deliberate or not echoes the so-called 'white flight' of mid-twentieth century America. Targeted and aggressive advertising is voiced overhead, incentivising exodus to the teeming masses at street level, "A new life awaits you in the Off-world colonies. The chance to begin again in a golden land of opportunity and adven-ture" (*Blade Runner* 2007). This indicates the prejudices held by the upper class towards those who may be categorised as 'other', such as the Replicants who have already been "declared illegal on Earth- under penalty of death". Just as the validation of their execution has been dulled down to the quant yet sinister term 'retirement', the promise of some off-world paradise (Figure 8) to the 'lower classes' takes class separation to spatial extremes with inhabitants being offered transfer to a new 'cell' under the false hope of escape from oppression.

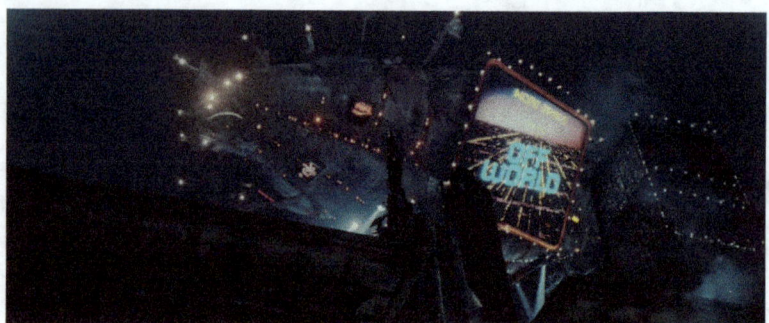

Figure 8: 'The chance to begin again', blimp advertising off-world life.
Blade Runner, 00.35.41

In summary, in the postmodern city we cannot analyse urban space, that is to say, in its singularity. The only conversation is that of isolated worlds, "framed within a frame- they appear as scenographic stage sets", the summation of which defies description (Boyer 1994, 471). However, an exclusively postmodern reading of this future is oversighted. This postulated city, despite all its complexity and confusion, remains divisible. This urbanism employs the same functionalist fantasy of predictable and rationalized spaces as that of modernism, offering containment as anticipatory control against dysfunctionality in the chaotic city, "it denies the underlying realities of the urban social fabric [...] Its porosity and permeability, where borders represent opportunities and not barriers." (Murray 2017, 37). Los Angeles 2019 then represents a modernist structuring of a postmodern condition. But perhaps this is not surprising or even avoidable. Postmodernism, being reactionary rather than original operates through, but in rejection of, the modernist remnants that lie at its core. The same co-dependency exists between utopia and dystopia:

> A utopian vision is necessarily singular and ideal, while a postmodern condition accepts that the ideal cannot be the same for everyone. Thus, while a postmodern utopia would appear to be impossible there is every possibility for a modernist utopia. Indeed, modernism —and especially the modernist urban experience as depicted in film— frequently regresses into utopianism. The postmodern condition then only appears dystopic when contrasted with the idealized modern experience (AlSayyad 2006, 123).

Seeing beyond the pejorative view of LA 2019 as a dystopia, we perceive a brighter, arguably more human trait of this city, one that Bukatman differentiates as 'a utopian vision' as opposed to 'a vision of utopia'; "What if the success of the city as an environment was not a function of its rational efficiency? What if the value of the metropolis derived from its status as an *irrational* space?" (1997, 52).

The layering of the city continues at an architectural scale in its visualisation of a retrofitted future, "a seemingly densely real creation which grafted futuristic imagery over the base of grittily textured leftovers" (Carper as quoted by Kerman 1991, 186). Similar in aesthetic, but wholly different in motivation, to the purposeful 'Bowellism' associated with Richard Rogers in the design of the Centre Pompidou, the Lloyds Building and the Rotterdam Library. Its buildings embody the synthesis of past, present and future; a hybrid city of eclecticism and an architecture of inclusivity which grounds the audience in a relatable, yet highly fantastical reality. This future world is the messy result of overproduction and accumulation; a logical extension from today's real world and a step away from past future-fictions which envisioned cities as implausible *tabulae-rasa* devoid of history. For example, the cities of George Lucas' *Star Wars* film series, which despite narratively taking place 'a long time ago in a galaxy far, far away', are evocative of a far distant and sinisterly unrecognisable *future*. The modernist utopian fantasy is "no longer economically, ecologically or politically supportable, even in dreams and fictions" (Bukatman 1997, 21).

In LA 2019, the retrofitting process is largely isolated to the 'basement' level of the city and is a consequence of an economically exhausted society. In this condition of depleted resources, survivalist architecture dominates as buildings have become impossible to maintain. It has become unaffordable to tear them down and start again; "Things have to work on a day-to-day basis and you do whatever is necessary to make it work. So you let go of style and it becomes pure function. The whole visual philosophy of the film is based on this social idea" (Mead as quoted by Kerman 1991, 202). In fact, it is by the same conditions that the films retrofit aesthetic was born; due to a tight production budget, sets could not be built from scratch and therefore detail had to be applied to the already existing New York Street set at Warner Bros. Studios in Burbank, California (Figure 9). A resonance exists here, that both the films production process and its resultant cinematic world, are consequences of the same financial context of necessity leading to the same architectural outcome.

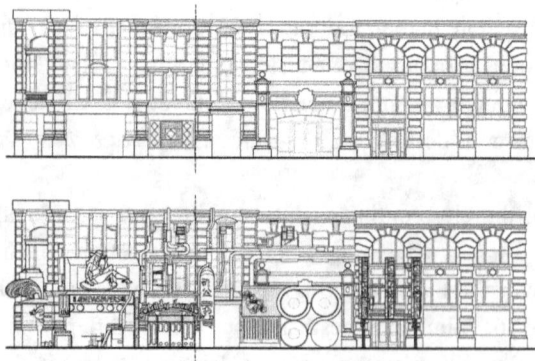

Figure 9: Set elevations before and after retrofitting process
(all drawings created by author)

> It is possible to make buildings by stringing together patterns, in a rather loose way. A building made like this, is an assembly of patterns. It is not dense. It is not profound. But it is also possible to put patterns together in such a way that many many patterns overlap in the same physical space: the building is very dense; it has many meanings captured in a small space; and through this density, it becomes profound [...] In this place, these two patterns exist in the same space; they are identified; there is a compression of the two, which requires less space, and which is more profound than in a place where they are merely side by side (Alexander 1977, 41-43).

Through this compression, temporality is manifest as a synergistic architectural narrative. The practice of retrofitting recognises the city as a continuum, an entity that has a before and an after and one that cannot be bound by or represented as a single event. When the city changes so much and so rapidly that we can no longer associate memory to it, we are disconnected from our environment, from each other and from our past selves; stumbling into an alien future we no longer identify as being part of. Just as postmodern film seeks to highlight the constructed nature of the screen, retrofitting exposes the city in all its vulnerability, making legible its constituent parts. The continued existence of the city and of its inhabitants are mutually dependent, and in *Blade Runner*, each sustains the survival of the other. In a city where buildings wear their hearts on their sleeve, its inhabitants are constantly exposed to the frailty of their world which is forever on the brink of collapse and ruin. Their experience of space is simultaneously one of safety and fear in a technologically saturated environment; "the sublimity of technology, an experience of its beauty infused with the anxiety that acknowledges its power" (Bukatman 1997, 25).

In the cinematic world, there is an analogous relationship between the planted memories of replicants and the retrofitted façades of buildings, which again relates to time. The grafting of these attachments to the 'origin' of either replicant or building are intended to imbue it with life. Additionally in both cases, this imbuing of time animates and locates its bearer in a temporal context. The source of memory becomes irrelevant, the imagined but 'felt real' past as Bastéa describes, becomes the new truth, indifferent to any argument that questions the definiteness of recollection (2005, 15). Even for humans, memories are not absolutes and therefore cannot be used as *a priori* evidence of humanity, as they are in *Blade Runner*. We choose, misremember and even consciously alter memories; we construct our past and in doing so remake ourselves in the present. In the postmodern city, memory whether actual or artificial, is a simulation of a lived but unrepeatable event. We experience a deep longing to go back, and the present becomes the perpetual past.

Los Angeles 2019 is a city that is self-aware. Early in the film, Deckard asks Tyrell, "How can it not know what it is?" when referring to Rachael's unawareness of her manufactured origin. Identity being a central theme of the films narrative, Rachael struggles with the news that her past has been given to her. But as the film progresses, she accepts that it is a part of her; her confrontation and acceptance of her constituent parts allow her to acquire identity in her own eyes, and humanity in the eyes of Deckard, as he begins to fall in love with her.

> **Rachael**: I didn't know if I could play. I remember lessons.
> I don't know if it's me or Tyrell's niece.
> **Deckard**: You play beautifully.

In the same way, the city openly plays on its constructed nature. In an almost self-deprecating way, it enables its inhabitants to participate in the mnemonic ritual of rebuilding the city around them; "Continuity between past and present creates a sense of sequence out of aleatory chaos and, since change is inevitable, a stable system of ordered meaning enables us to cope with both innovation and decay" (Harvey 1990, 86).

The retrofitted city of *Blade Runner* represents a sustained environment, both for its inhabitants and for the viewer who falls effortlessly into an alternate reality that is not only believable, but probable. The beauty of the city lies in its aesthetic of disinterest, where form no longer follows function, nor prescribes it, but emerges hand in hand. As utopia strives towards some hoped for but unreachable future, the dystopia of *Blade Runner* is simply the spatialisation of the desire to go back, "The true paradises are the paradises we have lost" (Proust 2003, 179).

> I never chuck away the set or the proscenium or the landscape. The set is the landscape. And to me in all my work, the landscape and proscenium is a character, sometimes to the irritation of some actors and always to the irritation of critics" (Scott 2007).

Places are established through the detailed *mise-en-scènes* of *Blade Runner* in such a way as to become an extension of the character that inhabits them. From the low ceilings and repetitive interiors of Deckard's apartment to Tyrell's temple-like penthouse, architecture and character are engaged in a formative dialogue, one building off the other. In many cases, the architecture itself is used to advance the narrative, finding expression in the moments between dialogue. It is not a passive backdrop but plays an active role, "space is never empty, it always embodies a meaning" (Lefebvre 1991, 154).

Ornament imparts meaning and identity to architectural space. In his essay *Ornament and Crime*, modernist architect Adolf Loos forcefully refutes the use of ornament, "The man of our day who, in response to an inner urge, smears the walls with erotic symbols is a criminal or degenerate. [...] *The evolution of culture is synonymous with the removal of ornament from utilitarian objects*" (As quoted by Conrads 1977, 19-20). While this criminalisation may be justified in the eyes of the modernist, it is a dishonest and incomplete reading of the significance of ornament. Furthermore it is contradicted within the same text, "What mankind created without ornament in earlier millennia was thrown away without a thought and abandoned to destruction [...] but every trifle that displays the least ornament has been collected and cleaned and palatial buildings have been erected to house it" (As quoted by Conrads 1977, 20). Ornament is not superfluous, and is no more saturated in its aesthetic than are the glistening white walls of Loos' modernism. The proposition of order and chaos, modernism and postmodernism, as binary opposites is a confused one and it is the argument of this research towards the value of ornament as a signifier of lived space.

The inescapable conversation between character and space is arguably at its strongest in the office of Dr. Eldon Tyrell. The audience inhabits this space for only five minutes of film time, yet it is one of the most striking of the forty-seven sets produced for *Blade Runner*.

The viewer's first experience is the vast scale of this space, which stands twenty feet high and eighty feet long (Figure 10) (Sammon, 124). This was a very deliberate move by production designer and art director Lawrence G. Paull. It serves as an architectural translation of Tyrell's character into lived space. As Pallasmaa describes "characters are etched into their spatial settings and the external spaces are the inner mental spaces of the characters. Man and space are one" (Pallasmaa 1999, 29). The space does not offer itself to the human scale, the body; it is inhuman as is Tyrell.

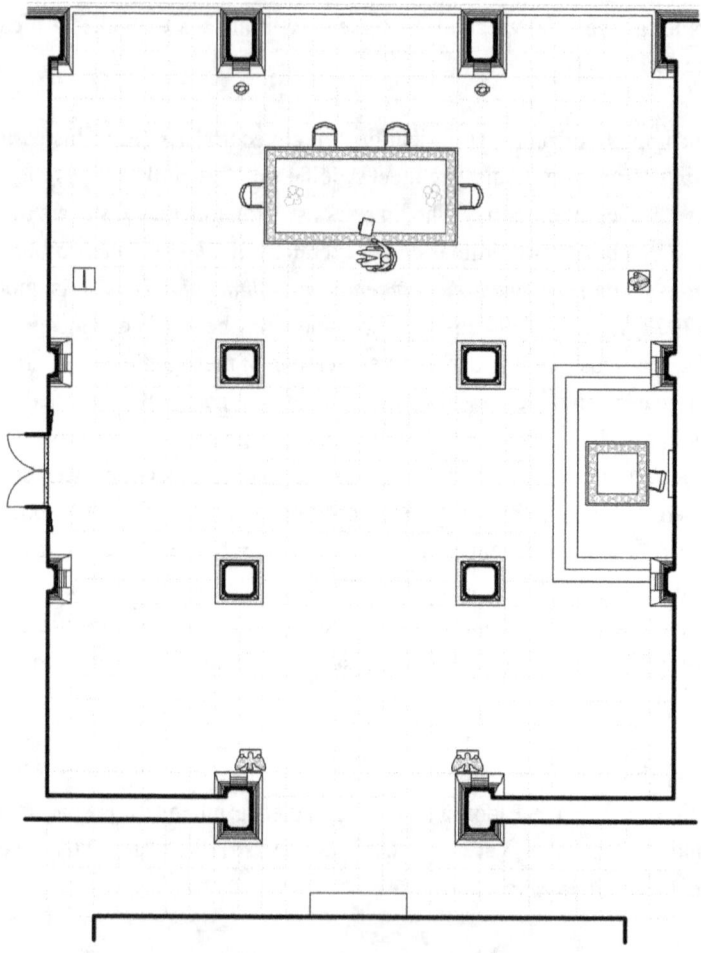

Figure 10: Plan drawing of Dr. Eldon Tyrell's office
(created by author)

Emphasising the magnificent scale of this space is the expansive picture window that frames the room. This is one of the most iconic scenes from *Blade Runner* and the only time we see the sun, or in fact any daylight, in the film. Light is one of the quintessential tools of both architects and directors, and is used to great effect here. The golden light of the rising sun gives strength and credence to the monumental, primal motifs of the interior (Figure 11). The window also presents an eye on to the city and reinforces the symbolism of the all seeing eye and the voyeuristic watch of Tyrell.

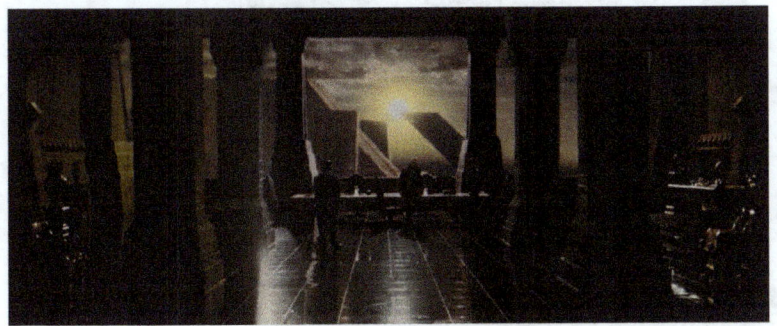

Figure 11: Tyrell's window on creation. *Blade Runner*, 00.18.42

Paull explains his design of the set, "I did a lot of research in the *moderne* style. I also wanted Tyrell's office to smack of a neofascist or 'Establishment Gothic' look, because that was the character of the man. He was omnipotent, a member of a rich, powerful class who had so cloistered himself away from the masses that he literally ran his empire from a tower" (Cited in Sammon 1996, 125).

A comparison can be drawn between Paull's linkage of character to space, and the work of Hitler's favoured architect Albert Speer. In particular, the spatial sequence of the now demolished Reich Chancellery built in 1938 mirrors the visual filmic progression through Tyrell's office (Figure 12). A grand entrance space leads to a vast, column-flanked hall. An ancient door demarcates a change in scale of space. The destination space is one which is of a more human scale and has an assigned function. In both cases, these spaces are more highly orna-mented and furnished allowing both the user and the viewer to associate per-sonal value to the space. In addition, both spaces are centred on a robust desk; Hitler's marble topped plinth and Tyrell's interrogatory alter. The transition of scales through a single space in Tyrell's office, in addition to the significance placed on furniture and objects are characteristic of postmodernism; structure and symbol carry the same visual weight.

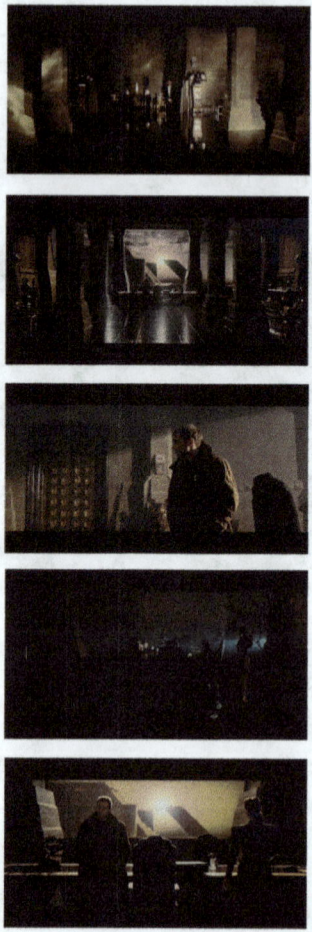

Figure 12: Progression through Tyrell's office mirroring the Reich Chancellery.

In many ways, interior space readily lends itself to a postmodern treatment. Both postmodernism and interior spaces embrace the smaller details; furniture and 'superficiality' become the punctuation of architectural space. Design theorist Christopher Alexander writes of the hierarchy and sequence of scale through which space is communicated, "moving always from the larger patterns to the smaller, always from the ones which create structures, to the ones which embellish those structures, and then to those which embellish the embellishments" (1977, 18). In studying the 'detail of the details' in Tyrell's office, arguably even characters become appliqué to the space. Tyrell's artificial owl, which we see in the first seconds of the scene, is a living ornament. By the simple act of traversing the width of the space it defines the frame (Figure 14). The other living ornament in this space is Rachael, Tyrell's replicant aide. Similarly to the owl, Rachael's movement in the space defines it, this time its length (Figure 15). It is worth alluding to the fact that both Rachael and the owl are artificial beings, fetish objects in a museum like space.

Primary values of postmodernism are exercised freely in this; historicism, classical ornament, colour, stylistic pluralism and a "simultaneity of multiple approaches, meanings, messages, historical inspiration and emotional content" (Güven 1993, 40).

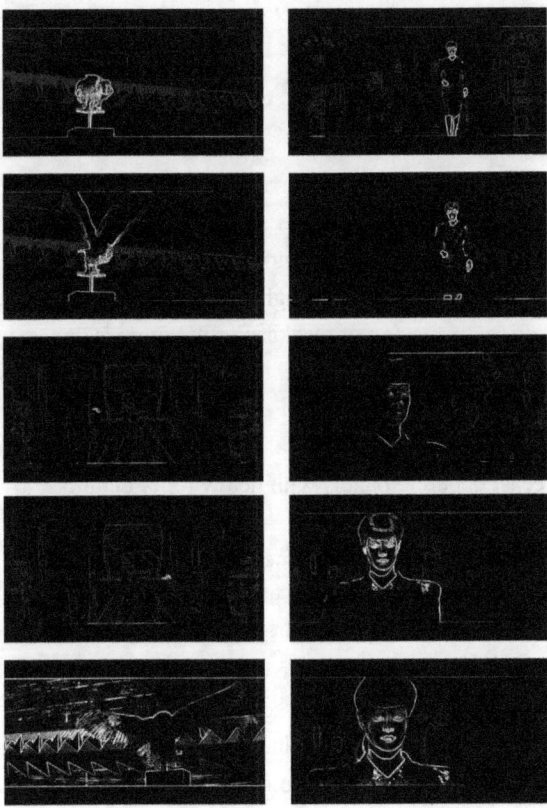

Figure 13: Edge detection of owl (left) and Rachael's (right) spatial progression.

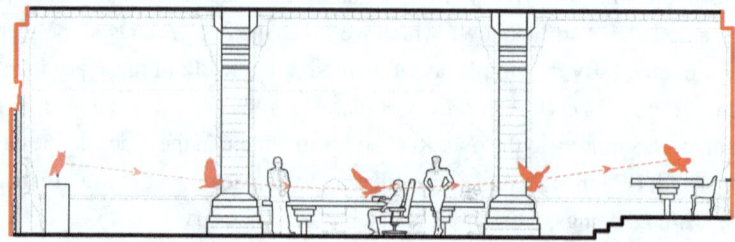

Figure 14. Cross section showing movement of artificial owl through space.

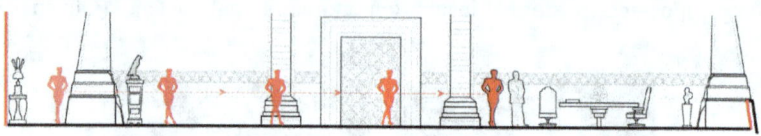

Figure 15: Longitudinal section showing movement of replicant
Rachael through space

As with Tyrell and his office, the same reciprocal relationship, where "characters, events and architecture interact and designate each other", exists between
the detective Rick Deckard and his high-rise apartment (Pallasmaa 1999, 23).
Unlike Tyrells office, the design of Deckard's apartment is drawn from real world
architecture, namely Frank Lloyd Wright's Ennis House built in 1924, a residential dwelling and landmark in the Los Feliz neighbourhood of Los Angeles. An
example of Mayan Revival architecture, its striking walls are constructed from
interlocking precast concrete panels with heavy relief detail.

As it appears in the film, Deckard's home is identified as apartment 9732; meaning apartment no.32 on the 97th floor. This information alone stimulates associa-
tive mechanisms between character and space. In the first of four scenes that take
place in Deckard's apartment, we see the weary *Blade Runner* returning home via
elevator, which despite having a video screen also appears to be made of stone.
This casual fusion of a primal material and future technology intensifies the latter,
perpetuating the suggestion that living off ground is now the norm and where the
97th floor may even be considered as one of the lower levels. Cinematic vertigo
reads as a cultural shift where disengagement and detachment have become synonymous with home life; "high-rise living takes people away from the ground,

and away from the casual [...] It leaves them alone in their apartments [...] The forced isolation then causes individual breakdowns" (Alexander 1977, 116).

Throughout its appearances in the film, Deckard's apartment is shown only in glimpses, relaying a series of fragmented images (Figure 16) which constitute a labyrinthine space. Again, this is in stark contrast to the space of Tyrell, which reveals itself and is understood at a single glance. These cauterized frames, which contain spaces rather than associate them, present the apartment as a prison-like enclosure; "I realised the way the concrete blocks were designed and broken out in coffers, it literally felt like a cave [...] That was the whole tip off for the whole set, for me design wise, was to make it feel totally claustrophobic" (Paull 2007). The narrative cage of Deckard's apartment becomes the empathetic release of the viewer whose eye is visually bound by the same walls. In a sense, the inner mental space of both character and viewer synchronise in a mutual inhabiting of existential and cinematic space respectively (Figure 17-18).

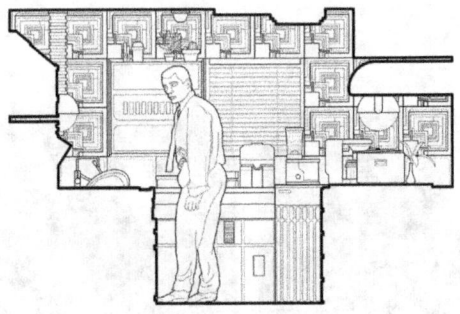

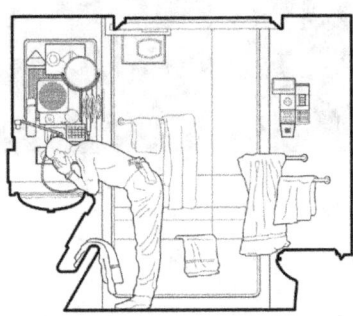

Figure 16: Sections of Deckards kitchen, top, and bathroom, bottom.

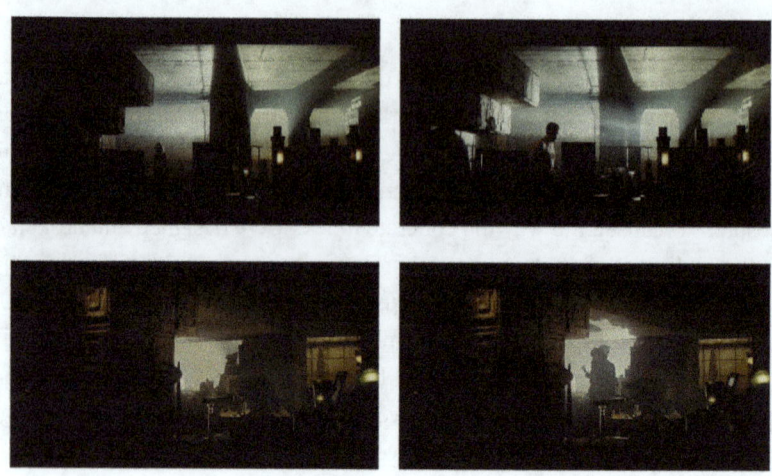

Figure 17: Film stills showing inhabited vs empty space.

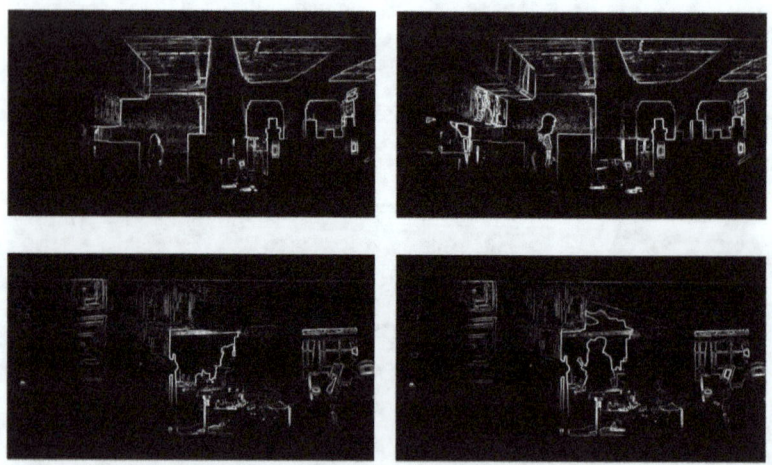

Figure 18: Edge detection of figure 16 stills showing changes
in architectural frame.

Consequently, the oppressive design of Deckard's apartment prompts speculation as to his relationship to Tyrell. The visual weight of the low ceilinged apartment with its bare concrete walls reflects the equally primitive monumentality of Tyrell's office. The Mayan theme also runs through both spaces. Architecture therefore not only relates character to space and vice versa, but informs relationships between characters, and in this case conveys Deckard's central struggle for identity; Is this the creators cage for his unaware creation? Is Deckard a replicant? Given the films celebrated ambiguity, it would be distasteful to argue for a definitive answer, however suggestions lie in the undecided *mise-en-scène*. The replicated and repeated pattern of the interior space highlights the danger of losing oneself in Deckard's monotonous profession. It is a space that looks the same no matter the vantage, where the individual cannot locate themselves. It characterises Deckard as the blasé, "an individual so hardened by the brutality of the metropolis that he must deaden his senses" (AlSayyad 2006, 238). Man is turned into machine by forced employment, as police captain Bryant threatens Deckard, "You know the score, pal! If you're not a cop, you're 'little people'" (*Blade Runner* 2007). With Deckard's humanity now in question, the viewer delves another layer deeper into the reading of his lived space. The precast concrete block can be seen under this new light as representative of industry, which in the filmic universe is dominated by the Tyrell Corporation. So too then does Deckard become associated as product of this industry, a factory made object with assigned function. The beams of light which pierce Deckard's apartment appear as prison bars through venetian blinds, emphasizing the unease of constant surveillance, a theme which saturates both postmodern theory and film (Figure 19). Void of any personality, Deckard has littered the apartment with photographs, many of which do not belong to him, in a desperate search for his own identity, "The art of memory depended on developing a mental construction that formed a series of places or 'topoi' in which a set of images were stored: images that make striking impressions on the mind." (Boyer 1994, 380). Finally, Deckard's abandonment of, and escape from, his apartment at the end of the film represents both the breaking of his contract to hunt down and retire replicants and release from a place of physical and emotional captivity. Whatever the reading, it becomes clear that the character of Deckard is both defined by and understood as an extension of architectural space. His identity is simultaneously kept from him and intensified by the reciprocal properties of lived space. As Koeck describes everyday life, of which the film centres around Deckard's, is characterized by "banal repetition and recurrence [...] However, analysed dialectically, the alienated everyday contains the seeds for its rehabilitation [...] a dual reading of the everyday that both rejects the culture produced by a technocratic capitalist rationality and attempts to unearth those opaque and ephemeral human characteristics which elude the instrumental logic of modernity" (2010, 115).

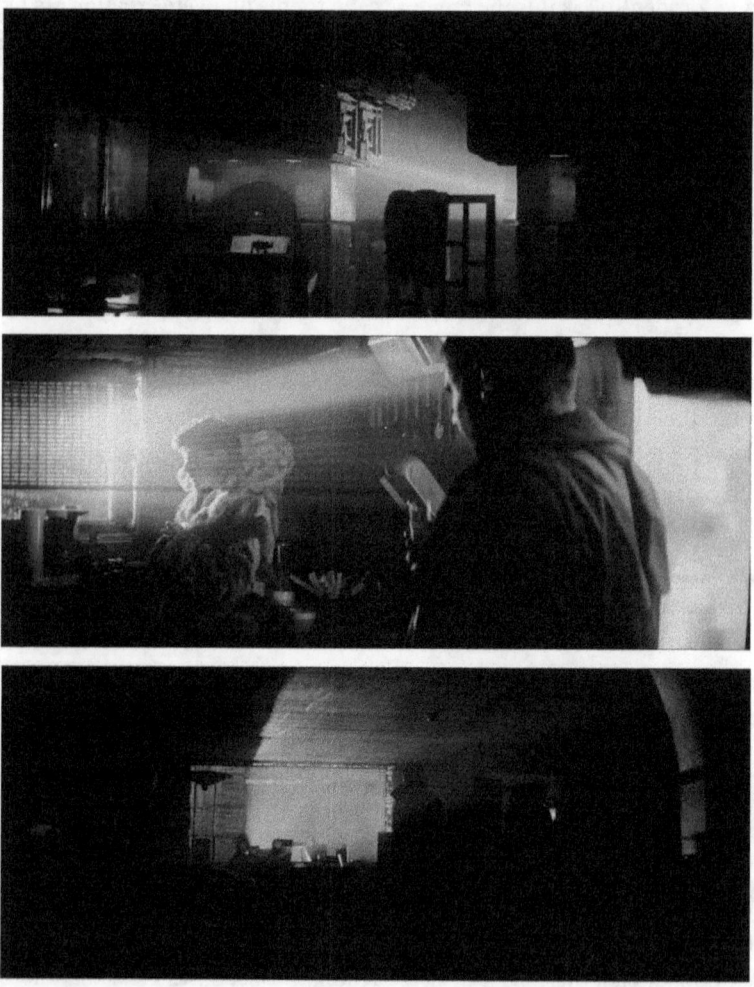

Figure 19: Light penetrates Deckard's apartment evoking the feeling of constant surveillance.

> Far below the Tyrell pyramid, the street-level masses jostle for every square
> inch of their own 'living room' (Sammon 1996, 125).

Through the previous analyses of interior spaces, namely that of Tyrell's office
and Deckard's apartment, it is has been established that character cannot be
separated from space. This relationship also holds true of the 'outside' room in
Blade Runner, the street, which rejects conservative boundaries of public and
private through the interweaving of interior and exterior space. As in Deckard's
apartment, a suffocating closeness of surfaces creates an intense atmosphere
that is distinctly interior; infinite yet intangible complexity conveys inescap-
ability, "I'd always known what the idea of the street was going to be, that
everything was going to be very claustrophobic, that the columns, the buildings
were going to be out to the edge of the sidewalk, and it was going to be very
heavy and heavy handed looking" (Paull 2007).

The character companion to the street is, like all other built space, the people
who inhabit it. In *Blade Runner*, this is the diverse and teeming crush of the
underprivileged. In this world, the poor have little control over the little space
they have been afforded, which in itself is nothing more than the abandoned
aftermath of a postindustrial condition. Paranoia pervades in the postmodern
city, where militarisation and surveillance are omnipresent and pose constant
threat to the ownership of city space; "This is the city of defensible spaces, fear
and distrust" as AlSayyad describes, where "all undesirable bodies are forced
to huddle together out of sight" (2006, 10, 123). Through forced habitation of
these depleted zones, the street has become domestic, a makeshift dwelling that
houses the overflow of society. As has been previously described, postmodernism regards the task of social engineering as beyond the scope of its intervention, it seeks only to accommodate post-industrial society rather than shape it
(Ellin 1999, 113). The street therefore, as a fortified space, closes around itself
and the distinction of outside over its antithesis no longer has any meaning.

A second force giving rise to the street as interior space is the films interpretation of a future held in perpetual night. As Dietrich Neumann exemplifies in
Architecture of the Night, artificial illumination holds the potential to create
illusionary interior space (Neumann 2002, 48). As an example, he references Speer's 'cathedral of light' created for the 1933 Nuremberg Rally, about

which Speer himself observed, "The feeling was of a vast room, with the beams serving as mighty pillars of infinitely light outer walls" (As quoted by Kitchen 2017, 35). Similarly in *Blade Runner*, the streetscape is flooded in neon lighting, the overall effect of which is perceived as a single glowing composition with defined edge, face and vertex. Additionally, as a less abstract notion, a space which requires constant illumination implies one where the sun cannot reach, an enclosure.

Finally, *Blade Runner* re-establishes the street as a social nexus as it is no longer held in abeyance as the thoroughfare of the automobile, which in this future city zooms overhead. Any remaining traffic on the street appears static, either because of severe congestion or abandonment, serving as little more than street furniture; during Deckard's pursuit of the replicant Zhora, we see him clamber over a sea of Metrokabs which line the street in yellow immobility, just another edge to navigate, a coffee table to trip on.

In this postmodern city, the street is a room which through spatial inversion once again pays homage to the pedestrian, whose walls, floor and ceiling compose the 'interior' city that the individual now calls home.

Conclusion

In a strange irony that is both appropriate and contradictory, this final section concludes the previous research on postmodernism and *Blade Runner*, both of which outwardly defy closure. Through a rounded study of postmodern theory, it has become clear that it is at once a reactionary force to the preceding context of modernism and, less obviously, a partial continuation of them. In the first instance, the term stands alone as an identifiable stylistic break which reincorporates symbolism, colour, ornament and by extension, memory and meaning into the syntax of urban and architectural design. A new and vivid aestheticisation reawakens the learnt and lived spaces of the city. Fragmentation, indeterminancy, contradiction and diversity hallmark postmodern values where the metropolis "'maintains, but only just maintains, a control over the clashing elements which compose it. Chaos is very near; its nearness, but its avoidance, give force' […] the built form inspired by this theory should suggest a climax but never reach it. This synthesis which is never final- the dialectic- is often regarded as the objective of art" (Filler and Hecksher as quoted by Ellin 1999, 113).

In the second case, and particularly following the analysis of the postmodern city in *Blade Runner*, postmodernism may be considered as a purposeful, or not, evolution of the defining traits of late modernism. Although its aesthetics suggest the antithesis to modernism, the underlying politics of social stratification and capitalism, with its new *modus operandi* of consumerism, remain resolutely unchanged. While liberated from the total space approach of modernism, its replacement with localised contexts while corrective in some regards, similarly disengages in acknowledging the needs of wider social and cultural cohesion. As is shown in *Blade Runner*, the greatest danger in this world of lost referents is dehumanisation, where a decentred and unmappable city perpetuates the loss of individual identity.

In the end, modernity and postmodernity exceed definition as periodised movements. They are supplementary political articulations of the tensions inherent in the processes or urbanization and of the conflicted psyche, which must constantly adapt to an ever changing built space.

As the long awaited sequel to the original is now released, *Blade Runner* 2049 has continued the cinematic legacy which reflects on identity, urban space, and humanities place in it. As an avid fan of *Blade Runner* it is of immense satisfaction, intrigue and admiration that the sequel has emulated the same tepid box office reception, intense scrutiny and uncompromising vision of the future as the 'original.'

> *Things fall apart; the centre cannot hold;*
> *Mere anarchy is loosed upon the world.*
> (Yeats 2000, 158)

REFERENCES

Akçay, Ayşegül. 2008. "The Architectural City Images in Cinema: The Representation of City in Renaissance as a Case Study." Unpublished Master's thesis, Middle East Technical University. https://etd.lib.metu.edu.tr/upload/12609699/index.pdf.

Alexander, Christopher. 1977. *A Pattern Language*. New York: Oxford University Press.

Amin, Ash. 2013. "Telescopic Urbanism and the Poor." *City* 17(4): 476-492.

Aumont, Jaques. 1987. *Montage Eisenstein*. Bloomington: Indiana University Press.

Avşar, Vahap. 1992. "A Pictorial Representation with a Postmodern Manner." Unpublished Master's thesis, Bilkent University. http://repository.bilkent.edu.tr/handle/11693/17422.

Bachelard, Gaston. 1969. *The Poetics of Space*. Boston: Beacon Press.

Barthes, Roland. 1977. "The Death of the Author." *In Image Music Text*, trans. Stephen Heath, 142-148. Great Britain, Fontana Press. https://grrrr.org/data/edu/20110509-cascone/Barthes-image_music_text.pdf.

Barthes, Roland. 1981. *Camera Lucida*, New York: Hill and Wang.

Bastéa, Eleni. 2005. *Memory and Architecture*. Albuquerque: University of New Mexico Press.

Baudrillard, Jean. 1983. *Simulations*, trans. Paul Foss, Paul Batton and Philip Beitchman. New York: Semiotext(e).

Becker, Louis, and Julian Chen. 2015. "A Tale of Tower and Cities: A Contextual Approach to Vertical Urbanism." *In The Middle East: A Selection of Written Works on Iconic Towers and Global Place-Making*, edited by Anthony Wood and Benjamin Mandel, 126-137. Chicago: Council on Tall Building and Urban Habitat. https://store.ctbuh.org/index.php?controller=attachment&id_attachment=24.

Bergson, Henri. 1922. *Creative Evolution*, trans. Arthur Mitchell. London: Macmillan and Co Limited.

Beshers. James M. 1962. "Urban Social Structure." *Social Forces* 41(1): 94-95. https://academic.oup.com/sf/article-abstract/41/1/94/2227855?redirectedFrom=fulltext

Bevan, Robert. 2006. *The Destruction of Memory: Architecture at War*. London: Reaktion Books.

Borden, Iain, Joe Kerr, Alicia Pivaro and Jane Rendell. 1996. *Strangely Familiar: Narratives of Architecture in the City*. London: Routledge.

Boyer, M. Christine. 1994. *The City of Collective Memory: Historical Imagery and Architectural Entertainments*. Cambridge: MIT Press.

Brooker, Will. 2006. *The Blade Runner Experience: The Legacy of a Science Fiction Classic*. New York: Wallflower Press.

Bukatman, Scott. 1997. *BFI Modern Classics: Blade Runner*. London: British Film Institute.

Burton, James Edward. 2015. *The Philosophy of Science Fiction: Henri Bergson and the Fabulations of Philip K. Dick*. London: Bloomsbury Academic.

Cameron Menzies, William. 1936. *Things to Come (Special Edition)*. DVD. Directed by William Cameron Menzies. Network.

Chan-Wook, Park. 2003. *Oldboy*. DVD. Directed by Park Chan-Wook. Palisade Tartan Cinema.

Chisholm, Dianne. 2001. "The City of Collective Memory." *Journal of Lesbian and Gay Studies* 7(2): 195-243. https://muse.jhu.edu/article/12163#%20FOOT2

Coiacetto, Eddo. 2005. "Urban social structure: a focus on the development industry." Paper presented at the 2ⁿᵈ *State of Australian Cities National Conference*, November 30- December 2, Brisbane, Australia, 2005. https://apo.org.au/sites/default/files/resource-files/2005-12/apo-nid60367.pdf.

Conrads, Ulrich. 1977. *Programs and Manifestoes on 20th-Century Architecture*. Cambridge: MIT Press.

Conway, Donald J. 1977. *Human Response to Tall Buildings*. Pennsylvania: Dowden, Hutchinson & Ross, Inc.

Cunningham, Chris. 2004. Interview with Mark Monaghan. March 15, 2004. http://www.telegraph.co.uk/culture/film/3613861/Film-makers-on-film-Chris-Cunningham.html.

De Lauzirika, Charles. 2007. *Dangerous Days: Making Blade Runner*. DVD. Directed by Charles de Lauzirika. The Blade Runner Partnership.

Debord, Guy. 1994. *The Society of the Spectacle*. New York: Zone Books.

De Certeau, Michel. 1988. *The Practice of Everyday Life*, trans. Steven Rendall. London: University of California Press.

Ellin, Nan. 1999. *Postmodern Urbanism*. New York: Princeton Architectural Press.

Fleischer, Richard. 1973. *Soylent Green*. DVD. Directed by Richard Fleischer. Warner Home Video.

Fussell, Paul. 1983. *Class: A Guide through the American Status System*. New York: Simon and Schuster..

Giedion, Sigfried. 2008. *Space, Time and Architecture: The Growth of a New Tradition*, 5ᵗʰ ed. Cambridge: Harvard University Press.

Güven, Yilmaz Burak. 1993. "Postmodernism as an Interior Design Approach." Unpublished Master's thesis, Middle East Technical University. http://repository.bilkent.edu.tr/handle/11693/17519.

Harvey, David. 1990. *The Condition of Postmodernity: An Enquiry into the Origins of Cultural Change*. Oxford: Blackwell Publishing.

Harvey, David. 2008. "The Right to the City." *New Left Review* 53(5), 23-40. https://newleftreview.org/issues/ii53/articles/david-harvey-the-right-to-the-city.pdf.

Hays, K. Michael. 2000. *Architecture Theory Since 1968*. Cambridge: The MIT Press.

Jacobs, Jane. 1992. *The Death and Life of Great American Cities*. New York: Vintage Books.

Jameson, Frederic. 1992. *Postmodernism or the Cultural Logic of Late Capitalism*. New York: Verso Books.

Kaufman, Charlie. 2008. *Synecdoche*, New York. DVD. Directed by Charlie Kaufman. Revolver Entertainment.

Kerman. Judith. 1991. *Retrofitting Blade Runner: Issues in Ridley Scott's Blade Runner and Philip K. Dick's Do Androids Dream of Electric Sheep?*. Ohio: Bowling Green State University Popular Press.

Kermode, Mark. 2000. *On the Edge of 'Blade Runner'*. Televised documentary. Directed by Andrew Abbott. United Kingdom: Channel 4 television Corporation. https://www.youtube.com/watch?v=NFAdUuqrlVU.

Kitchen, Martin. 2017. *Speer: Hitler's Architect*. London: Yale University Press.

Klotz. Heinrich. 1988. *The History of Postmodern Architecture*. London: MIT Press.

Koeck, Richard and Les Roberts. 2010. *The City and the Moving Image: Urban Projections*. Basingstoke: Palgrave Macmillan.

Koetter, Fred and Colin Rowe. 1984. *Collage City*. London: MIT Press.

Koolhaas, Rem. 1994. *Delirious New York*. New York: Monacelli Press.

Kuhn, Annette. 1990. *Alienzone: Cultural Theory and Contemporary Science Fiction Cinema*. London: Verso.

Landon, Brooks. 1992. *The Aesthetics of Ambivalence: Rethinking Science Fiction Film in the Age of Electronic (Re)Production*. London: Greenwood Press.

Lang, Fritz and Thea von Harbou. 1927. *Metropolis*. DVD. Directed by Fritz Lang. Eureka Entertainment.

Lavenne, François-Xavier, Virginie Renard and François Tollet. 2005. "Fiction, Between Inner Life and Collective Memory: A Methodological Reflection." *The New Arcadia Review* 3, 5. https://www.scribd.com/document/244118927/Fiction-Between-Inner-Life-and-Collective-Memory.

Lefebvre, Henri. 1991. *The Production of Space*. Oxford: Whiley-Blackwell.

Lefebvre, Henri. 2003. *The Urban Revolution*. London: University of Minnesota Press.

Lucas, George. 1999-2005. *Star War: The Prequel Trilogy (Episodes 1-III)*. DVD. Directed by George Lucas. 20th Century Fox Home Entertainment.

Lynch, David. 2001. *Mulholland Drive*. DVD. Directed by David Lynch. Studio Canal.

Lyotard, Jean-François. 1984. *The Postmodern Condition: A Report on Knowledge*. Manchester: Manchester University Press.

Murray, Martin J. 2017. *The Urbanism of Exception: The Dynamics of Global City Building in the Twenty-First Century.* Cambridge: Cambridge University Press.

Neumann, Dietrich. 2002. *Architecture of the Night: The Illuminated Building.* London: Prestel.

Okay, Damla. 2011. "The Dark Knight: Representing Urban Anxieties in Contemporary Superhero Films." Unpublished Master's thesis, Bilkent University. http://www.thesis.bilkent.edu.tr/0006439.pdf.

Olick, Jeffrey K., Vered Vinitzky-Seroussi and Dan Levy. 2011. *The Collective Memory Reader.* New York: Oxford University Press.

Oshii, Mamoru, Kazunori Itô and Shirow Masamune.1995. *Ghost in the Shell.* DVD. Directed by Mamoru Oshii. Manga Studios.

Pallasmaa, Juhani. 1999. *The Architecture of Image: Existential Space in Cinema.* 2ⁿᵈ ed. Helsinki: Rakennustieto.

Park, Robert Ezra 1967. "On Social Control and Collective Behaviour." *Social Forces* 41(1): 90. https://academic.oup.com/sf/article-abstract/47/1/90/2228896?redirectedFrom=fulltext.

Proust, Marcel. 2003. *In Search of Lost Time: Finding Time Again: Volume 6: Finding Time Again.* London: Penguin Books Ltd.

Rogers, Chris. 1977. "The City and the City: The architecture of Los Angeles, 2019." Chris Rogers. http://www.chrismrogers.net/#/architecture-blade-runner/4564812546.

Rossi, Aldo. 1984. *The Architecture of the City.* London: MIT Press.

Sacks, Oliver. 1995. *An Anthropologist on Mars: Seven Paradoxical Tales.* New York: Alfred A. Knopf.

Sak, Segah. 2013. "Cyberspace as a Locus for Urban Collective Memory." PhD thesis, Bilkent University. http://repository.bilkent.edu.tr/bitstream/handle /11693/15576 /0006303.pdf?sequence=1&isAllowed=y.

Sammon, Paul M. 1996. *Future Noir: The Making of Blade Runner.* London: Orion Media.

Saunders, Peter Robert. 1986. *Social Theory and the Urban Question.* London: Routledge.

Scott, Ridley. 2007. *Blade Runner: The Final Cut.* DVD. Directed by Ridley Scott. California: Warner Home Video.

Shepherdson, K.J., Philip Simpson and Andrew Utterson. 2003. *Film Theory: Critical Concepts in Media and Cultural Studies.* London: Routledge.

Shiel, Mark and Tony Fitzmaurice. 2001. *Cinema and the City: Film and Urban Societies in a Global Context.* Oxford: Blackwell.

Shiel, Mark. 2012. *Holywood Cinema and the Real Los Angeles.* London: Reaktion Books Ltd.

Sullivan, Louis H. 1896. "The Tall Office Building Artistically Considered" *Lippincott's Magazine* 57, March, 1896. https://ocw.mit.edu/courses/architecture/4-205-analysis-of-contemporary-architecture-fall-2009/readings/MIT4_205F09_Sullivan.pdf.

Tarantino, Quentin. 1994. *Pulp Fiction*. DVD. Directed by Quentin Tarantino. Lions Gate Home Entertainment UK Ltd.

Thomas, Martin. 1987. "A Future Turned Sour." *Worker's Liberty*, June, 1987. https://www.workersliberty.org/files/futureturnedsour.pdf.

Toy, Maggie. 1994. *Architecture and Film: Architectural Design*. Hoboken: John Wiley and Sons.

Varinlioğlu, Güzden. 2003. "The Fluid Experience of Space: Physical Body in Virtual Spaces over an Analysis of Osmose." Unpublished Master's thesis, Bilkent University. http://repository.bilkent.edu.tr/bitstream/handle/11693/29293/0002297.pdf?sequence=1&isAllowed=y.

Venturi, Robert. 1984. *Complexity and Contradiction in Architecture*. New York: The Museum of Modern Art.

Vidler, Anthony. 2000. *Warped Space: Art, Architecture, and Anxiety in Modern Culture*. Cambridge, London: The MIT Press.

Vidler, Anthony. 2008. *Histories of the Immediate Present: Inventing Architectural Modernism*. Cambridge: MIT Press.

Wachowski, Lana and Lilly Wachowski. 1999-2003. *The Matrix Trilogy*. DVD. Directed by The Wachowskis. Warner Home Video.

Wilson, Tony. 1990. "Reading the postmodernist image: a 'cognitive mapping." *Screen* 31(90), 390-407. https://academic.oup.com/screen/article-abstract/31/4/390/1649984.

Wolfe, Ross. 2017. "Architecture and Social Structure." *MAS Context*. https://www.mascontext.com/in-context/in-context-ross-wolfe/.

Yeats, William Butler. 2000. *The Collected Poems of W. B. Yeats*. Hertfordshire: Wordsworth Editions Ltd.

Yüksel, Pinar. 2014. "Reconstruction of Collective Memory through Spatial Prepresentations of Izmir Waterfront since the 1920s." Unpublished Master's thesis, Middle East Technical University. https://etd.lib.metu.edu.tr/upload/12619566/index.pdf.

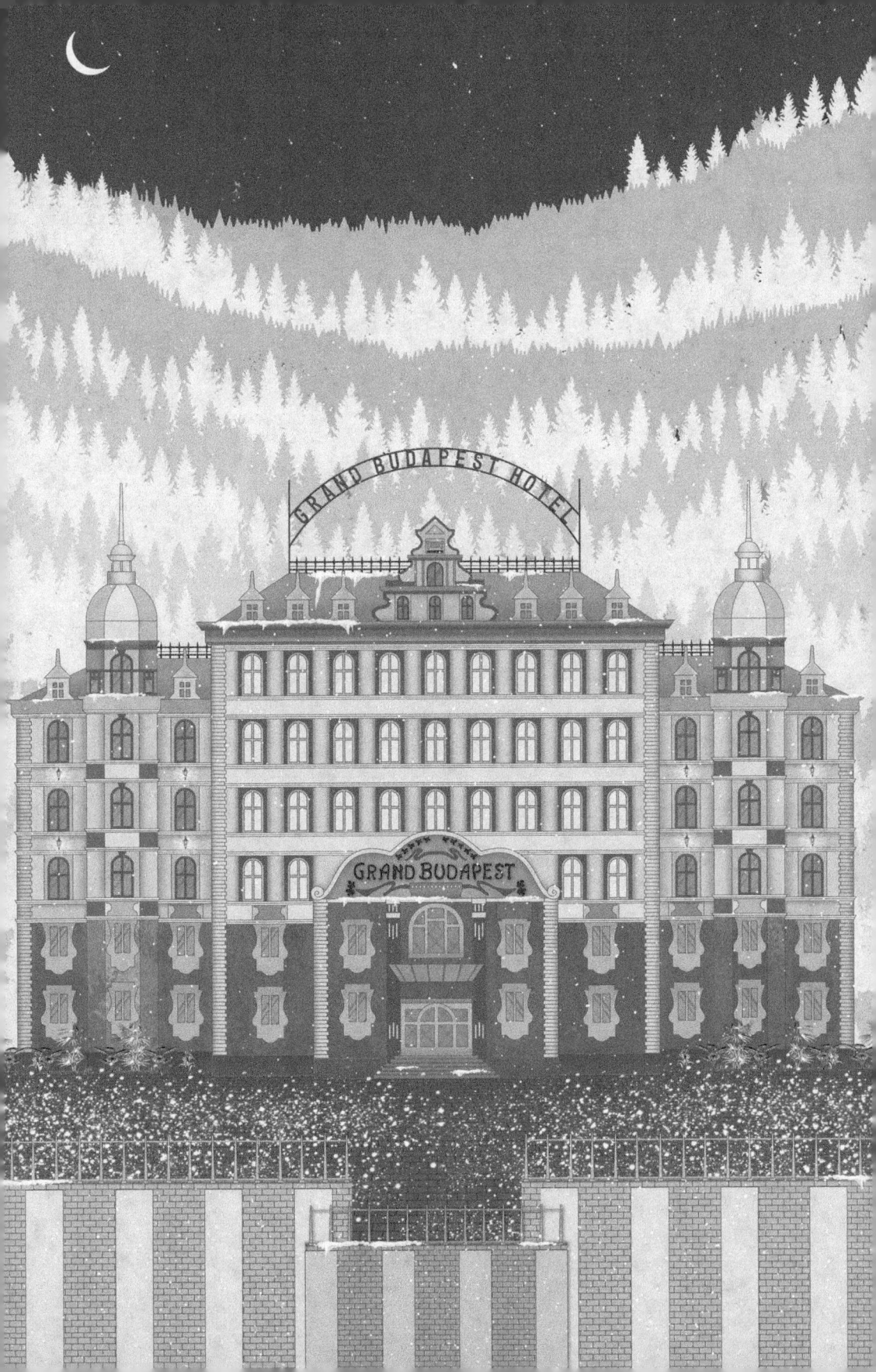

The Architecture of Wes Anderson

Liam Corcoran

LIAM CORCORAN, a native of his beloved County Tipperary, is finishing his thesis year at the School of Architecture, University of Limerick where his studies continue to test the intersection of architecture and his personal passions. Liam's pursuit of relevance in architecture has brought him to the great outdoors, introduced him to traditional crafts and immersed in cinema. He aspires to collate these thoughts in a worldly manner, drawing from his adventures within the volcanic valleys of Iceland or to the peaks of the French Alps.

Whenever Wes Anderson is mentioned, even someone who is not particularly familiar with his work will be aware of his framing. Renowned film scholar David Bordwell observes that Anderson's use of central perspective "helps drive your eye to the main items in the image" (2014). Anderson is adept at this. We are drawn to him and his cinema through expertly planned framed shots full of colour, endearing (mostly) offbeat characters and atmospheric locations and sets, which allows those characters to reveal themselves. Anderson believes that an unframed view lacks focus, that anything precisely framed will make us stop and look, examine what is framed and understand it more. Architects are no strangers to this. For years they have been in control of what is seen and unseen in their buildings. They guide your attention to what the building is 'about,' what the concept of the build is, stimulating your senses to fully appreciate and enjoy this building to the full. While architect and director may not be the same, they share an extreme amount of similarities, a final and complete work reflecting their sensibilities. Anderson's production designer Paul Harrod confirms this, citing the direct impact Frank Lloyd Wright had on the design of the stop motion picture *Isle of Dogs* (2018). "I think Frank Lloyd Wright has always been appealing to production designers because of his use of strong horizontal lines and layers are well served by a wide-aspect ratio" (Yalcinkaya 2018).

When viewing Anderson's third film *The Royal Tenenbaums* (2002), he demonstrates how innovative he is in the use of the framed shot. In the very first scene, of a slow pan down the front façade of the Tenenbaum's grand red-brick townhouse, we are introduced to the three main characters of the story, each sitting in a window attending to their respective hobbies: Margot (Gwyneth Paltrow) reading a play, Chas (Ben Stiller) perusing the financial times drinking his morning coffee, and Richie (Luke Wilson) painting a portrait of Margot.

Anderson tells us everything we really need to know of his characters in this simple pan. Three clearly gifted children, from a wealthy family, each working independently and who are quite beyond their years. Some directors can spend up to ten minutes in a film giving an introduction to each one of their characters, yet Andersen can present his ideas in a clear and concise way. His use of the framed shot focuses all of our attention on the characters, who sit neatly, perfectly symmetrically in each frame telling us who and what is important. Nearly every shot that Anderson wants us to focus on is framed with some sort of opening, be it a door, window or even a tent flap. This framing of openings becomes a regular index in Anderson's cinema. His continuous use of openings and facades of buildings has become an Anderson trope. The framed opening acts as a focal point of the movie, becoming the foundational idea of all his films.

If we analyse *The Royal Tenenbaums*, and look at major plot turns or devices, we find out that the film is separated into thirty segments, each framed and each driving the plot of the film. Within each segment a singular event will occur which will alter character development, the story and how we as the viewer feel while watching. Anderson cleverly links these thirty segments together by starting each scene with a shot of a threshold or opening. The camera never strays far from the opening in question where it proceeds to act as a negative space providing extra nuance and possibility.

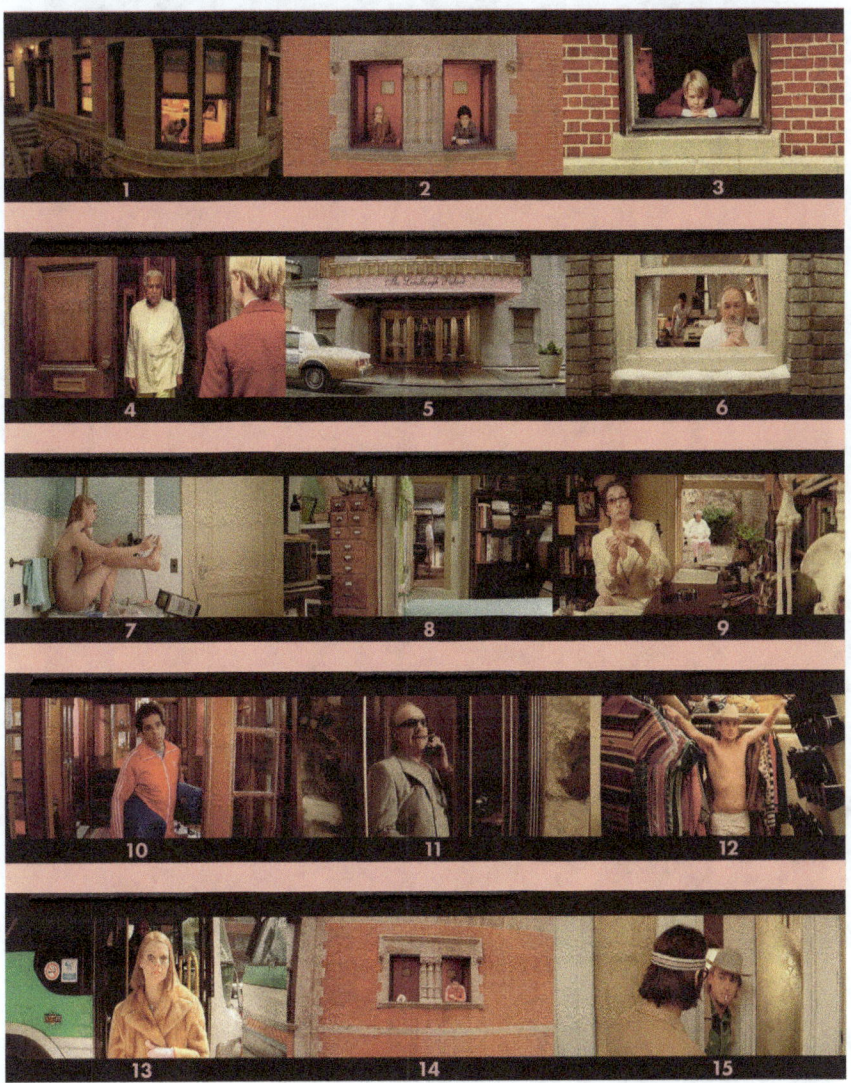

Figure 1: 1-15 frames within frames in *The Royal Tenenbaums*
(all film stills are captured by author, and all illustrations created by author.)

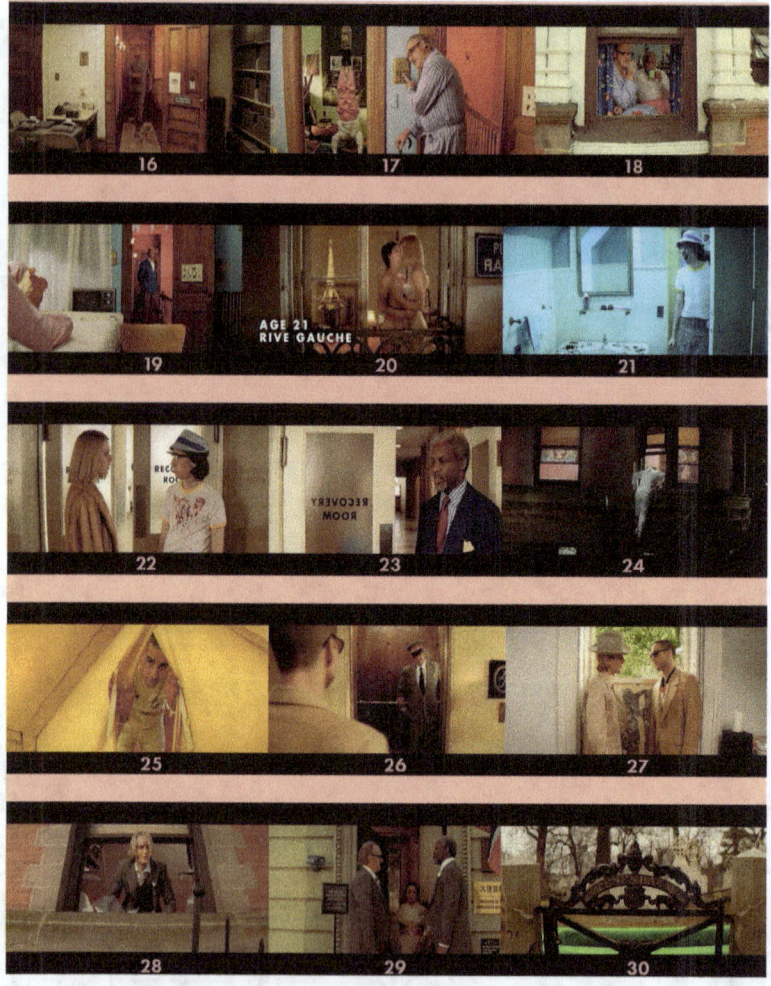

Figure 1: 1-15 frames within frames in *The Royal Tenenbaums*
(all film stills are captured by author, and all illustrations created by author.)

While windows and doors define the character of a structure, they also define the characters in Anderson's work. The symmetrical design of a perforated façade, such as the Tenenbaum townhouse, is a perfect representation of Anderson's cinematic worldview. It is fully symmetrical and conveys the viewers a feeling of calm. When something breaks this symmetry, be it a brightly clad Wilson brother it adds that unique excitement that we associate with his cinema. His use of negative space offers multi-dimensional layering to his characters which requires further view-ings to establish character determinants. Anderson knew that to define his movie he first had to define 'the place' as the central space, the central motivator of plot and character.

A later scene depicts how well the framed shot can be used. In this notable scene the guileful Royal Tenenbaum (Gene Hackman) opportunistically lies to his three adult children about having 'a pretty bad case of cancer.' The camera focuses on a paint-ing of a red-haired nurse against a blue background (presumably Royal's mother). She has a determined stare which penetrates the lens. The camera then pans down onto Royal, sitting at the head of the table, facing his three children Margot, Richie and Chas. The rest of the scene is one of the conflicts between Chas and Richie, shot from a lower angle, with the painting now out of view. In this casually framed shot, new information is simply and perfectly provided without need of narration or acknowledgment.

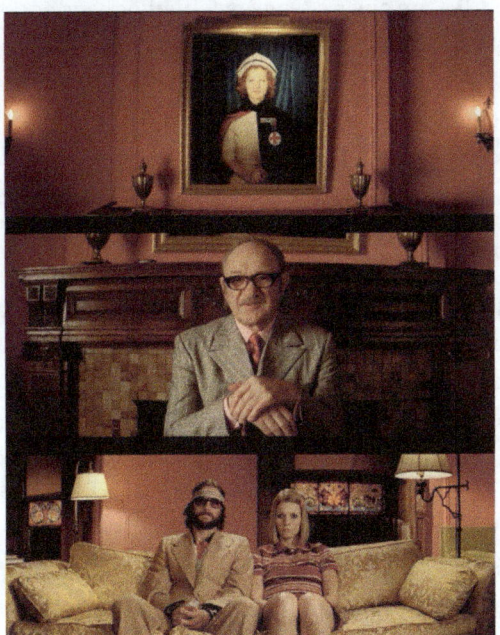

Figure 3: Gene Hackman as Royal Tenenbaum with his two children Richie and Margot (Luke Wilson and Gwyneth Paltrow) (00:27:39-00:29:12).

The presentation of Anderson's facades is a thread that can be followed in *The Royal Tenenbaums* but also in *The Grand Budapest Hotel, Moonrise Kingdom, Fantastic Mr. Fox, The Life Aquatic with Steve Zissou*, be they a hotel, townhouse, tent, an underground burrow or a submarine. All are designed to allow the characters a safe place, a refuge to read, consider, think, write and ultimately to become themselves. It is interesting to consider that, to-date at least, Anderson has not made a film, yet which is set in the age of digital communication and the internet. If he had, we would be deprived of all those wonderful scenes where the plot is devised by the use of the analogue telephone and two-way radios. In today's ultra-convenient modern and e-smart house design, the architect now has to consider the Wi-Fi capabilities of a site as a design feature and incorporate within the fabric the next generation smart house technology wherein the occupant (consumer) will never be alone. In *The Age of Surveillance Capitalism* (2019), Shoshanna Zuboff considers the sanctity of one's home or the buildings we live and work in under the surveillant eye of the net. She posits that the ever-watchful internet has become a digital iron cage within our homes. We are always 'engaged, 'willingly or not giving our digital fingerprints to 'the other.' We are never allowed to truly turn off and be on our own. An Anderson character needs the refuge of a safe place to be truly alone and then, to mature.

Section 2

Anderson as a director must decide what to film, how to film it and how to present any particular shots. In other words, he is a master of the implementation of *mise-en-scène*, a French term used to describe the design aspect of a theatre or film production. This essentially means "visual theme" that is presented in each film frame. The particular tools or codes that Anderson (or any director) employs to frame, create and present each shot are somewhat similar to those employed by an architect. In *Art and Visual Space*, film theorist Rudolf Arnheim identifies these tools as "balance, shape, form, growth, space, light, colour, movement, expression and tension," all easily recognizable within the architects' lexicon. It is "frame by frame" that a director "builds" a movie as it is brick by brick that the architectural vision advances (Arnheim 2011).

Anderson employs these same tenets to create his own auteur's style and to such an advantage and acclaim that his particular style has become much studied and identified as the 'Anderson' iconic and symbolic auteur signature. This style developed in Anderson as a young boy in his creation of dramatic, over-the-top school plays using wildly elaborate stage props and moving sets – *Rushmore* (1998), Anderson's second film, is actually based on this. From *Fantastic Mr. Fox* (2009) to *The Grand Budapest Hotel* (2014), Anderson shows us exactly how much elaborate design and detail are used to create each frame and scene. Whether it is the home of Mr. Fox (as based on Roald Dahl's Gypsy House) or to the custom created Zissou Adidas shoes in *The Life Aquatic with Steve Zissou* (2004), each particle of each frame is considered.

When it comes to Anderson, the Auteur Theory is absolutely applicable. This film theory emerged in the 1950s on the rise of the French New Wave of cinema. It regards the director as the complete creative force behind the movie and the film's rightful author. Consideration was given to the auteur's individual style through theme, subject matter, cast of actors, technical ability, knowledge of cinematic language, etc. (Cook 1990). Supporters of the auteur theory will further contend that the most cinematically successful films will bear the unmistakable personal stamp of the director. Prioritising the director's authority over screenwriters, cinematographers, studios or producers is perhaps the theory's major drawback.

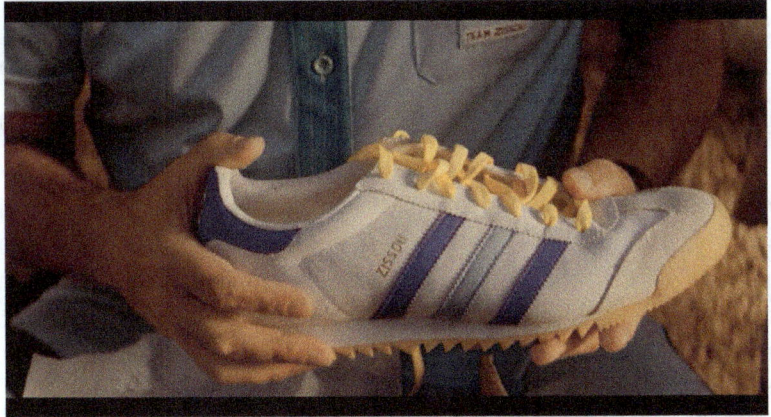

Figure 4: The Custom made "Zissou" Adidas shoe from
The Life Aquatic with Steve Zissou. (00:27:36)

The Darjeeling Limited (2007) is a prime example of how Anderson's particular *mise-en-scène* is an essential requirement of any one of his movies to tell the story. When we first meet the three protagonists, Francis, Jack and Peter (Owen Wilson, Jason Schwartzman and Adrien Brody), we are visually introduced to them and their mutual relationship by what is shown on screen through dialog or premise. All three are wearing expensive suits and carry the same bespoke luggage marked J.L.W., which was designed exclusively for the film by Marc Jacobs for Louis Vuitton. Francis is bandaged up with a ridiculous head bandage and has a walking stick. All three smoke cigarettes and pain-killing medication is strewn about their carriage. They smile and hug when they meet each other as they squeeze into a cramped train carriage; they appear to be in India. From this short scene we infer that these are three wealthy brothers who have not seen each other in some time. They are on some sort of journey through India, sporting inherited luggage and all requiring relief from their individual pains.

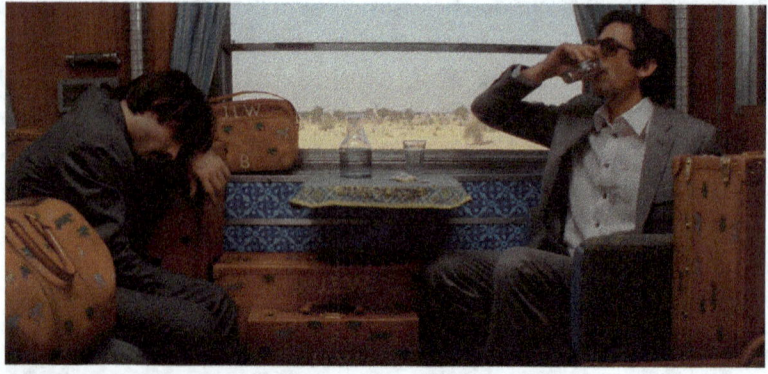

Figure 5: Adrian Brody as Peter on the Darjeeling Limited train. (00:04:01)

This amount of detail and precision continues throughout the film and the viewer as a result becomes an active participant, reading and interpreting each character's inner emotions. From scene to scene, the set acts as a mediator between the three brothers. The slightly cramped, brightly coloured train compartment with three beds and a sink is the setting for some of the most important scenes in the movie and also facilitates the viewers in an understanding of the problems these brothers face. We soon learn how frayed the communication between the brothers is. After a life of middle-class paranoia, the three brothers do not trust or talk to each other anymore, always talking about and scheming against each other. Anderson expertly uses the remarkable *mise-en-scène* of the train carriage on the Darjeeling Limited as a metaphor for the brothers' fading relationship and their inability to communicate.

The compartment's interior wall is broken up into three equally sized panels: a door, an interior window and a mirror. Anderson deliberately makes it difficult to tell the three apart. While the three brothers constantly critique each other, making each other feel as if they are worthless, we sometimes cannot tell where they are in the compartment or even where they are in life. The brothers think they are on a journey to heal the loss of their father, but really they are on a journey of self-discovery, about to find out who they really are after a life of wealth and hardship.

To present the three main characters in a challenging space like the train compartment and to do so, so subtly depicts Anderson's control over his technical abilities. When watching an Anderson movie, the viewers are always looking down the main line of symmetry; he is guiding the audience's gaze to look at what he wants them to see. But each scene, each movie has so much more to offer that will be delivered during multiple re-viewings, with every last detail, planned, thought out and delivered as designed.

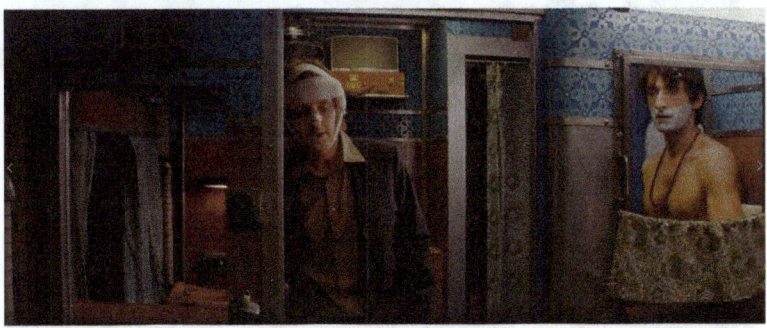

Figure 6: Owen Wilson and Adrian Brody arguing
in their cramped compartment. (00:18:53)

The Darjeeling Limited presents an example of another recurring theme of Anderson's films: the casting of the same actors. Bill Murray, Anjelica Huston, the Wilson brothers are but a few. Undoubtedly, these actors have formed a collaborative working relationship with Anderson who feels that they alone can best portray his characters on screen. This allows the actors, with the director, to create their cinematic vision time and time again. It also allows both actor and director to grow and mature together as the body of filmic work is created and released. The analogy with an architect is clearly their use of recurring ideas throughout a career: Frank Lloyd Wright's dedication to the built environment in nature, Le Corbusier's *pilotis*, roof gardens and open plan, and Frank Gehry's disjointed shapes, use of titanium cladding and abstraction, to name a few.

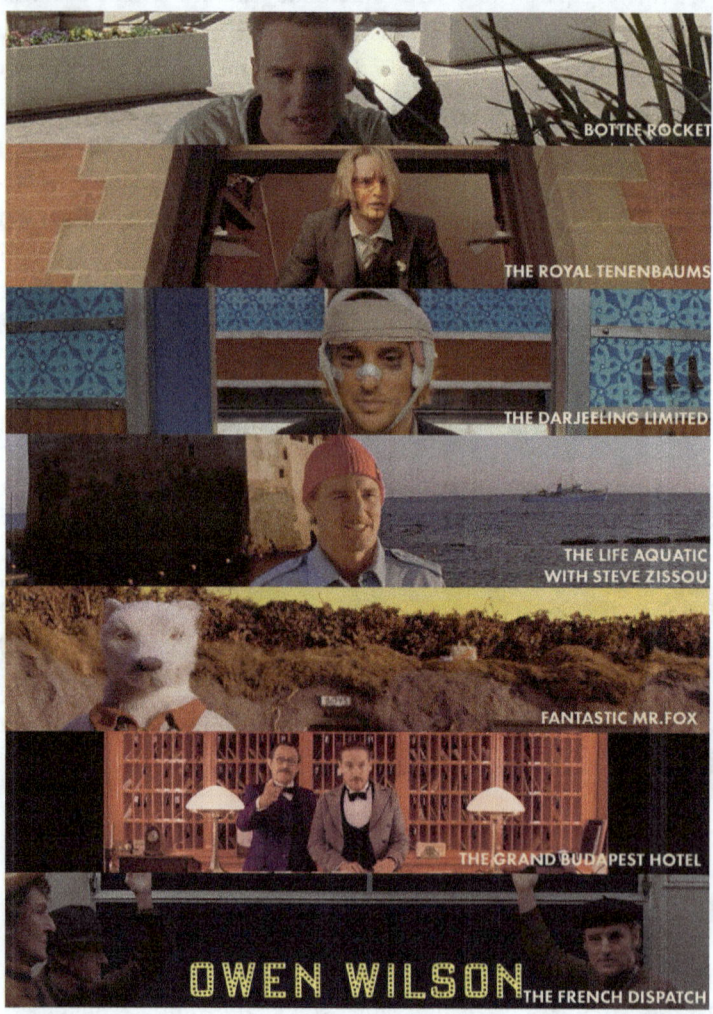

Figure 7: Owen Wilson's 7 appearances in Wes Anderson cinema.

Architecture employs similar principles that Anderson as a filmmaker has at his disposal. Take as an example the Case Study House No. 8, or the Eames House in California, which in its concept, design and presentation adopts an architectural version of *mise-en-scène*. Designed by architects and designers Ray and Charles Eames, the house is a landmark piece of architecture built in 1949. The house, a glass and steel box 45m in length clad in brightly coloured red and blues panels that were inspired by De Stijl architecture, acted as a studio and living space for the Eames. The couple wanted their house to be a representation of their lives and the love they shared for life.

The house soon filled up with ornaments and whimsical *objects d'art* which included an odd assortment of combs, pebbles found on the beach, Isamu Noguchi floor lamps, Chinese lanterns, objects from their childhood, and things of sentimental value and meaning that only they could understand and appreciate. The Eames House became a cabinet of curiosities that represented their remarkable lives. As if to show the world exactly this, Charles and Ray Eames made their directorial debut by making a short film, simply titled *House: After Five Years of Living* (1955), which showed their garden, exterior and interior of the house. With no narration but with a score written by the Eames' friend Elmer Bernstein, Charles and Ray set a camera up around different spots of the house, focusing on flowers in the garden and on the many assortments that the couple had picked up on their travels. They showed us how the home had become a vessel for their lives, becoming almost as important as the inhabitants. It was this functional but creative vitality that contributed to the success of the Eames House. Not only was the concept behind the house elaborate but it actually became fully functional, becoming a home, a workplace, a place to live, forever changing as the Eames' did. Through their vision of their *mise-en-scène*, they were able to convey a sense of their lives to anyone caring to watch. The film not only reveals the personal nature of the Eames House, it also allows rather intimate insights into the lives of its inhabitants and their approach to design. The careful construction of a visual theme for the film and the *mise-en-scène* of the house itself combine to create a narrative of love for the house, and a love story it became.

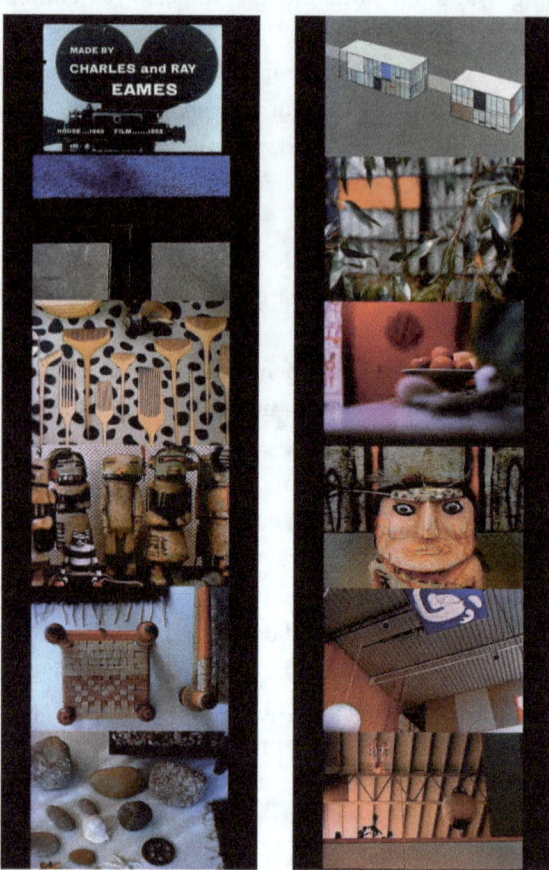

Figure 8: A sample of stills taken from *House: After Five Years of Living*.

SECTION 3

Wes Anderson's framing shots have become his defining aesthetic feature as a director. They are uniquely and visually original to him. As an unintended consequence of his unique style, he has even created a new schematic type of fashion, an architecture that can only be described as "Andersony." Anyone who has seen Anderson's work could immediately identify his style of hyper stylized symmetry, unique colour palette (usually pastel) and also a highly unusual and stimulating location. This is how "Accidental Wes

Anderson" was created. Early in 2017, Wally Koval, an 'Anderson fanboy' with a passion for travel and architectural design created an Instagram page *@accidentallywesanderson.com*. The premise of the page is that people are invited to venture out and find real world locations and architecture that might conceivably belong in one of Wes Anderson's sets. As noted by Elle Hunt of *The Guardian*, with anyone of these photographs you could imagine "Bill Murray or one of the Wilson brother's plausibly just out of shot" (Hunt 2018).

Whereas most people might think that these may be just 'likeable snapshots', Koval wanted them to be more. He would provide the entire history of the building in the photograph, "perspective, context and deeper insight into what these locations are really about – a bit more than just another pretty picture" (Koval 2019). He wishes to write what amounts to a manifesto into what truly makes something accidental Wes Anderson and not just an instagrammable picture of little worth. The page was an instant success, currently with 1. 4 million followers, brought together by a love of all things Anderson seeking the unique qualities of colour and symmetry, thereby offering a new and fresh insight and interest into what architecture means in this singular filmic approach. Whether we could call this a renaissance in architectural appreciation is premature, but it has spawned a unique style of awareness of the built world around us. People do not merely find these locations and offer them as a photograph but in addition they are architecturally identified, they are studied and analyzed for suitability, and often a detailed biography is offered.

The Anderson colour palette is worth further consideration. The specific use of colour is part of the Anderson vernacular and which is a major part of an architect's work and a critical design feature. Any design team will require a deep understanding of the colour principles and particularly so of the hue, saturation and absorption of the colours chosen. Designers need to consider the qualities of harmony, tone and emotional reaction and the site requirements of natural or artificial lighting.

To a project-driven director such as Anderson, the 'Anderson Palettes' have become synonymous with each film and its specific aesthetic. Recall the natural earth tones of *Moonrise Kingdom*, brown and khaki, a palette that was clearly chosen with discretion and that emphasizes in contrast the binary opposite colour of Suzi's character, including her dresses. Anderson's palettes are essentially monochromatic in tone, thus allowing for a pleasant viewing and presenting a somnambular quality to the characters that is in harmony with the gentle and non-threatening manner of their dialogue, the language used and its delivery. Each scene design is carefully coordinated with this scheme in mind so as to deny any visual jolt or irritant to the viewer. This then allows for the film's montage to flow with humanity and follow its natural course. Anderson chooses his colours to tell the story, to move the narrative along. They draw the attentive viewer's eyes to the specific details he wishes them to see. Colours set the overall tone of the film as it is created, acting as specific markers for the characters and their respective traits. Colours can and will indicate change in the narrative and in the evolution of the characters.

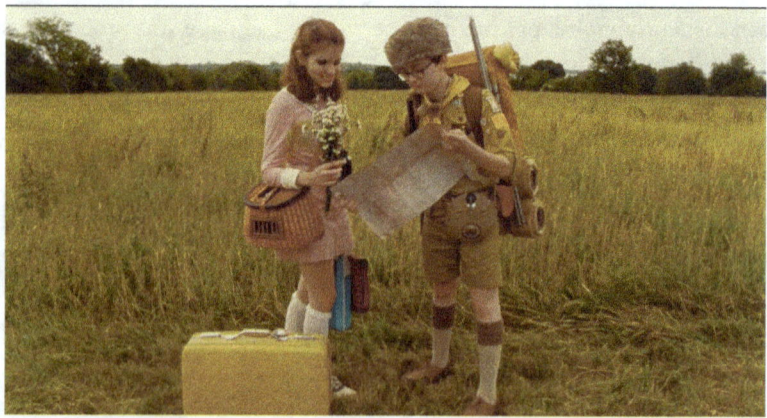

Figure 9. The colour palette in *Moonrise Kingdom*. (00:21:04)

The Anderson aesthetic is so particularly unique to him and as such makes an 'Anderson' movie immediately identifiable. At the same time, his influences are clearly referenced– French New Wave, Buster Keaton –and yet Anderson does not conform to anything that has been done before. His colour palette and symmetrical frames are parts of his signature, but the basis of every Anderson movie can be further considered as following Gottfried Semper's four elements of architecture.

In 1851, Gottfried Semper, a well-known German architect, wrote a book entitled *The Four Elements of Architecture*. The book was divided into four separate but essential elements, 'the hearth, the roof, the enclosure and the mound'. In this book Semper tried to universally define a theory for architecture. Beginning in prehistoric times, Semper studied and identified the methodology of building structure and attempted to define the basis of why we build the way we do.

Semper assumes the hearth to be the main element of the four, the beginning of architecture, with the remaining elements emanating from this center: "around the hearth the first groups formed: around the hearth the first groups assembled... around it were grouped the other three elements, the roof, the enclosure and the mound" (Semper, 1989). Semper does not research a single building typology but considers what systems and assemblies that are universal in all primitive structures so as to define his universal theory. If we take an Anderson movie and analyze it using these elements, we can clearly see that Anderson allows this system to guide him in his narrative construction. These central motifs play integral parts in Anderson's cinema and become the very foundation on which the film's structure and characters are built.

The Grand Budapest Hotel can be considered as an example in the employment of this system.

The Hearth: The atrium

The atrium within The Grand Budapest Hotel where Anderson allows the central and critical scenes to play out. In Semper's own words "The hearth is the germ, the embryo of all social institutions... It was a moral symbol" (1984). What Semper means is that the hearth is the focal point of any home or building. It is the fireplace (warmth and nourishment) around which you and your family gather around and if you wish may be the main studio space of any school of architecture.

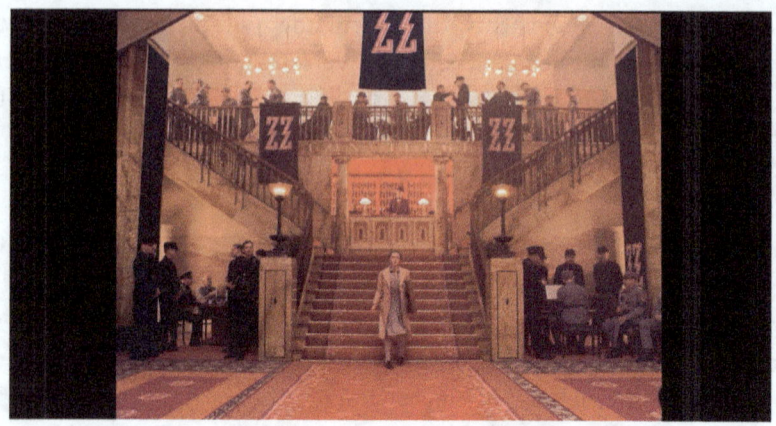

Figure 10: Saoirse Ronan in the atrium space in
The Grand Budapest Hotel. (01:22:52)

Each Anderson film revolves around one custom built highly detailed unit, whether it is the boat in *The Life Aquatic with Steve Zissou*, The Budapest Hotel or the beech tree in *Fantastic Mr. Fox*. This method has become a key aspect of his film's syntax.

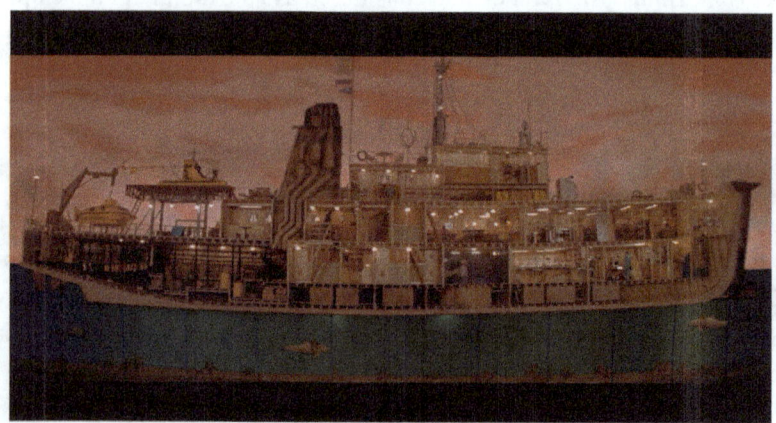

Figure 11: The section through the custom-made ship for
The Life Aquatic With Steve Zissou. (00:15:11)

Located in the fictional country of the Republic of Zubrowka, perched on top of an alp, accessible by funicular brightly coloured the Grand Budapest Hotel is actually a 2.7m tall model painstakingly made by Anderson and his dedicated team. The hotel atrium space, with its stained-glass ceiling and sweeping staircases was actually a splendid *Art Nouveau* department store, designed in 1913 by Austrian architect Carl Schumanns and situated in the East German town of Görlitz. Anderson trawled with great care through decades of archived pictures of now extinct buildings, sampling a staircase here and an elevator door there to try and make the hotel as 'real' to his reality as possible (Rose, 2014).

Throughout the film we follow the enfolding emotional relationship that each character has to this hotel. As the principal character Zero simply describes it, "The Grand Budapest, Sir? It's an institution" (*The Grand Budapest Hotel*, 2014). The love and regard that every character has for this space is reminiscent of that which we all have for our own hearths in our own homes. Anderson acknowledges this kinship and makes the hotel a main character in its own right, allowing the audience to create their own inevitable loyalty. Note again that the principal characters of any Anderson film are essentially quirky, funny, humane and emotionally moral. The atrium where some of the most important scenes take place is the beating heart of the hotel. Every critical scene takes place here. Recall your shudder when the Nazi-inspired militants make their headquarters there. It is in the atrium here where the film begins and ends.

The Enclosure: Anderson's use of free façade

Semper writes: "The Enclosure is said to have its origins in weaving. Just as fences and pens were woven sticks, the most basic form of spatial divider today is the fabric screen. Only when additional requirements are placed on the enclosure such as structural weight bearing elements does the materiality of the wall change to something beyond fabric" (1989). As mentioned earlier, Anderson's use of symmetry and elevations are revolutionary. Nowhere is this more utilized than in *The Grand Budapest Hotel*. The entire film focuses on the hotel but particularly the front façade of this building. Anderson understands fully that like a blank fabric sheet the materiality will change when you begin to change its structure. He designed every single window and ornamentation on the façade to give it this materiality. The enclosure is his signature element; it is the most unmistakable 'Anderson' in style and aesthetics.

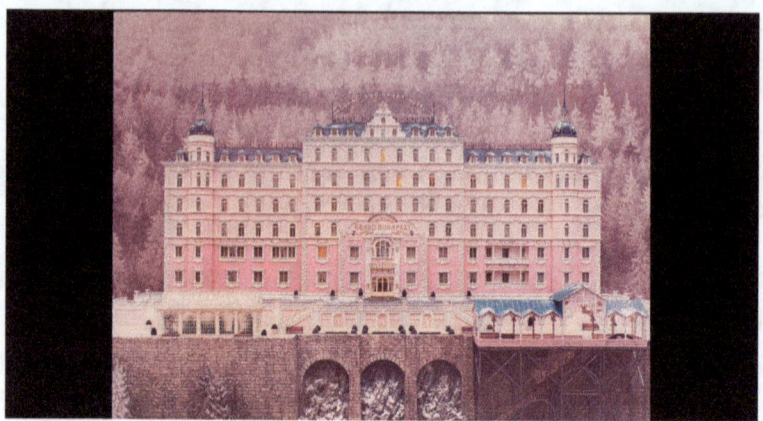

Figure 12: The front façade of the Grand Budapest hotel. (00:03:23)

The power over creating such a façade is evident from the cover of this chapter. Consider the expense on filming with and in a difficult location dealing with bad weather and studio demands,. when you can just create a studio model, bespoke piece, an architectural model that is suitable for purpose in and of itself. Models have been used in cinema before but never so blatantly as this. The iconic façade has since become a design landmark as to what can be achieved through innovative set design and an original idea.

It can be offered that Anderson also utilizes Le Corbusier's five points of architecture system, which includes the use of the' free design of the façade.' By separating the exterior of the building from its structural function this sets the façade free from its structural constraints. By incorporating a candy like pastel colouring to the continuous exterior, the façade is emphasized as separate but critically as a set design unit. Like Le Corbusier freeing the façade (use of horizontal windows), Anderson frees himself from the normal constraints of the 'filmed on location' process. He can create a childlike world that the viewer accepts and where we can switch-off in the dark and suspend our logical disbelief. His façades act as rose-tinted glass where we understand that not everything is real but which we can nonetheless still enjoy and fully appreciate.

The Mound: The characters

Semper defines 'mound' as rooted in the ground, stereo-metric wall making, protecting the hearth, allied to the materials and processes of the masonry. As every building needs a foundation, so does a film. For Anderson these are his characters. Although Wes Anderson's collection of whimsical, quirky characters may be there just for comedic effect or to blend into the pastel background, they add much more complexity and nuance than one may at first realise. They are the basis for the movie from which everything grows. Consider the story of Zero, played by Tony Revolori and F. Murray Abraham in *The Grand Budapest Hotel*: an orphaned boy running from civil unrest and war to find his place in the world as a lobby boy at The Grand Budapest. The rest of the film forms a love story between Zero and the hotel until, finally, all he has left is the hotel and a coterie of memories that fortifies him and which he can never forget.

As the 'mound' protects the 'hearth,' the same is relevant here as our protagonist reciprocates and does his utmost to protect, defend and keep his beloved hotel at all costs. He witnesses and suffers the gamut of human emotions and frailties: he falls in love in the hotel, he grows and is inspired by his mentor in the hotel, and he ultimately dies in this hotel.

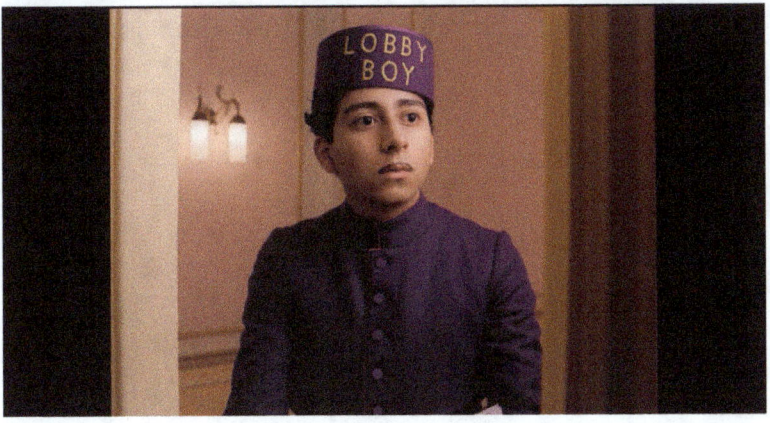

Figure 13. Zero played by Tony Revolori in
The Grand Budapest Hotel. (00:18:45)

The Roof: The Wes Anderson aesthetic

The one thing that really makes a Wes Anderson movie a Wes Anderson movie is his style. Overhead shots, Futura font, the pastel colouring, children that are adult-like, dysfunctional families, intricate set design, slow pans, symmetrical everything, these are but a few ingredients that amounts to a Wes Anderson aesthetic, his particular film grammar. It provides a covering for everything inside and brings with it a sense of protection and warmth. I offer that these are the feelings that are unearthed when experiencing one of his films. We are transported to this slightly surreal world that we know cannot be real, but we wish it was. Nostalgia for this bygone world of morality and mutual respect makes us crave more. His architectural inspiration and understanding provides him with a structure and process to allow him to create whole worlds that are believable and endearing.

Like truly great architecture, Wes Anderson captures humanity in a constructed world. From nothing he makes us feel connected to everything that we are watching, makes us feel what the characters are feeling. He does this solely by himself by starting with a simple idea that he keeps on developing until finally he has a masterpiece. At only 52 years of age he continues to influence the world be it through cinema, fashion or architecture.

Wes Anderson, a cultural icon of the twenty-first century, a director, a designer, an architect of cinema.

REFERENCES

Anderson, Wes. 1996. *Bottle Rocket*. DVD. Texas: Sony.

Anderson, Wes. 1998. *Rushmore*. DVD. Texas: Touchstone Pictures.

Anderson, Wes. 2001. *The Royal Tenenbaums*. DVD: New York: Buena Vista Pictures.

Anderson, Wes. 2004. *The life aquatic with Steve Zissou*. DVD. Italy: Buena Vista Pictures.

Anderson, Wes. 2007. *The Darjeeling Limited*. DVD. India: Fox Searchlight Pictures.

Anderson, Wes. 2009. *Fantastic Mr. Fox*. DVD. London: 20th Century Fox.

Anderson, Wes. 2012. *Moonrise Kingdom*. DVD. Rhode Island: American Empirical Pictures, Indian Paintbrush.

Anderson, Wes. 2014. *The Grand Budapest Hotel*. DVD. Germany: American Empirical Pictures.

Anderson, Wes. 2018. *Isle Of Dogs. DVD*. London: Fox Searchlight Pictures.

Andrew, Dudley. 1976. *The Major Film Theories*. London: Oxford University Press.

Arnheim, Rudolf. 2011. *Art And Visual Perception*. Berkeley: University of California Press.

Cook, Pam (ed). 2007. *The Cinema Book*. 3rd ed. London: British Film Institute.

Eames, Ch. 1955. *House: After Five Years Of Living*. Video.https://www.youtube.com/watch?v=CUc3kBpFUF0[accessed…]

Hermann, W. 1984. *Gottfied Semper*. London: MIT Press.

Hunt, E. 2018. "Accidentally Wes Anderson: Instagram Finds Stylised Symmetry In Real Cities". *The Guardian* (4 January). https://www.theguardian.com/cities/2018/jan/04/accidentally-wes-anderson-instagram-symmetry.

Koval, Wally. 2017. "Accidental Wes Anderson". *Accidental Wes Anderson*. https://www.instagram.com/accidentallywesanderson/.

Rawsthorn, A. 2019. *Image*. https://www.nytimes.com/2015/10/23/arts/international/the-eames-a-team-for-whom-design-was-a-way-of-life.html

Rose, Steve. 2014. "Wes Anderson: The Architectural Film-Maker". *The Architects' Journal*. https://www.architectsjournal.co.uk/news/wes-anderson-the-architectural-film-maker.

Semper, Gottfried. 1989. *The Four Elements Of Architecture And Other Writings*. 2nd ed. Cambridge: Cambridge University Press.

Semper, G. 1952. *Four Elements Of Architecture*. Image. http://nyitarch161.blogspot.com/2016/10/a_31.html.

Wise, L. 2018. "From Gucci Ads To Instagram Fads: How The Wes Anderson Aesthetic Took Over The World", *The Guardian*. https://www.theguardian.com/film/2018/

apr/07/from-gucci-ads-to-instagram-fads-how-the-wes-anderson-aesthetic-took-over-the-world.

Yalcinkaya, Gunseli. 2018. "Wes Anderson's Isle Of Dogs Film Sets Influenced By Metabolist Architecture". *Dezeen*. https://www.dezeen.com/2018/03/28/wes-anderson-isle-of-dogs-sets-metabolist-architecture-paul-harrod-interview/.

Zuboff, Shoshanna. 2019. *The Age of Surveillance Capitalism*. Profile Books.

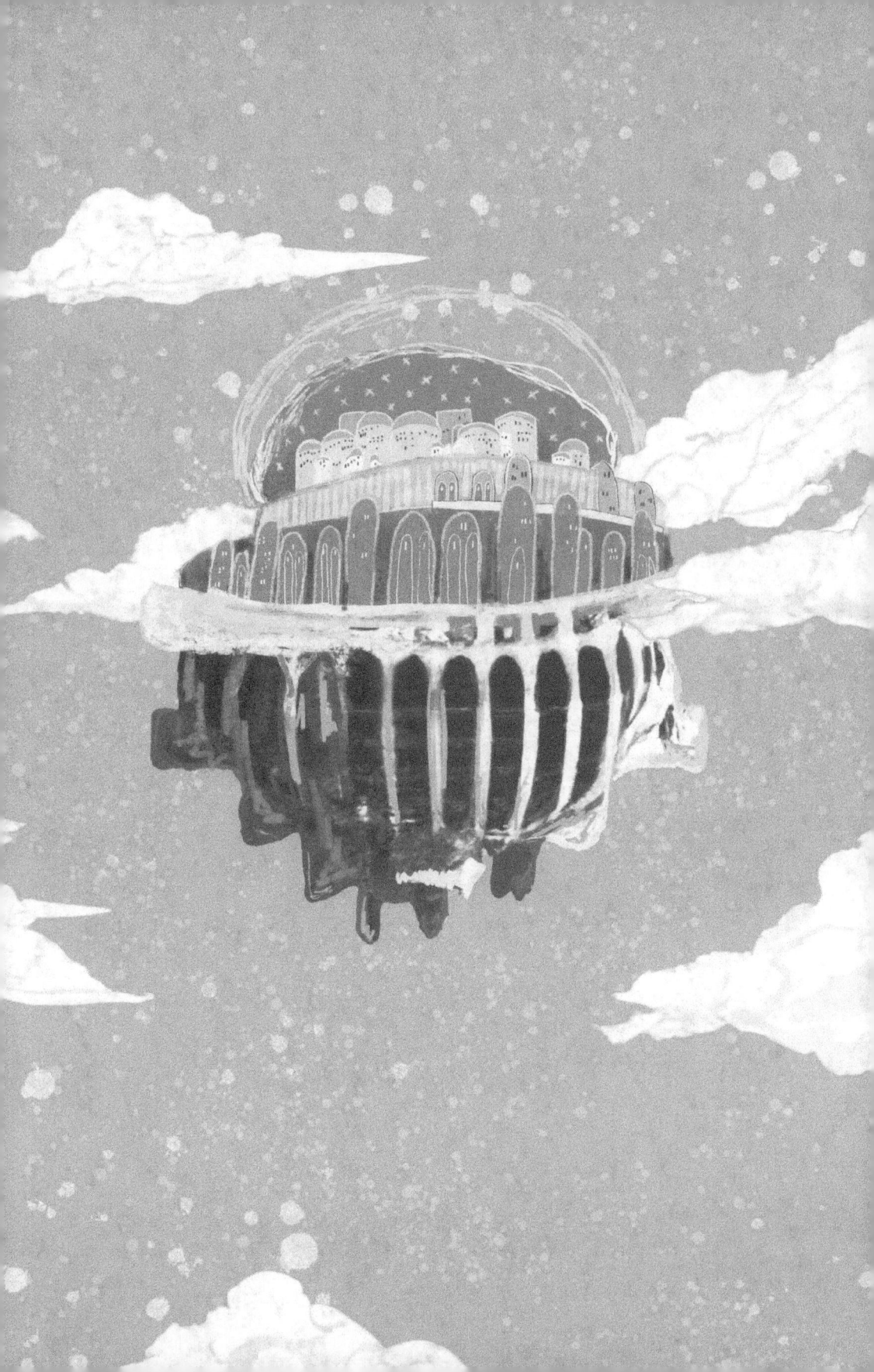

Frames of Fantasy: Fantasy Architecture in Hayao Miyazaki's Works with Studio Ghibli

Lara Clifford

LARA CLIFFORD studies architecture at the School of Architecture in the University of Limerick. She has a keen interest in the portrayal and impact of architecture in animation and in writing as an architectural medium. She has enjoyed the works of Studio Ghibli since first seeing the films as a child and feels they inspired early-on her love of art and design. When she finishes her degree, Lara hopes to continue writing in an architectural capacity.

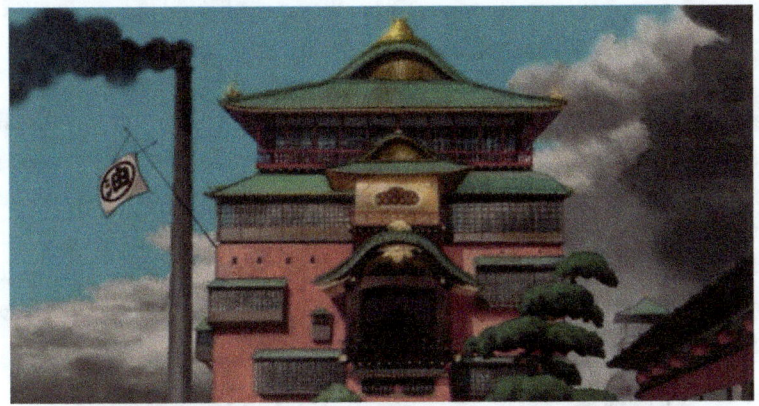

Figure 1 The Bathhouse in Spirited Away (2001)
(all film stills have been captured by the author)

Looming above the small frame of our protagonist Chihiro, the giant bathhouse looks unimaginably foreboding, amplified even more by a slow pan from the roof to the girl's eye level. The bathhouse is built in the traditional Meiji Japanese style with red flaking plaster and golden trims. Clouds of dark smoke billow from a tall chimney and windows rattle in tune with the wind. A gentle whoosh can be heard from the rocky pools of water below.

Chihiro leans over the bridge to see a train burst from a tunnel and then disappear quickly below her. The young heroine notices a boy ahead. "You're not allowed here!" he barks at her as a grey covering of clouds darkens the scene, "Go back – leave before it gets dark!" Chihiro gasps and runs from the bathhouse, glancing back in time to see the boy's white *kariginu* - traditional Japanese clothing, usually worn by nobles - flap as swirls of air wind around him. She stops to rub her eyes confused and then continues to run, passing flights of stone stairs flanked by oil lamps, tea houses and izakaya bars. A path of red lanterns guides her way through the ever-darkening streets. As she runs, storefronts begin to glow, shedding light on shadowy figures trailing gently through them. Chihiro keeps running, shying away from the figures until she returns to her parents. They are hunkered over giant plates. Piles of food and broken china surround them, grease drips from the tables and chairs. "Dad!" she screeches, "Let's go!" He lobs his head in her direction. His shirt has ripped around his now swollen body, there is a pink snout where his nose should be, ears have sprouted from his head. Chihiro reels back in horror as a slimy frogged arm grasping a spatula appears from the smoke behind the counter. It slaps the pig from cheek to cheek making it squeal and keel over.

Chihiro lets out a shriek and recoils, calling out for her parents again. She runs back to where she and her parents first entered the town as shadow figures glide past her. Lights glimmer ahead beckoning her. She stumbles her way down the steps to reach the path – except where the rest of the steps used to be, there is just water. A lustrous cruise ship hosting an array of glowing spirits and deities approaches. Dark shadow figures bob in the swarming water in front of her. Chihiro realises her way back is gone, her parents are gone. She is trapped here (Figure2).

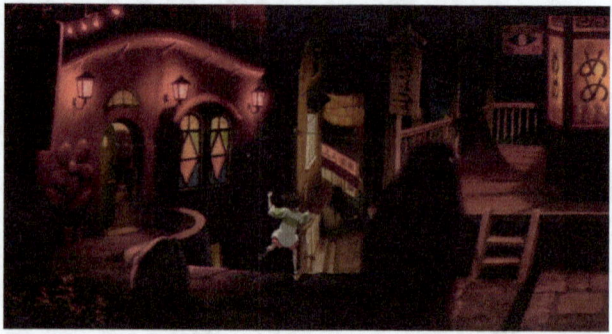

Figure 2: Atmospheric street scene with changing ground levels and shadow figures in *Spirited Away*.

Described here is an early scene in the 2001 Studio Ghibli film, *Sen to Chihiro no Kamikakushi*. In this scene, a young girl named Chihiro takes a shortcut on the way to her new house and gets trapped in witch Yubaba's bathhouse for spirits (Figure 1). She must sign away her name and commit to arduous, gruelling work if she wants to survive and have her parents turned back into humans – otherwise they will be eaten like the greedy pigs they now resemble.

The English version of this film was later released under the title Spirited Away and is referred back to frequently in this chapter. This film was pivotal for director Hayao Miyazaki and the anime industry as it became – and for almost two decades would remain – the most successful and highest grossing film in Japan (Kogyo Tsushinsha n.d.). On the international stage, it became the first hand-drawn and non-English language film to win an Oscar for Best Animated Feature at the 75th Academy Awards in 2003 (Oscars 2003).

Frames of Reference

Creating animation means creating a fictional world. That world soothes the spirit of those who are disheartened and exhausted from dealing with the sharp edges of reality.

Miyazaki (2014a, 25)

Born in Tokyo in 1941, Miyazaki was a young child during World War II. He was the second of four boys; his father was a successful but autocratic businessman and his mother was a woman of strong will but who was often hospitalised due to tuberculosis (Napier 2018, 24-26). Miyazaki's family was affluent, with much of their wealth derived from an aircraft manufacturing company who produced parts for the Mitsubishi Zero fighter planes. "The more the war went on the more money we made," Miyazaki remembered (Napier 2018, 11). He would for years feel the heavy burden of guilt for his family's relative affluence compared to their starving neighbours. Miyazaki did however have a lot of respect for flying machines. He fell in love with flight as a boy and would draw planes in incredible detail. Miyazaki's brother Arata says of him that even as a child he had an uncanny skill at "drawing everything correctly" (Napier 2018, 18). This love is clear in every film he has worked on, whether it is in the pirate planes of *Laputa, Castle in the Sky*, the fighter jets in *The Wind Rises* (2013) or the seaplanes in *Porco Rosso* (1992). Miyazaki draws impossible planes with detail so dense and carefully considered that they seem real.

Living in Tokyo, Miyazaki was exposed at an early age to the evacuations and bombings of the war. "I remember the air raids. I see my street burning" (Napier 2018, 2). He remembers his family fleeing from home in their truck during an air raid. Gasoline was rare and expensive at the time, so the family were fortunate to have access to it. In his memory, a mother with a baby hammered on the window of the truck and pleaded with his parents to allow her and her child to escape with them. They drove on without her. For Miyazaki, not begging his parents to let the pair into the crowded truck fills him with guilt, and he wonders if his pleas as their four-year-old son could have changed their minds (Napier 2018). The ethical underpinning of his filmmaking is a response to events such as this. He strives to encourage children to be brave and to stand up for what they believe in. They should find strength, happiness and value in themselves and their lives. It is as though he is paying off a debt to the child his family left behind.

Following the war, Japan came under American occupation. Miyazaki recalls how American soldiers would hand out sweets, hoping that by putting something in the bellies of hungry children, they would get on better terms with the defeated enemy. "After the war many Americans came and we would gather around. But I couldn't embarrass myself to the point of taking chocolate or chewing gum from them," he remembers (Napier 2018, 19). Miyazaki felt this act humiliating to his people, as it only stressed the difference between Japanese and Western culture. That said, Miyazaki did not harbour any hate for the Allies after the war. Occupation in the post-war period meant an overhaul in how schools were run. Suddenly militaristic drill was replaced by American-style teaching. "Occupation schooling emphasised democracy and democratic behaviour, with debate clubs and a free exchange of ideas. A vision was also promoted of recent Japanese history as a succession of terrible, indeed evil, actions," Napier observed (2018, 19). This new type of education had a pronounced effect on Miyazaki's cultural identity. As a child, he hated Japan. He hated militarism. He hated the country he was taught about in school – a Japan that limited individuality and placed a low value on happiness, on life. This may be why he puts such an emphasis on old traditions in his films. He strives to show young people the importance of the true Japanese traditions of the past--of forest spirits and gods of nature, not the militarist indoctrination of the 1930s and 40s (Napier 2018).

In 1963, shortly after graduating with a degree in Economics from Gakushuin University, Miyazaki became an animator for Toei Animation. He worked as an animator and producer for the company for years before moving on to other studios, building up a network of associates (Feldman 1994). In June 1985, together with Isao Takahata, Toshio Suzuki and Yasuyoshi Tokuma, Miyazaki founded Studio Ghibli, establishing his status as a filmmaker and director. Studio Ghibli is active to this day. It employs over one hundred and fifty employees and has produced twenty-four feature films and many more short films, commercials and music videos (Studio Ghibli 2017 b). Hayao Miyazaki has retired many times throughout his career, but each time has returned months later. Currently he is working on the film *How Do You Live*, which is rumoured to be premiering in 2022, and like countless times before, he has vowed that this will be his last (Loo 2017).

The Beginning of Movement

The films of Studio Ghibli strive to develop in children an understanding of culture, the environment and the value of curiosity and creativity. These films are a fantastical retelling of something the audience has already felt or experienced but could not make sense of. They use impossible fantastical creatures, huge but gentle tsunamis and thrilling adventures to represent the tribulations felt by children in an understandable way. This creates ideas so abstract that the individual can project meaning on them to relate to their own situations. The films acknowledge deeper themes than most children's entertainment. They treat children not as ignorant kids but as curious minds wishing to understand the confusing world they inhabit. They strive to inspire their inquisitive nature and unique thought. The films act as a point from which you begin to feel as though you are not just a replica of a parent or sibling but a seeing, feeling human with a narrative and an identity all of your own, created by everything that you experience. To create these powerful moments, Miyazaki and Studio Ghibli blend their love and understanding of film with intense craftsmanship.

Looking at Takei Shanshodo, one thing you immediately realise is that it was built by craftsmen. The glass doors, the walls, the merchandise racks – everything was handmade by craftsmen. You immediately sense a profound difference from current construction methods, where structures are assembled using labour-saving industrial components. When this building was made, craftsmen were inexpensive to hire, and there were probably very good ones available, too. If you were to build the same structures the same way today it would surely cost a small fortune, though the materials wouldn't be as good. It is an ironic aspect of the world then, that the craftsmen were, unfortunately, paid so little yet did such good work. (Miyazaki, 2014 a, 241)

The Takei Shanshodo referred to by Miyazaki is a stationery shop building in the Edo Open Air Architectural Museum. The interior of this building served as the basis for the design of the boiler room in *Spirited Away*. Miyazaki acknowledges the importance of craftsmanship and of investment in the creation and construction of good work. The studio is willing to spend significant time on their masterpieces, drawing each frame by hand – a labour-intensive process, but one that allows for meticulous specificity. Toshio Suzuki, one of the founders of the company spoke about their new film in a 2020 interview with *Entertainment Weekly*: "We are still hand-drawing everything, but it takes us more time to complete a film because we're drawing more frames." He continues, "Back when we were making [1988's] *My Neighbour Totoro*, we only had eight animators. *Totoro* we made in eight months. [For] the current film that Hayao Miyazaki is working on, we have 60 animators, but we are only able to come up with one minute of animation in a month. That means 12 months a year, you get 12 minutes worth of movie" (Romano 2020).

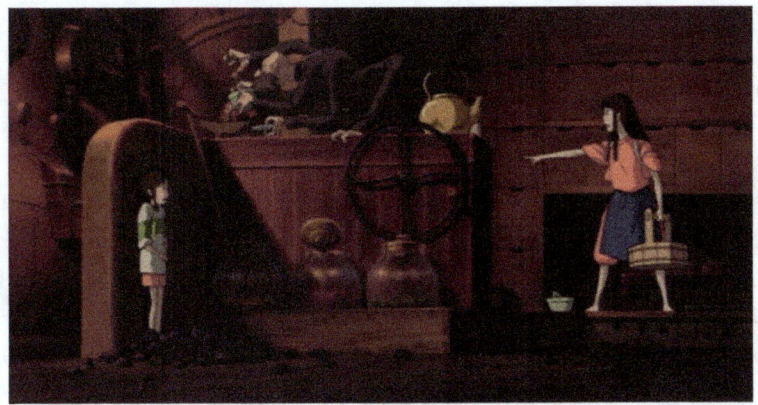

Figure 3: The boiler room in Spirited Away, based on an
Edo Tokyo stationery shop

Studio Ghibli's unique aesthetic is amplified by the desire to continue this decidedly traditional approach to filmmaking. Miyazaki's dedication to hand drawing has led him to admonish the use of computer-generated imagery (CGI). After having seen grotesquely moving computer-generated zombies with twisted limbs, he declares in a 2016 television documentary, "Whoever creates this stuff has no idea what pain is whatsoever. I am utterly disgusted. [...] I would never wish to incorporate this technology into my work at all." In the same context he adds that he strongly feels this was "an insult to life itself" (Arakawa 2016). This recourse to CGI belittles the conscious, emotive work of the animators and craftspeople he has been working with tirelessly throughout his life. A scene in *Spirited Away* (2001) reflects his attitude. Here, the good witch Zeniba is spinning her own threads by hand, and she says, *Mahō de tsukutta n ja, nan nimo naranai kara ne*, or "If you make it with magic, it has no meaning."

Although he publicly takes a strong position, Miyazaki has allowed small bits of CGI to creep into some of his works when necessary, such as in *Princess Mononoke* (1997) where it is used to animate a writhing demon boar (Team Ghiblink. n.d.). During his 2013 retirement period, Miyazaki himself even experimented with the use of CGI. In 2018, he released the short film *Boro the Caterpillar*, shown only at the Ghibli Museum in Mitaka. He created this almost entirely with CGI (Studio Ghibli 2017 b). The film does not so much embrace but acknowledge the medium. After meeting the team that created the CGI zombies, Miyazaki proclaimed (in the same TV documentary), "I feel like we are nearing the end of times. We humans are losing faith in ourselves" (Arakawa 2016). The use of CGI now feels bittersweet.

Whereas Miyazaki is hesitant to work with CGI, colour features strongly is his oeuvre. When working with colour, Studio Ghibli is incredibly dynamic. In the range of a single film – for example, *Howl's Moving Castle* (2004), we can see glistening blue seascapes with a colourful seaside town, a regal pastel city, the rolling hills of a blooming orchard, a grim grey wasteland and a war-torn hellscape (Figs.4–7). Some of the film's locations are closely related to real life such as the Franco-Germanic town based on a visit Miyazaki took to Colmar. Most other locations are more loosely based on a mixture of real and imagined places. Studio Ghibli incorporates deep rich colours to symbolise nature, brought to life by either especially bright or dark skies. They use smaller, bright elements to draw attention to a protagonist such as with *Ponyo*'s pink dress in Ponyo or Kiki's bright red bow in *Kiki's Delivery Service* (1989). Films such as *Porco Rosso*, *The Wind Rises* and *Princess Mononoke* target an older audience and have a more subtle palette to depict their cruel scenes of fire, disease, suffering, and death.

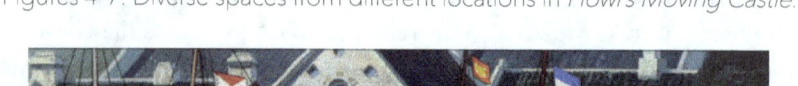

Figures 4–7: Diverse spaces from different locations in *Howl's Moving Castle.*

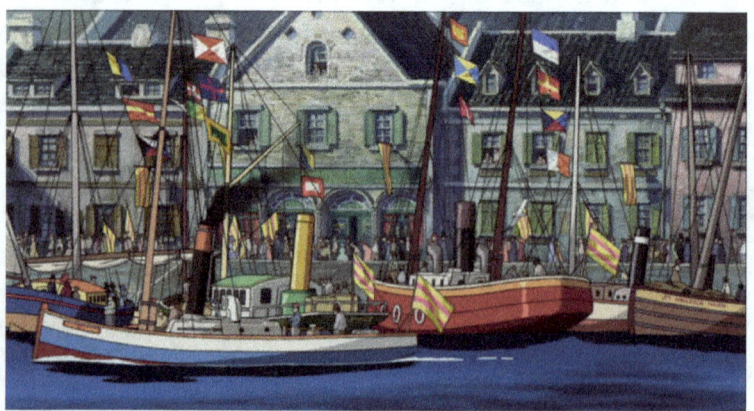

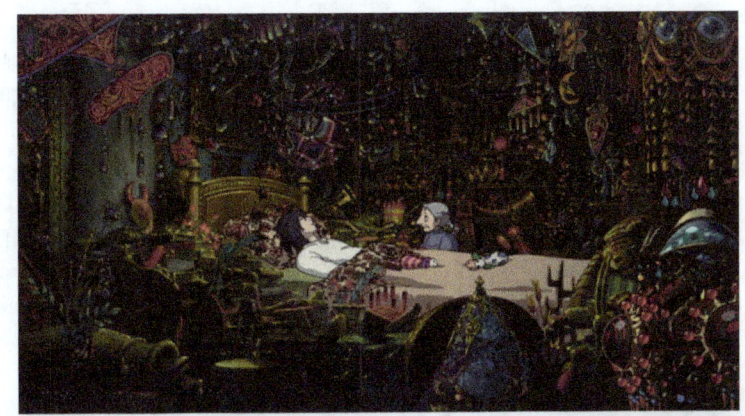

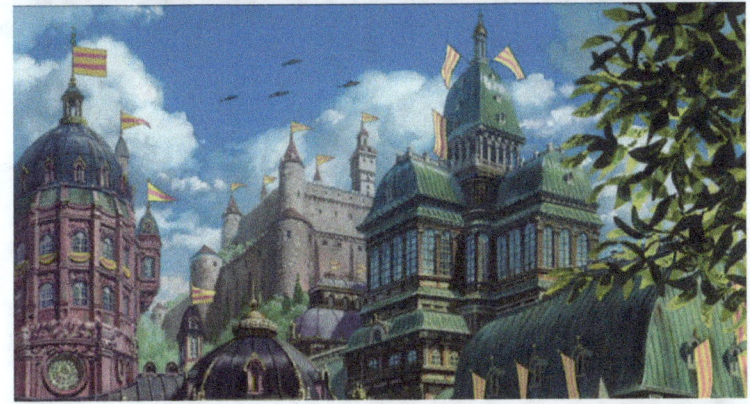

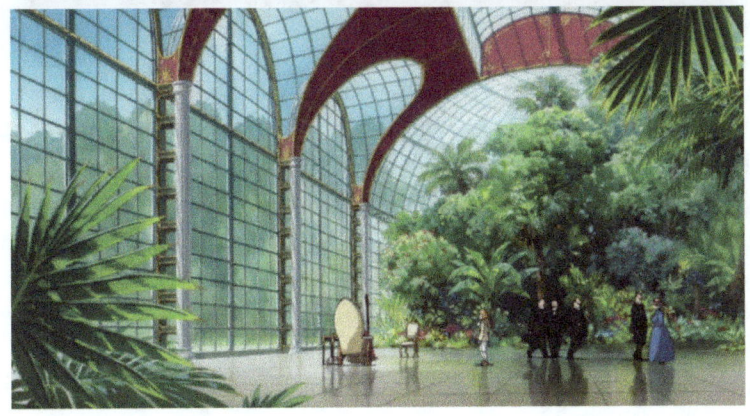

In *Porco Rosso*, the seaplane pilot protagonist takes the form of a pig man. Unlike the pigs of *Spirited Away*, his form is not that of magic or whimsy; it is subconsciously self-imposed, a reflection of his grief, regret and guilt. He tells of how he became this way after an ambush in World War I. All of his comrades were shot down by enemy planes, leaving him the sole survivor. In a painfully beautiful vision, he watches as his deceased friend's battered planes gently ascend into the sky, joining a stream of other fallen planes miles above. They are coloured in subtle hues with different patterns and symbols, some of them no more than a white speck in the distance, contrasted against the harsh blue sky, each plane representing a life lost to the war (Figure 8).

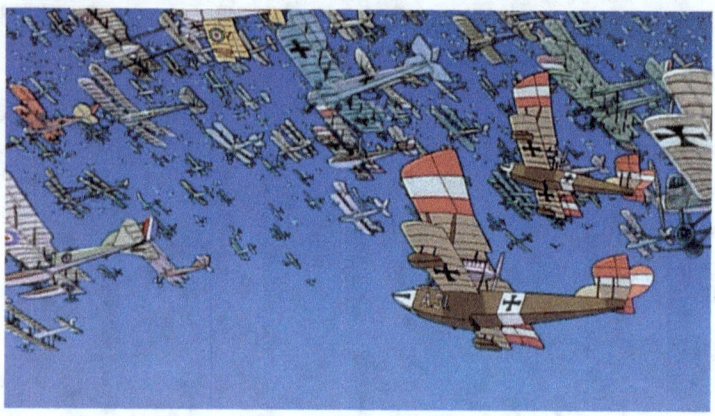

Figure 8: Plane heaven scene from *Porco Rosso*.

The use of colour in Studio Ghibli films can also be seen as a plot device. The opening sequence of *Spirited Away*, as detailed at the beginning of the chapter, is paramount to conveying Chihiro's character. In these scenes, light and colour take the place of dialogue. This allows the film to remain ambiguous with regard to its storyline and meaning, thus challenging viewers to make sense of the situation themselves. Chihiro's journey from car to the fantastical bathhouse is incredibly dynamic in terms of the quick succession of different light and colour conditions. The film begins in the family's Audi as they travel through the grey streets of a town. Your attention is drawn to the distinctly modern elements of urban life – wires, signposts, walls, all a bleak grey. It feels totally mundane (Figure 9). They lose their way as the scenery develops into a smothering green, tall telephones poles and wires are replaced by shrouds of trees, and concrete roads are left behind for moss covered stone roads. Their Audi seems unwelcome. The nature swells around them, darkening as their detour drags them further into a forest. They reach a gate with a façade of flaking vermillion plaster (Figure 10). Curious, they enter, drawn in by a light at the far end. It is even darker than the trees, and cooler. The family's footsteps echo as they walk through it. Piercing through the dark, coloured light from stained glass windows breaks up the heavy shadows (Figure 11). The family trundle through a picturesque green field, cross a rocky ditch and climb a flight of stone steps. Chihiro's parents stop on the steps as her father announces he can smell something delicious, that perhaps the small shopping district up ahead is still open. Following his nose, he leads them into a street (Figure 13). The lights of the buildings are off and their verandas, shaded from the sun, are nestled in darkness. The streets are deserted. Colourful and playful but ragged shops and restaurants line the streets. Red lanterns stretch between them. A timber clad steel bridge reaches out tempting her to cross. The camera pans down to show the depth of the valley below and a train roars past.

Kazuo Oga, the artist who painted the scenic countryside backdrops for *My Neighbour Totoro*, was hired to draw this scenery for this space outside of the spirit realm (Figure 12). The creative director, Yoji Takeshige, designed the following fantasy spirit realm (Miyazaki 2014 b, 61). Having these two clearly different artistic styles effectively separates the real world from the fantasy one.

As the sun sets, lanterns begin to light, the scene darkens and fills with shadow figures. Restaurants glow with a soft light (Figure 14). As she runs away from the shadows, it gets darker and darker, the red lanterns leading her back until Chihiro meets the water's edge on the stone steps. Moments later the scene is filled with the soft glow of the ship arriving. It is filled with colourful spirits and gods and, compared to them, Chihiro seems to fade. The parade of creatures shines in reds and yellows while she cowers in shadow (Figure 15). The boy from the description at the beginning of this chapter comes to help. He runs with Chihiro through the city via dark alleys and pigpens (Figure 16). Each space they run through in quick succession is lit by a single warm orange bulb placed somewhere in the frame.

When they arrive back at the bathhouse, it is glowing with light, steam is sitting like fog around it and spirit patrons are milling about the bridge and entrance

(Figure 17). The boy ushers her over the bridge and out of sight, he shows her a dream-like sequence of the route to the top floor where she will be able to get permission to be in this world until she is able to leave it. He leaves her and she scrambles out a side door of the bathhouse onto a cantilevered rickety timber platform (Figure 18). She climbs down a flight of stairs and enters the boiler room. Here, she gets escorted into the lavish bathhouse. The interior is shockingly bright and full of bridges and lifts of glistening gold or red; frescoes are painted on the walls and as a whole it feels as though it could be some sort of temple (Figure 19). When she finally reaches the top 'heaven' floor where the owner of the bathhouse resides, the feeling is much colder. The timber floors are replaced by marble, and large white columns make the space feel grand and regal (Figure 20).

Figure 9-20 Series of spaces from the first twenty minutes of *Spirited Away.*

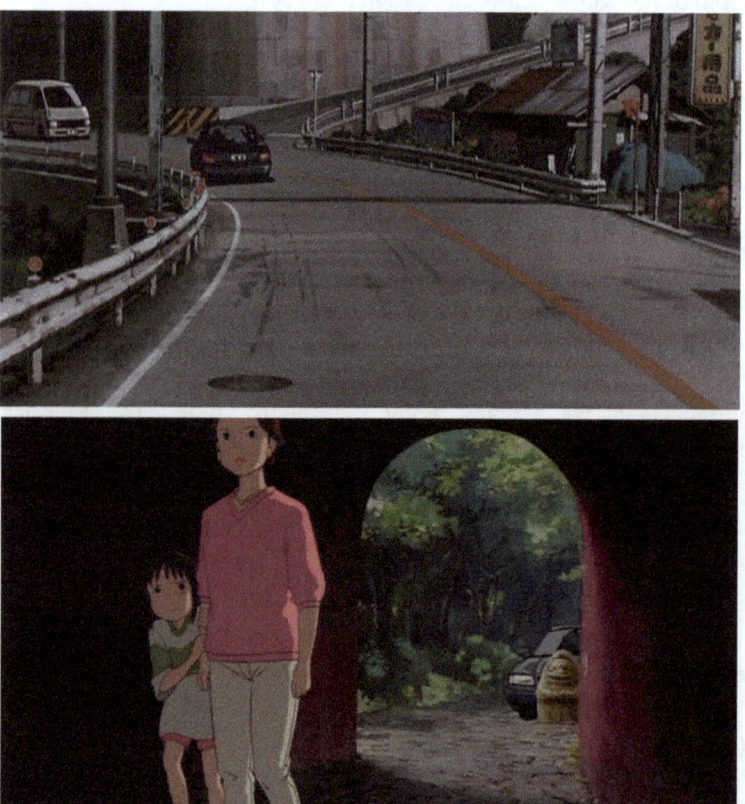

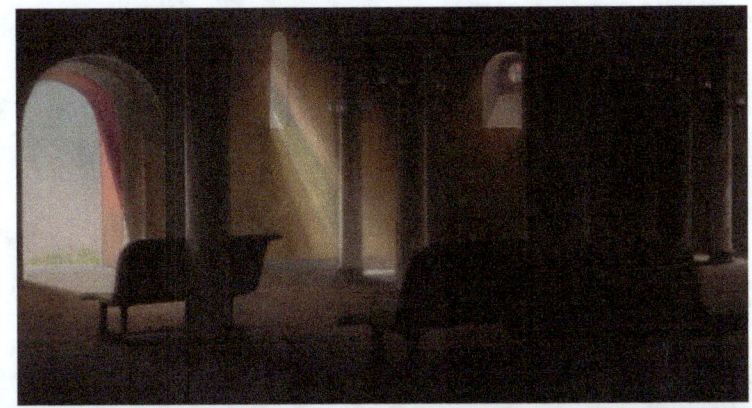

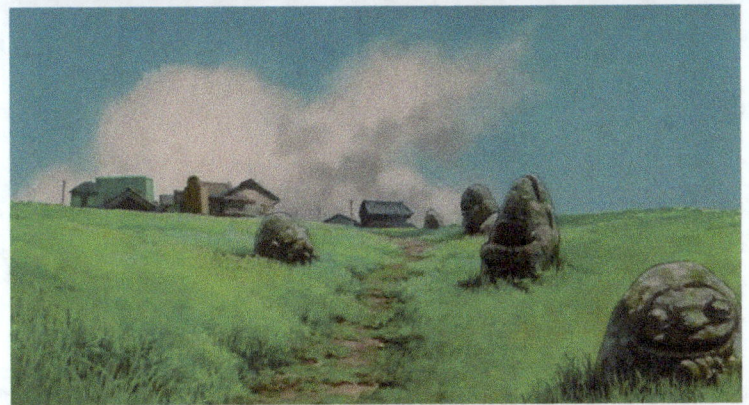

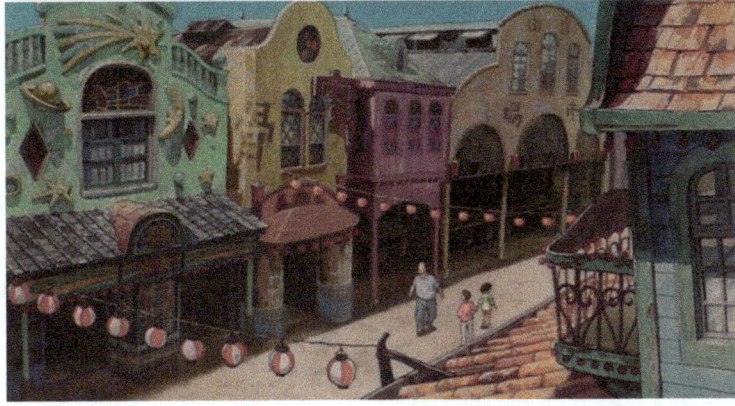

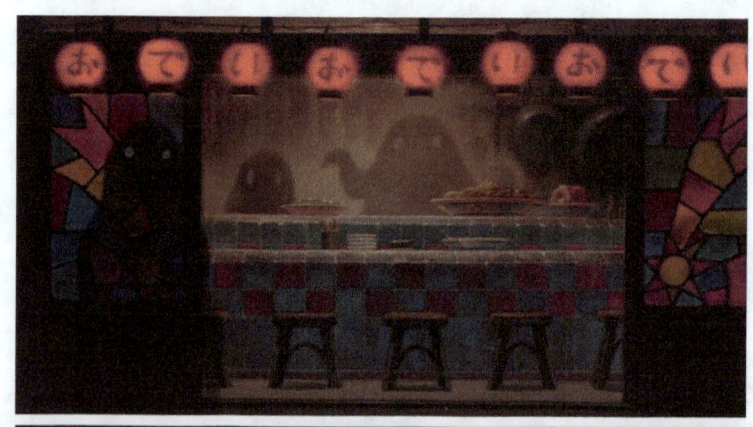

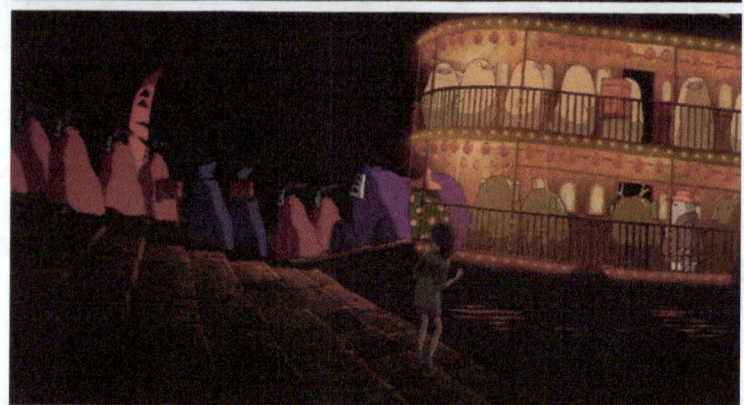

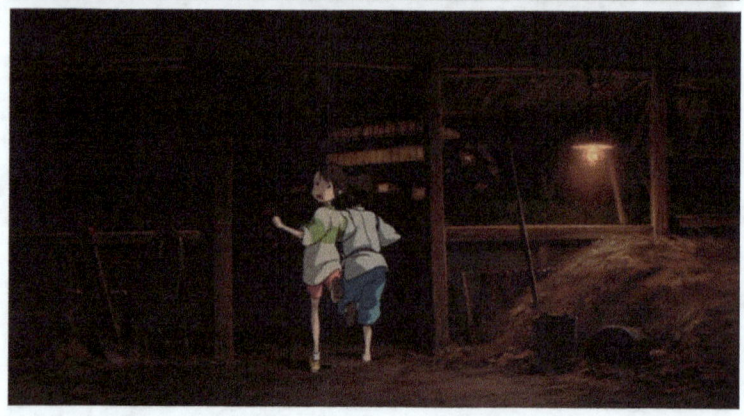

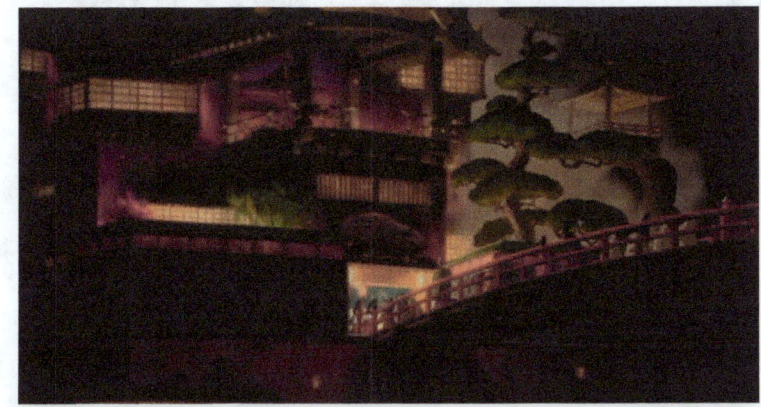

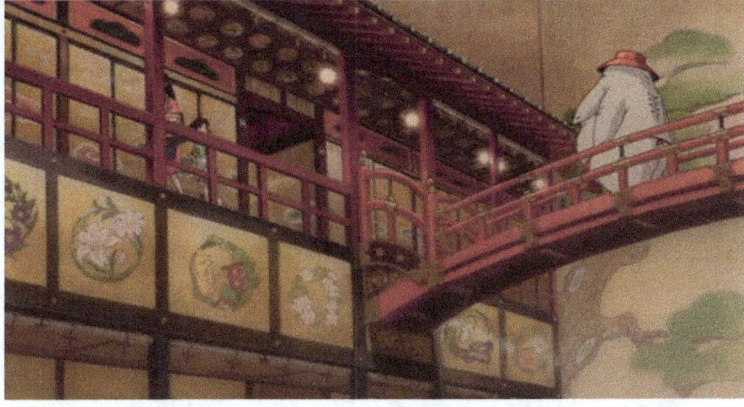

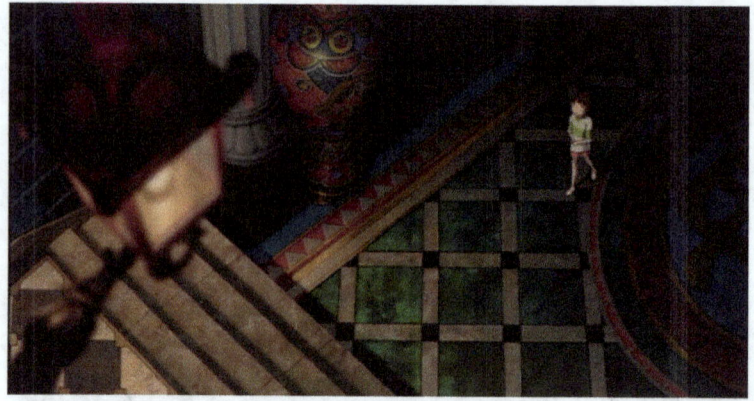

This sequence of scenes plays out over a timespan of around twenty minutes. In this time, the change in colour, lighting, and even artistic style has not only created a new world, but made the world we saw during the day look and feel entirely different at night. With so many different spaces created, a Studio Ghibli world could feel overly expansive, but the sequence of spaces is always so well presented that they are easily understandable. They allow the audience to explore the progression of spaces within the flow. Protagonists will generally move from one side of the screen to the other, the direction remaining consistent for much of the film to lead the audience comfortably through each area and showing how each space connects to the previous. By using this consistent progression in *Spirited Away*, the massive bathhouse whose winding corridors seem to continue endlessly become understandable for the viewer. You can trace Chihiro's path through the bathhouse and its different spaces with ease. In creating such deeply fantastical spaces but which connect so carefully and realistically, Studio Ghibli sets their worlds up in such a way that they could be real.

Where the World is Made

Every Studio Ghibli film is set in its own unique world. Some of these worlds feel similar to the one we live on like that of *My Neighbour Totoro* where two children explore their sylvian garden, finding whimsical creatures. Others are more detached like that of *Spirited Away* or the post-apocalyptic toxic jungle of *Nausicaä of the Valley of the Wind* (1984) where plants poison the air and giant shelled bugs frighten the humans. Each world created amplifies different aspects of society, highlighting problems and ethical questions. Studio Ghibli has created worlds for humans, spirits, flying machines, sea creatures, gods, and even witches. Worlds where there is a clear right and wrong and worlds where the line is blurred. Perhaps it would be more accurate to say that the studio did not create these worlds, rather it made wonderfully fantastical abstractions of our world, at different time periods and from different perspectives. These spaces are fantastical but have enough recognisable attributes that it feels as though these magical worlds could exist alongside you. Watching *My Neighbour Totoro* as a child would make you wonder if someday when you peered into the attic would you see the fabled Soot Sprites, or after watching *Laputa: Castle in the Sky*, you may wonder if when you were quiet, would the rocks speak to you as they did with Uncle Pom. Ironically, these films aim to inspire children to abandon the TV and have adventures of their own, exploring the grimy, dusty and potentially magical real world outside. And while it will probably never be as exciting or as terrifying as the films described, maybe someday we, too, would find ourselves staring up at a magical walking castle or discovering pools of ancient fish. The worlds exist to teach of friendship and love, of loneliness and loss and of bravery and a fighting spirit. Miyazaki's films fuel children's imaginations with magic and fantasy but also do not shy away from darker themes – the world around us is scary and unpredictable, but if the protagonists can fight their curses so can we.

By creating 'cartoon' or animated films, Studio Ghibli has released themselves from the limits of reality. Cartoons transport us to foreign worlds where we could never exist because we have been born here, in the now. In a 1983 interview, Miyazaki says, "To exist here, now, means to lose the possibility of being countless other potential selves." Cartoons allow us to imagine life if we free our complexes and relax our spirits. "Lies must be layered upon lies to create a thoroughly believable fake world" (Miyazaki 2014 a, 306). This is the importance of world building. Cartoons – as opposed to live action – can create characters with soft faces and a gentle presence. Since nothing feels entirely real, the viewer is disarmed and can be pulled into the world that might just evoke deeper longings within themselves. Although what the viewers are seeing is fake, it has been made by real people with real opinions and real biases and so there is truth in the work.

The bathhouse in *Spirited Away* is a cultural jumble, with architectural aspects from Showa, Heian and Edo Japan mixed with Western influences. It is a bathhouse for Japanese spirits and gods, most of whom have been forgotten about by modern Japan. Though it feels traditionally Japanese, there are often hints of Western ideals and propaganda throughout, their presence often subliminally forewarning of selfishness and greed. The bathhouse owner Yubaba is the embodiment of this. According to media scholar Ayumi Suzuki, Yubaba created a society where people "must work to be recognised as valuable human beings worthy of life" (Suzuki 2009). She forces Chihiro to labour to save her parents; her worth is in how quickly she can work. Yubaba lives on the top or 'heaven floor.' Her glistening chandelier, giant red vases on gold plated pedestals and cast metal door knocker are the image of wealth. She dons Western-style clothes and only when it will bring her more money does she wave fans imprinted with the rising sun to please patrons. Her servants live many floors beneath her, sleeping in Edo-style Japanese dormitories with *shoji* screens. They wear traditional garments and live and work amongst the spirits that frequent the bathhouse. The film speaks of Japan's struggle to retain its tradition in a country slowly adapting to Western ideals. In *Spirited Away*, masked Kasuga spirits reference a shrine in Nara, there is a river and radish spirit, and many of the bathhouse women have traditional Heian circular eyebrows (Figure 21). The fabled river spirit has been so long forgotten it is now a stink spirit. The river previously inhabited by the spirit is, like him, filled with dirt, metal and junk. Only when Chihiro pays attention to it, pulling what she believes is a thorn in its side and releasing a torrent of debris, is she able to free it from the weight of its pollution.

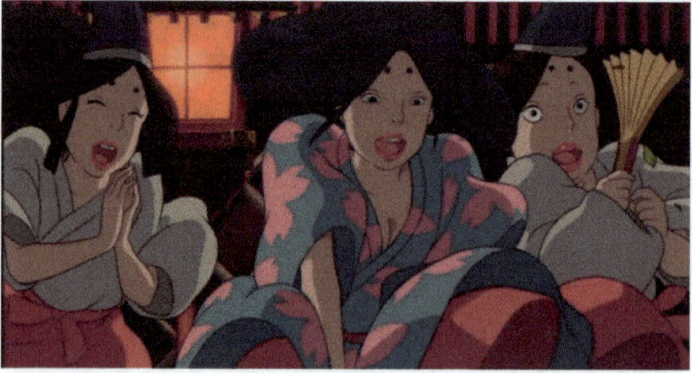

Figure 21: Workers in traditional dresses in *Spirited Away*.

Miyazaki not only seeks to preserve lost cultural traditions; his concerns embrace the full extent of the natural world. He puts nature at the forefront of many of his films to remind us of both its vitality and its vulnerability. He does not glorify it – nature is brutal and cruel, but it should thrive along with, and sometimes away from humanity. Humans have indisputably changed the course of nature and so one of the director's greatest dreams is for a Thousand-Year Forest to be constructed. Here, trees are planted, seeds are scattered, bugs and animals are let loose, and no matter what happens – if a runner chokes the trees, if a species devours another, still no human can interact with it. He would want it to be a place of heritage, with a sign at the front in every language in the world. A garden that cannot be touched for thousands of years so that when future humans find it, they will know this is a place of untouched nature, and they will know to leave well alone (Miyazaki 2014 a).

In a poem written for renowned composer Joe Hisashi in advance of him writing the soundtrack for the film, Miyazaki conveys the strength of the forest spirit in *Princess Mononoke*;

The forest has existed since the world was born

In this world of deep shadows filled with the essence of all creation [...]

Trees decay, animals die

The forest where the Forest Spirit lives is a world where life glistens and sparkles

It is a forest that denies entry to humans.

(Miyazaki 2014 b, 26)

In the world of *Princess Mononoke*, inspired by the Muromachi period in Japan (from 1336 to 1573), preservation of nature is at the forefront of San's mind, a girl who was raised by wolves and considers them her family. She believes killing Lady Eboshi, ruler of Irontown, will stop the deforestation of her land. San struggles with her own humanity, seeing humans as the enemy for their destructive nature. On the other side, Lady Eboshi culls the forest to make more space for her town's expansion. She is portrayed as a kind woman who values the lives of humans over nature. She provides homes and jobs for outcasts of society like brothel workers and those with leprosy. She has her people forge guns, cannons and *naginata* – a weapon similar to a glaive and traditionally used by women, requiring more skill than brute force. Ashitaka, the protagonist of the film is sympathetic to each side and reasons with both. Miyazaki admits in a short piece he wrote in April 1995 that the film does not try to solve the problems of the world: "There cannot be a happy ending. Yet, even amid the hatred and slaughter, there are things worthy of life" (Miyazaki 2014 a, 274). Nature is to be treated with respect, as are humans. Balancing these is one of life's greatest dilemmas.

In another film, *Laputa: Castle in the Sky*, it is rumoured that a floating castle exists somewhere in the sky with vast riches, an infinite energy core and a great tree at its centre (Figure 22). A series of events lead to protagonists Sheeta and Pazu landing on the island, only to witness antagonist Muska and his army looting it. When he discovers that the throne room has become overrun by nature, he snarls at the plants that have invaded the space, "What's happened here!? These filthy roots don't belong in this chamber! Horrible things, I'll have them burned." He considers himself superior to nature and destroys it with ease. His goal is to control the energy core and has no regard for anything else the island holds. Before Muska lands on the island, protagonists Sheeta and Pazu spend a short time exploring it, discovering gardens and pools filled with species like the Minonohashi, a mammal that became extinct in the seventeenth century and ancient fish from the Devonian period. We see Kitsune Risu – a mix between a fox and cat, symbols of luck in Japan – and a giant Laputian guardian robot that takes care of the gardens. Sheeta and Pazu treat the island respectfully, looking in careful awe at all the valuable species and plants on it (Figure 23). Despite their best efforts, however, even they cause the island damage. When they arrived on the island, their plane landed on a bird's nest and Pazu grappled with roots and branches while trying to save his friends. Ultimately, they cause the destruction of a large part of the island, although in doing so set it free to roam the skies away from human touch once more. The castle flies to preserve its species, for humans cannot help but interfere with nature. We should strive to create spaces where nature can play out as though untouched by humans. When building, the landscape and its species should always be respected.

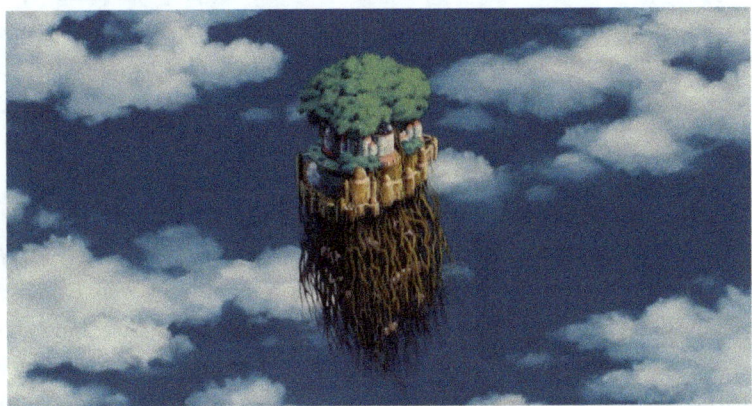

Figure 22: Floating Island from *Laputa: Castle in the Sky*.
Images sourced via animationscreencaps.com..

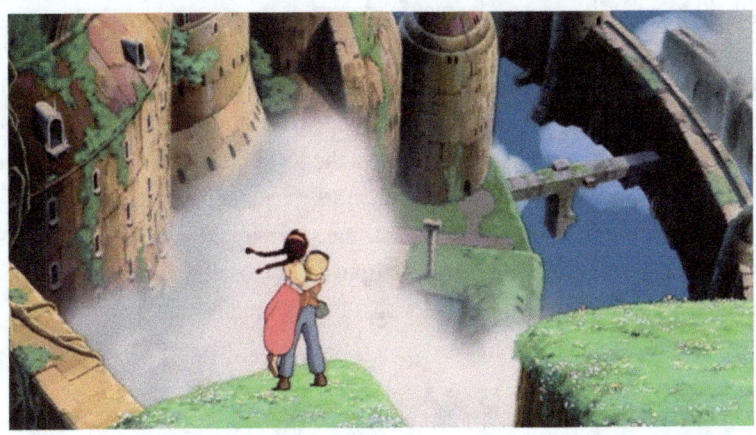

Figure 23: Sheeta and Pazu overlooking the Island in *Laputa: Castle in the Sky*.
Images sourced via animationscreencaps.com.

As every plant in the film feels inexplicably and innately real, the architecture in *Laputa: Castle in the Sky* feels impossibly fantastical while maintaining a sense of realism in its design. Pazu lives in a town set into the edges of a valley. Passages had to be drilled into the valley sides and houses were retained by timber beams jutting out from the cliff at precarious angles (Figure 24). Tall chimneys reach towards the sky, bridges stretch over the valley and a train on a stilted track runs through the gap. In young protagonist Pazu's house we see this more playful attitude towards architecture as the boy clambers up a ladder and through a trapdoor onto his pitched roof to feed peanuts to birds. When he later jumps off the roof he falls through the bricks on the ground, landing in his cellar. Robust animation makes up for a lack in health and safety.

The floating castle exists in part as a façade to protect the infinite energy core – which would have the potential to make any technology possible. Both the castle and tree were created by the people of Laputa to prevent the rock from being stolen and used to dominate the world. They knew that such energy would make technology redundant but would also have devastating effects on nature in the wrong hands. The castle is organised into tiers – In *The Art of Castle in the Sky* (2016), Miyazaki explains they were meant to represent a monarchical class system by the original townspeople. The architecture continues underwater where half the city is flooded. It has been abandoned by all but nature and a robot guardian. The castle is being held together by roots. The playful nature of this space comes to light when Pazu climbs along these roots and crawls under stones to navigate the maze of spaces, undetected by the military personnel that came to loot it. Everything about this castle should not exist – from its prehistoric creatures, the energy producing rock, its guardian robot soldiers and not least the fact that it floats in the sky. Yet the details within the turrets, the plants, the structure even, feels so intimately recognisable you cannot help but imagine it exists somewhere up there in the sky. This is the key to Miyazaki's success with fantasy. He pushes impossibility just far enough that it would never exist in real life, but it is possible to imagine that it could.

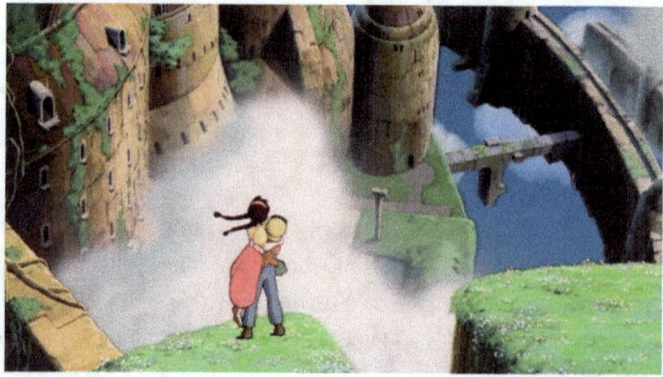

Figure 24: A train running through a populated valley in *Laputa, Castle in the Sky.*

Impossible Fantasy

Hayao Miyazaki's success in film led to the creation of one of his most tactile fantasy worlds yet. In 2001, the Ghibli Museum in Mitaka, Tokyo first opened its doors to showcase the work of the studio. The director played a huge role in conceiving its ethos and design. He created a sort of maze of spaces, stating "Visitors are not controlled with predetermined courses and fixed direction" (2017 a, 178). He believed it should be a place where children felt able to explore a magical fantasy world without limits, where they should "freely run about the museum" without their parents telling them to "stand over there!" for a photograph (Miyazaki 2014 b, 264). He wanted to treat children as if they were grown up and inspire them to "understand the artists' spirits" and to be interested in the animation process (Miyazaki 2014 b, 260). He wanted the building to be "put together as if it were a film, not arrogant, magnificent, flamboyant, or suffocating" (2017 a, 178). He wished it to be a translation of the fictional worlds of his films to the physical world we inhabit.

Although proud of the building, Miyazaki feels it is limited by laws and guidelines. He did not want to call it a museum except that he had to in order to satisfy regulations. Instead, he wished it would be called "an exhibition or a 'show-and-tell' hall" (Miyazaki 2014 b, 262). He needed it to differ from a regular museum – to be something experienced rather than seen. He wanted to avoid creating "a museum that treats its contents as if they were more important than people" (Miyazaki 2014 b, 261). He wanted to make the spiral stair narrower so it would not be boring to climb, to slant walls inwards creating nooks only children could get to, to place a pile of dirt children could clamber up and play in, where their mothers would yell at them to stop getting their clothes dirty! But the stairs were too narrow, the wall too crooked and the pile of dirt could only be a tenth of the desired size. He feels that the regulations which were "removing almost all elements of danger from this city" will not make children any safer, rather raise them to be unstable and weak from the absence of adversity to overcome (Miyazaki 2014 b, 272–273).

Despite this, he has created a space that feels truly fantastical (Figure25). In 2001, connoisseurs of architecture Terunobu Fujimori and Shimbo Minami were invited to the Ghibli Museum and asked to comment on it from an architectural point of view. Fujimori acknowledges the admirable craftsmanship of the space: "It is the very best quality that can be obtained in Japan (…) This type of space is a kind of fake or imaginary world, but when done this seriously, it doesn't look fake at all." He states that what makes it differ so drastically from a theme park is the materiality. Minami acknowledges the playfulness of the space – trick doors, low arches you had to duck under, a conical depression in the ground of the entrance. "Even on the walls inside, there is a row of wooden beams driven into one wall, seeming as if a person could climb it. Just imagining that gives a scary feeling, which is excellent." Like in the castle from *Laputa*, the rooftop is covered with what feels like a floating wild grassy field, with a life-size robot guardian to protect it. Both Fujimori and Minami consider this to be one of the strongest areas and would like to see it grow even wilder. Fujimori emphasises this; "People don't have to be able to go in!" He comments further on the transcendent quality of the building: "All parts of the building do not originate from any architecture from any period of time. Everything is shifted and off from a set point. In the world of architecture, usually, all architecture evolves from a certain style or aesthetic, but this does not fit in and is far off from any one of them… In short, this building has existed and been flowing inside Miyazaki-san's head since his childhood. People think of many kinds of things in their heads but to actually make it on this scale and in such an orderly fashion must be very rare. I was quite envious of this building" (Studio Ghibli 2017 a, 233).

The Ghibli Museum conveys an immediate sense of fun, something Fujimori says is usually absent. He considers the building to be greatly important although comments that it would rarely be understood in the architect's world. Perhaps Miyazaki's whimsy has distanced him too much from modern architecture, he muses. Fujimori suggests that a sense of fun is lost in modern architecture (Studio Ghibli 2017 a, 235). Does modern architecture put perhaps too much weight on subliminally clever spaces and see fun and enjoyment as something distracting? Could the two coexist? If architecture became more interested in fantasy and fun, it could make our lives more colourful and buildings more inhabitable. Public spaces are reduced to only a few activities – walking, sitting, reading. Adding elements of fantasy could create spaces that are not only more interesting to be in but that inspire more creative uses.

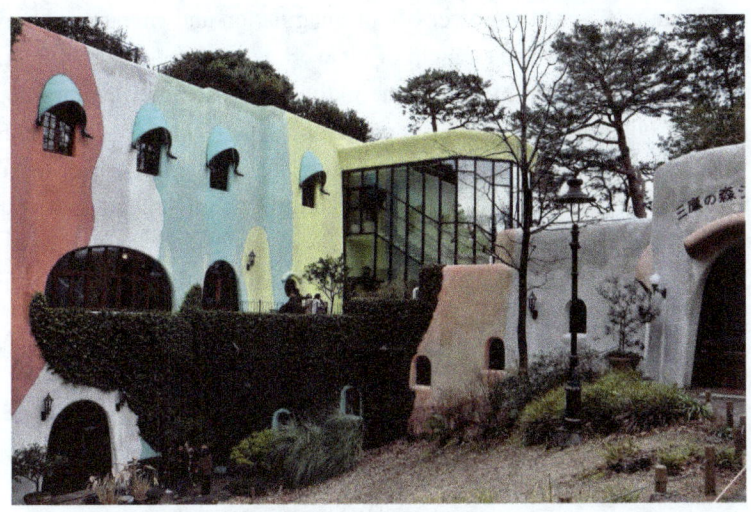

Figure 25: Ghibli Museum Exterior (photo by author)

As an animator, Hayao Miyazaki is widely considered one of the greatest. His unique visual style and vibrant storytelling make his films instantly recognisable. Through animation he has the ability to transport an audience of any age into a new world and in this way he promotes care – for each other and for all that is around us. Miyazaki tries to rescue and protect elements of a lost or threatened world – culture, nature and architecture. He values Japan's traditions, folklore and attention to craft, and he honours them not only through the messages of his films but also in the way they are produced. He tells of nature's intense vulnerability to blind technological progress and of his dream to preserve it as untouched by humans. His films show us architecture is as much about creating new environments as it is new spaces and a well-designed environment is a product of passion crafted with high quality detail. Shelley McNamara of Grafton Architects in her closing statement of their RIBA Gold Medal lecture referred to the Flying Island of Laputa from *Gulliver's Travels* by Irish novelist Jonathan Swift, illustrating it with an image from Miyazaki's *Laputa: Castle in the Sky*. McNamara linked the idea of a "floating world" to the present and pressing question of "where we are now and how we imagine ourselves optimistically with all the potential that architecture inherently has to make new worlds and to make new futures" (RIBA 2020, 1:51:10).

Miyazaki reminds us of the power of our imagination and encourages bravery in the face of adversity. The strength of his work is not necessarily in its translation into inhabitable reality, but in the individual lessons we can promote in our lives. Through the possibilities of animation, Miyazaki shows us visions of new worlds that are rooted in recognisable realistic detail and respect for tradition but their absence of real-life limitation allows its inhabitants to live more creatively and independently. These worlds show us how an environment can be both a carefully considered sequence of spaces and somewhere that inspires, awe and excites the human spirit.

REFERENCES

Arakawa, Kaku. 2016. *Never-Ending Man: Hayao Miyazaki.* Japan: NHK.

Feldman, Steven. 1994. "Hayao Miyazaki Biography, Revision 2." Nausicaa.net. http://www.nausicaa.net/miyazaki/miyazaki/miyazaki_biography.txt

Ghibli Museum. n.d. "All Films, Boro the Caterpillar." Ghibli-Museum.jp. Accessed May 21, 2021. https://www.ghibli-museum.jp/en/films/works/#boro_the_caterpillar.

Kogyo Tsushinsha. n.d. "Best 100 of the past box office." Kogyotsushin.com. Accessed April 14, 2020. http://www.kogyotsushin.com/archives/alltime/.

Loo, Egan. 2017. "Ghibli's Hayao Miyazaki Reveals His 'Final' Film's Title, Release Window." *Anime News Network.* https://www.animenewsnetwork.com/news/2017-10-28/ghibli-hayao-miyazaki-reveals-his-final-film-title-release-window/.123343

McNamara, Shelley, Yvonne Farrell. 2020. "RIBA Royal Gold Medal lecture with Grafton Architects." *RIBA Architecture.* https://youtu.be/OY85Nka40c0

Miyazaki, Hayao. 1997. *Princess Mononoke.* Netflix. CA: Netflix.

Miyazaki, Hayao. 2002. *The Art of Spirited Away.* San Francisco: VIZ Media.

Miyazaki, Hayao. (2001) 2004. *Spirited Away.* DVD. London: Optimum Releasing Ltd.

Miyazaki, Hayao. (1986) 2006. *Laputa Castle in the Sky.* DVD. UK: Optimum Releasing Ltd.

Miyazaki, Hayao. (1988) 2006. *My Neighbour Totoro.* DVD. London: Optimum Releasing Ltd.

Miyazaki, Hayao. (1989) 2006. *Kiki's Delivery Service.* DVD. London: Optimum Releasing Ltd.

Miyazaki, Hayao. (1992) 2006. *Porco Rosso*. DVD. London: Optimum Releasing Ltd.

Miyazaki, Hayao. (2004) 2006. *Howl's Moving Castle*. DVD. London: Optimum Releasing Ltd.

Miyazaki, Hayao. 2008. *The Art of Howl's Moving Castle*. San Francisco: VIZ Media.

Miyazaki, Hayao. (2008) 2010. *Ponyo*. DVD. London: Optimum Releasing Ltd.

Miyazaki, Hayao. (2013) 2014. *The Wind Rises*. DVD. London: Studiocanal Ltd.

Miyazaki, Hayao. 2014 a. *Starting Point 1979–1996*. San Francisco: VIZ Media.

Miyazaki, Hayao. 2014 b. *Turning Point 1997–2008*. San Francisco: VIZ Media.

Miyazaki, Hayao. 2016. *The Art of Castle in the Sky*. San Francisco: VIZ Media.

Napier, Susan. 2018. *Miyazakiworld – A Life in Art*. New Haven: Yale University Press.

Oscars. 2003. "The 75th Academy Awards 2003." Oscars.org. https://oscars.org/oscars/ceremonies/2003.

Romano, Nick. 2020. "Studio Ghibli co-founder teases Hayao Miyazaki's next 'big, fantastical' film." *Entertainment Weekly*. https://ew.com/movies/studio-ghibli-hayao-miyazaki-how-do-you-live/

Studio Ghibli. 2017 a. Ghibli Museum, Mitaka. Japan: The Tokuma Memorial Cultural Foundation for Animation.

Studio Ghibli. 2017 b. "History of Studio Ghibli." Studio Ghibli. https://www.ghibli.jp/history/

Suzuki, Ayumi. 2009. "A nightmare of capitalist Japan: *Spirited Away*." Jump Cut. https://www.ejumpcut.org/archive/jc51.2009/SpiritedAway/

Team Ghiblink. n.d. "Computer Graphics in Princess Mononoke (I)." Nausicaa.net. Accessed May 22, 2021. http://www.nausicaa.net/miyazaki/mh/cg.html.

SPACES OF
ACTUALITY

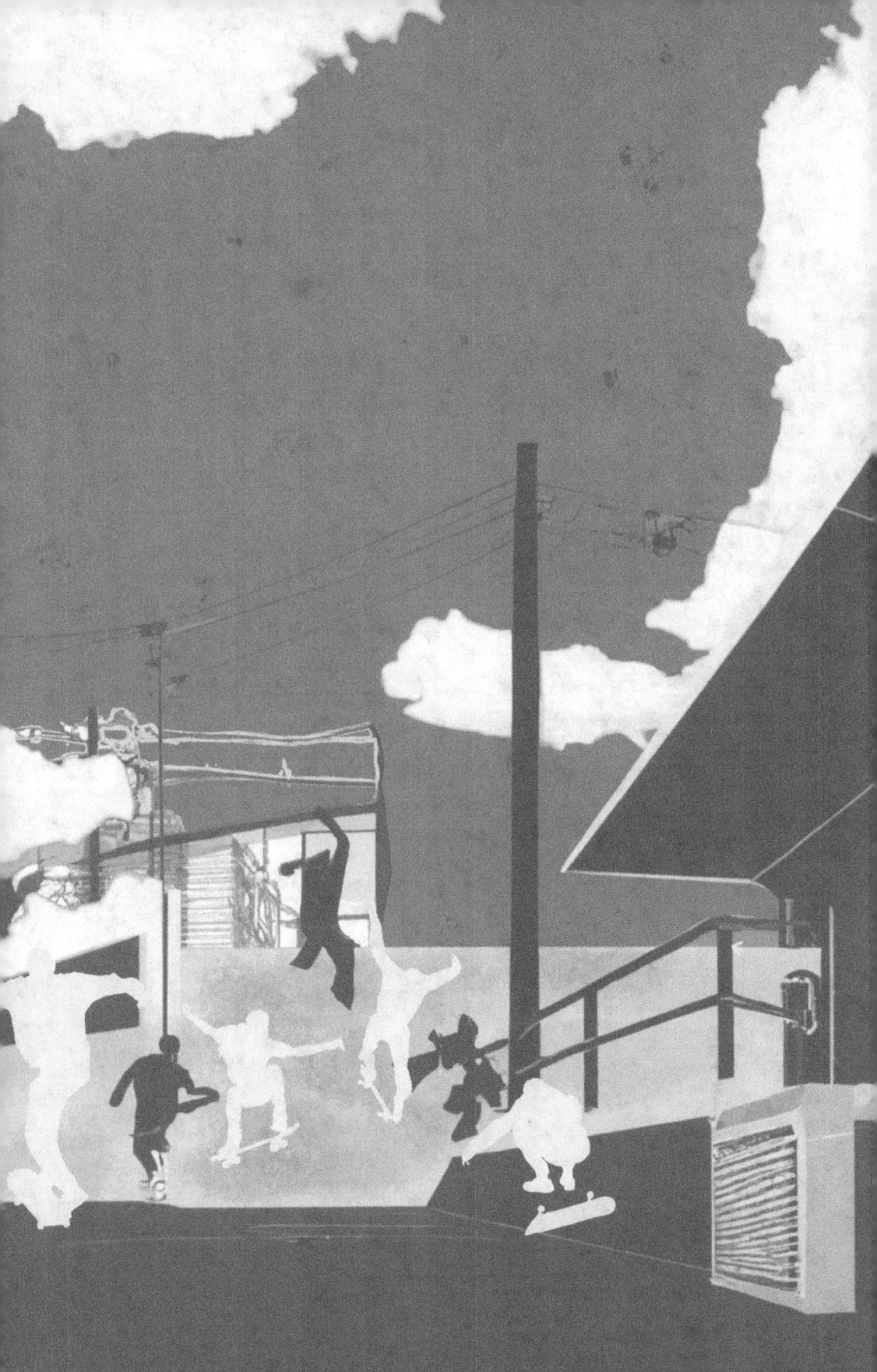

Skateboarding and Architecture:
Space, Time, and Social Being

Daniel Savage

DANIEL SAVAGE is an architectural technologist, with work/life experience in Ireland, UK, Belgium, and the Netherlands. Following his studies, he gained experience working in a professional practice delivering high-rise commercial projects across the UK. Having gained extensive technical knowledge and an interest in the progression of digital construction methods, he is currently specialising in using the latest digital innovations to deliver Hyperscale Data Centre projects across Europe.

The primary focus of this chapter concerns how skateboarders perceive the space they inhabit. Architectural Historian Iain Borden proposes the idea of 'super-architectural space' (2001, 23), the space beyond space, terrain, and tool (skateboard), the combination of which differentiates architecture as an object, drawing, or idea, and then presents it as a continual rhythmic procedure of the production of space. Skateboarders possess an altered perspective of the city to pedestrians; it is a pleasure ground, a place for the expression of energy, movement and representation, the conception of which is prescribed by addressing the physical architecture of the city, and responding to it with a dynamic presence.

The limits for the research are the experiences of pedestrians and skateboarders within a case study area in Belfast. This area is identified by applying Henri Lefebvre's principles on 'spatial zero degree' (1984, 184) spaces, with the study investigating how pedestrians and skateboarders experience such spaces. The analysis entails investigating the physical spaces of the city and the activities that occur within it, in particular, exploring how pedestrians and skateboarders perceive their generated experiences through their engagement with elements of the urban fabric.

The aim is to analyse the differences between pedestrians' and skateboarders' movement, experience, and perceptions of physical and created architectural space and time within the urban fabric of Belfast. The interaction of each spatial occupant embodies such processes within the architectural space and time. Subsequently, such experiential perceptions present themselves through these engagements within the social spaces projected within the city. By employing a comparative methodology of qualitative factors, the analysis enables a thorough comparison between the generated architectural spatial experiences.

While investigating how these engagements manifest them into generated perception, it is critical to bear in mind the underlying difference in the subconscious physiological process of each. This process dictates the perception and outlook towards space presented, to each, by the city. When pedestrians encounter functional or mundane elements such as a kerbstone or set of stairs, the skateboarder sees an opportunity for creative innovation. By redefining or creating new representational functional qualities, for such elements, their progressive manipulation of movement, rhythm, and performance achieves this.

Humans are inherently capable of sensual perceptions and it is through these that their resultant spatial experience is generated. To understand the spatial experience of each I investigate what sensual perceptions humans are subjected to, to create this. The basic human senses are:

1) Hearing
2) Sight
3) Smell
4) Taste
5) Touch

Their perceived spatial experience is dependent on various other senses. Some of which are time, temperature, pain, and kinesthetics. By determining the senses that are most pertinent to gain an understanding of spatial experience, an investigation of each determines the overall result. The research methodology for each sense is:

1) Hearing: Perception of sound. Does the interpretation of sounds give them a capacity to perceive the composition or provide an understanding of what occurs within spaces? Enabled by a written interpretation documentation process.

2) Movement: Representation of travelling through space. How do each move through space? Is there a subconscious predetermined route? Are there any restrictions of movement from elements of the urban fabric? How do they respond to this if such matters arise? Kinaesthesia - The perception generated through changing body position, weight, and movement while experiencing the space. Documented by mapping how each travels within the space and a written account of personal experience.

3) Serial Vision: Representation of the visual perception. What is seen by pedestrians and skateboarders during the performance of activities available in space? Documented through sketches of the significant points of view.

4) Time: Perception of duration. How does each perceive the period in events that unfold around them? This time aspect is linked to the movement aspect of the investigation by recording the time duration of the movement process.

5) Touch: Representation of the perception of feeling. What do they feel in terms of textures of the urban fabric? What reactions are provoked by this. Is the material's texture capable of providing any restrictions? To be recorded by drawn and photographic documentation.

This analytical methodology applies to both pedestrians and skateboarders. The comparison of the engagement of each within the urban fabric presents similarities and differences. It is the comparison of the production of perceived architectural spatial experience, derived through sensual perceptions that are the basis for my conclusions.

These conclusions are used to assess the validity of the hypothesis: The production of 'super-architectural space,' through the recreation and re-imagining of the city and their engagement with elements of the urban fabric, gives skateboarders a greater sense of space than pedestrians.

> I think skateboarding is a far more profound revolution that people give it credit for. The wonderful thing to me is that these young people discovered that they themselves would creatively adapt to the environment they already found. The whole notion of adapting to the environment, it is almost contrary to the basis of our civilisation (Edmund Bacon, *Freedom of Space*, 2006).

EXPERIENTIAL SENSING THROUGH
CONSCIOUS PERCEPTION

Being in time

What is "Being"? (Heidegger 1927, 10). This is the fundamental metaphysical problem in philosophy and what makes it possible? Martin Heidegger's endeavours to rationalise the question of 'Being' in his work "Being and Time" (Heidegger,1927) was to scrutinise ourselves. His starting point was not to look at what is perceptible but what is fundamentally a phenomenon, human "Da sein" (1927, 20). This analytical approach had put a new light on the question that had not been thought of by the Greek or any other philosophers, before or since. Heidegger postulated an approach that 'Dasein' is 'Being' that questions itself as to what is 'Being.' It is therefore a self-interpreting being, meaning existence is self-interpretation.

Furthermore, he believed resolving the question of 'Being' failed when transforming the subject, 'I,' into an object. His alternative thought was to imagine it as "Being-in-the-world" (1927, 23). A place for existence provides the opportunity for 'Dasein' and is filled with things, not objects. A thing can be defined in respect to two frames of thought:

1) It is what it is in terms of the projects within which it appears, and
2) It is what is in relation to other things also involved in such projects.

Heidegger classifies things as 'zeug' or gear to provide the achievement of 'projects.' In his account, the 'Being' of a thing is generated by the complete context of back-and-forth references created by some projects of 'Dasein' and by the other things simultaneously involved in that project, thus implicating that things always are what they are due to their placement beside other things, when referenced collectively.

Space

The definition of space is open to interpretation, depending on what line of intellectual thought it is utlising. If a theoretical approach is taken, then a "consideration of space permits reflection on the orderings of logics of simultaneity" (Löw, 2008), but space may also be examined in regards to social sciences as a "product of social actions" (Massey, 1999), the latter being pertinent to this investigation. Martina Löw states, in relation to social science, space "is better suited than any other to express the spheres of juxtaposition and coexistence" (Löw, 2008). Löw is describing the possibility of existing entities or space coinciding with, in close proximity, creating an effect on each other, while acting independently. While analysing space in this context "social sciences address inclusion/exclusion" (2008, 26) as a problem of dual nature that concerns both the 'symbolic' and 'material dimensions' found in the world. Therefore, space is generated through the consequential actions of experiencing objects in relation to each other.

While analysing space in this regard, it is crucial to refer to the work of Henri Lefebvre, in particular his writing *Production de l'espace* (1974). Ultimately, Lefebvre proposes two individual levels that space can be determined: "natural space, absolute/physical space" (Lefebvre 1995) which we inhabit, and "social space" (1995). An analogy is created that examines space as a produced element of society, and he states that "(Social) space is a (Social) product" (Lefebvre, 1995). A key aspect being that due to the resultant forces of capitalist conditions on societal processes of everyday life, it has been reduced to a standardised function of "individualization and particularization" (1995).

Lefebvre begins the investigation of "spatial practice" (2008, 28) by conveying three elements of conceptual contemplation:

1) Practice/perceived space
2) Representation of space/ conceived space
3) Space of representation/representational space/lived space (1991, 38).

He principally follows the work of Karl Marx who "examines the products of industry not in their material form but as the outcome of societal production process" (2008, 27) and operates under a Marxist tradition. The term 'spatial practice' is thus the spatially related manner of behaviour, i.e. the experiential perception of a body, produced everyday determined by the action of producing and reproducing space. An argument is proposed that through living under the restraints of capitalist conditions, a sense of prevailing monotony and repetition is established. This provides an underlying assertion over the experience of the occupant, predetermining a withdrawn possibility of representation, meaning "the user's space is lived – not represented (or conceived)" (1991, 362).

The apparent generation of 'spatial practice' is inundated with underlying complexities. The previously mentioned begins to explain the implied actions of bodies within spaces. This acts simultaneously with the perception of said bodies through "manipulated perceptions that point beyond the existing capitalist space," by virtue of "spaces of representation, imaginings [and] memories" (2008, 29), generating an overall perceptual experience of space. Another factor which is quintessential to the influential process of perception is the architecture of spaces, as its "mass and surface" (Le Corbusier, 1923), among other characteristics, portray the symbolic and materialistic realms.

Perception

Perception is the ability to develop an awareness of something through a sensory capacity. The inherent ability of human perception is of major significance in that it manifests itself into a state of conscious being, and exhibits a knowledge and recognition which enables humans to understand and question the space they inhabit. It is this consciousness that has brought us to acquire the dominant stance we have taken in harnessing the world.

"All knowledge takes its place within the horizons opened up by perception" (Mearleau-Ponty, 1989, 241). Maurice Merleau-Ponty, in his key work on perception *Phenomenology of Perception*, describes the "miracle of consciousness," in particular how a "re-establish[ment of] the unity of [an] object in a new dimension" is brought "to light, through attention [and] phenomena" (1989, 35). Here he refers to the capability of the conscience to create a new perception (meaning of an object) through what is physically sensed. Furthermore, as people and "social goods" (2008, 40) simultaneously occupy space through the engagement of everyday activities, this means, "that syntheses are formed" (2008, 40).

Perception "concentrates impressions into a process" (2008, 41), a physical sensing of what exists within the constraints of the body's vicinity. Löw's interpretation of this is, "a simultaneous process of social goods and people and the perceptual activity of bodily sensing" (2008, 41).

An inherent trait in humans controlled by the conscious state of mind is subjectivity. Niklas Luhmann comments that perceptions are open to interpretation and subject to a selection process.

In current perception as well as in the conception reactualized through imagination we are dealing with the outcome of the simultaneous processing of an abundance of impressions with the possibility of selecting focal points of attention without "losing sight" of others (Luhmann, 1998, 17).

Due to the copious amount of perceptible data available at any given moment, these are construed as pertinent factors to accommodate the wants of each individual. Therefore, perception does not abide by a "direct nature," (2008, 41) but as Löw suggests, "merely conveys the impressions of directness while being, in fact, a highly selective and constructive process." (2008, 41).

Spatial Zero Degree

This idea follows on from Roland Barthes' analytical approach to transformations in the writing of literature and his concept of "Zero point" (Barthes, 1958). These are spaces that are not symbolic in nature, a neutral point that is characterised by the conflicting presence and absence perceived by a "simple witness" (1984, 184). The symbolism inherited by such spaces is prescribed through their inherent expansivity of space, thus generating a monotonous spatial experience lacking in creative characteristics. Pedestrians are described as being "metropolitan dwellers [that] are simply witnesses to the functioning of the city, where the experience is like that of a museum" (Bennett, 1995). This is in contradiction to what Lefebvre states, "In such cities, creation of creations, everyday life would become a creation of which each citizen and each community would be capable" (Lefebvre, 1984).

An integral design aspect of the 1800s and early 1900s was consideration of how pedestrians inhabited these spaces. A prominent example of this is Central Park, New York, designed by Frederick Law Olmsted and Calvert Vaux. This park was designed to accommodate many users and activities, and they were concerned with enhancing the natural and organic green space, which contrasted the formal gridline structure that to which the city adhered. Restricting the amount of interference to the natural landscape through the interventions of roads or pathways was crucial to the process to reduce any impact on the natural beauty of the space. Open spaces and landscaping features heavily influenced the design of pedestrian pathways, creating interconnections between different areas visually and kinetically. The aim of the enhancement was to generate something that equated to the successful public gardens of Europe and Asia, confirming this global awareness to the importance that public space should be beneficial to the public. A place separate to the city, which encourages interactions amongst people, distracting them from the city to appreciate nature. (Olmsted and Fein 1967, 63-88). An example of such a space located within Belfast is the Botanic Gardens.

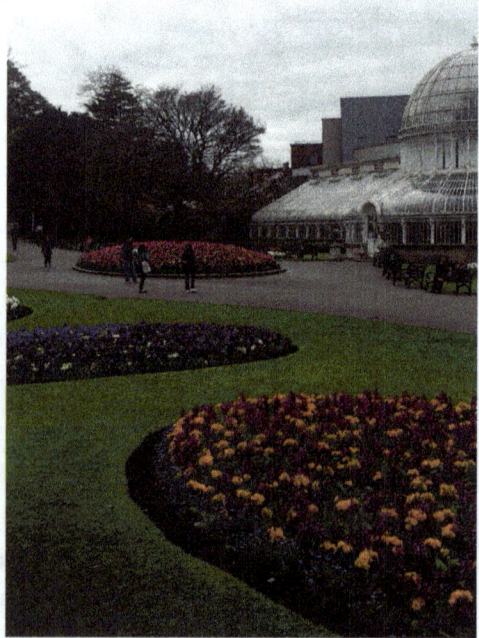

Figure 1: Botanic Gardens. 2014 (all photos and illustrations are by the author.)

This was the attitude adopted until the modernist movement beginning in the early 1900s and coming into full effect by the 1920s. The modernists created a more brutal and formal interpretational method to a design approach of outdoor public spaces constructing a reinterpretation of the relationships formed between people and spaces. The developed preconception that the city as a functionalist machine in which people operate, where "form ever follows function" (Sullivan. 1896) administered the treatment of urban public space as a homogenous entity inundated with a vast expansivity of space and defunct of "social activity and function" (Carmona et al., 2008, 38). These spaces were overpowered by the increasing demand to create buildings that were symbolic representations of power and monumentality, gestured by an ever increasing scale.

The Swiss-French architect Le Corbusier was at the forefront of this design narrative. His ideas of the modern city are documented in his publication *Towards a New Architecture*. He states that:

> The Plan is a generator. Without a plan, you have lack of order, and wilfulness. The Plan holds in itself the essence of sensation. The great problems of to-morrow, dictated by collective necessities, put the question of 'plan' in a new form. Modern life demands, and is waiting for, a new kind of plan both for the house and for the city (Le Corbusier, 1923).

According to Le Corbusier, architecture is "capable of the sublime, it impresses the most brutal instincts by its objectivity," "Architectural abstraction…is nothing more than a materialization of a possible idea," and "Mass and surface are the elements by which architecture manifests itself" (1923). It is easy to see his pragmatic thoughts towards architecture and, most notably, his unbuilt master plan for Paris embodies his ideas and is the personification of modernism on the grandest construction endeavours of humans, the city. It is also pertinent to mention an idea of an Italian architect, Antonio Sant'Elia. It is stated in the Manifesto of Futurist Architect 1914 that "the decorative value of Futurist architecture depends solely on the use and original arrangement of raw or bare or violent coloured materials." Although Sant'Elia was associated within a different architectural movement, the use of raw materials is very apparent in Le Corbusier's architecture, mainly in the vast use of concrete. This was through the modernist thoughts of being honest with the materials, but there are similarities to be drawn. Consequently, the construction during the modern movement relied mainly on concrete, steel and glass, another proclamation of Sant'Elia.

It is the planning ideas and use of materials that ultimately created the vast spaces between buildings for pedestrians who are diminished to anonymous beings of the functionalist machine which facilitates them, revoking the opportunity of social function. What resulted were vast expanses of space which could have little or no connection with other spaces of the city and could be left underused, only to be watched from the top of the high rise buildings or from car windows. In this sense, such space can be considered 'negative,' in that its role is entirely subservient to that of the buildings in which the "life; of the city is deemed to be" (Madanipour 2003, 202). This may have been the case for pedestrians, but for skateboarders this only opened up a whole new realm of possibilities. Modern architecture's inadequacy of providing functional public space was to inadvertently have a positive influence on the development of skateboarding.

The architect Tony Bracali, in his essay *Thanks Le Corbusier (...from the skateboarders)* comments on how skateboarders were the first to find positive aspects of "modernist urban design," which to a certain extent have post-rationalised the associated principles. The desired function of businessmen traversing through such spaces closing deals has not materialised. A genuine physical use for the "physical forms of modernist urban planning" had been discovered. The "wide open paved areas, low, simple benches," that were an extension of the architecture, usually constructed of concrete or granite slabs and "pure geometries of space" had presented a space that accommodated the performance of skateboarding (Bracali, 2003).

Bracali, who is interested in the relationship between skateboarders and public space comments that "Le Corbusier has the platonic ideal of a modernist architect....With his cool glasses and his love of concrete' and hails him as, 'the patron saint of skateboarding" (Roman Mars 2013).

Skateboarding as space production

There are various forces that exert themselves on architecture, these being elemental and social forces of time. These can be the effects of weather, physical decay, the actions of users, changing function, and economic viability, respectively. The fundamental force bearing on architecture is entropy, and it is due to the previously mentioned that cumulatively produce "entropic time" (Till, 2009). This inherently possesses a ubiquitous engagement with architecture, working in parallel with the design process, the resultant finished product, and continues to act past the point where the architect has finished their work, posing the question, can a finished product even exist? It is the social forces of time I elaborate on further, in particular how the users' engagement continues this idea of the unfinished (2009).

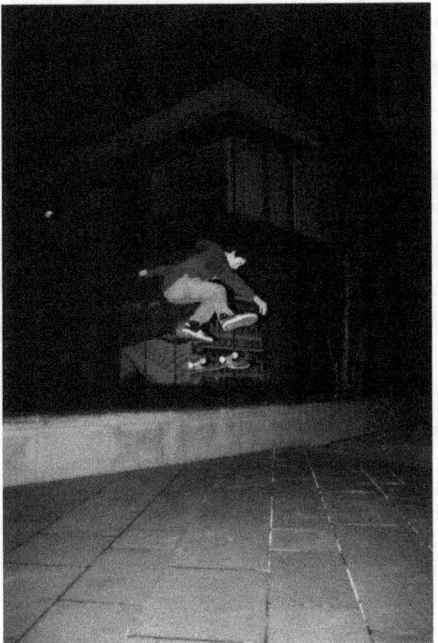

Figure 2: Re-defining space at Titanic Quarter. 2014

Skateboarding may not be a traditional form of study with regards to architecture, but it creates a different thought process in relation to the possibilities within architecture, such as its function as an external critique of architecture. The underlying origins of skateboarding were in the 1960s when Californian surfers took to the urban spaces to recreate the waves of the sea. Through this exploration of the city, they were exploiting the physical terrain in order to project themselves into abstract space and present new uses of the intended function of such terrain (Borden 2001, 29). This history is not in the conscious realm of the skateboarder as they immerse themselves in the present and immediate future, through addressing the physical architecture of the city, a number of distinct announcements and meanings resonate. It requires a tool (skateboard) that the body absorbs and "produces space, time and the self" (2001, 1). Such a body's representation is seen by those who take part in the act as a perceived alternative way of life. In this respect, it is not architecture of objects but a production of "space, time and social being" (2001, 1).

Furthermore, once you have had the introspective experience of what the nature of skateboarding presents, the desire becomes engrained in the sub-conscience. It becomes a visual performance through the response to objects "with a dynamic presence" (2001, 1) by expression of energy and movement, but also "refutes the reduction of the activity solely to the spectacle of the image" (2001, 1). There is a deeper psychological response that this act becomes a "projection of the self" (Borden, 2001, 100) into an endless realm of possibilities that could not be exploited without the tool (skateboard). It is somewhat reductive to refer to the skateboard as a mere tool, as it holds more premise than a simple commodity. Therefore, it is not just a tool but possesses characteristics of a "prosthetic device, an extension of the body as a fifth limb" (Borden, 2001, 100), or a better phrasing of this action, "Making your board an extension of your body is control over the soul" (Thrasher, 1997).

Super-architectural space

Borden suggests that the fundamental consideration of skateboarding is it "addresses the physical architecture of the modern city, yet responds to it not with another object but with a dynamic presence" (2001, 1). Skateboarding proclaims implicit announcements and meanings through its absorption of a tool into the body. "It produces space, but also time and the self" (Borden, 2001), allows "creativity and production of desires" (Borden, 2001) and possesses an internal contradiction of not reducing the highly visual aspect of the activity to mere display of imagery. Skateboarders have developed the act into a "complete and alternative way of life" (Borden 2001). In this sense it is therefore architecture, "not as a thing, but as a production of space, time and social being" (Borden, 2001). The contribution of skateboarding to architectural space is through its performative and representational characteristics. They are simultaneously space and projected space as well as an expression of energy, movement, and representation. Their space is therefore produced by a combination of body, terrain, and tool (skateboard), re-imagining architectural space to "recreate both it and themselves into super-architectural space" (2001, 89).

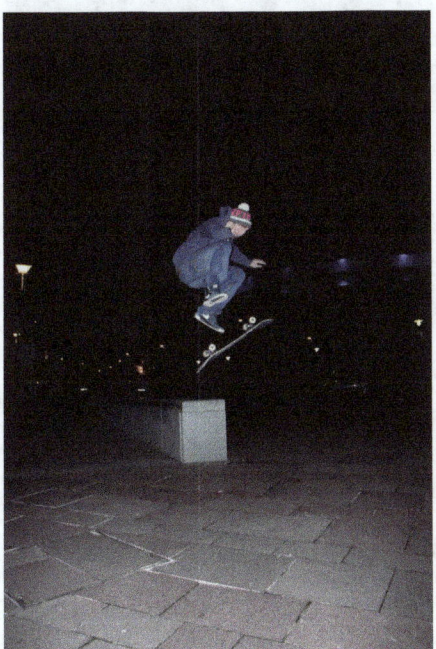

Figure 3: Implication through dynamic presence. 2014.

Skateboarders interact with the terrain through "gestural space of flow, of direct engagement with the terrain" (2001, 96). This describes the natural space conserved within abstract space, that of the space "within and around the body" (2001, 96) and is defined by Henri Lefebvre's "spatial architectonics" (Lefebvre, 1991). The spatial production partakes in a dual nature which is not derived from the conscience but from the occupation of space and the concise activity functions. The space is produced within the body, "co-ordinates of left-right, front-back, up-down, spinal rotation" (2001, 96), then outward as the body is subject to the dynamics of the movement provided. Such actions are comparable to what Len Lye achieved in his film Particles in Space (1979). In this work, there is no defined architectural subject apart from developing a sense of space.

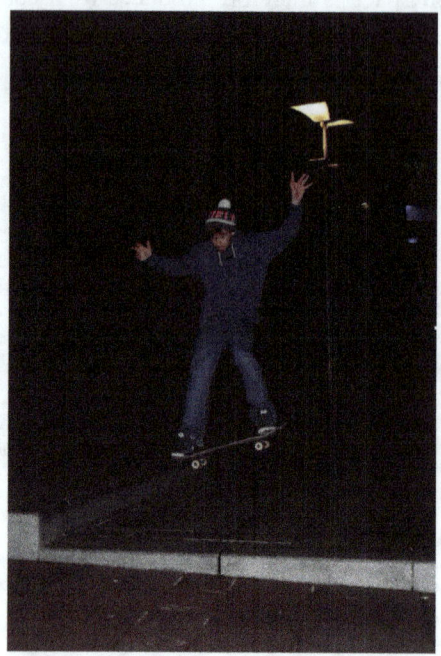

Figure 4: Gestural space of flow, noseslide the kerb. 2014.

Analysing how pedestrians and the skateboarders perceive the space which they inhabit focuses mainly on the particular movements that each exert on the space around them. Pedestrians' activities exert different demands on the physical architecture in three ways, as suggested by Jan Gehl:

1) "Necessary activities" (Gehl, 2001) are those predominantly associated with movement (walking) and everyone will participate in to some extent.

2) "Optional activities" (Gehl, 2001) allow pedestrians to engage in activities such as 'talking a walk to get some fresh air' and depend on the possibility provided from the place and time.

3) "Social activities" (Gehl, 2001) come about by the developed connection of activities within spaces and require an interaction with other bodies.

Such delimitation of space through activities is relevant to the pedestrian, but for the skateboarder, it is a different case. The skateboarder responds to the physical architecture with a "dynamic presence" (2001, 1). They inherit a creative production of space, time, and themselves through a sense of movement, performance, rhythm, and representation. The process of absorbing the tool (skateboard) into themselves and the corresponding actions of the combined entity of body, terrain, and tool, and subsequent engagement with the urban fabric creates an architecture that is a continual rhythmic procedure of the production of space and time. This greatly contrasts with that of the pedestrian. Their experience is dictated by the failure of the city to "replace the symbolisms, times, rhythms and different spaces of the traditional city" (1996, 127-8), and thus their experience is that of a bystander in a museum (Bennett, 1995) of the ominous functionalist city that engulfs them.

Research of a comparative nature can be utilised while investigating the generated architectural spatial experience of pedestrians and skateboarders. Comparative research covers an extensive range of quantitative and qualitative "comparisons of social entities" (Mills et al., 2006). Fundamentally, the principles behind comparative research are constructing an analysis that "searches for similarity and variance" (Mills et al., 2006). "Social entities" (Mills et al., 2006) again have numerous definitions. If investigating social relationships from an ontological stance, there is an assumption that they are "universal" (Mills et al., 2006), thus acting autonomously of "space and time" (Mills et al., 2006). Due to the underlying difficulty of a derivation of such "universal" relationships, comparative research offers a solution to segregating "more general" (Mills et al., 2006) relationships and can "isolate regularities from the context laden environment" Mills et al., (2006).

Max Weber suggests comparison can reveal variance in social relationships and expose a variation in distinctive traits possessed by a "particular entity" (Weber, 2006). His framework that "scientific knowledge of society and culture" (Levi-Faur, 2005) arises from various selective views of the subject matter at hand. This refuted Emile Durkheim by suggesting selectivity is determined by the "initiative of the investigator" (Levi-Faur, 2005) rather than the "nature of things" (Levi-Faur, 2005). John Creswell describes qualitative research as, "the means for testing objective theories by examining the relationship among variables" (Creswell, 2009), and it can therefore be said that it is:

a means for exploring and understanding the meaning individuals or groups as-
cribe to a social or human problem. The process of research involves emerging
questions and procedures; data typically collected in the participant's setting
(Creswell, 2009).

There are various philosophical attitudes regarding qualitative research, which
have a direct bearing on "the choice of theoretical framework and methodology" (Lemanski and Overton 2001) utilised to systematically conduct an investigation. One of these is constructivism, which "[h]olds the views that humans
generate and construct their own knowledge and understanding from their interactions with the world around them" (Matthews, 1993).

Research

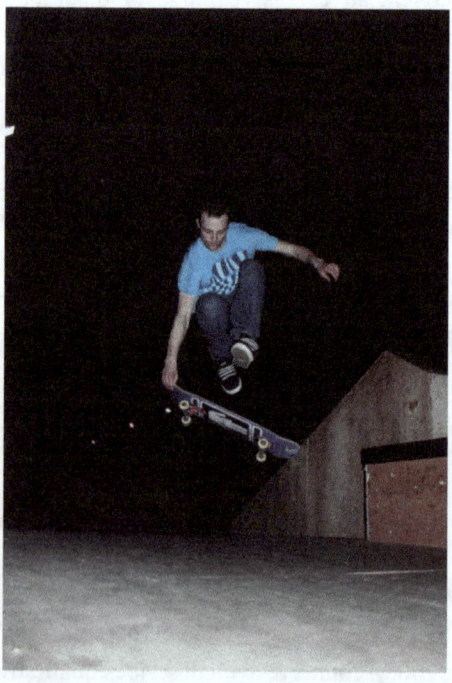

Figure 5: Projecting into new space at T13. 2014.

The popularity of skateboarding culture, like most things, is cyclical. Not only did this happen in Belfast, but has occurred throughout the history of skateboarding from its origins in the 1960s. Certainly in my memory, this spiked in Belfast around the early 2000s, but then experienced a recession. In recent years, interest has grown stronger, although there are some who will stay true to the cause. This has been facilitated by the construction of purpose built skate parks, Bridges (outdoor), and T13 (indoor). The fact that these facilities have been provided has not diminished skateboarders seeking spaces within the city to exploit the urban terrain. Such spaces are: Custom House Square, the Waterfront Hall, and Titanic Quarter. This list is endless as long as the skateboarder questions themselves, 'Can I skate this?'

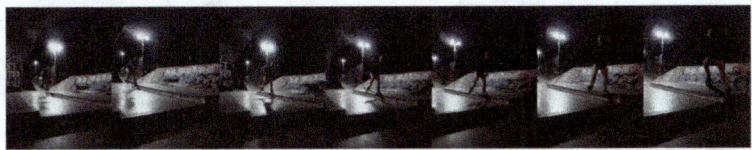

Figure 6: Sequential image of tailslide in Bridges. 2014.

The previously mentioned spaces are relevant as they can be defined as having what Lefebvre states as "spatial zero degree" (1984, 184). Each of these spaces characteristically lends itself to such a definition, and the design still follows the modernists' approach to, or lack of, public space design. These vast spaces evoke a diminishing effect, to the pedestrian, due to the scale of the buildings and their positioning in such spatial expansivity.

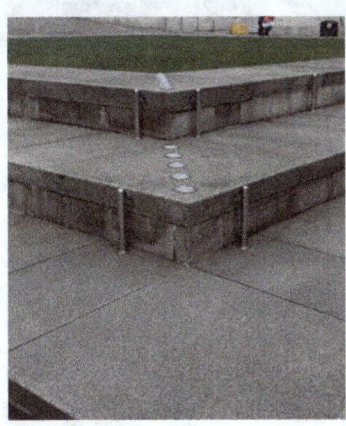

Figure 7: Interventions in the architecture at the Waterfront. 2014

Furthermore, post rationalisation for the absence of social function is found specifically at Custom House Square, by hosting an annual music festival and various other events. Although this may be perceived as a positive solution for an increase in social function, it does raise the question, are such post rationalisations of social function really justifiable when they remain socially functionless for the majority of the time? "In redefining space for themselves, skateboarders take over conceptually as well as physically and so strike at the heart of what everyone else understands by the city" (Borden, 2001, 247). As Borden suggests, pedestrians do not have an equivalent conceptual capacity for skateboarding; they see it as a threat, and generally speaking, it can be said that what people do not understand they do not like. Therefore, legislation and the repression of skateboarding are ever present in society. The interaction with the police or security guards is inevitable for a skateboarder.

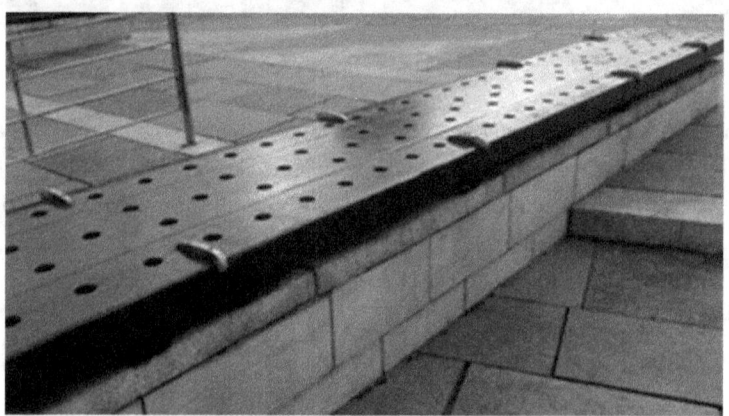

Figure 8: Skate stoppers incorporated into the architecture. 2014

One method of repression is the *skate stopper.* These are interventions within architectural elements designed to hinder the opportunity for something to be skated, some examples of which are shown in Figure 7 and Figure 8. They are somewhat successful in restricting the actions of skateboarders, but at what cost? Such actions directly contradict what Lefebvre states, "in such cities, creation of creations, everyday life would become a creation of which each citizen…would be capable of" (Lefebvre, 1984). Therefore, such interventions reduce these opportunities of creation but also arguably question the integrated architectural intent of the design.

The area of public space for the basis of this investigation is the Titanic Quarter. Bernard Ebbinghaus proposed the argument that the selection of cases or sampling is of paramount importance in relation to comparative research (Ebbinghaus, 2005). The decision of the sample size for the investigation is crucial. If a "relatively large N (i.e. sample size)" (2006, 622) is chosen, there is an underlying potential for construing "superficial...results [through] more general comparative variables" (2006. 622). Whereas, in "small-N case studies, the selection of case studies is often deliberate and theory-driven" (2006. 622).

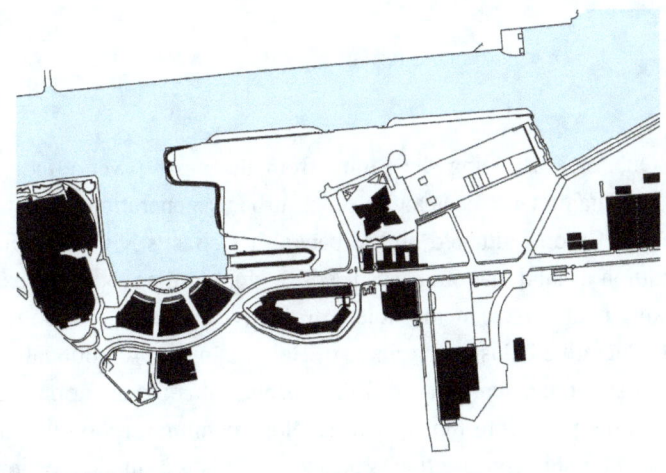

Figure 9: Map of the two areas of study in Titanic Quarter. 2014.

Therefore, the analytical process of identifying case studies in which to perform such analysis of movement in space has been determined by what Lefebvre refers to as "spatial zero degree" (1984, 184). This idea follows on from Roland Barthes' analytical approach to transformations in the writing of literature and his concept of "Zero point" (Barthes, 1958). These are spaces that are not symbolic in nature, a neutral point, that is characterised by the conflicting presence and absence perceived by a "simple witness" (Lefebvre 1984, 184).

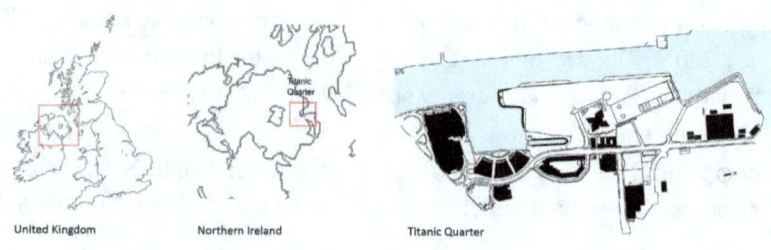

United Kingdom   Northern Ireland   Titanic Quarter

Figure 10: Location map of Titanic Quarter. 2014.

"Titanic Quarter... Building the future from the past" (twenty-first century icon, 2009). Titanic Quarter is an on-going urban regeneration project, one of the largest in Europe, situated on the banks of Belfast's River Lagan. It is a transformation of land that once was used for shipbuilding, but now exhibits a "high quality realm that is memorable, informative and legible" (2009) in celebrating the lucrative industrial heritage of Belfast. In the promotional brochure A twenty-first century icon, the idea that through this regeneration they have transformed the place into that which develops communities on the land that was one used for ship construction is presented. This is a subjective view to the promoter, but I scrutinize the public realm of Titanic Quarter in line with my investigation, based on ideas presented in the previous section.

Skateboarders' Sensual Experience of Space

Hearing

For skateboarders, there is an increased amount of noise produced by the skateboard on the ground. This produces different sound depending on the material. For them, it is all of the sound that they hear, as it is produced by the actions they are partaking in. This produces an introspective effect, and they are thefore less aware of other activities occurring in the space.

Movement

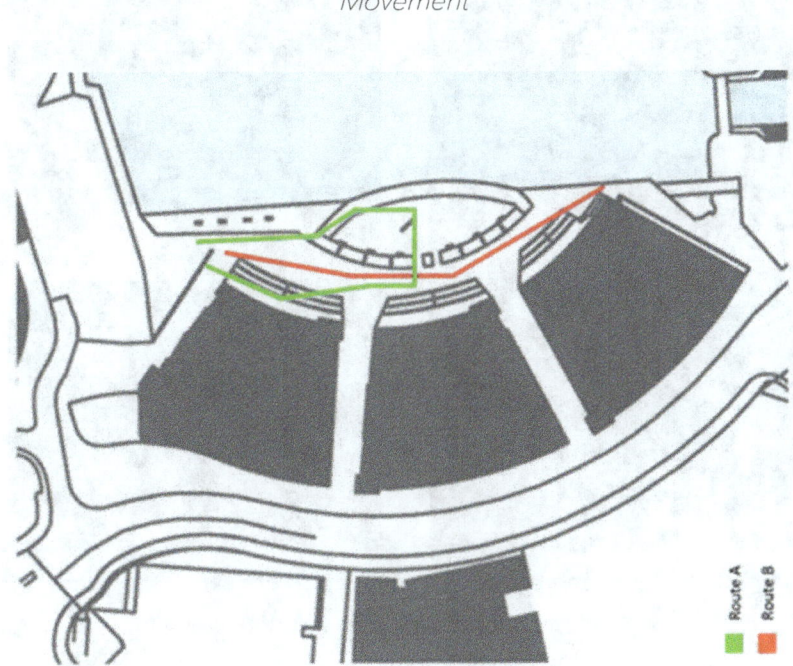

Figure 11: Route of movement around study area. 2014

Skateboarders do not adhere to a predetermined route. They move through the space as they wish and look for alternative routes or interactions to engage in. They are not restricted by elements of the urban fabric, as this presents a new challenge or opportunity to reinvent the function of such elements and generate new experiences. (Figure 12-13). Their perception is heightened by the constant shifting of body position while travelling and preparing for the next engagement. This is high priority, ensuring the correct body position and balance allowing them to stay on the skateboard.

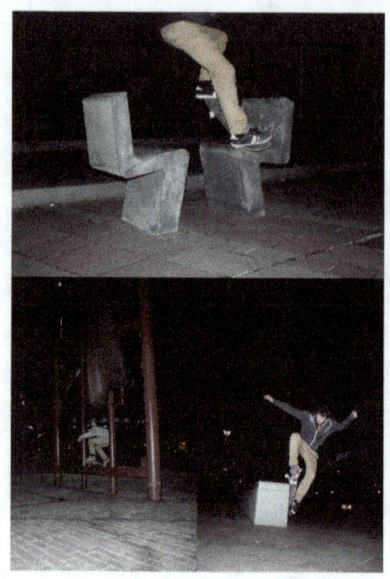

Figure 12: Movement and interaction
through study area. 2014.

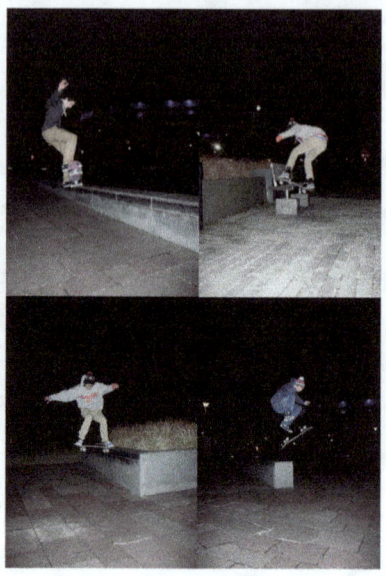

Figure 13: Movement and interaction
through study area. 2014.

Serial vision

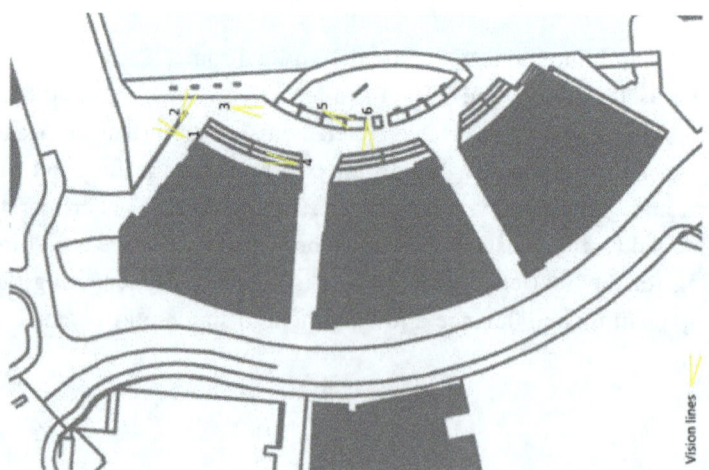

Figure 14: Map of study area with viewpoints for skateboarders. 2014

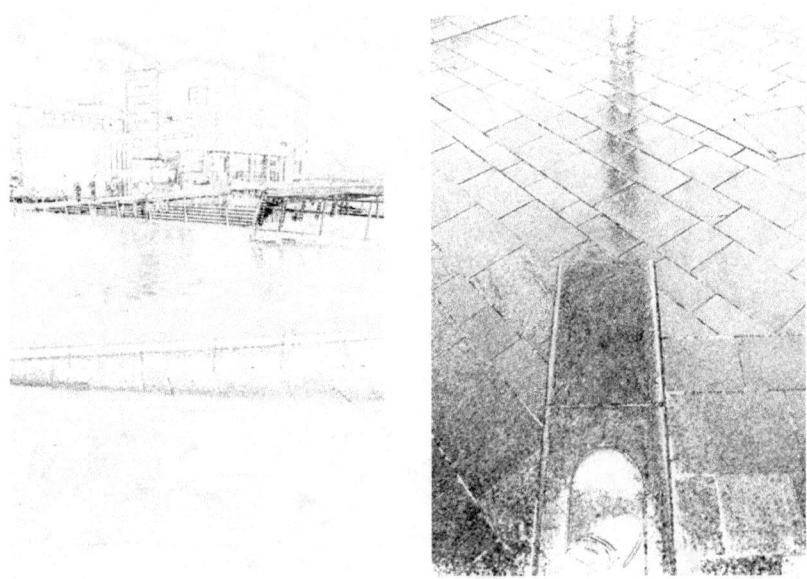

Figure 15: Sketch of view point 1. 2014.   Figure 16: Sketch of view point 2. 2014.

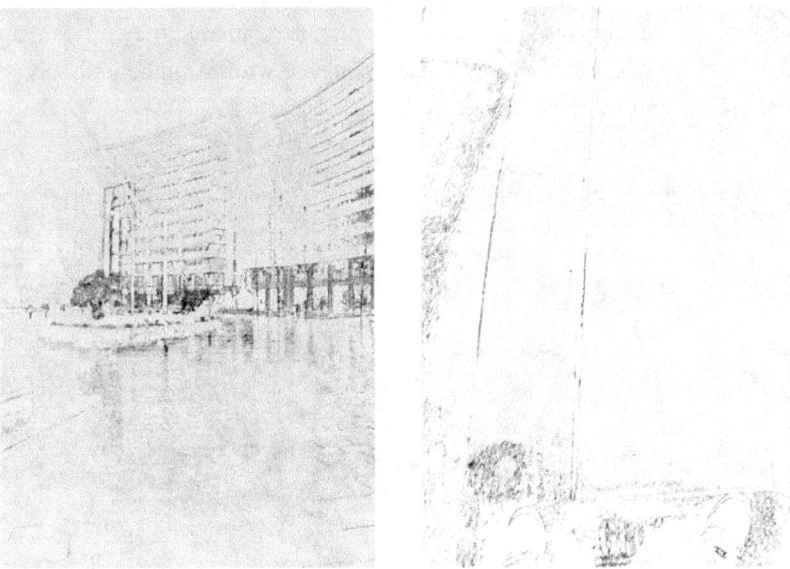

Figure 17: Sketch of view point 3. 2014.   Figure 18: Sketch of view point 4. 2014.

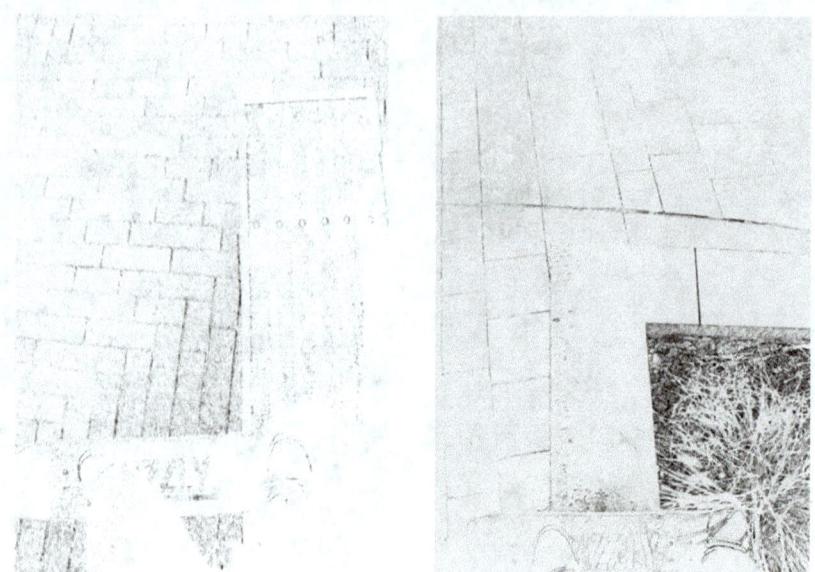

Figure 19: Sketch of view point 5. 2014.   Figure 20: Sketch of view point 6. 2014.

Skateboarders see the limits of the space which they inhabit; they focus mainly on the element of the fabric they intent to engage with. A tunnel effect is produced when approaching and performing an interaction.

Time

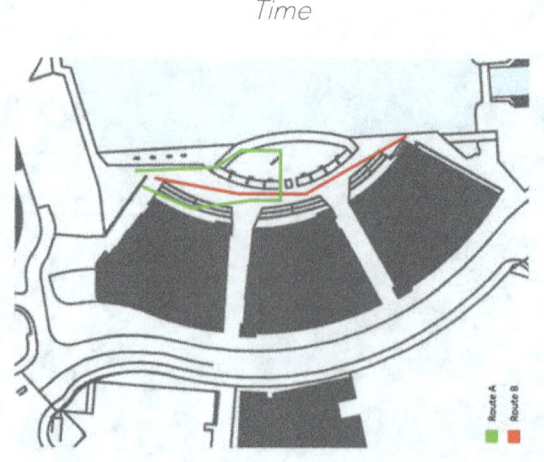

Figure 21: Route of movement around study area. 2014.

The time aspect increases the intensity of the experience the skateboarder undergoes when using the space as their actions happen at an increased rate relative to that of the pedestrian. This is due to the requirement of an increased speed to allow them to successfully perform the engagement of the urban fabric.

Route A: 56 seconds
Route B: 30 seconds

Touch

For skateboarders, the textures of the ground become more apparent. This occurs due to the interaction of the wheels of the skateboard being in constant contact with the ground, as opposed to pedestrians whose contact is broken up by the lifting of the feet between steps. Therefore, they are more aware of changes in the texture, which transfers itself through vibrations through the skateboard into the feet. The texture can directly impact the capability of the skateboarder, as if it is too rough it will impede the ability to allow a smooth flow of movement. Additionally, this smoothness will affect the speed at which skateboarders travel on a particular surface. If it is a rough texture, for instance, it will provide more resistance and therefore require more effort to move across it, as it will regularly slow them down.

Pedestrians' Sensual Experience of Space

Hearing

Pedestrians hear the sound produced by their footsteps, but it does not reduce the levels of sound from the other activities that may be occurring in and around the space. They are more aware of what is happening around them due to this.

Movement

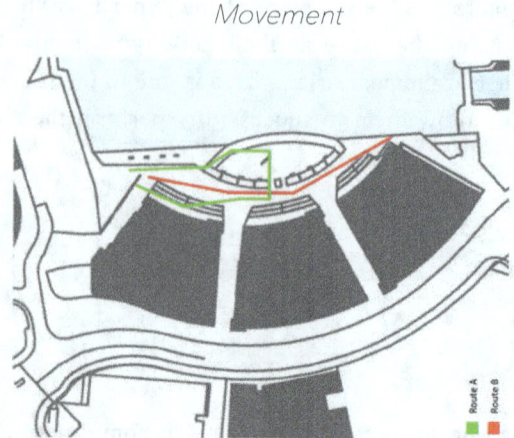

Figure 22: Route of movement around study area for pedestrians. 2014

For pedestrians, there seems to be a predetermined route which is straight across the space. Unlike the skateboarders who are seeking elements of the urban fabric to utilise them in new ways, such elements act as guidelines for the pedestrians.

In regard to body position, it is not as crucial for the pedestrian. As they are walking, which has become more of a reflex, they do not need to concentrate on body positioning to accomplish what they are trying to achieve.

Serial Vision

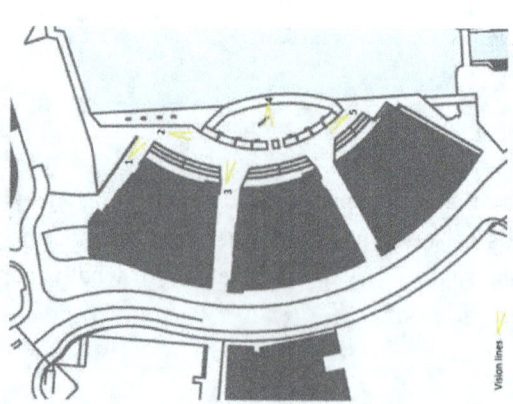

Figure 23: Map of study area with viewpoints for pedestrians. 2014.

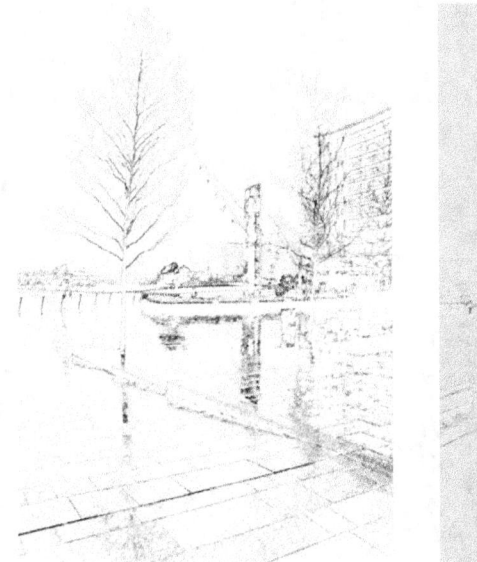

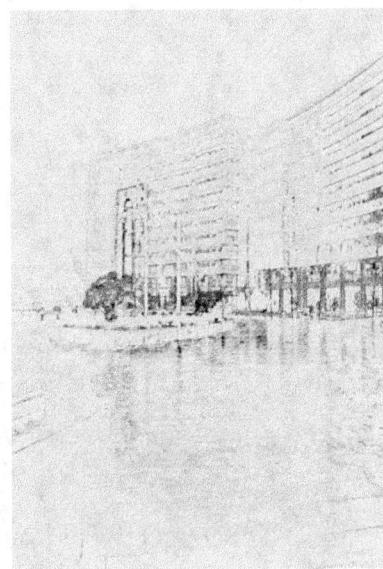

Figure 24: Sketch of view point 1. 2014 Figure 25: Sketch of view point 2. 2014

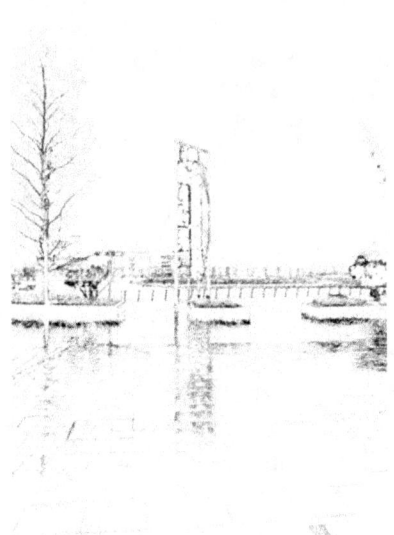

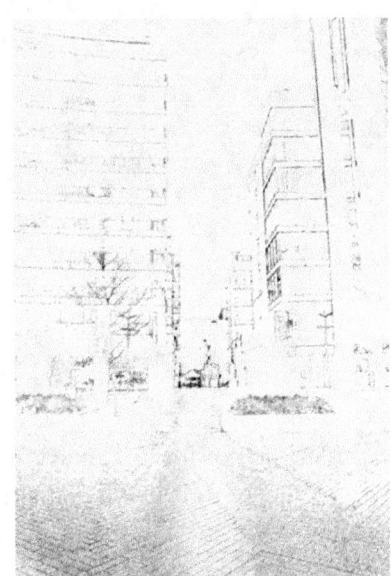

Figure 26: Sketch of view point 3. 2014 Figure 27: Sketch of view point 4. 2014

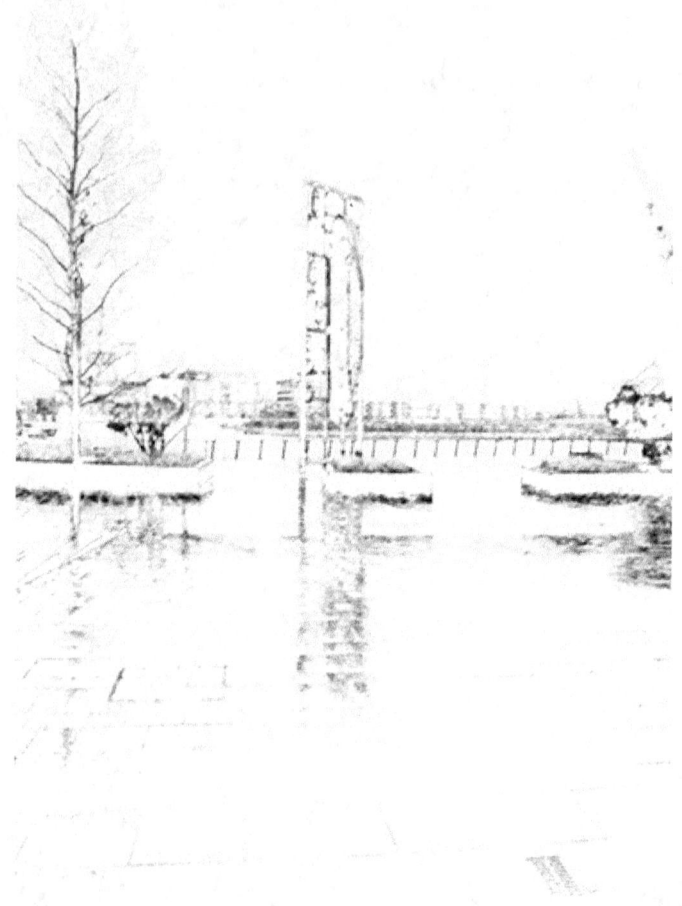

Figure 28: Sketch of view point 5. 2014

Pedestrians do not focus as much on the individual elements of the urban fabric but due to their intent in the space look at the overall composition in less detail. They are concerned with the end goal and to be able to see their desired destination rather than engaging on a more critical understanding of what the space actually consists of.

Time

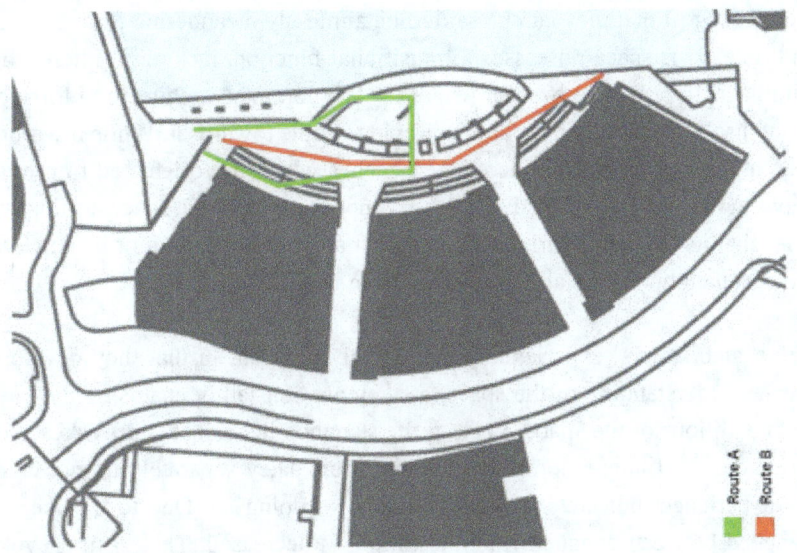

Figure 29: Route of movement around study area for pedestrians. 2014.

Due to the decreased speed at which the pedestrian travels through the space, the length of time taken is therefore increased. In both cases, for the route travelled, the time taken increases by over double that of the skateboarder.

Time taken to travel Routes
Route A: 130 seconds
Route B: 75 seconds

Touch

For the pedestrian, the textures of the ground are felt while moving over them, and differences can be distinguished. However, they do not experience every variance in the material, as their contact is broken at regular intervals from lifting their feet. The different textures do not impede how they travel through space, as it is possible to walk over either easily.

Analysis

From observation of how the pedestrians are occupying the Titanic Quarter area, I suggest that they can be said to be aimlessly meandering through space and time. This space possesses a transitional function, lacking in interest and stimulants to provide any other response. The dominant architectural force exerting itself is the Titanic building, drawing people towards it. While travelling, they may stop and sit on one of the benches which are orientated to provide views across the river. This in itself is reductive towards the space, as this suggests that its spatial qualities are redundant and not interesting or beneficial to the occupant but draws attention away from itself.

The skateboarders' experience is completely different in that they develop a greater understanding of the space, as they are constantly analysing the physical conditions of the space. Each of the skateboarder's senses provokes a different dialectal interaction than the pedestrian. They separately do not create the experience, but are intrinsically linked in doing so. Due to the increase of speed between engagements, the timing is decreased. This in turn evokes an increased awareness of body positioning, as before they engage, they must employ the correct foot positioning, ensure the body is in balance and check they are travelling at an appropriate speed. This becomes instinctive and occurs while focusing their sight on the object of intended interaction. The scope of serial vision, therefore, is of a more focal nature. A tunnel vision effect occurs at an increased rate of time. The skateboarder produces more sound than walking, and consequently a sense of materiality can be directly acquired by the sound response, and so qualities such as texture or even material composition is easily determined. Although there is no direct connection to the ground, a reading of the materiality can be determined through the vibrations felt in the feet of the skateboarder. As all of this happens simultaneously at a rapid rate; the skateboarder is more aware of themselves and the space, and adopt a more critical and analytical approach to how they inhabit such space.

Conclusion

This section uses the findings from the Case Study section to validate my hypothesis statement: The production of "super-architectural space" (2001, 1), through the recreation and re-imagining of the city and their engagement with elements of the urban fabric, gives skateboarders a greater sense of space than pedestrians. Through the implementation of the analytical methods used to construct a perception of the generated architectural spatial experience of pedestrians and skateboarders, I can conclude that skateboarders possess a greater sense of the space they inhabit. The various factors used to derive this conclusion are outlined below.

Skateboarders do not just occupy space and become another object in that space, which can be argued for pedestrians. Skateboarders see it as a blank canvas to create a personal projection of self-representation. They are inquisitive towards the boundaries and capabilities presented and utilise them in ways the pedestrian is incapable of understanding. Therefore, it is not something separate to them, but is something they become, and in turn becomes them. The inherent potential of the space can only be realised and brought to life by skateboarders who possess the ability to respond to it in such ways, but the skateboarder also requires space to offer such opportunities. Thus, this simultaneous juxtaposition of being and being in space gestures towards a harmonious co-existence of splendour, portraying a more romantic reflection of reality.

The overall experience of a body is in no doubt influenced by the physical experiences endured, as well as, their associated want for a feeling of belonging in their surroundings. This can be further explained by the juxtaposition of existing entities and space, specifically, how they coincide in close proximity, yet still bear an effect on each other, while acting independently. These experiences are further manifested by the capability of the conscience to create a new meaning for an object through physical sensory ability. This sensory capacity of people allows a manifestation of perception while simultaneously existing in the physical realms of space. Ultimately, this forms the synthesis of a generated architectural experience.

With each of the senses, the skateboarder provokes a different dialectal interaction than the pedestrian. The senses do not act independently but are intrinsically linked. The skateboarder produces more sound than walking and consequently a sense of materiality can be directly acquired by the sound response and so qualities such as texture or even material composition is easily determined. Although there is no direct connection to the ground, a reading of the materiality can be determined through the vibrations felt in the feet of the skateboarder. The timing between their interactions with elements is decreased due to the increase of speed. This in turn provokes them to have an increased awareness of body positioning as before they engage they must employ the correct foot positioning, ensure the body is in balance and check they are travelling at an appropriate speed. This becomes instinctive and occurs while focusing their sight on the object of intended interaction. The scope of serial vision, therefore, is of a more focal nature. A tunnel vision effect occurs at an increased rate of time. As all of this happens simultaneously at a rapid rate, the skateboarder is more aware of themselves and the space, and adopts a more critical and analytical approach to how they inhabit such space.

It is a prominent issue that the pedestrian is restricted to a bystander in the sense that they are conscious of the city's dictation with respect to the opportunities it presents. They develop a prevailing monotonous perception of an architectural spatial experience through falling into a repetitive meaning of cyclical functionalism, rather than striving to become the creator of their own experience. This should materialise through the scrutiny of the composition of their inhabited space and creative response to their engagement with elements of the urban fabric.

In this context of generated architectural spatial experience, it is not conclusive just to say that through revolting against what is perceived to be a normal use of space by the skateboarder, gives them a greater sense of inclusion in society as they are not restricted by "spatial zero degree" (1984, 184) spaces. They negate the restriction of their actions by opposing "spatial zero degree" (1984, 184) spaces through their possession of an ulterior motive to introduce new meanings and functional qualities to space.

Saying this, to define the overall position of where a pedestrian or skateboarder sits in the context of society would require additional investigation and a culmination of such additional studies to the conclusions in this investigation. A study of the empirical evidence of an aspect I give a brief prelude to in the previous section referring to the constant tension between non-skateboarding members of society and skateboarders would be a particularly pertinent line of inquiry, specifically, the resulting constant repression and legislation against the act. This would open up possible lines of investigation into how the dialect of skateboarding culture opposes what is perceived to be normative in socio-logical terms.

Furthermore, from this psychological mind frame, a relevant study could be pursued in the creation of the outdoor skate park Bridges. This is an interven-tion in what once could be described as a "spatial zero degree space" (1984, 184). It now is a functional space within the realms of the city and provides opportunity that was once devoid of such qualities. This consequently has re-duced the level of antisocial behaviour in this spot, which is in direct contrast to the adjacent car park. This would elaborate on a topic of the rise in antiso-cial behaviour as a direct result of modernist planning that focused on a more formal interpretational method to a design approach of outdoor public space. These methods of design created a vast expansivity of space, defunct of social activity and function. The primary aim of this line of inquiry would be in re-spect to how modern day society has responded to such problems through the intervention of space.

I have been asked numerous times by pedestrians (non-skaters), 'Why is a grown man on a skateboard?' This highlights the incomprehension of what the act of skateboarding actually is. They have a perception of it as a child's toy, and are incapable of understanding it as a means to a richer spatial experience. This is not always the case, as there are architects such as Tony Bracali and Edmund Bacon who understand the embedded psychological and social prov-ocations that skateboarding emanates. As a result, they are interested in the relationships between skateboarding and social space. I feel people ask this be-cause it is not perceived to be normal, and they are therefore perhaps ignorant, and in some ways disrespectful. For asking such a question is the equivalent of asking, 'Why do your read books?', 'why do you paint?' or 'why do you do anything you find interesting?' Everyone has their own virtues and desires they follow, to arguably find enjoyment or fulfilment, but it is also through such expressions of virtues that we define who we are. Each person is unique in their interests and opinions and I believe this is one of the humans' best traits. So through lack of understanding, who are we to question the interests of others who do not share the same as our own?

Furthermore, how can we decide what is normal? Is normality replicating the actions of your peers so that you 'fit in'? Or is normal being true to your beliefs and therefore yourself? I fear that it is the first that is true for the majority of people. Throughout history, creativity and innovation arguably do not arise from 'normal' behaviour or lines of intellect, but from those who were not afraid to reject and oppose such perceived constraints of normality, for if not, where as a society would we be today?

I return to Edmund Bacon to end with his profound statement which epitomises the narrative of this investigation;

> You – skateboarders - are the leading edge of a revolution of the human beings relation to his or her environment. What you already have done is to reinvent the idea that a human being can create spontaneously out of their own interior feelings a movement through whatever environment happens to catch their fancy, which is built on the creative application of the human body moving through an environment unrelating to it (Freedom of Space, 2006).

REFERENCES

Barthes, Roland. 1967. *Writing Degree Zero*. Translated from French by J. Cape. London: Jonathan Cape Ltd.

Bennett, Tony. 1995. *The Birth of the Museum*. London: Routledge.

Borden, Iain. 2001. *Skateboarding, Space and the City: Architecture and the Body*. Oxford: Berg.

Bracali, Anthony. 2003. *Thanks, Le Corbusier (...from the skateboarders)*. http://anthonybracali.com

Carmona, Matthew, Claudio de Magalhães, and Leo Hammond. 2008. *Public Space: The Management Dimension*. 1st ed., Oxon: Routledge.

Corbusier, Le. 1923. *Towards a New Architecture*. Translated by John Rodker. New York: Dover Publications, 1931.

Corbusier, Le. 1925. "[Plan Voisin for Paris]." Grand Paris Metropole. https://www.gpmetropole-infos.fr/quand-le-corbusier-prevoyait-de-raser-la-rive-droite-de-paris/.

Creswell, John W., and J. David Creswell. 2009. *Research Design: Qualitative, Quantitative, and Mixed Methods Approaches*. California. SAGE Publications Inc.

Ebbinghaus, Bernhard. 2005. "When Less is More: Selection Problems in Large-N and Small-N Cross-National Comparisons", *International Sociology*, 20(2), pp.133–52.

Flick, Uwe. 2009. *An Introduction to Qualitative Research*. London: SAGE Publications Ltd.

Olpin, Steve, and Tim Irvin. 2005. *Freedom of Space*. DVD. Directed by Steve Olpin. United States: Bluebrush Productions.

Gehl, Jan. 2001. *Life Between Buildings: Using Public Space*. 5th ed. Translated from Danish by Jens Koch. The Danish Architectural Press. 2001.

Gottdiener, Mark. 1985. *The Social Production of Urban Space*. Austin: University of Texas Press.

Harbour, Belfast. 2010. "[Titanic Quarter]." TQ Drumbeat. http://tq.drumbeat-server.co.uk/_assets/downloads/titanic_quarter.pdf

Heidegger, Martin. (1953) *Being and Time*. Translated by Joan Stambaugh. Albany: State University of New York Press. 1996

Lefebvre, Henri. 1984. *Everyday Life in the Modern City*. London: Transaction Publisher. pp 183-4.

Lefebvre, Henri. 1991. *The Production of Space*. Oxford: Blackwell Publishers.

Lefebvre, Henri. 1961. *Introduction to Modernity: Twelve preludes September*. Translated by John Moore. London: Verso. 1995.

Lemanski, Tom, and Tina Overton. 2011. *An Introduction to Qualitative Research*. http://www.heacademy.ac.uk/assets/ps/documents/primers/primers/qualitative_research.pdf.

Levi-Faur, David. 2005. *The comparative Strategies of Emile Durkheim and Max Weber: Between Positive and Interpretative Social Sciences*. http://poli.haifa.ac.il/~levi/durkheim.html/.

Low, Martina. 2008. "The Constitution of Space: The Structuration of Spaces Through the Simultaneity of Effect and Perception." *European Journal of Science*, 11 (1): 25-49.

Luhmann, Niklas. 1998. *Die Kunst der Gesellschaft*, 2nd ed. Frankfurt: Suhrkamp.

Madanipour, Ali. 2003. *Public and Private Space of the City*. New York: Routledge. pp 202.

Mars, Roman. 2013. "In and Out of LOVE." Ep 71. Audio Podcast. 99% Invisible. United States: 99% Invisible. https://99percentinvisible.org/episode/episode-71-in-and-out-of-love/

Massey, Doreen. (1999) "Space of Politics." In *Human Geography Today*, edited by Doreen Massey, John Allen and Phil Sarre, 279-94. Cambridge: Polity Press.

Matthews, Michael R. 1993. "Constructivism and Science Education: Some Epistemological Problems". *Journal of Science Education and Technology*, 2(1): 359–370. https://www.jstor.org/stable/40188457?seq=1.

Marton, Ference. 1981. "Phenomenography: Describing Conceptions of the World Around Us." *Instructional science*, 10(2): 177-200. http://dx.doi.org/10.1007/BF00132516.

Mearleau-Ponty, Maurice. 2013. *Phenomenology of Perception*. 1ˢᵗ ed. London and New York: Routledge.

Mills, Melinda, Gerhard G. van de Bunt, and Jeanne de Bruijn. 2006. "Comparative Research: Persistent Problems and Promising Solutions." *International sociology*, (21) 5: 619-631. https://doi.org/10.1177/0268580906067833.

Frederick Law Olmsted Jr, and Albert Fein. 1967. *Landscape and Cityscape*. Pennsylvania: Cornell University Press. 63-88.

Lye, Len (1979) *Particles in Space*. 16mm. Directed by Len Lye.

Simmel, Georg. 1951. "The Metropolis and Mental Life" In *The Blackwell City Reader*, edited by Gary Bridge and Sophie Watson. MA: Blackwell. ISBN: 0631225145.

Sullivan, Louis. H. 1896. "The Tall Office Building Artistically Considered." *Lippinicott's Magazine*. March, 1896.

Swenson, Eric, Kevin Thatcher, and Fausto Vitello. 1997. "Blast from the Past." *Thrasher*. March 1997.

Till, Jeremy. 2009. *Architecture depends*. Cambridge: MIT Press.

The Future of Chicago Movie Places

Antoine Trallero-Mindan

ANTOINE TRALLERO-MINDAN is an architect born in Le Mans, France in 1995. After internships shared between timber frame companies and architecture studios, he has been collaborating with BM Architects based in Paris and Le Mans since 2018. The workshop is mainly focused on contemporary wood buildings and offsite constructions. Antoine studied architecture at the Schools of Architecture of Brittany in Rennes (bachelor and master degrees) and Nantes (part III/HMONP). He also studied at the Queens University in Belfast, UK where he joined the Slicing Spaces project. The Chicago movie palaces subject came from a trip in Chicago in 2012 and his passion for architecture and cinema.

Movie palaces built in the early twentieth century in Chicago are mostly endangered and abandoned as well as their legacy forgotten. A large number of these theatres were demolished or converted into parking lots. This study develops arguments to support the importance of preserving movie palaces and the sustainable goals that it implies at the urban scale. Through a study of heritage preservation, the chapter also measures the importance of these buildings in their neighbourhoods and the evolution of the influence they have or could have on their surroundings in the twenty-first century.

In this sense, the research is based on historical analysis to understand the influence palaces used to have on their urban neighbourhoods as well as the evolution of their status in the public community during the twentieth century. The complex vocabulary of preservation provides a clarification concerning the actual issues of architectural and urban conservation. The study is supported by the analysis of two cases and also develops several examples of repurposed theatres in Chicago. Strengthened by local examples, the chapter illustrates the actual possibilities, and difficulties, to save these buildings. The study is supported with different kinds of sources including the library databases, books, journal articles, and interviews that I conducted as well as city institutions' websites such as the city of Chicago official website.

In order to set the boundaries of this research, the case study section focuses only on the city of Chicago, Illinois in the United States of America constructing a specific analysis on the evolution of the status of the movie theatres built at the beginning of the twentieth century, especially in the 1920s. The study is mainly based on library and online research and does not include on-site analysis because of timing and budget issues that a trip to Chicago would represent. Fortunately, I had the chance to interact with inhabitants of Chicago who were able to provide a local point of view concerning specific buildings and their preservation in this city.

Why preserve Chicago movie palaces from the 1920s? This reflection is divided into three major parts. In the first section following the introduction, through an historical review, the study synthesises the evolution of movie palaces and the film industry in Chicago throughout the twentieth century starting in the early 1900s. The writing reveals the beauty of the palace phenomenon and the sequence of spaces inside the buildings until the decline of 1920s theatres in Chicago in the 1970s. In the next section, the study defines the vocabulary of preservation and heritage in order to clarify the complexity of different terms. Through the viewpoint of different architects, we understand the aim of building preservation. Finally, the last section focuses on the actual status of movie palaces in Chicago through several examples of preservation, especially the case studies of the Central Park and the New Regal Theatres, and the influence they have on their neighbourhoods. We also review repurposed theatres and sustainable alternatives to understand the various possibilities of adaptability and how to preserve historic facilities.

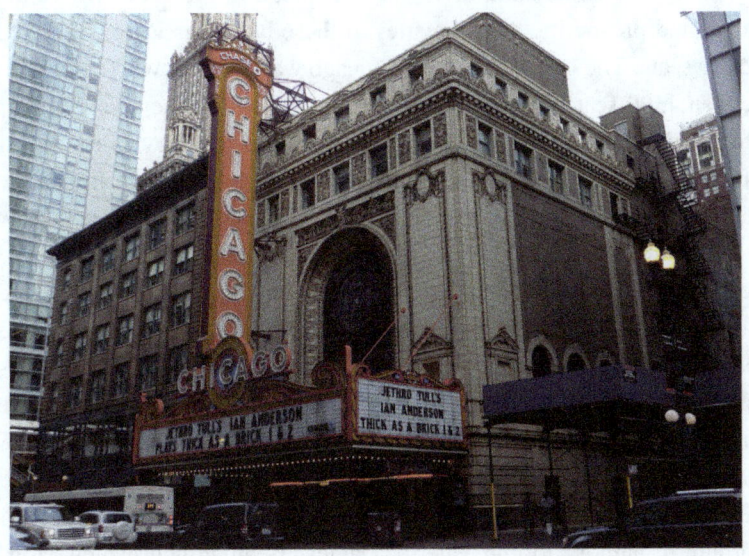

Figure 1: Marque of The Chicago Theatre,
Antoine Trallero-Mindan (Author, 2012)

Movie Palace's History

Chicago was a renowned place for the American movie industry in the early 1900s, as it was the principal central hub for motion picture production and exhibition before Hollywood's supremacy. Artists like Charlie Chaplin and Gloria Swanson were discovered as they were working for Essanay Studios founded by Goerge K. Spoor and Gilbert Anderson (Gloversmith 2010, par. 3). In 1907, the Chicago film industry owned 80% of the USA market, which influenced the development of movie theatres (Lindstrom 2016, par. 2). Chicagoans were getting used to the world of glitter and glamour which marked the beginning of a real architectural pattern. Unfortunately, the studios relocated to California in the 1920s because of the attractive weather for movie making. However, Chicago remained a large centre for the art of cinema with the construction of a significant number of movie palaces all around the city, especially the booming chain Balaban and Katz based there (Linstrom 2016, par. 7).

Inspired by the first Gaumont Palace built in Paris at the beginning of the twentieth century, the American movie palaces spread in the country. Symbols of grandeur and prosperity, the capacities of these buildings were between 1000 and 5000 seats. The largest palace in Chicago was the Uptown Theatre owning more than 4300 seats (Holubow & Ebert 2013, par. 8). They were principally located in downtown areas with the aim of promoting movies creating large community meeting venues. At this revolutionary era, with the Bauhaus, Einstein, Picasso, Nietzsche, Freud, the radio, cars, airplanes, and the end of World War I, people needed new forms of entertainment and fantasy/imagination. The palaces were truly an architectural phenomenon. The aim was to create enriching shows through perfumed air, changing coloured lighting, full orchestra, dancers and singers. The architectural elements of fantasy such as impressive decorations, olfactory sensations, lights and ascent contributed to the idea of cutting the public from daily life into a rich and impressive environment (Valerio *et al* 1982, 15).

According to authors Joseph Valerio, Daniel Friedman and Nancy Morrison, "every component of palace from street to screen is a part of this fantasy" (1982, 21). Every palace owns common properties. The facade has strong vertical lines, Classical pilasters, arch windows, eclectic towers, and the illuminated marquee. It is also made of material imitations such as marble and terracotta which reinforces the idea of the adornment facade. Then the entrance and the Baroque style grand staircase with, massive balustrades, low risers, elliptical treads, stairway, columns and pilasters invite the public to ascend, as seen in Figure 2, into a luxurious atmosphere. Finally, the main representation room embodies the paroxysm of fantasy in the building with impressive columns, niches, arches, ceiling vaulting and a main importance to light effects playing with the surfaces. The sections in Figures 2 and 3 illustrate the spaces within the building as well as the level of adornment, part of the fancy atmosphere.

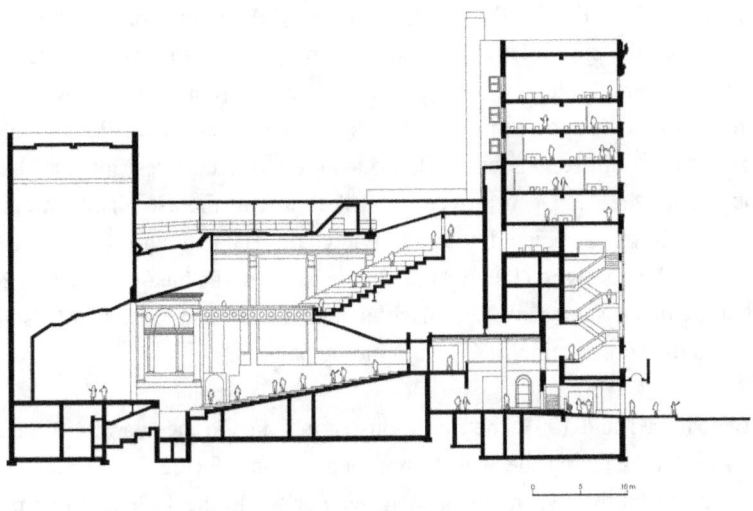

Figure 2: Section of a typical movie palace,
Antoine Trallero-Mindan (Author, 2016)

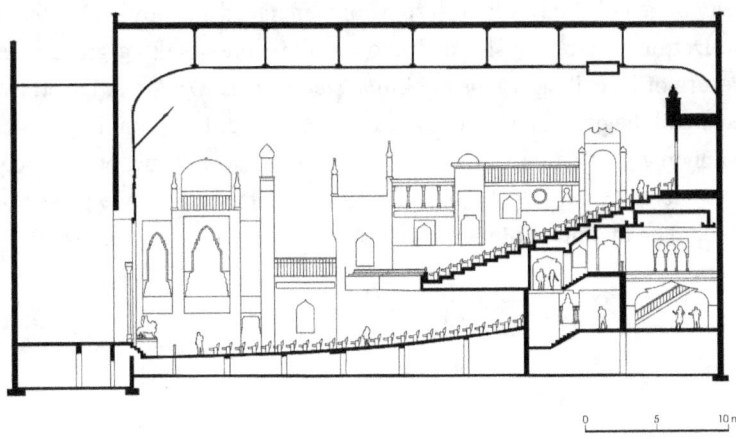

Figure 3: Section of the New Regal Theatre,
Antoine Trallero-Mindan (Author, 2016)

As an architectural style, the movie palaces had an influence on urban land-scape at the street level. The buildings became large popular venues at the heart of communities. Especially in Chicago, the Columbian World Exhibition in 1893 settled the principles to establish "a national building style" (Valerio *et al* 1982, 25). Cornelius and George Rapp brothers, the most popular movie palace architects of Chicago learned the basis of Neoclassicism in Paris Ecole des Beaux-Arts. With Renaissance, Baroque and exotic cultures' inspiration, they took part of the Art Deco movement. Like most of the established architects, Rapp and Rapp, associated with a movie chain, Balaban and Katz, from 1917 for which they designed the most elaborate palaces of Chicago (Balaban 2006). Other architects such as W.W. Ahlschlager, and Levy and Klein were also influ-ential in the construction of Chicago movie palaces.

Between 1931 and 1933, the film industry in Chicago faced a 25-40% decline to its revenues facing the world great depression. During World War ll, Hol-lywood passed through its most lucrative period. In the 1970s, movie palaces faced a real decline with many demolitions in Chicago and all over the US transmitting its legacy to "new popular culture" (Valerio *et al* 1982, 35) such as Disneyland World and Las Vegas casinos. Their huge size, which became inappropriate, faced competition from small suburban cinemas. With a large majority of demolished buildings, some of them faced inappropriate reuse, such as the Detroit theatre transformed into a multi-storey parking garage despite the beauty of its ceiling. In his book *American Picture Palaces*, David Naylor lists some of the palaces which were saved through different kind of reuse such as symphonic production, convention trade centre, synagogue, bowling centre, and commercial mall (1981). Introducing the theme of heritage preservation, what could be the future of the unused buildings and why saving them?

Preservation and Heritage

> It is the mark of an immature culture – a demonstration of a childish attitude
> to valuable and historic buildings – to assume that if new accommodation is
> required […] it can only be provided by demolishing […] and rebuilding on the
> same site. (James Richards, 1970)

The above quote from architectural writer James Richards introduces the third
part of my research. Indeed, to understand its relevance, it is important to have
in mind the context in which this statement was written. In 1970, at the heart
of the large demolition trend which ran across the world, Richards already
raised one of the major issues of this decade concerning building preservation.
Unfortunately, almost fifty years later, this quote is still valid even if minds
have evolved. How can we define sustainable preservation and heritage today?
Before focusing on the specific case of Chicago movie palaces, it is important
to understand the aims related to sustainable preservation and heritage. The
UNESCO defines heritage as "our legacy from the past, what we live with
today and what we pass on to the future generations" (2000). This interpretation
shows the implication of heritage about understanding the past, to live the present and draw the future. According to architect Dennis Rodwell, conservation
and sustainability have parallel meanings. They can be defined as the management of natural resources and the need of harmony between man and nature.
The conservation itself also contains a narrower signification when it deals with
architectural heritage. Indeed, it focuses on the management of the evolution of
buildings and as well as urban fabric (2007, 7). The definition of conservation
is often blurred with the synonyms preservation and restoration.

Based on the Burra Charter, preservation means maintaining the fabric of a
place in its existing state and retarding deterioration. Restoration means returning the existing fabric of a place to a known earlier state by removing accretions
or by reassembling existing components without the introduction of new material. Then conservation, as a broad discipline means all the processes of looking
after a place so as to retain its cultural significance, it means having in mind the
geocultural diversity and the local distinctiveness of a site (2013, art. 1). Furthermore, restoration appears to be an enhanced form of preservation bringing
the building to an original state. But it is not very relevant applied to historic
buildings in use where new material may be introduced. Then the Burra Char-

ter definition specifies that reconstruction means returning a place to a known earlier state. However, it is distinguished from restoration by the introduction of new material into the fabric. As demonstrated, the vocabulary of conservation and sustainability is variable and it is important to define these specific terms to lead the discussion in this research (2013, art. 1).

When we confront these statements to current issues, minimum intervention on existing buildings appears to be a principle (Rodwell 2007, 206). The architectural conservation is based on: safeguarding local distinctiveness, reuse of buildings and recycling of the materials, use of local materials and craft skills, understanding the environmental performance of historical structures as well as minimum intervention. In his review, James Richards, denounces actual measures on disused buildings: "heresy which afflicts old buildings increasingly [...] caused by the growth in the number of archaeologists [...] Good buildings are not archaeological sites, at least until they are ruins, and not always even then... Buildings are increasingly to be treated as documents, to be preserved for study, not as visual objects at all, and not for use" (1970). Buildings do embody a unique character, but what's next? Architects could find a compromise between conserving the soul of the facility but also allow it to open a new page to its history towards the future.

According to the previous statements, Dennis Rodwell defends conservation methods which are relevant to a sustainable approach. The adaptation of heritage buildings could allow a redefinition of the city which is relevant to the citizens' needs: live, work, shop, and play. The actual preservation scheme aims to include resources management, including an association between materials and cultural resources. In this way, conservation could be a main consideration regarding future sustainability. This research promotes architectural preservation as a whole. And this is where it is very linked to sustainability. Reusing a building focuses on the architecture itself. But as a broad discipline preservation is applied to the urban scale, to the neighbourhoods, and the community. Therefore, it could strengthen or regenerate these districts. A new function would transform an old building into the catalyst for the surroundings while preserving its heritage. An old movie palace can be transformed into a performing art live venue for instance as soon as it fits the needs of the community.

In France, architect Patrick Bouchain devoted his career to a sustainable and social approach of architectural reuse. Through *Construire Ensemble Le Grand Ensemble (Build Together The High Density Housing),* he proposes the reuse of the large social housing units built after World War II in France. Twenty years after the construction, the blocks did not fit the user's needs any more. In comparison to the movie palaces situation at the same period, these buildings faced a lot of demolitions because of their disuse. In this case heritage is not only applied to beautiful historical buildings but also to disused social large housing blocks. "Instead of demolishing [...] we could reuse, because history of architecture of the city is made of modifications and reinterpretation of the architecture" (Bouchain 2010).

In this sense, the preservation approach could help these underdeveloped neighbourhood by bringing social activity. The inhabitants reclaim the neigh-bourhood by densification, extension, new added elements. This sustainable approach could allow to look forward to the future while keeping the past her-itage in mind. The major part of Bouchain's work is based on the reconversion of industrial fallows into cultural centres. In Nantes, France, the architect has reused an old abandoned biscuit factory. Turned into a cultural centre includ-ing exhibition areas, restaurant, library and presentation stage and auditorium. More than just a conservation project, the building became an anchor for the neighbourhood in which it is located, a disused industrial island nearby the city centre. The district, through the work of planner Alexandre Chemetoff, is now one of the most dynamic and flexible parts of the city with a blend of cultural, business, housing and leisure places. Here again, preservation is first about the reuse of a building and its dedication to the fabric. But through these French examples, the conservationist approach uses the cultural significance of the historic environment, allied to its environment capital, in order to integrate this heritage as an actual part of the socio-economic and cultural life of the city. Today, we move toward progress, knowledge and enthusiasm exist as described by Rodwell (2007). But there are still large gaps in the scheme of preservation. What about a national strategy and the lack of urban coordination? In the city of Chicago, we try to understand the different landmark policies which can be applied to listed buildings, especially to movie palaces, in order to maintain and adapt the urban fabric. Back in the 1950s, in the context of race riots, Mayor Richard J. Daley established the basis of landmark policy in Chicago. (Blue-stone 2003, 2) After a few debates between architect Frank Lloyd Wright and poet Carl Sandburg about Chicago Renaissance and the danger of skyscraper's growth, they founded the Commission on Chicago Architectural Landmarks. The principles were to designate, mark, and educate the public as well as establishing specific policies for the concerned buildings. The Auditorium Theatre, designed by Adler and Sullivan in 1889, was part of this list for its role in Modernist genealogy. The famous Chicago Theatre only appeared thirty years later on this list (City of Chicago 2016, par. 1). When we look at the list today, only eight palaces out of forty listed in my study appear. Being designated as a landmark is not enough to be saved. Uptown Theatre, a very emblematic palace built in 1925 by Rapp & Rapp brothers is now in critical danger. The question is: "why preserve?" (Bluestone 2003, 1).

According to architect Philip Johnson, a building has to be saved if it has an architectural beauty. This type of judgement is "a slippery slope" (Bluestone 2003, 5) because the beauty of a building is not universal but personal. Johnson's statement echoes Richards' review from the 1970s; architectural sites are not archaeological sites to be protected under a transparent glass bell. About the Old Town in Chicago, at first, the committee did not find a rich architectural value to the existing buildings (Bluestone 2003, 5). They could have demolished every single building judged as non-architectural. Nevertheless, the eclectic design of the condos built by the local inhabitants gave the neighbourhood a certain (human) scale. In this case, preservation would help people to understand the borough because they are directly implicated through its use. According to authors Faia and Carlson, this process of sustainability is not only concerned by the environment but also by creativity, social engagement and "unique sense of place" (2015, par. 14). Indeed, preservation and sustainability are about people, and not only architectural beauty. Those two different examples illustrate two opposite reasons for preserving. First, the preservation of a site strong of its cultural and political significance. Second, the preservation of a building designated for its historical and architectural value without including the impact on its surroundings. Having in mind the objectives regarding heritage conservation and their importance to the actual urban goals for a sustainable future development, the study focuses on the specific case of movie palaces in Chicago.

The Future of Movie Palaces

The way we watch a movie has definitely changed. People have many alternative ways to experience cinema, such as television, the Internet, and large multi-screen movie theatres. They are not frequently looking for an evading sensation when they go to a theatre. Nevertheless, Chicago movie palaces in the early twentieth century used to be community centres for each neighbourhood in which they were located. All socio-economic groups were blending in those entertainment venues. When we think about the incredible size of these buildings, are they adaptable to our present society's needs? Do we have sustainable preservation schemes to propose?

Central Park Theatre and the New Regal Theatre are the two movie palaces analysed in depth in this chapter. Through these case studies, I had the chance to interview John Owens who wrote several articles for the Chicago Tribune concerning both buildings, which inspired me to write about this topic. Movie palaces still influence their surroundings despite the difficult character of their neighbourhood. Central Park Theatre, designed in 1917 by Rapp & Rapp brothers, was one of the first notable movie palaces in Chicago, but was also an iconic landmark for North Lawndale, a growing district with a doubled population during the 1910s. In the 1920s, the building was a gathering place for the community; all through the day, the Russian Jewish population made life vibrant. Following the great depression in the 1930s, the Jewish population moved away, replaced by a growing African-American working class population. In 1969, after the assassination of Martin Luther King Jr, a series of riots destroyed almost 75% of the businesses, worsening the situation of the neighbourhood (Owens 2015). In this particular context of poverty, riots. and high unemployment, the Central Park theatre re-opened in 1971 as a House of Prayer for the Church of God in Christ, created by Reverend Lincoln Scott. Bringing the community together, the place became the centre it used to be for the neighbourhood due to the reverend's involvement in turning it into a homeless shelter and food pantry. Unfortunately, because of building code violations, the church closed in 2013, and Rev. Lincoln Scott died two years later (Owens 2015). A new project reusing the building as a cultural centre and performance venue would connect art and community and bring synergy in the neighbourhood. Before this, however, it would need to raise money to address the violations. According to John Owens, the actual situation of North Lawndale is still challenging, and the landmark status of the building only maintains it under protection but does not allow modifications. This specific case raises the problems of listed buildings. The status of the theatre does not allow a large flexibility in order to bring modifications, especially when money is the main issue.

The New Regal Theatre, originally Avalon Theatre, was built in 1927 and designed by John Eberson. The auditorium with oriental decorations is unique. The section in Figure 3 illustrates the atmosphere, which was evading for the moviegoers, as described in the historical review. From the 1930s to the 1960s, the venue offered diverse shows and movies to its German and Irish working-class community. After a large population shift moving toward a majorly African-American community, as the Central Park Theatre, it closed in the 1970s. In 1987, the theatre reopened as a performing art venue dedicated to African-American culture as the New Regal Theatre in honour of the Regal Theatre, demolished at the beginning of the 1970s. Situated in Avalon Park Quarter close to South Chicago, this place was also a social centre for its neighbourhood, gathering people around the artistic milieu. The venue closed again in 2003 because of the lack of money to maintain and refurbish the structure. The building would need more than seven million dollars to re-open. For the future, there are several projects for a performing art centre and a jazz museum, but, with its small size and concurrence, the building is not attractive enough to convince important artist promoters (Owens 1998).

John Owens introduced me to Jerald Gary during the interview, the actual owner of the theatre who envisions a bright future for the building. Indeed, through the short exchange I had with Gary, I heard that in 2017, the renamed Avalon-Regal Theatre is due to re-open as a large venue for African- American performing arts. According to him, the building will become an "anchor for economic activity and a node for the revitalisation of South Chicago." Moreover, in synergy with the new Barack Obama Presidential Centre and Library nearby, the aim will be to "bring people together, creating opportunities, educating and empowering people and building community" (2017). In October 2016, I had the chance to attend a lecture by architect Billie Tsien in Belfast. With her partner Todd Williams, they were chosen by Barack and Michelle Obama as the architects for the presidential centre. Including the project of the Avalon-Regal Theatre, the centre will be part of the South Chicago regeneration. Bringing connection between community and architecture, the project embodies an economic boost for the neighbourhood. According to journalist Angela Caputo, "[…] residents view the proposed Obama library as of their best prospects for an economic renaissance of their impoverished neighbourhood" (2016, par. 1). The example of these theatres demonstrates that the community aspect is a major element in the preservation of the theatres. Both buildings own a central situation in each neighbourhood. The Central Park Theatre is close to a long green axis, and the pedestrian character of the neighbourhood could be a start to its regeneration. Moreover, the proximity to main city axes could bring people from beyond the border of the district. The Central Park is located on a main street which runs toward down-town Chicago, and the New Regal is positioned at a crossroad of a main street and the rail network. Beyond the architectural component that the theatre represents, the community appropriation is the main element of the process. The study has raised the need for extensive funds to renovate and maintain activity. Nevertheless, pictures of both auditoriums illustrate the buildings are in good shape even if restorations are required.

The next part of the study also analyses the economic aspect of preservation. We need to prove the relevance of this conservation to raise that money. Nevertheless, according to Owens, there is no controversy about new venues being built instead of refurbishing old ones. The example of the Oriental and the Chicago theatres are evocative. It proves that old venues are still adaptable to the present needs and that they still run daily shows. However, in an inner city, the need for this type of building has changed. Dawn Bilobran, Vice-President of Preservation Detroit states, "How this building can have a role in this community? It is not going to be in the same way. How can we be flexible with these structures?" (The H project interview 2016). The case of both theatres demonstrates that even and especially in a poor neighbourhood, a movie palace could be an anchor bringing activity and attractiveness. Through an adapted reuse, the community scale is one of the main arguments when we talk about building preservation. It is important to maintain the character of the neighbourhood and what made it vibrant. Then, as a manifesto for building preservation, the study analyses the different steps allowing the regeneration process to happen.

"User needs a facility and a facility needs a user" (Valerio, Friedman & Morrisson 1982). The preservation of a building requires two actors. Both catalysts are interdependent; the sponsor and the facility itself. According to the work of associations such as the League of Historic American Theatres (LHAT), we could understand the steps allowing the preservation process. How could we solve the threats raised through the case study of both Central Park and New Regal Theatres? As described by Valerio, the sponsors can be local citizens affected to the preservation project, but the owner and decision maker status needs to be clear as a basis of the project. In the case of the New Regal, Jerald Gary, young business man raised in the same neighbourhood, became that sponsor. In the other hand, after the death of the father owning the Central Park Theatre, the facility has been struggling to find someone and the project has not been going on. Old theatre owners might be interested in buying a new one, but so might private investors, non-for-profit organisations, and city governments.

The structural aspects often discourage decision makers, and most projects do not keep the existing structure. First, the structural analysis could approve the conditions and technical capacity of the building. The location and site of the theatre are key facts. Indeed, the process implicates the surroundings, the neighbourhood itself, the public transport and also parking facilities. Every of these parameters are part of the analysis. Then the market will define the feasibility: is there a demand for a performing art venue? Is it close to similar facilities? Are there financing opportunities? Is there an audience survey? Is there a mixed-use possibility? a project is supposed to bring activity to its surroundings but to achieve this goal, it needs to fit the existing needs and realities as we will develop in the following arguments. The building is not repurposed only as a piece of architecture but also on the urban scale of community and neighbourhood.

Once the sponsor has met the facility and the facility has met the sponsor, in order to start the process of reuse, the first task is to establish the development team for the project. In 2006, led by chair officer Jeffrey Gabel, owner of the Majestic Theatre in Gettysburg, PA, the LHAT released a broad manual explaining the process of preservation. First, the feasibility step will allow them to define the project vision to approach investors. To be able to create a strong proposal, the architect, teamed up with an architectural historian, draws the plans and sections and leads the theatre's reuse site work. To explain the importance of the building to the city and gain support, both the architect and the historian will be able to reveal the spirit of the facility and prove that the building tells its own story with a unique sense of attractiveness. In the case of the New Regal Theatre, the significance of the African-American culture, bringing activity around performing arts, makes it part of the regeneration of South Chicago. In addition, the economic analyst conducts financial studies and prepares reports on target markets. The goal is to show the relevance of the project to the community and insure the reality of its need and benefit to the neighbourhood. The engineering team assesses the theatre's physical condition with an accurate survey. The precision of this feasibility study will indicate to the investors the stability of the project. The fundraiser is very important with regard to researching and soliciting funding to allow the reuse of the building. The funding plan needs to be transparent, explaining each precise cost for each purpose. This list of actors illustrates the need of the large team in charge of the project. This large number of required actors demonstrates the importance of huge implications for the realisation of the project. Stephanie Meeks, director of the National Trust for Historic Preservation (NTHP), describes old buildings as allegories for identity, history and authenticity. This character represents a competitive advantage in today's economy (2016, 44).

Before starting any modifications in the building, all components of the theatre have to be evaluated. As described in the historical review, the journey and the components of the building are really specific, but for a new project some of them may have to be modified or adapted. First, the outside of the palace is characterised by a high-profile facade and an eclectic marquee and vertical sign. These components as visuals could be used throughout the reuse process to promote the project. They can show that the future of the facility is not the wrecking ball and that its story goes on energising the future and economy of the community. Sometimes it may be interesting to take a step back and look at surrounding properties in order to expand and adapt some of the functionalities such as the lobby, restrooms or food service areas allowing larger flexibility for the building. According to the NTHP, "New ideas and new economy thrive in older buildings" (2016 par. 8). Some of the most innovative companies of the twenty-first are choosing old buildings. The Sullivan Centre, built in 1889 in Chicago, hosts a mix of technology, information, marketing, and educational users. Moreover, in terms of flexibility, some theatres rent some of the previous spaces such as large lobbies, ballrooms or even parking areas when the facility is unused. Finally, still in terms of building composition and flexibility, some palaces, compose with mixed use facilities such as offices, restaurants or residences. As described by the LHAT, this sort of seven days a week, twenty-four hours a day use could also bring more strength to the project to obtain city funding. In her book, Meeks evokes the report made by the Green Lab in 2014, *Older, Smaller, Better*. The study led toward the conclusion that older districts are economic engines. Indeed, the neighbourhoods, with a blend of older and smaller buildings of diverse ages, create better economic levels and social activity. As a Jane Jacobs follower, Meeks states that old commercial districts and corridors could generate jobs, income, and attract families and businesses (2016, 44).

Once the survey of feasibility is made, the reuse development team can submit the project proposal. First, they have to explain the reuse project which sums up the concept, the goals, and development objectives. We are back to our research question; why preserve? Indeed, the project needs to prove the positive impact it could have for the community's lifestyle health. Concerning the market, the proposal has to show the number of competing facilities in relationship with economic demand and clarify the advantages of reuse instead of building a new facility. Indeed, preservation creates jobs because it requires skilled workers with knowledge of historical rehabilitation. Who will benefit from the reuse? Local retailers and restaurants will benefit from the pedestrian activity. Hotels will host visitors, and students could have more access to art and performance. Further than the market, the arguments need to be strong and clear to be included in city redevelopment plans. To the city, the preservation process could justify a sustainable and anti-sprawl investment, which are totally relevant to the actual urban issues. The project team needs to attend city council meetings to be aware of the decisions and always spread information about the project. Moreover, involving the community in the process, the project needs to illustrate the ideas that came from the public, which also develops a sort of feeling of ownership from them building the strength and success of the preservation project. Concerning the case of the Central Park Theatre, it used to serve a community purpose. Sheltering and feeding homeless people, it was a lot more than a church for the district.

The need has to come from this discussion and exchange benefiting the neighbourhood. Preservation does not concern saving individual buildings. According to Meeks (2016, 46), it is all about making blocks and dynamic streets. Through her book, we learn that preservation means turning old buildings into liveable places for people. Cities are not for vehicles. Places need to be sustainable. Districts have to own healthier lifestyles. Streets should allow people to walk or bike to stores, restaurants and work. Preservation is always about change in order to maintain the dynamic of the districts. In the *Re-Urbanism* manifesto, the NTHP states that places which are worth being saved, are those where communities choose to come together and that represent local stories they treasure. Preservation projects aim to provide people opportunities to "live, work and play in a diverse environment" (2016, par. 5). The project finally meets the definition of sustainability. First, its environmental capital is represented as embodied energy and materials in the existing building. Second, its dynamic capital acts for people's fulfilment. The maintained buildings create a low environmental impact and interact with their environment, the urban fabric, the neighbourhood, and the community.

Live performing art venues have a direct potential in reusing movie palaces because of the common spacial needs. The landmark Chicago Theatre is one of the most attractive live performing venues in the city. On the other hand, some palaces now have different uses. For example, the Diversey Theatre opened in 1925, was renamed Century Theatre in 1934, and became an eight story mall in 1973. Ironically, a new seven-screen cinema opened on the top floor of the building in 2000. (Cinema Treasures 2016). Less conventional, the Admiral Theatre, opened in 1927, went from films on screen to live entertainment in 1971 and became a "gentleman's club." Also related to sport and leisure, The Belmont Theatre, was reused as a bowling venue in the 1960s for twenty years before the main structure was torn down in 1996; only the original facade remains, combined with a new retail complex. Meanwhile, many theatres were turned into religious places, such as the Sheridan Theatre, which became a synagogue in the 1970s. The Iris Theatre, built in 1913, has also been used as a church for years (Melnick and Fuchs 2004). These examples show the flexibility and adaptability of the old facilities to fit new user needs. The Chicago movie palaces map inspired by the work of Micheal P. Conzen and Christopher P. Thale (Newberry Library Chicago), illustrates the evolution of the number of Chicago movie theatres between 1926 and the twenty-first century.

Some palaces, on the other hand, still need a new use. The Uptown Theatre is considered as the largest movie palace in Chicago with more than 4300 seats, and it embodies the spirit of the Uptown neighbourhood with a rich history (Latrace 2018, par. 1). Even with the huge implication for its community, John Owens told me about the bad structural condition of the building, which would need more than 70 million dollars to be refurbished. Fundraising, volunteer support, and marketing strategies could help to repurpose this National Historical Landmark. When we wonder about the reasons for preservation, we also have to think about the economic aspect. Indeed, the downtown situation of the palaces could bring job, business, patrons, and money back to the city. In the earlier discussion,, we had the example of the new regenerated island in Nantes, France. Fortunately, in June 2018, through a press release, Mayor Rahm Emanuel announced a $75 million restoration and redevelopment project for the Uptown Theatre. He stated that the Uptown Theatre has been a staple of the Uptown neighbourhood's past, and will be a strong asset for the community's future" (2018, par. 2). After more than a thirty-five year vacancy, this decision shows awareness from public deciders impulsed by a strong preservation community implication. The previous example of the Avalon-Regal theatre also aims to spread such activity and revitalise the neighbourhood in order to rediscover the original purpose of the palaces: "building community" (Gerald Gary 2017).

Conclusion

Browsing movie palaces' history throughout the twentieth century, this study has allowed me to develop arguments about the significance of building preservation and reuse. This architectural study has opened up a new perspective to the broader discussion of urbanism and preservation. Why preserve? First, it is important to conserve the architectural and social heritage movie palaces represent. The reason to save these buildings is not only for architectural quality and to restore them to their original condition. The challenge is to extend their activity instead of replacing them. The definition of the complex vocabulary of preservation has allowed me to identify the goals of each direction that could be taken when dealing with heritage buildings. Through this study, we have seen that a palace can be an important catalyst for neighbourhood activities. However, the need for this kind of building has also evolved. Keeping renewal and dynamism in the district is the priority. Reuse could bring coherence and strength to the community, linking people and places, especially in challenging neighbourhoods of Chicago. Theatres used to be vital centres for communities, and with adaptive reuse they can still become that anchor. The actual regeneration plans for South Chicago embody a bright perspective and illustrate the urban influence that heritage preservation could represent.

Even more than social and economic reasons, we have to see those buildings as materialised resources and energy in a century of sustainable development. Why build a new theatre for performing arts instead of using buildings we have? Reusing a building is more eco-effective than constructing a new building. Through the example of facadism defined by Rodwell, we understand the purpose of composing with the existing and make it relevant to the community instead of just throwing its heritage away and bringing a new component, which may not be helpful to the development of the urban fabric. Fortunately, the city of Chicago embodies a positive future with a large number of repurposed or refurbished theatres. But as Jacobs says, heritage buildings can be considered as a "dead corpse, nobody noticed this much until it began to smell" (1961, 198). This quote is relevant to the case of the Uptown Theatre and motivates us to make preservation a real priority.

This reflection has allowed us to reveal encouraging perspectives for preservation and building refurbishment which are two major issues of the twenty-first century concerning architecture and sustainability. Today we might wonder: is it too late for some of these buildings left too long aside? Does it mean we cannot build anymore? Maybe it is not just about reducing our activity, but as described by Rodwell, it might be about adapting and reorienting our activity so we could enhance what is existing and that we treasure.

REFERENCES

Australia ICOMOS. 2013. *The Burra Charter*. Accessed Jan. 2017. www.australia. icomos.org

Balaban, David. 2006. *The Chicago Movie Palaces Of Balaban And Katz*. Charleston, SC: Arcadia.

Bilobran, Dawn. 2016. *Preservation*, interviewed by Julie Drappier & Moanna Rosier, The H Project. Accessed Nov. 2016. www.thehproject.net

Bluestone, Daniel. 2003. *Why Preserve? Public Memory and Heritage Preservation*. University of Chicago, IL, unpublished.

Bouchain, Patrick. 2010. *Construire Ensemble Le Grand Ensemble*. Arles, FR : Actes SUD.

Caputo, Angela, and Dahleen Glaton. 2016. *Could Obama library turn tide on decades of neglect for Washington Park?*. Accessed Jan. 2017. www.chicagotribune.com

Cinema Treasures. 2016. *Movie Theatres in Chicago*. Accessed Oct. 2016. www.cine-matreasures.org

City of Chicago. 2016. *Commission on Chicago Landmarks*. Accessed Oct 2016. www. cityofchicago.org

Lindstrom, J.A. 2016. *Film*. Accessed Oct. 2016. www.encyclopedia.chicagohistory.org

Faia, Jean Carroon, and Ben Carlson. 2015. *Why old is the new green ?* Accessed Nov. 2016. http://www.archdaily.com

Gary, Jerald. 2017. *The Regal Theatre,* email conversation. Jan. 2017.

Gloversmith, Michael. 2010. *The Secret History of Chicago Movies*. Accessed Oct. 2016. www.whitecitycinema.com

Holubow, Eric, and Roger Ebert. 2013. *Chicago's Once-Grand Movie Places*. Accessed Oct. 2016. www.chicagomag.com

Jacobs, Jane. 1961. *The Death and the Life of Great American Cities*. New York, NY : Random House.

Latrace, Adrian. 2018. *Why the Uptown Theatre Restoration is a Big Deal*. Accessed Oct. 2018. www.chigacomag.com

League of Historic American Theatres. 2012. *Historic Theatre Rescue, Restoration, Re-habilitation and Adaptive Reuse Manual*. Accessed Jan. 2017. www.lhat.org

Meeks, Stephanie. 2016. *The Past and The Future City*. Washington, DC: Island Press.

Melnick, Ross, and Fuchs, Andreas. 2004. *Cinema Treasures*. St. Paul, MN: MBI.

National Trust for Historic Preservation. 2016. *Ten Principles for Re Urbanism*. Accessed Mar. 2017. www.savingplaces.org

Naylor, David. 1981. *American Picture Palaces*. New York, NY : Van Nostrand Reinhold.

Owens, John. 2015. *Owners of Chicago's Shuttered Historic Movie Palaces Hope for Revival*. Accessed Oct. 2016. www.chicagotribune.com

Owens J. (2015). *The Rev. Lincoln Scott, Who Resurrected West Side Movie Palace, Dies at 82*. Accessed Oct. 2016. www.chicagotribune.com

Owens, John. 1998. *The New New Regal*. Accessed Oct. 2016. www.chicagotreader.com

Richards, John. 1970. *Architectural Review*. London, UK : Architectural Press.

Rodwell, Denis. 2007. *Conservation and Sustainability in Historic Cities*. Oxford, UK: Blackwell Publishing.

UNESCO. 2000. *Heritage: A Gift From The Past To The Future, part of the mission statement of the World Heritage Centre*. Paris, FR: UNESCO.

Valerio, Joseph, Daniel Friedman, and Nancy Morison-Ambler. 1982. *Movie Palaces*. New York, NY: Educational Facilities Laboratories Division, Academy for Educational Development.

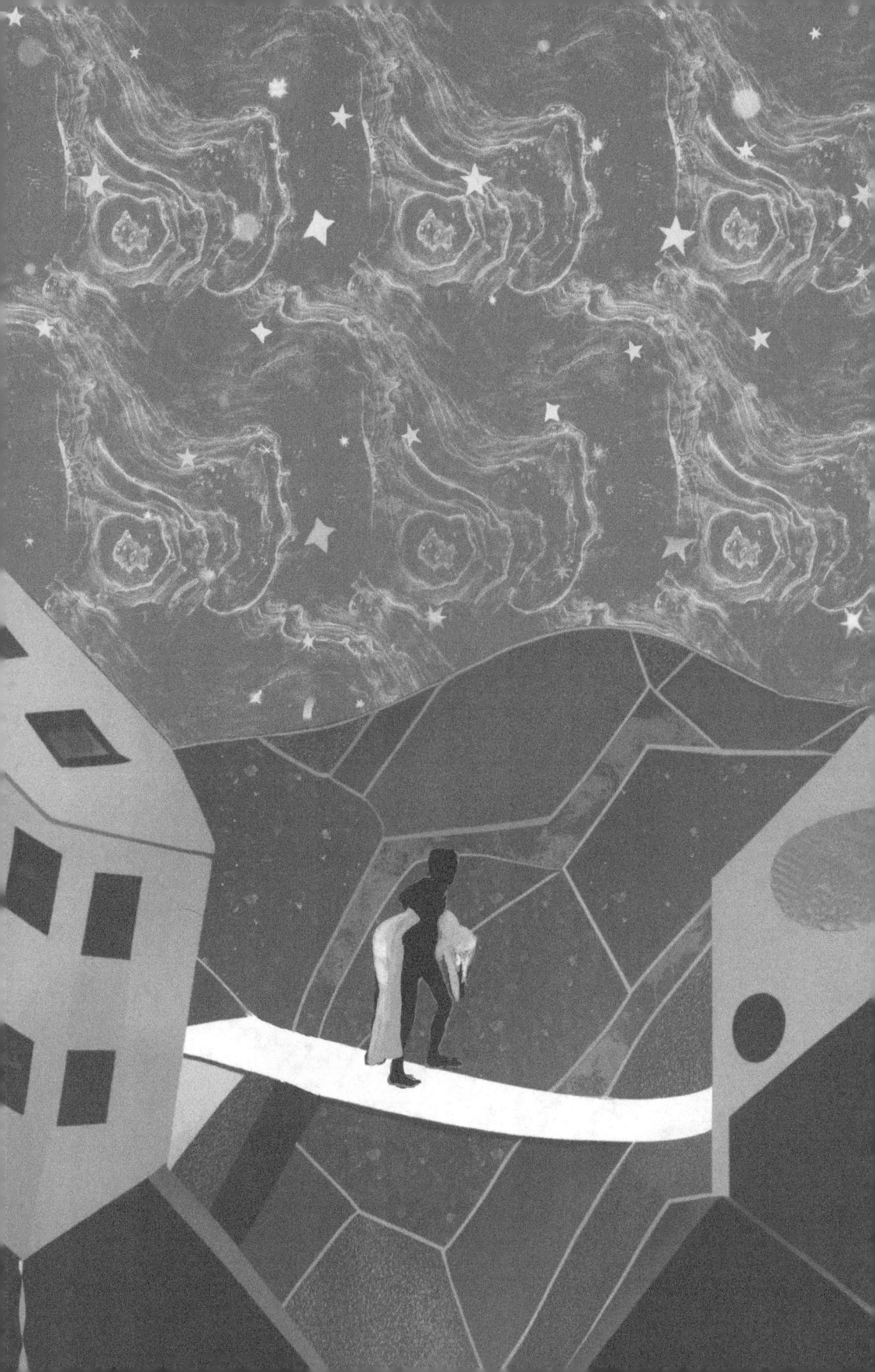

Pursuit of Architectural Ideas Through *The Cabinet of Dr Caligari, Psycho* and *The Crow*

Clarissa Moore

CLARISSA MOORE is an architectural assistant and Masters of Architecture graduate of Queen's University, Belfast. With work and life experience in Belfast and Dublin, she has been progressing her architectural career through education, with focus on 'architecture and cinema.' Before undertaking her Masters degree, Clarissa worked in professional practice in residential and educational architecture. Clarissa teaches part time skills to Bachelor's students and will continue to focus on cinematic architecture and design.

From the beginning of humankind, we have created ways to communicate information through different mediums. From caveman drawings on walls to the virtual reality that technology has allowed us to achieve today, we have always strived for better forms of communication with the help of technology. Since the nineteenth century, technological advances have facilitated the discovery of new methods of capturing images and sound, first through photography, then records, then through film. Monaco (2009, 578) discusses how we are entering a new phase in the history of media and describes how in this new phase, technology offers the promise of instant access to a universal catalogue of knowledge and art, which has been captured by a versatile set of media tools.

Film as a form of media allows us to use our visual and auditory senses. Through film, we can depict the surroundings of an object or character. Representation of space through film was a new and exciting concept for architects in the early twentieth century. Cairns (2013, 3) discusses how the use of film and the depiction of space offered new possibilities of understanding the representation of buildings. He further discusses how architects were presented with a "platform for experimentation" by working with different scales and designing for both interior and exterior spaces. Cairns remarks how over time experimentation of architecture through set design gave way to the conventions of the film industry and that filming then became standardised. In addition to this standardisation, film had become more about narrative, and as a result with the set being used as a tool, rather than a character within itself, the excitement of experimenting with new techniques and concepts had reduced.

Set design is a form of visualising the aesthetics of the theme of a film or show. It contains a variety of techniques, concepts, and materials to create an experience for the viewer to understand the space at a variety of scales. Pallasmaa (2007, 18) discusses the similarities between cinema and architecture as art forms. They are both used to depict lived space, which preserves images of culture and a way of life, highlighting the time it was made and the era it is trying to portray. Production designers and art directors throughout the years have developed techniques for designing architectural set designs. The process is similar to that of an architect designing a building in that it involves concepts, sketches, orthographic drawings, and model making, which, over time, develop into a final design. Pallasmaa also discusses how it is in the interest of the architect to expand the scope of architectural thought through different mediums, such as film and art.

This chapter focuses on the representation of architecture within film, specifically on set design. The techniques and processes used by designers to produce a set that represents a space is studied. Through the focus on three selected films, selected spaces are analysed, to investigate the use of set design and architectural techniques to design these spaces. The use of model making, sketching, and orthographic drawings that are used in the process to develop the set of the films are studied to gain a better understanding of the development of these techniques over time.

To begin this chapter, the concept of space is defined and I discuss how it is used within architectural techniques to portray environments in both the real world and the cinematic world. To continue from the definition of space, the following films are analysed: Robert Wiene's *The Cabinet of Dr Caligari* (1920), Alfred Hitchcock's *Psycho* (1960), and Alex Proyas' *The Crow* (1994). Each film has unique qualities within their productions; however, they have a similar style of conveying dark undertones that are shown through the use of camera techniques, sound, and set design, which have a mix of interior and exterior settings, allowing the viewer to experience the narrative of each story at different scales. While *The Cabinet of Dr Caligari* (1920) is a German Expressionist film, both *Psycho* (1960) and *The Crow* (1994) draw inspiration from the German Expressionist style, which is highlighted within the case study analysis. This chapter aims to achieve a better understanding of the spatial representation of the architecture within films, and how this is achieved through the design process of set designs.

To understand how space can be represented, it is important to understand what space is. Berkeley (2009, 75) discusses space as something that is distinctly discerned by our senses, and how it is relative to our bodies. Berkeley further discusses motion within space through the body, that there is space until resistance, in which there is a body. Through this definition, we conceive the idea of space to understand our surroundings.

Pallasmaa (2014, 231) discusses how our judgement of space calls on our physical and existential senses in a "peripheral and unconscious manner rather than through precise, focused and conscious observation." This discussion provokes the thought of space as not being just physical areas and forms, but a mental concept through which we show our connection to the metaphysical world. However, Lefebvre (1991), focusing on mental and real space, argues that these are highly abstract presumptions of the concept, which creates a void, making it difficult as an idea to understand.

Space has many different theories, mainly concerning the mental and physical aspects of it. Through our own experience of a space, we can connect emotions to certain spaces or associate objects with spaces that are familiar to us. Pallasmaa examines space and place as a multi-sensory singular experience that has a connection with our own existential experiences and perceptions. These experiences allow us to judge the situation of a space as well as showing attachment or dismay for certain settings.

We, as humans, make the connection of the space we are in to our mental cognition. However, Lefebvre discusses that the architect is meant to design a space that is to function for its needs as well as being furnished accordingly. The readability of space for the user is important, as this allows the user to create a mental impression based on their experience of space. The animated objects within the space are smaller connections; however, the space itself is what the user will judge more broadly. Zumthor (2009, 12) discusses his experience of walking into a space as, "I enter a building, see a room, and – in the fraction of a second – have this feeling about it." We make our first impressions of a space within a very short amount of time based on our own experiences and the room's atmosphere.

As architects, we draw and make models to communicate our ideas. Lefebvre describes architectural drawings as a language, which is a code of space. Architects have developed techniques over time for the representation of the spaces they are designing. From two-dimensional orthographic drawings to three-dimensional scale models, architects use a wide array of mediums for refining the process of design. These forms of communication allow the viewer to experience the space at different scales before the final production of the project. The techniques used by architects have also been used by art directors and production designers to design film sets for cinematic spaces. These techniques include the use of orthographic drawings and model making.

Though representative methods of architecture such as orthographic drawings, including plans, sections and elevations, can give us information on layout and measurement, it may limit itself in some ways of representing the space. Lefebvre discusses how forms of representation are bound to graphic elements such as the use of two-dimensional drawings, which act as a reducer of reality in which architects are representatives. These orthographic drawings may be difficult to interpret by someone unfamiliar with them compared to a three-dimensional image portraying the scale, atmosphere, and/or elements within the space.

Through the progression of technology, architects are now able to create orthographic drawings and 3D models on computers through the use of software. Graphic representation of space can also be achieved through software such as Adobe Photoshop and V-Ray to apply materials as well as light and shadow to give the user an idea of the layout of the space. Virtual reality may also be used to walk around and experience the vertices of the space. Technology has expanded the limits of architectural representation, allowing architects to design and represent space faster and more effectively. In an interview with the production designer of *The Crow*, McDowell (2021) discusses "CAD tools or all the Autodesk suite and any of those things that allow you to move volumetrically through space and then to use augmented reality to inhabit the space or virtual reality to inhabit space to design within a virtual space. So you're standing there moving things around. I mean the tools give you so much more extension, I think as an architect now".

Though technology has helped architects to improve the production of space graphically, Frascari (2009, 200-212) poses the question of our abilities to grasp and handle the new forms of graphic representation presented by computers. As computers use mathematical algorithms to assist with our drawings for accuracy, the question is posed to make us think if computers can give us the same materiality and sensuality as physical graphite drawing; is there a way that these two forms can be combined so that students and professionals can fully utilise the capabilities of digital media? The use of sketching in the early stages of a project helps to ground the ideas and develop the process, however, more recently, computers are being used to develop these drawings, and this interworking relationship of hand drawing and sketching proves well for many architects, as Stott (2015) has discovered when he asks the readers of ArchDaily what their preferences are for drawing technique.

From the beginning, cinema was a new and exciting way for architects and designers to experiment with space, as it allowed for more abstract concepts to portray space and the investigation of different structures at various scales. Architecture and space can be represented in many ways within cinema now, as from physical set designs to digital design, we are still finding new ways to convey space and architecture within the narrative. Barnwell (2017, 59) discusses how production designers devise visual concepts which can be depicted as space, whether interior or exterior, light, colour, and decoration of the sets. This is a similar process to which architects design, through which space as a concept can help explore the design for the story being told to the viewer.

Space is designed through both film and architecture, while film uses space as a tool, architecture uses space to design and build within. Kaçmaz Erk (2009) discusses how cinematic space can be representative of architectural space. As architecture represented within a film is not architecture itself, or a misapprehension, it is an interpretation of it and the space created by cinema is not an exact copy of architectural space. Penz and Thomas (1997) further discuss the point of cinematic space only being representational of that of architectural space. This means film sets are a representation of the real world as they also need to allow for the practicalities of filmmaking, using multiple cameras for example. The discussion of George Melies's awareness of the space portrayed on screen is not the same as space within the real world. The real world that is being portrayed on screen can be experienced only visually and audibly by the viewer, but it cannot be experienced physically. The space on the screen is a representation of what the viewer could experience, what is depicted will allow the viewer to imagine the feeling, but not physically feel what is being conveyed.

McDowell (2021) discusses how building architecture for a film is a different experience "it's very different considering you know the back of every piece of architecture is raw plywood." The cinematic space within films that give us a visual perception of an interior or exterior space is made up of singular modules and materials. This is in comparison to real space architecture which is designed to have wall build-ups and connections to other spaces. *The Cabinet of Dr Caligari* (1920), *Psycho* (1960), and *The Crow* (1994) all use techniques, such as drawings, sketches, and models, to portray both internal and external space which immerses us in the story and the atmosphere the director is trying to depict.

The Cabinet of Dr Caligari (1920) is a landmark German Expressionist film, which set the tone for film makers around the world. The film was made after the First World War when German Expressionism was at its peak. It had an overshadowing symbolism for the authoritarian dictatorship that Germany was experiencing at the time. As films from outside of Germany had been banned by 1916, there was an increase in the production of domestic films. These films conveyed feelings of alienation and political disillusionment – *The Cabinet of Dr Caligari* (1920) being one of the sources. Pallasmaa (2007, 18) discusses how German Expressionist films depict a city or a room as "fantasy architecture" walking on the line between reality and dream. He further explains how the three-dimensional, multi-sensory world, can be represented through two-dimensional imagery and how these films produce experiential fragments which leave an impression of the "continuous and real-world" through the use of the properties and limits of human perceptual mechanisms.

Walter Reimann, Walter Röhrig, and Hermann Warm were the art directors and production designers of the sets for the film. Vogt (2001, 92) discusses how the film's set design and decoration were initially meant to be shot with a more realistic style, however, the production team decided to use expressionist artwork. Walter Reimann suggested the film use painted sets on canvas, rather than using expensive construction materials. This in turn had the flexibility of depicting the urban space through perspective and layering of these set paintings. Vogt further discusses how the set design and the decoration depict the fragility and the instability of the painted city, which was an expression of symbolism for the mental state of the German people during those years. This symbolism and the Expressionist movement meant that the architecture being portrayed was reduced to its purest form, i.e. cubes, columns, cylinders, pillars, stairs, landings, arches, vaults, etc.

As previously mentioned, architecture within cinema allowed artists and architects to experiment with different shapes and forms without committing to a real working design, which could provide its constraints. Today we can depict a space, whether urban or domestic as purely cinematic, it can be depicted as true space, with little room for metaphorical analogies. *The Cabinet of Dr Caligari* (1920) however, can be considered as a depiction of metaphor, as the reflection of the troubling and upsetting experiences of the First World War are clear. Vogt (2001, 83) discusses how the forced anthropomorphism and psychologization led to a persistent darkening and demonization of these urban events. He discusses how the expression of the painted narrowness of rooms, squares, and streets gave a sense of the fear-filled, diffuse urban perception of life being experienced. The film shows how the depiction of physical reality morphed into the psychologised experience of the characters. This allows us to draw from our connection to the city and our perceptions and memories of experiences, which may be altered due to our state of mind at the time.

Though Walter Reimann suggested the use of painted canvases to portray the surroundings, this method followed the use of concept art which was drawn by the artists, mainly Hermann Warm. Figure 1 shows the patterns of light and shading taken from the film stills. The drawings were used to understand the space being represented and how different geometries would complement one another. It is with this flexible style of set design, that the restrictive and perverse nature of the architecture in which the characters interact can be seen.

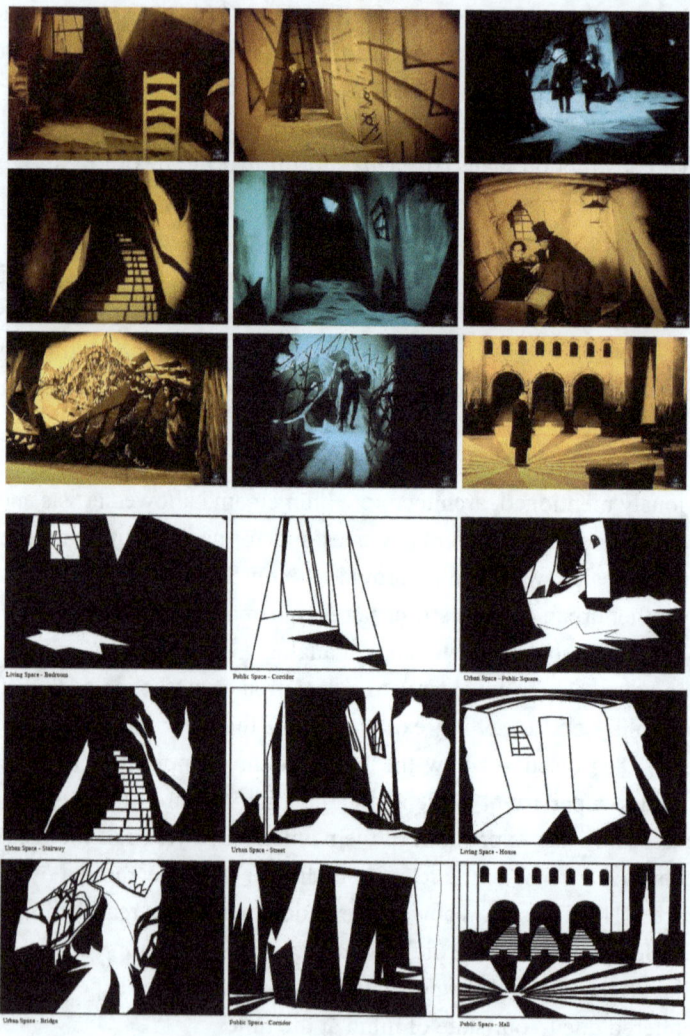

Figure 1: Exploration of geometries through light and shade in different spaces. *The Cabinet of Dr. Caligari* (00:06:04), (00:07:07), (00:21:48), (00:27:19), (00:31:35), (00:33:07), (00:38:56), (00:46:26), (00:52:51). (All film stills captured by the author).

Kurtz (2016, 66) discusses that when Hermann Warm read the script, he immediately thought of an anti-naturalistic design, and that the idea for an Expressionist painting design came from his colleague Walter Reimann. Kurtz further discusses that Warm is said to have declared, "The film image must become graphic." Which in turn, tended to give architecture its inner liveliness. Together with Walter Röhrig, the three artists then developed all the set designs and decoration sketches. Many set designs were sketched several times; they drew floor plans to prepare the planning in the studio more precisely. This finally led to the construction plans for the props and decorations to be made. The painting of the sets in 1920, illustrated the Expressionist artwork being painted onto large canvases. This allowed them to visualise the scale of the sets and the proportions used to form the geometries to show the contradictory nature of the scenes following the human scale and anatomy.

Hermann Warm, as the designer experienced in film production, was more responsible for the construction planning. (Vogt, 2001, 30) Röhrig was in charge of the painters' team that made the decorations. The techniques used for this were large sketches in charcoal and inked in colour. Walter Reimann assisted with the artistic realisation and was also responsible for the costume design and therefore also made costume sketches. Through time the set design and drawings of this iconic film were lost or destroyed, however, from the 1950s on, there have been repeated attempts to recreate the original sets for exhibitions in museums. A few of the original designers and director Robert Wiene were able to recreate some of the sets from their original drawings. Today, technology allows us to experience the set by using virtual reality in *Der Traum des Cesare (Cesare's Dream*, 2019). The viewer can be enthralled by the three-dimensional space and move freely around the set.

Ahi and Karaoghlanian (2020, 11) discuss how the German Expressionist films used designs and artwork that consisted of angular studio sets, rather than realistic set designs which portray the real world. With distorted buildings painted on canvas backdrops, the focus was on the internal and external surroundings, which reflected the distress of the characters. The film expresses interior (mental) reality through exterior means, with the use of extreme distortion in its production design. The sets created an architectural paradox. Claustrophobic spaces confine the characters, chaos, and confusion caused by the surreal perspectives which consist of distorted shapes and sharp angles. Ebert (2009) makes an astute observation about the directors' vision of the film and how Robert Wiene was making a film of "delusions and deceptive appearances" and how the characters within the story are madmen and murderers who "exist at right angles to reality." Through the use of angled and distorted sets inspired by the German Expressionist movement, these characters who are at "right angles to reality" are shaped by this world that has been created by the Expressionistic dream state.

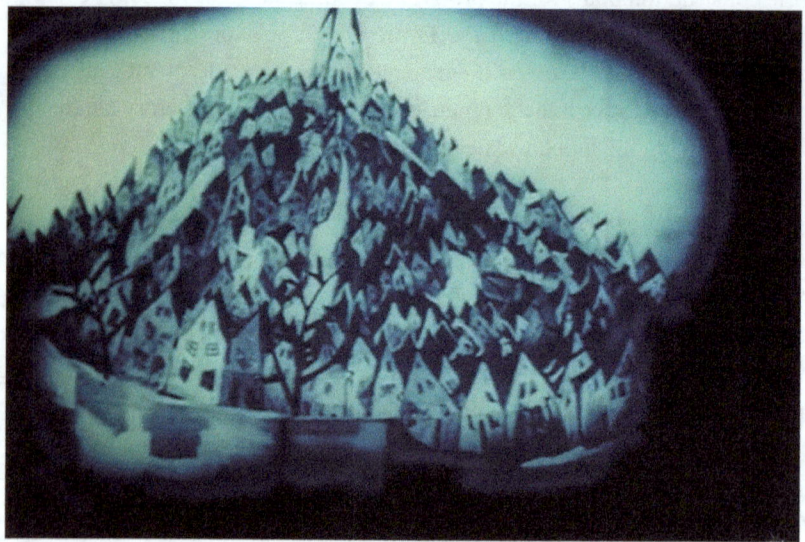

Figure 2: Film still (00:04:01) of the painted set of the Holstenwall, the village where *The Cabinet of Dr. Caligari* takes place, depicting the angular distortions of where the characters of the story live.

Through the use of cinematic plan, the space can be depicted to show the distortion of the interiors. Figure 5 shows the plans of Dr. Caligari's house, a main focal point within the film. It is a single room that is sparingly furnished, with the main feature being the coffin-like cabinet in which the somnambulist character, Cesare, rested. The angular nature of the space can also be seen in plan, as the walls have been cut, the walls are slanted to one side. Figures 3 and 4 are film stills, showing Dr Caligari's house and the characters interacting with the space. The Expressionist paintings on the walls of the interior, as well as the distorted, angular window reflected the view of the outside world that Dr Caligari had. Ahi and Karaoghlanian (2020, 13) examine how the shape and form of the house communicate the perverse nature of his being. They further comment on how the external shot of the house and the interior do not match in scale. The exterior of the house has a shorter width, whilst the interior appears to be wider, which further emphasises the unnatural design of the space.

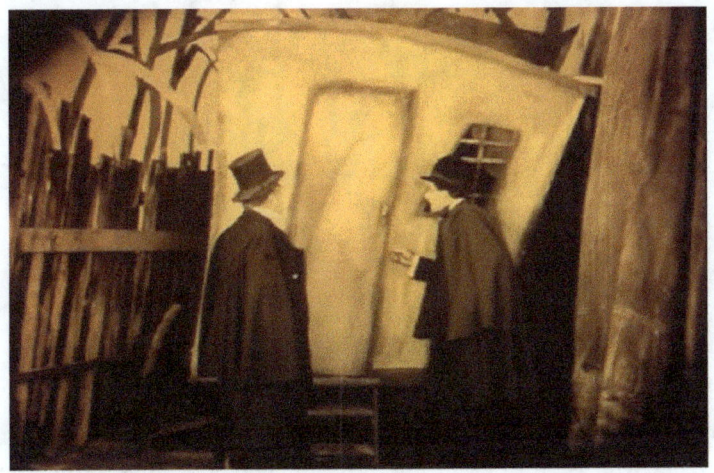

Figure 3: Film still showing the exterior of Dr. Caligari's house.
The Cabinet of Dr. Caligari (00 :23 :01)

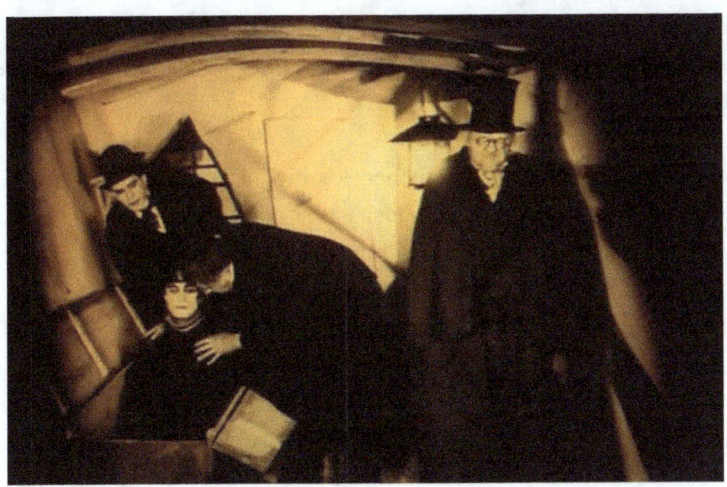

Figure 4: Film still showing interior of Dr. Caligari's house.
The Cabinet of Dr. Caligari (00 :35 :13)

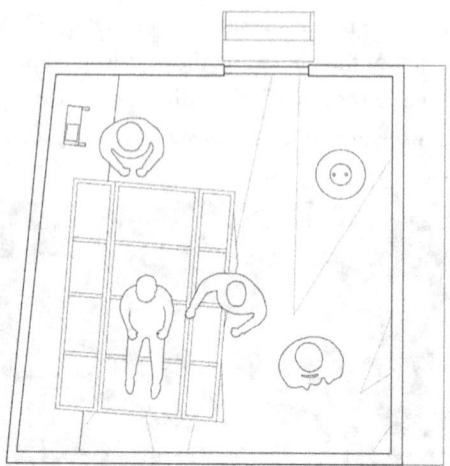

Figure 5: Floor Plan of Dr. Caligari's house
(all illustrations by author unless indicated otherwise)

Sir Alfred Hitchcock (1899-1980) was an English film director, producer, and screenwriter who is still one of the most influential filmmakers in cinematic history to this day. First entering the film industry in 1919, Hitchcock worked his way up to the title 'master of suspense,' which was earned by directing over 50 feature films and specialising in the horror/thriller genres. 'Hitchcockian Cinema' is a term given to the practice of using the camera to mimic the gaze of a person and capturing the audience by framing shots to maximise fear and anxiety.

McGilligan (2003, 63), Alfred Hitchcock's biographer, discusses how Hitchcock worked in the Berlin film industry and admired the visual style of the German Expressionist movement within cinema. McGilligan further discusses how German cinema was more architectural, with more emphasis on the design and atmosphere of the space. They loved shadows and glare as well as unusual angles and extreme closeups. These techniques and rigid design regimes became a trademark for the Hitchcockian style, as the influence of German cinema can be seen in many of Hitchcock's works.

Psycho (1960), a story inspired by the convicted murderer Ed Gein, was a horror/thriller novel published in 1959 by Robert Bloch, who then sold the book to Alfred Hitchcock for $9,500. The film had a low budget of $806,000, which was quite different from Hitchcock's usual budget that Paramount Pictures provided (*North by Northwest* (1959) cost $4 million and *Vertigo* (1958) cost $2.5 million). The budget did not deter Hitchcock from the film, but may have increased his incentive to prove that his art did not need a large budget to induce fear and anxiety into the viewer. Hitchcock had to make a series of decisions to constrain his spending. He used his camera crew from his television series *Alfred Hitchcock Presents* (1955-1965), and a quick turnaround, filming the movie within six weeks. Another way he saved money was by filming the film on black and white stock.

To create the Bates House in *Psycho* (1960), Hitchcock drew inspiration from artists such as Edward Hopper (1882-1967) and his artwork of "House by the Railroad" (1925). Barnwell (2017, 142) discusses how the painting was referenced with the style of a Gothic farmhouse with a mansard roof in an isolated landscape. The Bates house (Figure 6) resonates with this lonely aesthetic. Barnwell further discusses the use of the recurring themes of the artist, such as loneliness and entrapment, and how the people within these artworks are trapped by their own design. With the use of framing these people in windows or buildings, these qualities mirror the lonely and isolating qualities of Norman Bates.

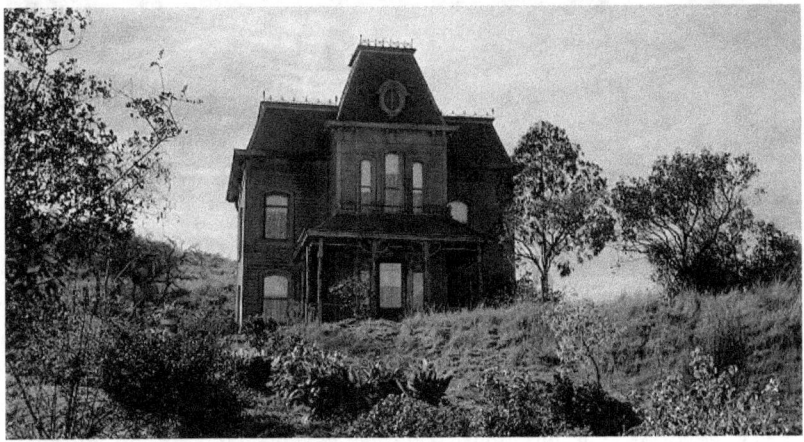

Figure 6: Norman Bates' house. *Psycho* (01:35:29)

In an interview with François Truffaut (1983, 269), Alfred Hitchcock discusses the architectural style of the set as well as the directional composition of the two buildings; the Bates house and the motel (Figure 7), and how they contrast each other. Hitchcock discusses how he did not set out to make an "old-fashioned Universal horror-picture" atmosphere, but instead wanted to be accurate. Where the film is set has an architectural style of 'California Gothic,' this helped Hitchcock reproduce authentic replicas of this style for the Bates house and kept the motel within this fashion. Truffaut mentions how the architectural contrast between the vertical house and the horizontal motel is quite pleasing to the viewer's eye, to which Hitchcock agreed.

Though it is pleasing to the eye, there are obvious reasons for Hitchcock to portray the vertical house as something quite ghostly, even sinister, which looms over the horizontal, flat motel. Within the rooms where guests are meant to feel comfortable on the interior of the motel, there is a sense of discomfort from the exterior with the view of the house, which adds to the suspense and allure of the dwelling from the viewer's perspective.

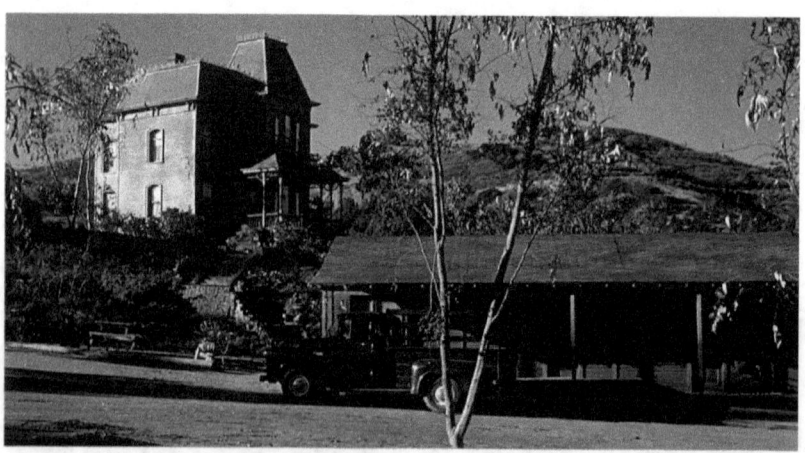

Figure 7: Bates Motel and House. *Psycho* (01:28:42)

The sets for *Psycho* (1960) were designed by Art Director's Joseph Hurley and Robert Clatworthy. The buildings of the house and motel had no interiors or back of house, so they acted as empty shells. The Bates house originally consisted of the left wall and the front façade, since these were the only sides visible on camera. But in 1963 the right side wall was added on and in 1983 the rear of the house had been added to close in the building. The interiors of the house and the motel were filmed on Stage 28 at Universal Studios, these did not need to be elaborate sets as Alfred Hitchcock mainly used close-up shots, which also allowed him to save money on the film production.

There are a few key themes in *Psycho* (1960), some of which include voyeurism and the audience take on a voyeuristic role for some of the key scenes within the film. This also allows the audience to be disturbed by Norman Bate's use of the peephole he created in the office parlour, to peep into room No.1, where Marion disrobes for her shower. As viewers, we are hypocritically disturbed by this action as Norman is in the same physical cinematic space as Marion. This means that this is a direct invasion of her privacy, whilst we as viewers are in real space, which is an indirect invasion of privacy. We are watching someone unaware they're being watched by someone else.

Norman discusses with Marion in the office parlour, "We're all in our private traps, clamped in them, and none of us can ever get out. We scratch and claw but only at the air, only at each other. And for all of it, we never budge an inch." (Hitchcock, 1960, 0:38:18) This chilling quote allows us to delve into the mind of Norman for a brief moment. It allows the audience to feel claustrophobic for the characters within these individual cell structures that Alfred Hitchcock created, and put together through montage. The theme of entrapment continues throughout the film with Norman moving between two spaces, both physically and mentally, which translates onto the other characters as their suspicions of him grow.

Jacobs (2007, 125) discusses the film's architecture and the use of sets to create cubicles which resonates the spatial compactness as well as the compression that characterises the film. From the earlier discussion of the vertical and horizontal compositions of the buildings, the house and motel also highlight the spatial layout and how they enclose cell-like rooms that entrap and imprison the characters. Whether they are physically there, or the memory of them, the characters do reflect the comments made earlier on Edward Hopper's artwork and how the subjects appear to be entrapped within the scene. Jacobs further discusses the comparison between the only two motel rooms shown within the film, Marion's room, No.1, and Lila and Sam's room, No.10 (Figure 15). Both rooms have undistinguished furniture such as the bed, wardrobe, lamps and nightstands. The main difference being that Marion's room had floral wallpaper on the wall adjacent to the office and office parlour, whilst Lila and Sam's room had plain walls. This difference could be that Norman used floral wallpaper to hide the peephole in the wall within the floral pattern.

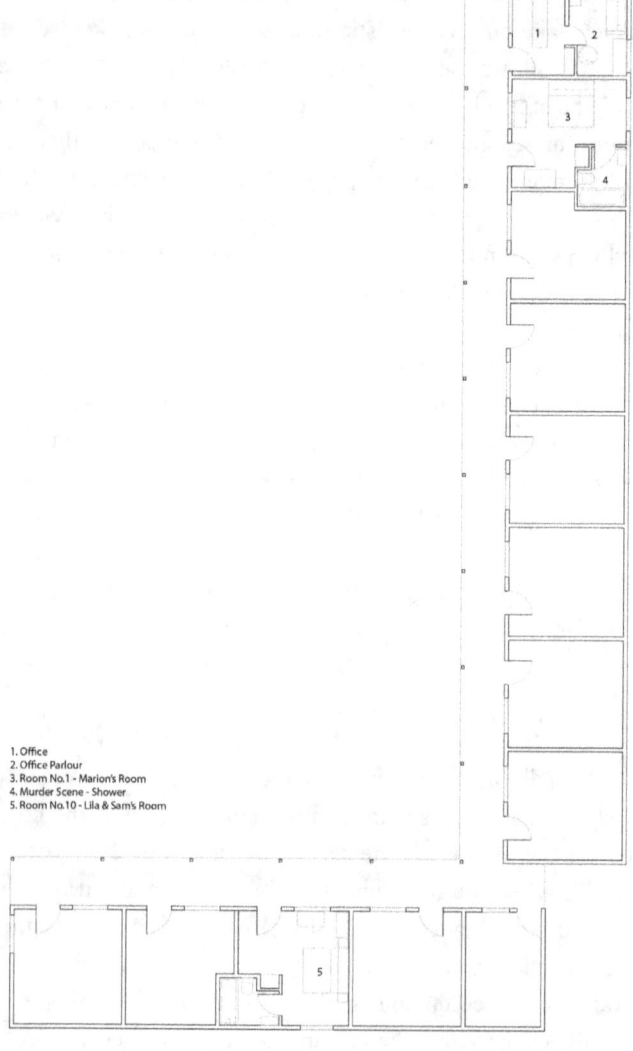

1. Office
2. Office Parlour
3. Room No.1 - Marion's Room
4. Murder Scene - Shower
5. Room No.10 - Lila & Sam's Room

Figure 8: Bates Motel layout floor plan drawn by the author

The Crow (1994) was based on a comic book, published in 1989 and written by James O'Barr who was inspired by a heartbreaking story of a young couple who were killed tragically over an engagement ring, which cost $30.00. Already coping with the grief of losing his girlfriend by the hand of a drunk driver, James poured this anger into his artwork for the comic. The story between the comic books and the film is quite different, as when the comics became of interest to producers, they wanted to align certain parts of the story to explain the concept better. However, the main concept remains the same.

The storyline of the comic was driven by music, with notes of music lyrics and quotes from artists such as Jim Carroll and Robert Smith from the rock band The Cure, as well as Joy Division. Alex Proyas, the director of *The Crow* (1994) wanted to draw reference from James O'Barr's use of music in the comics. Proyas found that making the soundtrack a more prominent character of the film made it feel more operatic and energetic. The use of rock music within the film is also reflected through the style in which the sets and costumes were designed and used to create a gothic and operatic atmosphere.

Conner and Zuckerman (1995, 86) discussed the influences of James O'Barr's work and the ideas for the look of the set design, which were considered with production designer Alex McDowell. The use of the comic book was a good starting point for the design team, as they could take the simplicity of the comic into the film. In a discussion with O'Barr, McDowell wanted to get the comic book's style across, by drawing on German Expressionist films such as *The Cabinet of Dr Caligari* (1920) and *Pandora's Box* (1929). O'Barr originally used these films as inspiration for the graphic style of the comic book with the sharp angles, and the use of dark lighting to emphasis the dark nature of the story.

Through a discussion with the assistant art director, Grimsman (2021) mentions the use of a storyboard artist: "We also had a seriously detailed storyboard artist who was a concept guy in his own right, Peter Pound. He drew the famous 'burning crow' camera angle which I took and extrapolated to become a ground layout for the actual set." The use of the storyboards allowed for the production team to draw inspiration from the comics in terms of the visual style and the designs for the architectural sets.

Whilst drawing inspiration from German Expressionism, mainly from films like *The Cabinet of Dr Caligari* (1920), the production team and the director wanted to keep the colour palette of the film monochromatic. Conner and Zuckerman quote Alex Proyas discussing the concept behind the visual style of the film and how they wanted to avoid the typical Hollywood fabrication, but instead go for a real-world feel. Proyas further discusses the stylization of Eric's new world and how it is stripped of life and colour, as his true life was taken from him. This allowed for the idea that Eric's flashbacks could be in vibrant colour, which hurt him to remember.

Grimsman (2021) further discusses the process involved in the set design for *The Crow* (1994). Grimsman mentions that at the beginning, the concept art for the film preceded the set design work, the concept art was predominately created by the Art Director Simon Murton. Simon did this for all the major sets for the film, with everything drawn by hand. Once the concept art had been completed and verified, Grimsman would take these drawings as reference. The drawing design specifications would be translated into orthographic architectural plans, sections, elevations, and detailed drawings. The process of these design decisions requires a lot of time and involvement, as set designers have to look at all factors of the design process. Grimsman mentions some of these decisions, material choices, engineering considerations, function for the shooting crew and the stunt work, and how it affects the set, i.e. removable set pieces, walls, windows, etc.

An example of the sets being planned and constructed was for the aforementioned 'burning crow' shot (figure 9), in which Geoffrey Grimsman explains how the scene was originally meant to be filmed outdoors, but due to the unreliability of the wind, the production team decided to do it on stage. The team screwed together about seventy sheets of gypsum sheetrock and then taped and mudded the joints. The sheets were then painted to look like asphalt, then the area of the burning crow was gridded out for the team to draw the outline of the bird. A keyway was then routed into the surface which was then painted and filled in with a rubber cement mix. Geoffrey suggested that pea gravel would be used to hide the surface of the gypsum sheet pattern, which was done in a single day as it was scheduled for a night shooting, which was shot from a high angle with raking light. In the end, the scene was only a one-take shot for the film which became an infamous scene for the film and was used for posters and promos. This scene was done by Brandon Lee's stunt double, as Brandon Lee sadly passed away earlier in production.

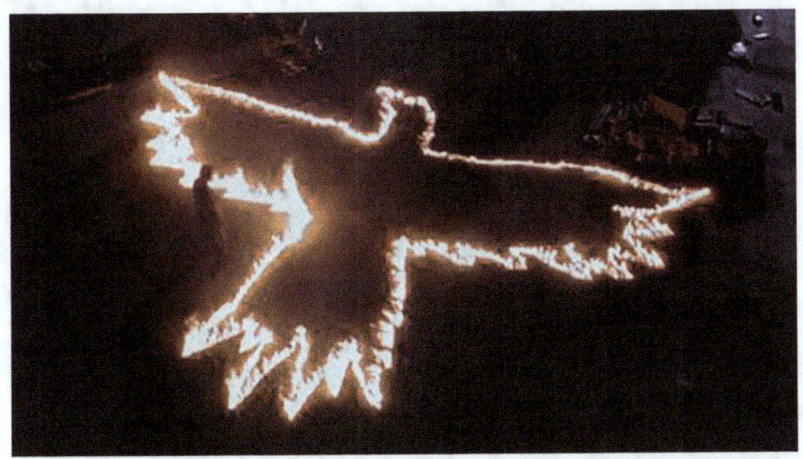

Figure 9: The "Burning Crow", *The Crow* (00:56:44)

To make the cityscape of *The Crow* (1994), Alex McDowell explored the city of Detroit, where the film was to be set. He took photos of the skyline to compose ideas for the set design with the concept art of Peter Pound. The concept art of the cityscape which Peter Pound drew, it shows the eery and dark scene of what is meant to be Detroit with Eric playing the guitar by himself. Pound portrays Eric as a lonely figure in the desolate city landscape. Figure 10 shows the development of the miniature models of the city, which were built by Gus Ramsden. In an interview with Alex McDowell, he discusses his technique of using the images of the city skyline and how it is not necessary to draw all of the buildings of a set, just the necessary interiors, and exteriors,

"So you go out and do research and you might photograph ... a bunch of skylines, and then you'll say, well, if you put these two things together, that's what we want. And that's very simple. You just put those two things side by side and then you say, well, how do I convert that into volume and you work with that and you can just give those two photos to a designer or model maker. And to an extent you don't need drawings, you can build from something like that" (McDowell, 2021).

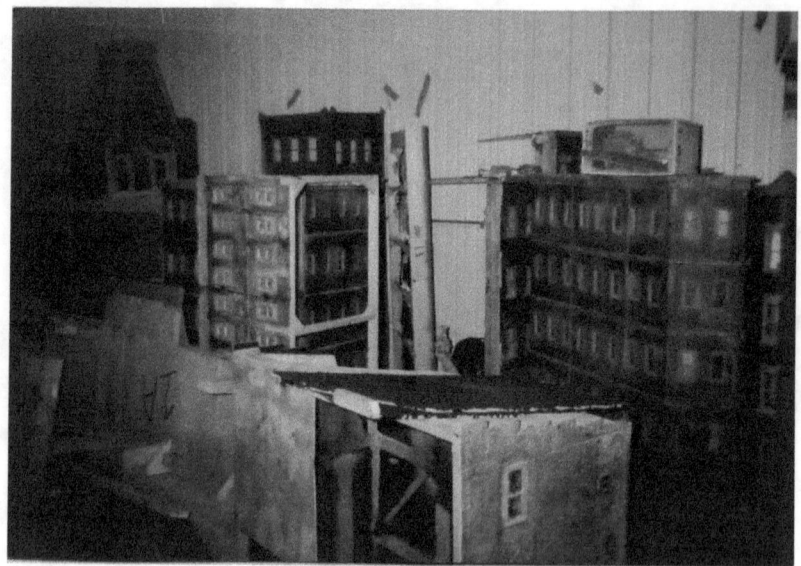

Figure 10: Models of the city set design.
Image Source: Geoffrey Grimsman

McDowell (2021) further discusses the techniques used in the set design process, and how it was very traditional. McDowell mentions the main sets were
constructed from wood and painted, with the set being lit from the ceiling.
These techniques could have been done at any time in the history of cinema,
but McDowell discusses how it is the ambition of the director and what they
want to achieve within a small timeframe and a restricted budget. Gus Ramsden was the leader of the model-making team with Eric Skipper. As previously
mentioned, Conner and Zuckerman (1995, 91) discuss Ramsden's use of Mc-
Dowell's photographs of the Detroit skyline and Peter Pound's concept art.
As well as other concept art from Darren Gilford and orthographic drawings
of the main interior and exterior spaces. They mention how Ramsden started
developing different parts for construction, i.e. bricks, stone, sheets of surface,
which in turn allowed for the development of around 10-15 buildings that had
multiple uses. They were able to rearrange buildings to give them different tops
and fronts which allowed more flexibility when it came to filming.

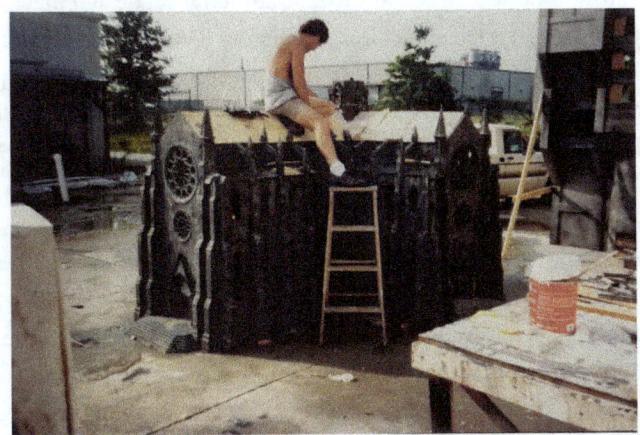

Figure 11: Cathedral model by Gus Ramsden.
Image Source: Geoffrey Grimsman.

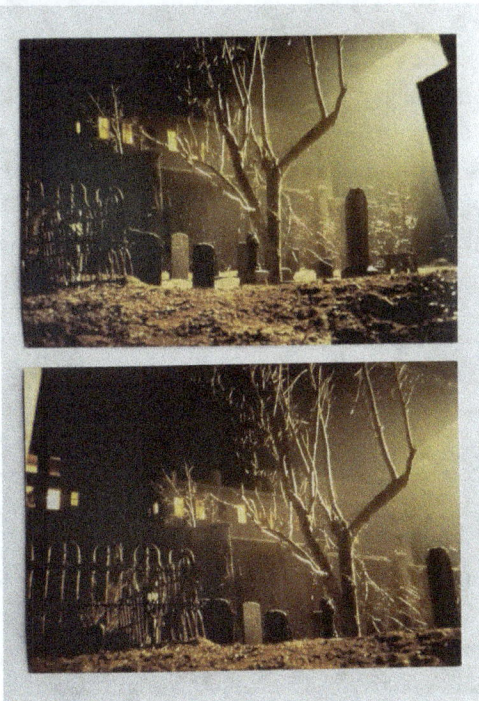

Figure 12: Graveyard where Eric was buried, this had to be built to allow for
camera angles to pick up on various angles of Eric 'rising' from the dead.

Although most of the sets were built from traditional set design materials, there was one set that was filmed in an already existing location. The nightclub, Club Trash in the film, was filmed on location in a deserted cement factory. As well as being a nightclub, this was Top Dollar's (the film's antagonist) lair. Alex McDowell is quoted by Conner and Zuckerman (1995, 89) saying, "The idea is that Top Dollar lives above the nightclub and we were able to do that with this space. We set his office four floors up and can look down." The use of an old cement factory meant that less money could be spent on materials for set building, as the factory was already used for filming. The building also gave another dimension to the sets, as music was a driving force for the film. The anarchic and apocalyptic sensibility that punk music has about it meant that the building was a great basis for the atmosphere the music was portraying. Through the use of hard materials such as concrete, it gave a grimy and industrial nature to the scenes when people were listening and dancing to music. Figure 13 shows the interior of the abandoned cement factory, which was adjusted for the set to have a perforated steel stage and added lighting for strobing.

Grimsman (2021) states in our correspondence that he designed the interiors for Top Dollar's lair which would be filmed on-site, but Gus Ramsden and Eric Skipper designed and built the exteriors as miniatures. These were then shot as 'crow vision,' this was used as a camera angle to simulate the crow flying over the city, which was made of these miniatures, and the crow was later added digitally. Figure 14 shows the exterior of Club Trash as a detailed model, with the crow superimposed into the shot, as the camera follows the crow's path.

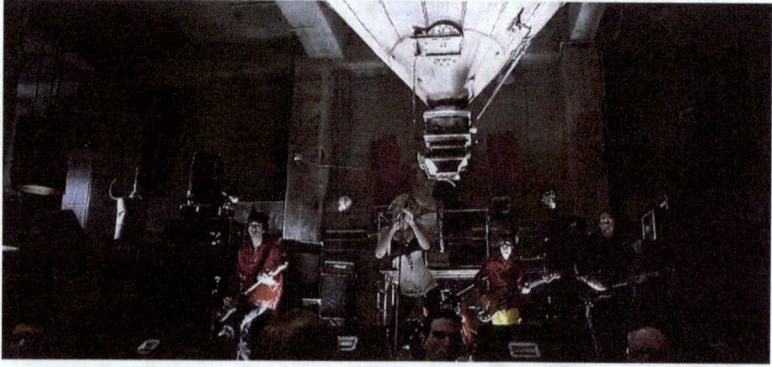

Figure 13: Interior of "Club Trash", filmed in an abandoned cement factory, *The Crow* (00:21:41)

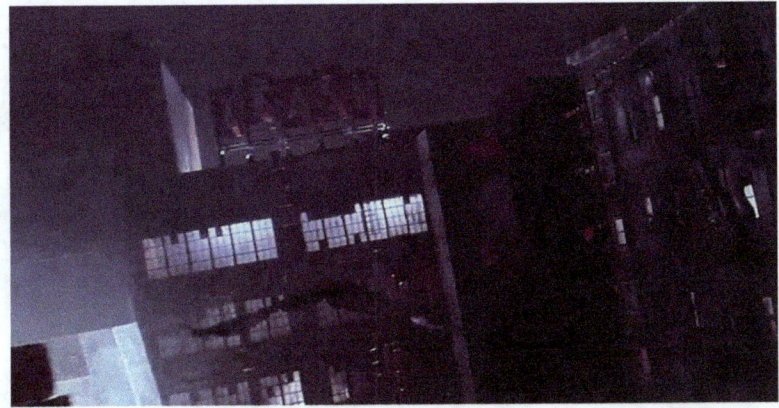

Figure 14: Exterior of "Club Trash", miniature built by Gus Ramsden and
Eric Skipper, *The Crow* (01:05:56)

The loft is one of the most iconic sets from the film. It is where the murder of
Eric and Shelly take place and it is where the crow guides Eric when he comes
back from the dead. Grimsman (2021) was the designer of the loft, and the look
of the interior and exterior was driven by the concept art done by Peter Pound
and Darren Gilford. The space is used for showing the memories of Eric, both
good and bad, and it is also used as a safe space for him to contemplate his previous life as he seeks vengeance on those who took that life from him. In Peter
Pound's concept art for Eric's loft, the artwork emphasises the character's layer
as it towers over the rest of the city with its dark, gothic style. Darren Gilford's
concept art for the interior of the loft highlights the structural nature of the loft,
making it look quite industrial, which is a recurring theme in the film, as the
influence of punk music was incorporated into the set design. The artwork still
draws its inspiration from German Expressionism through its use of angular
perspectives and dark undertones.

The interior of the loft was designed as a separate set from the exterior, as the
exterior was a miniature built by Gus Ramsden and Brandon Lee was digitally
added in after for when the camera zoomed out of the loft window. Figure 15
shows a section of the loft, the trusses were made from PVC and foam, with
hard coatings that were heavily painted to look like cast metal. The walls of the
loft were made from plywood that was painted and decorated by set designers.

Figure 16 shows the plan of the loft and the layout of the trusses. After the couple were murdered, the house had been barricaded off and their possessions taken away, showing only loose pieces of furniture, such as the dresser, where Eric first applies his face paint, which has been scattered to the centre of the room.

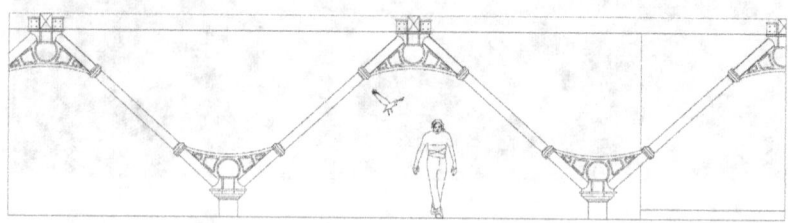

Figure 15: Section of Eric Draven's loft.

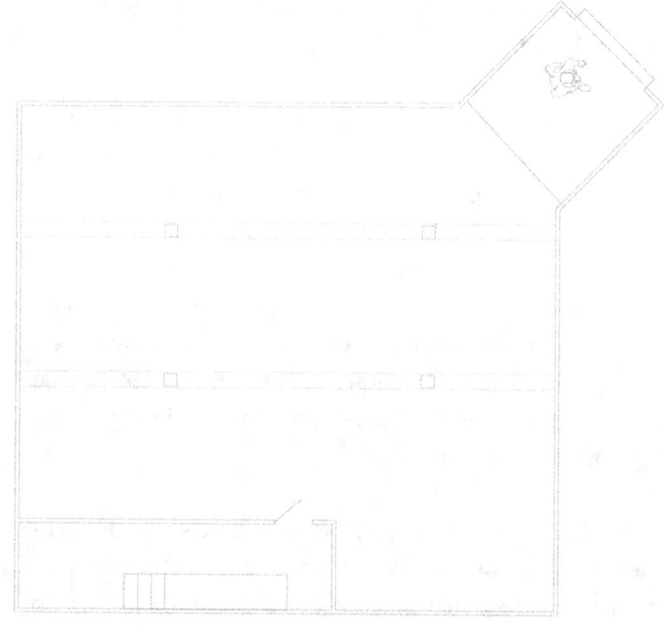

Figure 16: Plan of Eric Draven's loft. Image inspiration:
Geoffery Grimsman, reimagined by author.

Through research and analysis of the set designs, the connection between all three films has been highlighted. *The Cabinet of Dr Caligari* (1920) was filmed during the German Expressionist period which has left a lasting impression on directors to this day. *Psycho* (1960) and *The Crow* (1994) draw inspiration from *The Cabinet of Dr Caligari* and the Expressionist style. Alfred Hitchcock started in the film industry in Berlin during the German Expressionist movement and had adapted the techniques used by the directors of that time to become the 'Master of Suspense.' James O'Barr exemplified inspiration from Expressionist films for writing and drawing the comic, with the use of sharp angles, dark undertones, and symbolism which were incorporated into the film adaptation. These parallels show that even over a period of over seventy years, earlier films can set the basis for artists and directors to be inspired by their original techniques and experimentation of set design.

The architectural techniques used within the set designs of all three films, such as orthographic, sketches, and models, have been translated throughout their production into the final set design. The film production teams made the use of plans, sections, and elevations, as well as the use of models and concept art which depicted the spaces and atmospheres that the director wanted to portray. Through rigorous planning of the film and storyboarding, the director can decide on what the important shots are and how the camera needs to film them. This is how the production team knows the amount of detail that needs to go into specific parts of the sets. All three films used façades for exteriors with bracing behind them and built interior modules for filming. *The Crow* (1994) and *Psycho* (1960) both used similar methods of façade bracing, as scenes were being filmed outside they needed sturdier materials to cope with the weather. However, while *The Cabinet of Dr Caligari* (1920) also used bracing, it did so to a lesser extent as the canvases required for Expressionist paintings of the set would have been lighter. The set was also filmed on a stage indoors, so it would have not of had the same weathering conditions compared to *Psycho* (1960) and *The Crow* (1994). Figure 17 shows the elevation of bracing for façades designed for *The Crow* (1994). The similarities of the set design run in parallel with architectural practice, as even the smallest details need to be designed and thought through for the construction of a structure to work safely.

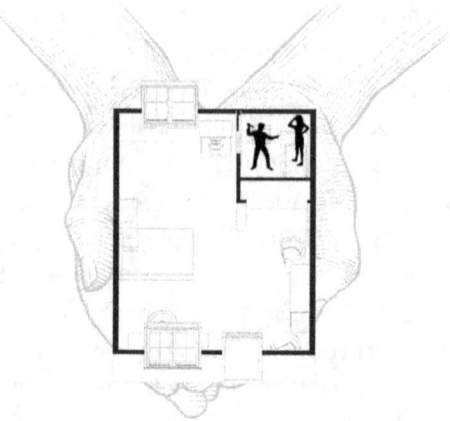

Figure 17: Bracing structure elevation for facades, *The Crow*.
Image inspiration: Tim Eckel, reimagined by author

Cinematic space is representative of what architecture is; it is used for experimenting, filming, and portraying what the director wants us to see, though it is only temporary. Architecture in real space can be either temporary or permanent but may have limitations on the experimentation that cinematic space allows for. This chapter demonstrates an understanding of the changes of architectural techniques within set design over a period of time and how this impacted the process of the set design. The research done on *The Cabinet of Dr Caligari* (1920), *Psycho* (1960) and *The Crow* (1994) has shown that the architectural techniques used in film set design over a period of time have not changed drastically, though there are some differences. The process of making the films has remained similar, as the director knows what shots they want to film, they focus on detailing those particular scenes through storyboarding and concept art. The production team is then able to design and build the sets to suit the needs of the film. One of the main differences is the use of technology. *The Crow* (1994) was the most recently produced film, though it was traditionally made in terms of set design, post-editing, and CGI was used for various touch-ups and scenes which entail the use of combining the miniature models with full-sized actors.

I have concluded that the set designs have not changed drastically for these three films over time, though this does not mean that set design hasn't changed for other films, due to the use of technology. Future films need to maintain the basis of these techniques that are used within the three discussed case studies. Films can benefit from understanding architectural space and how it can be represented in ways that don't require a lot of CGI, but rather, more focused storyboarding and techniques that don't require a large budget.

REFERENCES

Films

The Cabinet of Dr Caligari. (1920). Directed by Robert Wiene. Germany: Decla Film-Gesellschaft [Viewed 10 October 2020]. Available from Youtube.

Psycho. (1960). Directed by Alfred Hitchcock. America: Alfred Hitchcock [Viewed 04 December 2020]. Available from Amazon Prime.

The Crow. (1994). Directed by Alex Proyas. New York: Dimension Films [Viewed 01 November 2020]. Available from Youtube.

Books and Journals

Monaco, James. 2009. *How to Read a Film Movie, Media and Beyond.* 4th edn. New York: Oxford University Press.

McGloughlin, Stephen. 2001. *Multimedia Concepts and Practice.* New Jersey: Prentice Hall.

Cairns, Graham. 2013. *The Architecture of the Screen.* Bristol: Intellect.

Pallasmaa, Juhani. 2007. *The Architecture of Image Existential Space in Cinema.* 2nd edn. Helsinki: Rakennustieto Publishing.

Berkeley, George. 2009. *Principles of Human Knowledge and Three Dialogues.* 4th edn. New York: Oxford University Press.

Pallasmaa, Juhani. 2014. 'Space, place and atmosphere. Emotion and peripherical perception in architectural experience'. *Lebenswelt.* No. 4 p230-245. https://riviste.unimi.it/index.php/Lebenswelt/issue/view/571

Lefebvre, Henri. 1991. *The Production of Space.* 3rd edn. Oxford: Blackwell Publishing.

Zumthor, Peter. 2006. *Atmospheres Architectural Environments, Surrounding Objects.* 5th edn. Basel: Birkhauser.

Frascari, Marco. 2009. 'Lines as Architectural Thinking', *Architectural Theory Review*, 14(3). p200-212.

Stott, Rory. 2015. 'The Computer vs The Hand In Architectural Drawing: ArchDaily Readers Respond'. *ArchDaily.* https://www.archdaily.com/627654/the-computer-vs-the-hand-in-architectural-drawing-archdaily-readers-respond

Barnwell, Jane. 2017. *Production Design for Screen: Visual Storytelling in Film and Television*. 2nd edn. New York: Bloomsbury Visual Arts.

Kaçmaz Erk, Gül. 2009. *Architecture In Cinema A Relation of Representation Based on Space*. Germany: Lambert Academic Publishing AG & Co. KG.

Penz, Francois & Thomas, Maureen. 1997. *Cinema and Architecture; Melies, Mallet-Stevens, Multimedia*. London: British Film Institute.

Penz, Francois. 2018. *Cinematic Aided Design: an everyday life approach to architecture*. New York: Routledge.

Vogt, Guntram. 2001. *Die Stadt im Kino: deutsche Spielfilme 1900-2000*. Marburg: Schüren.

Kurtz, Rudolf. 2016. *Expressionism and Film*. 2nd edn. Bloomington: Indiana University Press.

Jon Ahi, Mehruss & Karaoghlanian, Armen. 2020. *The Architecture of Cinematic Spaces by Interiors*. Bristol, UK: Intellect.

Krohn, Bill. 2000. *Hitchcock at Work*. London: Phaidon Press Limited.

McGilligan, Patrick. 2003. *Alfred Hitchcock a Life in Darkness and Light*. New York: HarperCollins.

Truffaut, François. 1983. *Hitchcock Revised Edition*. 2nd edn. New York: Simon & Schuster Paperbacks.

Jacobs, Steven. 2007. *The Wrong House: The Architecture of Alfred Hitchcock*. Rotterdam: 010 Publishers.

Conner, Jeff & Zuckerman, Robert. 1995. *The Crow: The Movie*. London: Titan Books Ltd.

Websites

Ebert, Roger. 2009. 'A world slanted at sharp angles'. Accessed February 2020. https://www.rogerebert.com/reviews/great-movie-the-cabinet-of-dr-caligari-1920

Jon Ahi, Mehruss & Karaoghlanian, Armen. 2012. *Interiors; Psycho* (1960). Accessed March 2021. https://www.intjournal.com/1012/psycho

Interviews and Correspondence

McDowell, A. 2021. Zoom conversation with Clarissa Moore, 8th March.

Grimsman, G. 2021. Email to Clarissa Moore, 10th April.

Grimsman, G. 2021. Email to Clarissa Moore, 13th April.

Grimsman, G. 2021. Email to Clarissa Moore, 05th May.

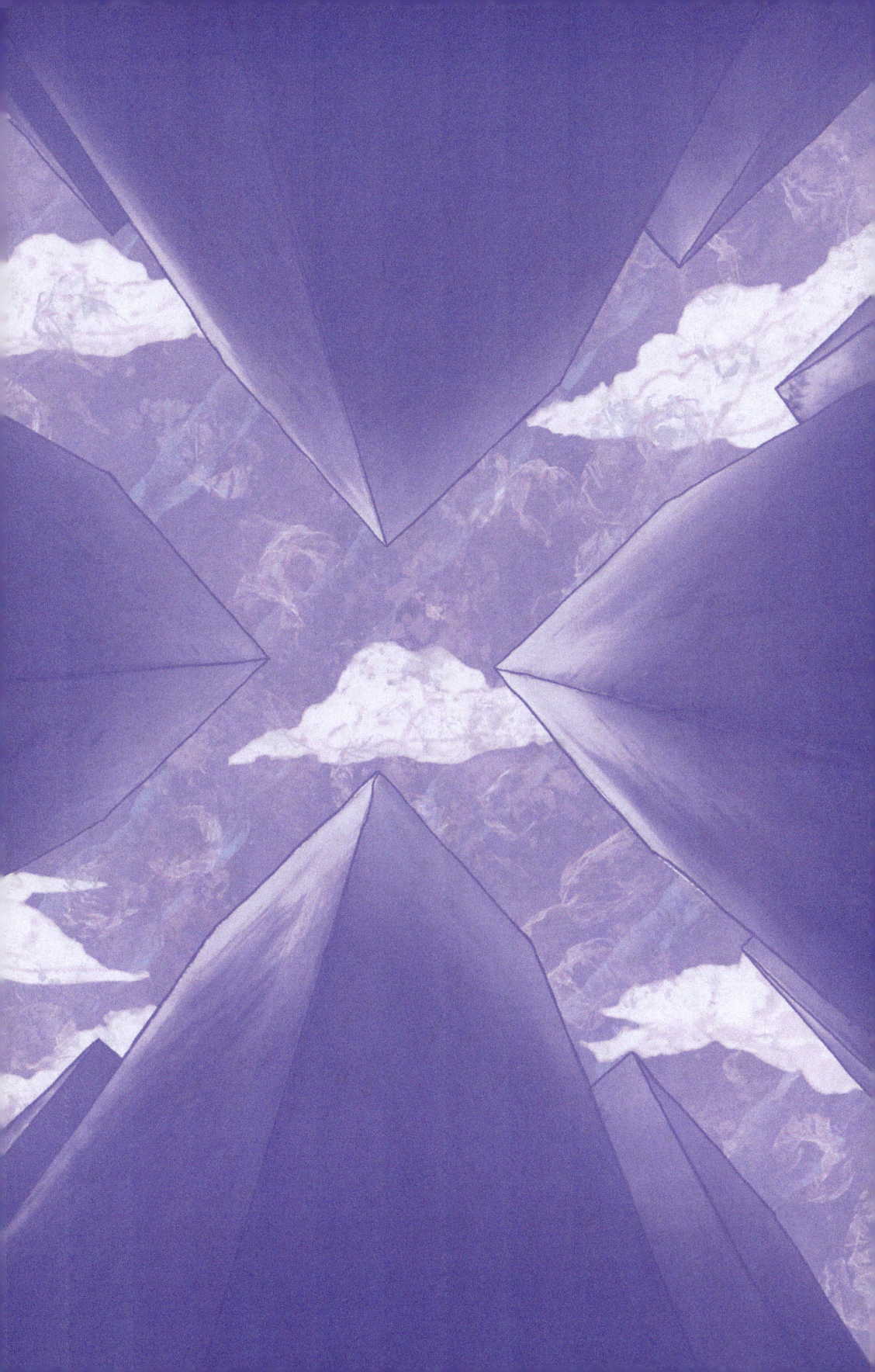

The Curious Case of Post-War Berlin: Dealing with Undesirable Hereditament

Fergal Rainey

FERGAL RAINEY is an award winning architect based in Northern Ireland, working over the UK and Ireland in a broad range of sectors (community, leisure, commercial, renewable energy, healthcare, housing, and residential) across a mix of different project scales, specialising in regeneration, retrofit and community focused projects. He is an active council member in the Royal Society of Ulster Architects (RSUA). Fergal was a Graduate Scholarship Winner with Common Ground Publishing in 2014 and has since won Young Architect of the Year in 2018 and was shortlisted for the RIBA Journal's Rising Stars in 2019.

This research focuses on how we deal with the past, particularly the aftermath of war. I have chosen Berlin as the focus of my investigation as it is a city shrouded in historical controversy and debate. How do you deal with the past? There is a significant amount of ambiguity surrounding the topic, especially in a historically contentious city like Berlin, and differing opinions have led to there being no finite approach that is to be taken. Should the slate be wiped clean and let Berlin start afresh? Should everything be left exactly as it is to act as a constant reminder of the past? The two options are polar opposites, but both have valid arguments; therefore, it is evident that a critical approach must be taken. It is important that the past is not forgotten, but equally it is important that we do not live in the past. The aim of my investigation is to study the undefined middle ground to find out if there is a way in which one can address the two main differing opinions of dealing with the past and find a middle ground that is appropriate to Berlin's past and future.

Memory is a difficult term when it comes to the curious case of post-war Berlin. It is not memory in the traditional sense as a positive term to remember a loved one or of an occasion. Memory in the case of post-war Berlin is then perhaps a misleading term because it is not necessarily something that we want to remember, but something that we have to deal with. This is where the German term that Professor Peter Fritzsche refers to as "Vergangenheitsbewaltigung" becomes useful. Roughly translated into English, this term means past coping or coping with the past; this resonates with German twentieth century history, and so is an appropriate term to describe the German past instead of 'memory.' After World War I (1914-1918) and Germany's defeat, the first German Republic was created and Berlin once again prospered and flourished into a cultural city. 1933 marked the darkest period of German history. Adolf Hitler gained power and appointed himself Chancellor in January 1933. Thus began his reign of terror, persecution against Jews, Communists, and political opposition. September 1st 1939 marked the beginning of World War II with Germany invading Poland. At this time Berlin had a population of approximately 4.5 million.

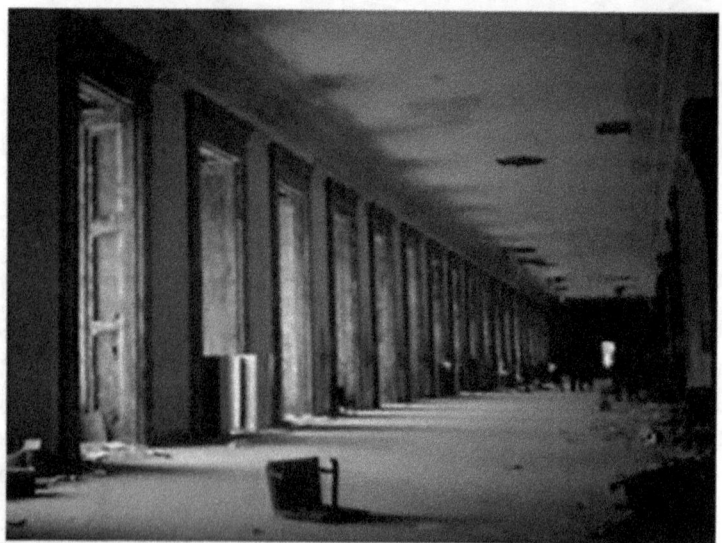

Figure 1: New Reich Chancellery after the fall of Berlin in
Fall of Berlin, 1945 (00:46:55).

The Russian Army halted Hilter's Eastern advances at Moscow and Stalingrad, and by 1943, the Allies began bombing Berlin. After D-Day in 1944, Germany's defeat was inevitable, and on May 7th 1945, Colonel General Alfred Jodl signed the unconditional surrender in Rheims, thus ending Nazi Germany's involvement in World War II. Berlin lay in ruins, with the population almost halved. The Allied Powers divided Germany and its Capital into four, each section controlled by one of the four victorious powers.

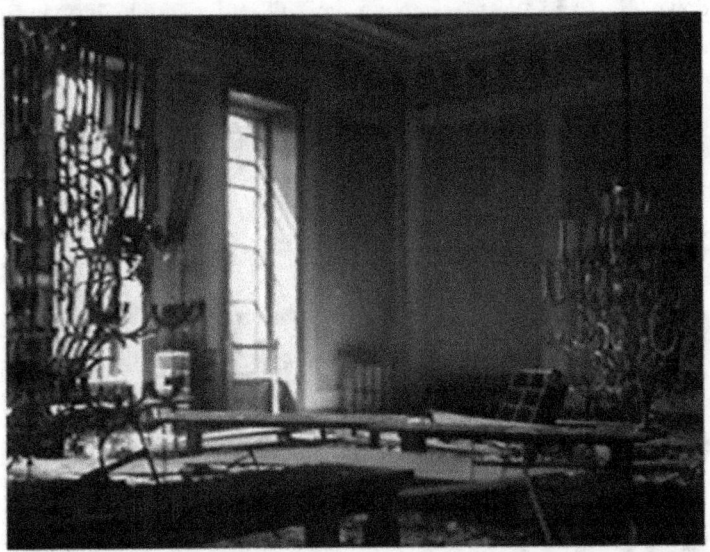

Figure 2: New Reich Chancellery after the fall of Berlin in
Fall of Berlin, 1945 (00:47:00).

After twelve years of Hilter's dictatorship, Germany's liberators had the chance to shape a new Germany and had a difficult job of dealing with the undesirable hereditament; the impact of Nazism, the physical and mental devastating effects on its streets and peoples.

The relationship between the Soviet Union and the other three Allied powers quickly disintegrated, turning Germany and its capital in the Soviet Sector into East versus West, communism versus democracy. Living conditions between the East and West were distinctly different; West Germany became a land of democracy, experiencing a growth in their economy. The East was a Communist society, the economy stagnated and individual freedoms were severely restricted. Many people in East Germany wanted out, no longer willing to accept the repressive living conditions. Having lost 2.5 million people since 1961, East Germany needed to stop the mass exodus. Berlin became the focal point, first barbed wire, but then a solid wall divided the city. Attempts to cross illegally from East to West were usually unsuccessful, even fatal. There were a few official crossing points, the most famous of which was Checkpoint Charlie on Friedrichstrasse which became the icon of the Cold War. After the Berlin Wall came down, East and West Germany reunified into a single German State on October 3rd 1990.

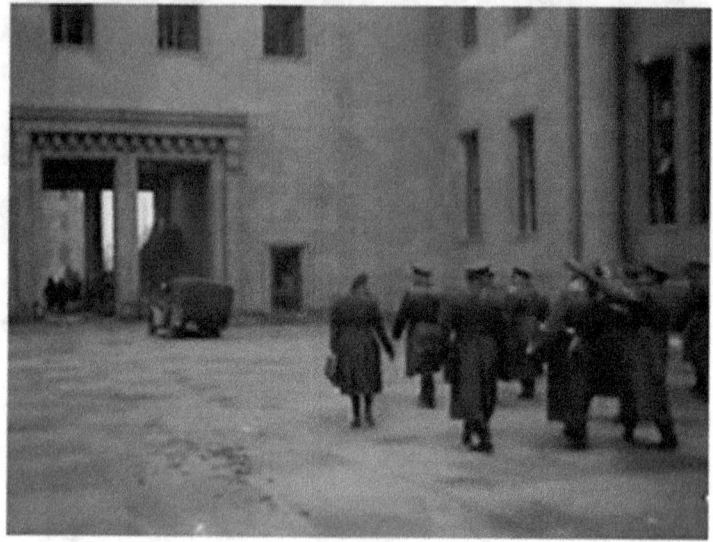

Figure 3: New Reich Chancellery after the fall of Berlin in
Fall of Berlin, 1945 (00:47:35).

The following research has been divided into four sections: demolition, restoration/re-use, preservation, and memorialisation. Within each, there are comparisons and contrasting examples of positive and negative past coping since the end of the war in 1945. This analysis allows us to understand the way history has been dealt with and formulates conclusions on whether the past has been dealt with 'correctly.' Has critical consciousness been maintained or have the changes failed to maintain the memory of the past? The changes that have been made post war are what have shaped Berlin into the city it is today. Have these changes shaped a city into a city for remembrance or a city looking towards the future?

Demolition

Demolition eradicates memory and removes the building from the present. This means it will be forever in the past, an opportunity to start anew and forget that building's legacy in history. As time passes, so too does our memory, forever getting distanced from the present, just to become another figure, statistic, or image in our history books, the only remaining reminder of times gone by.

New Reich Chancellery

New Reich Chancellery was damaged in the Battle of Berlin in April 1945. After the War, the Chancellery lay in what was East Berlin, the occupying Soviet troops were ordered to demolish the building that Hilter had commissioned Albert Speer to design five years after he declared himself head of state. Demolished after the liberation of Berlin, it represented all that Nazism stood for: a dominating, brutally powerful, oppressive party. This building was excessive in a multiplicity of ways; the scale of the building was excessive, the size of rooms and the oversized doorways made the visitor to Hilter's New Chancellery feel very small, overcome with its grandeur. This effect is furthered by the organised, symmetrical rhythm of oppressive large columns and huge windows which accentuate the reflective nature of the polished marble floor as can be seen in the marble gallery below. Excessively long corridors, rich materials covered in heavy ornamented detail all helped Albert Speer to create a Chancellery befitting a man, a political party and a nation who planned on world domination.

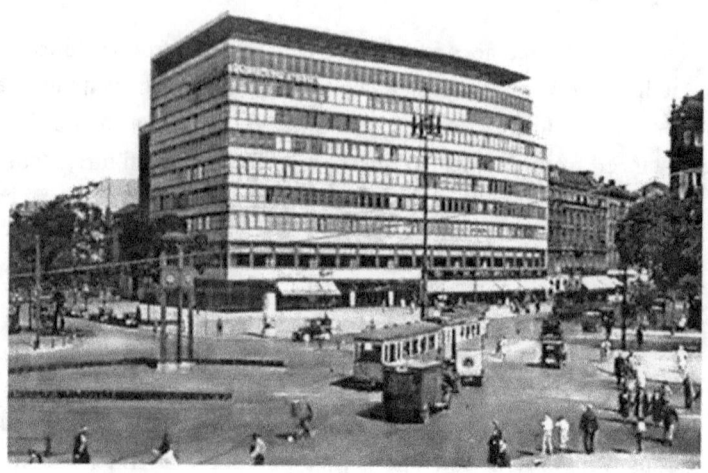

Figure 4: New Reich Chancellery after the marble was removed in,
Germany Year Zero, 1948 (00:28:30).

The building could not be kept to be a shrine to Neo-Nazism, but mainly it was a crucial process in representing to the people of Berlin that Nazism's reign of terror was over. But still, by doing this the concept of *Vergangenheitsbewältigung* is not correctly dealt with, as this method eradicates this memory as if it never happened. During demolition, the squared granite and marble were salvaged, these materials were used in new construction. The City of Berlin has shown here that Berliners have moved on from the past, but they have not lost the memory of what has happened. They have fractalised this building, this memory into parts and embedded them into modern society.

The squared granite was used by the Red Army to build the Soviet Cenotaph in 1946 to represent the liberation of Berlin. It does seem quite poignant that the material of a building that was the basis for decisions of the oppression of people was now a building used to represent the liberation of people.

The marble was used in the reconstruction of the Underground Station at Mohrenstrasse in 1950. The underground station was originally called Kaiserhof after the hotel at Wilhelmplatz which Adolf Hitler later moved into as headquarters. The station was destroyed in the Battle for Berlin in 1945. Five years later, it opened under the name Thalmannplatz. Professor Alan Balfour noted that the marble from the New Reich Chancellery, the same marble that Hitler had commented on when he first saw it, "That's exactly right… Diplomats should have to practice moving on a slippery surface," (Balfour 1990, 78) was now used for the floors, pillars, walls, and foundations of benches in the new station. A material once used to create a sense of unease and power now is being used in a completely different utilitarian way as part of everyday life.

This seems to symbolise the concept of *Vergangenheitsbewältigung* as this building is not something that wants to be remembered; it is a structure that cannot be forgotten and therefore had to find a way to represent that.

Columbus Haus at Potsdamer Platz

Columbus House was designed by Erich Mendelson, and the building was completed in 1932, one year before Hilter came to power. The building was designed for the maximum potential rental income, and passed through World War II relatively unscathed. "The steel structure of Columbus Haus withstood aerial bombing. The marks in its façade and damage to the terrace came from Russian shells" (Balfour 1990, 141).

Figure 5: (1936) Postcard of Columbas Haus [Postcard]

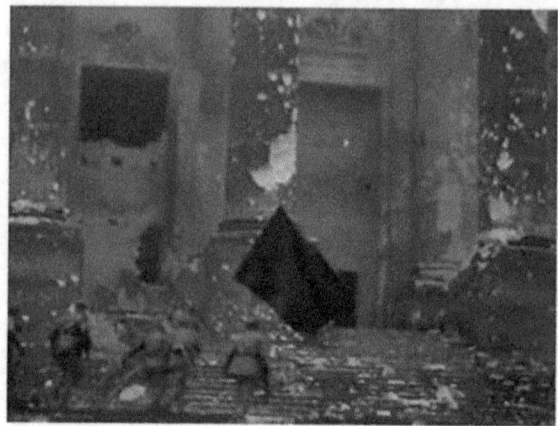

Figure 6: Soviet soldiers bringing the victory flag to the ruinous Reichstag
after the fall of Berlin in *Fall of Berlin*, 1945 (00:40:26).

After the war, Columbus Haus stood on a triangle of land under the jurisdiction
of East Germany that projected into West Berlin. The building became a state run
department store, replacing the old name with H.O Department Stores. In 1953,
the people of East Germany, led by angry construction workers, rioted against
raised work quotas and communism (Balfour 1990, 146). The focus of the action
was Columbus Haus due to its symbolic presence on the edge of the Eastern city.
The building was set on fire by the rioters; however, it was not badly damaged.

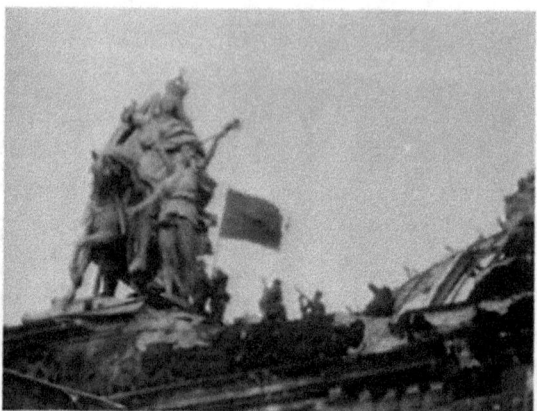

Figure 7: Soviet soldiers bringing the victory flag up the front steps of the
ruinous Reichstag after the fall of Berlin in *Fall of Berlin*, 1945 (00:40:38).

In 1954, the authorities closed H.O Department stores, boarding up all openings and removing the name from the exterior. Two years later the East Berlin authorities decided to demolish the building and in 1957 the military decision for permanent division occurred. The building was dismantled floor by floor, salvaging what materials they could, mainly steel. (Balfour 1990, 147)

This is a building that has survived through some of the most important historical events, not only in Berlin, but on a global scale. Surviving World War II, Hitler's dictatorship, it sat on the contentious border between East and West Berlin, in the firing line of the uprising against Communism. This building was one of the last major builds of democratic Berlin, embodying the resilience, defiance, and strength that is a democracy. The building was adaptable, being used in many different ways over its turbulent life, as shops like Woolworth's, restaurants, state department stores and serving as a billboard for peace propaganda. Such an anticlimactic ending for a building that endured so much does not seem right; to be stripped apart layer by layer, removing layer after layer of history, and for what? Not because it was not useful, not because it was unsafe; it was demolished because this was a building that was a thorn in the side of Communism and Dictatorship. Columbus Haus, stripped of its worth, just like a casualty of war, anything of worth taken away, melted down and used to build a Communist Utopia. It seems so wrong, all memory of this building is lost, no trace, no legacy, no memory, only photos now stored in an archive.

Restoration

A building can be restored rather than being demolished; to do so allows a new lease on life, while still remembering the old way of life, providing a contradictory relationship by maintaining a legacy of its historical past while creating a new way of life.

The Reichstag

In 1992, Norman Foster won an architectural competition for the reconstruction of the Reichstag. The original Reichstag building was designed by Paul Wallot in 1894. Since its opening in 1894, the building has had a notorious life, having been destroyed twice and restored twice. On February 27th 1933, the Reichstag Fire broke out in suspicious circumstances just under a month after Hitler had appointed himself Chancellor. Hilter never spoke at the Reichstag; he visited it once, calling it an 'old shack' that cost less to build than a single battleship (Foster 2000, 46). With its chamber destroyed, the Nazi regime abandoned the Reichstag. The building only served the purpose of propaganda for the Nazi party. In his book, Foster quotes the late Martin Pawley, one of the most insightful and provocative commentators on contemporary architecture and design: "It has been dogged by misconceptions: Kaiser Wilhelm held it in contempt; Hilter never spoke there; and the Red Army mistakenly targeted it as the bastion of Nazi power" (Foster 2000, 36). The Reichstag provoked much discussion in the 1940s and 1950s. What to do with it? In 1954, it was decided that the building was to be made safe by demolishing the dome.

'The scarred remains of Wallot's nineteenth-century interiors have tremendous poignancy; in the east corridor the cyclopean stone surrounding once elaborate doorways has an archaeological quality' to the building. (Foster 2000, 78)

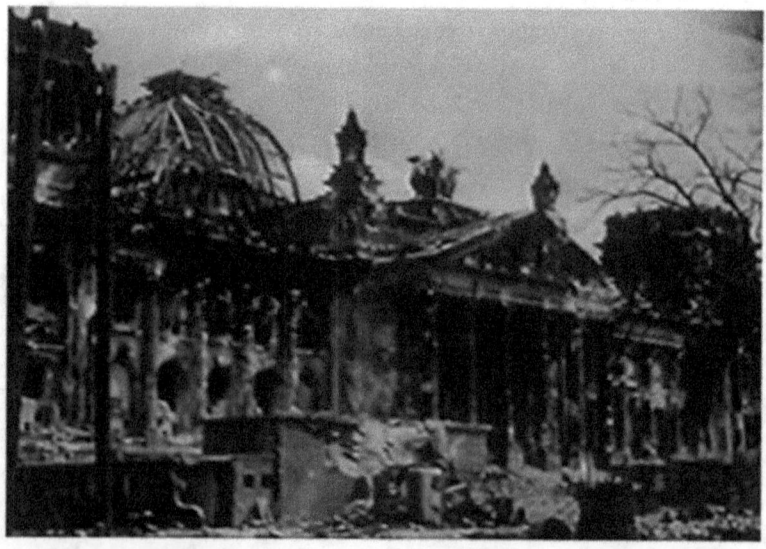

Figure 8: Soviet soldiers hoisting the victory flag on top of the ruinous Reichstag after the fall of Berlin in *Fall of Berlin*, 1945 (00:41:22).

The fabric of the Reichstag bears the imprint of time and events better than any exhibition ever could. The Reichstag is like a living museum, unlike the traditional museum that is a place to go and to view the past. The Reichstag differs from this, the building is not a museum, it is a parliament building, the home of German Democracy. The primary function of this building is therefore to govern the country, but when the politicians walk through the building they are surrounded by the scars of the past and layered identities. The contrast Foster creates between his modern architecture and these 'scars' and graffiti allows history to become part of everyday life in the parliament and invites visitors to have an insight into the history of the building and Berlin in a very palpable way.

The graffiti on the walls came from the Soviet soldiers after they liberated Berlin. The writing varied in medium according to rank, with soldiers writing in charcoal or chalk and officers wrote in coloured crayon (Foster 2000, 116). It was said that the Soviet Union secretly pleaded with the former West German government to limit the scope of work, as they did not want the graffiti of the Soviets to be removed as it acts as a memorial to their victory in 1945.

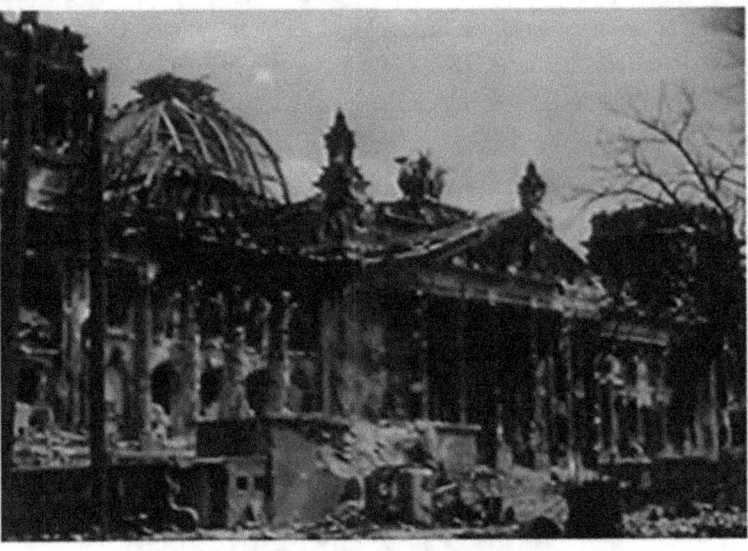

Figure 9: The ruinous Reichstag after the fall of Berlin in
Fall of Berlin, 1945 (01:00:39).

Foster adopted the scar and graffiti into his design at great expense and time, as the graffiti had to be cleaned using scalpels and glass paper. It is because of these design decisions and critical consciousness that the Reichstag has to some extent come to assume the role of a history book, but a history book that has no finish, as decisions made in this building continue to change and influence the future of democratic Berlin.

Foster quotes Peter Buchanan's view on the Reichstag; "Some of the twentieth century's most prominent architects have created landmark parliament buildings, which embody democracy in architecture itself. The new Reichstag forms part of this tradition, drawing lessons from the transparency and public accessibility of its predecessors" (Foster 2000, 164). This is true of the Reichstag; its success lies in its transparency, no attempts to cover over the past, but allow access to the past in a tactile and palpable way.

Hermann Göring's Air Ministry on Wilhelmstraße

The Reichsmarschall Hermann Göring's Air Ministry building on Wilhelmstraße is a classic example of Nazi Architecture. The architect of this building was Ernst Sagebiel who designed what was the largest office building in Europe. Constructed in a rigid limestone façade which encased the steel construction beneath, contemporaries saw this as a signal of nationalist socialist desire. (Haubrich 2006, 143)

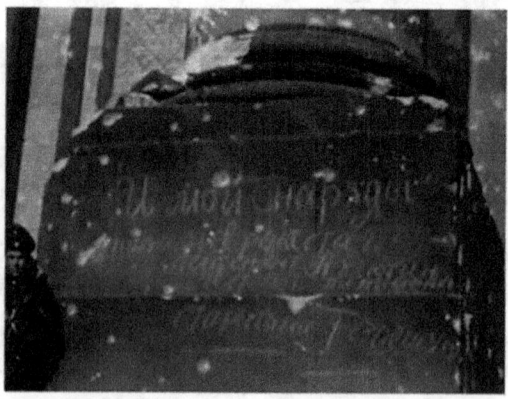

Figure 10: Soviet soldiers graffiti on the ruinous Reichstag after the fall of
Berlin in *Fall of Berlin*, 1945 (00:50:42).

During the war, this building was the centre where decisions on the Nazi's aviation attacks were implemented. Hermann Göring was in command of the Luftwaffe, and responsible for the devastating Blitzkrieg attacks on Poland and on Western Europe, including the Battle of Britain. It was in the neo-classical small festival room (Kleine Festsaal) that Göring made such decisions. (Haubrich 2006, 143) Somehow during the war, the building escaped damage, and after the War the East German government decided to restore the building to its original state minus the Eagles and Swasticas. The building is now the Ministry of Finance. There is no longer any suggestion as to the past of this building.

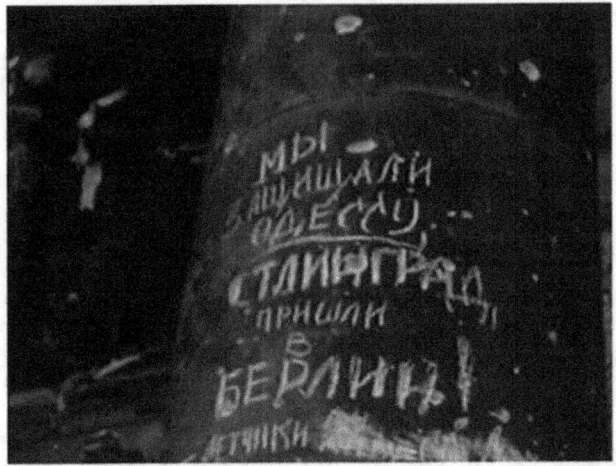

Figure 11, Soviet soldiers graffiti on the ruinous Reichstag after the fall of Berlin in *Fall of Berlin*, 1945 (00:50:56).

It is clear that this building has had an important impact on German history. A history that has become forgotten due to decisions made after the war, there is nothing left to suggest that this is a building of significant historical importance. A t the time, removing any Nazi paraphernalia was far from being a questionable decision, but years later, the decision now is one of disappointment, as this does not represent the concept of *Vergangenheitsbewältigung* (Fritzsche 2006, 25). The past is not being dealt with, it has just been removed, the viewer has no knowledge of past uses, of the devastating effect of the Blitzkriegs initiated here. There is no memory, and as time goes by, so increases the dilution of memory: no trace left, no knowledge and no critical consciousness is left.

Preservation

Unlike restoration, preservation does not create a new use for a building, but maintains the building or structure as it was for generations to come. This is done to allow future generations to have a physical connection to the past, to help them formulate ideas and memory of what the past might have been like for our ancestors. Our memory of the past today is mainly informed through media, such as documentaries, film, video games, photography, art, and literature. Modern digital memory can only go so far without physical memory. If chosen correctly, preserving historic buildings or structures can enforce our ideas of the past. This is because we can physically experience history as well as our modern experience through digital memory.

Berlin Wall

On August 13th 1961, the German Democratic Republic (GDR) closed the border by building the wall, imprisoning its own people and preventing migration towards West Berlin. Some through great courage still managed to flee. Many died trying to escape to freedom. One hundred and thirty six people lost their lives on the Berlin Wall.

Of the 155km barrier that surrounded West Berlin, a 220m strip has been preserved on Bernauer Strasse. The inner wall, signal fence, border control road, and guard tower all remain to help teach the inhumanity and cruelty that was the Berlin Wall. It is now preserved, documented and conveyed by this remaining strip of the Wall. Very little remains of the wall that divided Berlin, Germany and also divided the rest of Europe. Is this necessarily a bad thing? Would this site have the desired poignancy if there was a much greater expanse of wall? The Berlin Wall can be seen in fourteen different locations over Berlin, each of differing sizes and experiences, some more effective than others.

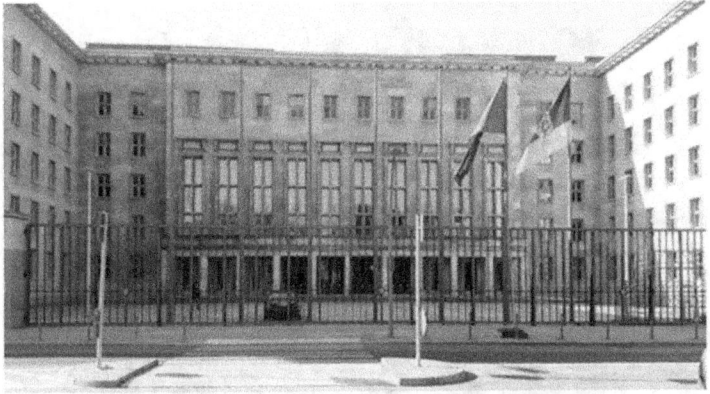

Figure 12: Air Ministry Building

The wall is represented in both an explicit and in an implicit way. The wall is explicitly preserved as it was so that people can learn without doubt what this location was like. Implicitly, only a small section of the wall remains, suggesting what was there before. It is the presence of an absence; it is obvious that there was more wall than there is today, and there is continuity even with the absence. Jacques Derrida talks about "trace" (1976), the metaphysical; these are the aspects of the design that encourage the viewer to make their own informed decisions based on what they have already observed. The wall as a memorial here would not be so successful without this idea of the metaphysical, as there would be no reason to think for ourselves and therefore the effect of completeness of memory would be lost.

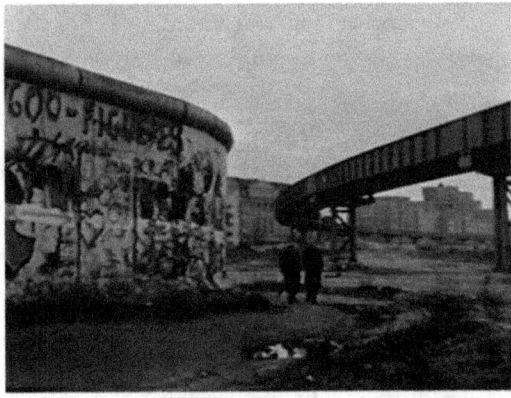

Figure 13: Walking along the Berlin Wall in *Wings of Desire*, 1987 0:42:21.

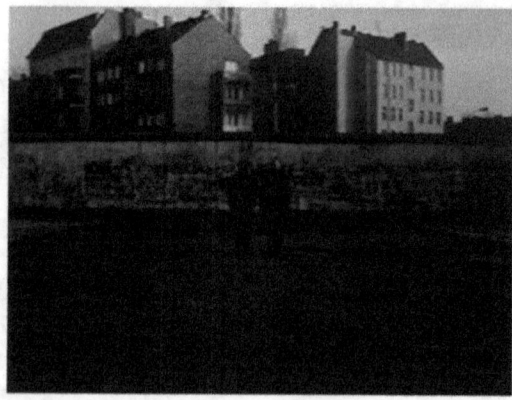

Figure 14: Walking along the Berlin Wall in *Wings of Desire*, 1987 1:05:43

Signs have been set up to mark the places along the wall where people escaped and indeed, where they failed. Another significant event on this location was the demolition of the Reconciliation Church. The church stood on the death strip until demolition in 1985, which marked the end of all hope to return. Fortunately, that was not the case as four years after the wall came down, and now where the Reconciliation Church once stood, there now stands the Chapel of Reconciliation. In commemoration to those who lost their lives during the war, memorial services are held here daily.

The East German Communist Party physically and mentally tortured those citizens deemed suspicious, denying them all basic human rights. The fact that this piece of East West German history from the Cold War has been preserved allows future generations the opportunity to experience this part of German history in a very tactile way.

Archaeological windows have been set up looking into the ground to reveal older layers of the wall and their relation to the city. These layered identities were all part of the housing and infrastructure that made up the city. It is now a memorial that embodies the benefits of fighting for freedom; walls are powerless to resist this desire. The statement here is clear; freedom and democracy are not a given, they are something to be fought for, this memorial now acts as a message to directly confront dictatorial systems.

Kaiser-Wilhelm Gedächniskirche (Memorial Church)

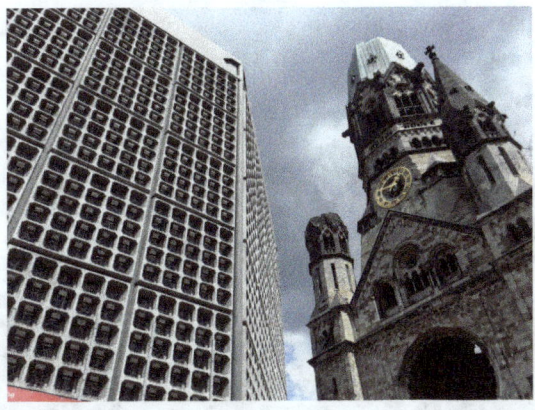

Figure 15: Kaiser Wilhelm Memorial Church

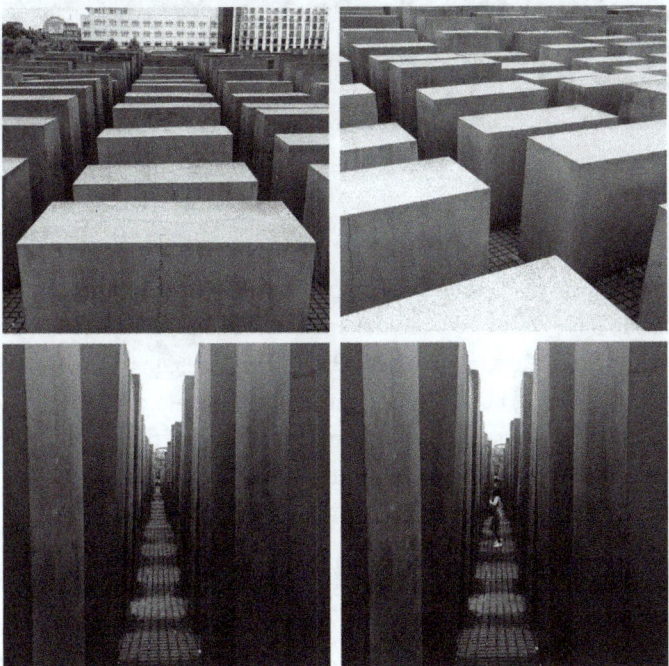

Figure 16: Peter Eisenman's Memorial to the Murdered
Jews of Europe, in Berlin.

Built between 1891 and 1895, the Kaiser Wilhelm Memorial Church was built on the orders of Wilhelm II who commissioned the building to commemorate his father. The church, built in the Romanesque revival style, was eventually completed in 1895. The building became one of Berlin's most beautiful and best known landmarks which had been built at great expense as a memorial to Kaiser Wilhelm.

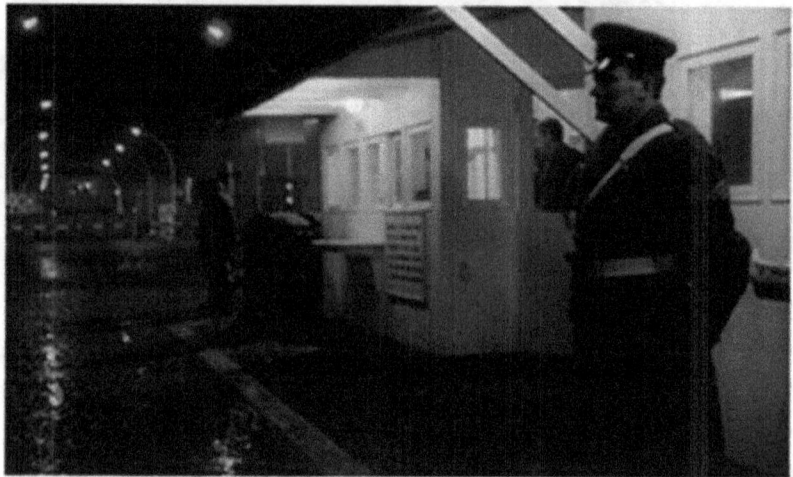

Figure 17, Checkpoint Charlie in *The Spy Who Came From The Cold,* 1965 (0:03:05)

During World War II, the church was badly damaged during the allied bombings, with the nave destroyed and the spire damaged. After the war, the fate of the memorial church was undecided. Preliminary designs were to completely reconstruct the church, but eventually after much debate, the option of preserving the church was chosen. Egon Eiermann's plans to build a modern church were chosen. His scheme was inherently about the contrast between old and new. Eiermann's new church was built between 1956- 63.

The exterior of the old church was preserved to make it safe and the interior underwent intensive work to repair the mosaic ceiling. The ground floor of the old church is used today as a visitor centre providing information about the buildings short, war ravaged history,with photographs, models and writing as well as information on the new church.

I believe the decision to preserve the ruins of the memorial church was a correct decision, as it allows the habitants and visitors to Berlin to see the destructive nature of the war and to remain as a permanent scar on an iconic Berlin landmark. The question I have posed is: Was Eiermann's design of the modern addition to the church conducive to the preservation of memory? I don't believe it is. Eiermann's scheme depends inherently on the contrast between old and new; however, I believe the contrast detracts attention away from the preserved old church towards the brutalism of the new concrete church. The new church and bell tower have a physical separation to the old church; Eiermann intended that the old church should be surrounded by the new church. This physical dislocation further separates that which is old from that which is new. The contrast creates a further separation. Even though the hexagonal shape of the building has been influenced by the shape of the spire in the old building, there still exists a presence of an absence; however this is not in the positive sense. The old and new buildings have now separate uses, the new construction functions as a 'working organ' in Berlin's society, functioning for church services and commercial tourism, while the old is now a 'failed organ' in Berlin's society, just remaining and deteriorating as a reminder of what used to be. Through this physical and theoretical gap the two buildings, which are related, become very separate and the relationship between the two becomes diluted.

It is true that a pastiche of the old building would not have been appropriate; it may have represented the grandeur of the building but would have been a copy, an unauthentic replacement. However, in 1895, the memorial church was criticised for the excessive expense, as the Romanesque revival church was finished to a high standard, so grand in scale and dominating Berlin's urban fabric. It would be the duty of the new church to emulate the qualities of what had been before without copying what had been there. When the visitor looks at the new church alongside the old remains, they do not see grandeur, they do not get the sense of the grand scale or high quality that the Kaiser Wilhelm Memorial Church embodied. What they see is something very different. They see three separate constructs, one old and two new. The new church has a heavy industrial concrete façade, in contrast to the light spiritual nature created on the inside, a very successful church in its own right. However, I do not believe that Eiermann's design successfully represents what came before, and without the visitor centre the viewer would have no idea of what the church was like, as the only reference to the past is the hexagonal shape that has been influenced by the

old building and it references not what is lost but what is still there, so much for
the legacy of Kaiser Wilhelm.

Memorial

Unlike all previous chapters, memorialization does not deal with existing buildings or structures; it deals with the creation of a new building or structure to
commemorate people or events in history. This conjures up the question, how
and what can be created to remember the past? Especially with Berlin's notorious past, this is a delicate and contentious topic. It is important that the
approach taken to memory is well considered and a fitting tribute to the past.

Peter Eisenman's Holocaust Memorial

In 2005, Peter Eisenman's controversial 4.6 acre holocaust memorial was
opened in the centre of Berlin just south of the Reichstag, North of Potsdammer
Platz where Columbas House was situated before its demolition.

This memorial had to rethink its approach to memorial, as the purpose was
not to celebrate but to commemorate suffering. It was important that the memorial accounted for collectivity of those affected by the Holocaust. It would
be impossible to represent the atrocities in a figurative way, as there were an
estimated 11 million killed during the final solution to the Jewish Question. It
would be impossible to figuratively represent each person. Peter Eisenman had
to account for the collective during his design as it was imperative that it was
all inclusive and did not leave anyone out.

Eisenman designed a field of 2,711 cubed concrete pillars on the 4.6 acre site,
separated by grey paving and grey gravel. The design has two different undulating planes, the first being the ground undulations and the second being the top
of the concrete pillars. The two undulate in different directions at different times
as can be seen below. There is no beginning and no end to the site, no inscriptions on the concrete, and the only information on the site is in an underground
visitor centre, which was installed later due to public demand.

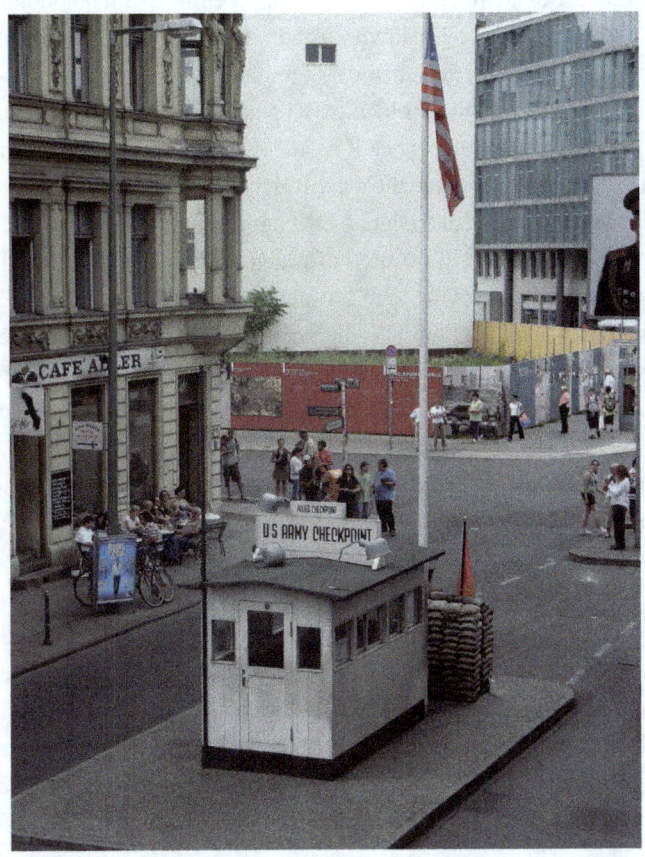

Figure 18: Checkpoint Charlie.

Explicit representation would not be right for such a design, as such an event in history speaks differently to each person who learns about it. The memorial does not preach, and since there are no inscriptions, and the site is bare of any symbol or images, it challenges the viewer to formulate their own decisions at their own speed and in their own time. "The memorial does not inculcate or preach. It challenges" (Eisenman 2004, 42). Walking through the 2,711 columns of various heights in this huge site makes the visitor think just how small and insignificant they are in comparison to this memorial; the visitor is made to feel as if they are just another number in this sea of concrete columns that represents the loss of millions of lives.

would be set in the past, and as time would go by, the memorial would slip even further into the past and would perhaps become like the Brandenburg Gate, having its function adopt a new role of becoming an icon of a particular location rather than the memorial it was meant to be. The power of memory would become dissolved over time. Eisenman uses French critic Marcel Proust (1871-1922) to explain this point in his writing; "Proust said the memory concerned not what was literally in the past but what we imagine the past to have been." (Eisenman 2004, 504)

Checkpoint Charlie

Checkpoint Charlie, along the Glienicker Bridge, is the best known crossing in Berlin from the Cold War days, a symbol of division in Germany. The well-known sign along the crossing reads, "YOU ARE NOW LEAVING THE AMERICAN SECTOR," with translations of this in French, German and Russian.

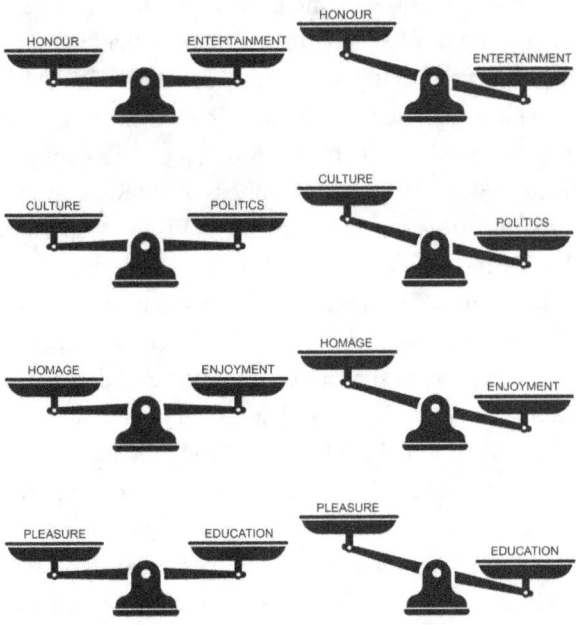

Figure 19: Diagram representing contradictory balance

When the Berlin Wall fell on November 9th 1989, the border opened between East and West, between Capitalism and Communism, replacing confinement with freedom. Today the crossing acts as a symbol of division, a place of historical and emotional poignancy.

"War tourism is a complex and multifaceted experience...internally contradictory in its ambivalence, pairing as it does, pleasure and education, honour and entertainment, homage and good fun." (Jarecka 2013, 155) After much debate, Checkpoint Charlie was left for visitors to come and enjoy and to boost tourism. The vetting barracks on the East was removed, and a copy of the US guardhouse and crossing sign were installed.

Although I agree with the decision to preserve the site as a memorial, I do not believe it is effective as a memorial. I understand that tourism is big business in Germany as in many countries, but is there not a line, past which, memorials may lose their capacity for memory?

In this instance, tourism has been exploited to its maximum potential, and financial revenue is the priority, not memory. Even the museum that accompanies the crossing has more focus on their gift shop than they do the crossing and historical information. Selling pieces of the Berlin Wall, it is no wonder history has become fragmented over time; it seems, in the case of Berlin, this fragmentation of memory is quite literal. Along the streets adjacent to the 'memorial' are street vendors selling cheap replicas of the Russian shapka-ushanka, fake medals, and other historical 'knock-offs.' Visitors can pay to have their photo taken beside the reproduction guard house and signs. The visitor may come away with the knowledge that this was a famous border between East and West, and that there was a wall here, but what sense do they get about what it must have been like to live in such a divided city, families separated overnight, the tension and oppression of such a high military presence, constantly being watched? School children and students are brought here to see the historical merit of the site, but instead, through no fault of their own, are overcome by commercialisation. "Social memory refers to the space that has the power to shape hearts and minds" (Jarecka 2013, 151). Yet it seems that the visitor has to sift through the commercial to get to the facts and the historical information that helps us to imagine what this place was like, to inform our decisions and to trigger our memory. If Peter Eisenman's Holocaust Memorial was financially motivated, would we perceive it in the same way? Eisenman's memorial has only the motivation of memory; this is one of the reasons for its success. This is why Checkpoint Charlie, in its role as a memorial, is not successful. There needs to be a pleasure in tourism that feeds on the honour of war and all those affected by it (Jarecka 2013, 157). It is successful as a business, due to its commercial prowess and souvenir sales, which are attractive to tourists, but the success as a business has led to Checkpoint Charlie's demise as a memorial removing its power to shape hearts and minds.

Critical consciousness for Berlin; allowing memory to occur but at the same time allowing the city to move on. Inherently contradictory in itself one could argue, is it really possible to remember and move on? This approach is inevitably contentious and its outcomes split opinion. However, it has to be done, and boundaries have to be pushed to try and achieve this critical consciousness. The eight different approaches of remembering or forgetting have illustrated this. The author's opinions may not be shared by all but that is part and parcel of the nature of this approach. Decisions had to be made, some of these decisions turned out to be success and others turned out to be failure. When the brief is to remember and to move on, this is an exceptionally difficult task and when memory is such a personal thing, this makes the job all the more difficult. When we delve deeper into the contradictory relationship with regard to memory, there are even more smaller sub sets of contradictory relationships like cultural or political, pleasure or education, honour or entertainment and homage or entertainment to name but a few.

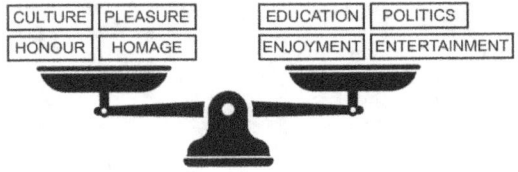

Figure 20: Diagram representing contradictory balance.

Handling these contradictions is a delicate balancing act. Too much emphasis on one contradictory element over another leads to imbalance. For example, if entertainment has a higher emphasis than homage, there is going to be an im balance, and therefore the ability for homage is greatly reduced. Success comes when the balance between the two contradictory elements is equal. When equal, in the example of homage versus enjoyment, then there is potential for both homage and entertainment.

If we combine all contradictory elements onto a balance, there will only be a balance if each contradictory element is equal; if even one of the elements is not balanced, the whole project becomes unbalanced. This is a simplified theoretical overview on balance; the reality is that a perfect balance will not be achieved, as it is impossible. This is because it is a very personal opinion of each person as to what an equal balance is. What one person may consider to be balanced, another may consider unbalanced. In each of the case studies under the four sections: Demolition, Preservation, Restoration, and Memorialisation, different approaches have been taken, and there are successful schemes and there are unsuccessful schemes. Since complete balance is purely theoretical, the challenge is getting as close to being balanced as possible. In these diagrams, the plinth that sits on the pivot represents *Vergangenheitsbewältigung* and maintains a critical consciousness of the past. The closer the balance is to level, the more successful *Vergangenheitsbewältigung* is.

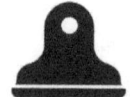 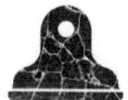

Longevity of Memory   No Longevity of Memory

Figure 21: Diagram to show the different pivots of longevity.

The pivot itself represents the longevity of memory. No matter how well balanced the contradictory scale is, if the future is not considered, then longevity of memory has not been dealt with, the scheme may be relevant today, but what about in five or ten years' time? Will the scheme be relevant anymore or will it decay with time? If the pivot of the contradictory balance fails, then so will the scheme, because without the pivot there can be no balance, just a bunch of elements remaining with no relevance anymore.

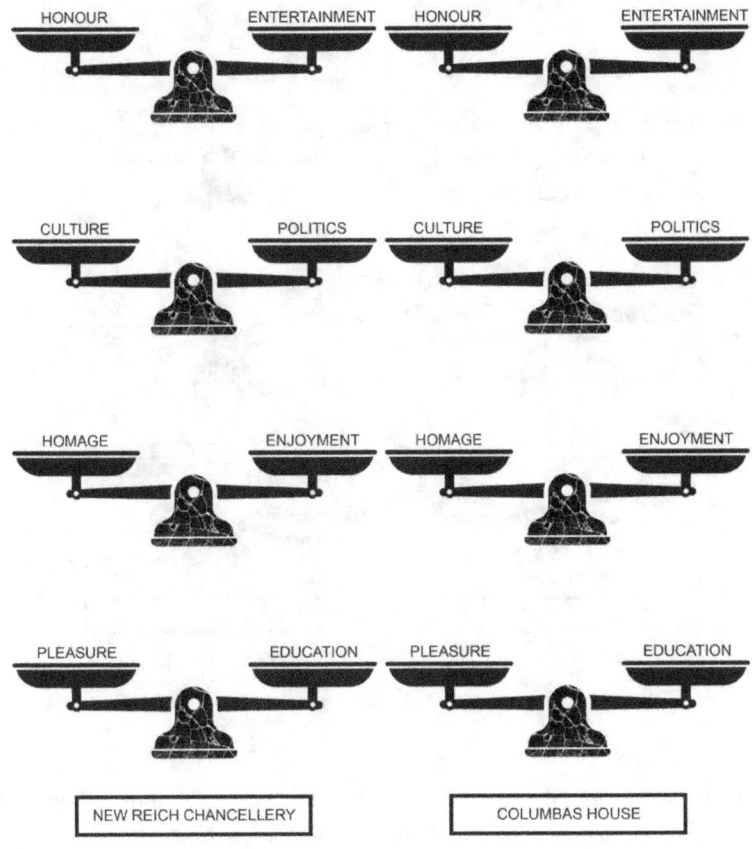

Figure 22: Balance of contradiction within demolition.

If a scheme does not consider the future, it is therefore set in the past, and this is all it will ever be, something old that does not hold the power to inform today or the future. It is important that the future is considered to provide a reference point for renewal and vigour of the German democratic process.

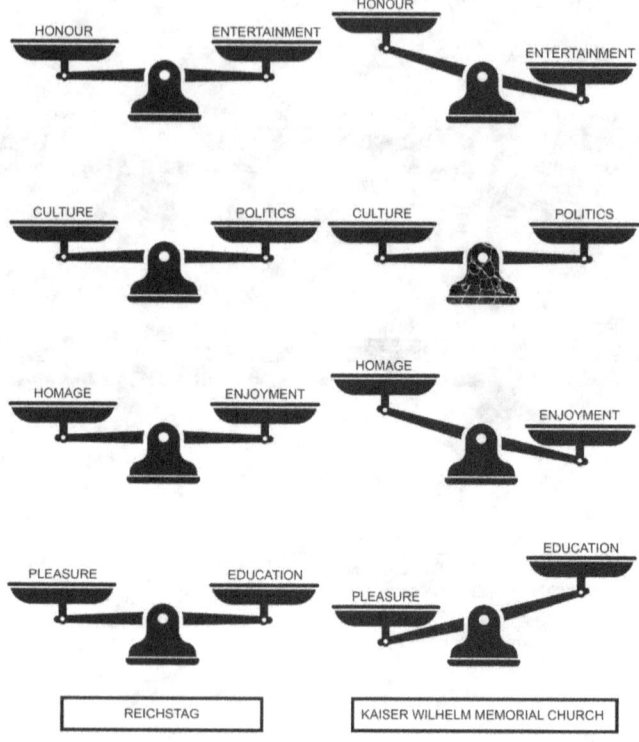

Figure 23: Balance of contradiction within preservation.

Within the category of demolition, the balance of contradictions will inevitably be balanced as there is nothing to balance. This is where the pivot is useful, as it represents the longevity of memory. Demolition is not about remembering; it is about forgetting and moving on. This is why, in the above diagram, (figure 23) all the pivots have no longevity of memory. As time goes by, the decay of the pivot (memory) increases until the pivot will fail and no longer work. At this stage, there will be little or no memory left of the building. However, the diagrams for the New Reich Chancellery and Columbas Haus are exactly the same, how can it be said that one is a failure and the other a success? The reason for this is because the New Reich Chancellery needed to be demolished to remove this symbol of Nazism and the destruction, oppression, and greed they created. The symbolic act of removing this building was intentionally done so that the longevity of memory would decay and be forgotten. On the other hand, Columbas Haus was a building built in 1932, one year before Hitler appointed himself Chancellor of Germany. This is a building that survived the war, one of the only buildings in Potsdamer Platz not destroyed. It sat on a conflict ground between East and West Berlin, a landmark building from pre-war democratic Berlin, just to be torn down later, leaving no trace of such a significant building. Like the Chancellery, memory decayed over time, and now there is no memory of such an undervalued, salient building at the focal point in twentieth century Berlin's history.

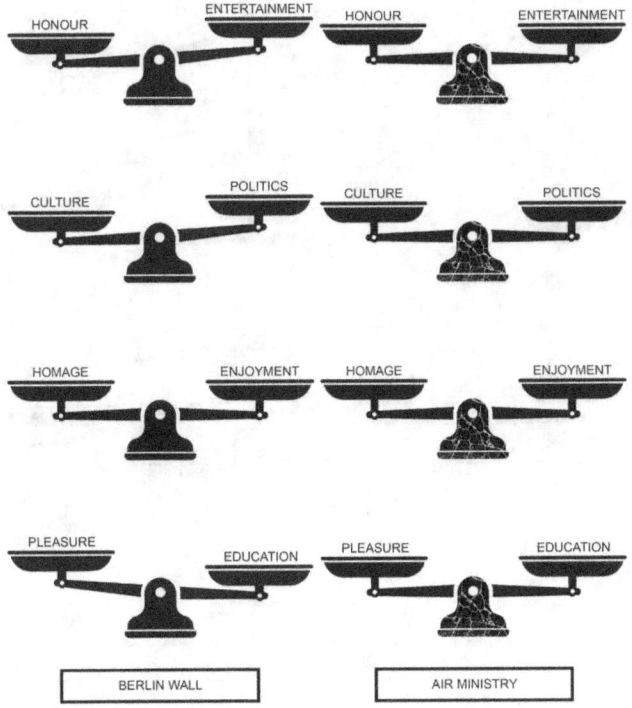

Figure 24: Balance of contradiction within preservation.

Within the category of restoration, it is plain to see the unbalance created in the Kaiser Wilhelm Memorial Church in comparison to the Reichstag. The reason for the Reichstag's success is that each contradicting measure has been considered with reference to their opposite member. Unlike the Kaiser Wilhelm

Memorial Church, which as can be seen above (Fig 24) which for all intents and purposes has become a tourist attraction more than a memorial church. The focus is on the pleasure of entertainment, enjoyment and pleasure rather than honour, homage, and education. Furthermore, longevity of memory has failed with regard to culture and politics as the new church seems to have turned its back on the past, just focusing on the future with the modern brutalist restoration approach that was taken. Over time, like memory, the pivot has become fragmented, and eventually there will be little left, thus, adding to the failure of the restoration of Kaiser Wilhelm Memorial Church.

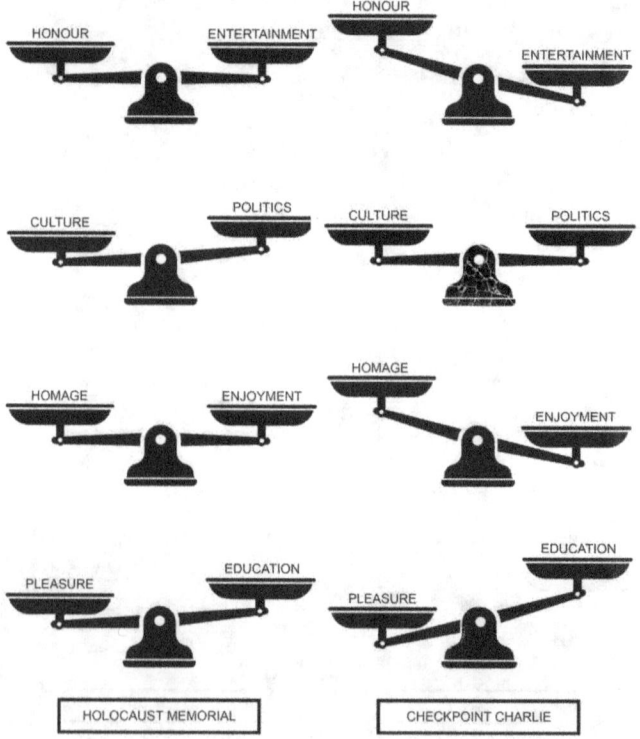

Figure 25: Balance of contradiction within memorialisation.

Within the category of preservation, we can see there is a very slight imbalance in the contradictory element within the Berlin Wall (Figure 25). There is a slight edge towards honour, culture, and education. However these are only very slight and therefore allow the balance to remain, contributing to its success as a preserved structure. One could even argue it is this slight imbalance that gives the wall its vitality and helps to provoke discussion. The Air Ministry building was preserved after the war just as it was apart from Third Reich and Nazi insignia, which were removed. To look at the building, the viewer would have no idea of what was or what had been. This is where the building fails, almost instantaneously memory has decayed after the symbols were taken off, leaving absolutely no longevity of memory, no consideration for culture, politics, or education.

The Holocaust Memorial, much like the Berlin Wall has a very slight imbalance in its contradictions, but still manages to remain balance (Figure 26). A similar effect is created; this slight imbalance causes the memorial's vitality and provokes conversation and debate. Checkpoint Charlie is very unbalanced as it has put pleasure, enjoyment and entertainment as very important issues. This is because the concern is higher for tourism than it is for memory. To add to this is that failure to address culture and politics; this is because any information on these have become lost in the commercialisation of the memorial, thus leading to the decay of longevity of memory and failure of the memorial.

Dealing with the leftovers from Nazism's effect on Berlin and further afield was never an easy task by any estimation. There is no remedy or formula to follow in order to deal with undesirable hereditament, but there is a method for dealing with such. A critical consciousness must be adopted in the approach. As shown, it is inherently contradictory, and to a certain extent provokes more questions than it answers. This is why dealing with undesirable hereditament is such a controversial topic, as everyone has contrasting and conflicting opinions. If there was a simple solution, there would be no contradiction, no debate, no opinion required. Like any good design, the research has to be undertaken, constant critique of design decisions, a rationale used to inform choices. It is not so much that a pursuit of perfection is desired, but rather a pursuit of balance. If we can find a balance, we have found the middle ground that we set out to achieve. A balance of contradictions; both physical and metaphysical contradictions, and the subsets within each must be comprehended in order to achieve balance. Complete balance, much like perfection is not possible in this sense, and to try and achieve such is counterintuitive and efforts may prove fruitless. Where balance differs from perfection is that perfection has no flexibility or room for manoeuvre; it is a singular entity and nothing else. Whereas balance has a flexibility and room to manoeuvre, because much like the scales, it can lean slightly to one side and still achieve a balance. It is this teetering on the edge of balance/unbalance that gives interest, opinion and sparks debate, thus leading to the success of *Vergangenheitsbewaltigung* (2006, p.25).

REFERENCES

Belfour, A. (1990). 'Berlin, the Politics of Order 1739- 1989'. Rizzoli International Publications Inc. p. 132- 210

Cermak, Laird S. (1972). Human Memory: Research and Theory. New York: The Ronald Press Company

D. Rosenfeld, G. (2000). Munich and Memory, Architecture, Monuments, and the Legacy of the Third Reich. California: University of California Press Ltd.

Eisenman, P, (2004). 'Notations of Affect. An Architecture of Memory', in Pathos, Affekt, Gefühl: die Emotionen in den Künsten. Berlin; New York; De Gruyter

Forty, A. (2005). 'Concrete and Memory', in Crinson, M. (ed.) Urban Memory History and Amnesia in the Modern City. Routledge Taylor and Francis Group p. 75- 95

Foster, N (2000). 'Rebuilding the Reichstag', London: Weidenfeld & Nicolson. p12-251.

Fritzsche, P. (2006). 'What Exactly Is Vergangenheitsbewaltigung? Narrative and its Insufficiency in Post War Germany', In: Fuchs, A and Cosgrove, M and Grote, G (ed.) German Memory Contests: The Quest for Identity in Literature, Film, and Discourse since 1990 (Studies in German Literature Linguistics and Culture). New York: Camden House. p25-40.

Haubrich, R. (2006). Berlin: The Architecture Guide. Braun: Braun Publishing.

Jarausch, K. (2008). 'Memory Wars: German Debates About the Legacy of Dictatorship', in Williams, JA. (ed.) Berlin since the Wall's End, Shaping Society and Memory. Cambridge: Cambridge Scholars Publishing. p. 90-109

Jarecka, U. (2013). 'War Tourism in Poland and Germany', in Niznik, J. (ed.) Twentieth Century Wars in European Memory. Frankfurt: Peter Lang International Academic Publishers.

Woods, R. (2006). 'On Forgetting and Remembering: The New Right since German Unification', in Fuch, A., Cosgrove, M. and Grote, G. (ed.) German Memory Contests, The Quest for identity in Literature, Film and Discourse since 1990. Suffolk: Camden House p. 271-286. http://beautifulberlin.blogspot.co.uk/2009/07/short-history-of-berlin.html

List of Illustrations

Figure 1, New Reich Chancellery after the fall of Berlin in, Fall of Berlin, 1945 (00:46:55).

Built in the heart of democratic Berlin, in the centre of the economic core, it is part of everyday life for Berliners in the city. Even the location of the site, without even studying the design shows the intent of the design. The statement is clear; the atrocities of the Holocaust will not be forgotten. The memorial's location symbolises the importance it has. It is very poignant that the memorial is built on the grounds of where the New Reich Chancellery was situated before its demolition in 1945; it is poignant because they removed a building that could have been considered a source of much suffering and replaced it with a site of memory and remembrance of those who lost their lives in the Holocaust. If the Chancellery had been left as a memorial in itself we would remember the people who were the cause of the anguish and pain rather than the people who were affected by the evil and inhumane decisions of the Final Solution.

What if the memorial was located away from Berlin? What if it was situated at one of the many concentration camps? The Holocaust occurred in sixteen different countries in many different concentration camps, work camps, and ghettos. Why would we not build at any of these locations? The answer is simple, and applies to all these locations; if the memorial was built there then there would be no account for collectivity and the critical consciousness would not be maintained. Through reconstitution of memorial back to Berlin, the source of many decisions on the Holocaust, also the capital of Germany, completeness of memory is achieved as the memorial is all inclusive of everyone affected by the Holocaust and therefore durability of memory is greater.

Peter Eisenman said "Memory is not nostalgia. Memory is an attempt to bring the past into the present as if it were the future" (Eisenman 2004, 504). The memorial is used as a thorough-fare, meeting point, seating, and a place to eat lunch or have a coffee by the public and tourists as well as a memorial. The journey through this sea of grey with its dual undulating surfaces, top and bottom, provokes thought and triggers involuntary memory even if this is just at a subconscious level. The memorial becomes an extension of the city's circulation, embedding it in and as a part of everyday life. The person walking through or engaging with the memorial becomes part of the memorial, as if they are an extension of the memorial. By doing so, Eisenman has brought this memorial into the present day and adaptable for the future; this could not be achieved if the public were not able to engage with the memorial as they do today. If the memorial was just a place that people came to visit and pay their respects, it

Figure 2, New Reich Chancellery after the fall of Berlin in, Fall of Berlin, 1945 (00:47:00).

Figure 3, New Reich Chancellery after the fall of Berlin in, Fall of Berlin, 1945 (00:47:35).

Figure 4, New Reich Chancellery after the marble was removed in, Germany Year Zero, 1948 (00:28:30).

Figure 5, (1936) Postcard of Columbas Haus [Postcard] Unknown

Figure 6, Soviet soldiers bringing the victory flag to the ruinous Reichstag after the fall of Berlin in Fall of Berlin, 1945 (00:40:26).

Figure 7, Soviet soldiers bringing the victory flag up the front steps of the ruinous Reichstag after the fall of Berlin in Fall of Berlin, 1945 (00:40:38).

Figure 8, Soviet soldiers hoisting the victory flag on top of the ruinous Reichstag after the fall of Berlin in Fall of Berlin, 1945 (00:41:22).

Figure 9, The ruinous Reichstag after the fall of Berlin in Fall of Berlin, 1945 (01:00:39).

Figure 10, Soviet soldiers graffiti on the ruinous Reichstag after the fall of Berlin in Fall of Berlin, 1945 (00:50:42).

Figure 11, Soviet soldiers graffiti on the ruinous Reichstag after the fall of Berlin in Fall of Berlin, 1945 (00:50:56).

Figure 12, Air Ministry Building [Photograph] [Own image]

Figure 13, Walking along the Berlin Wall in Wings of Desire, 1987 0:42:21

Figure 14, Walking along the Berlin Wall in Wings of Desire, 1987 1:05:43

Figure 15, Kaiser Wilhelm Memorial Church [Photograph] [Own image]

Figure 16, Peter Eisenman's Memorial to the Murdered Jews of Europe, in Berlin [Photograph] [Own image]

Figure 17, Checkpoint Charlie in The Spy Who Came From The Cold, 1965 (0:03:05)

Figure 18, Checkpoint Charlie [Photograph] [Own image]

Figure 19, Diagram representing contradictory balance [Own image]

Figure 20, Diagram representing contradictory balance [Own image]

Figure 21, Diagram to show the different pivots of longevity [Own image]

Figure 22, Balance of contradiction within demolition [Own image]

Figure 23, Balance of contradiction within preservation [Own image]

Figure 24, Balance of contradiction within preservation [Own image]

Figure 25, Balance of contradiction within memorialisation [Own image]

www.ingramcontent.com/pod-product-compliance
Lightning Source LLC
Chambersburg PA
CBHW072010230526
45468CB00021B/1175

* 9 781957 792101 *